Handbook of Research on Achieving Sustainable Development Goals With Sustainable Marketing

Iza Gigauri
St. Andrew the First-Called Georgian University, Georgia

Maria Palazzo
Universitas Mercatorum, Italy

Maria Antonella Ferri
Universitas Mercatorum, Italy

A volume in the Advances in Marketing, Customer Relationship Management, and E-Services (AMCRMES) Book Series

Published in the United States of America by
IGI Global
Business Science Reference (an imprint of IGI Global)
701 E. Chocolate Avenue
Hershey PA, USA 17033
Tel: 717-533-8845
Fax: 717-533-8661
E-mail: cust@igi-global.com
Web site: http://www.igi-global.com

Copyright © 2023 by IGI Global. All rights reserved. No part of this publication may be reproduced, stored or distributed in any form or by any means, electronic or mechanical, including photocopying, without written permission from the publisher. Product or company names used in this set are for identification purposes only. Inclusion of the names of the products or companies does not indicate a claim of ownership by IGI Global of the trademark or registered trademark.
   Library of Congress Cataloging-in-Publication Data

Names: Gigauri, Iza, 1979- editor. | Palazzo, Maria, editor. | Ferri, Maria
   Antonella, editor.
Title: Handbook of research on achieving sustainable development goals with
   sustainable marketing / edited by Iza Gigauri, Maria Palazzo, and Maria
   Antonella Ferri.
Description: Hershey, PA : Business Science Reference, [2023] | Includes
   bibliographical references and index. | Summary: "Achieving Sustainable
   Development Goals With Sustainable Marketing illuminates current
   developments in sustainable marketing and the new trends and tendencies
   concerning the concept in theory and practice. The book also explores
   the concept of sustainable marketing in today's context of the digital
   age, explains its boundaries and benefits, and describes the challenges
   and opportunities as well as the advantages and potential disadvantages
   of sustainable marketing and branding efforts. Covering key topics such
   as branding, marketing ethics, and corporate social responsibility, this
   premier reference source is ideal for marketers, business owners,
   managers, industry professionals, researchers, academicians, scholars,
   practitioners, instructors, and students"-- Provided by publisher.
Identifiers: LCCN 2023011122 (print) | LCCN 2023011123 (ebook) | ISBN
   9781668486818 (hardcover) | ISBN ISBN 9781668486832 (ebook)
Subjects: LCSH: Sustainable development. | Marketing.
Classification: LCC HC79.E5 A2668 2023 (print) | LCC HC79.E5 (ebook) |
   DDC 338.9/27--dc23/eng/20230324
LC record available at https://lccn.loc.gov/2023011122
LC ebook record available at https://lccn.loc.gov/2023011123

This book is published in the IGI Global book series Advances in Marketing, Customer Relationship Management, and E-Services (AMCRMES) (ISSN: 2327-5502; eISSN: 2327-5529)

British Cataloguing in Publication Data
A Cataloguing in Publication record for this book is available from the British Library.

All work contributed to this book is new, previously-unpublished material. The views expressed in this book are those of the authors, but not necessarily of the publisher.

For electronic access to this publication, please contact: eresources@igi-global.com.

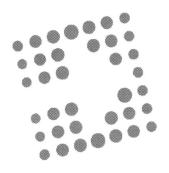

Advances in Marketing, Customer Relationship Management, and E-Services (AMCRMES) Book Series

Eldon Y. Li
National Chengchi University, Taiwan & California Polytechnic State University, USA

ISSN:2327-5502
EISSN:2327-5529

Mission

Business processes, services, and communications are important factors in the management of good customer relationship, which is the foundation of any well organized business. Technology continues to play a vital role in the organization and automation of business processes for marketing, sales, and customer service. These features aid in the attraction of new clients and maintaining existing relationships.

The Advances in Marketing, Customer Relationship Management, and E-Services (AMCRMES) Book Series addresses success factors for customer relationship management, marketing, and electronic services and its performance outcomes. This collection of reference source covers aspects of consumer behavior and marketing business strategies aiming towards researchers, scholars, and practitioners in the fields of marketing management.

Coverage

- Web Mining and Marketing
- Mobile Services
- Database marketing
- Cases on Electronic Services
- Electronic Services
- Social Networking and Marketing
- Telemarketing
- Online Community Management and Behavior
- Mobile CRM
- B2B marketing

IGI Global is currently accepting manuscripts for publication within this series. To submit a proposal for a volume in this series, please contact our Acquisition Editors at Acquisitions@igi-global.com or visit: http://www.igi-global.com/publish/.

The Advances in Marketing, Customer Relationship Management, and E-Services (AMCRMES) Book Series (ISSN 2327-5502) is published by IGI Global, 701 E. Chocolate Avenue, Hershey, PA 17033-1240, USA, www.igi-global.com. This series is composed of titles available for purchase individually; each title is edited to be contextually exclusive from any other title within the series. For pricing and ordering information please visit http://www.igi-global.com/book-series/advances-marketing-customer-relationship-management/37150. Postmaster: Send all address changes to above address. Copyright © 2023 IGI Global. All rights, including translation in other languages reserved by the publisher. No part of this series may be reproduced or used in any form or by any means – graphics, electronic, or mechanical, including photocopying, recording, taping, or information and retrieval systems – without written permission from the publisher, except for non commercial, educational use, including classroom teaching purposes. The views expressed in this series are those of the authors, but not necessarily of IGI Global.

Titles in this Series

For a list of additional titles in this series, please visit: www.igi-global.com/book-series

Global Developments in Nation Branding and Promotion Theoretical and Practical Approaches
Andreas Masouras (Neapolis University, Cyprus) Sofia Daskou (Neapolis University, Cyprus) Victoria Pistikou (Democritus University of Thrace, Greece) Dimitrios Dimitriou (Democritus University of Thrace, Greece) and Tim Friesner (University of Winchester, UK)
Information Science Reference • copyright 2023 • 320pp • H/C (ISBN: 9781668459027) • US $240.00 (our price)

Contemporary Approaches of Digital Marketing and the Role of Machine Intelligence
Afzal Sayed Munna (University of Sunderland in London, UK) Md Sadeque Imam Shaikh (University of Wales Trinity Saint David, UK) and Baha Uddin Kazi (Ryerson University, Canada)
Business Science Reference • copyright 2023 • 310pp • H/C (ISBN: 9781668477359) • US $250.00 (our price)

Origin and Branding in International Market Entry Processes
Carlos Francisco e Silva (Universidade Europeia, Portugal)
Business Science Reference • copyright 2023 • 320pp • H/C (ISBN: 9781668466131) • US $250.00 (our price)

Global Applications of the Internet of Things in Digital Marketing
Arshi Naim (King Kalid University, Saudi Arabia) and V. Ajantha Devi (AP3 Solutions, India)
Business Science Reference • copyright 2023 • 410pp • H/C (ISBN: 9781668481660) • US $250.00 (our price)

Applications of Neuromarketing in the Metaverse
Monika Gupta (Chitkara Business School, Chitkara University, India) Kumar Shalender (Chitkara University, India) Babita Singla (Chitkara Business School, Chitkara University, India) and Nripendra Singh (PennWest University, Clarion, USA)
Business Science Reference • copyright 2023 • 338pp • H/C (ISBN: 9781668481509) • US $255.00 (our price)

Influencer Marketing Applications Within the Metaverse
Rohit Bansal (Department of Management Studies, Vaish College of Engineering, Rohtak, India) Sikandar Ali Qalati (School of Business, Liaocheng University, Shandong, China) and Aziza Chakir (Faculty of Law, Economics and Social Sciences, Hassan II University, Casablanca, Morocco)
Business Science Reference • copyright 2023 • 334pp • H/C (ISBN: 9781668488980) • US $250.00 (our price)

Global Perspectives on the Strategic Role of Marketing Information Systems
Jose Melchor Medina-Quintero (Tamaulipas Autonomous University, Mexico) Miguel A. Sahagun (High Point University, USA) Jorge Alfaro (Universidad Catolica del Norte, Chile) and Fernando Ortiz-Rodriguez (Tamaulipas Autonomous University, Mexico)

701 East Chocolate Avenue, Hershey, PA 17033, USA
Tel: 717-533-8845 x100 • Fax: 717-533-8661
E-Mail: cust@igi-global.com • www.igi-global.com

List of Contributors

Amoako, George Kofi / *Ghana Communication Technology University, Accra, Ghana & Durban University of Technology, South Africa* 129, 170
Ampong, George Oppong Appiagyei / *Ghana Communication Technology University, Accra, Ghana* 170
Anuradha, A. / *Cambridge Institute of Technology, Bengaluru, India* 149
Bonsu, Gifty Agyeiwah / *Ghana Revenue Authority in Kaneshie Taxpayer Service Center, Accra, Ghana* 170
Booshan, Bharath / *Acharya Institute of Graduate Studies, Bengaluru, India* 149
Booshan, Shabista / *ISBR Business School, Bengaluru, India* 149
Cevher, Muhammed Fatih / *Munzur University, Turkey* 239
Chavadi, Chandan A. / *Presidency Business School, Presidency College, Bengaluru, India* 149
Chen, Yitong / *The University of Hong Kong, Hong Kong* 68
Chiu, Dickson K. W. / *The University of Hong Kong, Hong Kong* 68
Coffie, Isaac Sewornu / *Accra Technical University, Ghana* 129
Dalakishvili, Rusudan / *Davit Agmashenebeli National Defence Academy of Georgia, Georgia* .. 372
Darchia, Samson / *Georgian Technical University, Georgia* 189
Delgado, Catarina / *School of Economics and Management, University of Porto, Portugal* 41
Djakeli, Kakhaber / *International Black Sea University, Georgia* 271
Efremovski, Ivan Petre / *International Slavic University, Sveti Nikole, North Macedonia* 112
Ferri, Maria Antonella / *Universitas Mercatorum, Italy* 1
Gabrah, Antoinette Yaa Benewaa / *Academic City University College, Accra, Ghana* 170
Gigauri, Iza / *St. Andrew the First-Called Georgian University, Georgia* 1, 18
Grzymala, Zbigniew / *SGH Warsaw School of Economics, Poland* 288
Ionescu, Razvan / *School of Advanced Studies of the Romanian Academy, Bucharest, Romania* 18
Janjua, Laeeq Razzak / *WSB Merito University in Wroclaw, Poland* 255
Jganjgava, Kristina / *Ivane Javakhishvili Tbilisi State University, Georgia* 344
Malik, Firdous Ahmad / *National Institute of Public finance and Policy, India* 255
Marecki, Łukasz Jacek / *SGH Warsaw School of Economics, Poland* 326
Mızrak, Filiz / *Istanbul Medipol University, Turkey* 239
Mushkudiani, Zurab / *Guram Tavartkiladze Tbilisi Teaching University, Georgia* 218
Ocloo, Elikem Chosniel / *Accra Technical University, Ghana* 129
Padmapriya, S. / *CHRIST University (Deemed), Bengaluru, India* 149
Palazzo, Maria / *University of Salerno, Italy* 1
Pires, Paulo Botelho / *CEOS, Polytechnic of Porto, Portugal* 41
Pol, Naveen / *ISBR Business School, Bengaluru, India* 149

Popescu, Catalin / *Petroleum-Gas University of Ploiesti, Romania*	18
Raja, Maryum Sajid / *Southwest-Jiaotong University, China*	255
Razzak, Azeem / *Technical University of Munich, Germany*	255
Rodrigues, Ana Catarina / *School of Economics and Management, University of Porto, Portugal*	41
Rukhadze, Tamta / *Georgian Technical University, Georgia*	189
Sanli, Orhan / *Aydin Adnan Menderes University, Turkey*	255
Santos, José Duarte / *CEOS, ISCAP, Polytechnic of Porto, Portugal*	41
Shilpa, R. / *Garden City University, Bengaluru, India*	149
Stefanova, Dimitrina Petrova / *South-West University "Neofit Rilski", Blagoevgrad, Bulgaria*	112
Supramaniam, Gopalakrishnan / *Acharya Institute of Graduate Studies, Bengaluru, India*	149
Surmanidze, Natia / *The University of Georgia, Georgia*	218
Tabagari, Khatuna / *Guram Tavartkiladze Tbilisi Teaching University, Georgia*	218
Tchanturia, Nino / *Guram Tavartkiladze Tbilisi Teaching University, Georgia*	372
Tevdoradze, Medea / *Georgian Technical University, Georgia*	189
Tevdoradze, Sopiko / *Guram Tavartkiladze Tbilisi Teaching University, Georgia*	218
Thangam, Dhanabalan / *Presidency Business School, Presidency College, Bengaluru, India*	149
Thirupathi, M. / *CHRIST University (Deemed), Bengaluru, India*	149
Tskhadadze, Keti / *The University of Georgia, Georgia*	218
Ullah, A. S. M. Anam / *University of Wollongong, Australia*	303
Urbancová, Hana / *University of Economics and Management, Czech Republic*	92
Vasilev, Valentin Penchev / *Higher School of Security and Economics, Plovdiv, Bulgaria*	112
Vrabcová, Pavla / *Technical University of Liberec, Czech Republic*	92
Wójcik-Czerniawska, Agnieszka Jadwiga / *SGH Warsaw School of Economics, Poland*	355

Table of Contents

Preface xix

Section 1
Sustainable Marketing for the Sustainable Development Goals

Chapter 1
Intelligent Packaging: A Strategy for Boosting Sustainable Marketing and Contributing to the
Sustainable Development Goals 1
    Maria Palazzo, University of Salerno, Italy
    Iza Gigauri, St. Andrew the First-Called Georgian University, Georgia
    Maria Antonella Ferri, Universitas Mercatorum, Italy

Chapter 2
The Past, Present, and Future of Sustainable Marketing 18
    Catalin Popescu, Petroleum-Gas University of Ploiesti, Romania
    Razvan Ionescu, School of Advanced Studies of the Romanian Academy, Bucharest, Romania
    Iza Gigauri, St. Andrew the First-Called Georgian University, Georgia

Chapter 3
Green Cosmetics: Determinants of Purchase Intention 41
    Ana Catarina Rodrigues, School of Economics and Management, University of Porto,
        Portugal
    Paulo Botelho Pires, CEOS, Polytechnic of Porto, Portugal
    Catarina Delgado, School of Economics and Management, University of Porto, Portugal
    José Duarte Santos, CEOS, ISCAP, Polytechnic of Porto, Portugal

Chapter 4
Digital Marketing and Service Strategies for Sustainable Development of Visual Culture: A Case
Study of M+ Museum in Hong Kong 68
    Yitong Chen, The University of Hong Kong, Hong Kong
    Dickson K. W. Chiu, The University of Hong Kong, Hong Kong

Chapter 5
Setting a Sustainable Human Resource Strategy in the Context of Sustainable Business and
Marketing Principles 92
    Pavla Vrabcová, Technical University of Liberec, Czech Republic
    Hana Urbancová, University of Economics and Management, Czech Republic

Chapter 6
Re-Innovative Organizational Design: Sustainable Branding and Effective Communication – Applied Models in a World With New Borders/Without Borders 112
 Dimitrina Petrova Stefanova, South-West University "Neofit Rilski", Blagoevgrad, Bulgaria
 Valentin Penchev Vasilev, Higher School of Security and Economics, Plovdiv, Bulgaria
 Ivan Petre Efremovski, International Slavic University, Sveti Nikole, North Macedonia

Section 2
Marketing and Digitalization for Achieving Sustainability

Chapter 7
Social Media Communication and Sustainability Perception in Business: The Moderating Role of Social Media Influencers.. 129
 George Kofi Amoako, Ghana Communication Technology University, Accra, Ghana & Durban University of Technology, South Africa
 Isaac Sewornu Coffie, Accra Technical University, Ghana
 Elikem Chosniel Ocloo, Accra Technical University, Ghana

Chapter 8
Importance of Sustainable Marketing Initiatives for Supporting the Sustainable Development Goals 149
 A. Anuradha, Cambridge Institute of Technology, Bengaluru, India
 R. Shilpa, Garden City University, Bengaluru, India
 M. Thirupathi, CHRIST University (Deemed), Bengaluru, India
 S. Padmapriya, CHRIST University (Deemed), Bengaluru, India
 Gopalakrishnan Supramaniam, Acharya Institute of Graduate Studies, Bengaluru, India
 Bharath Booshan, Acharya Institute of Graduate Studies, Bengaluru, India
 Shabista Booshan, ISBR Business School, Bengaluru, India
 Naveen Pol, ISBR Business School, Bengaluru, India
 Chandan A. Chavadi, Presidency Business School, Presidency College, Bengaluru, India
 Dhanabalan Thangam, Presidency Business School, Presidency College, Bengaluru, India

Chapter 9
Digital Marketing and Sustainability Competitive Advantage: A Conceptual Framework 170
 George Kofi Amoako, Ghana Communication Technology University, Accra, Ghana & Durban University of Technology, South Africa
 Gifty Agyeiwah Bonsu, Ghana Revenue Authority in Kaneshie Taxpayer Service Center, Accra, Ghana
 Antoinette Yaa Benewaa Gabrah, Academic City University College, Accra, Ghana
 George Oppong Appiagyei Ampong, Ghana Communication Technology University, Accra, Ghana

Chapter 10
Design of Business Processes for Marketing Activity 189
 Medea Tevdoradze, Georgian Technical University, Georgia
 Samson Darchia, Georgian Technical University, Georgia
 Tamta Rukhadze, Georgian Technical University, Georgia

Section 3
Marketing and Digitalization for Achieving Sustainability: Country and Industry Context

Chapter 11
Digitalization of the Marketing Strategy as SMEs' Sustainable Development Guarantee 218
Natia Surmanidze, The University of Georgia, Georgia
Keti Tskhadadze, The University of Georgia, Georgia
Khatuna Tabagari, Guram Tavartkiladze Tbilisi Teaching University, Georgia
Sopiko Tevdoradze, Guram Tavartkiladze Tbilisi Teaching University, Georgia
Zurab Mushkudiani, Guram Tavartkiladze Tbilisi Teaching University, Georgia

Chapter 12
The Impact of Social Marketing and Corporate Social Responsibility on Energy Savings as a Competitive Strategy 239
Filiz Mızrak, Istanbul Medipol University, Turkey
Muhammed Fatih Cevher, Munzur University, Turkey

Chapter 13
The Threat of Unplanned Urban and Real Estate Expansion to Environmental Sustainability: A Fresh Insight From Pakistan 255
Azeem Razzak, Technical University of Munich, Germany
Orhan Sanli, Aydin Adnan Menderes University, Turkey
Firdous Ahmad Malik, National Institute of Public finance and Policy, India
Maryum Sajid Raja, Southwest-Jiaotong University, China
Laeeq Razzak Janjua, WSB Merito University in Wroclaw, Poland

Chapter 14
Sustainable Healthcare Reforming Model Based on Marketing: Case of Georgia 271
Kakhaber Djakeli, International Black Sea University, Georgia

Chapter 15
Circular Economy as a Sustainable Development Marketing Tool 288
Zbigniew Grzymala, SGH Warsaw School of Economics, Poland

Chapter 16
Unethical Outsourcing and Marketing of International Clothing, Fashion Brands, and Global Supply Chains: A Case Study of Bangladesh's RMG Industry 303
A. S. M. Anam Ullah, University of Wollongong, Australia

Section 4
Green, Digital, and Sustainable Marketing for Sustainable Development

Chapter 17
Green Marketing: Sustainability Is Already a Reality in Marketing 326
Łukasz Jacek Marecki, SGH Warsaw School of Economics, Poland

Chapter 18
Internet Marketing as an Effective Instrument for the Development of Companies in the Era of
Sustainable Marketing 344
 Kristina Jganjgava, Ivane Javakhishvili Tbilisi State University, Georgia

Chapter 19
The Role of Artificial Intelligence in Modern Finance and Sustainable Marketing 355
 Agnieszka Jadwiga Wójcik-Czerniawska, SGH Warsaw School of Economics, Poland

Chapter 20
Why Do We Need Sustainable Digital Marketing? 372
 Nino Tchanturia, Guram Tavartkiladze Tbilisi Teaching University, Georgia
 Rusudan Dalakishvili, Davit Agmashenebeli National Defence Academy of Georgia, Georgia

Compilation of References 387

About the Contributors 445

Index 452

Detailed Table of Contents

Preface xix

Section 1
Sustainable Marketing for the Sustainable Development Goals

Chapter 1
Intelligent Packaging: A Strategy for Boosting Sustainable Marketing and Contributing to the
Sustainable Development Goals 1
    Maria Palazzo, University of Salerno, Italy
    Iza Gigauri, St. Andrew the First-Called Georgian University, Georgia
    Maria Antonella Ferri, Universitas Mercatorum, Italy

Digitalization and sustainable development present a twin transition to the industry 5.0-based new normal. Companies try to achieve sustainability transformation through new business strategies in order to respond to the demand of their stakeholders. For this reason, food companies are striving to apply sustainability principles in product packaging design while considering the complete life cycle of a product. Therefore, intelligent packaging with sensor technologies and extended functions is emerging. It uses digital systems to package food to obtain real-time information on the features of goods during transportation or storage. While controlling the condition of food and the surrounding environment, it informs the manufacturer, retailer, or consumer of the state of the food. Therefore, the demand for intelligent packaging is growing in the food industry. This chapter explores intelligent packaging and defines the current trends in this innovative field.

Chapter 2
The Past, Present, and Future of Sustainable Marketing 18
    Catalin Popescu, Petroleum-Gas University of Ploiesti, Romania
    Razvan Ionescu, School of Advanced Studies of the Romanian Academy, Bucharest, Romania
    Iza Gigauri, St. Andrew the First-Called Georgian University, Georgia

Sustainable Development Goals have to be integrated into every aspect of modern society. Economic agents are transforming accordingly taking into consideration the economic, social, and environmental footprints of their activities. The marketing domain has devoted attention to sustainability issues for a long time. Organizations have applied social marketing, ethical and green marketing, as well as corporate social responsibility in their marketing strategies and programs. Sustainable marketing can center on sustainable communication, sustainable production and consumption, sustainable branding, and the promotion of sustainable behavior. The connection between marketing and sustainability can be contradictory as traditional marketing strategies induce overconsumption. Moreover, enhanced digitalization affects marketing and shapes the tools and strategies marketers are adopting. Digital transformation of marketing is expected to be based on sustainable development.

Chapter 3
Green Cosmetics: Determinants of Purchase Intention 41
    Ana Catarina Rodrigues, School of Economics and Management, University of Porto, Portugal
    Paulo Botelho Pires, CEOS, Polytechnic of Porto, Portugal
    Catarina Delgado, School of Economics and Management, University of Porto, Portugal
    José Duarte Santos, CEOS, ISCAP, Polytechnic of Porto, Portugal

This study examined the determinants of purchase intention of green cosmetics, and eight semi-structured interviews were performed to identify them. The determinants identified were environmental awareness, lifestyle, willingness to pay, ethical issues and social and economic justice, cosmetic quality, concern with health, certification labels, trust in the brand, and advertising. Environmental awareness, lifestyle, willingness to pay, quality issues, ethics, and social and economic justice, as well as quality expectations, health concerns, and product knowledge, are the most significant determinants in the intention to purchase green cosmetics. Determinants such as certification labels, brand trust, and advertising are less significant. The research is relevant for the cosmetics industry and its brands to adapt their strategy and product offering to meet consumers' needs and increase the consumption of green cosmetics and can also serve as a basis for the development of new quantitative studies on the purchase intention of green cosmetics.

Chapter 4
Digital Marketing and Service Strategies for Sustainable Development of Visual Culture: A Case Study of M+ Museum in Hong Kong 68
    Yitong Chen, The University of Hong Kong, Hong Kong
    Dickson K. W. Chiu, The University of Hong Kong, Hong Kong

Sustainability is an increasingly important topic internationally, but scant studies focus on the sustainability strategies of niche art museums, especially in Asia. Therefore, this study explores sustainable development strategies for niche art museums, with the M+ Museum of Visual Arts in Hong Kong as the case. The authors apply the PEST analysis to examine external influences on the sustainability of M+ based on the three pillars of sustainability to reveal the current problems of M+. The findings indicate the main sustainability problems of M+ include limited publicity, overpricing, lack of public cultural literacy, and limited coverage of social activities. Thus, the authors suggest strategies centered on building a multifunctional online community, including expanding online services for members, designing and selling electronic peripherals, developing online visual culture education programs, pushing events regularly, establishing a materials mall, inviting artists into the digital community, and designing a VR collection display.

Chapter 5
Setting a Sustainable Human Resource Strategy in the Context of Sustainable Business and Marketing Principles 92
    Pavla Vrabcová, Technical University of Liberec, Czech Republic
    Hana Urbancová, University of Economics and Management, Czech Republic

Human resources are valuable, including competencies, which are of key importance for achieving strategic targets. This chapter aims to summarize the findings and to expand the awareness of the professional and lay public about the possibilities of setting a sustainable human resource strategy. The chapter is based on the results of quantitative and qualitative research in the Czech Republic (n = 183). The results show that organizations place a permanent emphasis on the most effective involvement of people in work processes and the acceptance of all aspects of their activities. It is the only dignified way to ensure social responsibility and sustainability in a society-wide dimension, and modern trends in strategic human resources management, such as age management and diversity management. The chapter has a practical and theoretical contribution, as recommendations for setting internal processes of human resource management and marketing are presented, and the theory is also supplemented with other factors that influence the setting of human resource strategy.

Chapter 6
Re-Innovative Organizational Design: Sustainable Branding and Effective Communication – Applied Models in a World With New Borders/Without Borders 112
    Dimitrina Petrova Stefanova, South-West University "Neofit Rilski", Blagoevgrad, Bulgaria
    Valentin Penchev Vasilev, Higher School of Security and Economics, Plovdiv, Bulgaria
    Ivan Petre Efremovski, International Slavic University, Sveti Nikole, North Macedonia

Dynamics and crises in the present are inextricably associated with company growth and change management in the context of today. In this way, the question of innovation in management processes has evolved, and we now focus on re-innovative organizational practices that expand on and improve tried-and-true methods. In such a situation, the function of sustainable branding is that effective communications are essential tools for adapting to the climate and chaotic characteristics. Additionally, the long-lasting and unexpected pandemic crisis, a technologically advanced and globally integrated society and economy, and the hybridity of change all have a significant impact on marketing procedures. Although the subject is broad, the research's primary focus is on creating a dialogic, motivated, and productive management style, with new internal communication channels playing a key role as a component of branding.

Section 2
Marketing and Digitalization for Achieving Sustainability

Chapter 7
Social Media Communication and Sustainability Perception in Business: The Moderating Role of Social Media Influencers.. 129
    George Kofi Amoako, Ghana Communication Technology University, Accra, Ghana & Durban University of Technology, South Africa
    Isaac Sewornu Coffie, Accra Technical University, Ghana
    Elikem Chosniel Ocloo, Accra Technical University, Ghana

Achieving the 17 sustainable development goals (SDGs) has become very important in the survival of the human race and the earth's ecosystem. The purpose of this study is to see the effectiveness of social media communication and how it influences consumer behavior perception on environmental sustainability and the role of social media influencers. This chapter is a conceptual manuscript. The researcher used literature from good and reliable databases such as Emerald, Sage, Taylor & Francis, Web of Science, Elsevier, and others. Desk research was adopted and literature covering the relevant constructs in the title and model were reviewed and thoroughly discussed and meanings and implications were synthesized.

Chapter 8
Importance of Sustainable Marketing Initiatives for Supporting the Sustainable Development Goals 149
>	A. Anuradha, Cambridge Institute of Technology, Bengaluru, India
>	R. Shilpa, Garden City University, Bengaluru, India
>	M. Thirupathi, CHRIST University (Deemed), Bengaluru, India
>	S. Padmapriya, CHRIST University (Deemed), Bengaluru, India
>	Gopalakrishnan Supramaniam, Acharya Institute of Graduate Studies, Bengaluru, India
>	Bharath Booshan, Acharya Institute of Graduate Studies, Bengaluru, India
>	Shabista Booshan, ISBR Business School, Bengaluru, India
>	Naveen Pol, ISBR Business School, Bengaluru, India
>	Chandan A. Chavadi, Presidency Business School, Presidency College, Bengaluru, India
>	Dhanabalan Thangam, Presidency Business School, Presidency College, Bengaluru, India

Businesses that engage in sustainable marketing can benefit both the world and their bottom line. Earlier, companies could satisfy many customers by simply providing low pricing and high-quality goods. However, people's concern for the environment and other social concerns have grown, and so has their desire to support groups that share their beliefs. Because they often generate strong market returns and demonstrate durability during economic downturns, many investors want to support businesses that use sustainable business methods. Also, these businesses are more likely to comply with social and environmental laws. Several companies use sustainable marketing to succeed in today's ethical and ecologically sensitive marketplace. Organizations must finance sustainability programs in order to practice sustainable marketing. But, it can also improve employee engagement, promote regulatory compliance, raise revenues, and build brand loyalty.

Chapter 9
Digital Marketing and Sustainability Competitive Advantage: A Conceptual Framework 170
>	George Kofi Amoako, Ghana Communication Technology University, Accra, Ghana & Durban University of Technology, South Africa
>	Gifty Agyeiwah Bonsu, Ghana Revenue Authority in Kaneshie Taxpayer Service Center, Accra, Ghana
>	Antoinette Yaa Benewaa Gabrah, Academic City University College, Accra, Ghana
>	George Oppong Appiagyei Ampong, Ghana Communication Technology University, Accra, Ghana

The usage of digital marketing has significantly changed how firms, businesses, and marketers engage with their buyers. Digital platforms such as Facebook, Google, YouTube, Twitter, Instagram, and many others are utilized in an attempt to offer different kinds of personalized campaigns that companies can use to communicate with their customers. Many companies including retail, manufacturing, wholesale, and several others are exploiting digital marketing as a component of their overall sustainable marketing strategies to attain a competitive edge over their counterparts. Therefore, this research proposes that digital marketing relates to sustainability competitive advantage. The research argues that social media green marketing, ecological marketing orientation, social media corporate social responsibility, cause-related marketing, and digital marketing have a positive relationship with sustainability competitive advantage.

Chapter 10
Design of Business Processes for Marketing Activity 189
    Medea Tevdoradze, Georgian Technical University, Georgia
    Samson Darchia, Georgian Technical University, Georgia
    Tamta Rukhadze, Georgian Technical University, Georgia

As it is known, marketing plays a huge role in the activity of companies, which ensures the company's success in the market. Today the majority of companies have moved to process management, which because of some reason often is not applied to marketing activities and this has a negative impact on it. In order to correct the situation, this chapter serves the issues of design of business processes of marketing activities in the company. It is characterized by a marketing complex (4P model). Also, there are discussed holistic marketing features and marketing strategy issues, there are realized procedures which are necessary for management of marketing activities. But, the peculiarity of marketing activity is that, in addition to ERP-type programs, it is necessary to use a specialized marketing information system, which is due to the abundance and complexity of the models that must be used in the process of marketing evaluations. It is underlined that ERP-type and marketing information system must be used in the complex.

Section 3
Marketing and Digitalization for Achieving Sustainability: Country and Industry Context

Chapter 11
Digitalization of the Marketing Strategy as SMEs' Sustainable Development Guarantee 218
    Natia Surmanidze, The University of Georgia, Georgia
    Keti Tskhadadze, The University of Georgia, Georgia
    Khatuna Tabagari, Guram Tavartkiladze Tbilisi Teaching University, Georgia
    Sopiko Tevdoradze, Guram Tavartkiladze Tbilisi Teaching University, Georgia
    Zurab Mushkudiani, Guram Tavartkiladze Tbilisi Teaching University, Georgia

The chapter reviews and analyzes in depth the role and importance of marketing digitalization strategies in small companies, using the example of Georgian handmade accessories (bag manufacturer), where the problematic aspects of access to finance are considered vital for developing countries' entrepreneurship. Qualitative research was conducted on 90 respondents, the results of which and the comparative analysis of desk research confirmed the hypothesis that digital marketing strategy is a significant factor for SMEs to reach sustainable development. Besides, if the strategy is long-term, the company gets a guarantee to grow its size and obtain high competitiveness. The research solved the most critical problem, how small companies can implement marketing activities cheaply and qualitatively, and effectively, forming a brand and a loyal customer.

Chapter 12
The Impact of Social Marketing and Corporate Social Responsibility on Energy Savings as a Competitive Strategy 239
    Filiz Mızrak, Istanbul Medipol University, Turkey
    Muhammed Fatih Cevher, Munzur University, Turkey

In today's globalizing world, corporate social responsibility has become a necessity for businesses. The corporate social responsibility approach, which is based on the principles of giving back to the society what it has taken from the society and observing the benefit of the society in the activities of the enterprise, has an important place in terms of promoting the products and services they produce in the market under the best conditions and strengthening the brand image. From this point of view, corporate social responsibility is seen as a valid practice to make a difference. However, businesses mostly carry out social marketing activities for this purpose. Thus, while trying to find solutions to social problems, they can obtain a competitive strategy. In this context, the aim of the study is to show that the energy crisis, which is one of the most serious problems of today, can be solved by raising awareness in consumers with corporate social response activities and social marketing methods.

Chapter 13
The Threat of Unplanned Urban and Real Estate Expansion to Environmental Sustainability: A Fresh Insight From Pakistan 255
    Azeem Razzak, Technical University of Munich, Germany
    Orhan Sanli, Aydin Adnan Menderes University, Turkey
    Firdous Ahmad Malik, National Institute of Public finance and Policy, India
    Maryum Sajid Raja, Southwest-Jiaotong University, China
    Laeeq Razzak Janjua, WSB Merito University in Wroclaw, Poland

Urbanization is a complex and multifaceted process that positively and negatively impacts society and the environment. To promote sustainable and inclusive urban development, it is essential to adopt a holistic and interdisciplinary approach that takes into account social, economic, and environmental factors, as well as the needs and perspectives of local communities and stakeholders. By adopting sustainable real estate practices, Pakistan can create a more sustainable and prosperous future for all its citizens. Likewise, real estate firms that aim to promote environmental, social, and economic sustainability in their operations should consider adopting a sustainable marketing approach. Real estate organizations may contribute to a more sustainable future while also benefiting their business by integrating sustainable practices into all facets of their operations and promoting sustainability to their clients and stakeholders. Sustainable marketing gives real estate companies a competitive edge and long-term profitability in addition to helping to safeguard the environment and society.

Chapter 14
Sustainable Healthcare Reforming Model Based on Marketing: Case of Georgia 271
    Kakhaber Djakeli, International Black Sea University, Georgia

Discourse about sustainable marketing is not finished. The theme is very current, and it involves either business or government responsibility of sustainability, green marketing, and sustainable lifestyle. Sustainability marketing in healthcare reforming is oriented to societal goals and special type of approaches to society as a whole. The healthcare reforming must be totally devoted to people, but environmental and societal scanning is the business of societal marketing. What can be the special type of advantage of health marketing and reform marketing? If health reformers try to meet present goals of society and at the same time consider the environmental, green policies, societal problems, and meet the goals of next generation, such health reforming, they can be called sustainable health reforms.

Chapter 15
Circular Economy as a Sustainable Development Marketing Tool 288
Zbigniew Grzymala, SGH Warsaw School of Economics, Poland

The circular economy (also known as the circular economy and the circular economy) is one of the elements of the concept of sustainable development. Currently, it is most commonly described as an economy whose goal is to constantly maintain the highest value and utility of products, components, and materials in separate biological and technical cycles, and its task is ultimately to decouple economic development from the consumption of scarce resources. As humanity, we behave as if we have forgotten that we are part of the natural environment. The essence of assessing our progress has become the size of broadly understood consumption, which also pollutes our natural environment. In a sense, we have stopped observing nature, which can come to balance when it is out of balance. This chapter explores the circular economy as a sustainable development marketing tool.

Chapter 16
Unethical Outsourcing and Marketing of International Clothing, Fashion Brands, and Global Supply Chains: A Case Study of Bangladesh's RMG Industry 303
A. S. M. Anam Ullah, University of Wollongong, Australia

The exploitation of workers in global supply chains (GSCs) has been strengthened over the past 40 years, mainly since the emergence of globalization and neoliberalism. A primary ethical concern of outsourcing and marketing is labour exploitation in developing countries. In Bangladesh's RMG industry, workers are often paid low wages and forced to work long hours in unsafe conditions. Many international clothing brands have been criticized for outsourcing their production to factories that violate labor rights. As a result, unethical outsourcing and marketing of the global supply chains from Bangladesh's RMG industry has left millions of RMG workers in dire straits. Furthermore, this chapter focuses on theoretical interpretations and finds that globalization and neoliberalism exposed modern slavery in the global supply chain networks. Hence, this chapter suggests that international clothing and fashion brands must ethically outsource from a country like Bangladesh.

Section 4
Green, Digital, and Sustainable Marketing for Sustainable Development

Chapter 17
Green Marketing: Sustainability Is Already a Reality in Marketing 326
Łukasz Jacek Marecki, SGH Warsaw School of Economics, Poland

The marketing industry is struggling. The new consumers opt for green marketing products and strategies, more aware of the environment. After having grown 100% in the first quarter compared to the same period of the previous year, orders decreased significantly from March 2020 in large markets such as Spain, Germany, Italy, France, and EEUDE. It was a drop that affected the promotional marketing industry worldwide as a result of the coronavirus, which is why many companies are betting on green marketing. In the particular case of Sprout World, a pioneering company in sustainable merchandising with its plantable pencils, for example, the demand for writing products simply disappeared. And with this, it was experienced that the promotional products market was stagnating in the last year. Something that was also accompanied by a change of mentality in the consumer towards measures and products with a necessary environmental touch. Financial troubles are frequently a result of disasters, but businesses must carefully decide where to make savings.

Chapter 18
Internet Marketing as an Effective Instrument for the Development of Companies in the Era of
Sustainable Marketing... 344
 Kristina Jganjgava, Ivane Javakhishvili Tbilisi State University, Georgia

This chapter presents the results of studying the possibilities of using internet marketing technologies in the activities of modern companies focused primarily on the use of IT technologies and identifying related problems. The constituent elements of marketing activities performed using internet technologies are characterized, and the possibilities for the development of modern business structures focused mainly on digital marketing are described. The role of internet marketing in the promotion of goods and services by companies on the market is revealed, its effectiveness is assessed, and the possibilities for increasing the marketing competence of enterprises in the implementation of internet technologies are outlined.

Chapter 19
The Role of Artificial Intelligence in Modern Finance and Sustainable Marketing 355
 Agnieszka Jadwiga Wójcik-Czerniawska, SGH Warsaw School of Economics, Poland

Artificial intelligence (AI) is reshaping marketing and is becoming a capable assistant supporting many facets of the industry. Artificial intelligence plays a vital role in modern finance and sustainable marketing. AI can be utilized to improve sustainability and enhance financial services. The chapter begins with the assertion that contemporary finance and market viability are crucial components of every economy. The most recent disruptive technology is artificial intelligence (AI), which has the greatest potential to change marketing. International practitioners are trying to recognize the best AI results for their marketing functions. To build a more secure business and economic environment and lower human mistakes, the chapter demonstrates how artificial intelligence may combine contemporary finance and market sustainability with tech skills.

Chapter 20
Why Do We Need Sustainable Digital Marketing? 372
 Nino Tchanturia, Guram Tavartkiladze Tbilisi Teaching University, Georgia
 Rusudan Dalakishvili, Davit Agmashenebeli National Defence Academy of Georgia, Georgia

The conventional approach to business is not eco-friendly, and as the issue of climate change intensifies, consumers are becoming increasingly aware of the environmental impact of their preferred companies. Therefore, businesses need to evaluate their impact on the environment. Consumers are becoming more informed about how their purchases affect the environment and more selective about which companies they buy from. According to a survey by IBM, 57% of respondents are willing to alter their buying habits to decrease environmental impact. People want to contribute to ecological preservation, and one way to do so is by using their purchasing power. As a company, it is crucial to provide customers with the opportunity to support environmental sustainability by purchasing your products. This is where sustainable marketing can be beneficial.

Compilation of References 387

About the Contributors 445

Index 452

Preface

The prominent idea of Sustainable Development has influenced almost all disciplines, changing our understanding and behavior towards sustainability. In this respect, Marketing has been also transforming from the sustainability point of view as emerging social and ecological problems caused by exponential growth require sustainable solutions and joint efforts. Sustainable marketing intends to integrate ecological, social, and ethical concerns while creating value. Consumers along with other stakeholders expect that brands will contribute to Sustainable Development Goals. Consequently, companies need to redesign their marketing initiatives to create, promote, and deliver values that are in line with sustainability.

Moreover, Digitalization is transforming the future of Marketing and influencing sustainable marketing concepts. The constantly changing landscape in the past decades and the development of advanced technologies create demand for up-to-date research. The current sustainable marketing issues are required to be studied from different angles and various standpoints in order for scholars and professionals to stay informed.

Therefore, this book responds to the need for analyzing and evaluating the concept of sustainable marketing in the light of digitalization. In this regard, the book explores sustainable marketing from diverse contexts and intends to bridge marketing, sustainability, and digitalization.

This book provides valuable knowledge by covering the important components and aspects of Sustainable Marketing. It illuminates current developments in the insight of Sustainable Marketing, and the new trends and tendencies concerning the concept in theory and practice. While discussing significant concerns, it evaluates the advantages, progress, and contribution of sustainable marketing to sustainable development goals. Accordingly, this book integrates theoretical and practical frameworks, coupling conceptual views with applied examples providing case studies from particular countries including conducted empirical study results.

This book covers many academic topics including sustainable marketing, the role of marketing in the implementation of sustainable development goals, sustainable production and consumption, smart intelligent packaging for sustainability, corporate social responsibility, environmental sustainability, marketing ethics, green marketing, social marketing, sustainable branding, the impact of digitalization and artificial intelligence on sustainable marketing, sustainable human resources, and sustainable social media communications.

The book is structured into four main sections consisting of twenty chapters. The chapters were selected after a rigorous peer-review process. In addition, the book deliberately represents diverse regions in the world allowing readers insights into country-specific cases, examples, and nuances.

A brief description of each chapter follows.

Chapter 1, "Intelligent Packaging: A Strategy for Boosting Sustainable Marketing and Contributing to Sustainable Development Goals," discusses innovative solutions in packaging to extend the shelf-life of a product and decrease waste in order to contribute to sustainability. For this reason, the chapter focuses on the connection between packaging, sustainable development goals, and sustainable marketing strategy. To achieve its aims, the chapter first provides a conceptual background of packaging and identifies emerging trends in packaging, and then, it addresses the contribution of intelligent and sustainable packaging for sustainable development goals.

Chapter 2, "The Past, Present, and Future of Sustainable Marketing," further introduces the notion and expansion of sustainable marketing. It reviews the literature on sustainable marketing and follows the path of the development of the concept from the past to current trends while revealing future tendencies in this area. The chapter covers social, green, and ethical marketing, CSR, and analyzes Sustainable versus Sustainability marketing. It also examines the impact of technologies, such as virtual reality, virtual influencers, or digital marketing, on sustainable marketing.

Chapter 3, "Green Cosmetics: Determinants of Purchase Intention," comprehensively reviews the relevant literature and investigates sustainable production and consumption of cosmetics. The authors provide answers to the main research questions of what green cosmetics are, how consumers differentiate them, and what features they prefer in green cosmetics. The chapter is based on the qualitative interview method, the results of which are presented and academically discussed.

Chapter 4, "Digital Marketing and Service Strategies for Sustainable Development of Visual Culture: A Case Study of M+ Museum in Hong Kong," demonstrates digital marketing in the context of sustainable development through an in-depth case study to explore the sustainable development strategies for a niche art museum. The authors have established links between museum, digitalization, and sustainability and used PEST analysis for examining external impacts on the sustainability. The chapter identifies the opportunities and constraints of the external environment for niche museums' sustainability and discusses the role of digital technologies in museums to reach sustainability goals. Moreover, the authors elaborate strategies on how niche museums can contribute to sustainability based on the case study results of the M+ museum.

Chapter 5, "Setting a Sustainable Human Resource Strategy in the Context of Sustainable Business and Marketing Principles," presents the empirical study results based on quantitative and qualitative research methods in the Czech Republic. The authors have applied primary data to investigate sustainable human resource strategy, corporate responsibility, marketing, and sustainability for effective management in sustainable business organizations.

Chapter 6, "Re-Innovative Organizational Design: Sustainable Branding and Effective Communication – Applied Models in a World With New Borders/Without Borders," connects Human Resource Management and Public Relations to discuss sustainable employer branding. The authors provide an example of how HRM and PR can collaborate on the corporate communication plan and propose a "Waterfall" model for sustainable workplace branding.

Chapter 7, "Social Media Communication and Sustainability Perception in Business: The Moderating Role of Influencers," addresses the influence of social media on consumer behavior regarding environmental sustainability. It exhibits that consumers' perceptions and buying behavior can be shaped towards more environmental sustainability by the communication efforts of organizations. The chapter considers sustainability development in light of social media communication and proposes a conceptual framework while developing research propositions. The authors also mention the potential challenges

Preface

of social media influencers and discuss the sustainability perception of companies and consumers' perception of sustainability.

Chapter 8, "Importance of Sustainable Marketing Initiatives for Supporting Sustainable Development Goals," considers sustainable marketing practices to establish the significance and benefits of sustainable marketing. In addition, the authors describe strategies for the successful implementation of the concept in practice. The chapter is based on exploratory research methods with a special emphasis on examples and cases from worldwide reality.

Chapter 9, "Digital Marketing and Sustainability Competitive Advantage: A Conceptual Framework," seeks to contribute to the current knowledge of the effects of digital marketing and sustainable marketing on the competitiveness of companies. The authors comprehensively examine sustainable marketing activities, digital marketing, green and ecological marketing communication, CSR, and cause-related marketing communication as sources of sustainable competitive advantage and propose a conceptual model.

Chapter 10, "Design of Business Processes for Marketing Activity," proposes the development and modeling of the marketing business process. The chapter examines the structure of the marketing information system responsible for the processing of information for marketing. With the number of figures and diagrams, the authors explain business processes in marketing activities in a practical way. By using the special software tool, simulation modeling is presented enabling various scenarios and different initial parameter values for improving decision-making considering sustainable marketing requirements.

Chapter 11, "Digitalization of the Marketing Strategy as SMEs' Sustainable Development Guarantee," based on the qualitative research results emphasizes the significance of sustainable marketing strategies for small and medium companies. Specifically, through in-depth interviews conducted with the representatives of SMEs in Georgia, the authors analyze digitalization and digital marketing strategies and formulate recommendations for the implementation of sustainable marketing strategies.

Chapter 12, "The Impact of Social Marketing and Corporate Social Responsibility on Energy Savings as a Competitive Strategy," attempts to help resolve the energy crisis by raising awareness of consumers with CSR and social marketing activities. The chapter highlights that by engaging in such actions, especially big companies can, in turn, gain a competitive advantage. Furthermore, the authors overview the relationship between CSR, marketing, and social marketing and connection them to the energy sector.

Chapter 13, "The Threat of Unplanned Urban and Real Estate Expansion to Environmental Sustainability: A Fresh Insight From Pakistan," discusses urbanization issues in Pakistan from the sustainable marketing point of view. It explores sustainable marketing in real estate and suggests initiatives aiming to reduce the negative effects of urbanization while improving sustainability in the country. The chapter accentuates the power of sustainable marketing to inspire people towards sustainable behavior in urban areas.

Chapter 14, "Sustainable Healthcare Reforming Model Based on Marketing: Case of Georgia," reviews three waves of health reforms in the country from the sustainability and marketing perspective. Based on the marketing research findings using the Delphi method, the author describes the current state of the healthcare system and identifies the directions of the next reforms in accordance with the sustainable development goals considering sustainable marketing principles. In this regard, the chapter also offers recommendations.

Chapter 15, "Circular Economy as a Sustainable Development Marketing Tool," analyzes the concept of circular economy and illustrates valuable practical examples and case studies from the Polish organization.

Chapter 16, "Unethical Outsourcing and Marketing of International Clothing, Fashion Brands, and Global Supply Chains: A Case Study of Bangladesh's RMG Industry," investigates a critical issue of the Bangladesh garment sector from the ethical marketing perspective. RMG industry giving work to six million people has caused ethical concerns internationally. The chapter is based on qualitative semi-structured interviews and highlights the importance of ethical outsourcing. As a result, recommendations are made for fashion brands, employers, and the government in Bangladesh.

Chapter 17, "Green Marketing: Sustainability Is Already a Reality in Marketing," demonstrates the benefits of green marketing for brands and the communication advantages for organizations. It presents case studies and examples of successful green marketing initiatives and their positive influence on business performance. The chapter concludes with actionable insights and recommendations to implement green marketing and promote sustainability.

Chapter 18, "Internet Marketing as an Effective Instrument for the Development of Companies in the Era of Sustainable Marketing," once again indicates the effectiveness of the Internet marketing tools in sustainable marketing communication and shows the usage of artificial intelligence in digital marketing. Furthermore, the chapter includes practical examples from different countries.

Chapter 19, "The Role of Artificial Intelligence in Modern Finance and Sustainable Marketing," illustrates the potential of artificial intelligence in finance and market sustainability in order to decrease errors and achieve secure economic development. The chapter gives suggestions regarding the role of artificial intelligence in digital marketing and sustainable marketing.

Chapter 20, "Why Do We Need Sustainable Digital Marketing?" brings sustainable digital marketing into focus and investigates the sustainable digital marketing mix. The chapter summarizes the evolution of sustainable marketing and the advantages of its realization for companies while indicating obstacles as well.

Thus, this book also explores the concept of sustainable marketing in today's context of the digital age and explains its boundaries, benefits, challenges, and opportunities. This book will contribute to marketing, sustainability, and digitalization while taking into consideration the exponential growth on the planet that has limits. The book not only displays relevant theories, concepts, viewpoints, and practices of sustainable marketing but also proposes future research avenues, recommendations, and practical solutions.

The book can provide insight into the development of sustainable marketing and can serve as a source to comprehend interrelated conceptions of marketing, sustainability, and digitalization. By exploring this interrelationship, the book contributes to bridging theory and practice. Covering key topics, this book generates outputs for marketers, managers, business owners, industry professionals, researchers, academicians, instructors, and students in developed and developing countries as well as it can be considered a significant resource book for libraries and policymakers.

Iza Gigauri
St. Andrew the First-Called Georgian University, Georgia

Maria Palazzo
Universitas Mercatorum, Italy

Maria Antonella Ferri
Universitas Mercatorum, Italy

Section 1
Sustainable Marketing for the Sustainable Development Goals

Chapter 1
Intelligent Packaging:
A Strategy for Boosting Sustainable Marketing and Contributing to the Sustainable Development Goals

Maria Palazzo
University of Salerno, Italy

Iza Gigauri
https://orcid.org/0000-0001-6394-6416
St. Andrew the First-Called Georgian University, Georgia

Maria Antonella Ferri
Universitas Mercatorum, Italy

ABSTRACT

Digitalization and sustainable development present a twin transition to the industry 5.0-based new normal. Companies try to achieve sustainability transformation through new business strategies in order to respond to the demand of their stakeholders. For this reason, food companies are striving to apply sustainability principles in product packaging design while considering the complete life cycle of a product. Therefore, intelligent packaging with sensor technologies and extended functions is emerging. It uses digital systems to package food to obtain real-time information on the features of goods during transportation or storage. While controlling the condition of food and the surrounding environment, it informs the manufacturer, retailer, or consumer of the state of the food. Therefore, the demand for intelligent packaging is growing in the food industry. This chapter explores intelligent packaging and defines the current trends in this innovative field.

1. INTRODUCTION

The focus of the modern age is shifted towards the interaction between humans and manufacturing machines to urge economic and social welfare while contributing to sustainable development goals. Unprecedented

DOI: 10.4018/978-1-6684-8681-8.ch001

digitalization accelerates sustainable production and consumption as well as a novel perception of food products. Intelligent packaging not only enables tracing and monitoring the quality and safety of a product but also increases the shelf-life of a food product. Advancing technologies require new business strategies and hence, cutting-edge and expert insight to research this transition. Moreover, volatile, uncertain, complex, and ambiguous (VUCA) environment implies companies to center on consumers' needs and wants to recognize their power for their business models as customer relationship has become essential.

Intelligent packaging with sensor technologies includes extended functions and uses digital systems to package food, cosmetics, medicaments, and other kinds of products. It is also adopted by brands in healthcare, logistics, transport, consumer electronics, and home care industries. Intelligent packaging provides information on the product quality during shipping and storage. It monitors the state of food and the surrounding environment and notifies the producer, retailer, or consumer of the condition of the food. Such smart, and interactive packaging enables tracing, and monitoring functions to ensure the quality and safety of a product, and hence, can help increase the expiration date of foodstuffs. Therefore, the demand for intelligent packaging is growing in the food segment.

In accordance with the changes in consumption, lifestyle, and consumer preferences (Palazzo et al., 2022), packaging strategy should respond to consumers' needs for safe and quality of food products as well as recyclable or environmental-friendly packaging. Thus, food packaging is evolving by applying new technologies to improve the quality of the product, prolong shelf-life, reduce waste and beneficially impact the environment.

Intelligent packaging is an innovative field of research. The era of globalization and digitalization has given rise to innovative solutions in a wide range of domains. As a result, Intelligent packaging is offering commercial benefits and further expansion. The sales of electronic packaging are expected to increase to USD 1.45 billion by 2023 (Akhzar, 2021). The intelligent packaging market is anticipated to be worth USD 26.8 billion by 2028 (Globe Newswire, 2022).

In addition, globalization of the food industry has created logistical challenges to distribute food from manufacturers to retailers to end users while preserving its quality and safety. The packaging material must prevent foods from microbial contamination and decrease the risks of food-related illness. Consequently, innovative packaging devices should monitor the food quality and environment around the product to enhance the safety and shelf-life of a product. Intelligent packaging allows companies receive actual information about the product without taking the samples to the laboratory for a costly and time-consuming analysis. Such packaging facilitates the transportation of frozen food not only between countries but also to remote areas by monitoring the conditions of food without touching the product.

Furthermore, a low-touch economy has emerged as a consequence of the Covid-19 pandemic that accelerated digital transformation (Gigauri, 2021a). Brands need to adjust the altered behavior of keeping physical distance, and deliver safe and sustainable products. In this regard, digitalization, seen as a solution to many of the grand challenges, is adopted also by the food industry to develop innovative packaging. New technologies such as RFID, EAS, QR codes, Data loggers, and other emerging technologies give rise to extending functions of intelligent packaging.

2. LINKING PACKAGING, SUSTAINABLE DEVELOPMENT GOALS AND SUSTAINABLE MARKETING STRATEGY

Previous studies found that consumers waste more food compared with other subjects in the value chain (Müller & Schmid, 2019). Preserving food quality and minimizing waste are among global sustainable aims to enhance the standards of living worldwide (SDG 2). In addition, the demand for quality food is growing. Thus, innovative solutions to packaging can facilitate solving those issues (Kuswandi et al., 2011; Palazzo et al., 2023) by combining digitalization, Sustainable Development Goals and Sustainable Marketing Strategy.

To understand the new trends that are developing in the world of packaging (Prendergast & Pitt, 1996), it may be helpful to review the historical characteristics of packaging itself, analyzed by various authors especially in the field of marketing, logistics and communication (Rundh, 2013). In fact, packaging is used for four complementary functions (Yam et al., 2005):

1. protective - i.e., safeguarding the product from environmental risks and deterioration;
2. disclosure - i.e., providing the consumer with data of various kinds (e.g. nutritional values; origin of the goods; methods of use of the goods, information on the brand and the manufacturing company, etc.);
3. instructive - i.e., suggesting the simplest and/or best use;
4. practicality - i.e., providing differentiated packages both in terms of size and design (Mohebbi, 2014).

These packaging functions are usually summarized in the traditional "contain–protect–communicate–facilitate–convenience" model which briefly summarizes its characteristics (Lydekaityte & Tambo, 2020).

Traditional packaging, as considered in the model, has greatly influenced the development of distribution systems, especially in the food sector. However, the current evolutionary dynamics - social and economic - induce us to reflect more deeply on further and more consonant prerogatives that affect the sphere of protection and health; this market expectation is strengthened by increasingly stringent international and global regulatory requirements (Mumani & Stone, 2018; Palazzo et al., 2023).

The market's search for food products with fewer preservatives, capable of responding to more stringent regulatory requirements, consistent with the trends imposed by globalization and the threats of food bioterrorism have undoubtedly increased the added value of packaging (Priyanka & Parag, 2013).

It is therefore important to understand how the basic-traditional functions of a mature technical solution - such as that of packaging - can be enhanced to be dynamically in line with the new expectations/constraints imposed by the market, companies and relevant stakeholders. Probably to achieve this goal, there is a need to rethink and, perhaps, look towards a new paradigmatic horizon that need to include the Sustainable Development Goals.

For reaching its objectives, the chapter offers an overview of the current context that frames the "object-packaging" in the context of intelligent, active, interactive and smart packaging, reflecting on "how much" and "how" this assumption has raised the customers' expectations. Furthermore, the work proposes some insights on the use of packaging in line with technological and technical innovation. Finally, a research agenda is proposed, as a path for desirable best practice.

3. CONCEPTUAL BACKGROUND: AN EXCURSUS ON PACKAGING

Packaging, considered from a traditional perspective, has always performed a practical function of protecting products throughout the value creation chain, until the good is chosen by the end-user (Mason, 1958).

From a theoretical point of view, many authors have analyzed the functions performed by packaging (Short & Stovell, 1966; Palazzo et al., 2023). For example, considering conventional packaging, several scholars describe it as a simple container that not only encloses and protects the goods, but also classifies the product and simplifies its marketing, making it available to the final customer (Poyatos-Racionero et al., 2018). Furthermore, other researchers, broadening this description, state that the traditional role of packaging is not only to contain and protect, but also to 'show' the product on the shelf, at the point of sale (Butler, 2013; Palazzo et al., 2023). All the other functionalities fall, in a more general way, among the communication functions performed by the packaging. Therefore, the functions of packaging most frequently cited by the authors involve (i) protection, (ii) communication, (iii) convenience and (iv) containment of the product (Yam et al., 2005).

Starting from this perspective, several scholars also underline that packaging performs marketing tasks such as: drawing attention to the good, emphasizing the image of the product and helping customers make a decision regarding the purchase (Yam et al., 2005; Palazzo et al., 2023).

Especially whit traditional packaging, the purpose of this type of packaging is mainly linked to marketing. In fact, many purchase processes are influenced by the specific store environment, and it has been established that about 2/3 of purchases in supermarkets are decided in-store (Yam et al., 2005). Therefore, packaging becomes a critical success factor in guiding the consumers (Mohebbi, 2014).

This is even more true as, with the continuous changes taking place both in the field of study related to customers' behavior and in the supply chain area, many factors must be taken into consideration when it comes to considering the new role played by packaging (Rundh, 2013). For example, the reduction in the number of births and the tendency of young people to live in small households are driving companies to produce single packs and to prefer small packs instead of large family-sized packs. Based on these factors, scholars have identified some trends that are strongly changing the characteristics of packaging, such as: (i) the growing demand for transparency (to increase product visibility), (ii) the growing demand for packaging that is easier to open and close, and/or ready to use (e.g. oven or microwave packaging, etc.), (iii) the increased demand for packaging created with recycled and/or recyclable materials (Piergiovanni & Limbo, 2010). Designers and managers in general must take into account the fact that culture, usage and consumption habits strongly condition the way in which consumers, and the relevant stakeholders, see specific details of the packaging and whether or not they appreciate the way it is developed (Draskovic, 2007).

Therefore, from this need to make packaging evolve in compliance with the new trends in progress, new ways of understanding not only packaging, but also its definition and functions have arisen (Gerard & Leyland, 1996; Palazzo et al., 2023).

4. EMERGING TREND IN PACKAGING

Over the past years, the popularity of packaging, characterized by incremental functionality, has represented a paradigm shift in the packaging industry (Brockgreitens & Abbas, 2016). In fact, the main attribute of protection recognized to packaging has shifted from a typically 'passive' analysis perspective to an unquestionably 'active' one involving different players in the value creation chain (Ajwani-Ramchandani et al., 2021).

Traditionally, packaging materials were considered "passive", in the sense that they were seen only as a mere "container", useful for protecting the product from external agents, oxygen and humidity. Recently, new materials and new technologies have ensured "active" protection for the product, consistently responding to the expectations/requests of many stakeholders with whom the company interacts (Gobbo & Olsson, 2010): the new packaging concept has a systemic meaning in which the components, the packaging and the external environment are synergistically cohesive both in guaranteeing conservation, and in satisfying the ever greater information-communication purposes (Kerry & Butler, 2008; Palazzo et al., 2023).

In fact, active packaging is appropriately described as a "packaging system" able of adapting 'actively' according to the fashions-rules-constraints descending from the four defined functions: protective, informative, instructive and practical (Lydekaityte & Tambo, 2020). In fact, all the technologies present within the new generation packaging imply a physical/biological action, capable of influencing the connections within the packaging system between packaging/product/environment (Lebelo et al., 2021). Intelligent packaging can, for example, use technologies capable of absorbing vapors from the external environment or to release gases: in this way, the packaging creates a favorable habitat for the product and, therefore, prolongs its conservation and integrity time. Great attention, in this area, has been paid to the creation of antimicrobial and antioxidant packaging that is in great demand especially in the food or pharmaceutical sector (Li et al., 2020).

In consideration of the fact that the applications of new types of packaging have had profound repercussions in various markets, the meanings of intelligent packaging and smart packaging have increasingly found their place and significance in theoretical analysis and in concrete application.

Despite their importance being widely shared by now, converging and/or univocal definitions in this area are not yet available; in research and in managerial practice, intelligent packaging and smart packaging are considered by some authors, as interchangeable terms while others, however, use them with substantially different meanings.

Based on this assumption, Han et al., (2005) consider intelligent packaging as a system that aims to strengthen communication between the customer and the packaged product.

Yam et al., (2005) have described intelligent packaging as a "container" solution that includes functions useful for logistics.

Ghaani et al., (2016) assign to intelligent packaging the functionality to supervise on the condition of wrapped foods during transportation.

Consistent with these approaches, packaging with intelligent functions constitutes an essential prerequisite: being able to help those who use it to make correct decisions, also guaranteeing the possibility of developing effective communication, as well as, expanding the aptitude to acquire, store, and communicate with different types of stakeholders (Qin et al., 2022).

From this statement, it follows that intelligent packaging can make contributions to the development of the packaging sector, as a packaging system capable of implementing functions that can be seen, precisely, as "innovative technological-technical applications": detection, registration, tracking, communication, etc. (Kalpana et al., 2019). Ultimately, it is clear that the originality of intelligent packaging lies in its communicative potential due to the fact that package and product - physically and interpretatively - intersect along the entire supply chain cycle (Vila-Lopez & Küster-Boluda, 2020).

Such considerations allow us to state that: i) intelligent packaging is a "new vehicle" of communication; ii) smart packaging implies the protection and healthiness function of products (Palazzo et al., 2023).

It should be emphasized that, in applications and in operational practice, intelligent packaging and smart packaging are not alternatives: some packaging systems are classified as intelligent packaging or smart packaging, due to their functional prevalence, enhancing the added value in commercial and communicative terms (Voipio et al., 2020). However, a weakness in the scope of the definitions should not be overlooked (Rundh, 2016).

5. INTELLIGENT PACKAGING CONTRIBUTING TO SDGS

5.1. Intelligent and Sustainable Packaging for Sustainable Development

Sustainable transformation involves the packaging system to be altered as the packaging industry needs to move from leaving a negative footprint to having positive influence on the environment. The modern concepts of corporate responsibility, circular economy, and sustainable development attract attention of companies in the packaging industry, which take into account economic, social, and ecological facets moving towards sustainable packaging (Kozik, 2020). Technologies, playing a main part in this process, can change the packaging industry by not only preventing products to contact with environmental contaminants but also by communicating with the products inside packaging. Thanks to the technologies, product package functions - such as oxygen level can be controlled remotely. Besides, such digitization meets consumers' needs for transparency.

While urbanization is increasing, waste management becomes critical. Therefore, packaging components gains attention from retailers, consumers, manufacturers, as well as governments. Furthermore, in the globalized world, more and more goods flow through borders, which increases the demand for reliable packaging (Kozik, 2020). On the one hand, most products could get damaged rapidly without packaging; on the other hand, packages turns into waste. The concept of sustainable packaging can solve this tension by offering a balance between minimizing negative footprints and increasing packaging benefits. This is possible through involving recycled materials in packaging and make it easier to recycle or reuse. Thus, the circular economy model enables waste management to decrease ecological impact of packaging.

Moreover, changes in consumer lifestyle, emerging sustainability trend, and increased demand for lucidity facilitate the further growth of intelligent packaging industry. Producers are motivated create attractive packaging that is not discarded but rather will be useful in the future. Consumers are mindful of the effect of packaging waste on oceans and landfills (Apostu et al., 2023). As a result, they demand packaging that are made of natural, biodegradable, or recyclable materials (Restuccia et al., 2010).

In addition, accelerating E-commerce in recent years made packaging more important for customers as online shopping involves safe delivery. Consequently, in the current era of E-commerce, packaging is an integral part of the brand, which must ensure delivering products safely, but at the same time, be sustainable, functional, and easy to open.

Since consumers preferences are moving towards sustainability, companies have to adapt to this trend. Nowadays, consumers expect sustainable and biodegradable products and packaging with the option of reusing, recycling, or refilling them. Consumers prefer brands that support sustainable development goals, demonstrate social responsibility, and contribute to tackling global challenges (Martín-Cervantes et al., 2022a; Gigauri, 2021b). "Reduce, Reuse, Recycle" have become buzzwords. Likewise, the pandemic changed consumption and production trends in favor of sustainability encouraging sustainable lifestyle (Apostu et al., 2022). By the same token, intelligent packaging inspires consumers to sustainable behavior. For example, customers can return single-use plastics to get a refund. In this manner, companies can raise awareness and promote a circular economy concept.

Recent study revealed the correlation between food date label and food waste as consumers, misinterpreting the labels, discard safe and edible food products (Shamim et al., 2022). Globally, 795 million people i.e. one in eight suffer from hunger while a third of the food manufactured worldwide is lost yearly (FAO, n.d.). In 2021, 58 per cent of the online survey participants in Germany declared that they waste food products because they spoil quickly, while 37 per cent of the participants confirmed that they were not sure whether the discarded food was still fresh (Statista, 2021).

It is worth emphasizing that packaging is used by entrepreneurs as a marketing means to impress customers and satisfy their needs (Kozik, 2020). Packaging, through texts or illustrations, transmits information to consumers about a product or its usage, serves as a preservation tool for products to separate them from the environment, as well as ensures protected delivery of a product (Müller & Schmid, 2019). Since information impacts customers decision-making (Penagos-Londoño et al., 2022), intelligent packaging, as a marketing communication tool, delivers message to customers about a product (Zeng, 2022). Thereby, it can promote safety of a food product and hence, minimize wastage (Poyatos-Racionero et al., 2018).

Although consumers require information about the products, for instance, which ingredients are included in a food product, how to store it (Restuccia et al., 2010), how it was produced or transported, they are not always willing to pay more for intelligent packaging that ensures such information (Müller & Schmid, 2019). However, as studies show, consumers would use eco-design packaging if they knew that such packaging reduces food waste, but financial and social factors are still significant to decide on eco-packaging (Zeng, 2022). Yet, such packaging can increase brand loyalty among consumers who are environmentally conscious.

The main disadvantages of intelligent packaging systems are its costs and acceptance by companies; however, the benefits can overweigh (Müller & Schmid, 2019). Additionally, Intelligent packaging consists of various materials that makes it difficult to recycle. It should be noted that intelligent packaging cannot be used for all products, and hence, producers need to decide whether the technologies are worthwhile for their particular products to reduce waste, increase sales, or monitor the quality of perishable products (Poyatos-Racionero et al., 2018; Müller & Schmid, 2019). As an example, plastics applied for packaging food, beverages, medications and cosmetics for protecting these products, and due to their durability and lightness resulting in lower transportation costs, are mismanaged after use causing enormous waste (Kozik, 2020). Paper is widely used for labels, boxes, wrappings, and packaging, which, although is biodegradable, needs to be recycled in order to avoid greenhouse gases (Kozik, 2020). Glass is mainly used for packaging beverages and pharmaceuticals, production of which requires energy and causes greenhouse gases (Kozik, 2020).

Intelligent packaging types vary from product to product depending on a producer's intention and customer's demand. Mostly, it is used in foodstuffs industry but also in cosmetics as well as pharmaceutical industries (Müller & Schmid, 2019). Intelligent packaging in the food industry as a response to the modern sustainability trend ensures product safety and quality, communicating information with customers and producer at the same time (Lee & Rahman, 2014). This option of packaging reduces food loss and increases consumer satisfaction (Müller & Schmid, 2019). To avoid the food waste, intelligent packaging enables manufactures to monitor microbiological quality of the products in supermarkets and during transportation. Consequently, unnecessary food loss can be minimized while protecting consumers against spoiled food, thereby increasing efficiency of the food companies (Sohail et al., 2018). Accordingly, intelligent packaging adds value while extending expiration date, monitoring the quality of a product, and improving safety. In this regard, intelligent packaging helps reduce waste and increase customer satisfaction. Moreover, by addressing food waste and safety, intelligent packaging systems can decrease the environmental footprint.

In the same vein, intelligent packaging can address sustainability by, for instance, sustainable consumption of food. Since end users may throw out edible food due to the misunderstanding of labels indicating expire date, intelligent packaging will prevent this while communicating the actual condition of the food products. Consumers often throw safe foods away in fear that they might be decayed (Müller & Schmid, 2019).

Since all kind of food products need packaging to protect them during transportation and storage, the food and beverage industry strives to use new technologies to extend shelf-life and reduce damage (Restuccia et al., 2010). Additionally, food spoilage by microbes and microorganisms decreases their shelf life, which also increases the risk of food related sickness (Suppakul, 2012). Besides, the EU legislation requires food traceability, which obliges food companies to take responsibility for supply chain (Poyatos-Racionero et al., 2018). In this respect, intelligent packaging offers reliable solution to monitor products inside packaging noninvasively and evaluate their freshness in real time (Lee and Rahman, 2014). Through the information about internal (metabolites) and external (temperature, humidity) environmental factors, product biosecurity and quality are controlled automatically (Suppakul, 2012). Intelligent packaging detects any alterations in food quality and its environment and transmits this information to the producer, or consumer (Poyatos-Racionero et al., 2018). Two types of intelligent packaging controls the conditions (1) outside and (2) inside the packaging (Restuccia et al., 2010).

In order to improve packaging sustainability, the Sustainable Packaging Coalition support member companies as they believe "in the power of industry to make packaging more sustainable ... and are passionate about creating packaging that is good for people and good for the environment" (Sustainable Packaging Coalition, n.d.). Sustainable packaging can be described as one that considers environmental, economic and social aspects, while having better features, functionality, and quality (Kozik, 2020). Sustainable packaging uses renewable, responsible, and recycled source materials, increase recycling, utilize clean production technologies, enhance volume efficiency, use healthy materials, and minimize harmful materials (Figure 1).

Governments are trying to regulate packaging waste and initiate waste management activities. However, regulations regarding active and intelligent packaging are needed to hinder companies from abusing their power to advance in the market. Besides, active agents include toxic compounds that are used

Figure 1. Packaging sustainability goals
Source: Authors' elaboration based on Sustainable Packaging Coalition (n.d.) https://sustainablepackaging.org/

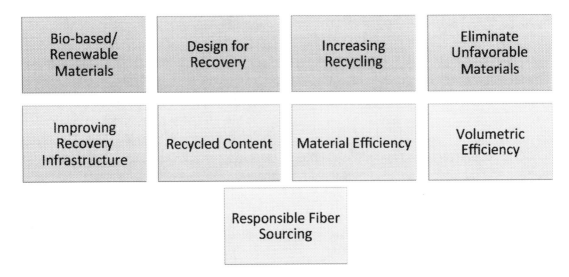

in intelligent packaging making them dangerous for health of customers in case those mixtures come in contact with foods. Though, it is worth mentioning that those actions may result in fewer packaging options on the market. As a result, packaging could cease to be a communication tool and become no more useful for marketing purposes.

5.2. The Contribution of Packaging to SDGs

Sustainable consumption and production try to separate economic growth from ecological deterioration, which can also facilitate poverty mitigation and the transition towards circular economy (SDGs, n.d.). The United Nations 17 Sustainable Development Goals concern various aspects of social, economic, and environmental issues. The packaging industry also plays a role in achieving those goals, as for example it includes food to be safe, water to be transported, and medications to improve people's health. The needed products for standards of living are enveloped in packaging materials to be delivered and protected.

Sustainable development aims to improve the living conditions globally (Manta et al., 2022; Gigauri & Vasilev, 2022; Martínez et al., 2022b). Consequently, the product quality is important to reach this goal. In addition, customers' demand for quality and safety is growing to which producers must respond to survive in the market. In this regard, packaging materials play a key role, especially, for food industries to track quality and safety in actual time (Kuswandi et al., 2011).

Due to the overconsumption (Montoro-Ríos & Rey-Pino, 2021), demand for products cause growing demand for packaging. Therefore, the concept of Sustainable Packaging aims to reduce waste, decrease negative impact, and increase efficiency throughout the supply chain from design to transportation to end users. The packaging industry needs to contribute to SDGs by integrating sustainability into their core business models. Sustainability needs to be considered throughout the value chain. In order to meet sustainability goals, the packaging system must regard its life cycle from the origin of materials, the design and manufacturing process to transportation to consumers as well as to recycling of packaging materials for preventing waste pollution and decreasing carbon footprint. In 2020, packaging wastage in the 27 EU member states was about 177 kg per citizen, and total packaging waste was estimated at 79.3 million tones (Eurostat, 2022). Paper packaging was around 33 million tons, glass materials waste was 15 million tons, and plastic packaging - 15.5 million tons (Eurostat, 2022). Figure 2 summarizes the generated packaging waste by materials during the year 2020.

The UN's Sustainable Development Goals aim to tackle global environmental, social, and economic challenges. Climate change, limited natural resources, deforestation, environmental degradation, or marine plastic pollution are among urgent ecological problems that need to be addressed by the governments and business. The SDGs contain 17 goals and 169 targets among which several goals and target are concerned to packaging. SDG 12 - Sustainable Consumption and Production intends to change a linear model of make-take-waste to more sustainable circular model (Figure 3). Targets under SDG 12 includes decreasing food waste through the supply chain and food losses through prevention, recycling, and reuse (UN, n.d.). In this respect, packaging must protect products against damage and consequently, waste. However, most packaging materials are used one time and are impossible to recycle. Thus, the energy resources needed for sourcing, transporting, and manufacturing packaging, which can negatively impact the environment, are wasted as the packages end up in landfills. Such unnecessary carbon emissions damage the environment and must be minimized.

Figure 2. Packaging waste in the European Union member countries
Source: Authors' elaboration based on Eurostat (2022).

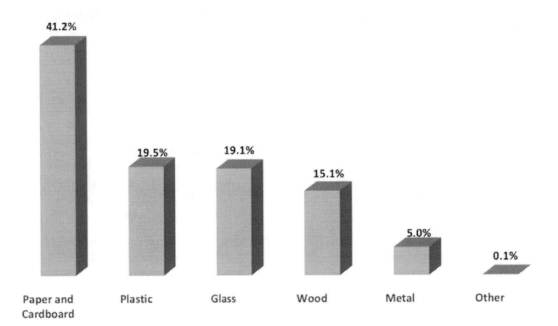

Moreover, packaging is related to more goals and consequently, companies should focus on the sustainability of their product packaging. Apart from SDG 12, sustainable packaging is important for achieving the following goals: 2, 3, 6, 11, 9, 13, 14, 15 (Figure 4).

Thus, Intelligent Packaging contributes to SDGs through improving product quality, and decreasing negative environmental impact (Fang et al., 2017; Müller & Schmid, 2019). Based on technological advancements, the packaging industry can switch towards more sustainable production and consumption of packaging.

5. CONCLUSION

Since the pandemic caused changes in customer behavior shifting towards more sustainable consumption and safety requirements, consumers devote more attention to health issues and demand quality products (Gigauri & Djakeli, 2021). Their shopping behavior changed towards more online channels leading to increased delivery services and hence, companies are seeking transportation solutions for all types of products. In addition, consumers in fear that a product might be spoiled throw edible food away causing needless waste on the one hand and overconsumption on the other hand as they buy the products again.

Moreover, customer awareness has also increased towards sustainability in conjunction with quality standards. Intelligent packaging has the potential to meet these requirements leading to reduced waste and increased consumer satisfaction. Sustainability development goals imply companies move towards sustainable use of resources while producing less waste, safe and quality products, and more recyclable and eco-friendly packaging. Increasing waste and resource exploitation leads to ecological and social problems.

Figure 3. SDG 12 targets
Source: Authors' elaboration based on Sustainable Development Goals (n.d). https://www.un.org/sustainabledevelopment/sustainable-consumption-production/

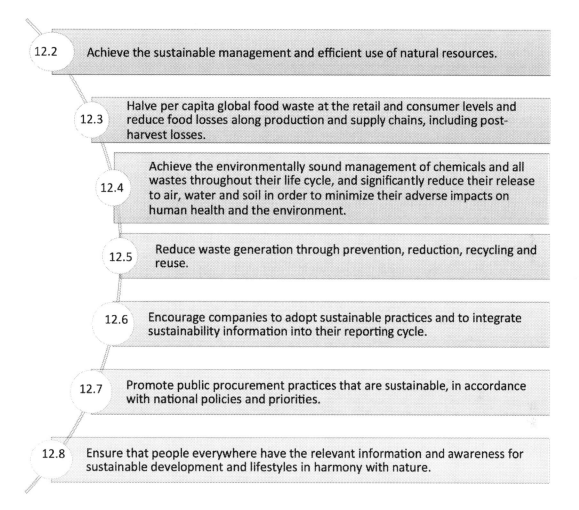

Consequently, companies through intelligent packaging can contribute to SDGs aiming to eliminate poverty (1) and hunger (2), ensure health (3) and sustainable consumption (12), foster innovation (9), and protect the environment (13, 14, 15).

However, the development and introduction of intelligent packaging in the market can be costly, and hence, brands and food manufacturers can avoid it by ignoring the advantages of the system. Therefore, further studies about intelligent packaging is essential to discover its potential, advantages, and innovation potential.

5.1. Limitations, Implications, and a Research Agenda

The chapter seeks to develop a first attempt to analyze the new role played by packaging with advanced features in the field of sustainable marketing and SDGs. The work briefly analyzes the characteristics of

Figure 4. Packaging for sustainable development goals
Source: Authors' elaboration based on: SDGs (n.d.) https://sdgs.un.org/goals and Plastic Soup Foundation (n.d.) https://www.plasticsoupfoundation.org/en/plastic-problem/sustainable-development/individual-sdgs/

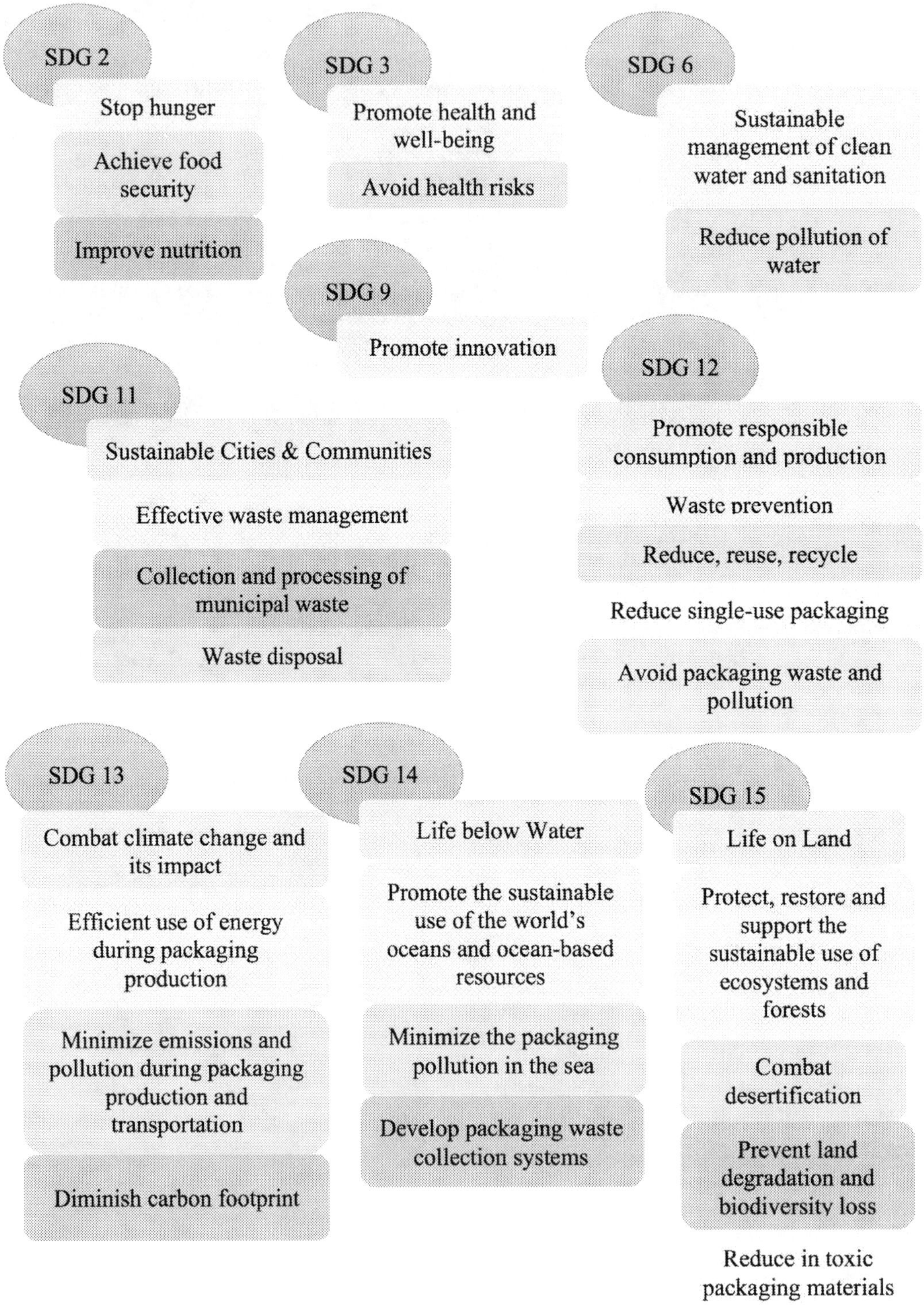

SDG 2
- Stop hunger
- Achieve food security
- Improve nutrition

SDG 3
- Promote health and well-being
- Avoid health risks

SDG 6
- Sustainable management of clean water and sanitation
- Reduce pollution of water

SDG 9
- Promote innovation

SDG 11
- Sustainable Cities & Communities
- Effective waste management
- Collection and processing of municipal waste
- Waste disposal

SDG 12
- Promote responsible consumption and production
- Waste prevention
- Reduce, reuse, recycle
- Reduce single-use packaging
- Avoid packaging waste and pollution

SDG 13
- Combat climate change and its impact
- Efficient use of energy during packaging production
- Minimize emissions and pollution during packaging production and transportation
- Diminish carbon footprint

SDG 14
- Life below Water
- Promote the sustainable use of the world's oceans and ocean-based resources
- Minimize the packaging pollution in the sea
- Develop packaging waste collection systems

SDG 15
- Life on Land
- Protect, restore and support the sustainable use of ecosystems and forests
- Combat desertification
- Prevent land degradation and biodiversity loss
- Reduce in toxic packaging materials

intelligent packaging and the different concepts connected to it which require, in the future, a detailed analysis both in theory and in practice.

The main limitations of this work are due to the fact that the literature on the selected topics is still limited and mostly recent. It must be said that professionals and managers are more interested in analyzing these topics than scholars and academic researchers. This has made it difficult to try to unambiguously define the concept of intelligent packaging, as today this technology is still in constant development. However, this theoretical gap can be seen as an interesting opportunity for researchers who would like to try to fill it by opening a new research area and exploring its potential practical implications in different entrepreneurial realities.

Actually, as the analysis of the case studies has shown, evaluating packaging with advanced functions could have several interesting implications.

The chapter therefore proposes a research agenda to explore and understand the applications of packaging with advanced functions, meant to develop an evolving environment that is increasingly attentive to the issues of sustainability and circular economy.

The chapter suggests: (i) Do not underestimate the direct contribution that 5G technologies can offer in helping organizations develop intelligent packaging. In fact, there is a need to evaluate how 5G applications can support the various players in the supply chain in finding an answer to the SDGs' questions; (ii) Use packaging to foster economic growth in a sustainable way. Economic growth will be strongly supported by intelligent packaging applications since the new digital changes will allow customers and organizations to draw from these types of packaging an enormous amount of data, not only relating to supply chain partners but also generated by the end user; (iii) Understand the role played by intelligent packaging in the sustainable development of medicines. The new way of packaging allows remote control of the quality of particular medicines, which are important for ensuring the health of patients around the world.

REFERENCES

Ajwani-Ramchandani, R., Figueira, S., De Oliveira, R. T., Jha, S., Ramchandani, A., & Schuricht, L. (2021). Towards a circular economy for packaging waste by using new technologies: The case of large multinationals in emerging economies. *Journal of Cleaner Production*, *281*, 125139. doi:10.1016/j.jclepro.2020.125139

Akhzar, P. (2021). *Advantages of Using Intelligent Packaging for Your E-Commerce Business*. Calcurates. https://calcurates.com/advantages-of-using-intelligent-packaging

Apostu, S. A., Gigauri, I., Panait, M., & Martín-Cervantes, P. A. (2023). Is Europe on the Way to Sustainable Development? Compatibility of Green Environment, Economic Growth, and Circular Economy Issues. *International Journal of Environmental Research and Public Health*, *20*(2), 1078. doi:10.3390/ijerph20021078 PMID:36673838

Apostu, S. A., Mukli, L., Panait, M., Gigauri, I., & Hysa, E. (2022). Economic Growth through the Lenses of Education, Entrepreneurship, and Innovation. *Administrative Sciences*, *12*(3), 74. doi:10.3390/admsci12030074

Brockgreitens, J., & Abbas, A. (2016). Responsive food packaging: Recent progress and technological prospects. *Comprehensive Reviews in Food Science and Food Safety*, *15*(1), 3–15. doi:10.1111/1541-4337.12174 PMID:33371571

Butler, P. (2013). Smart and interactive Packaging developments for enhanced communication at the packaging/user interface. In N. Farmer, Trends in Packaging of Food, Beverages and Other Fast-Moving Consumer Goods (FMCG) (pp. 261-286). Science Direct. doi:10.1533/9780857098979.261

Draskovic, N. (2007). The marketing role of packaging: A review. *International Journal of Management Cases*, *9*(3-4), 315–323. doi:10.5848/APBJ.2007.00034

Eurostat. (2022). *Packaging waste statistics*. Eurostat. https://ec.europa.eu/eurostat/statistics-explained/index.php?title=Packaging_waste_statistics

Fang, Z., Zhao, Y., Warner, R. D., & Johnson, S. K. (2017). Active and intelligent packaging in meat industry. *Trends in Food Science & Technology*, *61*, 60–71. doi:10.1016/j.tifs.2017.01.002

FAO. (n.d.). *Home*. Food and Agriculture Organization of the United Nations. www.fao.org

Gerard, P., & Leyland, P. (1996). Packaging, marketing, logistics and the environment: Are there trade-offs? *International Journal of Physical Distribution & Logistics Management*, *26*(6), 60–72. doi:10.1108/09600039610125206

Ghaani, M., Cozzolino, C. A., Castelli, G., & Farris, S. (2016). An overview of the intelligent packaging technologies in the food sector. *Trends in Food Science & Technology*, *51*, 1–11. doi:10.1016/j.tifs.2016.02.008

Gigauri, I. (2021a). New Economic Concepts Shaping Business Models in Post-Pandemic Era. *International Journal of Innovative Technologies in Economy*, *1*(33). doi:10.31435/rsglobal_ijite/30032021/7393

Gigauri, I. (2021b). Corporate Social Responsibility and COVID-19 Pandemic Crisis: Evidence from Georgia. [IJSECSR]. *International Journal of Sustainable Entrepreneurship and Corporate Social Responsibility*, *6*(1), 30–47. doi:10.4018/IJSECSR.2021010103

Gigauri, I., & Djakeli, K. (2021). Expecting Transformation of Marketing During the Post-Pandemic New Normal: Qualitative Research of Marketing Managers in Georgia. [IJSEM]. *International Journal of Sustainable Economies Management*, *10*(2), 1–18. doi:10.4018/IJSEM.2021040101

Gigauri, I., & Vasilev, V. (2022). Corporate Social Responsibility in the Energy Sector: Towards Sustainability. In S. A. R. Khan, M. Panait, F. Puime Guillen, & L. Raimi (Eds.), *Energy Transition. Industrial Ecology*. Springer. doi:10.1007/978-981-19-3540-4_10

Globe Newswire. (2022). Active and Intelligent Packaging Market Overview. *Globe Newswire*. https://www.globenewswire.com/en/news-release/2022/06/27/2469410/0/en/Active-and-Intelligent-Packaging-Market-Worth-USD-26-8-Billion-by-2028-at-6-51-CAGR-Report-by-Market-Research-Future-MRFR.html

Gobbo, J. A. Jr, & Olsson, A. (2010). The transformation between exploration and exploitation applied to inventors of packaging innovations. *Technovation*, *30*(5-6), 322–331. doi:10.1016/j.technovation.2010.01.001

Han, J. H., Ho, C. H., & Rodrigues, E. T. (2005). Intelligent packaging. *Innovations in food packaging*, 138-155. doi:10.1016/B978-012311632-1/50041-3

Kalpana, S., Priyadarshini, S. R., Leena, M. M., Moses, J. A., & Anandharamakrishnan, C. (2019). Intelligent packaging: Trends and applications in food systems. *Trends in Food Science & Technology*, *93*, 145–157. doi:10.1016/j.tifs.2019.09.008

Kerry, J., & Butler, P. (Eds.). (2008). *Smart packaging technologies for fast moving consumer goods*. John Wiley & Sons. doi:10.1002/9780470753699

Kozik, N. (2020). Sustainable packaging as a tool for global sustainable development. In *SHS Web of Conferences*, 74, 04012. EDP Sciences. 10.1051hsconf/20207404012

Kuswandi, B., Wicaksono, Y., Abdullah, A., Heng, L. Y., & Ahmad, M. (2011). Smart packaging: Sensors for monitoring of food quality and safety. *Sensing and Instrumentation for Food Quality and Safety*, *5*(3), 137–146. doi:10.100711694-011-9120-x

Lebelo, K., Masinde, M., Malebo, N., & Mochane, M. J. (2021). The surveillance and prediction of food contamination using intelligent systems: A bibliometric analysis. *British Food Journal*, *124*(4), 1149–1169. doi:10.1108/BFJ-04-2021-0366

Lee, S. J., & Rahman, A. M. (2014). Intelligent packaging for food products. In J. H. Han (Ed.), *Innovations in food packaging* (pp. 171–209). Academic Press. doi:10.1016/B978-0-12-394601-0.00008-4

Li, Y., Chu, F., Côté, J. F., Coelho, L. C., & Chu, C. (2020). The multi-plant perishable food production routing with packaging consideration. *International Journal of Production Economics*, *221*, 107472. doi:10.1016/j.ijpe.2019.08.007

Lydekaityte, J., & Tambo, T. (2020). Smart packaging: Definitions, models and packaging as an intermediator between digital and physical product management. *International Review of Retail, Distribution and Consumer Research*, *30*(4), 377–410. doi:10.1080/09593969.2020.1724555

Mahmoudi, M., & Parviziomran, I. (2020). Reusable packaging in supply chains: A review of environmental and economic impacts, logistics system designs, and operations management. *International Journal of Production Economics*, *228*, 107730. doi:10.1016/j.ijpe.2020.107730

Manta, O., Panait, M., Hysa, E., Rusu, E., & Cojocaru, M. (2022). Public procurement, a tool for achieving the goals of sustainable development. *Amfiteatru Economic*, *61*(24), 861–876. doi:10.24818/EA/2022/61/861

Martín-Cervantes, P. A., del Carmen Valls Martínez, M., & Gigauri, I. (2022a). Sustainable Marketing. In *Encyclopedia of Creativity, Invention, Innovation and Entrepreneurship*. Springer. doi:10.1007/978-1-4614-6616-1_200101-1

Martínez, M. D. C. V., Martín-Cervantes, P. A., & del Mar Miralles-Quirós, M. (2022b). Sustainable development and the limits of gender policies on corporate boards in Europe. A comparative analysis between developed and emerging markets. *European Research on Management and Business Economics*, *28*(1), 100168. doi:10.1016/j.iedeen.2021.100168

Mason, W. R. (1958). A theory of packaging in the marketing mix. *Business Horizons*, *1*(3), 91–95. doi:10.1016/0007-6813(58)90082-X

Mohebbi, B. (2014). The art of packaging: An investigation into the role of colour in packaging, marketing, and branding. *International Journal of Organizational Leadership*, *3*(2), 92–102. doi:10.33844/ijol.2014.60248

Montoro-Ríos, F. J., & Rey-Pino, J. M. (2021). Business Marketing Practices: Main Cause of Overconsumption. In W. Leal Filho, A. M. Azul, L. Brandli, P. G. Özuyar, & T. Wall (Eds.), *Responsible Consumption and Production. Encyclopedia of the UN Sustainable Development Goals*. Springer., doi:10.1007/978-3-319-71062-4_121-1

Müller, P., & Schmid, M. (2019). Intelligent Packaging in the Food Sector: A Brief Overview. *Foods*, *8*(1), 16. doi:10.3390/foods8010016 PMID:30621006

Mumani, A., & Stone, R. (2018). State of the art of user packaging interaction (UPI). *Packaging Technology & Science*, *31*(6), 401–419. doi:10.1002/pts.2363

Palazzo, M., Gigauri, I., Panait, M. C., Apostu, S. A., & Siano, A. (2022). Sustainable Tourism Issues in European Countries during the Global Pandemic Crisis. *Sustainability (Basel)*, *14*(7), 3844. doi:10.3390u14073844

Palazzo, M., Vollero, A., & Siano, A. (2023). Intelligent packaging in the transition from linear to circular economy: Driving research in practice. *Journal of Cleaner Production*, *135984*, 135984. doi:10.1016/j.jclepro.2023.135984

Penagos-Londoño, G. I., Ruiz-Moreno, F., Sellers-Rubio, R., Del Barrio-García, S., & Casado-Díaz, A. B. (2022). Consistency of Experts' Product Reviews: An Application to Wine Guides. *Wine Economics and Policy*, *11*(2), 51–60. doi:10.36253/wep-12400

Piergiovanni, L., & Limbo, S. (2010). *Food packaging: Materiali, tecnologie e soluzioni*. Springer Science & Business Media., doi:10.1007/978-88-470-1457-2

Plastic Soup Foundation. (n.d.). *Individual SDG's*. PSF. https://www.plasticsoupfoundation.org/en/plastic-problem/sustainable-development/individual-sdgs/

Poyatos-Racionero, E., Ros-Lis, J. V., Vivancos, J. L., & Martinez-Manez, R. (2018). Recent advances on intelligent packaging as tools to reduce food waste. *Journal of Cleaner Production*, *172*, 3398–3409. doi:10.1016/j.jclepro.2017.11.075

Prendergast, G., & Pitt, L. (1996). Packaging, marketing, logistics and the environment: Are there trade-offs? *International Journal of Physical Distribution & Logistics Management*, *26*(6), 60–72. doi:10.1108/09600039610125206

Priyanka, C. N., & Parag, D. N. (2013). Intelligent and active packaging. *International Journal of Engineering and Management Sciences*, *4*(4), 417–418.

Qin, X., Godil, D. I., Sarwat, S., Yu, Z., Khan, S. A. R., & Shujaat, S. (2022). Green practices in food supply chains: Evidence from emerging economies. *Operations Management Research : Advancing Practice Through Research*, *15*(1), 62–75. doi:10.100712063-021-00187-y

Restuccia, D., Spizzirri, U. G., Parisi, O. I., Cirillo, G., Curcio, M., Iemma, F., Puoci, F., Vinci, G., & Picci, N. (2010). New EU regulation aspects and global market of active and intelligent packaging for food industry applications. *Food Control, 21*(11), 1425–1435. doi:10.1016/j.foodcont.2010.04.028

Rundh, B. (2013). Linking Packaging to Marketing: How Packaging is Influencing the Marketing Strategy. *British Food Journal, 115*(11), 1547–1563. doi:10.1108/BFJ-12-2011-0297

Rundh, B. (2016). The role of packaging within marketing and value creation. *British Food Journal, 118*(10), 2491–2511. doi:10.1108/BFJ-10-2015-0390

SDGs. (n.d.). *The 17 Goals*. United Nations. https://sdgs.un.org/goals

Shamim, K., Ahmad, S., & Alam, M. A. (2022). Consumer understanding of food date labels: Preventing food wastage. *British Food Journal, 124*(10), 3116–3132. doi:10.1108/BFJ-06-2021-0672

Short, D., & Stovell, R. J. (1966). Packaging for people. *Human Factors, 8*(4), 307–315. doi:10.1177/001872086600800406

Sohail, M., Sun, D. W., & Zhu, Z. (2018). Recent developments in intelligent packaging for enhancing food quality and safety. *Critical Reviews in Food Science and Nutrition, 58*(15), 2650–2662. doi:10.1080/10408398.2018.1449731 PMID:29513558

Statista. (2021). *Umfrage zu Gründen für das Wegwerfen von Lebensmitteln in Deutschland 2021*. Statista. https://de.statista.com/statistik/daten/studie/486235/umfrage/umfrage-zu-gruenden-fuer-das-wegwerfen-von-lebensmitteln-in-deutschland/

Suppakul, P. (2012). Intelligent packaging. In D. W. Sun (Ed.), *Handbook of Frozen Food Processing and Packaging* (pp. 837–860). CRC Press.

Sustainable Development Goals (n.d). *Goal 12: Ensure sustainable consumption and production patterns*. United Nations. https://www.un.org/sustainabledevelopment/sustainable-consumption-production/

UN. (n.d.). *Sustainable Development Goals*. United Nations. https://www.un.org/sustainabledevelopment/

Vila-Lopez, N., & Küster-Boluda, I. (2020). A bibliometric analysis on packaging research: Towards sustainable and healthy packages. *British Food Journal, 123*(2), 684–701. doi:10.1108/BFJ-03-2020-0245

Voipio, V., Elfvengren, K., & Korpela, J. (2020). In the bowling alley: Acceptance of an intelligent packaging concept in European markets. *International Journal of Value Chain Management, 11*(2), 180–197. doi:10.1504/IJVCM.2020.106825

Yam, K. L., Takhistov, P. T., & Miltz, J. (2005). Intelligent packaging: Concepts and applications. *Journal of Food Science, 70*(1), R1–R10. doi:10.1111/j.1365-2621.2005.tb09052.x

Zeng, T. (2022). Impacts of consumers' perceived risks in eco-design packaging on food wastage behaviors. *British Food Journal, 124*(8), 2512–2532. doi:10.1108/BFJ-05-2021-0603

Chapter 2
The Past, Present, and Future of Sustainable Marketing

Catalin Popescu
https://orcid.org/0000-0002-8921-8123
Petroleum-Gas University of Ploiesti, Romania

Razvan Ionescu
School of Advanced Studies of the Romanian Academy, Bucharest, Romania

Iza Gigauri
https://orcid.org/0000-0001-6394-6416
St. Andrew the First-Called Georgian University, Georgia

ABSTRACT

Sustainable Development Goals have to be integrated into every aspect of modern society. Economic agents are transforming accordingly taking into consideration the economic, social, and environmental footprints of their activities. The marketing domain has devoted attention to sustainability issues for a long time. Organizations have applied social marketing, ethical and green marketing, as well as corporate social responsibility in their marketing strategies and programs. Sustainable marketing can center on sustainable communication, sustainable production and consumption, sustainable branding, and the promotion of sustainable behavior. The connection between marketing and sustainability can be contradictory as traditional marketing strategies induce overconsumption. Moreover, enhanced digitalization affects marketing and shapes the tools and strategies marketers are adopting. Digital transformation of marketing is expected to be based on sustainable development.

1. INTRODUCTION

Sustainable marketing, also known as *green marketing* or *environmental marketing*, is a concept that involves the development and promotion of products and services with the aim of reducing their environmental impact and promoting sustainability. The concept of sustainable marketing emerged in the

DOI: 10.4018/978-1-6684-8681-8.ch002

The Past, Present, and Future of Sustainable Marketing

1980s and 1990s, when environmental issues began to gain increased attention from both consumers and companies. Since then, sustainable marketing has become an increasingly important area of study and practice, as companies seek to respond to consumer demand for environmentally friendly products and services, and as consumers become more aware of the impact of their purchasing decisions on the environment.

Sustainable marketing is considered important for the next generations and for the future of the Earth because it addresses some of the most pressing environmental and social challenges facing the world today. Companies that adopt a sustainable marketing approach seek to promote environmental and social sustainability through their marketing activities, and to shape consumer behavior in ways that support sustainability.

One of the key reasons that sustainable marketing is considered important is because of the growing impact of human activities on the environment. Climate change, deforestation, pollution, and other environmental problems are having a significant impact on the health of the planet and on the well-being of future generations. In order to address these challenges, companies and consumers alike need to adopt more sustainable practices, and sustainable marketing can play an important role in promoting sustainability and shaping consumer behavior.

Another important reason that sustainable marketing is considered important is because of the growing awareness of the environmental impact of consumer behavior. As consumers become more conscious of the environmental impact of their purchasing decisions, they are increasingly seeking environmentally friendly products and services, and are making purchasing decisions based on environmental considerations. This shift in consumer behavior presents a significant opportunity for companies that adopt a sustainable marketing approach, as they can differentiate themselves from their competitors by promoting their environmental credentials, and by appealing to the growing number of consumers who are seeking environmentally friendly products and services.

An important contribution to the field of sustainable marketing was made by Kotler, who defined sustainable marketing as "the blending of marketing strategies and tactics with the principles of sustainability to create mutually satisfying exchange relationships and build long-term customer loyalty while maintaining the viability of natural systems" (Kotler et al., 2002).

In fact, according to Kotler, sustainable marketing involves a shift in focus from the traditional emphasis on product-centered marketing, to a more customer-centered and environmentally responsible approach. In a somewhat similar manner, some other authors have suggested that sustainable marketing requires a new type of marketing mix that includes elements such as sustainability communication, sustainability labeling, and sustainability education.

Over the last 30-40 years, there are studies that underlined the interaction between the economy and the environment. During this period there are identified different steps in developing the critical issues that are considered as main pillars for generating the sustainable marketing framework (Peattie, 2001).

Another useful contribution to the field was made by Elkington, who argued that sustainable marketing requires a new type of marketing that goes beyond the traditional "4 Ps" (product, price, promotion, and place) of marketing (Elkington, 2018). In fact, Elkington considered that sustainable marketing must also incorporate the "3 Ps" approach of people, planet, and profit.

This approach means not only is important to consider the economic and marketing aspects of a product or service, but also its social and environmental impacts. In this regard, Elkington has argued that sustainable marketing must be based on a "triple bottom line" approach, which considers the economic, social, and environmental impacts of marketing activities.

An issue that must be emphasized also refers to the criticisms of the field of sustainable marketing. Thus, some authors complained about the lack of rigor and the tendency of sustainable marketing to rely on vague and subjective concepts such as "sustainability" and "greenness". Thus, Carrigan and Attalla, argued that sustainable marketing is often based on unsubstantiated claims and that it is difficult to measure the effectiveness of sustainable marketing strategies and tactics (Carrigan & Attalla, 2001). Similarly, Peattie criticized the lack of consistency in defining and measuring sustainability and argued that sustainable marketing has to be based on a clear and consistent definition of sustainability (Peattie, 2001).

Despite these criticisms, the field of sustainable marketing continues to grow and evolve as companies and consumers become increasingly aware of the environmental and social impact of their purchasing decisions. In recent years, there has been a growing interest in the role that sustainable marketing can play in promoting sustainability and in developing new and innovative sustainable marketing strategies and tactics. As the field of sustainable marketing continues to mature, it is likely to become an increasingly important area of study and practice as companies seek to meet the growing demand for green products and services and as consumers become more aware of the environmental impact of their purchasing decisions.

In this regard, a useful contribution, made by Machova et al., explored the relationship between green marketing and consumer behavior (Machová et al, 2022). Their research highlights that green marketing can influence consumer behavior in a number of ways, including by increasing awareness of environmental issues, by providing consumers with information about the environmental impact of products and services, and by encouraging consumers to make environmentally responsible purchasing decisions.

In the same line can be mentioned the Barbu's et al article where are identified and declared the key factors that influence consumers' behavior toward green products: social norms, natural environmental orientation, company's perceived green image, green product characteristics, institutional trust, sociodemographic characteristics, and consumer confidence (Barbu et al., 2022).

Despite the growing body of research in the area of sustainable marketing, there is still much that is unknown about the relationship between sustainable marketing and consumer behavior. For example, there is a need for more research that explores the effectiveness of different types of sustainable marketing strategies and tactics, and that examines the impact of sustainable marketing on consumer attitudes and behaviors over time. There is also a need for more research that explores the impact of sustainable marketing on business outcomes, such as brand image, customer loyalty, and profitability.

Overall, the past of sustainable marketing can be traced back to the early 1990s, when a growing concern about the environmental impact of business activities led to the emergence of a new field of study and practice focused on promoting sustainability through marketing. During this time, a number of pioneering marketing scholars made important contributions to the field by exploring the relationship between sustainable marketing and consumer behavior, and by identifying the key factors that influence consumer-purchasing decisions with regard to environmentally friendly products and services.

In the present, sustainable marketing has become a critical issue for companies and consumers alike, as concerns about the environmental impact of business activities continue to grow, and as consumers become more conscious of the environmental impact of their purchasing decisions. In response to these trends, companies have increasingly turned to sustainable marketing as a way of promoting their environmental credentials, and of appealing to the growing number of consumers who are seeking environmentally friendly products and services.

In conclusion, sustainable marketing is a rapidly evolving field that has seen a growing interest in recent years, as companies and consumers become increasingly aware of the environmental and social impacts of their purchasing decisions. Although there have been a number of important contributions to the field of sustainable marketing, there is still much that is unknown about the relationship between sustainable marketing and consumer behavior, and the impact of sustainable marketing on business outcomes. As the field of sustainable marketing continues to mature, it is likely that it will become an increasingly important area of study and practice, as companies seek to respond to the growing demand for environmentally friendly products and services, and as consumers become more conscious of the environmental impact of their purchasing decisions.

Looking to the future it is clear that sustainable marketing will continue to play a critical role in promoting sustainability and shaping consumer behavior. As concerns about the environmental impact of business activities continue to grow, and as consumers become increasingly conscious of the environmental impact of their purchasing decisions, companies will need to invest in sustainable marketing to remain competitive and to respond to changing consumer demands. In addition, as the field of sustainable marketing continues to evolve, it is likely that we will see the development of new and innovative marketing strategies and tactics that are designed to promote sustainability and to shape consumer behavior in ways that are more effective.

2. THE PATH TOWARDS SUSTAINABLE MARKETING

2.1. From Social, Green, and Ethical Marketing to Sustainable Marketing

The evolution from social, green, and ethical marketing to sustainable marketing is an important development in the field of marketing. Actually, Social, Green, and Ethical Marketing are sub-categories of Sustainable Marketing and focus on specific areas of sustainability.

Social marketing emerged in the 1970s. More specifically, in 1971, the term Social Marketing was inserted in the fundamental article of the field, "Social Marketing: An Approach to Planned Social Change" (Kotler & Zaltman, 1971). From that moment on, the concept developed by focusing on promoting products and services that benefit society. During this time, social marketing campaigns might aim to promote healthy behaviors, such as exercise or seatbelt use, or to raise awareness about social issues, such as poverty or homelessness (Mir, 2016). In the idea of building an identity specific to the new concept, there were critical opinions that required separation from the concept of commercial marketing through the development of one's own vocabulary, some ideas and some distinctive tools in this sense. (Peattie & Peattie, 2003).

Green marketing emerged in the 1980s and 1990s, as companies started to recognize the importance of environmental protection and the potential benefits of promoting environmentally friendly products and practices. Green marketing strategies might involve promoting eco-friendly products, reducing waste and emissions, and encouraging environmentally responsible behavior among consumers (Kaur et al., 2022; Majeed et al., 2022).

Ethical marketing emerged in the 1990s, as companies sought to promote themselves as being socially responsible. Ethical marketing practices might involve avoiding controversial topics, such as tobacco or firearms, or promoting social causes, such as fair trade or human rights (Donaldson & Walsh, 2015; Welsh et al., 2015).

The evolution from social, green, and ethical marketing to sustainable marketing reflects a shift in the way companies approach their marketing strategies. Social marketing refers to the promotion of products and services that benefit society, while green marketing focuses on environmentally friendly products and practices. On this line, the most important issue for the companies' management is to identify an appropriate green marketing strategy as a part of efficient targeted communication of socially responsible activities (Nadanyiova et al., 2020). Ethical marketing refers to practices, which are morally and socially responsible.

Over time, these separate approaches have merged into the broader concept of sustainable marketing, which considers the long-term impact of marketing strategies on both the environment and society (Majeed et al., 2022; Nekmahmud & Fekete-Farkas, 2020). Sustainable marketing aims to balance economic, social, and environmental goals and create value for all stakeholders (Richardson, 2022). For example, a company that practices sustainable marketing might consider the entire life cycle of a product, from its production to its disposal, and seek to minimize its environmental impact. This might involve using sustainable materials, reducing waste and emissions, and promoting environmentally responsible behavior among consumers.

Sustainable marketing practices can take various forms, including eco-friendly product design, responsible packaging, and green advertising (García-Salirrosas & Rondon-Eusebio, 2022; Garg & Sharma, 2017; Maziriri, 2020). Companies that adopt sustainable marketing practices often aim to differentiate themselves from their competitors and appeal to consumers who prioritize environmental and social responsibility. Studies have shown that incorporating sustainability into marketing strategies can have positive effects on a company's reputation and financial performance, as well as on consumer behavior. For example, consumers are more likely to purchase products from companies that are seen as environmentally and socially responsible.

However, sustainable marketing practices can also face challenges and criticisms, such as greenwashing, where companies make false or exaggerated environmental claims, and the lack of clear and consistent sustainability standards (Nemes et al., 2022; Sun & Shi, 2022).

Overall, sustainable marketing represents an important shift in the way companies approach their marketing strategies, as they increasingly recognize the need to consider the long-term impact on the environment and society. As consumer preferences, continue to evolve and prioritize sustainability, companies that embrace sustainable marketing practices are likely to gain a competitive advantage (Moravcikova et al., 2017).

2.2. From CSR to Sustainable Marketing

Corporate Social Responsibility (CSR) has been a key concept in business for many decades, with companies increasingly seeking to balance their economic, social, and environmental responsibilities (Gigauri & Vasilev, 2022). CSR is often seen as a precursor to Sustainable Marketing, as it lays the foundation for companies to integrate sustainability into their overall business strategy and marketing practices. However, CSR has evolved into the broader concept of sustainable marketing, which considers the long-term impact of a company's marketing strategies on the environment and society (Sanclemente-Téllez, 2017).

As already mentioned in the chapter, sustainable marketing seeks to balance economic, social, and environmental goals and create value for all stakeholders. This approach considers the entire life cycle of a product, from its production to its disposal, and seeks to minimize its environmental impact. CSR, on the other hand, has traditionally focused on a company's social and environmental responsibilities, rather than on its marketing strategies (Vock, 2022). CSR activities might include philanthropic efforts, such as supporting local charities or environmental initiatives, such as reducing waste or emissions. In this line, Porter and Kramer described the main core of elements related to corporate philanthropy: the context for strategy and rivalry, factor conditions, supporting industries and demand conditions (Porter & Kramer, 2002).

The evolution from CSR to sustainable marketing represents a shift towards a more comprehensive approach to corporate responsibility, which takes into account a company's impact not only on society and the environment but also on its stakeholders, such as consumers and employees (Low, 2022; Costa & Fonseca, 2022).

In recent years, there has been a growing recognition of the need for companies to adopt a more comprehensive approach to corporate responsibility, which takes into account not only their social and environmental responsibilities but also their marketing strategies (Sanclemente-Téllez, 2017; Fallah Shayan et al., 2022). This is reflected in the growing trend of companies integrating sustainability into their overall business strategy and incorporating sustainable marketing practices into their operations (Maccarrone & Contri, 2021; Peters & Simaens, 2020; Rodrigues & Franco, 2019).

At the same time, the complex approach and the implementation of CSR must cover a multitude of activities at the community level, starting with green marketing and focusing on customers with disabilities, then continuing with aspects related to occupational health and safety and correct public information, ending with periodically auditing and reporting at the level of community (Zairi, 2000).

Despite the challenges and criticisms, the trend towards sustainable marketing is expected to continue in the future, as consumers continue to prioritize sustainability in their purchasing decisions and companies seek to gain a competitive advantage through their sustainability efforts (Alam & Islam, 2021; Mandaric et al., 2022; Moravcikova et al., 2017; Porter & Kramer, 2002).

3. CURRENT TRENDS IN SUSTAINABLE MARKETING

3.1. Social Media Marketing Shaping Consumer Behavior

The information age has been bringing changes in the marketing domain shifting its focus to digital marketing, digital content management, online Word-of-Mouth, mobile advertising, social media marketing, chatbots, and online marketing using artificial intelligence, as well as augmented reality marketing (Dwivedi et al., 2021). Consequently, consumer behavior has changed in terms of decision-making and shopping as they increasingly use digital technologies (Dwivedi et al., 2021). Mobile devices are integrated into customers' daily lives (Shukla & Nigam, 2018). Hand in hand with the development of digital technologies, companies try to use them to advance their brands through value creation and consumer engagement (Gartner, 2019).

Since social media have transformed consumer behavior, companies have to align with these changes by using social and digital marketing tools for increasing sales or enhancing their brands (Dwivedi et al., 2021). Besides, they need to deal with negative information that can be shared about their business on the Internet. Consumers have the power to spread information and be heard by a large audience through social media (Dwivedi et al., 2021).

Prior studies confirmed that online marketing influences a company's brand and its sustainability (Ahmed et al., 2019). In particular, social media marketing can positively influence brand loyalty, brand trust (Veseli-Kurtishi 2018), and the sustainability of business (Ibrahim & Aljarah 2018). Studies demonstrated that the motivations of belief, community participation, and psychological factors are important drivers of social media marketing as customers' approaches toward social media impact their opinions regarding a company brand (Dwivedi et al., 2021).

Consumer attitudes toward social media advertising are affected by their perception of its content, and their privacy concerns regarding targeted marketing promotions in social media (Gaber et al., 2019). In addition, consumer behavior is influenced by their perception of privacy control and the usefulness of online marketing ads (Gironda et al., 2018). For this reason, companies have to take into account the privacy concerns of their customers while applying online marketing tools in order to maintain the relationship with consumers (Mandal, 2019).

Using Artificial Intelligence in social media marketing involves some risks for both consumers and companies such as intrusion into privacy, cyber security threats, bias and mistakes, consumer data collection, fraud, and information leakage, hence, the social media data needs to be treated with cautiousness (Vayena et al., 2018; Martin & Murphy, 2017). Thus, ethical marketing procedures, regulations, and practices should be in place for successful, transparent, and fair social media marketing.

3.2. Sustainable Development Goals Reflected in Marketing

Contemporary grand challenges such as climate change, hunger, poverty, illiteracy, lack of clean water and sanitation, pandemic, access to energy sources, and social inequalities, which modern society is encountering, require innovative solutions and joint actions between various stakeholders. The UN's Sustainability Development Goals are regarded as a baseline also for marketing to transform its vision towards more sustainable programs, collaboration with consumers and suppliers, and engaging in innovative products and services (Bocken, 2021).

The 20th century has generated extraordinary economic growth and technological progress along with environmental and social problems (Belz & Peattie, 2012) that are summarized in Table 1.

Table 1. Current grand challenges

Population	The world population doubled in 2000 compared to 1960;
Poverty	Poverty has been increased with half of the world's population living less than 2 USD a day;
Hunger	Food shortage especially in developing counties caused by fertilizer costs, agricultural land use for biofuel production, weather conditions, and increased demand affecting food prices;
Education	More than a billion people was unable to read and write in 2000;
Health	Health issues threaten the quality of live, especially obesity and mental health problems are related to lifestyle globally;
Urbanization	Urbanization has been growing with half of the world's population living in cities by 2000;
Natural Resources	Resource depletion threatens ecosystem; More natural resources were used up in the 20th century than in all preceding centuries combined;
Ecosystem	Ecosystem destruction will leave future generations without necessary resources to survive;
Climate Change	Climate change caused by human activity, energy pollution, carbon dioxide (CO_2) emissions;
Water	Water scarcity due to pollution and climate factors;
Diversity	Destruction of cultural diversity due to globalization, tourism, technologies and other causes;

Source: Authors work based on Belz & Peattie, 2012.

Therefore, the millennium goals becoming Sustainable Development Goals emerged to solve the above-mentioned problems globally. 17 SDGs call for action to protect the environment and eliminate poverty (UN, n.d.). To achieve peace and prosperity, to improve lives for people, and to protect the planet, SDGs aim to promote economic growth while preserving the environment (Bocken, 2021). Accordingly, companies need to pursue a sustainability path in their business strategies and operations. In this regard, they need to move from gaining short-term financial profit toward long-term SDGs. Specifically, Goal 12 - responsible consumption and production - is closely related to the marketing field. From this perspective, the sharing economy and circular economy reinforce sustainable consumption. As a result, a production-consumption model is changing in favor of sustainability marketing in which novel technologies have a crucial role to play (Becker-Olsen & Moynihan, 2013).

Moreover, increasing competitiveness forces business to search for innovative ways, especially in terms of marketing. At the same time, sustainability concerns require adequate reactions from companies. Businesses should employ new technologies to contribute to the SDGs and improve the well-being of people. Sustainable business models are based on economic, social, and environmental pillars while using the triple bottom line concept of People, Profit, and Planet to measure performance, and taking into account all stakeholders including nature (Bocken, 2021).

Elkington (1994) introduced "the triple bottom line" to emphasize the significance of people, the planet, and profit. Furthermore, ESG - environmental, social, and governance aspects are measured by many companies to capture the impact and contribution. However, scholars note difficulties to capture "the interdependence of these domains" (Sikdar, 2019). The reporting based on the Global Reporting Initiative (GRI) is used for marketing aims to inform stakeholders about the sustainability achievements of a company (Calu et al., 2015). Prior studies explain that among 30 environmental and social indicators, companies mostly report the indicators reflecting positive aspects of business activities (Calu et al., 2015).

There is tension between SDGs and focusing on profit. Study results show that multinational companies engaging in the BoP (Base of the pyramid) approach find it challenging to address SDG 1 aiming to reduce or eliminate poverty and stay profitable (Borchardt et al., 2019). Although they improve the quality of life in the short- and medium-term, in the long-term perspective they have negative impacts as they are not able to balance sustainability outcomes and profit-making results (Borchardt et al., 2019).

Against this background, marketing plays a significant role in contributing to environmental and social well-being and facilitating the transformation toward sustainable development (Belz & Peattie, 2012). Companies need to understand how digital and social media marketing can help them achieve this purpose. Marketing plays a significant role to facilitate mindset change among consumers and stimulate more sustainable behavior as well as sustainable consumption.

3.3. Sustainable or Sustainability Marketing: Current Trends

Sustainable development goals gave rise to sustainability marketing. Marketing, as a combination of methods and techniques aiming to commercialize a product or service, has gained more and more attention from scholars and professionals in terms of its role in the sustainable development agenda.

The definition of sustainable marketing varies across years and authors. Sustainable marketing means satisfying consumer needs while considering ecological issues as well (Sheth & Parvatiyar, 1995). Other authors understand sustainable marketing as "creating, producing and delivering sustainable solutions" while meeting consumers' and other stakeholders' needs (Charter et al., 2006). Belz and Peattie (2009) focus on developing sustainable relationships with consumers, the environment, and society including ethical and sustainable development aspects. Bridges and Wilhelm (2008) proposed that a sustainability marketing concept integrates environmental, social, and economic facets into marketing strategies.

Scholars recognize the need of discussing sustainable marketing (Quoquab et al., 2020) and see the differences between the terms "Sustainable marketing" and "Sustainability marketing" (Quoquab et al., 2020; Belz & Peattie, 2012). Sustainable Marketing has become a common term but some researchers (e.g. Belz & Peattie, 2012) argue that Sustainability Marketing reflects the concept better as it conveys the spirit of Sustainability more accurately, while Sustainable describes durable, enduring, or long-term relationships with customers (Quoquab et al., 2020).

Until the twentieth century, Marketing aimed to gather buyers and sellers in the marketplace (Belz & Peattie, 2012). Since the beginning of mass production and mass markets, producers no longer have had direct interactions with their consumers to understand their preferences, and thus modern marketing emerged to study consumer's needs and the ways to satisfy them (Luo, & Bhattacharya, 2006; Belz & Peattie, 2012). Current technological advancements help marketers to achieve these goals. Globalization, e-commerce, as well as environmental concerns have directed marketing activities more towards focusing on the relationship "between markets, regulation and social welfare" (Belz & Peattie, 2012). Marketing needs to deliver values in a sustainable manner (Martin & Schouten, 2014).

According to Belz and Peattie (2012), marketing can focus on sustainability issues by integrating social, environmental, and ethical values into marketing programs and strategies, researching consumer preferences, and developing a sustainability marketing mix as the traditional 4P is company-oriented. Otherwise, marketing will contribute to global problems such as climate change, resource depletion, poverty, and hunger rather than tackling them (Belz & Peattie, 2012). In this sense, sustainable marketing can facilitate addressing sustainability issues.

Becker-Olsen and Moynihan (2013) suggest a sustainable marketing mix including products to be designed and developed sustainably, companies using renewable and recyclable resources, and engaging in recycling. Furthermore, through marketing communication, companies can inspire consumers to act more sustainably as marketing plays an essential role in shaping consumer values (Becker-Olsen & Moynihan, 2013).

Producer-oriented 4P - product, place, price, and promotion had to move towards customer-oriented 4Cs - "Customer solutions, Customer cost, Convenience, and Communication", which is regarded as the sustainability marketing mix (Belz & Peattie, 2012). A sustainability-focused concept of marketing should (Figure 1):

- Take into account the ecological concerns, and meet consumer needs without damaging the environment, consider the limits of the planet, and reduce negative footprints;
- Be viable in terms of technologies and competitive advantage;
- Behave ethically, respect social equity and promote social justice;
- Move towards relationship-oriented activities between the company and all its stakeholders, rather than solely focusing on economic exchange (Belz & Peattie, 2012).

Thus, sustainable marketing combines modern marketing including economic objectives of commercial transactions with relationship marketing, sustainable development goals, and environmental "green", ethical, and social marketing perspectives.

Marketing has placed the main emphasis on customer needs and wants in order to gain profit (Kotler & Armstrong, 2020). Yet to direct marketing efforts toward addressing environmental and social issues,

Figure 1. Sustainability-focused concept of marketing
Source: Authors work based on Belz & Peattie, 2012.

the fields of ethical, green, environmental, and societal marketing emerged, which are included in the sustainability marketing concept (Martín-Cervantes et al., 2022). Sustainability marketing pursues the long-run relationship rather than short-term transactions in a way that social and ecological problems are not seen as limitations but taken into consideration in the marketing activities, and hence customer behavior is learned, the marketing mix is modified, and the marketing programs are used to deliver changes (Peattie & Belz, 2010).

In contrast to traditional marketing that encourages overconsumption leading to environmental degradation, a sustainable marketing paradigm addresses ecological issues, and ethical consumption and production (Becker-Olsen & Moynihan, 2013), Sustainable marketing seeks to balance customers' needs and socio-ecological problems rather than concentrate on consumer wants. Sustainable marketing subordinates the needs of customers to sustainability goals in the marketing system of supply, production, and distribution (Calu et al., 2015). For this reason, unsustainable products and services are replaced by sustainable ones. For example, instead of outdoor heaters, blankets made of eco-friendly materials can be offered (Peattie & Belz, 2010), plastic in packaging can be reduced, new technologies in window production can be used to enable more solar heat into rooms, and negative transportation effects can be decreased through sustainable distribution systems (Olsen & Moynihan, 2013).

Ultimately, sustainable efforts of marketing promote environmentally friendly behavior, offer eco-products, and enhance brand value and competitiveness through responsible strategies (Becker-Olsen & Moynihan, 2013).

3.4. Sustainable Marketing Focus on Consumers

Studies suggest that sustainable marketing programs should target a company's efforts toward sustainable practices emphasizing environmental protection to increase consumer support for sustainable business (Peterson et al., 2021). However, there are costs associated with producing and purchasing sustainable products. In addition, there might be financial and sustainable marketing investment risks (Vollero et al., 2023). In many cases, traditional market competition may impede companies to integrate sustainability into business strategies. If consumers were not attracted by goods and services that are produced without considering environmental and social aspects, producers would be forced to shift towards more sustainable business, facilitating sustainability market competition. Since the main goal of a firm is to generate profit in the traditional marketplace, the focus is on customers' needs and wants (Calu et al., 2015). However, scholars confirm that the sustainable behavior of a company is imitated by competitors (Calu et al., 2015). Consumers' positive evaluation of sustainable products can encourage companies in the market to pursue sustainability practices (Peterson et al., 2021).

Since sustainability is related to corporate social responsibility (Wei et al., 2020; Panait et al., 2022; Palazzo et al., 2022) that is incorporated into a firm's strategy (Feng & Ngai, 2020) and affects the competitiveness of a company (Weber, 2008; Apostu et al., 2023), consumers' values and perceptions are essential. Consequently, companies take into account how consumers perceive their sustainability efforts. In general, consumers worry about ecological issues and prefer natural products over non-biodegradable ones, however, a higher price for such products prevents customers from purchasing sustainable products (Zhang et al., 2021). Therefore, sustainable marketing programs can be connected to consumer values and preferences (Peterson et al., 2021).

To achieve sustainability, all three sides need to be taken into consideration: supply (brands), demand (consumers), and regulations (government and industries) (Zhang et al., 2021). From the supply chain perspective, business-to-business buyers encounter challenges to evaluate the sustainability practices of their partners. A systematic literature analysis indicated that B2B marketing in connection with SDGs needs more attention from scholars and practitioners as there is a lack of studies in this field (Voola et al., 2022).

Recently, more emphasis is put on sustainable consumption shifting buying habits towards sustainability principles (Orîndaru et al., 2021). Especially, after the coronavirus pandemic outbreak, people and businesses begin to rethink their actions (Gigauri, 2021; Gigauri & Djakeli, 2021). The study accessing consumption habits quantitatively confirms that consumers' purchase behavior was shaken by financial uncertainty due to the pandemic and economic crisis, their desire for fresh products increased, and they begin purchasing locally produced goods (Orîndaru et al., 2021). In addition, ecological problems gained more interest, and consumers expressed a willingness to pay more for ethically made products (Orîndaru et al., 2021). Consumers tend to support companies with sustainability practices and make purchase decisions in favor of firms following environmental and social responsibility (Nikolaou et al., 2019).

The online survey conducted by Peterson et al. (2021) in the USA with 304 participants indicated that consumers' values and ethical concerns positively impact sustainable business. The survey of 289 young consumers in Vietnam illustrated that consumers decide on an organic food category taking into account food safety, health awareness, and information about products as these factors form their attitude towards food, while environmental concerns play a minor role (Pham et al., 2019). It is noteworthy that price, lack of accessibility, and poor labeling hinder a purchase decision of sustainable products in developing countries (Pham et al., 2019).

Previous research exploring the attitudes of consumers towards fast fashion in the United Kingdom through a survey of 128 young people illustrated that awareness of sustainability is not necessarily translated into purchase behavior (Zhang et al., 2021). The research of 750 educated consumers in India showed that sustainable purchase behavior is influenced by various factors including consumer attitudes, perceived marketplace stimulus, consumers' awareness about sustainability issues, and their environmental concerns (Joshi & Rahman, 2017).

It should be noted that consumer attitude toward sustainability is not always reflected in their behavior. People are not always making rational choices but emotional buying often takes place, though the young generation still considers sustainability important (Zhang et al., 2021). In other words, having a positive attitude towards sustainable products or brands does not mean that they will only purchase sustainable products, or will always take into account sustainability issues when making a purchase decision. Some other factors that influence a consumer's purchase decisions, for example, price or availability. Besides, buying sustainable products, for example, sustainable fashion can be categorized as complex buying as it requires high involvement of consumers in choosing between brands or products and decision-making can be a long process in comparison with routine rebuy that is habitual (Zhang et al., 2021). However, a favorable attitude and sustainability concerns more often shape consumers' decisions toward sustainable products and brands.

Although the current turbulent times are triggering a re-evaluation of values, marketing models still stimulate consumption, and beliefs, desires, perceptions, and behaviors are inspired by products that can serve as a declaration of identities (Orîndaru et al., 2021).

Sustainable marketing contributes to sustainable business through sustainable product development, production processes, customer relationships, raising awareness, and studying the marketplace (Claudy et al., 2016). Moreover, sustainable marketing can be beneficial for promoting sustainable practices, understanding how customers make choices, and connecting strategies to consumer values (Peterson et al., 2021). For sustainable marketing, communication plays a pivotal role as consumer behavior is formed by media tools and awareness of sustainability issues can be created. On the other hand, sustainable marketing communication must not be misleading.

The future tendencies will show the further development of sustainable marketing at both conceptual and practical levels.

4. FUTURE OF SUSTAINABLE MARKETING

4.1. The Impact of Internet on Marketing

As the Internet has become ubiquitous in the past decade, with 60% of the world's population having access to the World Wide Web, online marketing has seen exponential growth, with many companies focusing most of their advertising efforts on the digital space in an effort to attract younger, more savvy costumers. And while having a strong online presence is paramount to large companies worldwide, the digital realm, where opinions are voiced freely and mistakes are often costly, presents its own set of unique challenges, especially when it comes to the image a certain organization tries to project. Appealing to a younger, more informed crowd also implies addressing a generation that is much more concerned about the environment, climate change, pollution, and sustainability than the previous ones.

Traditional online advertising, with the same ads being served indiscriminately to all groups of Internet users, is considered to be largely obsolete and ineffective. The advent of big data and the ability to target individuals based on their own specific interests, concerns, views of the world, and online habits have led to the development of much more user-focused online behavioral advertising which doesn't try to convince potential customers to purchase a certain product or service but rather offers them one specifically tailored to their online behavioral pattern. For example, an Internet user which frequently visits web pages related to environmental protection, climate change, harmful effects of pollution while at the same time sharing eco-friendly content on their social media accounts will be profiled by big data analytics firms and served ads promoting products made from recycled and organic materials, eco-friendly products and services, alternative transport methods and so on. Online behavioral advertising exhibits a strong positive correlation to the usefulness, relevance, and credibility of an ad for the web user (Aiolfi et al., 2023). While behavioral advertising yields much better results for online marketing campaigns and has a greater return on investment for a company's ad budget, providing at the same time relevance to the Internet user, it also tends to have a polarizing and segregating effect, which in the context of sustainable marketing, pushes companies to create more environmentally conscious ads for products that often do not fit such a description.

The push for building a "green" image for a company or product online frequently faces scrutiny from Internet users that are quickly able to search for alternative sources of information and expose greenwashing practices. This has led to the advent of much more refined, often subversive greenwashing strategies. A January 2023, report by Willis and colleagues has identified six new forms of greenwashing that companies employ in an attempt to deflect public discontent for environmentally damaging business practices (Figure 2).

Greenhushing is the act of under-reporting or deliberately hiding certain aspects regarding an organization's sustainability track record in order to evade public scrutiny.

Greenrinsing refers to ever-changing ESG targets that a certain company sets, in order to distract attention from the fact that previously set targets were never achieved.

Greenlabelling is the practice of labeling certain products as "green" in a misleading manner.

Greenshifting is the act of shifting the blame for a company's environmentally unfriendly practices onto other stakeholders and, oftentimes, the consumer.

Figure 2. The new faces of Greenwashing
Sources: Authors work based on Willis et.al., 2023.

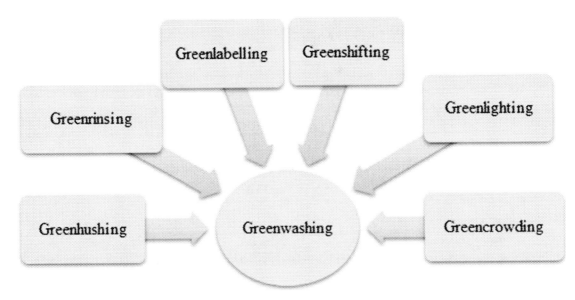

Greenlighting happens when a company's advertising campaigns focus on a certain green feature of its products or operations in order to draw attention away from its other, much bigger, environmentally harmful practices.

Greencrowding is the practice that focuses on building groups with large numbers of members in order to delay the implementation of sustainability policies, often by invoking lengthy processes and procedures associated with the group's size (Willis et al., 2023).

With greenwashing taking new forms, it's no surprise that the digital environment is flooded with false claims regarding the sustainability of products. A 2020 online sweep conducted by the Consumer Protection Cooperation Network of the European Union which examined 344 claims about the environmental characteristics of a product or a service sold online found that in 59% of cases, the vendor failed to provide clear evidence regarding the eco-friendliness which they claimed (Consumer Protection Cooperation Network, 2020).

Environmentally conscious consumers, concerned about the sustainability factor of the products and services they purchase and the companies they purchase them from, tend to be much more scrutinizing when it comes to advertising campaigns, exhibiting a higher level of ad skepticism than the general population and often seek detailed and specific green claims in advertising campaigns (Matthes & Wonneberger, 2014). Numerous online platforms now give Internet users the ability to verify the sustainability claims of advertisers and determine whether or not certain advertising campaigns are deceptive in nature. The fallout often associated with greenwashing practices that have been exposed to the general public can often lead to long-lasting and unpredictable negative effects for a company. A 2022 study by Neureiter and Matthes revealed the fact that even perceived greenwashing tactics in advertising can have a detrimental effect when it comes to the public's perception of a certain company, harming the brand both directly and indirectly (Neureiter & Matthes, 2022).

4.2. Virtual Reality, Virtual Influencers, and the Paradigm Shift of Digital Marketing

The digital space has seen profound transformations in the past few years. The emergence of novel technologies such as big data analytics, AI-generated content, virtual influencers, and tailor-made content has allowed online advertising to become more relevant to the individual.

Machine learning, allowing the automatic determination of optimal solutions to solve a certain problem without requiring human intervention (Dwyer et al., 2018), has empowered digital marketing companies to serve relevant ads, which have the maximum psychological effects on consumers. AI is taking things further with the advent of virtual influencers. Social media influencers have proven to be a valuable resource when it comes to digital advertising in the past few years and the growing market size for influencer marketing has reached 16.4 billion US dollars in 2022 (Figure 3).

Virtual influencers represent a metamorphosis of traditional online ads, that manage to communicate human-like emotions in a way no traditional display advertisement can. The contextual fit of an endorsement by a virtual influencer, without disclosure of sponsorship, tends to increase perceived transparency and credibility (Kim et al., 2023). Younger consumers seem to be attracted to virtual influencers and the latest data from the United States reveals that a staggering 75% of those aged between 18 and 24 follow at least one virtual influencer on their social media accounts (Figure 4).

The COVID-19 pandemic and the prolonged lockdowns have driven more people online than ever before. The search for an alternate reality has given rise to a completely new concept for a web-based

Figure 3. Influencer marketing market size worldwide
Source: Authors work based on data from Statista, 2023a: https://www.statista.com/statistics/1092819/global-influencer-market-size/

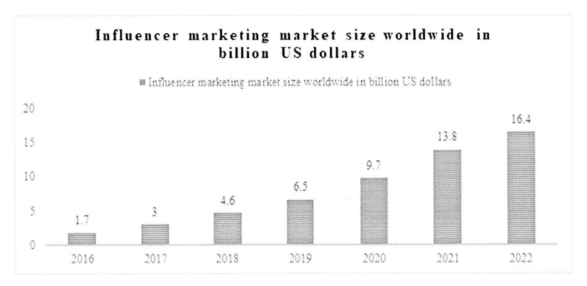

Figure 4. Share of consumers who follow at least one virtual influencer in the United States
Source: Authors work based on data from Statista, 2023b: https://www.statista.com/statistics/1304080/consumers-follow-virtual-influencers-age-us/

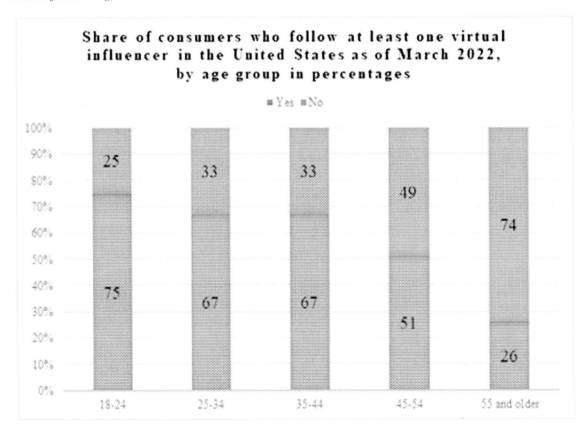

virtual society, manifested as the Metaverse. This new realm, completely digital in nature but populated by avatars of real-world individuals comes with unique opportunities but also unique challenges for advertisers. Turning virtual citizens into real-life consumers will require innovative use of marketing strategies that take into account the particularities and seemingly endless possibilities of the online world. With smart ad placements that are simply not possible in real life and a dynamic approach to advertising, the virtual city of the future will provide a more immersive experience than ever before (Vangelov, 2023). Metaverse shopping, however, does not necessarily have to translate to real-life purchases of goods and services. In game asset purchases have been on the rise in the past few years, with a market value estimated to reach 74.4 billion US dollars by the year 2025 (Kadry, 2022). Virtual assets that mirror real-world products but never materialize outside of the virtual space (such as clothes, furniture, vehicles, etc.) might prove extremely valuable as a way to convince digital shoppers to change their real-world purchasing habits. Products that are marketed as sustainable in the virtual world can translate to purchases of sustainable goods and services outside of the digital space.

5. CONCLUSION

In conclusion, Sustainable Marketing is a comprehensive approach to marketing that balances economic, social, and environmental goals and seeks to create long-term value for all stakeholders. It builds on the foundation of CSR and incorporates the principles of Social, Green, and Ethical Marketing, in order to create a more sustainable future for both businesses and society as a whole.

The implementation of Sustainable Marketing faces several challenges, including:

1. *Lack of consistent and unitary sustainability standards*: There is a lack of clear and consistent sustainability standards, which makes it difficult for companies to measure and report their sustainability performance. On the one hand, there is a need for a universally accepted and unitary standard on a global scale. At this point, the most well-known and used sustainability standards can be mentioned, which include different options such as Global Reporting Initiative, Sustainability Accounting Standards Board, ISO 14001 and Integrated Reporting. On the other hand, companies appeal to the so-called non-financial reporting instead, which has developed now (in some countries) from a voluntary to a mandatory highly standardized practice. At the same time, the companies must relate their activity to some critical issues such as Sustainable Development Goals and Science-Based Targets Initiative. In fact, this is necessary to ascertain the improvement of their productivity and efficiency and to establish to what extent the company generates a positive impact at the scale of the whole society;
2. *Resistance to change*: Some companies may be resistant to changing their traditional marketing practices and may be reluctant to embrace a more sustainable approach;
3. *Greenwashing*: The marketing of "green" or "eco-friendly" products can sometimes be misleading, with companies making false or exaggerated claims about their sustainability performance;
4. *Balancing conflicting goals*: Sustainable Marketing requires companies to balance competing economic, social, and environmental goals, which can be challenging.

Despite these challenges, the future of Sustainable Marketing is promising as consumers become increasingly concerned about the impact of their purchasing decisions on the environment and society.

Companies that embrace a more sustainable approach are likely to reap the benefits of improved reputation and financial performance, as well as a more sustainable future for all stakeholders.

However, for Sustainable Marketing to be successful, it is important for companies to continuously evaluate and improve their sustainability performance, and for stakeholders to hold them accountable for their actions. In addition, governments and industry organizations must work together to establish clear and consistent sustainability standards, and to educate consumers about the importance of sustainability in their purchasing decisions.

In summary, as an important idea, the future of Sustainable Marketing is promising, but it requires a collective effort from all stakeholders, including companies, consumers, governments, and industry organizations, to overcome the challenges and to create a more sustainable future for all.

REFERENCES

Ahmed, R. R., Streimikiene, D., Berchtold, G., Vveinhardt, J., Channar, Z. A., & Soomro, R. H. (2019). Effectiveness of online digital media advertising as a strategic tool for building brand sustainability: Evidence from FMCGs and services sectors of Pakistan. *Sustainability (Basel)*, *11*(12), 3436. doi:10.3390u11123436

Aiolfi, S., Bellini, S., & Pellegrini, D. (2021). Data-driven digital advertising: Benefits and risks of online behavioral advertising. *International Journal of Retail & Distribution Management*, *49*(7), 1089–1110. doi:10.1108/IJRDM-10-2020-0410

Alam, S. M. S., & Islam, K. M. Z. (2021). Examining the role of environmental corporate social responsibility in building green corporate image and green competitive advantage. *Int J Corporate Soc Responsibility*, *6*(8), 8. doi:10.118640991-021-00062-w

Apostu, S. A., Gigauri, I., Panait, M., & Martín-Cervantes, P. A. (2023). Is Europe on the Way to Sustainable Development? Compatibility of Green Environment, Economic Growth, and Circular Economy Issues. *International Journal of Environmental Research and Public Health*, *20*(2), 1078. doi:10.3390/ijerph20021078 PMID:36673838

Barbu, A., Catană, Ş.-A., Deselnicu, D. C., Cioca, L.-I., & Ioanid, A. (2022). Factors Influencing Consumer Behavior toward Green Products: A Systematic Literature Review. *International Journal of Environmental Research and Public Health*, *19*(24), 16568. doi:10.3390/ijerph192416568 PMID:36554445

Becker-Olsen, K., & Moynihan, K. (2013). Sustainable Marketing. In S. O. Idowu, N. Capaldi, L. Zu, & A. D. Gupta (Eds.), *Encyclopedia of Corporate Social Responsibility*. Springer. doi:10.1007/978-3-642-28036-8_105

Belz, F.-M., & Peattie, K. (2012). *Sustainability Marketing*. Wiley & Sons.

Bocken, N. (2021). Sustainable Business Models. In W. Leal Filho, A. M. Azul, L. Brandli, A. Lange Salvia, & T. Wall (Eds.), *Decent Work and Economic Growth. Encyclopedia of the UN Sustainable Development Goals*. Springer., doi:10.1007/978-3-319-95867-5_48

Borchardt, M., Ndubisi, N. O., Jabbour, C. J. C., Grebinevych, O., & Pereira, G. M. (2020). The evolution of base of the pyramid approaches and the role of multinational and domestic business ventures: Value-commitment and profit-making perspectives. *Industrial Marketing Management*, *89*, 171–180. doi:10.1016/j.indmarman.2019.05.013

Bridges, C. M., & Wilhelm, W. B. (2008). Going beyond green: The "why and how" of integrating sustainability into the marketing curriculum. *Journal of Marketing Education*, *30*(1), 33–46. doi:10.1177/0273475307312196

Calu, A., Negrei, C., Calu, D. A., & Avram, V. (2015). Reporting of Non-Financial Performance Indicators – a Useful Tool for a Sustainable Marketing Strategy. *Amfiteatru Economic*, *17*(40), 977–993.

Carrigan, M., & Attalla, A. (2001). The myth of the ethical consumer - do ethics matter in purchase behaviour? *Journal of Consumer Marketing*, *18*(7), 560–578. doi:10.1108/07363760110410263

Charter, M., Peattie, K., Ottman, J., & Polonsky, M. J. (2006). *Marketing and sustainability*. CSFD. https://cfsd.org.uk/smart-know-net/smart-know-net.pdf

Claudy, M. C., Peterson, M., & Pagell, M. (2016). The Roles of Sustainability Orientation and Market Knowledge Competence in New Product Development Success. *Journal of Product Innovation Management*, *33*, 72–85. doi:10.1111/jpim.12343

Costa, J., & Fonseca, J. P. (2022). The Impact of Corporate Social Responsibility and Innovative Strategies on Financial Performance. *Risks*, *10*(5), 103. doi:10.3390/risks10050103

Donaldson, T., & Walsh, J. P. (2015). Toward a theory of business. *Research in Organizational Behavior*, *35*, 181–20. doi:10.1016/j.riob.2015.10.002

Dwivedi, Y. K., Ismagilova, E., Hughes, D. L., Carlson, J., Filieri, R., Jacobson, J., Jain, V., Karjaluoto, H., Kefi, H., Krishen, A. S., Kumar, V., Rahman, M. M., Raman, R., Rauschnabel, P. A., Rowley, J., Salo, J., Tran, G. A., & Wang, Y. (2021). Setting the future of digital and social media marketing research: Perspectives and research propositions. *International Journal of Information Management*, *59*, 102168. doi:10.1016/j.ijinfomgt.2020.102168

Dwyer, D. B., Falkai, P., & Koutsouleris, N. (2018). Machine Learning Approaches for Clinical Psychology and Psychiatry. *Annual Review of Clinical Psychology*, *7*(14), 91–118. doi:10.1146/annurev-clinpsy-032816-045037 PMID:29401044

Elkington, J. (1994). Towards the Sustainable Corporation: Win-Win-Win Business Strategies for Sustainable Development. *California Management Review*, *36*(2), 90–100. doi:10.2307/41165746

Elkington, J. (2018). 25 Years Ago I Coined the Phrase "Triple Bottom Line." Here's Why It's Time to Rethink It. *Harvard Business Review*. https://hbr.org/2018/06/25-years-ago-i-coined-the-phrase-triple-bottom-line-heres-why-im-giving-up-on-it

Fallah Shayan, N., Mohabbati-Kalejahi, N., Alavi, S., & Zahed, M. A. (2022). Sustainable Development Goals (SDGs) as a Framework for Corporate Social Responsibility (CSR). *Sustainability (Basel)*, *14*(3), 1222. doi:10.3390u14031222

Feng, P., & Ngai, C. (2020). Doing more on the corporate sustainability front: A longitudinal analysis of CSR reporting of global fashion companies. *Sustainability (Basel)*, *12*(6), 2477. doi:10.3390u12062477

Frank-Martin, B., & Peattie, K. J. (2009). *Sustainability marketing: a global perspective*. Wiley.

Gaber, H. R., Wright, L. T., & Kooli, K. (2019). Consumer attitudes towards Instagram advertisements in Egypt: The role of the perceived advertising value and personalization. *Cogent Business & Management*, *6*(1), 1618431. doi:10.1080/23311975.2019.1618431

García-Salirrosas, E. E., & Rondon-Eusebio, R. F. (2022). Green Marketing Practices Related to Key Variables of Consumer Purchasing Behavior. *Sustainability (Basel)*, *14*(14), 8499. doi:10.3390u14148499

Garg, S., & Sharma, V. (2017). Green Marketing: An Emerging Approach to Sustainable Development. *International Journal of Applied Agricultural Research*, *12*(2), 177–184.

Gartner. (2019). 4 *Hidden forces that will shape marketing in 2019*. Gartner Research. https://www.gartner.com/en/marketing/insights/articles/4-hidden-forces-that-will-shape-marketing-in-2019

Gigauri, I. (2021). Corporate Social Responsibility and COVID-19 Pandemic Crisis: Evidence from Georgia. *International Journal of Sustainable Entrepreneurship and Corporate Social Responsibility*, *6*(1), 30–47. doi:10.4018/IJSECSR.2021010103

Gigauri, I., & Djakeli, K. (2021). Expecting Transformation of Marketing During the Post-Pandemic New Normal: Qualitative Research of Marketing Managers in Georgia. [IJSEM]. *International Journal of Sustainable Economies Management*, *10*(2), 1–18. doi:10.4018/IJSEM.2021040101

Gigauri, I., & Vasilev, V. (2022). Corporate Social Responsibility in the Energy Sector: Towards Sustainability. In S. A. R. Khan, M. Panait, F. Puime Guillen, & L. Raimi (Eds.), *Energy Transition. Industrial Ecology*. Springer. doi:10.1007/978-981-19-3540-4_10

Gironda, J. T., & Korgaonkar, P. K. (2018). iSpy? Tailored versus invasive ads and consumers' perceptions of personalized advertising. *Electronic Commerce Research and Applications*, *29*, 64–77. doi:10.1016/j.elerap.2018.03.007

Ibrahim, B., & Aljarah, A. (2018). Dataset of relationships among social media marketing activities, brand loyalty, revisit intention. Evidence from the hospitality industry in Northern Cyprus. *Data in Brief*, *21*, 1823–1828. doi:10.1016/j.dib.2018.11.024 PMID:30519601

Joshi, Y., & Rahman, Z. (2017). Investigating the determinants of consumers' sustainable purchase behaviour. *Sustainable Production and Consumption*, *10*, 110–120. doi:10.1016/j.spc.2017.02.002

Kadry, A. K. (2022). The Metaverse revolution and its impact on the future of advertising industry. *Journal of Design Sciences and Applied Arts*, *3*(2), 347–358. doi:10.21608/jdsaa.2022.129876.1171

Kaur, B., Gangwar, V. P., & Dash, G. (2022). Green Marketing Strategies, Environmental Attitude, and Green Buying Intention: A Multi-Group Analysis in an Emerging Economy Context. *Sustainability (Basel)*, *14*(10), 6107. doi:10.3390u14106107

Kim, D., Kim, E. A., & Shoenberger, H. (2023). The next hype in social media advertising: Examining virtual influencers' brand endorsement effectiveness. *Frontiers in Psychology*, *14*, 485. doi:10.3389/fpsyg.2023.1089051 PMID:36949930

Kotler, P., Kartajaya, H., Hooi, D. H., & Liu, S. (2002). *Rethinking Marketing: Sustainable Marketing Enterprise in Asia*. Pearson Education Canada.

Kotler, P., & Zaltman, G. (1971). Social Marketing: An Approach to Planned Social Change. *Journal of Marketing*, *35*(3), 3–12. doi:10.1177/002224297103500302 PMID:12276120

Kotler, P. T., & Armstrong, G. (2020). *Principles of marketing* (18th ed.). Person.

Low, M. P. (2016). Corporate Social Responsibility and the Evolution of Internal Corporate Social Responsibility in 21st Century. *Asian Journal of Social Sciences and Management Studies*, *3*(1), 56–74. doi:10.20448/journal.500/2016.3.1/500.1.56.74

Luo, X., & Bhattacharya, C. B. (2006). Corporate Social Responsibility, Customer Satisfaction, and Market Value. *Journal of Marketing*, *70*(4), 1–18. doi:10.1509/jmkg.70.4.001

Maccarrone, P., & Contri, A. M. (2021). Integrating Corporate Social Responsibility into Corporate Strategy: The Role of Formal Tools. *Sustainability (Basel)*, *13*(22), 12551. doi:10.3390u132212551

Machová, R., Ambrus, R., Zsigmond, T., & Bakó, F. (2022). The Impact of Green Marketing on Consumer Behavior in the Market of Palm Oil Products. *Sustainability (Basel)*, *14*(3), 1364. doi:10.3390u14031364

Majeed, M. U., Aslam, S., Murtaza, S. A., Attila, S., & Molnár, E. (2022). Green Marketing Approaches and Their Impact on Green Purchase Intentions: Mediating Role of Green Brand Image and Consumer Beliefs towards the Environment. *Sustainability (Basel)*, *14*(18), 11703. doi:10.3390u141811703

Mandal, P. C. (2019). Public Policy Issues in Direct and Digital Marketing – Concerns and Initiatives: Public Policy in Direct and Digital Marketing. [IJPADA]. *International Journal of Public Administration in the Digital Age*, *6*(4), 54–71. doi:10.4018/IJPADA.2019100105

Mandarić, D., Hunjet, A., & Vuković, D. (2022). The Impact of Fashion Brand Sustainability on Consumer Purchasing Decisions. *J. Risk Financial Manag.*, *15*(4), 176. doi:10.3390/jrfm15040176

Martin, D., & Schouten, J. (2014). *Sustainable marketing*. Pearson Prentice Hall.

Martin, K. D., & Murphy, P. E. (2017). The role of data privacy in marketing. *Journal of the Academy of Marketing Science*, *45*(2), 135–155. doi:10.100711747-016-0495-4

Martín-Cervantes, P. A., del Carmen Valls Martínez, M., & Gigauri, I. (2022). Sustainable Marketing. In *Encyclopedia of Creativity, Invention, Innovation and Entrepreneurship*. Springer. doi:10.1007/978-1-4614-6616-1_200101-1

Matthes, J., & Wonneberger, A. (2014). The skeptical green consumer revisited: Testing the relationship between green consumerism and skepticism toward advertising. *Journal of Advertising*, *43*(2), 115–127. doi:10.1080/00913367.2013.834804

Maziriri, E. T. (2020). Green packaging and green advertising as precursors of competitive advantage and business performance among manufacturing small and medium enterprises in South Africa. *Cogent Business & Management, 7*(1), 1. doi:10.1080/23311975.2020.1719586

Mir, S. N. (2016). Social marketing and its efficacy in creating responsible and respectful societies, *International Journal of Economics. Commerce and Management, 4*(3), 525–534.

Moravcikova, D., Krizanova, A., Kliestikova, J., & Rypakova, M. (2017). Green Marketing as the Source of the Competitive Advantage of the Business. *Sustainability (Basel), 9*(12), 2218. doi:10.3390u9122218

Nadanyiova, M., Gajanova, L., & Majerova, J. (2020). Green Marketing as a Part of the Socially Responsible Brand's Communication from the Aspect of Generational Stratification. *Sustainability (Basel), 12*(17), 7118. doi:10.3390u12177118

Nekmahmud, M., & Fekete-Farkas, M. (2020). Why Not Green Marketing? Determinates of Consumers' Intention to Green Purchase Decision in a New Developing Nation. *Sustainability (Basel), 12*(19), 7880. doi:10.3390u12197880

Nemes, N., Scanlan, S. J., Smith, P., Smith, T., Aronczyk, M., Hill, S., Lewis, S. L., Montgomery, A. W., Tubiello, F. N., & Stabinsky, D. (2022). An Integrated Framework to Assess Greenwashing. *Sustainability (Basel), 14*(8), 4431. doi:10.3390u14084431

Neureiter, A., & Matthes, J. (2022). Comparing the effects of greenwashing claims in environmental airline advertising: Perceived greenwashing, brand evaluation, and flight shame. *International Journal of Advertising*, 1–27. doi:10.1080/02650487.2022.2076510

Nikolaou, I. E., Tsalis, T. A., & Evangelinos, K. I. (2019). A framework to measure corporate sustainability performance: A strong sustainability-based view of firm. *Sustainable Production and Consumption, 18*, 1–18. doi:10.1016/j.spc.2018.10.004

Orîndaru, A., Popescu, M. F., Ceescu, S. C., Botezatu, F., Florescu, M. S., & Runceanu-Albu, C. C. (2021). Leveraging COVID-19 Outbreak for Shaping a More Sustainable Consumer Behavior. *Sustainability (Basel), 13*(11), 5762. doi:10.3390u13115762

Palazzo, M., Gigauri, I., Panait, M. C., Apostu, S. A., & Siano, A. (2022). Sustainable Tourism Issues in European Countries during the Global Pandemic Crisis. *Sustainability (Basel), 14*(7), 3844. doi:10.3390u14073844

Panait, M., Hysa, E., Raimi, L., Kruja, A., & Rodriguez, A. (2022). Guest editorial: Circular economy and entrepreneurship in emerging economies: opportunities and challenges. *Journal of Entrepreneurship in Emerging Economies, 14*(5), 673–677. doi:10.1108/JEEE-10-2022-487

Peattie, K. (2001). Towards Sustainability: The Third Age of Green Marketing. *The Marketing Review, 2*(2), 129–146. doi:10.1362/1469347012569869

Peattie, K., & Belz, F. M. (2010). Sustainability marketing—An innovative conception of marketing. *Marketing Review St. Gallen, 27*(5), 8–15. doi:10.100711621-010-0085-7

Peattie, S., & Peattie, K. (2003). Ready to fly solo? Reducing social marketing's dependence on commercial marketing theory. *Marketing Theory, 3*(3), 365–385. doi:10.1177/147059310333006

Peters, J., & Simaens, A. (2020). Integrating Sustainability into Corporate Strategy: A Case Study of the Textile and Clothing Industry. *Sustainability (Basel)*, *12*(15), 6125. doi:10.3390u12156125

Peterson, M., Minton, E. A., Liu, R. L., & Bartholomew, D. E. (2021). Sustainable Marketing and Consumer Support for Sustainable Businsses. *Sustainable Production and Consumption*, *27*, 157–168. doi:10.1016/j.spc.2020.10.018

Pham, T. H., Nguyen, T. N., Phan, T. T. H., & Nguyen, N. T. (2019). Evaluating the purchase behaviour of organic food by young consumers in an emerging market economy. *Journal of Strategic Marketing*, *27*(6), 540–556. doi:10.1080/0965254X.2018.1447984

Porter, M. E., & Kramer, M. R. (2002). The competitive advantage of corporate philanthropy. *Harvard Business Review*, *80*, 56–68. PMID:12510538

Quoquab, F., Mohamed Sadom, N. Z., & Mohammad, J. (2020). Sustainable Marketing. In S. Seifi (Ed.), *The Palgrave Handbook of Corporate Social Responsibility*. Palgrave Macmillan., doi:10.1007/978-3-030-22438-7_76-1

Richardson, N. (2022). How new sustainability typologies will reshape traditional approaches to loyalty. *Ital. J. Mark.*, 289–315. doi:10.1007/s43039-022-00047-y

Rodrigues, M., & Franco, M. (2019). The Corporate Sustainability Strategy in Organisations: A Systematic Review and Future Directions. *Sustainability (Basel)*, *11*(22), 6214. doi:10.3390u11226214

Sanclemente-Téllez, J.C. (2017). Marketing and Corporate Social Responsibility (CSR). Moving between broadening the concept of marketing and social factors as a marketing strategy, *Spanish Journal of Marketing - ESIC*, *21*(1), 4-25, doi:10.1016/j.sjme.2017.05.001

Sheth, J., & Parvatiyar, A. (1995). Ecological imperatives and the role of marketing. *Environmental marketing: Strategies, practice, theory, and research*, 3-20.

Shukla, P. S., & Nigam, P. V. (2018). E-shopping using mobile apps and the emerging consumer in the digital age of retail hyper personalization: An insight. *Pacific Business Review International*, *10*(10), 131–139.

Sikdar, S. K. (2019). Fractured state of decisions on sustainability: An assessment. *Sustainable Production and Consumption*, *19*, 231–237. doi:10.1016/j.spc.2019.04.004

Statista. (2023a). *Influencer marketing market size worldwide from 2016 to 2022*. Statista. https://www.statista.com/statistics/1092819/global-influencer-market-size/

Statista. (2023b). *Share of consumers who follow at least one virtual influencer in the United States as of March 2022, by age group*. Statista. https://www.statista.com/statistics/1304080/consumers-follow-virtual-influencers-age-us/

Sun, Y., & Shi, B. (2022). Impact of Greenwashing Perception on Consumers' Green Purchasing Intentions: A Moderated Mediation Model. *Sustainability (Basel)*, *14*(19), 12119. doi:10.3390u141912119

UN. (n.d.). *Sustainable Development Goals*. United Nations. https://www.un.org/sustainabledevelopment/

Vangelov, N. (2023). Ambient Advertising in Metaverse Smart Cities. *Smart Cities and Regional Development (SCRD). Journal, 7*(1), 43–55. doi:10.25019crdjournal.v7i1.175

Vayena, E., Blasimme, A., & Cohen, I. G. (2018). Machine learning in medicine: Addressing ethical challenges. *PLoS Medicine, 15*(11), e1002689. doi:10.1371/journal.pmed.1002689 PMID:30399149

Veseli-Kurtishi, T. (2018). Social media as a tool for the sustainability of small and medium businesses in Macedonia. *European Journal of Sustainable Development, 7*(4), 262–262. doi:10.14207/ejsd.2018.v7n4p262

Vock, M. (2022). Luxurious and responsible? Consumer perceptions of corporate social responsibility efforts by luxury versus mass-market brands. *Journal of Brand Management, 29*(6), 569–583. doi:10.105741262-022-00281-x

Vollero, A., Siano, A. & Bertolini, A. (2022). Ex ante assessment of sustainable marketing investments. *Italian Journal of Marketing,* 271-287. doi:10.1007/s43039-022-00052-1

Voola, R., Bandyopadhyay, C., Voola, A., Ray, S., & Carlson, J. (2022). B2B marketing scholarship and the UN sustainable development goals (SDGs): A systematic literature review. *Industrial Marketing Management, 101,* 12–32. doi:10.1016/j.indmarman.2021.11.013

Weber, M. (2008). The business case for corporate social responsibility: A company-level measurement approach for CSR. *European Management Journal, 26*(4), 247–261. doi:10.1016/j.emj.2008.01.006

Wei, A.-P., Peng, C.-L., Huang, H.-C., & Yeh, S.-P. (2020). Effects of Corporate Social Responsibility on Firm Performance: Does Customer Satisfaction Matter? *Sustainability (Basel), 12*(18), 7545. doi:10.3390u12187545

Welsh, D. T., Ordóñez, L. D., Snyder, D. G., & Christian, M. S. (2015). The slippery slope: How small ethical transgressions pave the way for larger future transgressions. *The Journal of Applied Psychology, 100*(1), 114–127. doi:10.1037/a0036950 PMID:24865577

Zairi, M. (2000). Social responsibility and impact on society. *The TQM Magazine, 12*(3), 172–178. doi:10.1108/09544780010320278

Zhang, B., Zhang, Y., & Zhou, P. (2021). Consumer Attitude towards Sustainability of Fast Fashion Products in the UK. *Sustainability (Basel), 13*(4), 1646. doi:10.3390u13041646

Chapter 3
Green Cosmetics:
Determinants of Purchase Intention

Ana Catarina Rodrigues
School of Economics and Management, University of Porto, Portugal

Paulo Botelho Pires
https://orcid.org/0000-0003-3786-6783
CEOS, Polytechnic of Porto, Portugal

Catarina Delgado
https://orcid.org/0000-0002-1494-0517
School of Economics and Management, University of Porto, Portugal

José Duarte Santos
https://orcid.org/0000-0001-5815-4983
CEOS, ISCAP, Polytechnic of Porto, Portugal

ABSTRACT

This study examined the determinants of purchase intention of green cosmetics, and eight semi-structured interviews were performed to identify them. The determinants identified were environmental awareness, lifestyle, willingness to pay, ethical issues and social and economic justice, cosmetic quality, concern with health, certification labels, trust in the brand, and advertising. Environmental awareness, lifestyle, willingness to pay, quality issues, ethics, and social and economic justice, as well as quality expectations, health concerns, and product knowledge, are the most significant determinants in the intention to purchase green cosmetics. Determinants such as certification labels, brand trust, and advertising are less significant. The research is relevant for the cosmetics industry and its brands to adapt their strategy and product offering to meet consumers' needs and increase the consumption of green cosmetics and can also serve as a basis for the development of new quantitative studies on the purchase intention of green cosmetics.

1. INTRODUCTION

Sustainable human behavior and consumption habits will determine the destiny of the coming generations in a time when environmental challenges are inescapable and their effects are evident, highlighting

DOI: 10.4018/978-1-6684-8681-8.ch003

among others climate change, air pollution, wildlife extinction, or soil degradation. Consequently, there is an increasing need for people to embrace behaviors that have the fewest negative effects on the environment (Doppelt, 2012). The cosmetics industry comprises a broad range of products that consumers use daily, including shampoo, shower gel, cream, and makeup, among others. In this industry, there are an increasing number of alternatives to traditional cosmetics being offered, with green cosmetics (also known as eco-friendly cosmetics) being the highlight. Yet, as Johnstone and Tan (2015) stated, there is a disparity between those who assert to be concerned about the environment and those who really exhibit pro-environmental consumption. This reveals a gap between customer behavior and their intention to make green purchases. The fact that many people have a level of skepticism and resistance toward green products compromises green purchasing (Goh & Balaji, 2016). The notion of green cosmetics is then explored in this research using qualitative analysis to identify the determinants that influence customers' decision to buy green cosmetics and it is designed to further examine and deepen the meaning of green cosmetics, a phrase that is seen by consumers as complicated and divergent, in addition to identifying the variables perceived as drivers or obstacles to the purchase of green cosmetics.

Therefore, the primary research question of this research is "What determinants impact the purchase intention of green cosmetics?". It will also explore and define "What is a green cosmetic from the consumer's perspective?" and review the idea of green cosmetics considering the literature that has already been published. The authors will particularly address "What features do consumers desire in a green cosmetic?" through the analysis of the determinants that influence customers' purchasing intentions.

2. LITERATURE REVIEW

Both quantitative and qualitative research need extensive use of the literature and therefore it is crucial to conduct a literature review to identify and define key constructs, deepen their understanding, and find data collection and analysis techniques that are useful for this research (vom Brocke & Rosemann, 2013). Therefore, a group of constructs and concepts from the literature review that has relevance to this research are described below.

2.1. Environmental Context

Society is significantly impacted by climate change and the contrary is also true. The severity and effects of natural catastrophes are also influenced by societal development and lifestyle choices. As a result, human behavior and their lack of environmental understanding and sensitivity raise concerns about sustainability and human existence (Borrego et al., 2010). Thus, it is imperative to raise public awareness about the need to protect the environment and ensure sustainability, as stated by Romero et al. (2018), since the environmental impact depends on the choices made by consumers in their daily lives, including their choices of consumer products. As a result, it may be possible for people to choose greener products. Despite being conscious of environmental changes, the controversy is that not everyone is aware of the connection between environmental change and individual behavior. Yet, to influence shifts in customers' purchasing behavior, it is critical to improve consumers' environmental education and also to raise their understanding (Wijekoon & Sabri, 2021). Pro-environmental behavior may thus be thought of as an action that reduces the adverse effects on the environment. Hence, reducing resource use, energy use, harmful compounds, and waste production are some examples of pro-environmental actions (Kollmuss & Agyeman, 2002). According to Rawof (2021), sustainability refers to the employment of environmentally friendly practices to ensure that resources will be available for future generations. These days, more and more customers are placing a high priority on sustainability. Parallel to this, they begin to give the environment more thought in their decisions and spending patterns, which raises their awareness of and demand for green products (Kahraman & Kazançoğlu, 2019).

2.2. Cosmetics

Regulation (EC) No. 1223/2009 of the European Parliament and of the Council defines a cosmetic product as any substance or mixture intended to be placed in contact with the external parts of a human body, teeth, or mucous membranes of the oral cavity with the sole or primary purpose of cleaning, perfuming, protecting, or maintaining good body odors. The words beauty and personal care products can also refer to items that are regarded as cosmetics, such as deodorants, hygiene products, scents, hair products, kits, skincare, and sun protection, as well as shower and bath products, as well as particular care items for newborns and children. Cosmetics have long been a part of society's life, claim Amberg and Fogarassy (2019). From Egyptian civilization, which already used cosmetics (colors and face and body oils), to modern society, people continue to use products that they view as essential for daily hygiene (such as shampoo, soap, and toothpaste), products that they view as essential for skin care and preservation (such as sunscreen and other lotions), and even other products that boost their confidence (such as make-up).

Amberg and Fogarassy (2019) revealed that the role of sustainable or natural products in the cosmetics industry is growing and becoming increasingly significant. Yet in the cosmetic business, many chemical components, including additives, fragrances, glosses, and stabilizers, are used in its production. As a result, the goal of these compounds is to improve the quality and shelf life of cosmetics. Yet, because of the broad and continuous exposure of food chains to these same bioactive compounds, they are prone to bioaccumulation, or the accumulation of hazardous substances along a food chain, which poses a risk to both human health and the environment (Bilal et al., 2020).

Some of the most dangerous ingredients found in synthetic cosmetics were identified by Csorba and Boglea (2011), including phthalates, lead found in hair dye, petroleum products like BHA (associated with cancer), mercury-containing products, fragrances, formaldehyde, propylene glycol, or para-aminobenzoic acid (PABA), a common ingredient found in sunscreens and known to have cancer-causing properties. As a result, more and more consumers are searching for advantages in natural and organic products without harmful ingredients and without the risk of damaging the skin, considering all the chemicals and preservatives present in traditionally used cosmetics (also known as traditional cosmetics).

2.3. Green Cosmetics

With promises like 100% natural ingredients, eco-friendly advantages, vegan, cruelty-free, sustainable packaging, sustainable production techniques, biodegradable formulation, and plastic-free packaging, among others, many companies are establishing new cosmetic product lines. Several definitions of the phrase green product are put forth in the literature. The absence of a comprehensive and precise definition for this word is highlighted by Sdrolia and Zarotiadis (2019) as a concern. Having said that, the authors offered a precise and comprehensive description of the definition of a green product based on a thorough examination of the literature. Using the authors' definition, a green cosmetic is a tangible product that, considering current technical and scientific advances, minimizes the environmental effects of the product during the various phases of its life cycle. The term green is used by the authors of various studies to refer to ecological, eco-friendly, environmental, or sustainable practices (Sdrolia & Zarotiadis, 2019).

The issue of the vagueness and complexity of the term green product is addressed by Durif et al. (2010). They define a green product as one whose design, attributes, production, and strategy use recycled, renewable, biodegradable, and toxin-free resources in a way that allows for improving the environmental impact or reducing the environmental toxic damage throughout the product life cycle. This definition is based on the codification of several academic definitions. In turn, Franca and Ueno (2020) define green cosmetics as products with ecological claims and appeals, manufactured under green chemistry principles, which strive to lessen or completely prevent the development of compounds harmful to ecosystems. Given that it might change over time because of advancements in science and technology, the term green can be seen as dynamic. According to this follow-up, a product that is viewed as a green alternative at one point in time may have an alternative that is viewed as significantly greener (having a lower impact on the environment) years later as a result of scientific advancement and the rise in green solutions available at the time (Ottman, 1992).

Csorba and Boglea (2011) state that for a product to be labeled as a green cosmetic, it must not be tested on animals, be referred to as natural, organic, or vegetarian by a trustworthy independent organization, contributes to environmental protection through research, donations, or other means, and have packaging that was created using efforts to save the planet like recyclable materials. According to the authors, an organic cosmetic is a product made using sustainable agricultural methods and free of toxic, chemical, pesticide, and herbicide substances.

Using natural components is frequently included in discussions of what constitutes green cosmetics. In light of this, Bom et al. (2019) contend that customers generally possess considerable misinformation. They claim that customers identify natural chemicals with something beneficial while negatively associating manufactured cosmetic elements. The authors do, however, contend that natural or purportedly organic cosmetics are not necessarily sustainable. Sustainability in this context refers to the interaction of social, environmental, and economic components. As a result, they believe that an item's natural status does not automatically qualify it as a sustainable ingredient. Many factors, including whether the chemical has been synthesized, extracted, or refined, as well as the source of the raw material from which it was removed, must be taken into consideration when determining if an ingredient is sustainable (whether synthetic, animal, or plant). Even if natural substances are preferred, they could be harmful to the environment.

There are, however, studies, in which the designation green cosmetics is a category composed of organic cosmetics and natural cosmetics. In the same vein, Furtado and Sampaio (2020) refer to green cosmetics or sustainable cosmetics as synonyms. For the authors, sustainable cosmetics are associated with cosmetics that encompass care with the composition, ingredients, or packaging and other social issues such as (better) working conditions, not using slave labor, or increasing the number of jobs for the community. For Franca and Ueno (2020) the concept of green cosmetics covers, in addition to the previous aspects, cosmetics with vegan compositions and free of animal testing.

Cinelli et al. (2019) emphasize that a cosmetic can also be considered more sustainable due to the materials that make up its packaging, such as packaging composed of bio-based and biodegradable materials, the use of circular economy policies that allow collecting and recycling the packaging in question, among other alternative solutions.

Thus, despite widespread calls for green products, the term green cosmetics still lacks a precise definition. The terms green cosmetics, organic cosmetics, and natural cosmetics don't quite match up, hence it's important to refer to the numerous certification programs that specify the criteria for designating a cosmetic as natural or organic. The study of the different certification programs for organic or natural products enables us to conclude that regulatory agencies generally define minimum percentages of organic ingredients, minimum percentages of natural ingredients or botanical ingredients, and maximum percentages of synthetic or naturally derived ingredients. Yet, depending on the certification system, different values and standards are shown. These products can be categorized differently depending on the certification system that is being used for the classification of the cosmetic because there is no government definition of green cosmetics or regulation in this order, as well as a difference in the criteria adopted by the certification systems (Franca & Ueno, 2020). Fonseca-Santos et al. (2015) strengthen this perspective, pointing out that there are several certification agencies in the world, each with its parameters defined at the level of certification and labeling of cosmetics. As a result, there is no harmonization of the guidelines and standards set by the different entities, so each product is classified as organic or natural, depending always on the regulation used. There are many different certification agencies, such as BDIH in Germany, NASAA in Australia, the Soil Association Organic Standard in the United Kingdom, IBD in Brazil, ECOCERT in France, ICEA in Italy, QAI and Oregon Tilth in the USA, and COSMOS (Fonseca-Santos et al., 2015). It is also relevant to add another certification. A recognized worldwide standard, ISO 16128 was developed to establish definitions and requirements for natural and organic cosmetic materials and products to define a common language on a global scale. However, unlike previous certification systems, this standard does not address issues such as lists of prohibited ingredients, product claims and labels, environmental safety, socio-economic considerations, storage characteristics, and cosmetic packaging, nor does it quantify a minimum percentage to define a product as organic or natural. It also allows the use of genetically modified organisms where these are permitted in the product's country of origin (Standardization, 2016). Although ISO 16128 defines natural ingredients, Carré (2021) reports that it only refers to the materials' origins and does not discuss their chemical changes or processes. As a result, there is debate concerning the standard and information contained in ISO 16218.

The EU Commission has announced the expansion of the EU Ecolabel to all cosmetics in 2021 to lessen cosmetic mislabeling. The EU Ecolabel, which has been used since 1992 for other product categories, encourages the use of ingredients that are more environmentally friendly and renewable by focusing on criteria that aim to lessen the environmental impact of products on water, soil, and biodiversity to help create a world free of toxic substances. The label is assumed by the European Commission as a voluntary label with environmental excellence and is recognized for its potential to inspire mandatory legislation, encourage producers to generate less hazardous chemicals, less carbon dioxide waste during manufacturing processes, and more durable, repairable, and recyclable products.

According to this literature review, the term green cosmetics is typically associated with a product that, in comparison to conventional cosmetics, has a lower environmental impact on ecosystems and the planet, and is also associated with the natural or organic component of the product. As there is no precise legislation that clearly defines the concept of green cosmetics, this research revealed that the designation is generally used to refer to products that are both natural and organic.

2.4. Intention to Purchase Green

Concerns about the environment and a desire to protect oneself and one's surroundings among consumers have started to influence their shopping behavior and enhance their propensity for environmentally friendly purchases. In this respect, terms like recycled, recyclable, oil-free, or cruelty-free animal for instance, have begun to be highlighted as attributes of various consumer products and drawing attention from consumers (Ottman, 1992). Consumers who are concerned about sustainability are looking for greener alternatives and this applies to cosmetics in the purchase decision, where consumers are more likely to buy sustainable alternatives than non-sustainable cosmetics (Rawof, 2021). Liobikienė and Bernatonienė (2017) conclude that in the purchase of green cosmetics, determinants such as health awareness, environmental concern, social factors, environmental knowledge, and product price stand out and that environmental attitude or concern is the most analyzed factor.

From another perspective, Johnstone and Tan (2015) suggested several barriers to green consumption: difficulty in being green, lack of money, lack of knowledge about the product and environment, lack of time, lack of self-discipline, and a green stigma. Green consumer reservations translate into uncertainty about the difference green consumption makes to the environment, making it difficult to promote behavior change.

2.5. Determinants of Green Cosmetics Purchase Intention

The key determinants that have been identified in the literature as influencing factors for consumer purchase intentions of green cosmetics will be discussed in the next sections.

2.5.1. Environmental Awareness

Environmental awareness is the propensity of a person to advocate for or oppose environmental concerns. As a result, Bedante (2004) highlighted that sustainable consumption is reliant on the consumer's level of environmental awareness in their research, which supported the impact of environmental knowledge on consumer behavior. Klineberg et al. (1998) prescribe four approaches to measure consumer environmental awareness or knowledge: 1) the seriousness an individual attaches to different types of environmental pollution; 2) the priority he gives to environmental issues compared to political and economic interests; 3) the degree of involvement in pro-environmental activities; 4) the assessment of his environmental outlook by how he relates human activity and the global environmental threat. Concern about purchasing items that do not hurt the environment arises among customers for whom environmental awareness is a basic value. Examples include personal care products free of synthetic chemicals, pesticides, and animal testing (Kim & Chung, 2011).

Chin et al. (2018) contend that customer perception of a product's environmental consciousness has a favorable impact on the attitude toward it. According to Patak et al. (2021), purchasing green consumer chemicals is largely influenced by environmental concerns. According to Tamashiro et al. (2014), ecological knowledge or awareness and ecological attachment are factors that determine the consumer's behavioral reaction to the environment. Paço and Raposo (2009) argue that although consumers are generally aware of environmental issues, they don't always act in an ecologically responsible way as a result of their worries. Although more environmentally concerned customers may be more inclined to purchase green cosmetics, Amberg and Fogarassy (2019) contend that their propensity to do so is influenced by other elements such as their level of education and information. Environmental awareness may be altered by education in ecological behavior, which can also help people understand the advantages and drawbacks of living sustainably (Wijekoon & Sabri, 2021). Given the above, the following research proposition is formulated:

- **RP1:** The individual's environmental awareness influences his or her intention to purchase green cosmetics.

2.5.2. Certification Labels

Environmental seals or labels serve as a representation of a product's or service's environmental qualities through declarations, symbols, or images that are placed on the product label or packaging. Increasing consumer trust in the brand's environmental sustainability is crucial. For this, the adoption of environmental labels, also known as eco-labels, is advised since they enable consumers to form positive connections with the environment in their minds. These help consumers have more faith in the environmental performance of a specific brand as well as the environmental messages or claims that the company communicates (Montoro Rios et al., 2006).

Liu et al. (2015) compared the effectiveness of two approaches to promote the purchase of carbon-neutral products. In the first approach, the carbon calculation was displayed on the product packaging, and in the second approach, the product contained only an eco-label. They found that consumer attitude and willingness to buy products with this environmentally sustainable feature increased when the eco-label was present, compared to if the product presented the carbon calculation in its composition. Similarly, Thøgersen (2021) emphasizes the value of labels in his research by arguing that the carbon footprint label may help customers who wish to make ecologically responsible choices. Also, Rawat and Garga (2012) indicate that green labels should be a trusted brand emblem for the majority of people. Moreover, Melović et al. (2020) stated that labels are one of the components that pull in customers and make it possible to distinguish between organic and conventional products. The authors emphasize the necessity of putting more effort into enhancing the credibility and recognition of official certifications of brands to help consumers distinguish between products and boost their consumption of organic products.

Janßen and Langen (2017) attempted to assess consumers' response to the vastness of labels, finding that they still do not understand the true meaning of the term sustainability. The plurality of labels representing green issues is not yet understood in all its complexity by consumers. It is suggested a universal sustainable label that covers the various aspects of sustainable production. It is important to build consumer confidence in green labeling. In essence, customers who are aware of green labels may understand what they mean and the benefits of purchasing products with labels (Wijekoon & Sabri, 2021). Parallel to this, Liu et al. (2012) found that just a small percentage of people recognize eco-labels. They suggest that their efficacy is unclear, particularly for consumers who lack a strong understanding of the surroundings and the meaning of the label. As a result, labels may become less effective due to a lack of understanding and trust, which results in labels that have no effect on customer purchasing decisions (Joshi & Rahman, 2015). In view of the above, the following research proposition is formulated:

- **RP2:** The presence of certification labels on cosmetics influences the intention to purchase green cosmetics.

2.5.3. Brand Trust

Chen (2010) defined green trust as the readiness to rely on a product or service because one believes or expects that company to be trustworthy, caring, and knowledgeable about how well it treats the environment. So, evidence of the transparency of green qualities enables customers to believe in the social responsibility of a specific company and to build a favorable brand image, which helps to build confidence in the green brand and the so-called green brand equity. The consumer's readiness to purchase green cosmetics is therefore impacted by developing green brand confidence (Lee & Chen, 2019). The same is confirmed by Yildirim (2021) who, when examining the purchase intention of cosmetics and personal care products, concluded that brand trust positively affects the purchase intention of personal care products. Similarly, Amallia et al. (2021) found that customer attitude has a strong positive impact on green brand trust, which in turn affects consumers' desire to make green purchases. Although trustworthy qualities are promised, a lack of confidence in the items being sold may reduce consumer purchase intention (Sun et al., 2021). Contrarily, increasing customer propensity to purchase green cosmetics is impacted by developing green brand credibility (Lee & Chen, 2019).

According to Morales et al. (2020), greenwashing is mostly to blame for customers' lack of faith in and skepticism about the firms' environmentally friendly business operations, which results in less environmentally friendly consumer behavior. Greenwashing is the practice of two behaviors: communicating and claiming to operate in an ecologically good manner while acting in an environmentally unfriendly manner (Delmas & Burbano, 2011). To put it another way, Jog and Singhal (2020) define greenwashing as a dishonest marketing strategy used by companies to deceive customers about the brand's environmental performance and the advantages of its products and services. As a result, greenwashing makes it more difficult for customers to recognize genuine green products, which affects how they perceive and feel about the product's green message (Johnstone & Tan, 2015). Kahraman and Kazançoğlu (2019) concluded that greenwashing when sensed by customers, negatively affects their perception, altering their trust, perceived risk, skepticism, and, as a result, the inclination to buy items marketed as environmentally friendly. A mention must also be made about the research of Rawat and Garga (2012), which found that people are dubious about the credibility of green claims made by brands. They advise that the green claim be supported by a reliable green certification label to win over consumers and potentially increase their desire to purchase green cosmetics for themselves and their families.

In conclusion, Jog and Singhal (2020) noted that the association between responsiveness to green advertising and green purchasing behavior is moderated by the amount of awareness of greenwashing. To enhance green purchasing intention, businesses must raise the perceived sustainable value, lower perceived environmental risk, and boost perceived environmental trust. Customers' skepticism about a product's sustainability promises may be raised by lowering their perceived risk, which will increase their confidence in eco-friendly items. Chen and Chang (2012) believe that green trust promotes green buying intention and behavior beneficially. In light of the foregoing, the following research proposition is made:

- **RP3:** Brand trust influences the purchase intention of green cosmetics.

2.5.4. Quality and Attributes

The perceived quality can be seen as the consumer's assessment of the brand excellence, based on its intrinsic value, namely in aspects such as its performance, and its extrinsic value, through aspects such as the brand name, knowing that the perceived quality of a product is a crucial factor with high influence on consumer behavior (Mohammad & Baharun, 2018). The perceived quality of the product is cited by Gleim et al. (2013) as a deciding factor for product purchase. For green products with higher pricing, the advantages highlighted in the product constitute a vital aspect to fulfill the consumer's quality expectation.

Green Cosmetics

According to Furtado and Sampaio (2020), perceived quality is a determining factor in consumer purchase motivation for cosmetics. Perceived quality has been demonstrated to positively affect customer brand loyalty in studies on green cosmetics. Because of this, customers respond favorably to functional advantages and product quality and tend to believe in the brand (Hwang et al., 2021). Al-Haddad et al. (2020) and Chen and Chang (2012) have also found that consumers tend to prioritize the attributes in a choice between product attributes or the level of sustainability of a product, suggesting that they are unlikely to compromise the value and quality they expect from a product. Chin et al. (2018) suggest that green product brands should focus on providing excellent functionality and consumer benefits, as well as a green factor and high perceived value, to increase consumer trust and green purchase intention.

Additionally, authors Romero et al. (2018) highlight aspects such as the sensory pleasantness of the cosmetic as a relevant attribute for consumers, and Wijekoon and Sabri (2021) concluded that products with functional and high-quality features strongly motivate purchase and foster positive consumer attitudes towards green Purchase intention. Consumers are more willing to engage in questionable moral behavior when they perceive that it brings them more net benefits (Sun et al., 2021). The following research proposition is offered in light of the aforementioned:

- **RP4:** Quality expectation influences the purchase intention of green cosmetics.

2.5.5. Lifestyle

According to Ribeiro and Veiga (2011), customers with organic eating habits or diets higher in vegetables and natural products have a stronger propensity to purchase natural and organic cosmetics. The individual's lifestyle and preferences have an impact on their purchasing intention because, according to Akkaya (2021), consumer purchasing behavior represents their identity. Patak et al. (2021) demonstrate that lifestyle affects the propensity to buy green consumer chemicals in their study on purchasing intentions. Kim and Chung (2011) conclude that a consumer's prior experience with organic personal care products can indicate their desire to make a purchase. The consumer's judgment of the items is influenced by experience, which also influences their decision to buy the same things. The authors provide evidence that a person's buying behavior reflects his lifestyle. In view of the above, the following research proposition is formulated:

- **RP5:** The lifestyle adopted by the individual in his daily routine, influences the intention to purchase green cosmetics.

2.5.6. Advertising

According to Ottman (1992), brands may inform customers, raise their understanding of environmental issues, alter their perspectives, and demonstrate the advantages of more environmentally friendly consumption. Advertisements that make claims about a product's green features or manufacturing procedures are referred to as green advertising. It promotes the ecological traits that make it possible to distinguish a product or service that helps to maintain or preserve the environment. Therefore, the primary goal of green advertising is to persuade people to purchase products or services by highlighting qualities (inherent to the product) that are environmentally friendly (Chan, 2004). It is crucial in advertising products with the green label. Sun et al. (2021) go a step further by proposing a connection between advertising and purchase intention for products with environmental labels. According to the authors, items with eco-labels highlight their environmental advantages, and consumers who are open to green advertising are more likely to buy products with eco-labels. Consumers who are influenced by green advertising are aware of environmental problems and are aware that their actions impact the environment. Amallia et al. (2021) acknowledged that green advertising should be used by companies, to increase consumers' perception of green brands and increase their green purchase intentions and decisions. Another contribution comes from Pop et al. (2020), who claimed that altruistic motivation, translates into a positive attitude that can formulate the intention to purchase green cosmetics by motivating their pro-environmental behaviors. The following study proposition is created in light of the aforementioned:

- **RP6:** Advertising influences the purchase intention of green cosmetics.

2.5.7. Willingness to Pay

Income was the most important demographic determinant for green purchasing in developing nations, according to Wijekoon and Sabri (2021) research. It was determined that raising consumer income has a beneficial influence on their green purchasing behavior since consumer income has a substantial impact on that behavior (Liu et al., 2012). Additionally, it was shown by Zahid et al. (2018) on the variables influencing green purchasing intention that price is not a deterrent for customers from socioeconomic classes with higher incomes or larger economic power, exhibiting more ecologically friendly behavior.

Rajput et al. (2022) assert that customers must accept higher prices for green marketing methods to be successful. Additionally, Lai and Cheng (2016) concluded that the desire to pay for environmentally friendly products predicts green consumer behavior. Amberg and Fogarassy (2019) concluded that customers are more prepared to spend extra on natural cosmetics than on other conventional cosmetics due to their concern for things like health and the environment. The cost of cosmetics is not a concern for customers, according to another study, since they believe that using green cosmetics protects them from potential harm to both them and the environment. As a result, they are prepared to spend a significant amount of money on these products (Rawat & Garga, 2012). Joung et al. (2014) found that age, monthly income, and whether or not they had children proved to be statistically significant factors for willingness to pay for environmentally friendly cosmetics. But Kaliyadan et al. (2021) reinforce that cosmetics need to be priced affordable to consumers' monetary availability. Kim and Chung (2011) determined that people's feeling of control over their ability to make purchases is higher and, as a result, their purchase intention increases. In this sense, how customers view the cost of a product and their capacity to purchase it affects how they feel about the decision to buy it. In view of the above, the following research proposition is formulated:

- **RP7:** Willingness to pay influences the purchase intention of green cosmetics.

2.5.8. Social Influence

Johnstone and Tan (2015) claim that the concept of green products is still not seen as a social norm. If the social norm is weak enough, green behavior will not be viewed as normal, and the customer will be less inclined to consider it since the social norm symbolizes morally right behavior. The propensity to buy green cosmetics is positively impacted by consumers' perceptions of social worth. Instead of focusing on the practical qualities of a product, consumers make purchases based on their social ideals, such as pride, respect, and social acceptability (Choi & Lee, 2019). Also, Zahid et al. (2018) cited social appreciation as a factor in consumers' green behavior. According to Wijekoon and Sabri (2021), social pressure and word-of-mouth can persuade consumers to choose environmentally friendly products. Before this, Klöckner (2013) developed a thorough psychology model of environmental behavior in which he showed that individuals typically respond and are impacted by what other people do. Social impact is therefore regarded as vital and important to the development of an aim. The acceptance of family and friends was discovered by the authors to be a factor affecting the purchase of sustainable cosmetics, albeit not a particularly important one. Along with the approval, the use and advice of loved ones may also influence a consumer's choice (Furtado & Sampaio, 2020). In this sense, communication from family, friends, close friends, or the media itself showed to be a potentially influencing aspect in the consumer's purchase decision within the context of social influence, independent of proximity. In view of the above, the following research proposition is formulated:

- **RP8:** Social influence impacts the purchase intention of green cosmetics.

2.5.9. Ethical Issues and Social and Economic Justice

Consumers' interest in acting ethically, which includes matters like animal welfare, using natural foods, being vegan, and using sustainable packaging, is growing steadily (Rawof, 2021). Chatterjee et al. (2022) conducted their study to determine how two ethical certifications affect consumers' purchasing intentions and readiness to pay a premium. The authors concluded that customers prefer products that have been certified as being free of animal cruelty and protecting children's rights (child-labor-free products). This indicates that having both certifications boost consumer confidence, buying intent, and willingness to pay for the cosmetic. Similarly to this, Furtado and Sampaio (2020) bring out the animal concern as one of the most important aspects for customers when choosing sustainable cosmetics as drivers of consumption. For some customers, the absence of guinea pigs and animal cruelty testing in a cosmetic adds to the appeal of the product. The authors also point out that social concern, or the desire to avoid hurting others and protect the environment, is often linked to environmental care. Consumers in this situation are worried about the ethical standards, social and environmental effect, and environmental impact of the brands of items they want to purchase. An important aspect influencing someone's decision to buy green cosmetics is their understanding of the environment and consumer ethics (Furtado & Sampaio, 2020). In this way, consumer behavior regarding the environment can be linked to a moral duty, more specifically, a personal standard. In other words, a person's moral character affects his or her purchasing decisions and may have positive or negative effects on the environment (Ölander & Thøgersen, 1995). Because of the above, the following research proposition is formulated:

- **RP9:** The inclusion of ethical and social and economic justice issues in cosmetics influences the purchase intention of green cosmetics.

2.5.10. Concern With Health

People are becoming more cognizant of the need of maintaining their health, which has led to a discernible rise in demand for food products that are seen as healthier (Mohammad & Baharun, 2018). When choosing green cosmetics, customers place a high priority on their health and care for others and their own well-being. Because they believe green products are better for their health, customers do not equate physical hazards with green cosmetic items (Durif et al., 2010). Due to the idea that green cosmetics are better or safer for the consumer's health, this association (perception) influences the consumer's intention to purchase. Still, in the same study, the authors discover that increased health consciousness makes consumers more conscious of what they eat and shapes their attitudes, which translates into a stronger predisposition to pick healthier, more sustainable alternatives (Furtado & Sampaio, 2020). Similarly, Kim and Seock (2009) also found a link between environmental knowledge and health. As a result, people who are more aware of and worried about their health are also more likely to care about the environment and try to make ecologically responsible choices. Given the above, the following research proposition is formulated:

- **RP10:** Health concern influences the purchase intention of green cosmetics.

2.5.11. Concern With Appearance

Furtado and Sampaio (2020) assert that, in addition to concerns for their health, consumers should also consider their concerns for their well-being as they relate to their self-esteem and care for beauty. Customers who are driven by their looks equate natural cosmetics with an advantage for their attractiveness and anticipate that using them will enhance the appearance of their skin and hair. In this regard, the authors highlighted the improvement of skin and hair, vanity, well-being, self-centeredness, and self-esteem as the second primary reasons for buying green cosmetics (Furtado & Sampaio, 2020). Strehlau et al. (2015) emphasize the significance of vanity for a person's sense of self-worth by showing a favorable correlation between vanity and the usage of cosmetics and treatment exposure. This leads the authors to the conclusion that vain people would use all means at their disposal to enhance and improve their beauty. Given the above, the following research proposition is formulated:

- **RP11:** Concern for appearance influences the intention to purchase green cosmetics.

2.5.12. Product Knowledge

Ribeiro and Veiga (2011) addressed the difficulty in distinguishing traditional cosmetics from organic and natural cosmetics, which stems from the lack of understanding of the label and the lack of knowledge of the ingredients and their respective benefits or harms. According to Wang et al. (2019), product knowledge can influence the entire decision-making process, where through product information, consumers with product knowledge form a cognitive judgment and evaluation about green products, which can translate into the consumer's green purchase intention. Furthermore, Ghazali et al. (2017) demonstrated how an improved understanding of personal care products tends to influence consumers' perceptions regarding the likelihood of making another purchase. Product knowledge is therefore seen as a predictor of attitude about purchase intention. Other research has unveiled that product knowledge proved to be the most important determinant in the purchase intention of green consumer chemicals. In addition to considering environmental concerns and green lifestyle, obtaining information about the product was the main factor in formulating their purchase intention (Patak et al., 2021). Similarly, Harahap et al.

(2018) concluded that there is a significant relationship between product knowledge and green purchasing behavior. Because of the above, the following research proposition is formulated:

- **RP12:** Product knowledge influences the purchase intention of green cosmetics.

3. RESEARCH OBJECTIVES AND METHODOLOGY

3.1. Research Question

Given the lack of understanding regarding the elements that boost the use of green cosmetics, the primary goal of the current study is to examine the variables that affect consumer purchase of green cosmetics, which translates into the following key research question: "What are the determinants of green cosmetics purchase intention?". Furthermore, due to the difficulty in defining the term green cosmetics, it became necessary to explore what consumers perceive as green cosmetics and how they differentiate it from other terms like traditional cosmetics, organic cosmetics, or natural cosmetics, to clarify the meaning of the term. The additional goals result in:

- What is a green cosmetic from the consumer's point of view?
- How do consumers distinguish green cosmetics from others?
- What attributes do consumers want from a green cosmetic?

3.2. Methodological Option

To do this, a study using a qualitative research methodology and an interview-based data-gathering strategy was used. A qualitative method, according to Carson et al. (2001), provides greater flexibility and open-mindedness and is suitable for marketing managers to understand the data. A small-sample, unstructured exploratory research process known as qualitative research offers comprehension and insights into the identified topic (Malhotra et al., 2006). Because the interviewee provides the interviewer with genuine knowledge during a dialogue with specific goals, interviews are a valuable tool for learning how people think, and the interview is one of the best ways to comprehend and get information from people, enabling researchers to examine the interpretations and meanings that people give to diverse experiences (Amado, 2017). The interview can be conducted between two persons or a group, depending on how many subjects are covered, and it can concentrate on one or several themes. Additionally, the extent of structure or predetermination of the topics it addresses allows for differentiation in its typology (Aires, 2011).

3.3. Sample and Sampling

A crucial component of characterizing the sample is defining the sample size. Between ten and fifteen interviewers was the initial goal in terms of sample size. Even though over 40 persons were contacted, only 8 of them were interviewed due to factors including poor response, their unavailability, or lack of attendance. As a result, the current study sample was limited to these eight participants who identify themselves as green cosmetics users. The interviewees were selected through an analysis of the social network profiles Twitter and Instagram. Interviewees were chosen who explicitly expressed their preference for green cosmetics. All interviews were recorded and the whole process of preparing and conducting the interviews followed the procedures prescribed in the bibliography.

3.4. Interview Structure

The interview was semi-structured, meaning that the questions were preplanned and there was a script with a logical order in which the fundamentals of what was wanted to be learned were defined. The interviewee is allowed complete freedom to respond, present his views, and draw attention to the things that are most significant to him by using the words that come to mind. In that there is some openness, the interview is therefore semi-directive.

In addition to allowing for the creation of new categories and the identification of other elements pertinent to the customer and their purchasing intention, a script was created to cover all the categories revealed in the secondary research that had been performed. It is possible to get the interview script, whose question-building is based on the literature reviewed, in Table 1.

3.5. Data Analysis

The data subject to analysis were obtained through the transcription of eight interviews with consumers of green cosmetics. The respective transcripts, organized by themes, can be requested from the authors. The following sections contain a summary of the results.

3.5.1. Green Cosmetic

More than four of the respondents defined a green cosmetic by aspects such as its natural ingredients, environmentally friendly composition, environmentally friendly production process, and packaging with less environmental impact. Finally, elements such as a production chain with economic and social justice, a reduced carbon footprint, less travel or transport, national production, and a positive contribution to health are the aspects mentioned to a lesser extent.

3.5.2. Environmental Awareness

Environmental awareness or concern and its possible impact on the desire to purchase green cosmetics were the first themes covered in the interviews. All respondents made it very clear that they care about environmental concerns, are ecologically sensitive, and are well aware of how their consumer choices affect the environment. All eight participants believe that being aware of the environment impacts their decision to buy green cosmetics favorably. They indicated that their starting point for using green cosmetics is the idea of the environmental effect of their decisions and the subsequent reflection on their consumption patterns when asked to explain the link between environmental awareness and purchasing intention.

Table 1. Interview script and respective support in the construction of questions

Dimensions	Questions	Authors
Green cosmetic	Q1: What is a green cosmetic for you?	Ribeiro & Veiga (2011)
Environmental Awareness	Q2: How would you describe your environmental awareness? Q3: What environmental concerns do you have for the planet? Q4: What relationship do you establish between your environmental awareness and your intention to buy green cosmetics?	Bedante (2004); Klineberg et al. (1998); Tamashiro et al. (2014)
Certification labels	Q5: Are you familiar with the concept of certification labels? Q6: What do you think about brands using certification labels? Q7: Are there any labels that are particularly relevant to you when buying products? Q8: What relationship do you establish between cosmetics bearing certification labels and your intention to buy green cosmetics?	Janssen and Langen (2017); Joshi and Rahman (2015); Liu et al. (2012; 2015); Sun et al. (2021)
Brand trust	Q9: How important is the trust you have in the brand when buying a green cosmetic? Q10: Are you familiar with the concept of *greenwashing*? Q11: In your opinion how do episodes of *greenwashing* affect your trust in green brands?	Kahraman and Kazançoğlu (2019); Morales et al. (2020); Yildirim (2021)
Quality and attributes expected	Q12: What is the quality of a green cosmetic for you? Q13: What attributes or features do you want to find in a green cosmetic? Q14: How does the expectation of quality in a cosmetic influence your choice of green cosmetics?	Chen and Chang (2012); Mohammad and Baharun (2018); Wijekoon and Sabri (2021)
Lifestyle	Q15: Apart from green cosmetics, what other healthcare environments or green behaviors are in your routine? Q16: Do you purchase or consume other products with environmentally friendly attributes?	Patak et al. (2021); Ribeiro and Veiga (2011)
Advertising	Q17: What do you think of the advertising of green cosmetics? Q18: How important is advertising in your decision to purchase a cosmetic with green attributes? Q19: Do you consider that product advertising increases, decreases, or does not change your likelihood of purchase?	Amallia et al. (2021); Sun et al. (2021)
Willingness to pay	Q20: How would you describe the price of green cosmetics? Q21: How does your income relate to your choice of green cosmetics? Q22: Are you willing to pay more for a cosmetic if it has green attributes?	Joung et al. (2014); Wijekoon and Sabri (2021); Kim and Chung (2011)
Ethical and social justice	Q23: When you buy cosmetics, apart from the component environmental, are there any ethical issues that are particularly important to you or that you are looking for? Q24: How do you view issues such as child labor, animal cruelty, fair trade, or other issues when buying a green cosmetic?	Chatterjee et al. (2022); Rawof (2021)
Concern with health and appearance	Q25: How would you describe your health concern? Q26: How do you rate the relationship between health and the use of green cosmetics? Q27: How does concern for your health influence your purchase of green cosmetics? Q28: What about appearance? Do you consider that vanity, the desire to care for your skin and hair, and to preserve your beauty has any influence on the purchase of green cosmetics?	Durif et al. (2010); Kim and Seock (2009); Ribeiro and Veiga (2011); Strehlau et al. (2015)
Social influence	Q29: How does the opinion of those around you (family, friends, and acquaintances) about green cosmetics affect your intention to buy? Q30: When advised to use a particular green cosmetic, how do you react? Q31: How important is public opinion in your intention to buy green cosmetics?	Choi and Lee (2019); Klöckner (2013)
Knowledge of product	Q32: How important is it for you to know the composition, the benefits, and what distinguishes a green cosmetic from traditional cosmetics? Q33: How does this knowledge impact your intention to buy green cosmetics?	Patak et al. (2021); Ribeiro and Veiga (2011)
Dimensions	**Finalization issues**	
Other motivations	Q34: Why do you buy green cosmetic products?	
The distinction between green and traditional cosmetics	Q35: How do you distinguish a green cosmetic from a cosmetic considered conventional?	
The distinction between green, natural, and organic cosmetics	Q36: Do you make any distinction between the concepts of green cosmetics, organic cosmetics, or natural cosmetics?	
Other factors	Q37: Apart from the factors mentioned, what other factors influence you at the moment of buying a green cosmetic?	
Finishing Question	Q38: To end the interview, are there any questions that should have been asked? There is an issue or topic that should have been discussed?	

3.5.3. Certification Labels

From the interviews, it can be inferred that six respondents generally concur that the presence of certification labels impacts their purchase of eco-friendly cosmetics in a good way. In this view, the labels are regarded as the cosmetic's initial call to attention, a tool for identifying cosmetic features, a source of preference or distinction, and a component that increases the consumer's sense of confidence or trust. Despite this favorable attitude, several interviewees said that they prefer other considerations over the label, such as reading up on the components and their provenance, having trust in the brand and the people behind it, and the impact of experts in the field. The lack of a label that certifies the entirety of the product, the enormous disparity between certification criteria, and the resulting lack of standardization between the various natural or organic certifiers are the final criticisms of green cosmetics. Therefore, interviews point out criticism such as the fact that labels can be bought and, can mislead the consumer when the cosmetic has an organic label without all the ingredients being organic.

3.5.4. Brand Trust

According to seven interviews, there is a strong consensus that brand trust affects consumers' intentions to buy eco-friendly cosmetics. This turned out to be crucial for the interviewees. As a result, they emphasize the importance they place on brand transparency, specifically on trust, as a major reason why there aren't enough certification labels and its role as a facilitator in spotting false or misleading promises. They also discuss the significance of learning about the brand and gathering customer feedback in this setting.

The increased faith in small brands or local businesses and mistrust of more well-known brands (or large brands) is another aspect that was mentioned by several interviewees. Regarding the effects of greenwashing, the interviewees explain the fraud with the difficulty in confirming the truth of the brand's green claims, indicating as consequences of the choice of only brands in which they have faith and are familiar with the work, the complete loss of faith in brands that exhibit episodes of greenwashing as well as greater attention, a more critical attitude, and greater selectivity when purchasing. The interviewees also identified a few factors that make them suspicious of greenwashing by some brands, including claims made by supermarket brands that their products are green, an overly appealing design, a composition with many ingredients, and assurances that carbon emissions are being offset by plantations in the Amazon.

3.5.5. Quality and Attributes

It is implied that there is consensus that the expectation of quality and attributes influence the buying intention of green cosmetics since the influence of the quality and attributes component on purchase intention received complete agreement from the eight interviewees. Several interviewees emphasized that quality was a deciding factor in whether they would repeat a purchase or not. The importance of product quality is discussed concerning difficulties like skin issues. On the other side, people are more likely to pay more for a green cosmetic since they perceive or anticipate excellence in it. The interviewees' perceptions of the quality of a green cosmetic include characteristics like longevity, skin feel, use of natural ingredients, cost-effectiveness, ingredients, packaging features, performance fulfillment, reduced water use, reduced waste, the green characteristics themselves (lower environmental impact, sustainable ingredients, and sustainable production methods), and finally, the sustainable part as a synonym for the three eco-friendly principles.

3.5.6. Lifestyle

It is confirmed that the eight respondents exhibit a lifestyle that includes actions that are inherently environmentally conscious, purchases and consumption of products with lower environmental impact, as well as other green initiatives. The intention of customers to purchase green cosmetics is thought to be influenced by their green lifestyle, given the range of pro-environmental actions that they all described throughout the interviews.

3.5.7. Advertising

There is some disagreement over the advertising factor. However, five of the interviewees acknowledge that advertising may have influenced their decision to buy, therefore it can be said that a relative majority accepts that advertising affects consumers' decisions to buy green cosmetics. Even still, the interviewees underline the lack of advertising for smaller firms, which they excuse by pointing to the latter's lack of resources as their preferred brands' lack of resources. The difficulty in separating authentic green claims from false ones due to the phenomenon of greenwashing has been mentioned as another critique of green cosmetics advertising. In contrast, emphasis is placed on the potential of advertising as a first call to attention and as a chance for the consumer to become familiar with the product. The interviewees underline their inclination to examine other criteria, such as product expertise, when confronted with this first appeal to attention. Finally, the interviewees stress the significance of advertising about things like its capacity for spreading information and the allure of the product's appearance.

3.5.8. Willingness to Pay

The results of the data analysis allow for the conclusion that the willingness to pay for the product affects the intention to purchase it. Despite the differences in how green cosmetics are described as being priced, the interviewees' responses indicate that factors such as cost-benefit, specifically the green cosmetics' longer lifespan, efficiency (which is higher than that of conventional cosmetics), conscious consumption (using only the necessary amounts), the sustainable perspective (environmental, economic, and social), and, possibly, their comfortable financial situation, affect their willingness to pay. The desire to pay a higher premium for green cosmetics is then expressed by every interviewee. It is therefore recommended that willingness to pay affects the intention to purchase green cosmetics.

3.5.9. Social Influence

Interviewees were environmentally aware, an awareness that dictates their choice of green cosmetics over conventional cosmetics, and therefore they are not permeable to opinions coming from people who are less environmentally aware, non-consumers, or non-connoisseurs of green cosmetics. On the other hand, consumers are receptive to and influenced by opinions coming from other consumers or experts in the field. It should be emphasized that the interviewees attempt to form their own conclusions and to give a cosmetic the benefit of the doubt in the face of such unfavorable feedback while discussing the thoughts of other customers who have tried a specific cosmetic. In this regard, it may be claimed that their immediate circle does not negatively affect them.

How much their purchasing decision is influenced also depends on whether they believe they know more or less than the people around them. Regarding public opinion, it is noted that social influence may exist depending on the subject matter; specifically, if the topic is a matter of good recommendations, a certain receptivity is seen. There is disagreement over the impact of a broad negative attitude on the decision to buy. One interviewee brought out the inclination to seek reviews or comments online before making a purchase, which is still a result of social influence on the side of the public. Given the above, it is not possible to validate a relationship between social influence and purchase intention for green cosmetics.

3.5.10. Ethical Issues and Social and Economic Justice

Data analysis allows us to declare that most respondents agree on the influence of ethical, social, and economic issues on their intention to purchase green cosmetics. As such, the importance of factors such as fair trade, i.e., adequate working conditions and fair rewards for all workers involved in the production chain, issues involving animal protection, and finally the preference for buying from local shops, artisans, or small producers, are relevant.

3.5.11. Concern With Health

All eight interviewees agreed that health concerns have an impact on their decision to buy eco-friendly cosmetics. Some interviewees even go so far as to say that this is the primary reason, they choose to buy green cosmetics. The interviewees' expectations of the health advantages of green cosmetics justify the association between the variables. They are confident that green cosmetics are healthier for their bodies because they include fewer hazardous chemicals, and more natural ingredients, fewer allergic responses could occur, and fewer skin issues.

3.5.12. Concern With Appearance

Five of the eight interviewees concurred that worry about their appearance did not influence their choice to buy green cosmetics. According to the interviews, worry about appearance is a factor that directly influences their decision to buy cosmetics and had little bearing on their decision to buy green cosmetics. The interviewees see green cosmetics more as a self-care tool than a fashion statement. One of the interviewees emphasizes how they prefer the discourse represented by green cosmetics, which emphasizes a discourse of change and improvement of qualities, to the discourse represented by conventional cosmetics, which emphasizes a discourse of the valorization of natural beauty.

3.5.13. Product Knowledge

All eight interviewees agreed that product knowledge is important and that it has an impact on their decision to buy. As a result, interviewees stated that they are interested in learning things like the ingredients in green cosmetics, where the raw materials come from, how the product affects the environment, and whether the claims made are accurate. As was already indicated, the interviewees also expressed interest in ethical and social justice concerns, which are a part of product knowledge. Because of this, the respondents show that this is an important consideration in their decision, demonstrating the effort they put forth to try to read the label and research the many components of the cosmetic, even though they lack a lot of chemical expertise.

3.5.14. Other Factors

Respondents mentioned two determinants: accessibility to green cosmetics (location and cheaper) and visual marketing. However, given the number of mentions of the two suggested factors, these could not be considered determinants in the intention to purchase green cosmetics.

3.5.15. Distinction Between Cosmetics

The definitions of cosmetics were found to be inconsistent and not entirely clear based on the literature review. Therefore, the purpose of the interview was to learn how respondents discern between natural, organic, and green cosmetics as well as how they set them apart from conventional cosmetics.

The primary factors to distinguish between a conventional and a green cosmetic include the ingredients and the environmental impact. The packaging and social issues are all listed as ways to differentiate between cosmetics.

Three of the interviewees disagree with the definitions provided in some of the articles evaluated in the literature and believe that green, organic, and natural cosmetics reflect distinct concepts with their own unique characteristics. In this field, the interviewees mention that green cosmetics go beyond natural and organic cosmetics in terms of their influence on the environment, whether it be through environmental protection during production, ingredient sourcing, or packaging. Two of the participants underline that organic cosmetics are distinguished by having a certification label as a requirement. Additionally, one of the interviewees points out that producing organic cosmetics requires using different methods and incurs higher expenditures than producing green cosmetics.

3.6. Research Propositions

The previous sections allowed us to assess the validity of the propositions, and a summary of the respective results is presented in Table 2.

4. CONCLUSION

Environmental issues such as global warming, deforestation, pollution, and species extinction are some of the concerns that jeopardize the sustainability of planet Earth. Encouragement of building consumption patterns with the lowest possible environmental impact is crucial since sustainable development can only be achieved with the right behaviors and decisions made by consumers throughout their lifetimes (Romero et al., 2018). The primary goal of this research was to identify and characterize the determinants that affect the purchase behavior of green cosmetics and given the growth potential of the cosmetics sector, it was thought vital to study the purchasing intention of green cosmetics.

Table 2. Summary of the results of the research propositions

Research proposition	Validity of the PR
RP1: The individual's environmental awareness influences his or her intention to purchase green cosmetics.	Validated
RP2: The presence of certification labels on cosmetics influences the intention to purchase green cosmetics.	Partially validated
RP3: Brand trust influences the purchase intention of green cosmetics.	Partially validated
RP4: Quality expectation influences the purchase intention of green cosmetics.	Validated
RP5: The lifestyle adopted by the individual in his daily routine, influences the intention to purchase green cosmetics.	Validated
RP6: Advertising influences the purchase intention of green cosmetics.	Partially validated
RP7: Willingness to pay influences the purchase intention of green cosmetics.	Validated
RP8: Social influence impacts the purchase intention of green cosmetics.	Not validated
RP9: The inclusion of ethical and social and economic justice issues in cosmetics influences the purchase intention of green cosmetics.	Partially validated
RP10: Health concern influences the purchase intention of green cosmetics.	Validated
RP11: Concern for appearance influences the intention to purchase green cosmetics.	Not validated
RP12: Product knowledge influences the purchase intention of green cosmetics.	Validated

Following a thorough investigation, it was found that the definition of green cosmetics is still not quite clear in the literature. Green cosmetics are, according to some authors, also concerned with economic, social, and animal ethics issues in addition to the decrease of their negative environmental effects. The relationship between natural, organic, and green cosmetics confirms the absence of legislation. As a result, to determine the requirements that characterize a cosmetic as natural or organic, one must turn to the definition provided by each certification system. The criteria of the various systems, however, did not appear to be uniform, but interviewees are aware of the differences between the three concepts and, for the most part, they agree that green cosmetics can be distinguished from natural and organic cosmetics by their increased attention to environmental impact during production, the source of the ingredients, and the composition of the packaging.

To address the primary goal of the work, the literature review set out to determine the variables that affect consumers' decisions to purchase green cosmetics. The following factors were revealed: environmental awareness; certification labels; trust in the brand; expected quality; lifestyle; advertising; willingness to pay; social influence; ethical issues and social and economic justice; health concern; concern with appearance; product knowledge. It was concluded that environmental awareness, lifestyle, willingness to pay, ethical concerns, social and economic justice, cosmetic quality, health concerns, certification labels, brand trust, and advertising are factors that affect consumer purchase intention based on exploratory research with a qualitative approach and data collection from eight interviews. In contrast, it was discovered that social influence and concern with appearance have little bearing on one's decision to buy green cosmetics. The interviewees also mentioned accessibility and visual marketing as important elements that affected their decision to buy. These are not regarded as predictors of the desire to buy green cosmetics, however, due to the small number of mentions. For the determinants that influence purchase intention, one can establish a hierarchy in which environmental awareness, lifestyle, willingness to pay, quality issues, ethics and social and economic justice, as well as quality expectations, health concerns, and product knowledge, are the most significant determinants in the intention to purchase green cosmetics. Determinants such as certification labels, brand trust, and advertising are less significant.

All survey participants agreed on some of the examined determinants, emphasizing their importance in affecting people's consumption of green cosmetics. With complete agreement from the interviewees, the following factors can be emphasized as influences on the use of green cosmetics: their level of environmental awareness, translated by the concern with the environment and the notion of the environmental impact of their actions, the pro-environmental lifestyle; measured by the consumer's environmental care in other actions and consumption areas; the expectation of product quality; the consumer's willingness to pay, essentially motivated by the high expectation of the product's cost-benefit; the fact that the product or brand incorporates components such as ethics and social and economic justice, translated by fair trade, the abolition of animal cruelty or being a local trade brand; the consumer's concern for her health and expectation that the product will be less harmful and safer; and the product's knowledge of the origin of the raw material, composition, veracity of the claims and environmental impact.

It is also important to highlight the identification of some of the attributes most sought by the interviewees in green cosmetics. Consumers seek to find attributes such as product durability, performance, skin and hair feel, scent, durable packaging, brand fair trade, natural ingredients, and reduced environmental impact in ingredients, production, packaging, and distribution. Thus, this information is pertinent for brands to review their product offer, reflect on their strategy and adapt it to the needs and preferences of consumers.

Given the gap between consumer beliefs and purchasing behavior, marketers must understand what motivates people to purchase eco-friendly cosmetics. This study is especially pertinent to the expansion of the green cosmetics market given the dearth of literature on the factors that influence the use of green cosmetics.

REFERENCES

Aires, L. (2011). Paradigma qualitativo e práticas de investigação educacional. Universidade Aberta.

Akkaya, M. (2021). Understanding the impacts of lifestyle segmentation & perceived value on brand purchase intention: An empirical study in different product categories. *European Research on Management and Business Economics*, *27*(3), 100155. doi:10.1016/j.iedeen.2021.100155

Al-Haddad, S., Awad, A., Albate, D., Almashhadani, I., & Dirani, W. (2020). Factors affecting green cosmetics purchase intention. *Journal of Management Information & Decision Sciences*, *23*(4).

Amado, J. (2017). *Manual de investigação Qualitativa em Educação (3ª ed)*. Imprensa da Universidade de Coimbra/Coimbra University Press.

Amallia, B. A., Effendi, M. I., & Ghofar, A. (2021). The effect of green advertising, trust, and attitude on green purchase intention: An evidence from Jogjakarta, Indonesia. *International Journal of Creative Business and Management*, *1*(1), 66–79. doi:10.31098/ijcbm.v1i1.4553

Amberg, N., & Fogarassy, C. (2019). Green consumer behavior in the cosmetics market. *Resources*, *8*(3), 137. doi:10.3390/resources8030137

Bedante, G. N. (2004). O comportamento de consumo sustentável e suas relações com a consciência ambiental e a intenção de compra de produtos ecologicamente embalados. Master Dissertation. Universidade Federal do Rio Grande do Sul.

Bilal, M., Mehmood, S., & Iqbal, H. M. (2020). The beast of beauty: Environmental and health concerns of toxic components in cosmetics. *Cosmetics*, *7*(1), 13. doi:10.3390/cosmetics7010013

Bom, S., Jorge, J., Ribeiro, H., & Marto, J. (2019). A step forward on sustainability in the cosmetics industry: A review. *Journal of Cleaner Production*, *225*, 270–290. doi:10.1016/j.jclepro.2019.03.255

Borrego, C., Lopes, M., Ribeiro, I., Carvalho, A., & Miranda, A. I. (2010). As alterações climáticas: Uma realidade transformada em desafio. *Revista Captar: Ciência e Ambiente para Todos*, *2*(2), 1–16.

Carré, P. (2021). Naturalness in the production of vegetable oils and proteins. *OCL. Oilseeds & Fats Crops and Lipids*, *28*, 10. doi:10.1051/ocl/2020065

Carson, D., Gilmore, A., Perry, C., & Gronhaug, K. (2001). *Qualitative marketing research*. Sage.

Chan, R. Y. (2004). Consumer responses to environmental advertising in China. *Marketing Intelligence & Planning*, *22*(4), 427–437. doi:10.1108/02634500410542789

Chatterjee, S., Sreen, N., Rana, J., Dhir, A., & Sadarangani, P. H. (2022). Impact of ethical certifications and product involvement on consumers' decision to purchase ethical products at price premiums in an emerging market context. *International Review on Public and Nonprofit Marketing*, *19*(4), 737–762. doi:10.100712208-021-00288-1

Chen, Y.-S. (2010). The drivers of green brand equity: Green brand image, green satisfaction, and green trust. *Journal of Business Ethics*, *93*(2), 307–319. doi:10.100710551-009-0223-9

Chen, Y. S., & Chang, C. H. (2012). Enhance green purchase intentions. *Management Decision*, *50*(3), 502–520. doi:10.1108/00251741211216250

Chin, J., Jiang, B. C., Mufidah, I., Persada, S. F., & Noer, B. A. (2018). The investigation of consumers' behavior intention in using green skincare products: A pro-environmental behavior model approach. *Sustainability (Basel)*, *10*(11), 3922. doi:10.3390u10113922

Choi, E., & Lee, K. C. (2019). Effect of trust in domain-specific information of safety, brand loyalty, and perceived value for cosmetics on purchase intentions in mobile e-commerce context. *Sustainability (Basel)*, *11*(22), 6257. doi:10.3390u11226257

Cinelli, P., Coltelli, M. B., Signori, F., Morganti, P., & Lazzeri, A. (2019). Cosmetic packaging to save the environment: Future perspectives. *Cosmetics*, *6*(2), 26. doi:10.3390/cosmetics6020026

Csorba, L. M., & Boglea, V. A. (2011). Sustainable cosmetics: A major instrument in protecting the consumer's interest. *Regional and Business Studies*, *3*(1, Suppl.), 167–176.

Delmas, M. A., & Burbano, V. C. (2011). The drivers of greenwashing. *California Management Review*, *54*(1), 64–87. doi:10.1525/cmr.2011.54.1.64

Doppelt, B. (2012). *The power of sustainable thinking: How to create a positive future for the climate, the planet, your organization and your life*. Routledge. doi:10.4324/9781849773232

Durif, F., Boivin, C., & Julien, C. (2010). In search of a green product definition. *Innovative Marketing, 6*(1), 25-33.

Fonseca-Santos, B., Corrêa, M. A., & Chorilli, M. (2015). Sustainability, natural and organic cosmetics: Consumer, products, efficacy, toxicological and regulatory considerations. *Brazilian Journal of Pharmaceutical Sciences, 51*(1), 17–26. doi:10.1590/S1984-82502015000100002

Franca, C. C. V., & Ueno, H. M. (2020). Green cosmetics: Perspectives and challenges in the context of green chemistry. *Desenvolvimento e Meio Ambiente, 53*, 53. doi:10.5380/dma.v53i0.62322

Furtado, B. A., & Sampaio, D. O. (2020). Cosméticos sustentáveis: Quais fatores influenciam o consumo destes produtos? *International Journal of Business Marketing, 5*(1), 36–54.

Ghazali, E., Soon, P. C., Mutum, D. S., & Nguyen, B. (2017). Health and cosmetics: Investigating consumers' values for buying organic personal care products. *Journal of Retailing and Consumer Services, 39*, 154–163. doi:10.1016/j.jretconser.2017.08.002

Gleim, M. R., Smith, J. S., Andrews, D., & Cronin, J. J. Jr. (2013). Against the green: A multi-method examination of the barriers to green consumption. *Journal of Retailing, 89*(1), 44–61. doi:10.1016/j.jretai.2012.10.001

Goh, S. K., & Balaji, M. (2016). Linking green skepticism to green purchase behavior. *Journal of Cleaner Production, 131*, 629–638. doi:10.1016/j.jclepro.2016.04.122

Harahap, A., Zuhriyah, A., & Rahmayanti, H. (2018). Relationship between knowledge of green product, social impact and perceived value with green purchase behavior. E3S Web of Conferences, Hwang, J. K., Kim, E.-J., Lee, S.-M., & Lee, Y.-K. (2021). Impact of susceptibility to global consumer culture on commitment and loyalty in botanic cosmetic brands. *Sustainability, 13*(2), 892.

Janßen, D., & Langen, N. (2017). The bunch of sustainability labels–Do consumers differentiate? *Journal of Cleaner Production, 143*, 1233–1245. doi:10.1016/j.jclepro.2016.11.171

Jog, D., & Singhal, D. (2020). Greenwashing understanding among Indian consumers and its impact on their green consumption. *Global Business Review*, 0972150920962933. doi:10.1177/0972150920962933

Johnstone, M.-L., & Tan, L. P. (2015). Exploring the gap between consumers' green rhetoric and purchasing behaviour. *Journal of Business Ethics, 132*(2), 311–328. doi:10.100710551-014-2316-3

Joshi, Y., & Rahman, Z. (2015). Factors affecting green purchase behaviour and future research directions. *International. Strategic Management Review, 3*(1-2), 128–143.

Joung, S. H., Park, S. W., & Ko, Y. J. (2014). Willingness to pay for eco-friendly products: Case of cosmetics. *Asia Marketing Journal, 15*(4), 33–49. doi:10.53728/2765-6500.1565

Kahraman, A., & Kazançoğlu, İ. (2019). Understanding consumers' purchase intentions toward natural-claimed products: A qualitative research in personal care products. *Business Strategy and the Environment, 28*(6), 1218–1233. doi:10.1002/bse.2312

Kaliyadan, F., Al Dhafiri, M., & Aatif, M. (2021). Attitudes toward organic cosmetics: A cross-sectional population-based survey from the Middle East. *Journal of Cosmetic Dermatology*, *20*(8), 2552–2555. doi:10.1111/jocd.13909 PMID:33355981

Kim, H. Y., & Chung, J. E. (2011). Consumer purchase intention for organic personal care products. *Journal of Consumer Marketing*, *28*(1), 40–47. doi:10.1108/07363761111101930

Kim, S., & Seock, Y. K. (2009). Impacts of health and environmental consciousness on young female consumers' attitude towards and purchase of natural beauty products. *International Journal of Consumer Studies*, *33*(6), 627–638. doi:10.1111/j.1470-6431.2009.00817.x

Klineberg, S. L., McKeever, M., & Rothenbach, B. (1998). Demographic predictors of environmental concern: It does make a difference how it's measured. *Social Science Quarterly*, *79*(4), 734–753.

Klöckner, C. A. (2013). A comprehensive model of the psychology of environmental behaviour - A meta-analysis. *Global Environmental Change*, *23*(5), 1028–1038. doi:10.1016/j.gloenvcha.2013.05.014

Kollmuss, A., & Agyeman, J. (2002). Mind the gap: Why do people act environmentally and what are the barriers to pro-environmental behavior? *Environmental Education Research*, *8*(3), 239–260. doi:10.1080/13504620220145401

Lai, C. K., & Cheng, E. W. (2016). Green purchase behavior of undergraduate students in Hong Kong. *The Social Science Journal*, *53*(1), 67–76. doi:10.1016/j.soscij.2015.11.003

Lee, Y.-H., & Chen, S.-L. (2019). Effect of green attributes transparency on wta for green cosmetics: Mediating effects of CSR and green brand concepts. *Sustainability (Basel)*, *11*(19), 5258. doi:10.3390u11195258

Liobikienė, G., & Bernatonienė, J. (2017). Why determinants of green purchase cannot be treated equally? The case of green cosmetics: Literature review. *Journal of Cleaner Production*, *162*, 109–120. doi:10.1016/j.jclepro.2017.05.204

Liu, L., Chen, R., & He, F. (2015). How to promote purchase of carbon offset products: Labeling vs. calculation? *Journal of Business Research*, *68*(5), 942–948. doi:10.1016/j.jbusres.2014.09.021

Liu, X., Wang, C., Shishime, T., & Fujitsuka, T. (2012). Sustainable consumption: Green purchasing behaviours of urban residents in China. *Sustainable Development (Bradford)*, *20*(4), 293–308. doi:10.1002d.484

Malhotra, N., Hall, J., Shaw, M., & Oppenheim, P. (2006). *Marketing research: an applied orientation. Frenchs Forest*. Pearson Education Australia. doi:10.1108/S1548-6435(2006)2

Melović, B., Cirović, D., Backovic-Vulić, T., Dudić, B., & Gubiniova, K. (2020). Attracting green consumers as a basis for creating sustainable marketing strategy on the organic market—Relevance for sustainable agriculture business development. *Foods*, *9*(11), 1552. doi:10.3390/foods9111552 PMID:33120944

Mohammad, N., & Baharun, R. (2018). Predicting the Purchase Intention for Organic Product: A Review and Conceptual Framework. *Advanced Science Letters*, *24*(6), 3849–3853. doi:10.1166/asl.2018.11496

Montoro Rios, F. J., Luque Martinez, T., Fuentes Moreno, F., & Cañadas Soriano, P. (2006). Improving attitudes toward brands with environmental associations: An experimental approach. *Journal of Consumer Marketing, 23*(1), 26–33. doi:10.1108/07363760610641136

Morales, P. A., True, S., & Tudor, R. K. (2020). Insights, challenges and recommendations for research on sustainability in marketing. *Journal of Global Scholars of Marketing Science, 30*(4), 394–406. doi:10.1080/21639159.2020.1803757

Ölander, F., & Thøgersen, J. (1995). Understanding of consumer behaviour as a prerequisite for environmental protection. *Journal of Consumer Policy, 18*(4), 345–385. doi:10.1007/BF01024160

Ottman, J. A. (1992). Industry's response to green consumerism. *The Journal of Business Strategy, 13*(4), 3–7. doi:10.1108/eb039498 PMID:10120307

Paço, A., & Raposo, M. (2009). "Green" segmentation: An application to the Portuguese consumer market. *Marketing Intelligence & Planning, 27*(3), 364–379. doi:10.1108/02634500910955245

Patak, M., Branska, L., & Pecinova, Z. (2021). Consumer intention to purchase green consumer chemicals. *Sustainability (Basel), 13*(14), 7992. doi:10.3390u13147992

Pop, R.-A., Săplăcan, Z., & Alt, M.-A. (2020). Social media goes green - The impact of social media on green cosmetics purchase motivation and intention. *Information (Basel), 11*(9), 447. doi:10.3390/info11090447

Rajput, N., Sharma, U., Kaur, B., Rani, P., Tongkachok, K., & Dornadula, V. H. R. (2022). Current global green marketing standard: Changing market and company branding. *International Journal of System Assurance Engineering and Management, 13*(S1, Suppl 1), 727–735. doi:10.100713198-021-01604-y

Rawat, S. R., & Garga, P. (2012). Understanding consumer behaviour towards green cosmetics. *Available at* SSRN *2111545*. doi: 10.2139/ssrn.2111545

Rawof, W. (2021). *Ethical and Sustainable Cosmetics and Their Importance on Consumer Purchase Behavior* (Publication Number Paper 746) [Undergraduate Honors Theses, ETSU.], https://dc.etsu.edu/honors/746

Ribeiro, J. A., & Veiga, R. T. (2011). Proposição de uma escala de consumo sustentável. *Revista ADM, 46*(1), 45–60.

Romero, V., Khury, E., Aiello, L. M., Foglio, M. A., & Leonardi, G. R. (2018). Diferenças entre cosméticos orgânicos e naturais: Literatura esclarecedora para prescritores. *Surgical & Cosmetic Dermatology, 10*(3), 188–193. doi:10.5935cd1984-8773.20181031087

Sdrolia, E., & Zarotiadis, G. (2019). A comprehensive review for green product term: From definition to evaluation. *Journal of Economic Surveys, 33*(1), 150–178. doi:10.1111/joes.12268

Strehlau, V. I., Claro, D. P., & Laban Neto, S. A. (2015). A vaidade impulsiona o consumo de cosméticos e de procedimentos estéticos cirúrgicos nas mulheres? Uma investigação exploratória. *Revista de Administração (São Paulo), 50*(1), 73–88. doi:10.5700/rausp1185

Sun, Y., Luo, B., Wang, S., & Fang, W. (2021). What you see is meaningful: Does green advertising change the intentions of consumers to purchase eco-labeled products? *Business Strategy and the Environment*, *30*(1), 694–704. doi:10.1002/bse.2648

Tamashiro, H. R. S., da Silveira, J. A. G., Mantovani, D. M. N., & de Abreu Campanário, C. R. A. (2014). Aspectos determinantes do consumo de produtos cosméticos verdes. *RAI Revista de Administração e Inovação*, *11*(1), 238–262. doi:10.5773/rai.v11i1.1206

Thøgersen, J. (2021). Consumer behavior and climate change: Consumers need considerable assistance. *Current Opinion in Behavioral Sciences*, *42*, 9–14. doi:10.1016/j.cobeha.2021.02.008

vom Brocke, J., & Rosemann, M. (2013). *Metodologia de pesquisa*. AMGH Editora.

Wang, H., Ma, B., & Bai, R. (2019). How does green product knowledge effectively promote green purchase intention? *Sustainability (Basel)*, *11*(4), 1193. doi:10.3390u11041193

Wijekoon, R., & Sabri, M. F. (2021). Determinants that influence green product purchase intention and behavior: A literature review and guiding framework. *Sustainability (Basel)*, *13*(11), 6219. doi:10.3390u13116219

Yildirim, K. (2021). The determinants of purchase intention and willingness to pay for cosmetics and personal care products. *Marketing i menedžment innovacij*.

Zahid, M. M., Ali, B., Ahmad, M. S., Thurasamy, R., & Amin, N. (2018). Factors affecting purchase intention and social media publicity of green products: The mediating role of concern for consequences. *Corporate Social Responsibility and Environmental Management*, *25*(3), 225–236. doi:10.1002/csr.1450

ADDITIONAL READING

Dini, I., & Laneri, S. (2021). The new challenge of green cosmetics: Natural food ingredients for cosmetic formulations. *Molecules (Basel, Switzerland)*, *26*(13), 3921. doi:10.3390/molecules26133921 PMID:34206931

Lin, Y., Yang, S., Hanifah, H., & Iqbal, Q. (2018). An exploratory study of consumer attitudes toward green cosmetics in the UK market. *Administrative Sciences*, *8*(4), 71. doi:10.3390/admsci8040071

Liobikienė, G., & Bernatonienė, J. (2017). Why determinants of green purchase cannot be treated equally? The case of green cosmetics: Literature review. *Journal of Cleaner Production*, *162*, 109–120. doi:10.1016/j.jclepro.2017.05.204

Pop, R.-A., Săplăcan, Z., & Alt, M.-A. (2020). Social media goes green—The impact of social media on green cosmetics purchase motivation and intention. *Information (Basel)*, *11*(9), 447. doi:10.3390/info11090447

Suphasomboon, T., & Vassanadumrongdee, S. (2022). Toward sustainable consumption of green cosmetics and personal care products: The role of perceived value and ethical concern. *Sustainable Production and Consumption*, *33*, 230–243. doi:10.1016/j.spc.2022.07.004

KEY TERMS AND DEFINITIONS

Eco-label: This is a certification or label awarded to products or services that meet specific environmental standards. These labels are intended to provide consumers with information about the environmental impact of a product or service, allowing them to make informed purchasing decisions. Eco-labels may be awarded by third-party organizations or government agencies and may cover a wide range of environmental criteria, such as energy efficiency, carbon footprint, water conservation, and sustainable sourcing.

Green Cosmetics: Also known as eco-friendly cosmetics, they are produced using sustainable and environmentally friendly practices. These products are formulated with natural or organic ingredients that are responsibly sourced, and the manufacturing processes used to produce them are designed to minimize waste and reduce environmental impact. Green cosmetics typically use eco-friendly packaging and avoid the use of harmful chemicals and ingredients that can harm the environment.

Natural Cosmetics: These are cosmetic products that are made from naturally occurring ingredients such as plants, minerals, and other organic substances. These products are free from synthetic chemicals and are often minimally processed to retain their natural properties. Natural cosmetics are marketed as being gentle and safe for use on the skin, as they do not contain harsh chemicals that can cause irritation or other adverse effects. However, it is important to note that not all natural ingredients are necessarily safe or effective, so it is important to research and choose products carefully.

Organic Cosmetics: These are cosmetic products made from natural ingredients that are grown and processed without the use of synthetic chemicals or harmful pesticides. These products typically contain high-quality plant-based ingredients such as essential oils, herbs, and botanical extracts that are sustainably sourced and harvested. Organic cosmetics are often marketed as being better for the environment and for personal health, as they are free from potentially harmful chemicals commonly found in non-organic cosmetic products.

Social Influence: Refers to how people affect the attitudes, beliefs, and behaviors of others. This influence can be intentional or unintentional and may occur in various forms, such as through persuasion, conformity, obedience, or socialization. Social influence can be exerted by individuals, groups, or institutions, and can occur through various channels, such as face-to-face communication, mass media, or social networks.

Chapter 4
Digital Marketing and Service Strategies for Sustainable Development of Visual Culture:
A Case Study of M+ Museum in Hong Kong

Yitong Chen
The University of Hong Kong, Hong Kong

Dickson K. W. Chiu
The University of Hong Kong, Hong Kong

ABSTRACT

Sustainability is an increasingly important topic internationally, but scant studies focus on the sustainability strategies of niche art museums, especially in Asia. Therefore, this study explores sustainable development strategies for niche art museums, with the M+ Museum of Visual Arts in Hong Kong as the case. The authors apply the PEST analysis to examine external influences on the sustainability of M+ based on the three pillars of sustainability to reveal the current problems of M+. The findings indicate the main sustainability problems of M+ include limited publicity, overpricing, lack of public cultural literacy, and limited coverage of social activities. Thus, the authors suggest strategies centered on building a multifunctional online community, including expanding online services for members, designing and selling electronic peripherals, developing online visual culture education programs, pushing events regularly, establishing a materials mall, inviting artists into the digital community, and designing a VR collection display.

INTRODUCTION

Hong Kong is a city that encourages sustainable development, aiming to strike a balance between environmental, social, and economic needs to maintain a high quality of life (Chung et al., 2020; Ho et al.,

DOI: 10.4018/978-1-6684-8681-8.ch004

2018). At the same time, Hong Kong, as one of Asia's cultural centers, is rooted in traditional Chinese culture and builds bridges between East and West (Hong Kong Cultural, Sports, and Tourism Bureau, 2022). With a total of about 60 museums as of December 2022, Hong Kong has become an important hub for public cultural industries (Wong & Chiu, 2023; Deng et al., 2022), with the global responsibility of Sustainable Development Goals (SDG) 11.4 to encourage the preservation of the world's cultural and natural heritage (Xu et al., 2023; Sun et al., 2022; Zuo et al., 2023). UNESCO (2020) recommends unleashing the power of culture, from improving education through cultural activities to enhancing social justice and promoting sustainability on multiple dimensions.

Given that the main task of museums is to "preserve cultural resources and make them available to present and future generations" (Moldavanova, 2014), they are considered entities with "a key role in shaping a sustainable future" (Blagoeva-Yarkova, 2012). However, there are many types of museums in Hong Kong (Jiang et al., 2019; Cho et al., 2017), and different types of museums in sustainability may require different goals and actions. The contribution of niche art and culture museums to sustainability is often overlooked compared to traditional subject museums (e.g., history and science museums). Therefore, this study focuses on the existing sustainability strategies and potential problems of niche art and culture museums in Hong Kong and suggests corresponding technical recommendations.

To better understand the sustainable development strategies of niche art and culture museums, this study selected the M+ Museum of Visual Culture in Hong Kong, one of the world's largest museums of visual culture under the West Kowloon Cultural District Authority and exhibited art and design collections from the 20th to the 21st century. While fulfilling its function of promoting and educating the visual arts, M+ has formulated a series of sustainability goals and action plans, aspiring to contribute to sustainable development (M+ Museum, 2021). Since M+ already has a more established vision and action plan in the area of sustainability, and it is one of the largest visual arts museums in Asia, it was selected for this case study.

A framework that can identify opportunities and threats is essential for organizations "to develop, implement, control, and improve sustainability strategies" to enhance their sustainability performance (Baumgartner, 2013). We apply PEST as the basic framework for external environment analysis (Jiang et al., 2023) to reveal the external opportunities and threats to M+ sustainability. Further, we analyze the status and sustainability issues within M+ with the three pillars of sustainability to highlight the contribution of niche art museums to sustainability and future development. Our findings then provide suggestions for the sustainability of niche art museums to promote sustainable development by combining digital and commercial approaches. Based on the fiercely competitive environment of the West Kowloon Cultural District (Wong & Chiu, 2023), M+ faces many opportunities and challenges for sustainable development in the context of the rapid advancement of digital technology and the continuous expansion of its application areas. Therefore, it is critical to review M+'s current external environment and sustainability vision and actions to meet the needs and expectations of sustainable development in its environmental, social, and economic aspects.

LITERATURE REVIEW

Visual Cultural Museum and Value

As the main institution for collections, museums play the role of collection, promotion, education, and research (Peng, 2022). Museums can be classified into different types, focusing on history, science, art, stamp, etc. Most research on tourism treats different types of museums as cultural attractions with the same "label" (Brida et al., 2012). However, each museum demonstrates its uniqueness by offering its visitors different types of engagement and experiences (Brida et al., 2012; Chen et al., 2018; Lo et al., 2019). M+ belongs to the museum of visual culture among art museums, which puts popular visual culture objects into museums and becomes an important subject of attention for modern museums to provide their sustainability (Çıldır and Karadeniz, 2015). Stephen (2001) argues that museums aim to benefit the general public today based on their symbolic and practical role. Therefore, "museums need to develop their public service function by understanding visitors' needs and providing more enjoyable and valuable services" (Hooper-Greenhill, 1994).

Sustainable Development

In the 1950s and 1960s, the environmental and social resource pressures associated with economic growth led people to question the "development = economic growth" paradigm and to conduct research (Hess, 2016). In 1961, the United Nations (UN) adopted its first resolution on development, the United Nations Development Decade, which proposed that economic growth was not the same as development and shifted development focus from quantitative to qualitative improvement. In 1972, Ward and Dubos provided a shadow report, "Only One Earth: The Care and Maintenance of a Small Planet," to the UN, which analyzed the impact of environmental pollution on different countries and regions from different perspectives and called for attention to the protection of the earth (Ward, 2013). In 1982, the "World Charter for Nature" was adopted at the 48th Plenary Session of the UN (Wood, 1985), which proclaims five "principles of conservation by which all human conduct affecting nature is to be guided and judged." Our Common Future (Keeblem, 1988), published by the World Commission on Environment and Development (WCED) in 1987, describes the future of sustainable development and how to achieve it. The article states that the goal of sustainable development is "development that meets the needs of the present without compromising the ability of future generations to meet their own needs." Since then, the concept of sustainable development has gradually come into the public eye. In 2016, the 17 Sustainable Development Goals (SDGs) for 2030 came into effect at the UN Summit, which is historical and sets the basic framework for future sustainable development (Biermann et al., 2017).

Three Pillars of Sustainability

The concept of three pillars of sustainability (social, economic, and environmental) is increasingly used by sustainability researchers. Purvis et al. (2018) opined that the "three pillars of sustainability do not have a single point of origin" but rather a gradual emergence. The earliest related literature is Our Common Future, published by the WCED in 1987, suggesting sustainability should be assessed from three main perspectives: economy, environment, and ecology, which form the basis of three pillars: economic viability, environmental protection, and social ecology. After this, researchers have generally adopted three interrelated "pillars" to describe "sustainable development" (Pope et al., 2004; Gibson, 2006; Waas et al., 2011).

Researchers in related fields have further elaborated on the three pillars of sustainability. Murphy (2012) analyzed the relationship between the social and environmental pillars and identified four social frameworks: public awareness, equity, participation, and social cohesion, to examine the organizational understanding of the relationship. Dalampira and Nastis (2020) simplified the UN SDG map by linking the three pillars of sustainability to the UN SDGs and further helped the public understand sustainable development awareness.

Museum, Digitalization, and Sustainability

A key museum function is conducting scientific research on collections and providing cultural, educational, and connoisseurship services to the public (Peng, 2022). It has thus been given a natural mission of cultural sustainability (Pop, 2019). The multifunctional, socio-cultural complex properties have made museums appear as a group with "a key role in shaping a sustainable future "(Blagoeva-Yarkova, 2012). The role of museums in sustainable development has also been extended to the wider arts and other fields (Perera, 2013). The international museum community is also beginning to acknowledge its ecological responsibility and obligation to cultural landscapes as essential resources for a sustainable future (Siena Charter, 2016). The broader role of museums in the field of sustainability is premised on the idea that "museums can provide places for communities to meet, work, share and mediate ideas, build social sustainability and promote individual and collective wellbeing for the common good" (Brown, 2019).

Digitalization has reconfigured many areas of businesses and social life with various information and communication technologies (ICT) and digital storage infrastructures (Chiu & Ho, 2022a, 2022b; Li, Lam, & Chiu, 2023; Tse et al., 2022; Wu et al., 2023; Lo et al., 2020). Raimo et al. (2021) suggest "the adoption of digital technologies stems from the desire to attract more visitors, reduce costs, improve the visitor experience, and adapt to competitors. Further, digital transformation, which helps to improve organizational performance and expand its reach, requires a higher level of socio-technical transformation than just the digitization of resources (Liao et al., 2020). Museums and archives store objects to provide information about the objects themselves, their types, their contexts, and their relationships to other objects (Buckland, 1991; Chung et al., 2016; Ng et al., 2022; Li & Chiu, 2022). Thus, the form and function of museums are similar to other information institutions, such as libraries and archives, and digitalization facilitates the development of museums as other information institutions (Lo et al., 2017; 2019).

However, integrating emerging technologies into museums to promote the treasures of human civilization is not as simple as supporting them with technology but should start with a comprehensive and holistic consideration (Peng, 2022). At the same time, the COVID-19 pandemic has brought massive lockdown of cultural organizations and thus accelerated the adoption of digital technologies (Raimo et al., 2021; Yu, Lam, & Chiu, 2023). Although some museums had already deployed digital solutions for visitors before the coronavirus pandemic, museums have significantly increased digital channels since early 2020 to sustain their operations and services (Meng et al., 2023).

Digitalization is not a drastic mandatory external change but a dynamic process that should be shaped to transition to a sustainable and low-carbon society, and digitalization helps sustainable development and resilience during unprecedented times (Yu, Chiu, & Chan, 2023; Ho et al., 2023). In addition, the sustainable governance model also helps reduce the friction and "costs associated with information collection and processing, management" (Aksin-Sivrikaya and Bhattacharya, 2017), thus reaching the interplay of sustainability and digitalization, showing promising opportunities to shape a greener economy and society, and paving the way to achieve the SDGs (Castro et al., 2021). In addition, enhancing the sustainability of museums through digitization is feasible, as museums can achieve more sustainable livelihoods using digital resources (Liao et al., 2020).

PEST Analysis

Aguilar (1967) first introduced PEST analysis in his book Scanning the Business Environment, a basic framework for macro-environmental analysis consisting of four main external environmental elements: political, economic, social, and Technological. PEST analysis identifies changes in the external macro-environment and the impact on the organization's competitive position for making better business decisions (Aguilar, 1967). Through PEST analysis of external factors, organizations can make pre-emptive strategies to mitigate the impact of external factors and take advantage of opportunities to create new competitive positions (Jiang et al., 2023).

Research Gap

Despite previous research on museums and sustainability, scant studies explore how digitization can contribute to the museum's sustainability, especially in niche museums in Asia. With the development of digital technology and increased informatization in society, digital methods to help museums store information and improve sustainability are interesting topics for investigation. Therefore, our study can help niche museums better integrate digital solutions into their development while allowing them to better understand their role in sustainability. Therefore, the following research questions guide this study.

RQ1. *What are the opportunities and constraints of the external environment for niche museums' sustainability?*

RQ2. *What are the contributions of niche museums in sustainability, as exemplified by M+?*

RQ3. *How can digital technologies help niche museums reach their sustainability goals?*

PEST ANALYSIS

PEST analysis (Aguilar, 1967) is a basic framework for macro-environmental analysis, which consists of four main external environmental elements: Political, Economic, Social, and Technological. Political refers to the political factors that help or hinder business development, such as policies, regulations, etc. Economic refers to the external economic factors that affect business development, such as economic growth or recession, cost of living, etc. Social refers to the related social factors, such as work attitude, culture, etc. Technological refers to the external factors of technology, such as technological innovation. This study will use PEST analysis to discuss the external factors affecting M+'s sustainability.

Political

Cultural Policy

Hong Kong, as one of the cultural centers in Asia, is rooted in traditional Chinese culture while blending Eastern and Western cultures to form a unique and distinct cultural content (Wang et al., 2022). The Hong Kong government has always aimed to develop Hong Kong as a cultural exchange center between the East and the West and has formulated policies in various aspects such as cultural preservation, talent training, and cultural exchange (Yu et al., 2023).

According to the Hong Kong Culture, Sports and Tourism Bureau (CSTB), the Hong Kong government allocated $5.7 billion for arts and culture in 2021-2022, mainly to promote arts education and fund arts groups and venue support (https://www.cstb.gov.hk/en/policies/culture/culture-and-the-arts.html). Currently, the West Kowloon Cultural District Authority (WKCDA), where M+ is located, has been allocated $21.6 billion to develop the West Kowloon Cultural District (WKCD) to support the development of arts and culture in Hong Kong (https://www.westkowloon.hk/en/our-story).

In addition, the Hong Kong Government has established a wider cultural network in recent years through a series of steps to promote cultural exchange and development between the regions. For example, the Hong Kong government has organized the Asian Cultural Cooperation Forum (ACCF, https://www.accf.org.hk/) since 2003 to exchange views on arts and cultural development policies. A series of cultural exchange policies are conducive to the further spread of M+ and visual culture, creating favorable conditions for M+ to expand its influence in the cultural field in Asia.

Sustainable Policy

At the beginning of the 21st century, the Hong Kong government began focusing on sustainable development, which aligns with the WCED's aim to develop toward present needs without compromising future generations' ability to meet them (Keeblem, 1988). In March 2003, the Hong Kong Council for Sustainable Development was established to advise the government on sustainable development and related strategies. For example, the Hong Kong Environmental Protection Department has implemented the ISO14001 Environmental Management System to continuously reduce pollution caused by daily work. In addition, the promulgation of regulations such as the Outdoor Lighting Charter and the Clean Air Charter has also helped Hong Kong achieve environmental protection and sustainable development from several perspectives. A series of sustainability policies and plans regulate the daily behavior of businesses, individuals, and communities in Hong Kong and enhance public understanding of sustainable development (Fu & Lu, 2020).

In addition, the Hong Kong government has established Sustainable Development Fund (SDF) to provide financial support for developing sustainability awareness among the Hong Kong public, encouraging Hong Kong companies, individuals, and communities to explore and practice sustainable development (Das, 2020). These policies and strategies have been developed to influence all aspects of public life in Hong Kong, to limit the actions of companies, individuals, and communities that threaten sustainable development in multiple dimensions, and to provide policy and financial support for sustainable development exploration and practices. In addition, the implementation of the policy influences the public perception of sustainability to a certain extent and facilitates the implementation of the organization's sustainable development strategy.

Economic

Hong Kong's economy has experienced its most difficult year since Covid-19 in 2020. According to the World Bank, Hong Kong's GDP per capita fell from US$48,356.1 in 2019 to US$46,107.8 in 2020. In 2021, GDP per capita rose back to US$49,800 (see: https://tradingeconomics.com/hong-kong/gdp). The annual growth rate of Hong Kong's per capita final consumption expenditure decreased from -1.5 in 2019 to -10.2 in 2020. With the enactment of a series of government measures to stimulate consumption (e.g., the government issues consumption vouchers), the figure grew to 6.3 in 2021. The economic rebound means that the Hong Kong region's population has renewed access to disposable funds for recreational and cultural activities (Yu et al., 2023), which has a favorable impact on the sustainable development of the M+ and cultural sectors.

Since M+ opened in 2021 and lacks data from previous years, this study references other museums' visits in Hong Kong. According to the Hong Kong Census and Statistics Department's Statistics (https://www.censtatd.gov.hk/), Hong Kong Science Museum and the Hong Kong Heritage Museum were severely affected by the epidemic and economic fluctuations, showing a downturn in attendance in 2020 and failed to return to the 2019 visitation level by 2021. This shows economic factors might impact people's cultural and recreational consumption participation. A poorer economic environment constrains people's spending on cultural activities, while a rebounding economy helps cultural and entertainment activities be promoted, profitable, and further developed. Therefore, as Hong Kong's economy recovers, M+ has a large market and potential consumer base in the long run. However, since the museums exemplified above all use a lower pricing strategy than M+, their situation may not apply to M+. In the current economic environment, it is doubtful that this market and consumer base will be willing to spend heavily in the cultural and entertainment sector (Li, Lam, & Chiu, 2023).

Social

In today's society, the public's appreciation of art is inadequate, and art museums are reduced to photo ops. Compared to museums of history, science, and technology, art museums are losing their intellectual impression, especially to the younger generation (Deng et al., 2022; Lo et al., 2019). People consider art museums more as photo material than an attempt to understand and learn about art. However, it is difficult to quickly solve the problem of a lack of public art appreciation. Therefore, art museums represented by M+ may face inefficiency regarding cultural export and influence expansion.

In addition, the lack of public art appreciation and the characteristics of visual culture evaluate visual culture museums tend to be polarized. The abstract expressions and unique visual effects of visual culture have led to mixed reviews from the public. Negative user reviews may cause potential users to lose interest in visual culture and, in the long run, may lead to user attrition (Chen et al., 2018), thus negatively impacting the sustainable development of visual culture.

Due to young people's curiosity and receptiveness to new things, the younger generation should gradually be the main audience of visual culture, but there is a lack of systematic education on visual culture in Hong Kong and many Asian countries (Jiang et al., 2019; Lo et al., 2021). The lack of visual culture education may cause these young people to miss the opportunity to learn about visual culture, thus limiting the further development of visual culture education and preventing the development of visual culture sustainability.

Yet, young people's widespread use of social media could be a potential booster for visual culture promotion (Mak et al., 2022; Deng & Chiu, 2023; Lam et al., 2023; Chan et al., 2020). Many young people share their lives and experiences visiting tourist attractions on social media (Cheung et al., 2023; Cheng et al., 2023; Ni et al., 2022). Such sharing helps more young people understand the visual culture and M+, laying the foundation for cultural and economic sustainability.

The Hong Kong region has a rich cultural heritage, which has led to competition from museums similar to M+, such as the Hong Kong Museum of Art and the Hong Kong Palace Museum (Wong &

Chiu, 2023). Competition within these sectors has led to the need for M+ to fully exploit its characteristics and identify competitive advantages to achieve sustainable economic development.

As the economy grows, society faces increasing pressure from the environment, resources, and other sources (Chung et al., 2020). Promoting sustainability in Hong Kong has led to a growing public awareness of the importance of sustainability and attempts to incorporate the concept of sustainability and green lifestyles into all aspects of life (Ho et al., 2018; 2023). The public gradually has a higher recognition of companies with good sustainability policies and is more willing to support the development of such companies. Therefore, a good sustainability policy may build a better public image for the company and attract potential user groups for long-term growth.

Technological

Technology for Museum Development

Digital and information technology has developed rapidly in recent decades, laying the foundation for the digitization of museums and other cultural organizations (Meng et al., 2023; Sun et al., 2022). Improvements in digital technology have facilitated museums to store exhibits and information. From traditional storage methods to digital and cloud storage (Hui et al., 2023; Zhuang et al., 2014), digital technology has greatly reduced the cost and potential risk of exhibit storage, improving economic and cultural sustainability.

In addition, information technology improvements have allowed museums to bring richer experiences to users, such as online exhibits, digital interactive works, animations, and more (Deng et al., 2022; Lo et al., 2019). Whereas in the past, such content often required extensive time and high costs for specialized technical staff, information technology developments now allow such content to be easily applied to the daily operations of museums. The development of these technologies has helped to increase the impact of visual culture, allowing users who cannot visit offline to appreciate the appeal of visual culture. In particular, virtual reality (VR) and augmented reality technologies can easily engage the younger generation (Lo et al., 2019; Suen et al., 2020).

Technology for Sustainable Development

Developing new technologies and materials has led to more ways to create visual culture artworks, and materials and technologies less constrain artists. The invention of environmentally friendly materials allows artists and museums to create and exhibit works of art with less environmental damage, thus promoting environmental protection and sustainability (Wong & Chiu, 2023).

In addition, information and computer technology improvements have made the sustainability vision traceable and measurable. Enterprises can design reasonable goals for sustainable development through information and computer technology and quantify the content and process of tasks to monitor sustainable development actions reasonably. Regarding environmental protection, the development of information technology facilitates accurate recording and tracking of the amount of energy consumed, how it is consumed, and the trends of changes (Ho et al., 2023). Regarding economic and cultural promotion, information such as changes in revenue and website visits can be clearly recorded to assist the museum in making decisions (Deng & Chiu, 2023; Liu et al., 2023; Lam et al., 2019).

THREE PILLARS OF SUSTAINABLE DEVELOPMENT

This section uses the three pillars of sustainability (economic viability, environmental protection, and social equity) to further analyze sustainability and potential issues within M+. According to the M+ Impact Framework, (M+ Museum, 2021) released in November 2020, M+ "are committed to social and cultural wellbeing, and environmental and financial sustainability" and has articulated one vision and seven key intentions related to sustainability for all aspects of M+ operations and to be integrated into its work in exhibitions, programs, collection maintenance, research, and visitor experience. The seven main intentions contain A Role Model, An Advocate, Experimental, Trustworthy, Embedding Sustainability, A Platform for Collaboration, and Giving Back. Table 1 explains the seven visions for presenting the relevant sustainability strategies implemented by M+ in detail from each of the three pillars of sustainability.

Environmental Protection

According to the M+ Sustainability Document, M+ will work on several fronts to achieve environmental and climate sustainability goals (e.g., the Hong Kong government's goal of reducing carbon emissions by 60 to 70 percent by 2030).

Architecture

Herzog & de Meuron, in collaboration with TFP Farrells and Arup, designed the M+ building in the West Kowloon Cultural District. It incorporates sustainable architectural design features and follows the Green Building EIA environmental assessment program whenever possible. Throughout the architectural design process, the M+ building utilizes an Integrated Sustainable Building Design (ISBD) approach that integrates architectural, construction, mechanical, electrical, and other technical disciplines "to minimize energy consumption and reduce greenhouse gas emissions" (M+ Museum, 2021).

Table 1. M+'s 7 visions of sustainable development

Vision	Explanation
A Role Model	Consciously act sustainably and be seen as a key opinion leader in sustainable museum practices in Hong Kong and across Asia
An Advocate	Leveraging the museum's strengths to work with communities to co-imagine, design, and create a sustainable future for all.
Experimental	Become a pioneer, innovating and experimenting in the fight against climate change
Trustworthy	Focus on transparency, action, and accountability to increase trust. Goals and actions will be publicly reported.
Embedding Sustainability	Adopt a holistic and sustainable approach, paying attention to sustainability and emissions in every decision and action taken.
A Platform for Collaboration	Supporting sustainability-related action and education through collaboration and the exchange of ideas.
Giving Back	Contribute with expertise to help individuals, community organizations, and our peers respond to climate and sustainability issues

Façade

M+ participates in the Hong Kong Environment and Ecology Bureau's Outdoor Lighting Charter and will close the M+ facade after 23:00 each night to minimize light damage and energy waste.

Materials

According to the M+ Sustainability Document (M+ Museum, 2021), M+ focuses on environmental protection and sustainability of materials, challenging common museum industry practices and critically evaluating the materials it uses. Managers draw on the expertise of the museum's in-house professionals to seek breakthroughs and innovations in materials. At the same time, M+ actively seeks input from external partners such as artists, manufacturers, and the community.

Pollution

M+ Muesm (2021) focuses on identifying major sources of emissions and investing time in researching, exploring, and testing new solutions to polluting emissions. The scope of research and investigation includes and is not limited to internal systems, policies and procedures, and work practices. These findings on emission sources will be documented and committed to reviews. M+ agrees on transparent and achievable measures and commits to such yearly improvements. Sustainability will be included in M+'s planning discussions and reflected in annual goals and budgets.

Promotion

M+ encourages its partners and service providers to act sustainably through their relationships and agreements. At the same time, environmental advocates are invited to lead and contribute to sustainability discussions with M+, both internally and across the cultural sector. M+ convenes international sustainability events and brings together museums across Asia to discuss their responses to climate emergencies. In addition, M+ executives attend museum-led forums such as CIMAM (International Council of Museums and Collections of Modern Art), IEO (International Exhibition Organizers), and Bizot (The International Group of Organizers of Major Exhibitions) to ensure M+ plays an active role in global discussions.

Overall, M+ is well prepared in the environmental pillar of sustainability and has integrated the vision into various aspects of its daily operations. However, due to its museum nature, there are limitations to expanding its reach, thus limiting M+'s role in broader sustainability advocacy activities. The pillar's sustainability strategy may lack advocacy for sustainability within the larger community, such as its user groups and visual culture artists outside of Asia.

Economic Viability

Ongoing Exhibit Acquisition

M+'s collections are mainly derived from purchases, gifts, bequests, exchanges, and transfers. For museums, the quantity and quality of the collection determine the sustainability of its users to some extent

(Cho et al., 2017; Jiang et al., 2019). Since visual culture collections are updated quickly, M+ needs to acquire new collections more frequently than other types of museums (e.g., history museums) to ensure the richness of the collections. On this basis, the control of the quality of exhibits and the development of budgets are of paramount importance for the economic sustainability of M+. Since purchases are one of the main means of acquisition for M+, M+ needs to have a reasonable budget control and purchase plan to ensure financial sustainability while maintaining users' sustainability and thus continuing the sustainable cycle of economic income from the users.

Tickets

Standard admission to M+ is HK$120 (1US$=7.8HK$ approximately) for standard tickets and HK$60 for concession tickets, excluding special exhibitions. Special exhibitions, such as the recent Yayoi Kusama exhibition, are priced at HK$240 and HK$150, respectively. Compared to the Hong Kong Museum of Art's HK$10 admission fee, M+'s high admission price somewhat limits the possibility of visiting the museum to those not financially well-off. Due to its high ticket price, it is difficult for users to form a repeat clientele, while most visitors will only visit once. As a result, users' sustainability may be constrained, leading to economic sustainability problems.

Membership

M+ membership provides users with special services such as priority booking, M+ Lounge, and M+ Private Viewing. The annual membership system allows M+ to obtain a large cash flow in advance for its exhibits and operation costs. This approach effectively alleviates the problem of insufficient cash flow. At the same time, M+ is more deeply tied to its users through this approach, enhancing their stickiness and repeat business and promoting the sustainability of the economic pillar (Wang et al., 2022).

Shopping

M+ offers shopping for products surrounding the exhibition, allowing users to choose their favorite products, with prices ranging from tens to hundreds of dollars. Most products feature relevant visual culture graphics printed on daily life items, costing 5 to 10 times more than regular products. The high prices are consistent with the pricing of tickets to exhibitions, limiting the possibility of purchasing favorite peripheral products for the less well-off or average user. Since peripheral products can, to some extent, stimulate users' memories of museum exhibits (Deng et al., 2022), a lower peripheral purchase rate is not conducive to an increase in museum user stickiness, thus reducing the sustainability of the economic pillar.

In summary, M+ has some results in the economic pillar of sustainability, but the overall high cost makes it lack the stickiness of the average user, which affects economic sustainability. In addition, collection selection and budget control is another focus of M+ to ensure the economic pillar is sustainable.

Social Equity

Promotion

M+ infuses sustainability into how partners, employees, and communities do things through action. M+ will increasingly invest in sustainable solutions and practices by reaching out to groups such as employees, artists, creator communities, service providers, partners, and communities to develop awareness, understanding, and responsibility for sustainability (Yu, Chiu, & Chan, 2023).

Education

M+ offers a range of kindergarten, elementary, secondary, and teacher programs to promote museum and visual culture education. Depending on the audience, M+ has carefully created appropriate programs for different age groups and levels of knowledge. For example, in the kindergarten school program, students learn about the Museum of Visual Culture through fun in-library learning and interactive activities, and M+ provides students with tactile materials and tools to help them explore the M+ exhibits, as well as learning kits and tutorials after the visit as an extension of this experience. In the secondary program, M+ is designed to complement the local school curriculum and expand students' holistic learning, focusing on promoting critical thinking, cultural awareness, and visual literacy. M+ also facilitates the exploration of the intersection of museum and school teaching through teacher roundtables comprised of teachers from the Hong Kong region, providing expert advice and support for museum projects.

Communities

The M+ Community Precursors Program is M+'s representative contribution to the social pillar of sustainable development. The program is socially oriented, exploring more possibilities for social service by engaging artists, social workers, and communities in cultural and creative practices, providing new opportunities for communities to develop social capital (Fong et al., 2020; Leung et al., 2022) and contribute to a sustainable future. In addition, M+ regularly offers charitable community events that foster social relationships, such as the Community Festival: Holding Hands (https://www.mplus.org.hk/en/events/community-festival-joining-hands/), which invites people to reconnect with old friends through a series of events. This no-strings-attached event is designed to help community members explore the arts and maintain a creative and open mind.

From a social perspective, M+ has contributed to community service, visual culture dissemination, and education, but its coverage is narrow, with most of its activities covering only the West Kowloon Cultural District and restricted parts of Hong Kong. The nature of offline activities limits the possibility of these activities being further promoted to a wider audience (Lu et al., 2023). Therefore, M+ has contributed to the social pillar of sustainable development, but there is still room for further improvement at the level of society as a whole.

DISCUSSION

Based on the results of the PEST analysis and the analysis of the three pillars of sustainability, Table 2 includes the opportunities and threats of the external environment of M+ and the related issues highlighted by the internal strategy. In response to the highlighted issues, solutions centered on digital communities are recommended to enhance M+'s contribution and impact on sustainable development and improve organizational sustainability so that M+ can better survive and provide a sustainable future for future generations. M+ can create new collections presentations and promote museum sustainability by using creative digital products based on the collections, such as virtual/online communities, VR, etc.

M+ Online Community

Online communities refer to groups of people who interact in a virtual environment to conduct common activities in a virtual form anytime, anywhere (Wang et al., 2022; Deng & Chiu, 2023). Thus, we propose related technical suggestions to help M+ achieve sustainability with the online community as the focus. M+ online community is a multifunctional virtual community for visual culture enthusiasts, forming a community of practice (Lei et al., 2021; Jiang et al., 2023). Participants have no prerequisites, and any visual culture enthusiast can find common interest enthusiasts, learn about visual culture, experience virtual exhibitions, etc., through the community. In the pre-release stage of the online community, M+

Table 2. Issues and suggestions

	External Opportunity and Threats	Suggestions
Political	Opportunity: Favorable cultural and sustainable development policies.	Grasp the favorable policies and establish a sustainable development system
Economic	Opportunity: The rebound of the Hong Kong economy may bring new markets and opportunities.	Using digital strategies to improve competitiveness
Economic	Threats: Public acceptance of high pricing is unclear and may undermine development advantages	Adjust pricing to cover a larger customer segment
Social	Opportunity: Young people love to use social media, which can be used to promote visual culture and M+ and expand the potential customer base	Promote the use of social media and digital technology
Social	Threats: The public lacks visual culture literacy, and visual culture education needs to be improved. Competition for similar museums in West Kowloon Cultural District.	Design and promote online education courses on visual culture to enhance public understanding of visual culture
Technological	Opportunity: The rapid development of information technology, the reduction of costs, and the increase in efficiency of digital development	Sustainability through digitalization and information technology
Issues highlighted by the internal strategy		
Environmental Protection	There is a lack of promotion of sustainability in the larger community, such as its user groups and visual culture artists, museums, etc., outside of Asia.	Further promotion through digital, online, and social media
Economic viability	The overall high cost makes it lack the stickiness of the average user. Collection selection and budget control is another focus of M+ to ensure the sustainability of the economic pillar.	Adjusting the cost range and increasing user dependency through digital means. Seek user opinions to acquire more popular collections.
Social Equity	The coverage is narrow, and most events are only held in the West Kowloon Cultural District and parts of Hong Kong. The nature of offline events limits the possibility of these events being further promoted to a broader audience.	Further expand the coverage of social welfare activities through the Internet and digitalization for more people to participate.

needs to increase publicity and expand its influence through effective relationship management (Chan & Chiu, 2022; Chin & Chiu, 2023). A large group of potential users is a key factor for the success of an online community, which can be promoted and implemented with social media (Wang et al., 2021; 2022).

Profit Model

Unlike offline exhibitions, the M+ online community attracts more users to participate through a ticket-less approach, with the purchase of membership by users as the primary way to generate profit (Li, Lam, & Chiu, 2023; Wang et al., 2022). Users can enjoy most of the community's content for free, except for a range of content provided for members, such as visual culture education courses (Yu et al., 2023; Deng & Chiu, 2023). There are two types of membership: regular members can use all the functions of the online community, while premium members can enjoy the benefits and special privileges of offline exhibitions on top of the regular members, like the current M+ members. Current M+ members will enjoy Premium membership benefits directly after the online community's launch.

M+ Membership Feature Expansion

M+ membership helps increase user stickiness, but due to its lack of online functionality, users have no pressing need for membership. The online community expands the functionality of membership and increases its usefulness (Deng & Chiu, 2023). Users can buy tickets, attend online exhibitions, meet friends with common interests, learn about visual culture, and use the creative section to design their visual culture works through the online community (Lei et al., 2021). The online community largely makes up for the lack of membership functions and activities. Its practicality and long-term nature can attract more groups interested in visual culture to participate in purchasing, improving the sustainability of the M+ economy and operation.

Online Exhibitions and Pricing

The M+ online community provides users with additional online exhibitions at lower pricing to make visual culture accessible to lower-income groups, overseas members, and future lockdowns (Meng et al., 2023; Li, Lam, & Chiu, 2023). Since online communities are far less expensive to maintain than museums, M+ can use online communities as a secondary business, catering to various income groups. Lower-income groups can visit the M+ Museum through the online community, while those who can afford the high price of tickets can continue to visit offline exhibitions, and those in this group who are interested in the online community section may also activate their online community membership. Categorical pricing allows both online and offline exhibitions to maintain profits, thus contributing to the sustainability of M+.

Technological Analysis

The Technological analysis in the PEST analysis shows that the development of outside technology has reduced the technical difficulties of establishing an online community. M+'s existing experience in website creation and digital interactive game design has provided a good foundation for M+ to establish an online community, enhancing its technical feasibility (Fung et al., 2016). Further development of mobile apps may be useful to attract younger and overseas members (Chan et al., 2022; Fan et al., 2020; Yip et al., 2021; Wai et al., 2018).

Visual Culture Education Courses

By designing and releasing the section on visual culture education, the M+ online community allows more people who have not been systematically educated in visual culture to access visual culture education (Yao et al., 2023; Cheng et al., 2022; Li, Xie, Chiu, & Ho, 2022). Thus, users interested in visual culture can genuinely understand the knowledge of visual culture and maintain long-term interest (Jiang et al., 2023; Deng & Chiu, 2023), thus increasing the influence of visual culture, expanding the user market for M+, and establishing sustainable development.

Online Social Welfare Activities and Sustainable Development Promotion

To address the problem of narrow coverage of social welfare activities, M+ can increase the coverage of social welfare activities through online communities. Thus, social welfare activities can cover the West Kowloon community and be connected to any part of the world through the Internet, enhancing the social capital of M+, improving social influence, and strengthening the sustainable development of social pillars. In addition, the online community can further promote sustainable development by regularly sending sustainable development policies and articles to users, which can effectively improve the problem of narrow publicity and low publicity impact of sustainable development and environmental protection (Chung et al., 2020).

Online Store

The M+ online community also features an online store (Meng et al., 2023) that provides users with environmentally friendly materials for visual arts design. Since the M+ online community may attract many new visual culture enthusiasts who may lack access to purchase design materials. M+, as an influential museum in the field, M+ can purchase high-quality materials at a relatively lower price. This approach lowers the threshold for users' visual culture creation and helps increase user stickiness, expanding M+'s influence and the development of visual culture. From the perspective of environmental protection, the sale of environmentally friendly materials can respond to Hong Kong's environmental protection policy and promote environmental sustainability. In addition, the program provides a new revenue source for M+ and promotes sustainable development in terms of the economic and financial aspects of M+.

Digital Periphery

Online communities can increase user stickiness and generate additional revenue by selling digital peripherals. Peripherals help enhance users' memories of their museum visit experience and increase user stickiness, making the design and sale of peripherals necessary. However, the pricing of M+ exhibit peripherals is too high for the average user to afford. The concept of digital peripherals has been increasingly admired by young people in recent years, for example, digital badges, digital illustrations, etc. M+ could design and sell the digital periphery with a thin pricing strategy. The lower price makes users, especially the younger demographic, willing to pay for it, and the virtual nature makes it easy for users to make remote purchases and multi-purchases. Whenever users see a purchased digital peripheral, they are reminded of the experience of seeing the exhibition. Thus, it brings new profit avenues to M+, enhances user stickiness, and improves the economy's and visual culture's sustainability.

Artist and Collection Selection

M+ can invite visual culture artists to reside in the M+ online community (Lei et al., 2021; Deng & Chiu, 2023). Their participation can attract more young people to communicate and interact with their favorite artists, cultivate users' visual art literacy, enhance their interest in visual culture, and promote sustainable cultural development. In addition, the artist's presence in the community strengthens their relationship with M+, and the good relationship benefits M+'s purchase of works and copyrights. At the same time, M+ can obtain users' opinions on the collection through questionnaires and other methods in the online community and select the collection they like more while ensuring the quality of the collection, promoting repeated participation of users, and enhancing financial sustainability.

VR and AR

The development of AR and VR technologies is also a potential opportunity for M+ to expand its influence. These technologies have become increasingly advanced, and the eco-chain of related products has been gradually developed. M+ can further explore the application of new technologies in visual culture by designing VR exhibitions and producing VR interactive games for visual cultures so that potential users in more regions can experience the charm of visual culture.

CONCLUSION, LIMITATIONS, AND FUTURE WORKS

In this case study, the current situation of the sustainable development of M+ is reviewed through the joint analysis of PEST analysis and the three pillars of sustainable development. The PEST analysis allows for a better understanding of the impact of the external environment on M+ sustainability; the analysis of the three pillars of sustainability allows for a better understanding of the actions and limitations of M+ sustainability. Specifically, the main issues of M+ sustainability include (1) limited publicity, (2) overpricing, (3) lack of public cultural literacy, and (4) narrow coverage of social events. As one of the largest visual culture museums in the world, M+ needs to continuously improve its strategies to meet the needs and expectations of sustainability to establish good sustainability and contribute to global sustainable development. Based on the findings, some recommendations centered on building a multifunctional online community were made, including (1) expanding online services for members, (2) designing and selling electronic peripherals, (3) designing online visual culture education programs, (4) pushing events regularly, (5) establishing a materials mall, (6) inviting artists into the digital community, and (7) designing VR collections displays.

Although this study covered a variety of information sources, such as M+'s sustainability documents, Hong Kong government information, and M+'s website, many of M+'s internal records and documents were not available, so the comprehensiveness of the findings needs to be further examined. In addition, the standard technical framework of PEST does not adequately support the interrelationship of the four dimensions, and it mainly provides a general concept of the macro-environmental conditions and situations of the company. Furthermore, the technical recommendations made in this study need further practical verification, such as technology development, cost considerations, and other potential problems. Regarding the above issues, further internal information can be obtained through questionnaires, interviews, etc., to make a more comprehensive research investigation. In addition, the technical recommendations proposed in this study can be further evaluated by establishing technical teams and interdisciplinary collaboration with technical disciplines to investigate their feasibility, for example, through value chain analysis (Wong & Chiu, 2023; Cheung et al., 2021). We are also interested in the change of habits in information consumption behavior due to the impact of technologies (Ding et al., 2021; Ezeamuzie et al., 2022; Xue et al., 2023; Xie et al., 2023; Zhang et al., 2021) and pandemics (Dai & Chiu, 2023; Yi & Chiu, 2023; Sung & Chiu, 2022; Huang et al., 2021; 2022; 2023).

REFERENCES

Aguilar, F. J. (1967). *Scanning the business environment*. Macmillan.

Aksin-Sivrikaya, S., & Bhattacharya, C. B. (2017). Where digitalization meets sustainability: Opportunities and challenges. *CSR, Sustainability*. Ethics & Governance. doi:10.1007/978-3-319-54603-2_3

Baumgartner, R. J. (2013). Managing corporate sustainability and CSR: A Conceptual Framework combining values, strategies and instruments contributing to sustainable development. *Corporate Social Responsibility and Environmental Management*, *21*(5), 258–271. doi:10.1002/csr.1336

Biermann, F., Kanie, N., & Kim, R. E. (2017). Global governance by goal-setting: The novel approach of the UN Sustainable Development Goals. *Current Opinion in Environmental Sustainability*, *26*, 26–31. doi:10.1016/j.cosust.2017.01.010

Blagoeva-Yarkova, Y. I. (2012). The Role of Local Cultural Institutions for Local Sustainable Development. The Case-study of Bulgaria. *Trakia Journal of Sciences*, *10*(4), 42–52.

Brida, J. G., Disegna, M., & Scuderi, R. (2013). Visitors of two types of museums: A segmentation study. *Expert Systems with Applications*, *40*(6), 2224–2232. doi:10.1016/j.eswa.2012.10.039

Brown, K. (2019). Museums and local development: An introduction to museums, sustainability and wellbeing. *Museum International*, *71*(3-4), 1–13. doi:10.1080/13500775.2019.1702257

Buckland, M. K. (1991). Information as thing. *Journal of the American Society for Information Science*, *42*(5), 351–360. doi:10.1002/(SICI)1097-4571(199106)42:5<351::AID-ASI5>3.0.CO;2-3

Castro, G. D. R., Fernandez, M. C. G., & Colsa, A. U. (2021). Unleashing the convergence amid digitalization and sustainability towards pursuing the Sustainable Development Goals (SDGs): A holistic review. *Journal of Cleaner Production*, *280*, 122204. doi:10.1016/j.jclepro.2020.122204

Chan, M. M. W., & Chiu, D. K. W. (2022). Alert Driven Customer Relationship Management in Online Travel Agencies: Event-Condition-Actions rules and Key Performance Indicators. In A. Naim & S. Kautish (Eds.), *Building a Brand Image Through Electronic Customer Relationship Management*. IGI Global. doi:10.4018/978-1-6684-5386-5.ch012

Chan, T. T. W., Lam, A. H. C., & Chiu, D. K. W. (2020). From Facebook to Instagram: Exploring user engagement in an academic library. *Journal of Academic Librarianship*, *46*(6), 102229. doi:10.1016/j.acalib.2020.102229 PMID:34173399

Chan, V. H. Y., Ho, K. K. W., & Chiu, D. K. W. (2022). Mediating effects on the relationship between perceived service quality and public library app loyalty during the COVID-19 era. *Journal of Retailing and Consumer Services*, *67*, 102960. doi:10.1016/j.jretconser.2022.102960

Chen, Y., Chiu, D. K. W., & Ho, K. K. W. (2018). Facilitating the learning of the art of Chinese painting and calligraphy at Chao Shao-an Gallery. *Micronesian Educators*, *26*, 45–58.

Cheng, J., Yuen, A. H., & Chiu, D. K. (2022). Systematic review of MOOC research in mainland China. *Library Hi Tech*. Advance online publication. doi:10.1108/LHT-02-2022-0099

Cheng, W., Tian, R., & Chiu, D. K. W. (2023). Travel vlogs influencing tourist decisions: Information preferences and gender differences. *Aslib Journal of Information Management*. Advance online publication. doi:10.1108/AJIM-05-2022-0261

Cheung, T. Y., Ye, Z., & Chiu, D. K. W. (2021). Value chain analysis of information services for the visually impaired: A case study of contemporary technological solutions. *Library Hi Tech*, *39*(2), 625–642. doi:10.1108/LHT-08-2020-0185

Cheung, V. S. Y., Lo, J. C. Y., Chiu, D. K. W., & Ho, K. K. W. (2023). Predicting Facebook's influence on travel products marketing based on the AIDA model. *Information Discovery and Delivery*, *51*(1), 66–73. doi:10.1108/IDD-10-2021-0117

Chin, G. Y. L., & Chiu, D. K. W. (2023). RFID-based Robotic Process Automation for Smart Museums with an Alert-driven Approach. In R. Tailor (Ed.), *Application and Adoption of Robotic Process Automation for Smart Cities*. IGI. Global.

Chiu, D. K. W., & Ho, K. K. W. (2022a). Special selection on contemporary digital culture and reading. *Library Hi Tech*, *40*(5), 1204–1209. doi:10.1108/LHT-10-2022-516

Chiu, D. K. W., & Ho, K. K. W. (2022b). Editorial: 40th anniversary: contemporary library research. *Library Hi Tech*, *40*(6), 1525–1531. doi:10.1108/LHT-12-2022-517

Cho, A., Lo, P., & Chiu, D. K. W. (2017). *Inside the World's Major East Asian Collections: One Belt, One Road, and Beyond*. Chandos Publishing.

Chung, A. C. W., & Chiu, D. K. (2016). OPAC Usability Problems of Archives: A Case Study of the Hong Kong Film Archive. [IJSSOE]. *International Journal of Systems and Service-Oriented Engineering*, *6*(1), 54–70. doi:10.4018/IJSSOE.2016010104

Chung, C., Chiu, D. K. W., Ho, K. K. W., & Au, C. H. (2020). Applying social media to environmental education: Is it more impactful than traditional media? *Information Discovery and Delivery*, *48*(4), 255–266. doi:10.1108/IDD-04-2020-0047

Çıldır, Z., & Karadeniz, C. (2014). Museum, Education and visual culture practices: Museums in Turkey. *American Journal of Educational Research*, *2*(7), 543–551. doi:10.12691/education-2-7-18

Culture, Sports and Tourism Bureau. (2022). *Culture and the arts*. CSTB. https://www.cstb.gov.hk/en/policies/culture/culture-and-the-arts.html

Dai, C., & Chiu, D. K. W. (2023). (in press). Impact of COVID-19 on reading behaviors and preferences: Investigating high school students and parents with the 5E instructional model. *Library Hi Tech*. doi:10.1108/LHT-10-2022-0472

Das, A. (2020). Low Carbon Growth, Climate Change and Sustainable Development Nexus: The Tale of Hong Kong. *Journal of Environmental Engineering and Its Scope*, 2(3), 1–10.

Deng, S., & Chiu, D. K. W. (2023). Analyzing Hong Kong Philharmonic Orchestra's Facebook Community Engagement with the Honeycomb Model. In M. Dennis & J. Halbert (Eds.), *Community Engagement in the Online Space*. IGI. Global. doi:10.4018/978-1-6684-5190-8.ch003

Deng, W., Chin, G. Y.-l., Chiu, D. K. W., & Ho, K. K. W. (2022). Contribution of Literature Thematic Exhibition to Cultural Education: A Case Study of Jin Yong's Gallery. *Micronesian Educators*, 32, 14–26.

Ding, S. J., Lam, E. T. H., Chiu, D. K. W., Lung, M. M., & Ho, K. K. W. (2021). Changes in reading behavior of periodicals on mobile devices: A comparative study. *Journal of Librarianship and Information Science*, 53(2), 233–244. doi:10.1177/0961000620938119

Ezeamuzie, N. M., Rhim, A. H. R., Chiu, D. K. W., & Lung, M. M. (2022). (in press). Mobile Technology Usage by Foreign Domestic Helpers: Exploring Gender Differences. *Library Hi Tech*. Advance online publication. doi:10.1108/LHT-07-2022-0350

Fan, K. Y. K., Lo, P., Ho, K. K. W., So, S., Chiu, D. K. W., & Ko, K. H. T. (2020). Exploring the mobile learning needs amongst performing arts students. *Information Discovery and Delivery*, 48(2), 103–112. doi:10.1108/IDD-12-2019-0085

Fong, K. C. H., Au, C. H., Lam, E. T. H., & Chiu, D. K. W. (2020). Social network services for academic libraries: A study based on social capital and social proof. *Journal of Academic Librarianship*, 46(1), 102091. doi:10.1016/j.acalib.2019.102091

Fu, J., & Lu, X. (2020). *Sustainable Energy and Green Finance for a Low-carbon Economy: Perspectives from the Greater Bay Area of China*. Springer. doi:10.1007/978-3-030-35411-4

Fung, R. H. Y., Chiu, D. K. W., Ko, E. H. T., Ho, K. K., & Lo, P. (2016). Heuristic usability evaluation of university of Hong Kong Libraries' mobile website. *Journal of Academic Librarianship*, 42(5), 581–594. doi:10.1016/j.acalib.2016.06.004

Hess, P. N. (2016). *Economic Growth and Sustainable Development*. Routledge. doi:10.4324/9781315722467

Ho, C. Y., Chiu, D. K. W., & Ho, K. K. W. (2023). Green Space Development in Academic Libraries: A Case Study in Hong Kong. In V. Okojie & M. Igbinovia (Eds.), *Global Perspectives on Sustainable Library Practices* (pp. 142–156). IGI. Global.

Ho, K. K. W., Takagi, T., Ye, S., Au, C. K., & Chiu, D. K. W. (2018) The Use of Social Media for Engaging People with Environmentally Friendly Lifestyle – A Conceptual Model. *SIG Green Pre ICIS Workshop*. AISEL. https://aisel.aisnet.org/sprouts_proceedings_siggreen_2018/2/

Hooper-Greenhill, E. (1994). *Museums and their visitors*. Routledge.

Huang, P. S., Paulino, Y., So, S., Chiu, D. K. W., & Ho, K. K. W. (2021). Editorial - COVID-19 Pandemic and Health Informatics (Part 1). *Library Hi Tech, 39*(3), 693–695. doi:10.1108/LHT-09-2021-324

Huang, P.-S., Paulino, Y. C., So, S., Chiu, D. K. W., & Ho, K. K. W. (2022). Guest editorial: COVID-19 Pandemic and Health Informatics Part 2. *Library Hi Tech, 40*(2), 281–285. doi:10.1108/LHT-04-2022-447

Huang, P.-S., Paulino, Y. C., So, S., Chiu, D. K. W., & Ho, K. K. W. (2023). Guest editorial: COVID-19 Pandemic and Health Informatics Part 3. *Library Hi Tech, 41*(1), 1–6. doi:10.1108/LHT-02-2023-585

Hui, S. C., Kwok, M. Y., Kong, E. W. S., & Chiu, D. K. W. (2023). (in press). Information Security and Technical Issues of Cloud Storage Services: A Qualitative Study on University Students in Hong Kong. *Library Hi Tech*. doi:10.1108/LHT-11-2022-0533

Jiang, T., Lo, P., Cheuk, M. K., Chiu, D. K. W., Chu, M. Y., Zhang, X., Zhou, Q., Liu, Q., Tang, J., Zhang, X., Sun, X., Ye, Z., Yang, M., & Lam, S. K. (2019) 文化新語:兩岸四地傑出圖書館、檔案館及博物館傑出工作者訪談 [New Cultural Dialog: Interviews with Outstanding Librarians, Archivists, and Curators in Greater China]. Hong Kong: Systech publications.

Jiang, X., Chiu, D. K. W., & Chan, C. T. (2023). Application of the AIDA model in social media promotion and community engagement for small cultural organizations: A case study of the Choi Chang Sau Qin Society. In M. Dennis & J. Halbert (Eds.), *Community Engagement in the Online Space* (pp. 48–70). IGI Global. doi:10.4018/978-1-6684-5190-8.ch004

Keeble, B. R. (1988). The Brundtland report: 'Our common future'. *Medicine and War, 4*(1), 17–25. doi:10.1080/07488008808408783

Lam, A. H. C., Ho, K. K. W., & Chiu, D. K. W. (2023). Instagram for student learning and library promotions? A quantitative study using the 5E Instructional Model. *Aslib Journal of Information Management, 75*(1), 112–130. doi:10.1108/AJIM-12-2021-0389

Lam, E. T. H., Au, C. H., & Chiu, D. K. W. (2019). Analyzing the use of Facebook among university libraries in Hong Kong. *Journal of Academic Librarianship, 45*(3), 175–183. doi:10.1016/j.acalib.2019.02.007

Lei, S. Y., Chiu, D. K. W., Lung, M. M., & Chan, C. T. (2021). Exploring the aids of social media for musical instrument education. *International Journal of Music Education, 39*(2), 187–201. doi:10.1177/0255761420986217

Leung, T. N., Luk, C. K. L., Chiu, D. K. W., & Ho, K. K. W. (2022). User perceptions, academic library usage, and social capital: A correlation analysis under COVID-19 after library renovation. *Library Hi Tech, 40*(2), 304–322. doi:10.1108/LHT-04-2021-0122

Li, K. K., & Chiu, D. K. W. (2022). A Worldwide Quantitative Review of the iSchools' Archival Education. *Library Hi Tech, 40*(5), 1497–1518. doi:10.1108/LHT-09-2021-0311

Li, S., Xie, Z., Chiu, D. K. W., & Ho, K. K. W. (2023). Sentiment Analysis and Topic Modeling Regarding Online Classes on the Reddit Platform: Educators versus Learners. *Applied Sciences (Basel, Switzerland), 13*(4), 2250. doi:10.3390/app13042250

Li, S. M., Lam, A. H. C., & Chiu, D. K. W. (2023). Digital transformation of ticketing services: A value chain analysis of POPTICKET in Hong Kong. In J. D. Santos & I. V. Pereira (Eds.), *Management and Marketing for Improved Retail Competitiveness and Performance*. IGI. Global.

Liao, H.-T., Zhao, M., & Sun, S.-P. (2020). A literature review of Museum and Heritage on Digitization, digitalization, and Digital Transformation. *Proceedings of the 6th International Conference on Humanities and Social Science Research (ICHSSR2020)*. Atlantis Press. 10.2991/assehr.k.200428.101

Liu, Y., Chiu, D. K. W., & Ho, K. K. W. (2023). Short-Form Videos for Public Library Marketing: Performance Analytics of Douyin in China. *Applied Sciences (Basel, Switzerland)*, *13*(6), 3386. doi:10.3390/app13063386

Lo, P., Allard, B., Anghelescu, H. G. B., Xin, Y., Chiu, D. K. W., & Stark, A. J. (2020). Transformational Leadership and Library Management in World's Leading Academic Libraries. *Journal of Librarianship and Information Science*, *52*(4), 972–999. doi:10.1177/0961000619897991

Lo, P., Chan, H. H. Y., Tang, A. W. M., Chiu, D. K. W., Cho, A., Ho, K. K. W., See-To, E., & He, J. (2019). Visualising and Revitalising Traditional Chinese Martial Arts – Visitors' Engagement and Learning Experience at the 300 Years of Hakka KungFu. *Library Hi Tech*, *37*(2), 273–292. doi:10.1108/LHT-05-2018-0071

Lo, P., Cho, A., Law, B. K. K., Chiu, D. K. W., & Allard, B. (2017). Progressive trends in electronic resources management among academic libraries in Hong Kong. *Library Collections, Acquisitions & Technical Services*, *40*(1-2), 28–37. doi:10.1080/14649055.2017.1291243

Lo, P., Hsu, W.-E., Wu, S. H. S., Travis, J., & Chiu, D. K. W. (2021). *Creating a Global Cultural City via Public Participation in the Arts: Conversations with Hong Kong's Leading Arts and Cultural Administrators*. Nova Science Publishers.

Lu, S. S., Tian, R., & Chiu, D. K. W. (2023). (in press). Why do people not attend public library programs in the current digital age? *Library Hi Tech*. doi:10.1108/LHT-04-2022-0217

M+ Museum. (2021) *M+Sustainable Document*. M+ Museum. https://webmedia.mplus.org.hk/documents/M_Sustainability_Document_EN_Accessible_Version.pdf

Mak, M. Y. C., Poon, A. Y. M., & Chiu, D. K. W. (2022). Using Social Media as Learning Aids and Preservation: Chinese Martial Arts in Hong Kong. In S. Papadakis & A. Kapaniaris (Eds.), *The Digital Folklore of Cyberculture and Digital Humanities* (pp. 171–185). IGI Global. doi:10.4018/978-1-6684-4461-0.ch010

Meng, Y., Chu, M. Y., & Chiu, D. K. W. (2023). The impact of COVID-19 on museums in the digital era: Practices and Challenges in Hong Kong. *Library Hi Tech*, *41*(1), 130–151. doi:10.1108/LHT-05-2022-0273

Moldavanova, A. (2014). Two narratives of Intergenerational Sustainability. *American Review of Public Administration*, *46*(5), 526–545. doi:10.1177/0275074014565390

Ng, T. C. W., Chiu, D. K. W., & Li, K. K. (2022). Motivations of choosing archival studies as major in the i-School: Viewpoint between two universities across the Pacific Ocean. *Library Hi Tech*, *40*(5), 1483–1496. doi:10.1108/LHT-07-2021-0230

Ni, J., Chiu, D. K. W., & Ho, K. K. W. (2022). Information search behavior among Chinese self-drive tourists in the smartphone era. *Information Discovery and Delivery*, *50*(3), 285–296. doi:10.1108/IDD-05-2020-0054

Peng, J. (2022). Research on digitalization of the museum industry in china- based on SWOT-pest model. *Asian Journal of Social Science Studies*, *7*(1), 31. doi:10.20849/ajsss.v7i1.982

Purvis, B., Mao, Y., & Robinson, D. (2018). Three pillars of sustainability: In Search of Conceptual Origins. *Sustainability Science*, *14*(3), 681–695. doi:10.100711625-018-0627-5

Raimo, N., De Turi, I., Ricciardelli, A., & Vitolla, F. (2021). Digitalization in the cultural industry: Evidence from Italian museums. *International Journal of Entrepreneurial Behaviour & Research*, *28*(8), 1962–1974. doi:10.1108/IJEBR-01-2021-0082

Stephen, A. (2001). The Contemporary Museum and leisure: Recreation as a museum function. *Museum Management and Curatorship*, *19*(3), 297–308. doi:10.1080/09647770100601903

Suen, R. L. T., Tang, J., & Chiu, D. K. W. (2020). Virtual reality services in academic libraries: Deployment experience in Hong Kong. *The Electronic Library*, *38*(4), 843–858. doi:10.1108/EL-05-2020-0116

Sun, X., Chiu, D. K. W., & Chan, C. T. (2022). Recent Digitalization Development of Buddhist Libraries: A Comparative Case Study. In S. Papadakis & A. Kapaniaris (Eds.), *The Digital Folklore of Cyberculture and Digital Humanities* (pp. 251–266). IGI Global. doi:10.4018/978-1-6684-4461-0.ch014

Sung, Y. Y. C., & Chiu, D. K. W. (2022). E-book or print book: Parents' Current View in Hong Kong. *Library Hi Tech*, *40*(5), 1289–1304. doi:10.1108/LHT-09-2020-0230

Tse, H. L., Chiu, D. K., & Lam, A. H. (2022). From Reading Promotion to Digital Literacy: An Analysis of Digitalizing Mobile Library Services With the 5E Instructional Model. In A. Almeida & S. Esteves (Eds.), *Modern Reading Practices and Collaboration Between Schools, Family, and Community* (pp. 239–256). IGI Global. doi:10.4018/978-1-7998-9750-7.ch011

UNESCO. (2022, September 5). *Culture & Sustainable Development*. UNESCO. https://en.unesco.org/culture-development

Wai, I. S. H., Ng, S. S. Y., Chiu, D. K. W., Ho, K. K., & Lo, P. (2018). Exploring undergraduate students' usage pattern of mobile apps for education. *Journal of Librarianship and Information Science*, *50*(1), 34–47. doi:10.1177/0961000616662699

Wang, J., Deng, S., Chiu, D. K. W., & Chan, C. T. (2022). Social network customer relationship management for orchestras: A case study on Hong Kong Philharmonic Orchestra. In N. B. Ammari (Ed.), *Social customer relationship management (Social-CRM) in the era of Web 4.0* (pp. 250–268). IGI Global. doi:10.4018/978-1-7998-9553-4.ch012

Wang, W., Lam, E. T. H., Chiu, D. K. W., Lung, M. M., & Ho, K. K. W. (2021). Supporting Higher Education with Social Networks: Trust and Privacy vs. Perceived Effectiveness. *Online Information Review*, *45*(1), 207–219. doi:10.1108/OIR-02-2020-0042

Ward, B. (2013). *Progress for a small planet*. Routledge. doi:10.4324/9781315066202

Wong, A. K.-k., & Chiu, D. K. W. (2023). Digital Transformation of Museum Conservation Practices: A Value Chain Analysis of Public Museums in Hong Kong. In R. Pettinger, B. B. Gupta, A. Roja, & D. Cozmiuc (Eds.), *Handbook of Research on the Digital Transformation Digitalization Solutions for Social and Economic Needs* (pp. 226–242). IGI. Global. doi:10.4018/978-1-6684-4102-2.ch010

Wood, H. W. (1985). The United Nations World Charter for Nature: The Developing Nations' Initiative to Establish Protections for the Environment. *Ecology Law Quarterly*, *12*(4), 977–996.

Wu, M., Lam, A. H. C., & Chiu, D. K. W. (2023) Transforming and Promoting Reference Services with Digital Technologies: A Case Study on Hong Kong Baptist University Library. In: B. Holland (Ed.) Handbook of Research on Advancements of Contactless Technology and Service Innovation in Library and Information Science. IGI. Global. doi:10.4018/978-1-6684-7693-2.ch007

Xie, Z., Chiu, D. K. W., & Ho, K. K. W. (2023). (in press). The Role of Social Media as Aids for Accounting Education and Knowledge Sharing: Learning Effectiveness and Knowledge Management Perspectives in Mainland China. *Journal of the Knowledge Economy*. doi:10.100713132-023-01262-4

Xu, C., Lam, A. H. C., & Chiu, D. K. W. (2023). Antique Bookstores Marketing Strategies as Urban Cultural Landmark: A Case Analysis for Suzhou Antique Bookstore. In M. Rodrigues & M. A. M. Carvalho (Eds.), *Exploring Niche Tourism Business Models, Marketing, and Consumer Experience*. I.G.I. Global.

Xue, B., Lam, A. H. C., & Chiu, D. K. W. (2023). Redesigning Library Information Literacy Education with the BOPPPS Model: A Case Study of the HKUST. In R. Taiwo, B. Idowu-Faith, & S. Ajiboye (Eds.), *Transformation of Higher Education Through Institutional Online Spaces*. IGI Global.

Yao, L., Lei, J., Chiu, D. K. W., & Xie, Z. (2023). Adult Learners' Perception of Online Language English Learning Platforms in China. In A. Garcés-Manzanera & M. E. C. García (Eds.), *New Approaches to the Investigation of Language Teaching and Literature*. IGI Global.

Yi, Y., & Chiu, D. K. W. (2023). Public information needs during the COVID-19 outbreak: A qualitative study in mainland China. *Library Hi Tech*, *41*(1), 248–274. doi:10.1108/LHT-08-2022-0398

Yip, K. H. T., Chiu, D. K. W., Ho, K. K. W., & Lo, P. (2021). Adoption of Mobile Library Apps as Learning Tools in Higher Education: A Tale between Hong Kong and Japan. *Online Information Review*, *45*(2), 389–405. doi:10.1108/OIR-07-2020-0287

Yu, H. H. K., Chiu, D. K. W., & Chan, C. T. (2023). Resilience of symphony orchestras to challenges in the COVID-19 era: Analyzing the Hong Kong Philharmonic Orchestra with Porter's five force model. In W. Aloulou (Ed.), *Handbook of Research on Entrepreneurship and Organizational Resilience During Unprecedented Times* (pp. 586–601). IGI Global.

Yu, P. Y., Lam, E. T. H., & Chiu, D. K. W. (2023). Operation management of academic libraries in Hong Kong under COVID-19. *Library Hi Tech*, *41*(1), 108–129. doi:10.1108/LHT-10-2021-0342

Zhang, X., Lo, P., So, S., Chiu, D. K. W., Leung, T. N., Ho, K. K. W., & Stark, A. (2021). Medical students' attitudes and perceptions towards the effectiveness of mobile learning: A comparative information-need perspective. *Journal of Librarianship and Information Science, 53*(1), 116–129. doi:10.1177/0961000620925547

Zhuang, Y., Jiang, N., Wu, Z., Li, Q., Chiu, D. K., & Hu, H. (2014). Efficient and robust large medical image retrieval in mobile cloud computing environment. *Information Sciences, 263*, 60–86. doi:10.1016/j.ins.2013.10.013

Zuo, Y., Lam, A. H. C., & Chiu, D. K. W. (2023). Digital protection of traditional villages for sustainable heritage tourism: A case study on Qiqiao Ancient Village, China. In A. Masouras, C. Papademetriou, D. Belias, & S. Anastasiadou (Eds.), *Sustainable Growth Strategies for Entrepreneurial Venture Tourism and Regional Development*. IGI Global. doi:10.4018/978-1-6684-6055-9.ch009

Chapter 5
Setting a Sustainable Human Resource Strategy in the Context of Sustainable Business and Marketing Principles

Pavla Vrabcová
Technical University of Liberec, Czech Republic

Hana Urbancová
University of Economics and Management, Czech Republic

ABSTRACT

Human resources are valuable, including competencies, which are of key importance for achieving strategic targets. This chapter aims to summarize the findings and to expand the awareness of the professional and lay public about the possibilities of setting a sustainable human resource strategy. The chapter is based on the results of quantitative and qualitative research in the Czech Republic (n = 183). The results show that organizations place a permanent emphasis on the most effective involvement of people in work processes and the acceptance of all aspects of their activities. It is the only dignified way to ensure social responsibility and sustainability in a society-wide dimension, and modern trends in strategic human resources management, such as age management and diversity management. The chapter has a practical and theoretical contribution, as recommendations for setting internal processes of human resource management and marketing are presented, and the theory is also supplemented with other factors that influence the setting of human resource strategy.

INTRODUCTION

The majority of organizations worldwide, whether they are small family businesses or large organizations, strive to maximize profit based on the fundamental principle of the invisible hand of the market that leads individual actors to efficient results, to the efficient use of scarce resources within the economy and

DOI: 10.4018/978-1-6684-8681-8.ch005

society as a whole. However, there is not sufficient non-monetary appreciation of the context. A narrow focus on monetary profit alone can lead to consequences that are in direct conflict with the concept of sustainable development, which respects the social and environmental aspects of life on the planet of Earth and observes human rights. The development of sustainability perception is evolving very rapidly, seeking to react to the turbulent environment and to flexibly respond to changes.

Stakeholders´ expectations as well as changing business conditions are forcing organizations to respond and build their activities on the principles of sustainable business and sustainable human resource management (SHRM).

The ubiquitous paradigm of development brings increasing disillusionment related to its unclear meaning and especially its practical implications. This threatens to change the concept of sustainable development and SHRM into a fashionable and rhetorical phrase. In the absence of practical examples and identification of practices on how to fulfill the content of theoretical declarations, this development paradigm will only remain an academic concept (Mensah, Casadevall, 2019).

The importance of SHRM increases every year, the reason being quite simple - quality employees are a valuable resource that can ensure the desired performance, success, and achievement of the set goals. And for this reason, the importance of human resources marketing is also increasing, when its focus can be seen in ensuring and supporting the creation of a "good reputation of the organization", thanks to which it is possible to stand out from the competition and thus increase your attractiveness as an employer. Human resource marketing can be said to sell the organization as an employer in the labor market. This then helps promote the sustainability of human resources and the need for a strategic view of human resource management. Due to the current war for talent, the modern approaches of organizations and their attractiveness are essential. Employees no longer only want to identify with the job itself, but also with their employer. Diversity management is one of the primary directions of focus of current employers for acquiring and retaining quality employees

Diversity management is a concept and part of human resource management strategy that is based on respecting a range of differences and diversities of employees (cultural, sexual orientation, racial, religious, etc.). Age management plays an important role. Addressing the age distribution of employees in organizations and their management is very important, not only due to the growing proportion of 50+ people in the population (Urbancová, 2017). Learning and development play a pivotal role in the running of the organization, they are included in both the organizational strategy and the organization´s vision. The current situation implies the need for quite significant changes related to the setting of intergenerational cooperation and organizational culture and climate. The following sub-chapters present the procedures and examples of good practices in the Czech Republic.

LITERATURE REVIEW

SHRM in the Context Of Sustainable Business and Social Responsibility Principles

Sustainability consists of the concept with three pillars (Joyce, Paquin, 2016). It is a way of doing business that aims to achieve: economic, social, and environmental profit. The sustainable business represents creating customer and social value through the interaction of business, social, and environmental activities. It is an essential source of competitiveness (Geissdoerfer et al., 2018), improving performance (Ahi, Searcy, 2013), reputation (Esteban-Sanchez et al., 2017), and cost reduction (Hung et al., 2019).

Sustainable entrepreneurship in organizations can be based on the following principles (Vrabcová, 2021):

- integrating sustainability into all management activities at all levels of management,
- producing environmentally friendly products that are relevant alternatives to less sustainable ones,
- channeling sustainable business as a fundamental path to competitiveness and economic performance, and
- respecting environmental principles.

In the business environment, the balanced saturation of social, environmental, and economic requirements and needs represents an important source of competitiveness, or competitive advantage, and a solid foundation for sustainable business. According to Baumgartner, Rauter (2017), the economic pillar consists of all economic activities, the interactions between them, and the interactions between the environment and society. It involves the correct setting of processes in the organization, and the experience and knowledge of managers who draw on quality underlying documents (conceptual, planning, and strategic).

the following elements can be mentioned in the economic pillar:

- the ethical code,
- strategic documents observing human rights and fighting against corruption and bribery,
- after-sales services to customers,
- the protection of intellectual property.

Corporate Social Responsibility (CSR) has close and effective links to stakeholders. CSR also enhances reputation, which improves competitiveness, sustainability, and market position. One of the basic assumptions of the social pillar is poverty eradication (Sengupta, 2018; Kang et al., 2020), both within and between regions, and in a global context between individual countries and geopolitical units (Cobbinah et al., 2015). This category includes equal access to basic sanitation and medical care, and the suppression of discrimination, racism, xenophobia, and religious intolerance (Cobbinah et al., 2015). A social area is a group of external and internal elements. The internal group includes the issues of occupational health and safety, employee training, job satisfaction, equal opportunities, the balanced composition of employees by gender, ethnicity, age, and otherwise, employee turnover rate, non-discrimination of any type, etc.

The external social area includes corporate donorship, volunteering at the level of organizations, social integration and helping disadvantaged groups, employment development, debt prevention, supporting education, local community support, consumer protection, and many others. Bansal et al. (2015) have evidenced that during recessions, organizations withdraw their CSR activities due to a severe lack of resources and increased uncertainty resulting from adverse market conditions. Corporations should have a duty to work on improving social welfare (Prates et al., 2015). Analyzing the strategic impacts of social responsibility is hindered by certain cultural differences in organizations that have a cross-border reach (McWilliams, 2015), as organizations operating in several countries or cultures have a more complicated process of determining which activities to engage in and how much to invest.

The environmental pillar affects both the social and economic levels (Tröester, Hiete, 2018) because it is based on the fact that unlimited growth is not possible in a constrained system. Within the environmental area, some important factors can be mentioned (Sengupta, Sahay, 2017): waste in organizations, negative impact on the environment, the consumption of renewable and non-renewable resources, water and energy consumption, environmentally friendly production process, hazardous chemicals, and their handling, using energy-saving appliances, greenhouse gas emissions, ecological footprint, carbon footprint, insulation of buildings, biodiversity conservation. The areas of voluntary tools in the context of sustainability and SHRM are summarized in Table 1 below.

As Table 2 indicates, in the context of the economic pillar, tools are based on knowledge, skills, and compliance and improve the competitiveness of the organization by compiling strategic documents and sharing key content with employees to help achieve the strategic goals of the organization. The concerned research in the framework of social sustainability focuses on the concept of CSR and the support of HR development also concerning the current challenges in social innovations, while coping with the barriers in the field of HR is necessary.

Based on the above, it can be summarized that the time has come when people perceive the attitude of companies towards the environment, perceive quality products, companies' relationships with local

Table 1. Voluntary activities, tools, and approaches in the context of the pillars of sustainable business and sustainable human resource management

Pillar	Voluntary activity, tool, approach	Integrating elements
Economic	Ethical code and other strategic documents	Improving relations with stakeholders, e.g., Stakeholder Engagement Standard AA1000SES Non-financial and sustainability reporting, for example, Global Reporting Initiative Integrating quality, health, safety, and environmental management systems, etc. Examples and sharing of good practices of sustainable business Associations and institutions of organizations: the World Business Council for Sustainable Development (WBCSD); CBCSD in the Czech Republic etc.
Economic	Activities beyond compliance with legislation and guidelines	
Economic	Quality management	
Economic	Protection of intellectual property	
Economic	Observing human rights and combating corruption and bribery	
Social	Age management	
Social	CSR report	
Social	Occupational health and safety management systems	
Social	Talent management	
Social	Diversity management	
Social	Knowledge management and knowledge continuity management	
Social	Social innovation	
Environmental	Environmental management	
Environmental	Life Cycle Assessment	
Environmental	Environmental Accounting	
Environmental	Carbon footprint management	
Environmental	Environmental auditing	
Environmental	Environmental labeling	
Environmental	Environmental performance assessment	
Environmental	Environmental communication	

Source: Vrabcová et al. (2022)

communities and public benefit projects, and how good are employers. Society has begun to take these factors seriously, and companies that won't react will be punished shortly by loss of reputation, loss of customers, and finally, losses on tangible assets. Many smaller companies do not believe in the positive impacts of CSR for the company and society sees only costs and no benefits, which are often intangible. However, medium-sized and large enterprises see the positives and are developing both human resource marketing and SHRM settings in this direction.

Because Czech organizations have yet to make the transition to sustainable business and sustainable human resource management, the authors believe it is important to further communicate this fact while defining current strategic trends related to sustainable business. No similar research has been conducted at the level of Czech organizations; the selected aspects have been addressed at the level of the Czech Republic by Mikušová (2017); similar research has been conducted in Eastern European countries, for example, in Poland (Šebestová, Sroka, 2020) and Slovakia (Rajnoha et al., 2016). Considering the current developments in the market of goods and services, as well as in the labor market, it can be noted that more and more Czech organizations are engaged in sustainable business and sustainable management of human resources. However, this is not always their direct activity, but rather the pressure of the external environment, whether global or national. The main factors driving the management of organizations towards sustainability principles to gain a competitive advantage are the current tight labor market, buyers demanding ethical or environmental principles from their suppliers or new legislation.

At the level of the organization, it is then the recognition of the needs and wishes of both existing and potential employees as one of the key strategic tasks, because by identifying them and subsequently satisfying them, the organization can achieve a significant competitive advantage and competitiveness on the labor market.

In the last two decades (Chams, García-Blandón, 2019; Macke, Genari, 2019), a new approach to human resource management has been developed, namely sustainable **human resource management (SHRM)**. Jaerlström et al. (2018) identified four dimensions of SHRM: Equity and equality, transparent HR practices, profitability, and employee welfare. It can be seen as an extension of strategic human resource management, with SHRM adding a new aspect to the discussion of corporate social responsibility (Bombiak, Marciniuk-Kluska, 2018). SHRM is based on the following approaches, among others (Vrabcová, Urbancová, 2022, p. 118):

"*a)* **green HRM**, *which can be seen as support for environmental management and the adoption of environmentally friendly practices (Bombiak, Marciniuk-Kluska, 2018; Järlström et al., 2018),*

    b)   **age management** as the business management concerning the age of employees (Urbancová, 2017; Urbancová, Vrabcová, 2020; Garavaglia et al., 2021),

    c)   **diversity management** as the effective management of a diverse workforce to foster organizational equality (Dennissen et al., 2020),

    d)   **sustainable work systems** (Järlström et al., 2018),

    e)   **Ehnert´s model** (Ehnert, 2009) and Kramer's model (Kramar, 2014), which complement Ehnert´s model with ecological outcomes;

    f)   **the theory of stakeholders** (Järlström et al., 2018; Ren et al., 2018)."

There is no consensus in the literature on what SHRM should include (Chams, García-Blandón 2019); therefore, Table 2 lists definitions of SHRM.

Table 2. Definitions of sustainable human resource management

Definition of SHRM	References
"A model of sustainable human capital starts with pre-hiring processes (raw materials), on-boarding (design stage), training and development (production stage), developing external partnerships and integrating individual employees into the system (distribution stage), building internal relationships through mentoring (use and maintenance stage), and employee's exit through succession planning (recovery stage)."	(Banerjee, 2013, p. 216)
"Sustainable HRM could be defined as the pattern of planned or emerging HR strategies and practices intended to enable the achievement of financial, social and ecological goals while simultaneously reproducing the HR base over a long term."	(Kramar, 2014, p. 1084)
"Adoption of HRM strategies and practices that enable the achievement of financial, social and ecological goals, with an impact inside and outside of the organisation and over a long-term time horizon while controlling for unintended side effects and negative feedback."	(Ehnert et al., 2016, p. 90)
"Sustainability of an organization depends on the exploration of the external environment for opportunities, changes, trends and risks involved and the balance between economic, social and environmental arenas in an organization."	(Tooranloo et al., 2017, p. 1253)
"This is a new approach to the realization of the HR function, the nature of which is to include ecological objectives in all HRM sub-areas, from employment planning, through recruitment, selection, employee motivation and development, to their evaluation and influence on working conditions."	(Bombiak, Marciniuk-Kluska, 2018, p. 5)
"SHRM and sustainability are two paradigms that converge toward a common organizational benefit, not only satisfying shareholders´ objectives but also operating responsibly while taking into consideration collective welfare and the preservation of natural resources."	(Chams, García-Blandón, 2019, p. 113)
"The SHRM model points out that human resource management enables the promotion of social welfare, considering that individuals and organizations can work together, reciprocally and sustainably, seeking long-term benefits."	(Macke, Genari, 2019, p. 813)

Source: Vrabcová, Urbancová (2022, p. 119)

This implies that SHRM involves strategic practices that reflect the triple bottom line principle by developing partnerships with all stakeholders to ensure sustainable competitive advantage and social well-being. According to Tooranloo et al. (2017), key dimensions and factors that influence the implementation of sustainable human resource management include corporate social responsibility (CSR), availability of career opportunities, green management of employee health and safety, green workforce planning, human resource efficiency, management commitment to economic sustainability, and employment guarantee.

Because of the current demographic trends, it is important to ensure knowledge continuity between the older generation and the next generation, not only in agriculture and forestry (Hitka et al., 2018). Age management is corporate management concerning the age of employees (Garavaglia et al., 2021). The implementation of age management is one of the tools that can be used to support a human resources strategy and the implementation of the Common Agricultural Policy in terms of knowledge transfer, both at the national and European level (Urbancová, 2019). Garavaglia et al. (2021) suggest adopting an action research approach to facilitate the implementation of these practices. Research by Urbancová, Vrabcová (2020) identified three key explanatory factors for implementing age management in the primary sector, namely building the internal employer brand by applying current management trends, building the external employer brand, and ensuring knowledge continuity, which ties into the social factor identified by Earl, Taylor (2015). The conditions under which today's employee teams of all generations are formed and function are undergoing dynamic change (Skibiński et al., 2016), and the COVID-19 pandemic reinforces this statement due to the need for social distance (Hartley et al., 2020).

The activities carried out within SHRM in cooperation with human resources marketing can subsequently as a whole lead to an increase in customer satisfaction, to building and subsequently maintaining strong and friendly business relationships, and all this to improve the efficiency and results of the company. An organization that correctly uses the personnel marketing strategy and its tools is open to the needs and expectations of its employees because the fulfillment of these needs is subsequently reflected in the above-mentioned customer satisfaction and improvement of the organization's image.

METHODOLOGY

The research analyzed primary data obtained using a survey, using the CAPI (Computer Assisted Personal Interviewing) data collection technique, from organizations of all economic sectors of the Czech Republic. The sample file was exported from the Albertina database (more than 2,700,000 organizations in the Czech Republic).

850 Czech organizations were contacted, and the basic identification questions of the survey include the variables (Vrabcová, Urbancová, 2022; Vrabcová et al., 2022): the operation sector of the organization, the size of the organization, majority ownership, the type of the organization, annual turnover (see Table 3).

The chi-square test was performed for the selected nominal variables depending on selected identification variables. The results were analyzed using the dependence test ($\chi 2$) and the power of dependence test (Cramer's V) at a given level of significance $\alpha = 0.05$.

To find the hidden factors, factor analysis was applied, which is used to reduce the number of variables and to reveal the structure of relationships between variables using the principal components method and orthogonal rotation by the Varimax method, which maximizes the sum of all factors' variances. The IBM SPSS Statistics 24 was used for this statistical analysis. The prerequisites are (Vrabcová, Urbancová, 2022; Vrabcová et al., 2022):

- cardinal variables,

Table 3. Basic data – selected characteristics

Characteristics	Categories		
The operation sector of the organization	Primary	Secondary	Tertiary
	4.5%	40.2%	55.3%
The size of the organization	≤50	51–250	>250
	26.8%	27.9%	45.3%
Majority ownership	Domestic	Foreign	
	45.3%	54.7%	
The type of the organization	Private	Public	Non-profit
	86.0%	11.2%	2.8%
Annual turnover	≤10 mil. EUR	11–50 mil. EUR	>50 mil.
	38.5%	38.0%	23.5%

Source: Vrabcová, Urbancová (2022); Vrabcová et al. (2022)

- low cross-correlations,
- the Kaiser-Meyer-Olkin (*KMO*) measure of sampling adequacy greater than 0.7, and
- non-zero correlations.

Synthesis, induction, and deduction were also used to create the chapter.

RESULTS

The Setting of Sustainable Business in Czech Organizations

In most cases, the direction is set by large, international organizations, while small and medium-sized organizations are just beginning to apply the principles of sustainability. However, one must realize that nowadays every organization should address the issues of responsible business conduct in a comprehensive way, namely by formulating a long-term strategy with specific strategic objectives that will lead to continuous process improvement, fair behavior, and active problem-solving through the management of organizations. The presented research concentrated, inter alia, on the surveyed organizations´ focus on the individual pillars of sustainable business. Table 4 presents the attitudes of the surveyed organizations ($n = 183$) concerning their focus on the pillars of sustainable business.

A total of 9% of the organizations surveyed use voluntary tools and approaches (outside the legal framework) aimed at protecting the environment, preventing pollution, and pursuing economic goals. 27% of respondents (especially in the tertiary sector, namely 15%) pay close attention to the social and economic aspects of doing business (outside the legal framework), especially to issues of health and safety at work and relations with the community and other relevant stakeholders. 41% of respondents describe themselves as socially responsible because, in addition to pursuing economic goals, they undertake projects that benefit the environment, employees, the site, or other relevant stakeholders) 23% of respondents believe that the concept of sustainable development is a government issue and that companies should primarily comply with the law.

The concept of sustainable business builds on these efforts by identifying several fundamental ways in which economic, social, and environmental activities can be closely linked to organizational and

Table 4. The focus of the surveyed organizations in terms of the three pillars of sustainability

The focus of the organization	Sector			In total
	Primary	Secondary	Tertiary	
All activities are assessed for their economic and environmental aspects and impacts.	0%	4%	5%	**9%**
The main focus is on economic and social objectives. The approach to the environment is in line with environmental protection laws.	2%	10%	15%	**27%**
The main focus is on economic objectives. The social and environmental objectives are achieved following the applicable laws.	0%	8%	15%	**23%**
All processes and projects are assessed concerning their economic, environmental as well as social aspects and impacts.	2%	20%	19%	**41%**
Total	**4%**	**42%**	**54%**	**100%**

Source: Vrabcová et al. (2022)

functional strategy (or strategies). The results related to the strategic trends leading to sustainable business and the realization of sustainable human resource management, the conditions affecting knowledge sharing in organizations, which are one of the most important prerequisites for management systems, have been subjected to several statistics, namely factor analysis using the principal component method and the Varimax method, which can be evaluated as one of the most commonly used methods for the verification function of factor analysis in the field of management.

The focus group ($n = 8$) has identified 15 strategic trends that organizations in the Czech Republic view as the most important and most frequently implemented in strategic management (Vrabcová et al., 2022). The identified strategic trends by the Varimax method are listed in Table 5.

The results have shown that the trends most highlighted by the representatives of the organizations are related to the definition of processes, in the areas of quality, OHS, environment, and their reporting, including CSR. The coefficients range from 0.4 to 0.6, and the first factor can be called an "integrated management system", as these organizations emphasize effective and high-quality process definition and process approach, including compliance with legal measures, risk management, continuous improvement, and consistent documentation of information.

CSR is not a new matter, the definition of social responsibility in the context of business was introduced in the professional literature as early as 1953, and currently, this phenomenon is viewed as a trend that appeals to a change in business orientation from short-term to long-term objectives and from maximum to optimum profit. It is associated with a category that has also undergone a significant shift within the economic theory, namely innovation. Contextual business helps organizations predict and manage risks, reduce costs, and increase their success by helping customers live more responsibly, win

Table 5. Factors related to strategic approaches and trends

Variables	Factor 1	Factor 2	Factor 3	Factor 4	Factor 5	Factor 6
Knowledge continuity	-0.099	0.372	-0.073	0.373	0.358	**0.408**
Talent management	0.145	-0.231	**0.343**	-0.089	**0.602**	-0.327
Age management	0.297	0.301	0.333	-0.306	0.206	**0.363**
Diversity management	0.195	**0.576**	**0.490**	-0.174	-0.006	-0.007
Career management	0.264	**0.427**	-0.426	-0.395	-0.014	0.051
CSR report	**0.454**	0.100	0.259	0.087	-0.501	-0.084
Ethical code	**0.532**	-0.009	-0.301	-0.196	0.256	-0.165
Flat organizational structure	-0.160	0.291	0.183	**0.582**	0.256	0.046
Quality management systems	**0.568**	-0.236	-0.137	0.322	-0.040	-0.013
Occupational health and safety management systems	**0.422**	-0.005	-0.194	0.164	-0.238	0.505
Environmental management systems	**0.683**	-0.218	0.181	0.142	0.119	0202
Environmental Accounting	**0.523**	-0.379	0.363	-0.095	-0.015	0.048
Non-financial reporting	0.084	**0.476**	0.258	0.068	-0.265	-0.346
Product life cycle assessment	**0.435**	0.299	-0.402	-0.086	0.233	-0.158
Innovation including digitization	0.383	0.197	-0.177	**0.442**	-0.015	-0.443
Factor	Integrated management system	CSR reporting	Employee development	Conditions for innovation development	Succession	Knowledge continuity

Source: Vrabcová et al. (2022)

new markets, etc., through innovation. The transition to an innovative society entails the automation of many work processes, which implies new risks and pressure on organizations to regularly retrain and educate their employees.

The sustainability of an organization is not possible without an adequate management system or mechanism. Management in organizations, regardless of the area of implementation, has also been undergoing major changes over the last decades. Numerous factors that were associated with smaller entities a few years ago are now permeating all segments without exception. These include the issue of succession, which could currently be characterized as the process of ensuring the continuity of management in the context of sustainability of the position in the market, or, more precisely in the business environment. This process covers both the formulation of objectives and the entire area of management and its elements. Planning is a living, continuous, dynamic process and a purposeful succession formation, the basis of and starting point for which is the quality of human resources.

Ensuring the continuity of the existence of the organization, and the management of the organization also means the need to ensure the continuity of knowledge transfer. The continuity of knowledge, skills, and competencies is a challenge especially in the context of transformation processes and the associated mobility of employees at all levels and in all processes. It can be deduced that the principles of sustainable business in the Czech organizations interviewed focus on three core areas, namely the labor market (demographic change and migration, diversity, education, flexibility, and equality), the circular economy (shifting the economy from dependence on fossil resources to the "circular" or "recycling" approach through innovation), and the existence of sustainable communities (voluntarism, giving, and partnership). This was also confirmed in the focus group ($n = 8$), with stakeholders emphasizing the need to ensure continuity of knowledge across generations and employee groups (age management). Developing employee potential through the use of age management can work differently in different settings. In some cases, separating generations into different departments may work better, while in other cases, the collaboration between generations is most effective. Thank cooperation, new ideas, and innovations can emerge that gain originality by combining the theoretical school knowledge of the younger generation with the many years of experience of the older generation. It is this intergenerational connection that can weed out mistakes that are not obvious to the younger generations. Last but not least, the dependence of selected variables on the identifying characteristics (industry, size by several employees, type, and annual turnover) is examined, see Table 6.

Considering the results obtained, it can be concluded that a strategic approach to CSR and corporate sustainability translates into a better return on investment for the entire company. Focusing companies on sustainability helps to reduce costs, increase profits and improve the company's reputation, as well as generate positive social and environmental impacts. By leveraging the core pillars of sustainability, companies can achieve sustainable competitive advantage and be financially sustainable. The integration of organizational, social, and environmental policies into the traditional strategy model is supported by the well-known assertion, nearly thirty years old, that social interactions in organizations "*should be strategically linked to the economic interests of the organization*" (Carroll, Hoy, 1984, p. 55). According to Baumgartner, Rauter (2017), integrating sustainability concerns into the strategic context is essential for creating business value. These are approaches by organizations that go beyond their interests and legally mandated activities to work for a specific social good, incorporating social attributes or characteristics into products and production processes. The mentioned voluntarism is very closely related to proactivity, especially to the extent that it presupposes the absence of the mentioned regulatory and legal measures (Tröester, Hiete, 2018). These activities relate to the role of entrepreneurship in ensuring

Table 6. The orientation of organizations under the principles of sustainable business: testing the dependencies between the selected qualitative variables

Variable	Sector p-value/ Cramer's V	Size p-value/ Cramer's V	Type p-value/ Cramer's V	Annual turnover p-value/Cramer's V
Orientation to results	0.003/0.248	0.114/–	0.181/–	0.260/–
Customer orientation (i.e., market value)	0.781/–	0.647/–	0.064/–	0.609/–
Quality orientation (products and services)	0.981/–	0.354/–	0.017/0.207	0.172/–
Innovation orientation (adaptability and flexibility)	0.647/–	0.042/0.183	0.593/–	0.268/–
Corporate processes	0.038/0.186	0.002/0.255	0.388/–	0.040/0.185
Innovation	0.267/–	0.502/–	0.006/0.231	0.594/–
Customers	0.234/–	0.527/–	0.411/–	0.296/–
Employees	0.178/–	0.854/–	0.091/–	0.697/–
Financial results	0.322/–	0.568/–	0.251/–	0.482/–
Increasing the organization's performance	0.798/–	0.096/–	0.267/–	0.542/–
Increase in profits	0.126/–	0.910/–	0.347/–	0.587/–
Maximizing sales	0.344/–	0.999/–	0.096/–	0.574/–
Cost reduction	0.544/–	0.488/–	0.759/–	0.034/0.189
Introducing new ways of working	0.020/0.202	0.149/–	0.338/–	0.044/0.182
Creating new market opportunities	0.548/–	0.382/–	0.149/–	0.023/0.199
Unique product/service	0.373/–	0.482/–	0.000/0.286	0.840/–
Unique financial/material resources	0.030/0.193	0.004/0.241	0.412/–	0.007/0.227
Unique human resources (competencies)	0.964/–	0.794/–	0.154/–	0.892/–
The largest market share	0.790/–	0.211/–	0.128/–	0.387/–
Returns to scale	0.700/–	0.740/–	0.545/–	0.490/–

Source: Vrabcová et al. (2022)

sustainable development by maintaining equitable and appropriate relationships with various stakeholders, which is particularly important given the limited capacity of state organizations to meet all social needs (Prates et al., 2015).

The Setting of Sustainable Human Resource Management in Czech Organizations

First, the research investigated the extent to which the surveyed organizations apply age management, see Table 7. It can be stated that the majority of the surveyed organizations are engaged in age management (55%) and more than 80% have information on how the age composition of their employees develops over time.

However, the results of the quantitative survey also show that the majority of respondents (55%) overall have no plans for the age structure of the workforce in the next 3 to 5 years. As shown in Table 7, the majority of respondents indicated that they are concerned with age management, but on the other hand, they also indicated that there has been no difference in the attitude of department managers towards

Table 7. Contingency table (relative frequencies in %): applying age management and the size of agricultural and forestry enterprises

Applying age management	The size of the organization			Total
	< 50 employees	51–249 employees	≥ 250 employees	
The company applies age management	13	18	24	**55**
The organization does not apply age management	13	10	22	**45**
Total	**26**	**28**	**46**	**100**

Source: Vrabcová, Urbancová (2022)

young or older employees in the last 12 months (77%). It is therefore evident that while the respondents paint a positive picture of their organization with the application of age management, their responses do not indicate that they have taken active steps to implement age-oriented human resource management. This is also evidenced by the fact that 67% of the organizations surveyed do not have any training programs related to management considering the age of employees and intergenerational cooperation.

The results of the quantitative questionnaire survey show a relatively high level of corporate social responsibility related to the promotion of employees' health (regardless of their age), as 77% of respondents contribute to activities that promote physical activity. At the same time, 80% of the companies surveyed indicated that they have procedures in place to transfer the knowledge and skills of older and more experienced employees to less experienced ones (peer consulting, task sharing, etc.). Table 8 presents the results of testing the qualitative variables (industry, size by several employees, ownership, type, and annual turnover).

Based on the results, it can be summarized that the majority of the monitored activities are not statistically affected by the studied variables at the 0.05 significance level, i.e., it can be concluded that all activities can be performed by any organization, regardless of size, focus, or turnover, with the same benefit. The activity most influenced by the variables studied is the approaching of their former employees with the offer to continue working or collaborating with them despite their departure, by the organizations' management (depending on the size, owners, and annual turnover).

The results obtained are then subjected to multidimensional statistics (factor analysis), as shown by the application of the principal components method in Table 9. The factor analysis identifies 4 significant factors that combine the variables related to the benefits of age management for organizations.

The survey results showed that both external and internal trends that improve the HR marketing of the organization are most emphasized by the representatives of the organizations. These are processes to improve the motivation and performance of existing employees, employer branding, and prestige building to gain a competitive advantage. The coefficients range from 0.527 to 0.685. The first factor can be called "**emphasis on HR marketing**", as it can be assumed that these organizations have a certain strategy aimed at gaining a competitive advantage through effective human resources management. HR marketing is currently formed as a separate area that combines the field of human resources management with marketing and considers employees as customers.

The second factor focuses on **stabilizing the internal environment**, especially organizational climate (0.586) and culture (0.707). Companies emphasize proactive resolution of workplace conflicts that could lead to employee demotivation, discontinuity, or a threat to the company. The third factor, labeled "managing job performance," identifies organizations whose strategy is based on the resource-based

Table 8. The results of the qualitative variables testing

Variable	Sector p-value/ Cramer's V	Size p-value/ Cramer's V	Ownership p-value/ Cramer's V	Type p-value/ Cramer's V	Annual turnover p-value/ Cramer's V
The management monitors the development of the employee age composition over time.	0.300/-	0.182/-	0.756/-	0.804/-	0.585/-
The management plans for the employee age structure within 3–5 years.	0.422/-	0.733/-	0.624/-	0.507/-	0.709/-
The organization has noted different attitudes of department heads towards junior or senior employees in the last 12 months.	0.341/-	0.437/-	0.737/-	0.038/0.186	0.012/0.214
The training program takes into account the age of employees and emphasizes intergenerational cooperation.	0.097/0.274	0.331/-	0.016/0.176	0.403/-	0.094/0.159
The organization contributes to activities that help improve the physical fitness of employees (regardless of their age).	0.375/-	0.146/-	0.382/-	0.408/-	0.259/-
The organization has procedures in place aimed at transferring the knowledge and skills of older and more experienced employees to less experienced ones (peer consultations, task sharing, etc.).	0.297/-	0.517/-	0.510/-	0.771/-	0.444/-
The organization allows for flexible working hours as employees' life roles change.	0.087/0.276	0.012/0.215	0.421/-	0.059/0.173	0.099/0.157
The organization approaches its former employees with an offer to continue working or becoming involved in the running of the organization after their retirement.	0.200/-	0.033/0.190	0.009/0.190	0.385/-	0.002/0.256

Source: Vrabcová, Urbancová (2022)

Table 9. The resultant factors by the Varimax method, factors affecting the cooperation of all employee generations

Variables	Factor 1	Factor 2	Factor 3	Factor 4
Retaining key employees	0.292	0.125	**-0.747**	0.152
Acquiring talented employees	0.279	0.060	-0.010	**0.783**
Improving motivation and performance	**0.527**	0.246	0.018	-0.534
Improving the organizational climate	0.030	**0.586**	0.262	-0.228
Improving the organizational culture	-0.067	**0.707**	-0.027	0.275
Improving the organization's prestige	**0.592**	-0.058	-0.052	0.065
Employer brand building	**0.639**	-0.131	0.091	0.170
Gaining a competitive advantage	**0.685**	0.199	-0.030	-0.024
Improving crisis management	0.051	**0.590**	-0.067	-0.068
Increasing the organization's performance	0.282	0.178	**0.746**	0.137
Factor	Emphasis on HR marketing	Emphasis on stabilizing the internal environment	Job performance management	Emphasis on recruiting qualified employees

Source: Vrabcová, Urbancová (2022)

approach, in which employees with key knowledge play an important role in enhancing the organization's performance. However, it is necessary to ensure knowledge sharing, especially in today's world (COVID-19). The fourth factor, **"emphasis on hiring professionals,"** emphasizes the knowledge, skills, and abilities of employees and the sharing of knowledge among them. Organizations emphasize continuous and regular retraining, continuing education, and the development of employees. The above findings can help reduce intergenerational conflict, mitigate ageism in organizations, and increase the willingness to share knowledge among employees. The systems approach was applied to identify possible factors influencing the aforementioned process, namely improving HR marketing, stabilizing the internal environment, continuity of knowledge, and attracting qualified employees, which is becoming increasingly difficult not only in agriculture and forestry. However, sustainable employability is crucial both for the workers who find employment and for the success of the companies and thus for the prosperity of the state.

Based on the author's long-term research, it can be summarized that the benefits of human resources marketing can be characterized as supporting the long-term competitiveness of the organization on the market, in connection with the high quality of human resources; an increased level of employee engagement, which has a positive effect on both work productivity and the profitability of the entire organization; higher employee retention (lower turnover, minimal loss of qualified employees, and thus talent); reduction of financial and time demands associated with the recruitment process; improvement of intra-company communication and overall relations in the organization; strengthening the employer brand, improving the good reputation of the organization on the labor market; the stronger and more stable position of the personnel department. Support of human resource marketing with the help of CSR, and modern trends in SHRM is a possibility for the organization and its employees to stand up in the ring with the competition.

Recommendations to Organizations on How to Set Sustainable Business and SHRM

Taking into account the theoretical background and the research results in the Czech organizations, it can be summarized that one of the pillars of a sustainable and responsible company and sustainable human resources management is the readiness of the organizations for demographic change, training, and development of employees, offering flexible working hours or focusing on equal opportunities and diversity. It is imperative to recognize that the success of companies will always depend on diverse and motivated employees who are loyal and enjoy working for their employer. Companies are beginning to learn how to manage the generations, but more importantly, how to address the individual needs of employees through the application of age management.

Organizations can benefit from age diversity in the workplace. Employees of different generations can offer unique perspectives and bring different benefits. It depends on the management of organizations what system they set, however, considering the results achieved, the following can be recommended to the management of organizations (Vrabcová et al., 2022):

- Since every generation has its approach to problem-solving, the presence of employees from several generations can be very useful when it comes to identifying opportunities for innovation and new ways to solve everyday problems.

- Understanding the requirements of different customers: every generation is unique, which is a great advantage for the organization. You can better understand different target groups through people of each generation. Determining the way feedback is given will bring clarity and ease managers of the workload. Generation Y employees do not want to be constantly monitored and Generation Z employees want immediate feedback on their work.
- Learning opportunities: different generations at work open up learning opportunities for all employees. Colleagues can pass on new approaches and more efficient ways of doing business to each other. For example, a more technologically advanced employee can suggest how a member of the older generation can quickly manage a tiring task.
- Mentoring: the multi-generational workforce is an ideal environment for mentoring. Many organizations run mentoring and internal training programs that provide opportunities for employees to coach each other. This not only helps employees learn new skills and gain information, but it also improves collaboration.
- To stimulate relationship development: the better your employees know each other, the more likely they are to communicate and work together effectively. Being able to communicate and build relationships outside of the day-to-day workplace within individual processes will provide team members with the opportunity to increase collaboration. If you understand the qualities of each generation, you can not only create a convenient workplace for everyone but also benefit from this advantage. Together, three generations will be able to guide the organization to outstanding results. In practice, the existence of differences between generations may not be important, but people are convinced that such differences exist.

Therefore, organizations should consider implementing the discussed HRM practices (talent management, diversity management, knowledge management, and knowledge continuity management), whether as a benefit to themselves (changing organizational culture and creating a better position in the market due to the diversity of interpersonal skills), but mainly as a benefit to their employees (self-satisfaction, maintaining socialization and mutual interaction).

The above-recommended intergenerational cooperation in the form of mentoring or coaching will help make better use of the potential of all employees. Older employees will guide new graduates, thus getting the opportunity to provide them with know-how as well as counseling that comes from their years of experience. In the meantime, graduates will have the opportunity to acquire tacit knowledge that they cannot read in books. Furthermore, there is a need to focus on job restructuring, with jobs being matched to the skills of individuals - either in terms of graduates progressing from simple to more complex work, or for the benefit of the older employee who would be relieved of physically demanding work. However, success depends on the quality of management and their education in effective human resource management.

Based on the research findings, sustainable business is a specific business approach taken by managers and owners of companies, where companies incorporate the aspects of the three pillars into their business operations. Efforts to protect the environment have led to the current form of sustainable development, which emphasizes the social and economic dimensions. Focus group results indicate that a good relationship between employees and the company creates a positive link between responsible human resource management practices and the company's perceived commitment to its employees. The changed approach is similar in many ways to the philosophy of total quality management, where the main goal is to be competitive and excel in business.

One can conclude that sustainable entrepreneurship and its principles influence (and will increasingly influence in the future) Czech organizations of all sizes and will cause a radical change compared to the changes in the 1980s and 1990s. Radical changes can be expected in quality systems and business management.

DISCUSSION

Not only organizations, but also entire countries compete in the globalized environment, which is characterized by high competition: their competitiveness no longer depends only on material resources, but primarily on the knowledge of employees (Vrabcová et al., 2021), which is used for innovations to develop the entire organization. Continuous development, enhancing individual knowledge, skills, qualifications, and experience will improve the innovation potential of individuals, teams, and organizations in all types of innovation, which is confirmed by authors (Bocken et al., 2014; Hollensbe et al., 2014; Stachová et al., 2017; Leopold, 2019).

Age management plays an important role in addressing the age distribution of employees in an organization and their management, namely as a result of the growing proportion of 50+ people in the population. Organizations must inevitably adapt to this trend and coping with demographic changes is one of the partial objectives of age management. Urbancová (2017); Urbancová, Vrabcová (2020); Garavaglia et al. Urbancová (2017), Urbancová & Vrabcová (2020), and Garavaglia et al. (2021) deal with resistance to the implementation of age management associated with the persistence of stereotypes and barriers related to the age of employees and the presence of hostile organizational cultures in their research. Management plays a very important role in sustainable human resource management (Chams, García-Blandón, 2019; Macke, Genari, 2019), especially in the context of legitimizing human resource practices and resource allocation (Järlström et al., 2018). Stakeholders in age management have different ambitions at different levels. At the organizational level, however, the development of human potential through continuous learning and increasing labor productivity must be emphasized. Management taking the age of employees into account can be viewed as an organization´s social responsibility.

Based on the research conducted, the following recommendations can be formulated in the context of the CSR phenomenon:

- to devote time to knowledge transfer upon retirement and the onboarding of new employees,
- to use the existing potential of older employees in such a way that business continuity is not disrupted, productivity is not reduced, or performance does not decline,
- to optimize the level and forms of training, to use modern methods of development - mentoring, including the so-called "reverse mentoring" and to use coaching effectively,
- to listen to experienced employees and managers with respect and to avoid negative stereotypes (ageism),
- to respect experience, loyalty, long-standing contacts, responsibility, discipline, and especially decency and humility of this category, and
- to understand their customers who are also ageing.

Based on the previous research results on the issue of age management, one can conclude that due to the pandemic, there have been unsystematic steps in setting human resource strategies because of frequent financial problems, increased employee sickness including short-term (the turnover of skilled employees) and long-term shortages of skilled labor in the labor market. The pressure to cut costs has caused an increase in the number of redundancies without systematic practices (without emphasis on identifying knowledge employees in the organization), which has led to destabilizing teams, and demotivating employees who remain in the organization. Management of companies is no longer paying attention to the necessity of sustainable human resource management; however, without this condition, sustainable business cannot be ensured, and it may even lead to threatening the existence of organizations.

Globalization and new communication technologies create a very favorable environment for the emergence of multicultural teams in the workplace. This implies the emergence of social changes and room for new possibilities. Within the European Union, diversity management is becoming an important and inevitable aspect of organizational strategy. Digitized organizations have simpler decision-making processes, are more inclined towards diversity, and are also more attractive to job candidates. A digitized workplace can quickly attract quality talent. The overall employee satisfaction that drives greater engagement has a direct impact on organizational performance and customer satisfaction. However, the concept of diversity management is sometimes criticized (Mousa et al., 2020) because of its focus on minorities and simple practices such as training, communication, coaching, or mentoring. These practices seek to mitigate cultural clashes and discrimination in the workplace resulting from differences in religion, gender, age, political ideologies, etc. Diversity management is sometimes pointed to as a driver of divisions, prejudices, stereotypes, and classifications within groups.

CONCLUSION

As the results of the qualitative survey have shown, people are the most valuable factor in organizations, and despite the fluctuations in the labor market, goods, and services markets that accompany the financial instability of organizations, employees need to be treated in a non-discriminatory, humane, and stimulating way, as well as more support for intergenerational cooperation and continuous sharing of knowledge and experience must be given.

With this in mind, it can be summarized that the primary impetus for applying age management at the organizational level was the need to respond to population demographics; however, this is now augmented by increasing the ability of organizations to deal flexibly with the social and professional interactions of each generation of employees and to ensure knowledge sharing between generations. This sub-strategy of human resource management is consistent with CSR and helps to shape effective organizational processes and interactions with the organization's stakeholders. The main barriers to research include the relative lack of awareness of the concept of age management among the public and management, and the unavailability or incompleteness of some publicly available data (CSO, Eurostat, etc.) in the field of CSR.

Concerning the presented current state of the issues addressed, one can conclude that sustainable human resource management has undergone a fundamental transformation (the transition from learning organizations to talent management, knowledge management, and knowledge continuity management, from homogeneous work teams to agile teams supporting diversity, targeted employer branding, the use of ICT in HR activities and emphasizing sustainability, etc.) and is currently influenced by the current trends in HR practice including the systematic care of employees which is one of the most effective tools for stabilizing employees and creating harmonious working relationships and thereby influencing the performance of the organization.

Further research will focus on developmental changes in this area with regard to current challenges and specifics of the Czech economy.

REFERENCES

Ahi, P., & Searcy, C. (2013). A comparative literature analysis of definitions for green and sustainable supply chain management. *Journal of Cleaner Production, 52*, 329–341. doi:10.1016/j.jclepro.2013.02.018

Bakker, S., Maat, K., & Van Wee, B. (2014). Stakeholders' interests, expectations, and strategies regarding the development and implementation of electric vehicles: The case of the Netherlands. *Transportation Research Part A, Policy and Practice, 66*, 52–64. doi:10.1016/j.tra.2014.04.018

Baumgartner, R. J., & Rauter, R. (2017). Strategic perspectives of corporate sustainability management to develop a sustainable organization. *Journal of Cleaner Production, 140*, 81–92. doi:10.1016/j.jclepro.2016.04.146

Bocken, N. M. P., Short, S. W., Rana, P., & Evans, S. (2014). A literature and practice review to develop sustainable business model archetypes. *Journal of Cleaner Production, 65*, 42–56. doi:10.1016/j.jclepro.2013.11.039

Bombiak, E., & Marciniuk-Kluska, A. (2018). Green human resource management as a tool for the sustainable development of enterprises: Polish young company experience. *Sustainability (Basel), 10*(6), 1739. doi:10.3390u10061739

Carroll, A. B., & Hoy, F. (1984). Integrating corporate social policy into strategic management. *The Journal of Business Strategy, 4*(3), 48–57. doi:10.1108/eb039031

Chams, N., & García-Blandón, J. (2019). On the importance of sustainable human resource management for the adoption of sustainable development goals. *Resources, Conservation and Recycling, 141*, 109–122. doi:10.1016/j.resconrec.2018.10.006

Dennissen, M., Benschop, Y., & van den Brink, M. (2020). Rethinking diversity management: An intersectional analysis of diversity networks. *Organization Studies, 41*(2), 219–240. doi:10.1177/0170840618800103

Ehnert, I. (2009). *Sustainable human resource management*. Physica-Verlag. doi:10.1007/978-3-7908-2188-8

Esteban-Sanchez, P., de la Cuesta-Gonzalez, M., & Paredes-Gazquez, J. D. (2017). Corporate social performance and its relation with corporate financial performance: International evidence in the banking industry. *Journal of Cleaner Production, 162*, 1102–1110. doi:10.1016/j.jclepro.2017.06.127

Garavaglia, E., Marcaletti, F., & Iñiguez-Berrozpe, T. (2021). Action research in age management: The quality of ageing at work model. *Work, Aging and Retirement, 7*(4), 339–351. doi:10.1093/workar/waaa025

Geissdoerfer, M., Vladimirova, D., & Evans, S. (2018). Sustainable business model innovation: A review. *Journal of Cleaner Production*, *198*, 401–416. doi:10.1016/j.jclepro.2018.06.240

Hartley, D. M., Reisinger, H. S., & Perencevich, E. N. (2020). When infection prevention enters the temple: Intergenerational social distancing and Covid-19. *Infection Control and Hospital Epidemiology*, *41*(7), 868–869. doi:10.1017/ice.2020.100 PMID:32234091

Hitka, M., Balazova, Z., Gražulis, V., & Lejskova, P. (2018). Differences in employee motivation in selected countries of CEE (Slovakia, Lithuania and the Czech Republic). *Inžinerinė ekonomika*.

Hollensbe, E., Wookey, Ch., Hickey, L., George, G., & Nichols, C. V. (2014). Organizations with Purpose. *Academy of Management Journal*, *57*(5), 1227–1234. doi:10.5465/amj.2014.4005

Hung, S. W., Li, C. M., & Lee, J. M. (2019). Firm growth, business risk, and corporate social responsibility in Taiwan's food industry. *Agricultural Economics*, *65*(8), 366–374.

Järlström, M., Saru, E., & Vanhala, S. (2018). Sustainable human resource management with salience of stakeholders: A top management perspective. *Journal of Business Ethics*, *152*(3), 703–724. doi:10.100710551-016-3310-8

Joyce, A., & Paquin, R. L. (2016). The triple layered business model canvas: A tool to design more sustainable business models. *Journal of Cleaner Production*, *135*, 1474–1486. doi:10.1016/j.jclepro.2016.06.067

Kramar, R. (2014). Beyond strategic human resource management: Is sustainable human resource management the next approach? *International Journal of Human Resource Management*, *25*(8), 1069–1089. doi:10.1080/09585192.2013.816863

Leopold, H. (2019). Innovation through culture and communication. *E&I Elektrotechnik und Informationstechnik*, *136*(3), 225–225. doi:10.100700502-019-0730-z

Macke, J., & Genari, D. (2019). Systematic literature review on sustainable human resource management. *Journal of Cleaner Production*, *208*, 806–815. doi:10.1016/j.jclepro.2018.10.091

Mensah, J., & Casadevall, S. R. (2019). Sustainable development: Meaning, history, principles, pillars, and implications for human action: Literature review. *Cogent Social Sciences*, *5*(1), 1653531. doi:10.1080/23311886.2019.1653531

Mikušová, M. (2017). To be or not to be a business responsible for sustainable development? Survey from small Czech businesses. *Economic Research –. Ekonomska Istrazivanja*, *30*(1), 1318–1338. doi:10.1080/1331677X.2017.1355257

Mousa, M., Massoud, H. K., & Ayoubi, R. M. (2020). Gender, diversity management perceptions, workplace happiness and organisational citizenship behaviour. *Employee Relations*, *42*(6), 1249–1269. doi:10.1108/ER-10-2019-0385

Prates, C., Pedrozo, E., & Silva, T. (2015). Corporate social responsibility: A case study in subsidiaries from Brazil and China. *Journal of Technology Management & Innovation*, *10*(3), 131–142. doi:10.4067/S0718-27242015000300014

Rajnoha, R., Lesnikova, P., & Krauš, A. (2016). From financial measures to strategic performance measurement system and corporate sustainability: Empirical evidence from Slovakia. *Economics & Sociology (Ternopil)*, *9*(4), 134–152. doi:10.14254/2071-789X.2016/9-4/8

Ren, S., Tang, G., & Jackson, S. E. (2018). Green human resource management research in emergence: A review and future directions. *Asia Pacific Journal of Management*, *35*, 769–803. doi:10.100710490-017-9532-1

Šebestová, J., & Sroka, W. (2020). Sustainable development goals and SMEs decisions: Czech Republic vs. Poland. [JEECAR]. *Journal of Eastern European and Central Asian Research*, *7*(1), 39–50.

Skibiński, A., Sipa, M., & Gorzeń-Mitka, I. (2016). An intergenerational cooperation in the organization-view from the age perspective. *Procedia: Social and Behavioral Sciences*, *235*, 412–419. doi:10.1016/j.sbspro.2016.11.051

Stachová, K., Stacho, Z., & Vicen, V. (2017). Efficient involvement of human resources in innovations through effective communication. *Business: Theory and Practice*, *18*(0), 33–42. doi:10.3846/btp.2017.004

Tooranloo, H. S., Azadi, M. H., & Sayyahpoor, A. (2017). Analyzing factors affecting implementation success of sustainable human resource management (SHRM) using a hybrid approach of FAHP and Type-2 fuzzy DEMATEL. *Journal of Cleaner Production*, *162*, 1252–1265. doi:10.1016/j.jclepro.2017.06.109

Tröester, R., & Hiete, M. (2018). Success of voluntary sustainability certification schemes–a comprehensive review. *Journal of Cleaner Production*, *196*, 1034–1043. doi:10.1016/j.jclepro.2018.05.240

Urbancová, H. (2017). *Age management in organisations*. Wolters Kluwer.

Urbancová, H. (2019). Organisation of Working Time for Senior Workers in Agricultural Companies with a Focus on Age Management. *Studies in Agricultural Economics (Budapest)*, *121*, 161–165.

Urbancová, H., & Vrabcová, P. (2020). Age management as a human resources management strategy with a focus on the primary sector of the Czech Republic. *Agricultural Economics*, *66*, 251–259.

Vrabcová, P. (2021). Udržitelné podnikání: dobrovolné nástroje (nejen) zemědělských a lesnických podniků. Praha: Grada Publishing, 192 s.

Vrabcová, P., & Urbancová, H. (2022). Holistic Human Resource Management as a Tool for the Intergenerational Cooperation and Sustainable Business. *Agricultural Economics*, *68*(4), 117–126.

Vrabcová, P., Urbancová, H., & Hudáková, M. (2022). Strategic Trends of Organizations in the Context of New Perspectives of Sustainable Competitiveness. *Journal of Competitiveness*, *14*(2), 174–193. doi:10.7441/joc.2022.02.10

Vrabcová, P., Urbancová, H., & Petříček, M. (2021). Knowledge and its transfer–key prerequisite for long-term competitive advantage and sustainable business. *Knowledge Management Research and Practice*, 1–11.

Chapter 6
Re-Innovative Organizational Design:
Sustainable Branding and Effective Communication – Applied Models in a World With New Borders/Without Borders

Dimitrina Petrova Stefanova
South-West University "Neofit Rilski", Blagoevgrad, Bulgaria

Valentin Penchev Vasilev
Higher School of Security and Economics, Plovdiv, Bulgaria

Ivan Petre Efremovski
International Slavic University, Sveti Nikole, North Macedonia

ABSTRACT

Dynamics and crises in the present are inextricably associated with company growth and change management in the context of today. In this way, the question of innovation in management processes has evolved, and we now focus on re-innovative organizational practices that expand on and improve tried-and-true methods. In such a situation, the function of sustainable branding is that effective communications are essential tools for adapting to the climate and chaotic characteristics. Additionally, the long-lasting and unexpected pandemic crisis, a technologically advanced and globally integrated society and economy, and the hybridity of change all have a significant impact on marketing procedures. Although the subject is broad, the research's primary focus is on creating a dialogic, motivated, and productive management style, with new internal communication channels playing a key role as a component of branding.

INTRODUCTION

Scientific study is structured using a series of both theoretical and empirical analysis, logical thinking, and model building. By reconsidering hierarchical structures in „networked" models based on collabo-

DOI: 10.4018/978-1-6684-8681-8.ch006

ration between two functional areas of the organization, the study advances its defense of the thesis.

In order to establish and sustain productive relationships and the viability of the employer brand, the authors' research aim was to give a model of the connection between "Human resource management" (HRM) and "Public relations" (PR). The central idea of the chapter is that, in the digital world, both inner and external perfection are closely linked and are driven by one another. The „human-centric" paradigm is oriented toward Society 5.0, a society that integrates the digital, physical, and social spheres. In this sense, Society 5.0 is viewed as a community that prioritizes people. Society 5.0 is described as „a human-centric society that combines economic development with solving social problems through a system that firmly combines cyberspace and physical space" by the Japanese cabinet, from which the idea of Society 5.0 originated. In order to promote a society where people lead various lives and seek happiness in their own special ways, digital technologies and data must be used. (Keidanren, Japan Business Federation, 2016).

The need for innovative two-way communications and relationships with citizens and businesses in the context of successful branding presented another of this model's old „enemies" to it. The new ways of collecting and sharing information are changing how people live, think, and operate in organizations. At all levels in society, demands and claims are increasing. Any organization's management must be ready for every possibility; in other words, we take a deep breath and prepare for the unexpected! Following Nasim Taleb's guide, a prepared mind did much better with the black swans of daily living. This calls for a reevaluation of a number of management models that were previously unquestioned, as well as the creation of fresh organizational beginning points, marketing strategies, and a clearer picture of management process efficiency.

Current dynamics and crises are closely linked to organizational growth and change management in a contemporary setting. Evolutionarily speaking, the problem of innovation in management processes has changed, and we are now focusing on re-innovative organizational practices that build on and strengthen tried-and-true methods. Effective communications are crucial tools for adapting to the environment's pressure situations in such a context, and sustainable branding plays an important part in this.

Additionally, the long-lasting and uncertain pandemic crisis, a technologically advanced and globally integrated society and economy, and the hybridity of change all have a significant impact on marketing procedures. Although the subject is broad, the research's primary focus is on creating a dialogic, motivated, and productive management style, with new internal communication channels playing a key role as a component of branding. The need for creative two-way communications and relationships with citizens and businesses in the context of successful branding presented this model of re-innovation with yet another old „enemy" of its own. The new ways of collecting and sharing information are changing how people live, think, and operate in organizations. At all levels in society, demands and claims are increasing. Any organization's management must be ready for every eventuality; in other words, we take a deep breath and plan for the unexpected! According to Nasim Taleb, a prepared mind can handle the black swans of daily living much better. This calls for a reevaluation of a number of management models that were previously unquestioned, as well as the creation of fresh organizational beginning points, marketing strategies, and a greater understanding of management process efficiency.

At the heart of the development is the author's idea that there is a significant connection between the trends to complicate marketing processes, especially strong in the current world, which we can define with the term "world with borders / without borders", because there are a number of characteristics associated with this trend, such as financial markets and flows, Internet of Things, smart technologies, chatbot and others. The authors pose the research question – what are the components of balance in these new processes and whether they can be combined into a management model. An attempt is made to look scientifically for these relationships and to present an author's model aimed at optimizing marketing processes in the context of sustainable development of organizations.

Increasing responsibility by gaining individual buy-in, a feeling of purpose, prompt and convincing action for a balanced approach to duties and people are the key components of modern human resource management. These components also include a purposeful linking of objectives and performance measures. On the other hand, the crisis context and organizational changes bring about high levels of stress and anxiety, decreased staff motivation, and staff turnover. They also cause uncertainty about the future, a loss of confidence, and new demands on organizations. That has been done on embedding sustainability into organizational design and structure including guidance on basic steps that should be taken including incorporating sustainability into mission and vision statements, creating an executive position with responsibility for sustainability, providing sustainability training to employees, collecting and reporting data on sustainability performance and incorporating sustainability into financial and non-financial rewards programs (Gutterman, 2020).

It can be summarized that the processes of sustainable development are related to effective human resource management and communication processes, and in this area there are prerequisites for improving the classic management models.

Previously, organizations competed mainly for a single market, but today they must demonstrate and defend their places in front of numerous stakeholders and organizations by utilizing cutting-edge market strategies. Organizations that are adaptable and take advantage of the digital era become more competitive and establish themselves not only in domestic but also foreign markets. Today's organizations are constantly faced with a variety of changes, and as a result, management plays a crucial role in both the organization's survival and success. Furthermore, assets like a company's identity, reputation, and image are receiving more notice as a significant component in the pursuit of competitive advantages. They give us an opportunity to demonstrate our competitiveness in the context of global competition, in addition to providing a way toward a potential solution. The management of a company in a world that is constantly changing requires a reputation strategy. „The chances of any corporation today, regardless of its size, are in the cleverly designed corporate identity and the stable relationship created through it with the target audiences and all relevant individuals, in focusing the uniqueness not only of the products and services but, more importantly, of the organization in its entirety. One of the company's competitive factors, a strong reputation offers strategic advantages and sustainability in the company's investment strategy.

The ideas presented in the development would be useful in the work of specialists in marketing, public relations, human resource management and managers in the field of sustainable development, and the use of the presented ideas in their practice would significantly enrich their management capacity and efficiency.

An Empirical View of Social Context

The Edelman Trust Barometer and the Edelman Trust Barometer Special Reports (2023) from Edelman Data & Intelligence offer an incredibly wide empirical base for analysis and inference to the creation of theoretical-practical models for organizational design. They help us describe the situation in terms of the gap between the desired (ideal) state and the present state more simply. On the basis of extensive research, we identify various aspects of confidence in various types of organizations. Due to their similarity, organizations are subject to a number of sharing common demands from stakeholders, customers, workers, and society. The Covid-19 pandemic and current crises are altering values for workers, making higher pay ineffective as a motivator to work longer and tougher hours. The employee now chooses and stays with the business based on his values, just as the consumer chooses and sticks with the employer brand. The modern era is characterized by social care, flexible work schedules and remote work, increased power delegation, and company dedication to acting in the best interests of both employees and society. A new agreement between employee and employer requires business to adopt a more ambitious social role while essentially reconsidering employee motivations. An agreement that calls for more active two-way communication to accomplish mutual interests, which prompts a reevaluation of the top priorities in leadership communication. Implications for academics are the starting point for understanding the foundations of approaches of the design of sustainable organizations, providing guidance for the future. This study provides practitioners with an overview of the importance of organizational design to realize the strategy that they have formulated with their sustainable business model, as well as a set of approaches that could already apply in their firms. (Lemus-Aguilar I, Morales-Alonso G, Ramirez-Portilla A, Hidalgo A.; 2019).

Organizations must make additional promises for both their customers and employees as a result of the decline in public confidence in public institutions, business, government, non-governmental organizations, and the media. The analysis concludes that this paradox can be explained by people's worries about the future and their place in it, which serve as a wake-up call for our institutions to implement a new strategy for successfully fostering trust: balancing competence with moral behavior. A growing feeling of systemic injustice creates mistrust. Organizations are seen as increasingly prioritizing the goals of a select few. Fairness in economic systems causes people to worry about the future, including the possibility of employment losses, an impending recession, a shortage of skills, automation, and general partnerships. Although there are different kinds of trust, they all depend on how confident and ready one is to act on the words, deeds, and decisions of another person. The majority of respondents say they expect CEOs to take the lead in promoting inclusion, social care, sustainable employment, and public health problems rather than just speak about social reform. With that confidence comes high expectations. The key to driving social transformation is empathy. Leaders who have a thorough understanding of the critical role of empathy in problems like encouraging inclusive cultures, addressing vaccine hesitancy, or encouraging innovation to address needs and requirements are those who can be trusted. However, in the Edelman Trust Barometer special report, respondents were questioned on how much their political views, social opinions, and personal values influence their purchasing behavior. Customers who are motivated by belief and faith in this respect. Even if a company's product was the one they preferred best, customers frequently would not switch brands or purchase it if they disagreed with the organization's position on significant social issues. The decision to purchase or not to buy is a significant way in which these opinions are expressed, as is an organization's attention to or position on a contentious public issue. Along with social responsibility, dialog, and commitment to employees, public leadership is now the fundamental skill in business. However, the employer continues to be the organization that people value the most. My workplace is the only respected organization, even among those who believe that our nation is divided. It is clear that having high expectations puts the company at greater risk. People want business to be more involved in social issues, but when it takes on contentious topics, it runs the risk of becoming politicized. Businesses should take every opportunity to reassure the public about the existence of economic dangers as well as the strategies for minimizing them. Retraining, employment possibilities, levels of pay, inclusive work environments, minimizing environmental effect, and ethical behavior all help to calm some of the dividing forces at work in societies all over the world.

The modern digital era is powerful enough to channel communication towards individuals or consumers through various platforms - mass media, social media, websites, blogs or applications. (Kusá, Alena & Urmínová, Marianna; 2021)

Here, it's important to note that in parallel with technology and change processes, talent attraction, growth, encouragement, training, and integration are taking on new dimensions. Following the COVID pandemic's breath of fresh air, a new cycle of crisis phenomena, including the Russian invasion, the ongoing widespread dissemination of fake news, and cognitive anxiety, which has an indirect and direct impact on managers and workers, started to appear. I.e., elements that cause daily uncertainty and force one to reevaluate their goals. The principles of perception, retention, and processing of information—whether it is connected to knowledge, training, persuasion, or pleasure—are altered for all the reasons mentioned above, which results in an improvement in organizational communications.

Communication processes are undoubtedly a key basis for effective human capital management in a digital environment. The communication barriers to effective communication are numerous, and in order to achieve an effective communication process, it is necessary to know these barriers well and to develop effective communication strategies. Therefore, it is important to monitor whether the messages are received and interpreted correctly and to take timely measures in the direction of overcoming them and managing communication crises in a timely manner. Striking the right balance between centrality and distinctiveness is critical, because a company's choices influence not just how the brand will be perceived, but how much of it will be sold and at what price—and, ultimately, how profitable it will be. (Niraj Dawar and Charan K. Bagga; 2015)

We would emphasize the need to update this well-established model of overcoming resistance to change. We want to believe that recent years have shown that the role of information and smart technologies is becoming increasingly important in management. Something more. They establish themselves leaders in every change. Therefore, in our opinion, a key component in overcoming resistance to change is technological innovations, of course with proper testing and communication. (Vasilev, V.; 2020, p.228).

The impact of globalization has changed the nature of work and employment through digitalization. Globalization represents a breakthrough with the introduction of new knowledge, cutting cross countries boundaries and increasing digitalized advancement. Technological advancement has improved the nature of work and the conditions of how this work are being carried out.

Along with the benefits of digitalization, there poses some challenges such as information workload, job loss and several other issues. Thus, it is pertinent that managers develop skills and attitudes to face these changes, and also supports the employees during this change period.

According to the summary of the strict sense, the organization's success is driven by confidence, leadership, empathy, commitment, and responsibility towards its members as well as the society. In such an environment, interpersonal connections become more important, and communication and action are themes that are eventually intended to produce better results for both sides. An increased focus is seen on the manner in which leaders interact with staff members, as well as how they affect organizational authenticity (i.e., the degree of sincerity, openness, consistency, and dedication that staff members perceive about their organization) and organizational identification. The concepts of empathy, emotional intelligence, interpersonal communication, confidence, and responsible leadership are being reinvented. Since it is obvious that employees are not only the primary and most important component of the organization, but also the change direction in maintaining organizational strategies during a time of instability and uncertainty, crisis factors have forced managers to prioritize internal communication in which, in recent years, it had previously been focused primarily on customer-related matters. In the new environment, reducing the effects of uncertainty and boosting trust are necessary. To do this, leaders must get involved, employees and all stakeholders must practice active listening, and a response that foresees a genuine two-way communication process structured in a strategic plan is required.

It can be categorically summarized that effective communication processes have an essential impact on sustainable branding, and their presentation in a conceptual model greatly facilitates their adoption and application in practice.

An Example of How Human Resource Management (HRM) And Public Relations (PR) Should Work Together as Part of a Cooperative Communication Plan

The efficacy of theories regarding the function of public communication in organizational and social transformation is being established. They represent a successful organizational design that depends on both internal and external factors in the present. The proposed method has intuitive potential and is applicable to the current social changes; it is a tool for trust-building, effective transformation, quick growth, and sustainability. Organizational sustainable development is a process, based on knowledge from theory and practice, and through which the organization develops its internal capacity and resources to be able to more successfully realize its mission, intentions and goals. It is a series of consistent and systematically planned activities, accepted and initiated by the management and aimed at all levels of the organization, including in the direction of effective development of human capital. Here, a general goal is the full development of the people working in the organization, improving its capabilities for solving problems, planning changes and meeting the needs of the interested parties, as well as the search for innovative solutions in motivating human resources. This, in turn, requires a simultaneous understanding of individual and organizational needs, as well as highly effective communication processes, both internal and external.

The presented author's model „waterfall" model is interacting with the components of the management system and the data related to them. It is shown below graphically and progressively from top to bottom. All of these are combined into one information pool that forms the internal relationships within the organization and its image as part of its vision, understanding, and functioning. It is defined by methodology, process, structure, principles, roles, techniques, and management, just like each „step" is. As a result, the system clearly demonstrates the organizational relationships and functional structure that come together to create a system for communications, the creation and implementation of management decisions, and the understanding and support of information. The development of helpful in developing is viewed as an up or down activity because each element that must be finished builds upon and expands upon the findings of the one that came before it. This is because the methodology for going from one level to another and then to the highest level must correspond to the objectives.

1. Strategic management of information (strategic communication management)
2. The „Change-story" paradigm, emotional intelligence, and leadership motivation
3. The „storytelling" model and organizational ethos
4. Sustainable growth and sustainable branding

Following the overarching principle of strategic management of information (strategic communication management) is the waterfall model. On the one hand, it should be viewed as a strategy for creating a PR or communication plan that is unified, follows the concepts of collaboration and integration. When

Figure 1. "Waterfall" model for re-innovation management
/Stefanova; Vasilev; Efremovski; 2023/

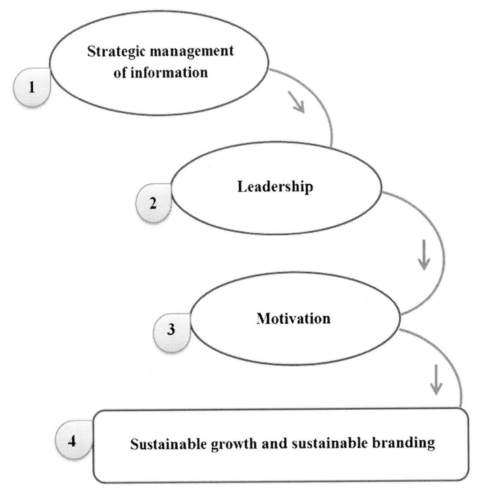

applying these principles, it is also crucial to take into consideration the specifics of the organizational structure of the business or institution. Each company is divided into levels, each of which includes departments, offices, and services that vary according to a range of factors, including how specific tasks are carried out. The interaction between divisions and services at a particular organizational level is defined by coordination. A business organization's departments, services, and other units that are located at various levels of the organizational structure interact with one another as part of integration. The creation of a strategic plan, budget, and procedures (campaigns or actions), which can be thought of as medium and short-term plans, is also indicated by the implementation of the strategy. Here, PR strategy is defined as a broad, overarching plan that expresses the primary course of action in both the organization's overall course of action and in a particular specialized area (PR). Complex actions are referred to as „strategy" in PR or PR strategy. These actions begin with an idea, a concept, a stage, and decisions about how to combine and use resources to achieve a specific goal or strategies for the fundamental PR directions (internal communication strategy, Internet strategy, media strategy, strategy for working with specific audience), as well as the viewpoint of particular actions.

A sequence of actions that are coordinated with the interaction's objective or goals is included in the strategic plan in PR. (Stefanova, D.; 2016; p.12).

On the other hand, the three major sections that compose the conceptual framework for internal communications describe the specifics of managing internal communications.

ü Conceptual framework OC: Organizational Communication is measured by Strategy, Structure, System, style
ü EC: Effectiveness of communication is measured by Communication-skill, Organization Culture. Communication Methods, Organization Structure.
ü EP: Employees Productivity is measured by shared values, skills, and staff

Effective organizational communication can lead organization in a successful way, only if exists. Without proper information and planning any deliberated decision cannot occur. There is a vast literature on organizational communication and productivity of employees. However this research looks over the influence of effectiveness of internal communication on employees' productivity. The core concentration in this study is level of communication in organization and how employees perceive communication, and what are the effects of internal communication on their work capability. Therefore after recognizing the effectiveness of communication the employee's productivity flourishes in organizational communication. Flow of effective communication in organizations develops the strong bonding between staff and management, then employees get trusted, that make them more productive.

It is a conceptual basis that demonstrates the structural connections between worker output, OC, and efficient internal communication. Understanding the different organizational communication characteristics and how they affect efficient internal communication and the productivity of the workforce is crucial.

The plan can fully perform the role of strategic internal PR in helping to establish and carry out corporate and business strategies once the focus is on a shared vision and mission. This will shape both strategic and downstream levels of operational and management decisions to work together from the very beginning in communication programs, which as a result build and maintain the employer brand.

Figure 2. Internal communication management
Adapted by: Aysha, Berhannudin, Kadir, Sanif, 2016

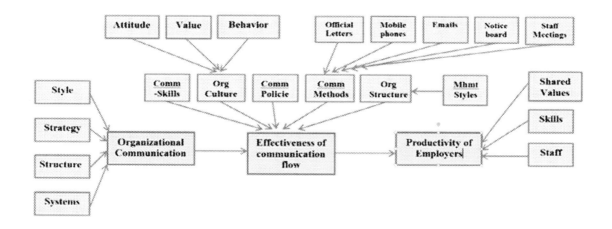

The waterfall model's suggested components are linked to a process of input analysis, goal planning, coordinated communication, outcomes, and efficiency rather than being chosen at random. Parallel organizational requirements and communication actions are the process's objects. On the other hand, the ongoing digital revolution, which has been reducing frictional, transactional costs for years, has accelerated recently with tremendous increases in electronic data, the ubiquity of mobile interfaces, and the growing power of artificial intelligence. Together, these forces are reshaping customer expectations and creating the potential for virtually every sector with a distribution component to have its borders redrawn or redefined, at a more rapid pace than we have previously experienced. (Venkat Atluri, Miklós Dietz, and Nicolaus Henke; 2017)

In keeping with Berger's statement (Berger, 2008), we can sum up that strategic internal communications play a connecting role in giving workers critical information about their regular tasks, the company, their surroundings, and themselves. Activities involving communication are also intended to support motivation, trust-building, identity-building, and a stronger feeling of responsibility. Building an environment that encourages the expression of ideas, opinions, and feelings, the sharing of dreams and aspirations, and the celebration of accomplishments requires the application of the understanding, support, and feedback approach. The basis for understanding an organization, what it actually is, what it signifies, and being able to work effectively for it is communication.

This process of collecting information must be planned and arranged in a way that makes the most effective use of communication tools, strategies, and messages. These tools should help leaders manage change and transformation processes while also having an impact on society as a whole. The overflowing internal and external communication processes get a basic boost from digitization, which has a noticeable effect on relationships and the reputation of the company. According to the intuitive viewpoint, effective external relationships with customers, partners, the local community, and other groups depend on successful internal relationships and their position, which have developed into a stronger capability.

Today, there is a culture of sharing and continuous development that is growing, and any employer branding initiative cannot be successful in a company that hides itself or refuses to share its best management practices with the public. Nowadays, many companies engage in „false" modesty by discouraging or openly forbidding managers from sharing information about best practices. Previous to the 1990s, when the value of PR was fairly valued and the models for calculating the monetary value of such publicity were more theoretical, such an attitude might have been acceptable. But in an era where technology can monitor increases in market value and sales that correspond with such publicity, public relations has taken on a life of its own at top companies like GE, Cisco, Southwest Airlines, and Wal-Mart. Senior management must realize the importance of employer branding and promote the sharing of best practices if a company doesn't want to fall behind and lose ground year after year. A top management team that promotes, evaluates, and rewards the development and spread of best practices is therefore the essential component of a strong employment brand. The creation of procedures to allow quick sharing of best practices between business units strengthens this element. (Sullivan; 2004).

This means that both the image of the company and the opinions in public groups can be directly impacted by the information that workers share and express in external social media. Some groups have noticed that social networks complement and strengthen one another by influencing how society as a whole develops.

However, there's still no guarantee that the conversation will be appropriate, prepared, and meaningful. The main task is for people to adjust to the new social and technological realities without losing their humanity, value systems, or social interaction.

The strategic communication model was created in tandem with the HRM model and is based on the idea that employees aren't just recipients of performance feedback; they're also proactive communicators who try to make sense of their surroundings and have a say in how the employer brand is built and maintained.

Depending on the company, strategic communication management can be developed in planned variations.

Communication is effective when it understands, responds, educates, and influences employees as well as when it understands the organization's goals and can be shown to have an impact. Communication is not effective because it is attractive, uses contemporary methods of communication, or because the materials are well written and illustrated. It must be designed in accordance with the requirements of the organizational design, have genuine interaction to better the processes, and be based on a strong foundation of the strategic vision of human resource management and coordination in their tactical activities.

Knowledge exchange and conversation are crucial components of the workplace for the sector. The suggested model is based on the assumption that „human" maturity follows digital maturity.

As a consequence, a management tool for the organization with an information structure should be created: an internal communication system. Due to its lean structure, it will be possible to integrate and optimize the work process as well as achieve something crucial in times of crisis: rapid and high-quality information flow.

In reality, the cross-functional cooperation between public relations (PR) and human resources (HR) has a beneficial impact on the accomplishment of goals. The fundamental tools (PR) for optimum information sharing in a particular direction, of a certain caliber, and for a particular purpose with open feedback support HR goals.

Through the interaction of objects and subjects in the administration of the organization, this connection supports overcoming communication and organizational barriers in the digital age and emergency environment.

As psychological phenomena that are connected and challenging to isolate and differentiate, barriers are increasingly being understood to be the core and foundation of an effective communication process. This establishes the requirement for their comprehension, significance, and function, as well as for accurate interpretation in a specific organizational context. Here, a parenthesis must be opened to reflect the following: „The administration of human resources is crucial to the growth and transformation of organizations. It provides a way for management and employees to converse in order to improve organizational evaluation and staff acceptance of management changes,, (Gigauri, I., 2020, p. 26). The amount of data that needs to be shared within and outside of the company, the dedication of leaders, and how they act and think as part of the communication process, have all increased in importance and complexity. If there is no effort made to learn about and get past obstacles in human relations in a professional setting, the existence of an effective communication system within the company does not ensure effective communication between human resources. (Vasiliev & Stefanova, 2021; p.30)

Taking a close look at these barriers may enable management to spot and remove them in order to improve dialogue with subordinates. Many groups of communication barriers linked to the personal relations of the participants in the effective communication, the ways of perception and interpretation, the levels of listening, and status characteristics have been taken into account in recent years in scientific advances. There are many communication barriers that are unique to each company. It's challenging to have effective conversation. Barriers can be supplemented with the power of the direct impact of social context, trust, and online communications as well as and in particular with their specific reflex by applying the international perspective in summarizing knowledge and research from the field of human resource management and public relations, through the view of today's reality and organizational challenges. This is not meant to minimize or deny the many benefits of online communication, particularly in a context where technology is the primary tool for remote work, but rather to take a „inside" look at the obstacles it raises or to examine modernity from a different perspective. The efficacy of „real communication" that is automatically transferred to online communication is lost. In the internet age, we tend to overvalue things that undergo change, like technology, and undervalue things that also play a significant part but are constant, like water or interpersonal relationships. The new generations are more open to technology and experiment more, but they do so frequently in inappropriate ways. As Nasim Taleb describes them, technologies are primarily „fragile and perishable" (Taleb, N., 2019, p. 417-419).

According to research, overcoming obstacles is one of the requirements for implementing an organizing and communication process that is focused on people in-person and on developing or enhancing their soft skills.

"Waterfall" Model for Re-Innovation Management Interaction With Sustainable Workplace Brand Components

Arguments are given in support of the thesis that the organization's reflection of work and communication with human resources appears to be an intelligent answer in influencing the sustainability of an employer brand during the discussion.

A business that lacks a brand management plan is totally at the control of customers and other stakeholders. Audiences form opinions and adopt certain attitudes toward organizations, their goods and services, whether the business likes it or not. „Branding, in its ideal state, satisfies audiences' needs, wants, and expectations, leaving [the business] with a positive brand image" (Yastrow, 2003, p. 76).

There are numerous brand definitions, branding components, and forms to choose from in the academic literature. Additionally, in the Journal of Brand Management from 1996, the subject of the company brand was covered (Ambler & Barrow, 1996).

The application of brand management methods to human resource management is the author's stated thesis in that article. The foundation for this idea is a study's findings, which provide the most clear explanation of the relationship between „the best people," „the best stores," and the „best image" (best word of mouth). „Top applicants" who will work for the company. This defines the employer brand's image as a component of marketing, one of its most crucial qualities.

The following definitions serve as an overview of how the perspectives and aspects of the employer brand have evolved:

1. Employer branding, in its traditional sense, aims to cultivate an organization's reputation as a „employer of choice" in the eyes of current and prospective employees as well as other partners, such as customers and potential employees. In addition to providing them with concrete advantages, the objective is to create an emotional bond with them. The organization's values, people strategy, HR policies, and two-way communication should all be reflected in and tied together by a powerful employer brand to create a distinctive identity for the business. The process of positioning a business or organization as a desirable workplace to a target audience that the business needs to draw in and keep is known as employer branding. The business strategy of the company is made

possible by top talent. A workplace brand is defined by Ambler and Barrow (Ambler & Barrow, 1996) in terms of the advantages it offers staff members.

2. „A purposeful, long-term strategy for managing the awareness and perceptions of employees, potential employees, and related stakeholders about a specific business," according to the definition of employer branding. It also states that corporate strategy can be developed to coordinate efforts in hiring, keeping employees, and managing performance, and that developing an employer brand is a targeted long-term strategy for controlling perceptions among current employees, prospective employees, and pertinent stakeholders. mindset of a specific company. (Sullivan; 2004)

3. A company's employer brand, according to Rosethorn (Rosethorn, 2009), is „the two-way transaction between an organization and its people - the reason they choose to join and the reasons they choose - and are allowed - to remain.

4. A set of qualities that distinguish and appeal to those who will identify with a company and give it their best effort constitute an employer brand. (CIPD, 2006);

5. A sophisticated idea founded on a number of difficult elements, such as perception, the ability to distinguish between one's image and one's identity, and other similar concepts (Randstad, 2013).

The employer brand implies a long-term commitment between the „seller and the buyer," which goes beyond financial interests and is based on: commitment (Geyskens et al., 1999, p. 223-238), trust (Sividas and Dwyer, 2000, p. 31-49), cooperation (Morgan and Hunt, 1994, p. 20-38), keeping commitments (Gronroos, 1994, p. 4-20), the ability to resolve conflicts A growing number of companies are positioning themselves as „clean, green, and socially responsible" as of late (Clegg, 2007, p.23). These brands, which represent the current society's pursuit of social, economic, and environmental justice and are defined as „the brands of the future," were created as a result of the altered paradigm of traditional marketing and beyond it (Nieto, 2009).

Or, to put it another way, the organization's unique offer, which stands for a particular promise of values to both current and prospective workers, is what genuinely distinguishes the company's reputation as an employer. In her presentation, she gave one of the simple yet perfectly accurate explanations of the term „employer brand," which is defined as the perception of the company as an employer, primarily in the eyes of its current employees and prospective employees, but also in the eyes of other interested parties and society. Basically, a notion of a route to a standard company. And if branding is concerned with a name, term, sign, symbol, design, or a combination of these in order to identify a seller's or group of sellers' goods and services and set them apart from those of competing firms in branding to separate physical products, it has also evolved over time to apply differentiation of people, places, and organizations in the perception of the employer it presents on the job market. The organization's reputation as an employer will be established and highlighted through employer branding. This complex includes the organization's value system, policies, and behavior with regard to the goals of bringing in, inspiring, and keeping the company's current and prospective employees, as well as leadership, trust, empathy, CSR, attitude, and relationship. Building an employer brand takes a time-intensive effort. When a brand is thriving, one cannot rest entirely on one's laurels. In order to adapt to a target audience's changing needs, it must continuously get better and change. A key point is the perception of human resource development with a focus on the importance of so-called „soft skills" in today's leaders. In recent years, some leading research centers have focused on them and laid the foundations for a broad debate in academia and practicing managers in this direction (Chankova, Vasilev, 2020; p. 210).

Building a powerful employer brand is a process that has an impact on both talent retention and establishing the brand as a trustworthy, dependable, and sought-after partner in the marketplace. Here, a two-way process contributes to creating a strong employer brand, which helps the company become recognized and communicate its values, purpose, and vision. Additionally, the labor market is included, with a focus on the dedication and satisfaction of the present workforce.

In summary, if there is no effective communication that is clear and well-targeted, the objectives cannot be reached. We are all aware that communication is successful if the objectives we have established are met. There is a best company out there for a particular candidate, profile, and set of abilities. Here, having clear messages and potential segments to interact with is crucial. Investing in communication channels that are not used by our defined target audiences is not financially viable. Every interaction we have with prospective workers has the power to tip the scales in our favor or turn the tables. Because of this, it is crucial that the company's strategy is consistent in all of its communications. Consider a business that has been the subject of conflicting online reviews. Or the vision and message are drastically different when you read and observe manager interviews, but when you speak with present employees, you get a different impression. It is crucial to clearly define the route your applicant will take when creating a communication plan and to ensure that his experiences at each point where he interacts with your brand will be at the necessary level. This causes a reevaluation of conventional models and a push for a deliberate, long-term approach to managing communications, employee and prospective employee views, and other related stakeholders who have or will have an interest in the organization. Not to mention, developing an employer identity is a continuous process. The fact that a certain tactic is written down but fails to produce the desired results in reality does not preclude its adaptation and modification. We operate in a dynamic environment where the labor market, supply, and demand are all changing, the impact of the crisis is felt, and audience expectations are high. Every component of the plan for developing the employer brand needs to have room for growth and the potential for adaptation in our approaches. It still forms a part of a dynamic ecosystem where the importance of people and their perceptions of what makes an employer good or evil prevails.

CONCLUSION

A crucial component of the sustainable employer brand is public involvement, which necessitates analyzing and assessing the term „sustainable" in light of various factors. In today's world of digitization, changes are required at all organizational levels, and it seems that change has replaced all other societal constants. In an increasingly competitive workplace, employer branding is emerging as a comparatively new strategy for attracting and keeping the best human talent. Employer branding could be a useful idea for managers, employees, and researchers equally. Employer branding is a tool that managers can use to direct various hiring and retaining initiatives into an unified HR strategy. The results of integrating hiring, employment, training, development, and career management under one umbrella will be very different from the results of each process operating independently. Not only must this positivity be urgently cultivated in the thoughts of stakeholders and external customers, but it must also be cultivated in the minds of employees. The reputation built must be watched over and maintained in a way that promotes growth in sales as well as a sense of pride, self-actualization, and genuine dedication expressed in words and deeds. The value of the Waterfall idea of sustainable employer branding for management, HRM and PR researchers is paralleled by the value it has for the development of the 'human-centered society'.

Employer branding is a tool that management scholars can use to unify a variety of concepts that have been explored in the literature on recruitment, selection, and retention. When creating the organizational structure and design for strategic human resource management, the idea of workplace branding can be especially helpful. The following objectives, which seem to be of high added value in the implementation of changes, during times of crisis, and in maintaining the employer brand, can be accomplished by the organization with the creation of an internal communication strategy:

1. An environment that is pleasant to work in and helps people perform their jobs well;
2. Psychological advantages like belonging, identification, and recognition;
3. Keeping the genuine talents that the public group has invested in;
4. Maintaining the employer brand over time (employer branding);
5. Using employees to create successful social responsibility.

As a result of higher levels of a positive organizational and communication climate, the relationship between internal communication and employee engagement is significant and related to motivation levels for improved outcomes for both employees and the company.

"Waterfall" model for re-innovation management „invests" in establishing a long-term relationship between the parties and an unity for improved interaction between management's objects and subjects in the framework of the overall employer brand, according to the suggested theoretical prism.

The presented author's model for sustainable branding through effective communications is in full relation with the ideas of the concept of sustainable development of organizations and innovative marketing. The model could be useful to experts in the field of marketing, sustainable development, human resources management, communication specialists, experts in the field of strategic management and others. Also, the ideas of the development would be useful in the training of students in the field of marketing and sustainable branding.

The use of communication management, which incorporates fundamental procedures like problem-solving research and definition, planning and programming, action and communication, assessment and monitoring in relation to collaboration and engagement with HRM, will produce outcomes that have been demonstrated to be advantageous for organizations and communities.

REFERENCES

Ambler, T., & Barrow, S. J. (1996). The Employer Brand. *Journal of Brand Management*, 4(3), 185–206. doi:10.1057/bm.1996.42

Atluri, V., Dietz, M., & Henke, N. (2017). Competing in a world of sectors without borders. McKinsey Quarterly, July, 2017. https://www.mckinsey.com/capabilities/quantumblack/our-insights/competing-in-a-world-of-sectors-without-borders

Aysha, S. B. MohdSalleh, Z. Abdul Kadir, S. Sanif (2016). The Relationship between Organizational Communication and Employees Productivity with New Dimensions of Effective Communication Flow, *Journal of Business and Social Review in Emerging Economies*.

Berger, B. (2008, November 17). Employee/Organizational Communications. *Institute for Public Relations*.

Chankova, D. & V., V. (2020). Leadership and deliberative democracy in the changing world: compatible or reconcilable paradigms. *Perspectives of Law and Public Administration, 9*(2).

Clegg, A. (2007). *Unlock the power of brands.* Marketing Week Edelman Trust Barometer (2023). https://www.edelman.com/trust/2023/Trust-Barometer/navigating-a-polarized-world

Dawar, N., & Bagga, C. K. (2015). A Better Way to Map Brand Strategy. Figure out where you are on the distinctiveness-centrality spectrum. *Harvard Business Review*, (June), 90–97. https://hbr.org/2015/06/a-better-way-to-map-brand-strategy

Geyskens et al., (1999). A meta – analysis of satisfaction in marketing channel relationships. *Journal of Marketing Research*, 36 (2), ;

Gigauri, I. (2020). Implications Of Covid-19 For Human Resources; Management SSRG. *International Journal of Economics and Management Studies, 7*(11).

Gronroos, C. (1994). From marketing mix to relationship marketing. *Management Decisions, 32* (2)

Keidanren (Japan Business Federation). (2016). *Toward Realization of the New Economy and Society, Reform of the Economy and Society by the Deepening of 'Society 5.0'.* Keidanren. https://www.keidanren.or.jp/en/policy/2016/029.html

Kusá. (2021). *Alena & Urmínová, Marianna.* Innovative Approaches in Marketing Communication in Sustainable Fashion Business. doi:10.34190/EIE.20.183

Lemus-Aguilar, I., Morales-Alonso, G., Ramirez-Portilla, A., & Hidalgo, A. (2019). Sustainable Business Models through the Lens of Organizational Design: A Systematic Literature Review. *Sustainability (Basel), 11*(19), 5379. doi:10.3390u11195379

Morgan, R., & Hunt, S. (1994). The commitment – trust theory of relationship marketing. *Journal of Marketing, 58*(3), 20–38. doi:10.1177/002224299405800302

Randstad, (2013). *Results Randstad Award 2013.* Randstad. www.randstadt.com

Rosethorn, H. (2009). *The Employer Brand. Keeping Faith with the Deal.* Gower Publishing Limited.

Sividas, E., & Dwyer, F. (2000). An examination of organizational factors influencing new product success in internal and alliance-based processes. *Journal of Marketing, 64*(1), 31–49. doi:10.1509/jmkg.64.1.31.17985

Stefanova, D. (2016). Features of PR strategy and its implementation in stages. *Rhetoric and Communications Journal, 24*. Advance online publication. doi:10.13140/RG.2.2.19020.85128

Sullivan, J. (2004). The 8 Elements of a Successful Employment Brand. *ER Daily*. https://www.ere.net/the-8-elements-of-a-successful-employment-brand/

Taleb, N. (2019). *Antifragile; InfoDar.* Sofiq.

Vasilev, V. (2020). From a crisis of confidence to effective crisis management in the public administration. *KNOWLEDGE - International Journal, 43*.

Vasilev, V., & Stefanova, D. (2021). Complex communication barriers in the organization in a crisis context. *International Journal (Toronto, Ont.)*, *49*(1). https://ikm.mk/ojs/index.php/kij/article/view/4617

Yastrow, S. (2003). *Brand Harmony: Achieving Dynamic Results by Orchestrating Your Customer's Total Experience*. Select Books Inc.

Section 2
Marketing and Digitalization for Achieving Sustainability

Chapter 7
Social Media Communication and Sustainability Perception in Business:
The Moderating Role of Social Media Influencers

George Kofi Amoako
Ghana Communication Technology University, Accra, Ghana & Durban University of Technology, South Africa

Isaac Sewornu Coffie
Accra Technical University, Ghana

Elikem Chosniel Ocloo
https://orcid.org/0000-0003-4729-3093
Accra Technical University, Ghana

ABSTRACT

Achieving the 17 sustainable development goals (SDGs) has become very important in the survival of the human race and the earth's ecosystem. The purpose of this study is to see the effectiveness of social media communication and how it influences consumer behavior perception on environmental sustainability and the role of social media influencers. This chapter is a conceptual manuscript. The researcher used literature from good and reliable databases such as Emerald, Sage, Taylor & Francis, Web of Science, Elsevier, and others. Desk research was adopted and literature covering the relevant constructs in the title and model were reviewed and thoroughly discussed and meanings and implications were synthesized.

INTRODUCTION

Achieving the 17 sustainable development goals (SDGs) has become very important in the survival of the human race and the earth's ecosystem. Social media platforms have quickly emerged as a formidable

DOI: 10.4018/978-1-6684-8681-8.ch007

communications tool, exerting significant influence not just in urban centres but also in rural areas (Ahmad et al., 2019; Golmohammadi et al., 2023). The digital revolution has affected businesses and how individuals communicate and made the globe more accessible. How people communicate has been profoundly altered by the rise of social media, which has also become an indispensable component of people's everyday life. To ensure the continued health and prosperity of future generations, it is the duty of all of us (businesses and individuals) to ensure the conservation of natural resources and the protection of global ecosystems. Sustainability is also described as preserving and improving environmental quality over the long term to prevent the exhaustion or degradation of natural resources (Bruno & Dabrowski, 2016). Environmental sustainability is, thus, the practice of not compromising future generations' ability to satisfy their requirements while also providing for the current population's needs. Firms that practice activities that are friendly to the environment will eventually will more customers because society is growing in awareness of the environment (Okuah et al., 2019). Social media communication can therefore be used effectively to draw society's attention to the benefits of sustainability practices. *The use of social media can make businesses, individuals, and society change their behaviour positively towards brands, products and firms to protect humanity and the environment (Radi & Shokouhyar, 2021).*

A new type of consumer influencer that has emerged on the seen in the past few decades and growing rapidly due to the proliferation of social networking sites, social media and billions of users on the internet is called social media influencers (SMIs) (Qalati et al., 2021; Radi & Shokouhyar, 2021). SMIs are social media users who have acquired many followers and achieved a certain level of credibility, both of which can lead to an impact or a level of persuasion in their interactions with their followers (Malik et al., 2023). Based on their popularity, many brands and marketers use them to promote and create awareness of their products and services (Ho & Rezaei, 2018; Malik et al., 2023). Given their popularity and ability to influence their followers, SMI could be an effective tool to help engage with the public to influence their perception to adopt pro-environmental behaviour and buy environmentally friendly products. SMIs have become an excellent source for reaching target audiences credibly and efficiently due to their capacity to grow a considerable number of followers and generate influence, confidence, and trust among followers (Malik et al., 2023). Despite their increasing growth and wide usage among marketers and brands, little is known about how SMIs are used to influence consumer perception towards social and environmentally sustainable products.

LITERATURE REVIEW

Evolution of Social Media

Social media sites like Facebook, Twitter, Instagram, and WeChat have changed from being a platform for direct electronic information exchange to a globally connected circle, photo-sharing websites, virtual meetings, instant global news, and a retail platform in less than a few decades (ElAlfy, Darwish, et al., 2020; van Zanten & van Tulder, 2021). Social media has occupied a significant portion of our lives and is progressively attracting the attention of businesses (Voorveld, 2019). However, when did social media begin, and what does it mean? How did the quick transition from print media like newspapers and magazines to digital media like computers and smartphones happen?

The exponential growth of social media platforms at the turn of the 20th century was notable. In the 1940s, the first supercomputers were developed; shortly after that, scientists and engineers began to work on methods for connecting individual computers to form networks; this was the initial step toward the development of the Internet (Malik et al., 2023). The networking technology had advanced to the degree by the 1970s that it was able to build UseNet in 1979, allowing users to connect through a digital newsletter (Charoensukmongkol & Sasatanun, 2017). This was made possible due to the advancements made in networking technology throughout the 1970s. When computers became more prevalent, social media became more sophisticated by the 1980s (Charoensukmongkol & Sasatanun, 2017). The emergence of blogging and messaging platforms in the late 1990s marked the beginning of social media, which is still a rapidly growing phenomenon globally today (Charoensukmongkol & Sasatanun, 2017; Ho & Rezaei, 2018). As time progressed, social networking programs expanded beyond personal computers and into mobile devices like smartphones and tablets. This, coupled with the increasing availability of high-speed internet coverage, has led to the rapid growth of social media (Ahmad et al., 2019).

The advent of blogging can directly be attributed to the spectacular surge in the popularity of social media (Floreddu & Cabiddu, 2016). At the beginning of the twenty-first century, social networking sites such as MySpace and LinkedIn emerged. Others, such as Photobucket and Flickr, were also introduced to encourage online sharing of digital photographs (Bruno & Dabrowski, 2016; Floreddu & Cabiddu, 2016). When YouTube was made available to the general public for the first time in 2005, it marked the start of an age of remarkable ingenuity in how people communicate with one another and exchange knowledge across tremendous distances (Ahmad et al., 2019; Voorveld, 2019). Facebook and Twitter, which are still among the most popular social networking sites, were introduced a year later in 2006.

Currently, 4.76 billion or 59.45 of the world's population, are using social media worldwide (Statista, 2023). The proliferation of social media applications has occurred exponentially, and each has particular goals.

SOCIAL MEDIA COMMUNICATION

Although the term "social media" can mean different things to different people, for this chapter, we will refer to it as a collection of web-based applications developed around the Web 2.0 standard that allows users to produce and share user-generated content and engage in two-way communication (Schaltegger & Burritt, 2018; Silva, 2021). The significance of social media in shaping communication between customers and companies has undergone a dramatic transition over the previous decade. For example, statistics have shown that the number of people who use the internet exceeds five billion, equivalent to around 64 per cent of the world's total population (Statista, 2023). In addition, one out of every seven people has a Facebook profile, and around 80% of all Internet users use social media at least once every month (Trivedi et al., 2020; Statista, 2023). The use of social networking sites has grown to become a standard component of most people's habits. It is projected that 2.62 billion people worldwide will utilize a social media site at least once a month in 2022, with each user spending an average of 135 minutes interacting with their chosen network (Statista, 2023). Facebook, YouTube, WhatsApp, Messenger, WeChat, and Instagram are the world's most widely used social media platforms as of the beginning of 2019 (Ahmad et al., 2019; Statista, 2023). For instance, as of February 2023, Facebook had 2.96 billion active users, Twitter 353.90 million users, Instagram 2.35 billion and WeChat 1.3 billion active users. The idea that we are in the Web 2.0 era, when user-generated content (UGC) may establish potent communities that facilitate the connections of people with similar interests, has arisen as a result of the expanding importance and popularity of these websites (Ahmad et al., 2019; Cantele & Zardini, 2020;

Charoensukmongkol & Sasatanun, 2017). In addition, social media platforms make it easier for customers to communicate with one another and speed up conversations that already exist among customers (Charoensukmongkol & Sasatanun, 2017; Chen et al., 2023). Almost every major consumer brand now has a social media presence, and advertisers and marketers are excitedly incorporating social media into their digital strategy to capitalize on its widespread adoption (Cantele & Zardini, 2020).

The proliferation of social media platforms has radically altered the nature of communication, shifting it from a one-way broadcast to a two-way, interactive exchange between individuals (Li et al., 2020; Malik et al., 2023). Because of the multifaceted nature of social media platforms, they make it possible for customers to communicate with other customers (Tajudeen et al., 2018). Thus, businesses no longer have a monopoly over brand communication. Businesses are increasingly turning to social media to connect with their customers and build lasting relationships (Charoensukmongkol & Sasatanun, 2017; Ho & Rezaei, 2018). Social media now present both businesses and their customers with new opportunities to interact with one another.

Consequently, the social media content generated by the company is now also seen as a vital component of the company's overall marketing strategy (Malik et al., 2023; Qalati et al., 2021). Marketing managers now use these social media platforms to build strong customer relationships and alter their views or how people think about their products (Ahmad et al., 2019; Li et al., 2020). In contrast to more conventional methods of company-generated communication, social media communications have been recognized as a mass phenomenon with appeal across a wide range of demographic categories (Floreddu & Cabiddu, 2016; Tajudeen et al., 2018).

SUSTAINABILITY DEVELOPMENT GOALS AND ITS RELEVANCE TO BUSINESSES

The concept of sustainability, also known as sustainable development, refers to the process of developing, producing, and consuming goods and services such that the requirements and preferences of the current generation are satisfied without compromising the ability of subsequent generations to fulfil their requirements and preferences (Ordonez-Ponce et al., 2021). Sustainable development has recently been in the limelight due to rising environmental and climate change concerns and growing societal inequalities. Businesses are increasingly under pressure from key stakeholders, including national and international authorities and society at large, to incorporate social and environmentally responsible values into their strategies, structures, policies, and management systems (Cantele & Zardini, 2018; Kong et al., 2021). In light of this, it has become increasingly important for businesses in recent years to pursue and implement strategies and operations that consider social and environmental concerns in a more comprehensive manner if they wish to be successful.

The United Nations, in September 2015, adopted a set of 17 Sustainable Development Goals (SDGs) as a global plan to attain sustainable development issues by 2030 (Ordonez-Ponce et al., 2021; Schaltegger & Burritt, 2018). The 17 SDGs (see table 2), which were tagged "Transforming Our World: The 2030 Agenda for Sustainable Development", were adopted by all 193 Member States. The SDGs explicitly emphasise the need for all stakeholders to work together to achieve a sustainable society and incorporate the 5Ps: People, Planet, Prosperity, Peace, and Partnership (Khaled et al., 2021; Ordonez-Ponce et al., 2021). Demands for corporations to take on a more prominent role in sustainable development have been made several times (Mio et al., 2020). Even though all businesses want to make money, they may not be able to do so in the long run if they do not care about their social and environmental problems. For this purpose, the sustainability agenda should encompass the entire firm and all stakeholders in the value chain (Ghosh & Rajan, 2019). Szabo and Webster (2021) further argue that given corporate bodies' unique and specific capabilities, such as financing, sector-specific expertise and knowledge, and managerial and enforcement capabilities, they play a critical and unique role in achieving the SDGs. This suggests that the private sector's partnership, collaboration and participation are very significant to achieving the 2030 agenda for the SDGs. In addition, Schramade (2017) have emphasised that Goal 12, which is about ensuring sustainable consumption and production, places a renewed emphasis on businesses' role in attaining sustainable development.

Current State of Sustainability Practices Among Corporate Organisations

Despite the call for a collaborative stakeholder approach to achieve shared sustainable prosperity, past studies and reports suggest that the current state of sustainability practices and corporate organisations' involvement in achieving this goal is relatively slow (Van der Waal & Thijssens, 2020; van Zanten & van Tulder, 2021). For example, the report of PricewaterhouseCoopers (PwC, 2019) shows that even though 72% of companies talk about SDGs in their public reports, only 20% set quantitative goals for achieving them. Only 8% of these companies (about 1% of the total sample) report quantitative measures to show their progress toward achieving those goals. Thus, although more and more companies are thinking and speaking sustainability, a lot of them are lacking when it comes to implementation. Accenture's study on Reaching Net Zero by 2050 shows that only 5% of European companies are on track to achieving their net-zero targets (Accenture, 2022). Net-zero is a company's commitment to reduce its emissions of CO_2 and other greenhouse gases to zero. Using the Fortune Global Top 500 corporations, the findings of Song et al. (2022) reveled that although 304 of the 500 corporations had presented relevant content regarding sustainability on their websites, only 22.8% of these corporations developed specific action or strategies for specific SDGs, and only 0.2% developed methods and stools to evaluate progress. According to Song et al. (2022) the low implementation of sustainability initiatives could be attributed to lack of adequate engagement with corporate organisations and CEOs on sustainability strategies.

However, a study by Boston Consulting Group in 2022 of 850 companies globally provides hope for the future as their findings show that more than 80% of companies planned to increase their investments in sustainability programs and products (Boston Consulting Group, 2022). This is an indication that sustainability issues are becoming top of the agenda for most corporate organisations. Additionally, a survey by McKinney in 2021 of 2,475 company leaders worldwide representing a range of industries and company sizes shows that company leaders are increasingly increasing their commitment in sustainability as they expect to generate profits from these sustainability programs by attracting more environmentally conscious consumers (McKinsey, 2021). Almost one-third (30%) of Europe's largest listed companies have also pledged to reach to net-zero by 2050. In UK, 37% of the listed companies have also pledge their commitment to achieving the net-zero target (TravelPerk, 2023).

As indicated earlier, given the growing concern for social and environmental sustainability among consumers and other key stakeholders, businesses that adhere to sustainability concerns are more likely to gain a competitive advantage in today's competitive business environment. For instance, the work of Foroudi et al. (2022) shows that more consumers are willing to purchase products and services from organisations deemed or perceived as environmentally sustainability conscious. Focusing on SDGs 8, 9, 12,13,15, and 17, the findings of a study conducted in Spain by Mozas-Moral et al. (2021) provide empirical evidence to show that alignment of business activities with SDGs positively and significantly enhances business performance. Cantele and Zardini (2018) also assert that the game changer in dynamic, complex, demanding and competitive environments is likely to be sustainable social and environmental behaviour. As asserted by Pedersen (2018), businesses, in general, are successful when they can satisfy their customers' needs with solutions that they desire. Consumers are continually demanding that their needs be satisfied in a socially and environmentally sustainable manner. Businesses that provide solutions with this mindset are more likely to succeed in today's fiercely competitive business environment. Findings from other scholars (e.g., Ordonez-Ponce et al., 2021; Silva, 2021) further show that sustainable behaviour is rapidly becoming a significant means of attaining corporate reputation, competitive advantage and survival of businesses.

The Proposed Conceptual Framework and Development of Propositions

Social Media Communication and Business Performance

The question is, does social media communication have any influence on the performance of businesses? Will the adoption of social media communication have a positive or negative influence on businesses?

With the advent of social media technologies, companies now have an inexpensive means of communicating with their customers and responding to their competitors (ElAlfy, Darwish, et al., 2020; Foroudi et al., 2022). For companies that already have access to the internet, adopting social media requires little or no investment of resources (ElAlfy, Palaschuk, et al., 2020). Because of its low cost and limited technical requirements, social media can be adopted and implemented by small and medium-sized businesses (SMEs) (Reyes-Rodríguez, 2021). As a consequence, the usage of social media within organisations is continuing to increase at an exponential rate, and it is swiftly becoming a phenomenon that is essential to the practice of business management in both small and large companies (Ho & Rezaei, 2018; Kapoor et al., 2021). Businesses may favour social media more than ever before because it facilitates interactions between large groups of people rather than just an individual (Li et al., 2020; Qalati et al., 2021). In addition, social media features offer very inexpensive solutions for analytics, automatic posting, content management, conversion tracking, and customer targeting.

The answer to the earlier questions is that when social media communication is used strategically and effectively, it can or can potentially improve various areas of company activities. This is because social media platforms enable users to contribute and share their user-generated content. Building relationships with customers, maintaining active customer participation, and effectively sharing and managing information are examples of company activities that could be impacted by using social media effectively (Bruno & Dabrowski, 2016; Golmohammadi et al., 2023). The impact of social media communication on business performance has been the subject of several studies in the past (Chen & Lin, 2019; Chen & Wei, 2020). From the Danish SMEs' context, Reyes-Rodríguez (2021) work, for instance, shows a significant positive relationship between social media communication and competitive advantage. The finding of Ho and Rezaei (2018) also showed that using social media as a communication tool has a direct positive and significant impact on the economic performance of businesses. The empirical evidence by Tajudeen et al. (2018) further demonstrates the significant role of social media communication on the performance of business organisations. Table 1 provides a summary of some studies conducted to examine the impact of social media communication on the performance of businesses. Though not exhaustive, the summary of studies in the table provides some important insight into how social media communication influences the performance of businesses. Based on the above discussion, we give proposition that:

P1: social media communication will positively influence business performance.

Social Media Communication and Sustainability Perception of Business Organizations

What is the perception of businesses with regard to their engagement in social and environmental sustainability? Why should a business with a share value orientation engage in socially and environmentally sustainable behaviour? Can social media communication play a role in shaping the perception of a business to embark on sustainability behaviour?

To attain a sustainable level of development from social, environmental, and economic viewpoints, the collaboration of a wide range of stakeholders, including businesses, governments, and individual

Table 1. Summary of findings on the impact of social media communication on the performance of businesses

Author	Model	Title	Findings
(Ahmad et al. (2019)	TOE	Social media adoption and its impact on firm performance: the case of the UAE	Adoption of social media communication has no significant impact on performance of businesses.
(Ahmad et al. (2018)	Social presence theory	Reflections of entrepreneurs of small and medium sized enterprises concerning the adoption of social media and its impact on performance outcomes: Evidence form the UAE	No impact
(Bakri, 2017)	Integrated model	The impact of social media adoption on competitive advantage in small medium enterprises	Adoption of social media has no significant influence on competitive advantage of SMEs
Tajudeen et al. (2017)	TOE	Understanding the impact of social media usage among organisations	SM has a positive impact on cost reduction, customer service and relationships enhanced information accessibility about customers.
(Chen & Lin, 2019)	Second order construct	Understanding the effect of social media marketing activities: The mediation of social identification, perceived value, and satisfaction	No direct effect of social media marketing on performance
(Chatterjee & Kumar Kar, 2020)	TAM and UTAUT2	Why do small and medium enterprises use social media marketing and what is the impact: Empirical insights from India	SM has positive impact on business performance.
(Tajvidi & Karami, 2021)	RBVS	The effect of social media on firm performance	No positive relationship was found
Qalati et al. (2020)	TOE	A mediated model on the adoption of social media and SMEs' performance in developing countries	Positive influence on performance
(Li et al., 2020)		The impact of social media on the business performance of small firms in China	There significant effect
Chen and Wei (2020)	Theory of virtuality	The impact of social media use for communication and social exchange relationship on employee performance	Positive significant impact on employee performance
(Gruner et al., 2019)	Reactance theory	Supporting new product launches with social media communication and online advertising: Sales volume and profit implication	Positive significant relationship.

citizens, is very important (Kapoor et al., 2021). Thus, the achievement of the SDGs (reducing poverty, ending hunger, and protecting biodiversity) is heavily reliant on the commitment and active participation of corporate organizations, given their critical role in the production of goods and services, as well as creativity and innovation to create value for the common good. As major stakeholders, corporate organizations are expected to integrate and implement these SDGs as part of their business strategy.

Although the increasing demand from stakeholder constituencies puts enormous pressure on businesses to behave sustainably and contribute positively to achieving the SDGs, studies have shown that while some business organizations consider the common good as their business objectives, most businesses clearly do not (Foroudi et al., 2022). For some organizations, the increasing concerns for social and environmental protection and high expectations from stakeholders are an opportunity to achieve reputation and competitive advantage (Kapoor et al., 2021; Ordonez-Ponce et al., 2021; Taylor et al., 2003). For others, striving for sustainable behaviour is a cost that may be difficult to transfer to consumers (Cantele & Zardini, 2018, 2020; ElAlfy, Darwish, et al., 2020). Thus, the way and manner businesses perceive or think about sustainability issues will greatly influence their willingness and readiness to adopt and implement sustainability values into their business operations. They may be reluctant to incorporate these values into their operations and business strategies if they think attaining the SDGs and sustainable environmental issues are not worth pursuing (ElAlfy, Darwish, et al., 2020). For instance, the findings of an empirical study by Cantele and Zardini (2020) to measure the perception of SMEs and their responses to the current requirements of environmental best practice shows that though most SMEs believe that environmentally sustainable behaviour positively affects their businesses, most SMEs perceive it as a business cost which is difficult or impossible to transfer to consumers. Their finding also shows that, given this consideration, only a few SMEs believe that environmentally sustainable behaviour leads to competitive advantage.

The work of Schaltegger and Burritt (2018) explores the likely factors that could motivate business managers to embark on different types of CSR initiatives and provides four business cases that drive management perception towards engagement in sustainable social and environmental behaviour. First, their finding show that business engagement in sustainable behaviour could be driven by a reactionary business case where the managers of the business believe that engaging in a particular sustainable behaviour at a particular point in time will lead to an increase in their financial performance in the short term. Second is the reputational business case, where management embarks on social or environmental sustainability behaviour to achieve a reputation from stakeholders through media sensitivity. The third factor is the responsible business case for sustainability, where sustainability is considered a measure of excellence that guides and challenges management to improve the efficiency and quality of products and processes. The final factor is the collaborative case for sustainability which is more of a dialogue-based perspective where management engages with relevant stakeholders to provide stakeholder-oriented sustainable products from the perspectives of stakeholders.

As corporate organizations are increasingly responding to the increasing demand to behave sustainably, they need to communicate how they respond to this call to stakeholders effectively. Effective communication of CSR and other sustainability initiatives has become extremely important. Research has shown a positive correlation between stakeholders' awareness of these initiatives and their willingness to patronize sustainability products. We, therefore give proposition as follows:

P2: social media communication will positively influence sustainability perception of business organizations

Social Media Communication and Sustainability Performance of Businesses

The sustainability performance of a business is the ability of a business to contribute to societal well-being and perform financially strong (Khaled et al., 2021). Previous studies have shown the importance of effective corporate communication in informing company stakeholders about their CSR and sustainability initiatives (ElAlfy, Darwish et al., 2020; Khaled et al., 2021; Taylor et al., 2003). One of the most basic tools for supporting organisational change is communication. Over the past decade, companies have increasingly communicated with their external stakeholders about their CSR and sustainability initiatives (Reilly & Hynan, 2014; Reilly & Larya, 2018). According to Kyu Kim et al. (2020), reputation can be boosted by reporting on effective participation in nonmarket matters, like social and environmental programs, that are not considered core company activity. Since the number of consumers that desires or consider sustainability issues when making a purchase decision is steadily growing, sustainability reporting has also become a major strategic issue and top priority in most organisations.

Given past studies' findings, which show that environmental management practices have favourable consequences for business performance, explicitly expressing or communicating efforts and commitments made towards sustainability is extremely important (Reilly & Hynan, 2014). This is because the implementation of environmental management practices can be considered a manifestation of commitment to sustainable development (Silva, 2021). However, it should be stressed that evidence of the implementation of actual practices is required in order to make such environmental communication more meaningful and trustworthy; otherwise, the company can be culpable of greenwashing (Heras-Saizarbitoria et al., 2022; Reyes-Rodríguez, 2021). Engaging in greenwashing is when an organisation exaggerates its efforts in embarking on environmentally sustainable behaviour or does not embark on any sustainable behaviour but claims it does (Reyes-Rodríguez, 2021). Consequently, many researchers have attempted to comprehend how receptive customers are to environmentally friendly advertising and have revealed that consumers continue to be somewhat sceptical of environmentally friendly advertising (Gil-Soto et al., 2019; Kapoor et al., 2021). So, successfully communicating and interacting with the sceptical green consumer remains a challenging goal for marketers to solve.

Since informing stakeholders about environmentally sustainable behaviour is very strategic and crucial to reaping the benefits of embarking on sustainable behaviour, social media communication will play a very significant role in this regard. Due to the unique characteristics of social media communication, it has the potential to create highly persuasive green messages to effectively deal with the increasing consumer scepticism about firms' involvement in sustainable behaviour or green behaviour (Charoensukmongkol & Sasatanun, 2017; Ho & Rezaei, 2018; Kapoor et al., 2021). As shown by Voorveld (2019), family, friends and important others such as opinion leaders or influencers have a more substantial influence on the adoption of green consumption behaviour. This implies that environmentally friendly messages created and shared by friends are more likely to be trusted and received than information from the organisation. The following proposition was formulated based on these discussions:

P3: Social media communication will significantly influence sustainability performance of businesses

Social Media Communication and Consumers' Perception of Sustainability

There has been an astronomical jump in the use of social media by consumers in recent times. The influence of social media on individual lives and the survival and performance of businesses can no longer be ignored. Consumers are increasingly turning away from traditional communication through television, radio, billboards, newspapers, and magazines (Foroudi et al., 2022; Ho & Rezaei, 2018; Radi & Shokouhyar, 2021). The introduction of social media has significantly changed traditional one-way communication, where firms primarily were the sole source of brand communication, into a largely multi-dimensional, two-way and peer-to-peer communication (Trivedi et al., 2020). Internet users and consumers have greatly experienced a large amount of online exposure and social networking primarily due to the domineering influence of Web 2.0 technologies and social media.

Research has shown that consumption patterns and behaviour individual consumers is one of the major factors negatively affecting the ecosystem and the environment (Gil-Soto et al., 2019; Sun & Wang, 2020; Szabo & Webster, 2021). This suggest that consumers' consumption pattern and demand for unsustainable products is one of the major contributor to climate change issues. Thus, changing consumers' behaviour and consumption pattern is likely to influence the sustainability of the environment positively. The question however, is, are consumers aware of sustainability issues? What is the current level of awareness and perception of sustainability among consumers? Can social media communication influence their perception about the need for sustainable consumption?

Current State of Sustainability Awareness Among Consumers

As indicated earlier, there is an increasing demand for environmentally friendly products from stakeholder constituencies which is putting pressure on corporate organisations to behave sustainably. This suggest that the higher the consumer demand and pressure for environmentally sustainable products, the higher the likelihood that corporate organisations will be committed and have the intention to adopt sustainability behaviour. However, findings from past studies and surveys show that although majority of consumers are willing to take action to protect the environment, most of them, particularly those in less developed economies, are unaware of the gravity of environmental challenges facing the world and their role as consumers in curbing the dangers posed by unsustainable production and consumption (Simon-Kucher, 2021; Song et al., 2022; TravelPerk, 2023). For example, 85% of respondents surveyed in 2021 by Simon-Kucher (2021) said that though consumers are willing to be more loyal to companies that are socially and environmentally responsible, they had little knowledge about sustainable consumption. The same survey report shows that only 29% of consumers see themselves as major actors towards achiveing positive environmenta change. The survey findings of (Accenture, 2019) also shows 81% of consumers have little knowledge or unaware of sustainability issues, although willing to pay more if they are aware of such products. From a developing country perspective, the findings of (Wang et al., 2019) also point to lack of knowledge about sustainability and perceive high price for sustainable products as major factors contributing to low intention among consumers to purchase environmentally sustainable products.

These findings suggest that communications seeking to raise awareness and educate stakeholders, particularly consumers, about sustainability, the SDGs and the need to consume environmentally sustainable products may significantly enhance pro-sustainability behaviour and achievement of the SDGs. And social media will play a critical role in this regard, given its wide coverage and the large number of users in recent times. The work of Radi and Shokouhyar (2021) on consumers' willingness to engage in environmentally sustainable consumption, for instance, shows that awareness creation enhances pro-environmental behaviour among consumers. For instance, Yamane and Kaneko (2021) conducted a study on the impact of raising awareness of the SDGs on eliciting stakeholders' preference for corporate behaviour towards the SDGs. In other words, would awareness creation about the SDGs and sustainability affect stakeholders' preference or support for products or companies that positively contribute to achieving the SDGs and environmental sustainability? Their findings empirically demonstrate that when consumers are aware and understand the purpose or why the need for sustainability, they are more likely to have a positive attitude and perception towards sustainable products and a positive attitude towards companies that produce those products.

Like corporate organizations, the perception and understanding of consumers about the need for environmental sustainability issues are likely to significantly influence their appreciation and willingness to purchase environmentally friendly products. Corporate organizations may be committed more to environmental sustainability and invest huge sums of resources in terms of time and money to produce environmentally sustainable products or services if they know consumers will appreciate and buy those products. Conversely, the huge investment may go waste if consumers do not appreciate and buy those products and services. The findings of Gil-Soto et al. (2019), for instance, shows that though hotel managers in the Canary Islands (Spain) spent a substantial amount of resources to acquire environmentally friendly products and practices, it does not significantly influence guests' perceptions and review experience. The empirical findings of Sun and Wang (2020) also show that consumers' price consciousness negatively influences purchase intention.

We give proposition as follows:

P4: social media communication will positively influence consumers' perception of sustainability

The Role of Social Media Influencers in Shaping Sustainability Perception of Both Consumers and Organizations

With the introduction and rapid growth of social networking and social media platforms such as Facebook, Twitter, WeChat, Instagram, etc., a new type of consumer influencer has emerged: social media influencers (SMI) (Ahmad et al., 2019). An individual who has built up an extensive social media network of followers due to the online content they provide and has consequently acquired the ability to exert influence over those followers is known as a social media influencer (Malik et al., 2023). These social media influencers promote themselves to their followers by sharing their views, areas of expertise, and frequently endorsed products. Because of the large number of followers they usually enjoy and their ability to exert influence on these followers, many top organizations most often call on them to promote or enhance the awareness of their brands (Malik et al., 2023; Voorveld, 2019). Due to the proliferation of social media platforms and the billions of people using the internet for entertainment and other reasons daily, the social media influencer industry has become the most popular and effective means of shaping consumer perception and purchase intention (Okuah et al., 2019). The industry's estimated value as of December 2022 was more than doubled from 2019's value to 16.4 billion U.S. dollars (Statista, 2023). The astronomical and strong growth of SMI could be attributable to their great influence on their followers as experts (Malik et al., 2023). The survey report by Statista (2023), for instance, shows that about 70% of teenagers prefer SMI to traditional celebrities, and 53% of women are likely to buy products recommended by these SMI. Study by Szabo and Webster (2021) also points to how celebrities do influence their followers purchase intentions.

Findings from empirical studies have also shown the significant influence of SMI on consumer purchase intention (Lim et al 2017). From the grounded theory's perspective, the findings of Okuah et al. (2019), for instance, shows that the characteristics and techniques used by SMI are an effective avenue that could be used to create awareness and influence public perception about positive environmental behaviour and purchase intention of environmentally friendly products and services. The findings of Kim and Kim (2020) shows that social media influencers are significant marketing communication tool for promoting sustainable fashion. The empirical findings of Yıldırım (2021) also demonstrate that green women social media influencers have more power to change consumption patterns of consumers towards green foods, sustainable travel, green cosmetics, sustainable lifestyle, and choices through digital platforms. Practically, there are some evidence to show how social media and social media influencers are being used to promote sustainability behaviour. For example, using the hashtag #econfession campaign, Ocean Bottle and their partner Plastic Bank are harnessing the potential of TikTok to achieve their objective of preventing 80million kg of plastic from entering the sea (Peel-Yates, 2022). Leah Thomas, who is a well-known eco-friendly and sustainability social media influencer utilizes her platforms to talk to her followers about environmental justice and equality (the good grade, 2022). Additionally, Kathryn Kellogg, an Instagram celebrity has used her famous blog to gather a significant following by posting helpful hints on achieving waste-free lifestyle in addition to her work with corporations on sustainability marketing (Peel-Yates, 2022). Corporate organisations that have successfully used social media to promote sustainable practices or environmentally friendly products include Allbirds, Everlane, Starbuck, Johnson & Johnson, Patagonia, TOMS, TRIBE, Tentree, etc. For example, Allbirds, a Sillicon Valley startup company in sportswear took the industry by surprise by focusing on sustainability and appealing to consumers through social media (Peel-Yates, 2022). The company uses natural sustainable materials such as merino wool and eucalyptus to produce its shoes and use social media to amass large following of eco-friendly conscious users. Allbirds also leverage on social media influencers and content creators to appeal to Millennials and generation Z (Peel-Yates, 2022).

Given their potential to influence the sustainability perception of consumers, there is the need for more empirical studies to validate its influence on actual purchase behaviour of eco-friendly and sustainable consumption. Based on the above discussion, we give propositions as follows:

P5 – P8: SMI will moderate the relationship between social media communication and business performance, sustainability perception, sustainability performance, and consumers' perception of sustainability

Potential Drawbacks or Challenges of Social Media Influencers

Although social media influencers can be a powerful tool for shaping consumers' perception and purchase behaviour about sustainable products and promote sustainability, there are equally potential drawbacks or challenges about its usage that must be considered. Given the ability, persuasive power, and influence these SMIs exert on their followers, they could rather be promoting unethical or unsustainable products for personal gain instead of promoting sustainable products and consumption. For instance, instead of promoting healthy eating lifestyle, a SMI could rather be promoting fast weight loss drinks and products. There is the possibility of sustainable social media influencers may end up engaging in greenwashing (a situation where an influencer may be promoting unsustainable product but presenting it to his followers as a sustainable product). An influencer, may be over ambitious to promote sustainable product and make false claims in the campaign that could hurt the brand or bring negative backlash for both the brand and the influencer. There is also the danger of choosing the wrong SMI to promote a product.

Companies should be careful when selecting or choosing who they want to use as social media influencer for their brands because, choosing the wrong SMI could be harmful to their brand.

Implication for Managers and Sustainability Promoters

The chapter looked into how social media communication could be used to influence the perception of both corporate organisation bodies and consumers towards sustainable production and consumption to fast track the achievement of the SDGs as well as the role social media influencers could play in achieving these objectives.

The result shows that though there is an increasing demand and pressure on corporate organisations to produce environmentally sustainable products, majority of consumers are still unaware about the need to consume sustainably. This suggest that much is required of organisations and sustainability promoters to achieve the sustainability objectives and the SDGs. Social media communication could play a significant role with this regard given its wide coverage and the large number of users in recent times. Therefore, organisations and individuals seeking to promote sustainability behaviour among consumers could leverage on or take advantage of social media communication to encourage consumption of sustainable products. Producing sustainable product alone is not enough to achieve the SDGs. Consumers must equally be aware of the need for sustainability and be willing to patronize sustainable products. This is because as shown in the chapter, corporate organisations may be discourage from producing or engaging in sustainable behaviour if their efforts are not appreciated by consumers in terms of patronizing those sustainable products.

The role of social media influencers cannot be underestimated as they play a critical role in shaping their followers' perception and buying behaviour of sustainable products. Influencing the perception and intention of consumers towards environmentally sustainable products is extremely important because these sustainable products are likely to be more expensive than unsustainable products and SMIs stands tall in shaping the perception of consumers' sustainable behaviour. Despite their potentiality, care must be taken in selecting the right SMI to avoid miss-match and possible greenwashing. Contents created by the SMIs should also be carefully scrutinized to ensure that it is congruent with the brand and intended impression the organisation sought communicate.

CONCLUSION

The objective of this study was to see the effectiveness of social media communication and how it influences consumer behaviour perception on environmental sustainability and the role of social media influencers. The findings showed that effective communication about efforts and commitments made by the organisation towards environmentally sustainable behaviour is extremely important to shape consumers' perceptions about the organisation and influence their purchase intention of the company's products and services. The findings also showed that though a substantial amount of work has been done about factors influencing the perception of businesses to engage in sustainable social and environmental behaviour, the influence of social media communication on organisation's intention to embark on sustainable behaviour has received little attention in the literature.

Since the advent of social media and the increasing influence of social media, scholars for many decades have examined the field of social media communication to understand how it affects or influences the performance of brands and organisational performance. This interest has led to the production of so many research topics, such as social media communication and electronic word-of-month (eWOM) (Radi & Shokouhyar, 2021), social media and brand love (Voorveld, 2019), social media communication and brand performance (Ahmad et al., 2019), virtual brand engagement and relationship building (Bruno & Dabrowski, 2016), virtual brand communities and fan pages (Chen & Lin, 2019), and user-generated contents (Ho & Rezaei, 2018). Recently scholars (e.g., Golmohammadi et al., 2023; Trivedi et al., 2020) have also examined how user-generated and firm-generated contents influence the performance of businesses. Nevertheless, despite the increasing interest and empirical research into how social media influence business performance, attention given to how social media communication influences the sustainability perception of both consumers and organisations, and the role of SMIs in shaping these perceptions needs to be more in the literature.

FUTURE RESEARCH DIRECTION

The chapter provides some important insights on how social media communication could be used to shape the perception of both corporate organisations and consumes towards sustainability behaviour as well as the role of SMIs in achieving this objective. We however, could not cover everything and therefore, provide the following suggestions for future research direction.

1. There is the need for future studies to provide guidelines for identifying credible social media influencers or strategies for creating effective social media campaigns.
2. While the use of SMIs is presented as a promising tool for promoting sustainable behavior and products in this chapter, the chapter also presents some potential negative consequences or challenges of using social media influencers (SMIs) to promote sustainable products. Future research is required to examine how these negative consequences of SMIs could be addressed to ensure that influencers are genuinely committed to promoting sustainability rather than simply seeking financial gain or damaging the corporate brand.
3. Additionally, future research could explore alternative or complementary strategies for promoting sustainable behavior and products, such as education campaigns or partnerships with environmental organizations. Another potential area for improvement is to examine the intersectionality of sustainability issues and how different social, economic, and cultural factors may impact the success of sustainability initiatives. For example, low-income communities may face different barriers to adopting sustainable practices than affluent communities, and cultural attitudes towards sustainability may differ between different regions or demographic groups. Acknowledging these differences could provide more nuanced and effective strategies for promoting sustainable behavior and products across diverse communities.

REFERENCES

Accenture. (2019). *More than Half of Consumers Would Pay More for Sustainable Products Designed to Be Reused or Recycled, Accenture Survey Finds*. Newsroom. https://newsroom.accenture.com/news/more-than-half-of-consumers-would-pay-more-for-sustainable-products

Accenture. (2022). Almost One-Third of Europe's Largest Listed Companies Have Pledged to Reach Net-Zero by 2050, Accenture Study Finds. *Travel Perk*. https://www.travelperk.com/blog/business-sustainability-statistics/

Ahmad, S. Z., Abu Bakar, A. R., & Ahmad, N. (2019). Social media adoption and its impact on firm performance: The case of the UAE. *International Journal of Entrepreneurial Behaviour & Research*, 25(1), 84–111. doi:10.1108/IJEBR-08-2017-0299

Ahmad, S. Z., Ahmad, N., & Abu Bakar, A. R. (2018). Reflections of entrepreneurs of small and medium-sized enterprises concerning the adoption of social media and its impact on performance outcomes: Evidence from the UAE. *Telematics and Informatics*, 35(1), 6–17. doi:10.1016/j.tele.2017.09.006

Bakri, A. A. (2017). The impact of social media adoption on competitive advantage in the small and medium enterprises. *International Journal of Business Innovation and Research*, 13(2), 255–269. doi:10.1504/IJBIR.2017.083542

Boston Consulting Group. (2022). *More than 80% of companies plan to increase their investments in sustainability*. BCG. https://www.prnewswire.com/news-releases/more-than-60-of-companies-prioritize-esg-in-their-digital-transformations-301514352.html# Bruno.

Cantele, S., & Zardini, A. (2018). Is sustainability a competitive advantage for small businesses? An empirical analysis of possible mediators in the sustainability–financial performance relationship. *Journal of Cleaner Production*, 182, 166–176. doi:10.1016/j.jclepro.2018.02.016

Cantele, S., & Zardini, A. (2020). What drives small and medium enterprises towards sustainability? Role of interactions between pressures, barriers, and benefits. *Corporate Social Responsibility and Environmental Management*, 27(1), 126–136. doi:10.1002/csr.1778

Charoensukmongkol, P., & Sasatanun, P. (2017). Social media use for CRM and business performance satisfaction: The moderating roles of social skills and social media sales intensity. *Asia Pacific Management Review*, 22(1), 25–34. doi:10.1016/j.apmrv.2016.10.005

Chatterjee, S., & Kumar Kar, A. (2020). Why do small and medium enterprises use social media marketing and what is the impact: Empirical insights from India. *International Journal of Information Management*, 53, 102103. doi:10.1016/j.ijinfomgt.2020.102103

Chen, Q., Zhang, Y., Liu, H., Zhang, W., & Evans, R. (2023). Dialogic communication on local government social media during the first wave of COVID-19: Evidence from the health commissions of prefecture-level cities in China. *Computers in Human Behavior*, 143(3), 107715. doi:10.1016/j.chb.2023.107715 PMID:36846271

Chen, S. C., & Lin, C. P. (2019). Understanding the effect of social media marketing activities: The mediation of social identification, perceived value, and satisfaction. *Technological Forecasting and Social Change*, 140, 22–32. doi:10.1016/j.techfore.2018.11.025

Chen, X., & Wei, S. (2020). The impact of social media use for communication and social exchange relationship on employee performance. *Journal of Knowledge Management*, 24(6), 1289–1314. doi:10.1108/JKM-04-2019-0167

El Alfy, A., Darwish, K. M., & Weber, O. (2020). Corporations and sustainable development goals communication on social media: Corporate social responsibility or just another buzzword? *Sustainable Development (Bradford)*, *28*(5), 1418–1430. doi:10.1002d.2095

El Alfy, A., Palaschuk, N., El-Bassiouny, D., Wilson, J., & Weber, O. (2020). Scoping the evolution of corporate social responsibility (CSR) research in the sustainable development goals (SDGS) era. *Sustainability (Basel)*, *12*(14), 5544. doi:10.3390u12145544

Floreddu, P. B., & Cabiddu, F. (2016). Social media communication strategies. *Journal of Services Marketing*, *34*(1), 1–5.

Foroudi, P., Marvi, R., Cuomo, M. T., Bagozzi, R., Dennis, C., & Jannelli, R. (2022). Consumer Perceptions of Sustainable Development Goals: Conceptualization, Measurement and Contingent Effects. *British Journal of Management*, *00*, 1–27. doi:10.1111/1467-8551.12637

Ghosh, S., & Rajan, J. (2019). The business case for SDGs: An analysis of inclusive business models in emerging economies. *International Journal of Sustainable Development and World Ecology*, *26*(4), 344–353. doi:10.1080/13504509.2019.1591539

Gil-Soto, E., Armas-Cruz, Y., Morini-Marrero, S., & Ramos-Henríquez, J. M. (2019). Hotel guests' perceptions of environmental friendly practices in social media. *International Journal of Hospitality Management*, *78*, 59–67. doi:10.1016/j.ijhm.2018.11.016

Golmohammadi, A., Gauri, D. K., & Mirahmad, H. (2023). Social Media Communication and Company Value: The Moderating Role of Industry Competitiveness. *Journal of Service Research*, *26*(1), 120–135. doi:10.1177/10946705211072429

Gruner, R. L., Vomberg, A., Homburg, C., & Lukas, B. A. (2019). Supporting New Product Launches With Social Media Communication and Online Advertising: Sales Volume and Profit Implications. *Journal of Product Innovation Management*, *36*(2), 172–195. doi:10.1111/jpim.12475

Heras-Saizarbitoria, I., Urbieta, L., & Boiral, O. (2022). Organizations' engagement with sustainable development goals: From cherry-picking to SDG-washing? *Corporate Social Responsibility and Environmental Management*, *29*(2), 316–328. doi:10.1002/csr.2202

Ho, R. C., & Rezaei, S. (2018). Social Media Communication and Consumers Decisions: Analysis of the Antecedents for Intended Apps Purchase. *Journal of Relationship Marketing*, *17*(3), 204–228. doi:10.1080/15332667.2018.1492322

Ilicic, J., & Webster, C. M. (2011). Effects of multiple endorsements and consumer–celebrity attachment on attitude and purchase intention [AMJ]. *Australasian Marketing Journal*, *19*(4), 230–237. doi:10.1016/j.ausmj.2011.07.005

Kapoor, P. S., Balaji, M. S., & Jiang, Y. (2021). Effectiveness of sustainability communication on social media: Role of message appeal and message source. *International Journal of Contemporary Hospitality Management*, *33*(3), 949–972. doi:10.1108/IJCHM-09-2020-0974

Khaled, R., Ali, H., & Mohamed, E. K. A. (2021). The Sustainable Development Goals and corporate sustainability performance: Mapping, extent and determinants. *Journal of Cleaner Production, 311*(May), 127599. doi:10.1016/j.jclepro.2021.127599

Kim, K. H., & Kim, E. Y. (2020). Fashion marketing trends in social media and sustainability in fashion management. *Journal of Business Research, 11*(7), 1–2. doi:10.1016/j.jbusres.2020.06.001

Kong, H. M., Witmaier, A., & Ko, E. (2021). Sustainability and social media communication: How consumers respond to marketing efforts of luxury and non-luxury fashion brands. *Journal of Business Research, 131*, 640–651. doi:10.1016/j.jbusres.2020.08.021

Kyu Kim, Y., Yim, M. Y. C., Kim, E., & Reeves, W. (2020). Exploring the optimized social advertising strategy that can generate consumer engagement with green messages on social media. *Journal of Research in Interactive Marketing, 15*(1), 30–48. doi:10.1108/JRIM-10-2019-0171

Li, X., He, X., & Zhang, Y. (2020). The impact of social media on the business performance of small firms in China. *Information Technology for Development, 26*(2), 346–368. doi:10.1080/02681102.2019.1594661

Lim, X. J., Radzol, A. M., Cheah, J., & Wong, M. W. (2017). The impact of social media influencers on purchase intention and the mediation effect of customer attitude. *Asian Journal of Business Research, 7*(2), 19–36. doi:10.14707/ajbr.170035

Malik, A. Z., Thapa, S., & Paswan, A. K. (2023). Social media influencer (SMI) as a human brand – a need fulfillment perspective. *Journal of Product and Brand Management, 32*(2), 173–190. doi:10.1108/JPBM-07-2021-3546

McKinsey. (2021). *How companies capture the value of sustainability: Survey findings*. McKinsey. https://www.mckinsey.com/capabilities/sustainability/our-insights/how-companies-capture-the-value-of-sustainability-survey-findings

Mio, C., Panfilo, S., & Blundo, B. (2020). Sustainable development goals and the strategic role of business: A systematic literature review. *Business Strategy and the Environment, 29*(8), 3220–3245. doi:10.1002/bse.2568

Mozas-Moral, A., Fernández-Uclés, D., Medina-Viruel, M. J., & Bernal-Jurado, E. (2021). The role of the SDGs as enhancers of the performance of Spanish wine cooperatives. *Technological Forecasting and Social Change, 173*(9), 121176. doi:10.1016/j.techfore.2021.121176

Okuah, O., Scholtz, B. M., & Snow, B. (2019). A grounded theory analysis of the techniques used by social media influencers and their potential for influencing the public regarding environmental awareness. *ACM International Conference Proceeding Series*. ACM. 10.1145/3351108.3351145

Ordonez-Ponce, E., Clarke, A., & MacDonald, A. (2021). Business contributions to the sustainable development goals through community sustainability partnerships. *Sustainability Accounting. Management and Policy Journal, 12*(6), 1239–1267. doi:10.1108/SAMPJ-03-2020-0068

Pedersen, C. S. (2018). The un Sustainable Development Goals (SDGs) are a Great Gift to Business! *Procedia CIRP, 69*(May), 21–24. doi:10.1016/j.procir.2018.01.003

Peel-Yates, V. (2022). *5 Sustainability Social Media Campaigns that Rocked*. The Sustainable Agency. https://thesustainableagency.com/blog/sustainability-social-media-campaigns-that-rocked/

PwC. (2019). *Creating a strategy for a better world*. PwC. doi:10.2307/j.ctvc77cxj.37

Qalati, S. A., Yuan, L. W., Khan, M. A. S., & Anwar, F. (2021). A mediated model on the adoption of social media and SMEs' performance in developing countries. *Technology in Society*, *64*, 101513. doi:10.1016/j.techsoc.2020.101513

Radi, A. S., & Shokouhyar, S. (2021). Toward consumer perception of cellphones sustainability: A social media analytics. *Sustainable Production and Consumption*, *25*, 217–233. doi:10.1016/j.spc.2020.08.012

Reilly, A. H., & Hynan, K. A. (2014). Corporate communication, sustainability, and social media: It's not easy (really) being green. *Business Horizons*, *57*(6), 747–758. doi:10.1016/j.bushor.2014.07.008

Reilly, A. H., & Larya, N. (2018). External Communication About Sustainability: Corporate Social Responsibility Reports and Social Media Activity. *Environmental Communication*, *12*(5), 621–637. doi:10.1080/17524032.2018.1424009

Reyes-Rodríguez, J. F. (2021). Explaining the business case for environmental management practices in SMEs: The role of organisational capabilities for environmental communication. *Journal of Cleaner Production*, *318*, 128590. doi:10.1016/j.jclepro.2021.128590

Schaltegger, S., & Burritt, R. (2018). Business cases and corporate engagement with sustainability: Differentiating ethical motivations. *Journal of Business Ethics*, *147*(2), 241–259. doi:10.100710551-015-2938-0

Schramade, W. (2017). Investing in the UN Sustainable Development Goals. *The Bank of America Journal of Applied Corporate Finance*, *29*(2), 87–99. doi:10.1111/jacf.12236

Silva, S. (2021). Corporate contributions to the Sustainable Development Goals: An empirical analysis informed by legitimacy theory. *Journal of Cleaner Production*, *292*, 125962. doi:10.1016/j.jclepro.2021.125962

Simon-Kucher. (2021). *Global Sustainability Study 2021 - Consumers are key players for a sustainable future*. Simon-Kucher.

Song, L., Zhan, X., Zhang, H., Xu, M., Liu, J., & Zheng, C. (2022). How much is global business sectors contributing to sustainable development goals? *Sustainable Horizons*, *1*, 100012. doi:10.1016/j.horiz.2022.100012

Statista. (2023). *Number of internet and social media users worldwide as of January 2023*. Statista. https://www.statista.com/statistics/617136/digital-population-worldwide/#:~:text=Ofthistotal%2C4.76 billion,population%2C were social media users.

Sun, Y., & Wang, S. (2020). Understanding consumers' intentions to purchase green products in the social media marketing context. *Asia Pacific Journal of Marketing and Logistics*, *32*(4), 860–878. doi:10.1108/APJML-03-2019-0178

Szabo, S., & Webster, J. (2021). Perceived Greenwashing: The Effects of Green Marketing on Environmental and Product Perceptions. *Journal of Business Ethics*, *171*(4), 719–739. doi:10.100710551-020-04461-0

Tajudeen, F. P., Jaafar, N. I., & Ainin, S. (2018). Understanding the impact of social media usage among organizations. *Information & Management*, *55*(3), 308–321. doi:10.1016/j.im.2017.08.004

Tajvidi, R., & Karami, A. (2021). The effect of social media on firm performance. *Computers in Human Behavior*, *115*, 1–10. doi:10.1016/j.chb.2017.09.026

Taylor, N., Barker, K., & Simpson, M. (2003). Achieving "sustainable business": A study of perceptions of environmental best practice by SMEs in South Yorkshire. *Environment and Planning. C, Government & Policy*, *21*(1), 89–105. doi:10.1068/c0219

The Good Grade. (2022). *11 Sustainability Influencers Inspiring Us To Do A Little Better Every Day*. The Good Grade. https://www.thegoodtrade.com/features/sustainability-influencers/

TravelPerk. (2023). *Are companies becoming more sustainable?* Travel Perk. https://www.travelperk.com/blog/business-sustainability-statistics/

Trivedi, J., Soni, S., & Kishore, A. (2020). Exploring the Role of Social Media Communications in the Success of Professional Sports Leagues: An Emerging Market Perspective. *Journal of Promotion Management*, *27*(2), 306–331. doi:10.1080/10496491.2020.1829774

Van der Waal, J. W., & Thijssens, T. (2020). Corporate involvement in Sustainable Development Goals: Exploring the territory. *Journal of Cleaner Production*, *252*, 119625. doi:10.1016/j.jclepro.2019.119625

van Zanten, J. A., & van Tulder, R. (2021). Improving companies' impacts on sustainable development: A nexus approach to the SDGS. *Business Strategy and the Environment*, *30*(8), 3703–3720. doi:10.1002/bse.2835

Voorveld, H. A. M. (2019). Brand Communication in Social Media: A Research Agenda. *Journal of Advertising*, *48*(1), 14–26. doi:10.1080/00913367.2019.1588808

Wang, X., Pacho, F., Liu, J., & Kajungiro, R. (2019). Factors Influencing Organic Food Purchase Intention in Developing Countries and the Moderating Role of Knowledge. *Sustainability (Basel)*, *11*(1), 209–221. doi:10.3390u11010209

Yamane, T., & Kaneko, S. (2021). Impact of raising awareness of Sustainable Development Goals: A survey experiment eliciting stakeholder preferences for corporate behavior. *Journal of Cleaner Production*, *28*(5), 125291. doi:10.1016/j.jclepro.2020.125291

Yıldırım, S. (2021). Do green women influencers spur sustainable consumption patterns? Descriptive evidences from social media influencers. *Ecofeminism and Climate Change*, *2*(4), 198–210. doi:10.1108/EFCC-02-2021-0003

KEY TERMS AND DEFINITIONS

Business Performance: Overall business performance can be defined as the ability of a business to implement a strategy to achieve organizational objectives and is considered as an important tool for businesses to analyze how effective management is at achieving business goals.

Consumers' Perception Of Sustainability: This is how consumers perceive sustainability with particular product or service provider engagement.

Social Media Influencer: An influencer is a person who can influence the decisions of their followers because of their relationship with their audience and their knowledge and expertise. Influencers in social media are people who have built a reputation for their knowledge and expertise on a specific topic

Social Media: Social media refers to the means of interactions among people in which they create, share, and/or exchange information and ideas in virtual communities and networks. It is an internet-based form of **communication.** In 2019, Merriam-Webster defined *social media* as "forms of electronic communication (such as websites for social networking and microblogging) through which users create online communities to share information, ideas, personal messages, and other content (such as videos)."

Sustainability Perception Of Business: This refers to how business firms and their activities are perceived to be eco friendly.

Sustainability Performance: It is the harmonization of environmental and financial objectives in the delivery of core business activities to maximize value.

Chapter 8
Importance of Sustainable Marketing Initiatives for Supporting the Sustainable Development Goals

A. Anuradha
https://orcid.org/0000-0003-1026-3798
Cambridge Institute of Technology, Bengaluru, India

R. Shilpa
Garden City University, Bengaluru, India

M. Thirupathi
https://orcid.org/0000-0001-7976-6073
CHRIST University (Deemed), Bengaluru, India

S. Padmapriya
CHRIST University (Deemed), Bengaluru, India

Gopalakrishnan Supramaniam
https://orcid.org/0000-0002-2158-7483
Acharya Institute of Graduate Studies, Bengaluru, India

Bharath Booshan
Acharya Institute of Graduate Studies, Bengaluru, India

Shabista Booshan
ISBR Business School, Bengaluru, India

Naveen Pol
https://orcid.org/0000-0002-6113-4665
ISBR Business School, Bengaluru, India

Chandan A. Chavadi
https://orcid.org/0000-0002-7214-5888
Presidency Business School, Presidency College, Bengaluru, India

Dhanabalan Thangam
https://orcid.org/0000-0003-1253-3587
Presidency Business School, Presidency College, Bengaluru, India

ABSTRACT

Businesses that engage in sustainable marketing can benefit both the world and their bottom line. Earlier, companies could satisfy many customers by simply providing low pricing and high-quality goods. However, people's concern for the environment and other social concerns have grown, and so has their desire to support groups that share their beliefs. Because they often generate strong market returns and

DOI: 10.4018/978-1-6684-8681-8.ch008

demonstrate durability during economic downturns, many investors want to support businesses that use sustainable business methods. Also, these businesses are more likely to comply with social and environmental laws. Several companies use sustainable marketing to succeed in today's ethical and ecologically sensitive marketplace. Organizations must finance sustainability programs in order to practice sustainable marketing. But, it can also improve employee engagement, promote regulatory compliance, raise revenues, and build brand loyalty.

INTRODUCTION

Sustainability has grown in importance as a topic in the modern world. Customers are searching for businesses that reflect their values as they become more conscious of the environmental and social effects of their shopping decisions. To combat this, businesses have started using sustainable marketing techniques that take into account the effects that their operations have on society and the environment. This kind of marketing sometimes referred to as eco-friendly marketing or green marketing, aims to strike a balance between the requirements of the company and those of society and the environment. Because of this, using sustainable marketing can help companies connect with their target market and set themselves apart from rivals (World Economic Forum, 2021).Moreover, environmentally responsible corporate practices and reduced environmental impact can be achieved with the aid of sustainable marketing. Businesses can make decisions that improve both their bottom line and the environment by thinking about the long-term effects of their marketing operations. In general, sustainable marketing is important because it enables companies to be more accountable and transparent while also establishing connections with customers who are interested in eco-friendly goods and services. Sustainable marketing may also aid in addressing some of the most important ecological and social issues of our time, such as social injustice, deforestation, and climate change (outlook, 2023). Businesses can accelerate the shift to a more sustainable and just future by promoting sustainable products and practices. Using the following measures will help organizations adopt sustainable marketing;

Companies must use Packaging and promotional items made from environmentally friendly materials. Concentrating more on goods and services' durable advantages rather than temporary sales. Assisting neighborhood and eco-friendly companies. Companies should diminish waste by switching from conventional print materials to digital marketing strategies like email marketing and social media advertising. Need to find some compensating ways and means for carbon emissions caused by business operations like manufacturing and transportation. Educate the consumers about environmentally friendly options and how to minimize their impact (IMD, 2022).Furthermore, because many of the Sustainable Development Goals (SDGs) are directly tied to marketing activities, sustainable marketing is strongly aligned with the SDGs established by the United Nations. SDG 12, which strives to make sure accountable consumption and manufacturing, is an illustration of how marketing strategies are directly connected to this goal.

The SDGs SDG 3 (excellent health and well-being), SDG 7 (cheap and clean energy), and SDG 13 are also pertinent to sustainable marketing (climate action). Companies may help accomplish the SDGs and increase their long-term sustainability and prosperity by aligning their marketing strategies with these global objectives (Anwar & El-Bassiouny, 2019). This can promote client trust and loyalty as well as a more favorable perception of the business among stakeholders.

Similarly to this, businesses must embrace sustainable marketing strategies, but it is also crucial to teach the next wave of management experts. Future management professionals should understand the value of sustainable marketing since it enables companies to uphold their moral and environmental commitments while simultaneously improving their bottom line. It will be crucial for people to comprehend and apply sustainable marketing strategies in their careers as management experts. This can assist them in positioning their businesses as industry leaders in sustainability and in developing more environmentally and socially conscious business strategies (Thangam &Chavadi, 2023).

METHODOLOGY

This current chapter is solely based on secondary data sources, and it was created after analyzing scientific journals from authoritative sources like Google Scholar, MDPI journals, Wiley Online Library, Sage Journal System, Science Direct, and Springer Link. Together with these sources, the keywords Sustainable marketing, Evolution of Sustainable Marketing, Advantages of Sustainable Marketing, and Significance of Sustainable Marketing have also been used in online sources.The most recent data about sustainable marketing and its measures to achieve sustainable development has been gathered from the search. Accordingly this chapter has been structured. The second section of the chapter deals with the progression of sustainable marketing, third section deals with importance of sustainable marketing, sustainable marketing practices and its contribution towards sustainability in the fourth section, fifth section explains the benefits of sustainable marketing, strategies for successful sustainable marketing placed in the seventh section, stages and levels of sustainable marketing strategy has explained in the eight section and final section concludes the work with suggestions.

The Progression of Sustainable Marketing

Organizations' environmental, social, and governance (ESG) activities are at the heart of sustainable marketing. The idea originated from green marketing, a subset of advertising that primarily emphasizes the environment (Diez-Martin, Blanco-Gonzalez& Prado-Roman, 2019). When the environmental repercussions of the industrial revolution became more obvious, green marketing began to take shape. In the 1960s, there were minimal environmental controls in place, which led to an increase in air and waterway pollution. To encourage more ethical business practices, the U.S. and European Union (EU) put into effect significant environmental restrictions at the beginning of the 1970s. While many company executives saw it as a niche activity, several firms employed green marketing methods during this time to gain the trust of environmentally sensitive consumers (Park et al, 2022).

The 1990s saw an upsurge in public interest in climate issues as a result of moremedia attention given to the subject. As a result, there was a little increasein interest in green marketing. Some businesses developed environmentallyfriendly marketing campaigns to promote recycling and energy-saving products.The majority of businesses, however, continue to view environmental preservationand green marketing as optional and expensive efforts. Later, in 2004, the UNissued a report urging governments, investors, and financial analysts to givefirms' ESG practices more attention. Many businesses then started ESGinitiatives and sustainable marketing campaigns. Since the middle of the 2000s,customers' awareness of environmental and social issues has grown, andsustainable marketing has spread among corporations (Thangam &Chavadi,2023).

Importance of Sustainable Marketing

Consumers may hold brands accountable for the state of the environment to the tune of up to 33%. Companies need to implement sustainable marketing strategies to achieve these expectations. Around 95% of the decisions to buy are made subconsciously. Emotion has a significant influence on whether or not customers will make a purchase. By stepping up your sustainability efforts, you can sway customers' purchasing decisions by appealing to their emotions. Yet, exceeding client expectations comes before the significance of sustainable marketing. Society requires a general change towards sustainable marketing if society is to survive as living things. The effects on the environment of carrying on as the society is today could be disastrous (Athwal, Wells, Carrigan&Henninger, 2019). Hence society must change economic practices to have less of an adverse effect on the environment. Although there are many advantages to sustainable marketing, they can be categorized into three groups and explained the same in Figure.1.

People

Any corporation or business is composed of the public and created to give out people as well. Devoid of people, no one would be around to purchase goods. Sustainable marketing facilitates achieving this by building a community and surroundings where people may thrive in this generation and the one after. A flourishing business must support its employees (Kemper &Ballantine, 2019). Furthermore, by giving

Figure 1. Sustainable marketing categories

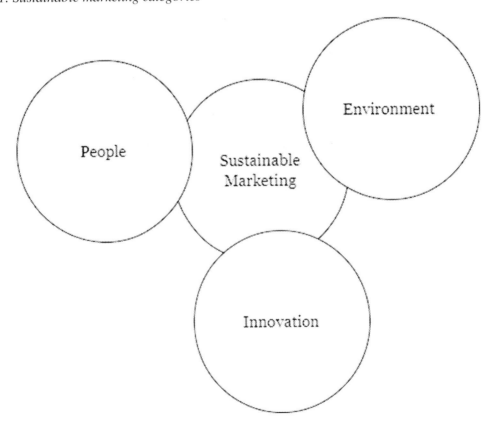

customers a shared cause to support by buying specific brand items, sustainable marketing improves the bonds between businesses and consumers. Sustainable marketing strategies combine action with truthful messaging, appealing to the conscientious consumer of today (Martha Kendall, 2021). A company will have the chance to build solid, long-lasting relationships with its customers when it offers them high-quality, environmentally friendly products.

Environment

Despite the planet's vital importance to economic processes, multinational enterprises significantly harm the condition of our world. By using these behaviors as a competitive advantage, businesses can use sustainable marketing to transform their negative impacts into positive ones. The objective is to identify the environmental issues that the target audience of the business is passionate about, the business' impact on those issues, and what the business can do to bring about positive change (Martha Kendall, 2021).

Innovation

Due to the positive effects that innovation has on consumers, businesses that place a high priority on it frequently experience increased customer loyalty. Businesses are rewarded with a competitive advantage, higher market share, and favorable press when they apply innovation to reduce their carbon footprint and contribute to the ecosystem. Sustainable marketing strategies focus on long-term goals rather than just short-term financial gains (Martha Kendall, 2021). Consumers favor businesses with forward-thinking, long-term objectives that give back to their communities.

Sustainable Marketing Practices and Its Contribution Towards Sustainability: A Collection of Worldwide Reality

Humans have been using natural resources for years, which have resulted in problems including climate change, air pollution, waste generation, and biodiversity loss. Failure to solve these problems would harm the environment irreparably and may jeopardize the survival of future generations. 17 goals have been set by the UN to achieve sustainability, some of which include gender equality, responsible consumption and production, climate action, and excellent health and well-being (Amoako, Dzogbenuku, Doe &Adjaison, 2022). These objectives demand that businesses, governments, and individuals start operating more sustainably right away.

Creating, conveying, and providing value to customers in a way that both natural and human capital are conserved or improved throughout is what is meant by sustainable marketing (Martin & Schouten, 2014). Cassman and Grassini (2020) define sustainable marketing as "planning, organizing, implementing and controlling marketing resources and programs to satisfy consumers' demands and requirements, while considering social and environmental factors and meeting company objectives". Both definitions emphasize how sustainable marketing works to protect or improve the environment and human capital, but Cassman and Grassini also stress how it works to help businesses achieve their goals.

Society must unite and take action to create a sustainable future to meet long-term sustainability goals. To bring about behavioral changes in society, marketing may play a crucial role in delivering innovative and compelling information. Social marketing and green marketing are two marketing sub-disciplines that could be used to hasten sustainability and sustainable development (Gordon, Carrigan, and Hastings,

2011). Social marketing is the theory and practice of promoting an idea, cause, or behavior, according to Kotler and Zaltman (1971). Social marketing could be used to encourage consumption and demand reduction to create a sustainable future. Many examples from the recent past demonstrate how successful brands have promoted their environmental initiatives.

Air pollution harms many cities throughout the world. A study on the Chinese tourism industry, (Huang, 2012) revealed that every 1% rise in air pollution might reduce visitor arrivals by 1.24% and negatively affect the tourism and hospitality sectors, underscoring the devastating effects that air pollution can have on contemporary economies. In 2017, Madrid was one of the cities that experienced significant levels of air pollution. The Madrid city council established measures to minimize the number of vehicles on the road by encouraging people to use car-sharing services and lower their carbon footprint to address this issue by utilizing public policies and social marketing (Melović, Cirović, Backovic-Vulić, Dudić, &Gubiniova, 2020). The "Truth Campaign," which ran from 1998 to 2003 in Florida, prejudiced youngsters not to smoke by making them conscious of the actuality of the tobacco industry and how millions of dollars are exhausted on marketing tobacco products to deceive young people (Trivedi, Trivedi, &Goswami, 2018). This is similar to how social marketing played a significant role in motivating people to start adapting to concepts like carsharing and consumption reduction in Madrid (Peattie and Peattie, 2009). The Truth campaign offers yet another viewpoint on social marketing and its influence on consumer behavior. It makes the case that marketers should stress reality and the reasons for the change needed rather than instructing their target audience on what to do.

Boundaries that apply to both consumers and corporations might be set by public policies. Governments could battle resource scarcity by employing demarketing tactics to induce a demand decrease. For instance, one local regime in California had to utilize a demarketing approach to cut back on industries' and consumers' water consumption to address a persistent water scarcity (Kotler, 2011). Demarketing efforts may help address issues like energy squandering, overfishing, and corpulence, among many others that impede sustainable development, as indicated by Kotler(2011).

Also, marketers have the chance to reconsider the four Ps of marketing and adjust to the idea of the circular economy, which is a production and consumption model that prioritizes sharing, renting, recycling, revamping, renovating, and reuse of pre-existing resources and goods (European Parliament, 2015). To reduce trash and carbon footprints, firms may develop biodegradable and reusable products in a nearby production facility, price them according to their level of ecological responsiveness, and advertise them online by rethinking the four Ps of marketing (Kotler, 2011). IKEA, a Swedish furniture retailer, is an illustration of it. It produces furniture using more than 10% recycled and 60% renewable materials, and by 2030 it wants all of its goods to be circular.

While increasing profits and economic return is still a common goal for many firms (McDonagh, Prothero, 2014), it can be argued that incorporating social and environmental value into business proposals will eventually lead to an increase in a company's overall performance and profitability. According to research (Menon and Menon, 1999), innovation is significantly influenced by sustainability. For instance, if companies challenged the traditional ways that people function by bringing cutting-edge, environmentally friendly technologies, such an effort would open new markets that had never existed before and provide opportunities to make more money (Nidumolu, et al., 2009).

Tesla, an electric vehicle manufacturer that is reinventing the automotive industry, is a shining example of how to seize an opportunity by developing innovations that could address major environmental and sustainability issues. Traditional road vehicles utilize fuel, which contributes to noise and air pollution, but Tesla's electric automobiles offer a greener alternative to traditional vehicles. Many people may aspire to own an electric car, but the infrastructure needed to recharge the vehicle is one of the major issues making it challenging for consumers to adapt. Tesla saw this as an opportunity and set about building the largest network of charging stations in the United States (Andries and Stephan, 2019). This resulted in significant upfront fixed costs, but the business attempted to address the main issues that discouraged consumers from choosing electric cars over conventional vehicles. Tesla released the Model 3 in 2016, and it was an immediate success, garnering more than 400,000 pre-orders so far (Fernandes, Ferreira, Lobo &Raposo, 2020). Market acceptance of Tesla's unorthodox products is high. Its success can be ascribed to the fact that businesses can ultimately construct novel markets in their desire to make the planet more sustainable. One important take away from this instance is that Tesla focused on the three sustainable marketing pillars of economic success, social responsibility, and environmental responsibility (Ahmad, & Khan, 2019). As a result, Tesla was able to develop skills that increased profits and gave it an edge over rivals.

Consumers may increasingly be aware of the effects of unsustainable corporate practices, according to a previous study. Consumers today "carry fresh concerns, questions, and fears," according to Kotler (2011). Will they still be employed? Will they be able to retire with adequate money? Will the amount of traffic worsen? Will the air become increasingly contaminated? Such actions show a shift in attitudes toward the demand for goods and services that would contribute to a sustainable future. This might also be a factor in the positive reception Tesla's first electric vehicle received from the general population. Unilever developed a marketing effort to allay consumers' worries about the sustainable conduct of business: A short film called Project Sunshine showcases some of Unilever's sustainability initiatives. According to Marc Mathieu, senior vice president of marketing, "We aim to leverage the Unilever brand as a Trustmark for sustainable living" (Ziolo, Bak, &Cheba, 2021). Such a brand's incorporation of sustainability-based values into its fundamental principles may foster closer ties with customers who share these goals for the advancement of society. In five different nations, the Project Sunlight ad campaign produced 77 million views and 3 million website visits (Think With Google, 2014). Project Sunshine serves as an illustration of how marketers may leverage ethical business practices to enhance brand perception.

It's a win-win situation for businesses and the environment because firms can justify charging more for their products by supporting green projects (Peterson, Minton, Liu & Bartholomew, 2021; Gordon, Carrigan, and Hastings, 2011). From a public or practitioner standpoint, "green marketing refers to the marketing of products and services that are perceived to be ecologically preferable to others," Another study by Wymer and Polonsky (2015) demonstrates that higher profitability and ongoing sustainable production are positively correlated. So, companies can charge higher prices for their products and increase their profitability if they engage in activities like green marketing and sustainable production.

It is no secret that unethical business activities can cause customers to turn against a specific company. According to Kotler (2011), "word of mouth is impacting consumer decisions with increasing vigor. Customers may email, blog, and tweet positive or negative comments about a business to their friends and acquaintances. For instance, Nestle faced harsh criticism for working with a company that was connected to deforestation on YouTube, Facebook, and Twitter. Nestle stopped its collaboration with the vendor to protect its brand reputation (Metz, Burek, Hultgren, Kogan, & Schwartz, 2016). As a result, businesses that employ sustainable methods not only gain a competitive edge but also prevent consumer backlash that could harm their brand's reputation.

Some brands focus on increasing demand for their products to increase consumption, which therefore results in greater sales, while others use transactional activities just to maximize profits. Even if these companies produce and market green products, rising use will eventually lead to environmental degradation (Kotler, 2011). Selling environmentally friendly goods alone would not meet sustainability goals, thus businesses must also encourage consumption reduction. Doing demarketing initiatives to reduce consumption volume can lead to a conflict of interest within a company because marketers are the ones who develop sales volume (Kotler and Levy, 1971). This could be cited as another disadvantage of using a sustainable strategy.

There is some evidence to support the idea that companies find a middle ground where they can engage in sustainable practices and yet make money. (Berrone& Gomez-Mejia, 2009) proposed a few explanations for this behavior, including the possibility of bankruptcy, a decline in profitability, or the potential to discontinue profit-based remuneration incentives. This restricts how far a company may act sustainably and outside the bounds of its profitability levels. However, this result runs counter to the notion that profitable marketing practices should be sustainable. Due to the potential negative effects on short-term profitability, corporations do not want to address environmental concerns that call for changes in manufacturing technology or the creation of environmentally friendly alternatives. This elucidates why major automakers chose not to mass produce electric cars despite having the means to do so, as opposed to Tesla, which specialized in the production of electric vehicles and invented a market that had never been before (Trivedi, Trivedi&Goswami, 2018). So, brands won't be able to develop a distinct competitive edge that would eventually translate into larger profits unless they spend more on technical advancements to boost sustainable manufacturing.

Benefits of Sustainable Marketing

Organizations' relationships with the environment and their stakeholders can be strengthened through sustainable marketing. Additionally, this tactic can assist businesses in enhancing customer loyalty, enhancing staff satisfaction, achieving regulatory compliance, and boosting revenue. Consumers that are socially and ecologically sensitive might develop brand loyalty for businesses that sincerely practice sustainable marketing (Murphy, 2005). Brand loyalty is a dedication to a company or product based on the brand's values and perceived reliability. Businesses may see a rise in customer retention rates if they successfully tie their brand image to a more important environmental or social cause, such as the battle against discrimination or climate change. Even when competitors offer lower pricing, brand-loyal customers generally make repeated purchases. Recurring business can provide a sizable amount of revenue and costs businesses less in advertising than acquiring new customers (Danciu, 2013).Martek et al, (2019) Employees want to believe that the job they perform has a good impact, just as customers prefer to spend money with companies that share their values. Sincere sustainable marketing calls for firms to enhance their (Environmental, Social, and Governance) ESG procedures, which can increase employee motivation. Those who work for companies that place a high priority on ESG may have a sense of fulfillment as they appreciate sustainability. The social component of ESG, social sustainability, is another tool organizations can use to potentially enhance employee quality of life. For instance, a company might adopt a flexible paid time off policy to put long-term success ahead of employee work-life balance. Such a social sustainability program can lower turnover and raise employee satisfaction (Jain, Sharma, &Srivastava, 2019).

Business executives need to think about the social and environmental impacts of their enterprises before launching sustainable marketing efforts. Before engaging in sustainable marketing, a company could, for instance, lower its greenhouse gas emissions and freely report them. A rising variety of ESG regulations can be complied with by firms using these procedures. For instance, the corporate sustainability reporting requirement, which increased the number of firms needed to publicly disclose their ESG data, was finalized by the EU in January 2023. Similar to this, in March 2022 the U.S. Securities and Exchange Commission suggested an extended version of its reporting standards, which it may have finalized by spring 2023. Large U.S. organizations would have to publish environmental information, like greenhouse gas emissions, in regular reports under the enhanced standards (Makenzie Holland, 2022). Organizations are encouraged by sustainable marketing to enhance their social and environmental business practices, which can assist them in complying with the rules that are in place now and those that may be implemented in the future (Nekmahmud, &Fekete-Farkas, 2020).Because they often necessitate expensive upfront investments, sustainability programs have historically been seen by many corporate leaders as barriers to success. Sustainable business methods, however, can boost an organization's earnings. A sustainable marketing campaign, for instance, can focus on how much energy and water an organization uses. Organizations can save operational expenses by implementing more energy-efficient technologies, appliances, and procedures. ESG ratings, which measure an organization's long-term exposure to environmental and social hazards, are another tool used by investors to find successful investments (Gil-Gomez, Guerola-Navarro, Oltra-Badenes& Lozano-Quilis, 2020).Investor investment may be more generous for companies with strong ESG ratings than for others, which may open up prospects for expansion and boost earnings. Organizations can increase their competitiveness in their marketplaces by implementing sustainable marketing strategies. Yet if companies deliberately or unintentionally misrepresent their sustainability measures, a technique known as "greenwashing," their campaigns may suffer (Tim Murphy, 2023). Companies can engage with sustainability consultants to discover how to implement efficient ESG efforts before launching sustainable marketing campaigns. Apart from these, a company can enjoy the benefits presented in Table 1;

Enhances Brand Recognition and Gives Companies a Competitive Edge

The best companies are those that can out-compete their rivals. Only those that differentiate themselves can successfully build and extend their businesses when there are so many business owners vying for the same clientele. Making sure the company has a better offer than its rivals is one of the simplest methods to keep clients coming back to the business. Make sure to position the brand so that potential clients and buyers find it impossible to resist. Even if promotion is great, it is simpler to get results when buyers are aware that products consistently offer the cheapest prices. For instance, knowing what pleases our clients is helpful as a business. Some clients will only purchase goods or visit the business if the company adheres to following the environment essential measures. When consumers and clients have enough faith in a brand, it can quickly become sustainable. Once clients are persuaded of this, conduct-

Table 1. Benefits of sustainable marketing

10.Ensures the Survival of the Company	1.Enhances Brand Recognition and Gives Companies a Competitive Edge	2.Reduces Expenses and Boosts Productivity	3.Makes it Simple for the Company to Adhere to Rules
9.Sustainable Marketing Helps and Encourages Innovation	**Benefits of Sustainable Marketing**		4.Helps to Attract Investors and Employees
8.Minimization of Waste	7.Customers are drawn To Businesses for the Indented Purpose	6.Enhances Worker Retention	5.Tax Advantages

ing business becomes simple (Christensen, 2013). Invest in the appropriate channels to advance your company to this level.

Reduces Expenses and Boosts Productivity

Our overarching objective should be to make sure that our firm becomes sustainable, regardless of whether we are physically present or are thinking about acquiring the greatest virtual office in one location. The company will eventually reach a point where earnings flow easily, which is one of the major benefits of operating an eco-friendly corporation. When an industry achieves financial stability, it can continue to grow and expand without necessarily needing more resources. As processes are already optimized and the necessary paths to success are ensured, it translates to outstanding productivity. Because it has previously determined what works and what doesn't, a sustainable firm rarely goes through trial and error phases. As a result, managing growth is simple because the influencing factors are widely known. The business's profit margins inevitably increase as production costs decrease. Although it may appear expensive at first, business owners should be prepared to invest significantly more when testing solutions (Atz, Van Holt, Douglas & Whelan, 2021). It will eventually pay off and increase profitability after everything is closed, therefore it is worth the effort.

Makes it Simple for the Company to Adhere to Rules

Several of the legislative standards set forth by the government for the sector are simple to implement when a company concentrates on its sustainability and long-term performance. Most governments are moving in to fix the issues as a result of the ongoing uproar regarding environmental degradation and the role that corporations play in this deterioration. As a result, several regulating measures that support the safe operation of enterprises and industries without harming the environment have been introduced. As a result, several rules have been developed. Such standards are simple to follow for businesses that concentrate on developing a sustainable business because they allow for such occurrences. Such businesses deliberately choose to follow guidelines that would lead them to the subsequent level (Atz, Van Holt, Douglas & Whelan, 2021).

Helps to Attract Investors and Employees

Sustainability is typically a good thing that offers the business many benefits. Most people today choose to do business with organizations that are concerned about the environment and the benefits society can provide. Hence, having sustainable methods for resolving client difficulties makes it simple to draw in talented and energetic staff as well as possible investors. This is one of the components that any company requires. Employees that are capable and well-intentioned can easily advance your company and support success. After all, nobody wants to be associated with irresponsible businesses that worsen the effects on the environment and nearby communities (Marcel &Dragan, 2014). It becomes simple for employees to decide to work for a company once they are aware of how well-regarded and cherished it is in the neighborhood. Make sure this is the image your company projects by opting to use sustainable production techniques. A straightforward action like organizing regular neighborhood cleanups as one of your company's community service activities will assist develop the proper mindset. Also, the neighborhood where your company operates is likely to support you. Having such a serene workplace attracts potential employees. Since your business is not involved in any complicated legal disputes or lawsuits, investors will likewise feel secure investing with the company (Nkamnebe, 2011). Nevertheless, profitable shareholders typically result from sustainable enterprises. Profits are considered to rise when a business' operating expenses are typically low. As a result, shareholder profit margins increase and the risks are decreased. When a profitable business informs an investor that such potential success will be profitable, they won't shy away from it.

Tax Advantages

Eco-friendly practices and the use of renewable energy boost your likelihood of obtaining numerous tax advantages. This is among the most significant advantages of sustainability in business. According to research titled "Going Green in Canada," a firm can take advantage of the Income Tax Act's accelerated Capital Cost Allowance (CCA) by deducting expenses related to the production of sustainable energy.

Enhances Worker Retention

Sustainable business practices are said to make employees happier, feel better-taken care of, and be more productive at work. As a positive byproduct of this, businesses can use sustainable practices as a powerful tool in their personnel retention strategy. According to a global study, 46% of professionals will only work for companies that follow sustainable business practices, and 61% of professionals believe that firm sustainability is essential (AmitGhodasara, 2022).

Customers Are Drawn to Businesses for the Indented Purpose

Due to their green purchasing and consumption habits, Generation Z and Millennials, who now have purchasing power, are pressuring companies to push their sustainability goals. Customers now take into account a product or service's social and environmental impact in addition to its exterior features. Sixty-five percent of all consumer goods sales that were monitored internationally were produced by brands whose marketing demonstrated a commitment to social and/or environmental value.

Minimization of Waste

The likelihood of resource waste is also decreased when companies use sustainable production methods. Recycling would be one of the best practices for a company to undertake to make sure that all resources are used effectively. Since all business managers need to pinpoint places where recycling might benefit the system and operations, fortunately, this is a simple task to complete. To further ensure that fewer resources are consumed at all times, the recycling process should be generally prioritized. Also, it is important to promote among employees the use of efficient methods to reduce waste (AmitGhodasara, 2022).

Sustainable Marketing Helps and Encourages Innovation

Redesigning products, processes, or systems to accommodate new approaches may be necessary as a company makes the transition to more sustainable business practices. By doing this, businesses can encourage innovation and originality among their staff members and vendors.

Ensures the Survival of the Company

All different sorts of businesses use natural resources in one way or another. Both water and the land on which businesses are built are essential. If natural resources become scarce or if disasters strike the business sector, businesses will struggle to survive and grow. Consequently, adopting sustainable practices promotes business continuity by saving or replenishing available resources and putting in place plans for catastrophe prevention and preparation (AmitGhodasara, 2022).

Thus it could understand that sustainable marketing is a great one not only for the business but also for all the stakeholders. This does not imply that it can be accomplished fast. Companies might reach a point where they are recognized as sustainable if they work hard, are committed, and are persistent. Since it pays off, patience is a virtue. Using sustainable methods in their everyday operations can benefit staff, investors, and business owners alike. Businesses that care about the environment should concentrate on obtaining this degree of sustainability for future development.

Strategies for Successful Sustainable Marketing

With traditional marketing, gaining the public's trust is crucial, but in sustainable marketing, it is everything. Marketers must interact with clients in a way that strengthens their ties with them while simultaneously promoting the company brand. There are some other ways a company can be sustainable in its brand beyond simply sticking a sticker on the item. Figure.2 explains the successful sustainable marketing strategies.

Figure 2. Successful sustainable marketing strategies

Use a Customer-Focused Strategy

Making sure that your sustainable marketing plan is customer-centric is the first step. This entails comprehending the meaning of sustainability to your target market and adjusting your sustainable marketing strategies accordingly. In contrast to conventional marketing techniques, consumer-oriented marketing involves more than simply forcing a product down the audience's throat. It involves paying attention to and figuring out what your customers want from your business and the values they expect the business to prioritize. For instance, you can provide the information on your website and marketing materials if the audience requests additional clarity or openness regarding the company's sustainability policies or carbon emissions (Rudawska, 2019). When companies attempt to capitalize on the "sustainable boom," those who don't listen frequently end up being labeled as tone-deaf. Make sure that the entire pipeline is carefully built to listen to and apply what consumers genuinely want to see in the organization's sustainability initiatives.

Establish a Goal

Sustainability marketing promotes a company's broader objectives and vision rather than concentrating on a specific product. Instead of focusing just on advertising the company's goods or services, a green marketing plan should be developed around effectively communicating the sustainability objective of the organization. By establishing a mission, the company may provide the audience with a coherent story by centering the narrative on a single objective. This enables the company to better engage with environmentally conscious customers, who frequently seek out businesses that share their values and aspirations for leaving a lasting impact (TrivediTrivedi&Goswami, 2018). Companies with a more conventional, product-focused marketing strategy will have an advantage over the company if the company conveys that its business is in it for the long run. Starbucks is one business that has a great sustainability objective. It seeks to become resource-positive or to contribute more to the environment than it consumes. The coffee chain accomplishes this by obtaining its coffee beans ethically and responsibly, lowering its water usage and carbon emissions, and minimizing the amount of garbage it dumps in landfills (Hitesh Bhasin, 2021).

Be Dependable

The defined goal is expanded upon by this tactic. Having a unified message to convey is necessary for consistency. When a company's efforts to promote sustainability are intermittent or half-hearted, it gives the appearance that it only practices sustainability when it is advantageous or profitable. Businesses must align their sustainability marketing with their business operations to gain the audience's trust. Customers will recognize the deception if a company's marketing touts a product as being environmentally friendly even when its business operations are everything. Say, for instance, that the company promise to lower its carbon emissions. For the same, the company must demonstrate that the organization is making the necessary preparations (Jung, Kim, & Kim, 2020). Customers expect to see proof of companies' dedication, whether that means putting solar panels in factories or moving to other sustainable energy sources. Wolven is a fantastic illustration of a business that backs up its claims. The company's strategy is to "make sustainability sexy" by creating fashionable apparel from recycled plastics.

Be Truthful

Consumers place a premium on authenticity. Consumers that care about sustainability are searching for businesses they can rely on to be open and honest about their sustainable practices. This calls for being open and truthful about both the company's strengths and its areas for development. For instance, if a business strives for environmentally friendly packaging but continues to use non-recyclable materials, be upfront about it in the company's marketing. The company can take advantage of this to demonstrate to the audience that the business is aware of the problem and is trying to find a solution. For instance, an individual could admit that their business still has a ways to go before fully adopting sustainable packaging, but that the organization's ultimate objective is to eliminate all plastic from its supply chain by 2030. The target audience can be reached through social media, which is a crucial route (Jessica La, 2022).

Aim Higher

A company shouldn't simply latch onto any environmental popular subject on Twitter. The secret to sustainable marketing is to take an internal and external perspective. What issues are current in the field you work in? Which issues is your business best suited to address? This enables the business to create long-lasting campaigns as well as sustainable marketing tactics that are socially and environmentally responsible. One of the existing instances of eBay's sustainable marketing is the toilet paper manufacturer who gives a Crap. It concentrates its charitable activities and marketing initiatives on challenges related to sustainable health and global sanitation that are unique to its sector. As a result, the marketing for the brand is more relevant and well-intentioned (Ottman, 2011).The company's sustainability claims are actionable and driven by intent when the firm sets its eyes on creating longer-lasting plans that are concentrated on bringing about change in the organization's immediate environment. This gives the promises more credibility and provides consumers a more realistic metric to assess your success against than a generic "make the world a better place" desire. In a society that prioritizes consumption, marketers must not only convey the benefits of their goods and services but also take into account the global impact of those goods and services. Marketers can change the focus away from what makes the most money and towards what makes the most difference. Because of the consumer's increasing clout, marketers are now in a position to start significant, observable change. Becoming green is just one aspect of sustainability. It entails creating more durable structures that improve rather than harm the environment (Major sustainability, 2022).

Stages and Levels of Sustainable Marketing Strategy

Marketing was born out of the need to make a profit and stay competitive. Indeed, the importance of sales and income generation will not change. Yet, contemporary marketing tactics also involve encouraging customers to move to more ecologically responsible usage. Ballantine and Kemper's 2019 analysis of more than 200 papers on the topic revealed three layers of interaction that constitute sustainable marketing strategy such as;

- Causing Less harm
- More positive action
- Doing things differently

Causing Less Harm

This kind of sustainable marketing strategy "encapsulates the bulk of sustainability marketing viewpoints as it focuses on change inside existing structures or arrangements," according to Ballantine and Kemper. Examining three characteristics of products is part of the Doing Less Wrong method (Griffin LaFleur, 2023).

- Production circumstances - how products are made, e.g. child labor, working conditions, emissions from production.
- Product attributes - what the product contains and what it does
- Exposures and dangers - how product use affects people and the environment.
- The concepts of private consumption and product ownership are not questioned by Causing Less harm. These factors are related to Doing things differently and More Good.

More Positive Action

More Positive Action "acknowledges that current consumption levels are unsustainable, reflecting often either the unequal distribution of wealth between wealthy and developing countries or the Earth's limiting resources." More Positive Action is centered on encouraging sustainable lifestyles as opposed to Doing Less Bad, which is focused on promoting sustainable products (Tollin, & Christensen, 2019). Moving from the more positive action phase of sustainable marketing strategy involves three significant changes:

- From exclusive proprietorship to renting and sharing
- Shifting from a focus on the needs of the consumer to those of external stakeholders.
- From a sales orientation to an education orientation

Doing Things Differently

According to Ballantine and Kemper, Doing things differently "seeks to transform the institutions that impede the transition to a sustainable society... prioritizing sustainability over profit and tackling the obstacles to sustainable purchasing that consumers encounter, such as our persuasive consumption mindset, institutional hurdles, and societal conventions. Together with sustainable lives and products, Doing Different is committed to advancing sustainable systems and institutions. Although Doing Different is aware that many products and consumption paradigms need to be disrupted, there is a focus on promoting and supporting social enterprise. The disruptions brought about by start-ups looking for lucrative solutions to social and environmental problems can be supported through marketing (Major sustainability, 2022).

CONCLUSION

Sustainable marketing is not just a crucial component; it is also a requirement and the only path forward. Companies should concentrate on obtaining their raw materials from sustainable sources and should support the community in any manner they can. To expand the company, they must concentrate on the three bottom lines of the firm. Every company should use sustainable marketing as a long-term plan to ensure their future viability, rather than as a short-term goal.Patagonia is a best example for its green business practices.Patagonia is concerned about climate change and works to produce its products in more environmentally responsible ways. Additionally, it is truthful with customers by admitting that the jackets' outer shells are made of less-than-green fossil fuels. This fact won't have an impact on the brand's reputation as long as the neighbourhood can sense the company's sincere desire to preserve our planet.One of the business's most effective environmental programmes is the Common Threads Recycling Programme. Its objective was to provide customers more ways to utilise products they had already purchased.Patagonia has been a registered B Corporation for the past five years and has consistently received a "outstanding" rating (151). The Fashion Transparency Index gave the Ventura, California-based business a 60 percent acceptability grade after conducting an audit of it in 2020.For the same this company has planned to not touse virgin petroleum fibre by 2025. To oppose Big Oil, recycled polyester is used to make Better Sweater® coats. They have stopped the atmospheric release of 14.6 million pounds of CO_2 since autumn 2019. By 2025, the packaging will be 100 percent recyclable, biodegradable, and reusable. On hangtags and packaging, they are using algal ink, reducing plastic, and using QR code technology to reduce paper by 100,000 pounds annually. The company will have zero net debt by 2030. In order to reduce their carbon footprint to 1.5 C, they are first creating less harmful products. With the conversion to post-consumer recycled polyester insulation in 2020, emissions from the Nano Puff® jacket were cut in half (Lizzie Davey, 2022).One of the factors driving the growth of sustainable marketing is customers' raising awareness of and concern for environmental issues. They are therefore more inclined to look for goods and services that are sustainable and kind to the environment. To appeal to environmentally sensitive consumers, this trend has prompted corporations to embrace more sustainable business practices and engage in sustainable marketing. Another factor driving the expansion of sustainable marketing is the mounting demand for businesses to embrace environmentally friendly practices and lessen their negative effects on the environment. TOMS is suitable example for this case. The well-known company TOMS is known for their comfortable footwear. The business's profits are used to benefit the community and the environment. On the company's website, you can see that TOMS has worked to advance sustainable practises in significant areas of its operations over the past five years. Examples of environmentally responsible marketing strategies include included using renewable cotton and waste and energy reduction strategies. The organisation behind the company also provides packaging made from recycled materials to its clients.In 2021, TOMS received a B Corp score of 121.5, which was about 30 points higher than their last evaluation from 2018. They surpass the minimum standard for a B Corporation by approximately 70 points when compared to the overall median score of all firms. According to the company's website, they have no plans to slow down (TOMS, 2021).Companies are under increasing pressure from regulators, customers, and other stakeholders to be more accountable in their business practices and supply chains. Due to this, businesses now publicly display their dedication to sustainability and set themselves apart from their competitors. Technology advancements that have made it simpler and more affordable for businesses to adopt sustainable practices can also be blamed for the expansion of sustainable marketing. Starbucks is a best example as it is one of the rare companies that has not only adopted but also remained committed to ecologically responsible business practises. Solar energy helps Starbucks use less energy overall.In addition, they have made a point of using environmentally friendly building materials in their stores. They organised a very successful Facebook effort to get people to help paint the pavements and plant trees for the city's streets. This green marketing case study was praised as a success all over the world. They're now making an effort to use recyclable cups in an effort to reduce the quantity of trash they produce.The Greener Store Framework, created in 2018 in collaboration with WWF, intends to hasten the shift of retail to lower-impact stores that cut down on carbon emissions, water use, and landfill waste. By 2025, 10,000 Greener Stores will have been developed and converted outside of North America, where Starbucks currently operates more than 2,300 Greener Stores (Starbucks, 2018).As a result, it has become more and more profitable for businesses to use green marketing and to tell customers about their environmental initiatives. In conclusion, sustainable marketing is essential to contemporary firms since it encourages consumers to make more sustainable decisions and works to increase consumer knowledge of environmental issues. Companies can not only lessen their environmental impact by promoting eco-friendly products and activities but also help society as a whole move towards sustainability.In terms of future study, a more drastic intervention might be necessary. By focusing more on integrated time rather than events, authors encourage marketing academics to better explore and problematize studies in this area. The marketing academy will succeed in enabling and guiding change in people, the environment, and larger society if it does this.

REFERENCES

Ahmad, S., & Khan, M. (2019). Tesla: Disruptor or Sustaining Innovator. *Journal of Case Research*, *10*(1).

Amit, G. (2022). 10 Advantages Of Being A Sustainable Business. Available at: https://www.ismartrecruit.com/blog-advantages-sustainable-business

Amoako, G. K., Dzogbenuku, R. K., Doe, J., & Adjaison, G. K. (2022). Green marketing and the SDGs: Emerging market perspective. *Marketing Intelligence & Planning*, *40*(3), 310–327. doi:10.1108/MIP-11-2018-0543

Andries, P., & Stephan, U. (2019). Environmental innovation and firm performance: How firm size and motives matter. *Sustainability (Basel)*, *11*(13), 3585. doi:10.3390u11133585

Anwar, Y., & El-Bassiouny, N. (2019). Marketing and the sustainable development goals (SDGs): A review and research agenda. The Future of the UN Sustainable Development Goals: Business Perspectives for Global Development in 2030, 187-207.

Athwal, N., Wells, V. K., Carrigan, M., & Henninger, C. E. (2019). Sustainable luxury marketing: A synthesis and research agenda. *International Journal of Management Reviews*, *21*(4), 405–426. doi:10.1111/ijmr.12195

Atz, U., Van Holt, T., Douglas, E., & Whelan, T. (2021). *The Return on Sustainability Investment (ROSI): Monetizing financial benefits of sustainability actions in companies. Sustainable Consumption and Production* (Vol. II). Circular Economy and Beyond.

Berrone, P., & Gomez-Mejia, L. R. (2009). Environmental performance and executive compensation: An integrated agency-institutional perspective. *Academy of Management Journal*, *52*(1), 103–126. doi:10.5465/amj.2009.36461950

Cassman, K. G., & Grassini, P. (2020). A global perspective on sustainable intensification research. *Nature Sustainability*, *3*(4), 262–268. doi:10.103841893-020-0507-8

Christensen, C. M. (2013). *The innovator's dilemma: when new technologies cause great firms to fail.* Harvard Business Review Press.

Danciu, V. (2013). The contribution of sustainable marketing to sustainable development. *Management & Marketing, 8*(2), 385.

Diez-Martin, F., Blanco-Gonzalez, A., & Prado-Roman, C. (2019). Research challenges in digital marketing: Sustainability. *Sustainability (Basel), 11*(10), 2839. doi:10.3390u11102839

European Parliament. (2015). *Circular economy: definition, importance and benefits.* European Parliament. https://www.europarl.europa.eu/news/en/headlines/economy/20151201STO05603/circular-economy-definition-importance-and-benefits#:~:text=The%20circular%20economy%20is%20a,reducing%20waste%20to%20a%20minimum

Fernandes, C. I., Ferreira, J. J., Lobo, C. A., &Raposo, M. (2020). The impact of market orientation on the internationalisation of SMEs. *Review of International Business and Strategy*.

Gil-Gomez, H., Guerola-Navarro, V., Oltra-Badenes, R., & Lozano-Quilis, J. A. (2020). Customer relationship management: digital transformation and sustainable business model innovation. *Economic research-Ekonomskaistraživanja, 33*(1), 2733-2750.

Gordon, R., Carrigan, M., & Hastings, G. (2011). A framework for sustainable marketing. *Marketing Theory, 11*(2), 143–163. doi:10.1177/1470593111403218

Gordon, R., Carrigan, M., & Hastings, G. (2011). A framework for sustainable marketing. *Marketing Theory, 11*(2), 143–163. doi:10.1177/1470593111403218

Griffin, L. (2023). 5 best practices for a sustainable marketing strategy. *Tech Target.* https://www.techtarget.com/searchcustomerexperience/tip/Best-practices-for-a-sustainable-marketing-strategy

Hitesh, B. (2021). Sustainable Marketing – Strategy, Importance and Principles. *Marketing 91.* https://www.marketing91.com/sustainable-marketing/

Huang, C. (2012). *The impact of local environmental quality on international tourism demand: The case of China.* University of San Francisco.

IMD. (2022). Why all businesses should embrace sustainability. IMD. https://www.imd.org/research-knowledge/articles/why-all-businesses-should-embrace-sustainability/

Jain, M., Sharma, G. D., & Srivastava, M. (2019). Can sustainable investment yield better financial returns: A comparative study of ESG indices and MSCI indices. *Risks, 7*(1), 15. doi:10.3390/risks7010015

Jessica, La. (2022). Sustainable Marketing Basics: 5 Strategies for Greener E-Commerce. *Spiralytics.* https://www.spiralytics.com/blog/sustainable-marketing-strategies-for-greener-ecommerce/

Jung, J., Kim, S. J., & Kim, K. H. (2020). Sustainable marketing activities of traditional fashion market and brand loyalty. *Journal of Business Research, 120*, 294–301. doi:10.1016/j.jbusres.2020.04.019

Kemper, J. A., & Ballantine, P. W. (2019). What do we mean by sustainability marketing? *Journal of Marketing Management, 35*(3-4), 277–309. doi:10.1080/0267257X.2019.1573845

Kotler, P. (2011). Reinventing marketing to manage the environmental imperative. *Journal of Marketing*, *75*(4), 132–135. doi:10.1509/jmkg.75.4.132

Kotler, P., & Levy, S. J. (1971). Demarketing, yes, demarketing. *Harvard Business Review*, *79*, 74–80.

Kotler, P., & Zaltman, G. (1971). Social marketing: An approach to planned social change. *Journal of Marketing*, *35*(3), 3–12. doi:10.1177/002224297103500302 PMID:12276120

Davey, L. (2022). 15 Green Marketing Examples to Inspire You in 2022. *Givz*. https://www.givz.com/blog/green-marketing-examples

Major Sustainability. (2022). Sustainability Marketing Strategy: Engaging Consumers in Responsible Consumption. *Major Sustainability*. https://majorsustainability.smeal.psu.edu/five-principles-of-sustainability-marketing/

Holland, M. (2022). SEC's proposed climate rule a game-changer for sustainability. *Tech Target*. https://www.techtarget.com/searchcio/news/252515034/SECs-proposed-climate-rule-a-game-changer-for-sustainability

Marcel, M., & Dragan, M. (2014, June). Sustainable marketing for sustainable development. In *Proceedings of the 11th International Academic Conference in Reykjavik* (pp. 230-248). ACM.

Marketing, S. (2014). *Schouten* (International Edition). Sustainable Marketing. D. M. J. Pearson New.

Martek, I., Hosseini, M. R., Shrestha, A., Edwards, D. J., & Durdyev, S. (2019). Barriers inhibiting the transition to sustainability within the Australian construction industry: An investigation of technical and social interactions. *Journal of Cleaner Production*, *211*, 281–292. doi:10.1016/j.jclepro.2018.11.166

Kendall, M. (2021). Sustainable Marketing: What It Is, Why It Matters, & How to Get It Right. *Unstack*. https://www.unstack.com/sustainable-marketing-what-it-is-why-it-matters-how-to-get-it-right

McDonagh, P., & Prothero, A. (2014). Sustainability marketing research: Past, present and future. *Journal of Marketing Management*, *30*(11-12), 1186–1219. doi:10.1080/0267257X.2014.943263

Melović, B., Cirović, D., Backovic-Vulić, T., Dudić, B., & Gubiniova, K. (2020). Attracting green consumers as a basis for creating sustainable marketing strategy on the organic market—Relevance for sustainable agriculture business development. *Foods*, *9*(11), 1552. doi:10.3390/foods9111552 PMID:33120944

Menon, A., Menon, A., Chowdhury, J., & Jankovich, J. (1999). Evolving paradigm for environmental sensitivity in marketing programs: A synthesis of theory and practice. *Journal of Marketing Theory and Practice*, *7*(2), 1–15. doi:10.1080/10696679.1999.11501825

Metz, P., Burek, S., Hultgren, T. R., Kogan, S., & Schwartz, L. (2016). The Path to Sustainability-Driven Innovation: Environmental sustainability can be the foundation for increasing competitive advantage and the basis for effective innovation. *Research Technology Management*, *59*(3), 50–61. doi:10.1080/08956308.2016.1161409

Murphy, P. E. (2005). Sustainable marketing. *Business & Professional Ethics Journal*, *24*(1/2), 171–198. doi:10.5840/bpej2005241/210

Nekmahmud, M., & Fekete-Farkas, M. (2020). Why not green marketing? Determinates of consumers' intention to green purchase decision in a new developing nation. *Sustainability (Basel)*, *12*(19), 7880. doi:10.3390u12197880

Nidumolu, R., Prahalad, C. K., & Rangaswami, M. R. (2009). Why sustainability is now the key driver of innovation. *Harvard Business Review*, *87*(9), 56–64.

Nkamnebe, A. D. (2011). Sustainability marketing in the emerging markets: imperatives, challenges, and agenda setting. *International Journal of Emerging Markets*.

Ottman, J. A. (2011). *The new rules of green marketing: Strategies, tools, and inspiration for sustainable branding*. Berrett-Koehler Publishers.

Outlook. (2023). *Sustainable Marketing: A Key Priority for Management Professionals Explains Dr. Adya Sharma, Director of SCMS Pune*. Microsoft. https://www.outlookindia.com/outlook-spotlight/sustainable-marketing-a-key-priority-for-management-professionals-explains-dr-adya-sharma-director-of-scms-pune-news-245162

Park, J. Y., Perumal, S. V., Sanyal, S., Ah Nguyen, B., Ray, S., Krishnan, R., Narasimhaiah, R., & Thangam, D. (2022). Sustainable Marketing Strategies as an Essential Tool of Business. *American Journal of Economics and Sociology*, *81*(2), 359–379. doi:10.1111/ajes.12459

Peattie, K., & Peattie, S. (2009). Social marketing: A pathway to consumption reduction? *Journal of Business Research*, *62*(2), 260–268. doi:10.1016/j.jbusres.2008.01.033

Rudawska, E. (2019). Sustainable marketing strategy in food and drink industry: a comparative analysis of B2B and B2C SMEs operating in Europe. *Journal of Business & Industrial Marketing*.

Starbucks. (2018). *Starbucks Announces Global Greener Stores Commitment*. Starbucks. https://stories.starbucks.com/press/2018/starbucks-announces-global-greener-stores-commitment/

Thangam, D., & Chavadi, C. (2023). Impact of Digital Marketing Practices on Energy Consumption, Climate Change, and Sustainability. *Climate and Energy*, *39*(7), 11–19. doi:10.1002/gas.22329

Murphy, T. (2023). Why is sustainable marketing important? *Tech Target*. https://www.techtarget.com/searchcustomerexperience/feature/Why-is-sustainable-marketing-important#:~:text=Sustainable%20marketing%20can%20improve%20how,with%20regulations%20and%20increase%20profits

Tollin, K., & Christensen, L. B. (2019). Sustainability marketing commitment: Empirical insights about its drivers at the corporate and functional level of marketing. *Journal of Business Ethics*, *156*(4), 1165–1185. doi:10.100710551-017-3591-6

TOMS. (2021). *Overall B Impact Score*. BC Corporation. https://www.bcorporation.net/en-us/find-a-b-corp/company/toms

Trivedi, K., Trivedi, P., & Goswami, V. (2018). Sustainable marketing strategies: Creating business value by meeting consumer expectation. [IJMESS]. *International Journal of Management, Economics and Social Sciences*, *7*(2), 186–205.

World Economic Forum. (2021). *The global eco-wakening: how consumers are driving sustainability.* WEF. https://www.weforum.org/agenda/2021/05/eco-wakening-consumers-driving-sustainability/

Wymer, W., & Polonsky, M. J. (2015). The limitations and potentialities of green marketing. *Journal of Nonprofit & Public Sector Marketing, 27*(3), 239–262. doi:10.1080/10495142.2015.1053341

Ziolo, M., Bak, I., & Cheba, K. (2021). The role of sustainable finance in achieving Sustainable Development Goals: Does it work? *Technological and Economic Development of Economy, 27*(1), 45–70. doi:10.3846/tede.2020.13863

Chapter 9
Digital Marketing and Sustainability Competitive Advantage:
A Conceptual Framework

George Kofi Amoako
Ghana Communication Technology University, Accra, Ghana & Durban University of Technology, South Africa

Gifty Agyeiwah Bonsu
Ghana Revenue Authority in Kaneshie Taxpayer Service Center, Accra, Ghana

Antoinette Yaa Benewaa Gabrah
Academic City University College, Accra, Ghana

George Oppong Appiagyei Ampong
Ghana Communication Technology University, Accra, Ghana

ABSTRACT

The usage of digital marketing has significantly changed how firms, businesses, and marketers engage with their buyers. Digital platforms such as Facebook, Google, YouTube, Twitter, Instagram, and many others are utilized in an attempt to offer different kinds of personalized campaigns that companies can use to communicate with their customers. Many companies including retail, manufacturing, wholesale, and several others are exploiting digital marketing as a component of their overall sustainable marketing strategies to attain a competitive edge over their counterparts. Therefore, this research proposes that digital marketing relates to sustainability competitive advantage. The research argues that social media green marketing, ecological marketing orientation, social media corporate social responsibility, cause-related marketing, and digital marketing have a positive relationship with sustainability competitive advantage.

DOI: 10.4018/978-1-6684-8681-8.ch009

INTRODUCTION

The usage of digital marketing has significantly changed how firms, businesses and marketers engage with their buyers. According to Dwivedi et al. (2021), buyers utilizing digital resources in the purchasing process normally depend on social media platforms to patronize their products, goods and or services. Digital platforms such as Facebook, Google, YouTube, Twitter, Instagram and so on are offering different kinds of personalized campaigns that companies can use to communicate with their customers and the general public as well. The online platforms driving traffic synchronized with analytics allow firms to track as well as configure various options on how to attract including converting leads into new customers. Being creative and knowledgeable about digital marketing can have an impact on the outlook of the company whether is a startup business or a corporate institution (Dwivedi et al., 2021; Rizvanović et al., 2023). Hitchen et al. (2017) propose that businesses that fully explore the benefits of online or social media marketing have strategies that focus on the coevolution of innovation as well as resources whiles sharing their vision including providing a framework for innovation.

Currently, social media has a significant positive influence on business innovation outcomes thus online involvement has become a platform for exchange between learning as well as innovation (Corral de Zubielqui & Jones, 2020). For instance, digital marketing ensures digital transformation in terms of creating new or modify existing business process, changes organizational culture, and helps to improve the experiences of customers in that it helps to meet the changing business and market requirements satisfactorily and profitably. Thus, to say that digital marketing enhances efficiency and modernizes the process of doing business as well as strengthens the competitiveness of the firm. It makes it easier for firms to implement their business innovation at all levels to create value and increases the overall business performance (Melovic et al., 2020). According to de Zubielqui and Jones (2020) and de Zubielqui, Fryges and Jones (2019), digital marketing impact significantly on innovation of businesses as digitization changes the face of how organizations interact, exchange information as well as other business practices (Zhang, Liu, Li & Wu, 2023). Muninger, Mahr and Hammedi (2022) and Rizavanovic et al. (2023) collaborate to this that the use of digital marketing include social media usage leads to the effective implementation of innovation since such a process requires information, big data, and a two-way communication mechanism. They argue that digital tools are leverage to access knowledge from external actors, including customers to facilitate the business innovation process and the overall performance of firms. Similarly, Ogink and Dong (2019) add that user feedback from the various marketing digital platforms is used to stimulate innovation.

In this sense, knowing which determinants can lead to higher-value interactions activated by data analytics, including the process of gaining insight from digital channels (Kaur & Kumar, 2020), can be the key to enabling successful customer relationships in the short and long-term which can lead to sustainable competitive advantage. According to Ancillai et al. (2019), online marketing is becoming more unique in its impact as well as does not include only buying and selling but other initiatives connected with digitalization together with upcoming technologies when applied to social media marketing is a facilitator for cross-dimensional organizational impact and sustainable competitive edge. In this digital marketing competition, the firm with more resources, and effective strategies have higher availability of interpreting their data as well as targeting their buyers to achieve competitive advantage over their rivals. According to Sidek et al. (2020), de Zubielquii and Jones (2022) and Pan, Bai and Ren (2022), digital marketing is identified as a technological driver of a sustainable competitive edge, as it is the quickest as well as the most convenient method of branding products, goods, and services, including conveying information and ideas directly through the internet.

Moreover, Saura and Palos-Sanchez (2020) asserted that online marketing is a medium for understanding how buyers behave as well as involving themselves with the company through the Internet has become significant for communication including promoting the firm's sustainable activities. Chaffey and Ellis-Chadwick (2019) argue that many companies including retail, manufacturing, wholesale, and several others are exploiting digital marketing as a component of their overall sustainable marketing strategies to attain a competitive edge over their counterparts. As sustainability has emerged as one of the most significant concerns of today's business, many current businesses from developed countries have already managed to include sustainability initiatives in all their marketing efforts, including traditional and digital marketing strategies, communications, and other strategies (Dumitriu et al., 2019). Sheikh et al. (2018) suggest that digital marketing adoption has reduced the tangible including intangible expenses of communication, thus allowing firms' marketing managers to connect with prospective buyers, thereby leading to sustainable performance which in the long term turns to sustainable competitive advantage. Lastly, some scholars posit that the size of a company, its profitability as well as growth are strongly associated with its high volume of investment in the firm's sustainability. Therefore, profitable businesses may invest extensively in sustainability programs, as they help to sustain their competitiveness.

2.0. LITERATURE VIEW AND HYPOTHESIS DEVELOPMENT

2.1. Sustainability Competitive Advantage

The level to which a company, business or organization has a competitive advantage can be directly connected with how well they perform within a particular industry. Sustaining a competitive edge is seen as a result of increased productivity (Asante, 2018; Keong & Dastane, 2019). Competitive advantage is when companies use value creating as a strategy that no competitor is using at the same time. Sustainability competitive advantage is a situation where a company's sustainability practices and initiatives create a competitive advantage that distinguishes it from its competitor and enhances its financial as well as market position in the long run. Firms have a sustainable competitive advantage if it is pursuing a value-creation strategy that is different from what their rivals are pursuing both current as well as potential, and if those competitors lack the necessary resources to copy the strategy successfully (Job et al., 2020). Some researchers believe that the maintenance of a company's competitive advantage depends on the probability that it will be copied by other rivals in the same sector. Sustainable competitive advantage can be maintained only if a company survives after many efforts to manufacture goods or products when finishes.

Practically, sustainable competitive advantage can last for a longer period. The difficulty of both current as well as potential rivals to copy the same strategy is what makes a competitive advantage sustainable but not the passage of time. According to Huang et al. (2015), a sustainable competitive edge does not indicate that a company or business will last forever. Furthermore, sustainable competitive advantage is recognized by the structural school of thought. A sustainable competitive edge as well as the corresponding advanced organizational performance is viewed as not only possible but also acceptable by advocates of industrial organizations including the market-led view as well as the resource-based approach. Moreover, the market-led view of business-level strategy proposes that companies, as well as businesses, can keep records of competitive advantage by identifying as well as exploring opportunities in existing including emerging markets, in niches within markets and thereby putting the company's strategy to the most efficient use of their resources and capabilities, for instance, core competencies and so on (Asante, 2018; Huang et al., 2015). Lastly, for a company's advantages to last over time, the limited resources it depends on must be original, rare as well as difficult for competitors to copy. The firm must also continually innovate and involves incorporate sustainability practices and initiatives into the firm's operation, products, and services.

2.2 Digital Marketing

Digital marketing is the selling of goods, products, and services through the use of digital technologies such as display marketing, web, and mobile marketing as well as other social media platforms, for instance, Facebook, Instagram, YouTube and so on. Again, digital marketing is a form of marketing that involves the promotion of products and services using digital networks to communicate with buyers and other stakeholders. It also helps companies to implement their marketing strategies more effectively (Veleva & Ttsvetanova, 2020). According to Wang et al. (2020a), digital marketing holds great importance as well as the growth of a business depends on its effectiveness to manage its online presence. Kim (2020) asserted that digital selling, and online shopping including delivery are constantly growing very fast. Any business that promotes a good or service using Internet media or the network "www" is said to be engaging in Internet marketing, often known as e-marketing or online marketing (Meria et al., 2021).

Marketing is one of the most vital components of any business, company, or organization because it is the management process that strives to maximize shareholder and stakeholder returns by building relationships with valued customers as well as achieving competitive advantage. Kumar (2020) asserts that the cost of marketing was very high before digital and social media marketing and the profit margin was also low however, now marketing has become incredibly cost effective as well as influential and all that is needed is a mobile phone with fast internet connectivity. Facebook, Twitter, Whatsapp, and YouTube together with Instagram are examples of online or social media networks including virtual platforms. For instance, webpages, microblogs, and search engines are all forms of digital marketing tools that firms can deploy to reach out to their customers. Rai (2018) assert that digital marketing has expanded its importance to increasing sales of products and services, companies are constantly using these new forms of digital marketing strategy to advertise their products and services. The emergence of digital marketing has changed how companies, businesses and marketers use digital technology and channels in their marketing efforts.

The literature proposes that digital marketing includes an additional comprehensive scope to expand businesses in the future (Alzyoud, 2018). Thus, buyers are happy doing online shopping as well as recognizing that online or social media marketing is safer and better than traditional marketing. Tirpude and Kombade (2018) suggest that digital marketing has changed the story of traditional marketing. Digital marketing saves valuable resources like time, money, and other resources for both firms and customers (Ghazie et al., 2018). Furthermore, Clarke and Nelson (2012) identify that social media platforms like Twitter, YouTube, Instagram and Facebook can successfully function as a channel. Again, Chaffey (2012) recognizes the application of the web including other connected digital technologies with standard communication to achieve marketing or advertising objectives.

2.3. Sustainable Development Goals and Sustainable Marketing Activities

Sustainable marketing has been set in motion by public concern including pressure with regard to problems facing the world today such as environmental deterioration, poverty, hunger, disease, and lack of education (Jones et al., 2018). Thus, for marketing to be able to address these sustainable development problems, companies should have a realistic as well as appropriate meaning of sustainable development goals. The real definition of sustainable development is in terms of the goals it seeks to achieve as well as the indicators that can be used to measure it. According to Jones et al. (2018), within the year 2000 and 2015 the United Nations established the Millennium Development Goals (MDGs), a set of eight global goals that acted as a guide mainly on poverty reduction in developing countries. Although the Millennium Development Goals (MDGs) were recognized as having produced the most successful anti-poverty movement in history (Jones et al., 2018, p. 2), it failed to align several issues for instance the environment (Sachs, 2012) as well as unsustainable utilization and manufacturing of goods, and services (Le Blanc, 2015).

Moreover, engaging companies in the implementation of these goals was insufficient (Jones et al. 2018). Through examination some weakness of MDGs was identified making the international community notice the importance of setting goals that can cover the trip's bottom line which aims to achieve economic development, environmental sustainability, and social equity. This led to the creation of Sustainable Development Goals (SDGs) by the United Nations in the following years, with a time range reaching up to 2030 (Jones et al., 2018; Scheyvens et al., 2016). The SDGs constitute 17 goals with 169 associated targets (Jones et al., 2018). Company's engagement with Sustainable Development Goals (SDGs) has been increasing year by year (Eccles & Karbassi, 2018; Jun & Kim, 2021). Business organizations can use SDGs to create their marketing activities to achieve long-term goals by building brand trust and reputation, which could lead to overall profitability (De Luca et al., 2022). Marketing activities such as green marketing, ecological marketing, CSR, and cause-related marketing are considered pillars used to achieve sustainability.

2.4 Green marketing Communication and Sustainability Competitive Advantage

Green marketing is a crucial concept that aims to bring companies' activities into a closer and more harmonious relationship with the environment. According to Zafar et al. (2020), green marketing is a marketing practice that raises environmental issues. Borenstein et al. (2019) propose that green marketing is characterized by the practice of incorporating considerations of the environment into a variety of aspects of a business's operations, including its products, marketing places, promotion activities, pricing strategy, as well as choices regarding how buyers will be served (market selection). The practice of green marketing which was still a relatively novel idea when the 1990s rolled around, is experiencing phenomenal expansion in India right now (Masocha, 2021). To satisfy buyers who have grown more discerning and environmentally conscious, many companies and businesses that engaged in green marketing are now focusing on producing genuine green goods, and services. This is done to satisfy consumers who have now become more conscious of their impact on the environment (de Freitas Netto et al., 2020).

The primary goal of integrating green marketing into firms' marketing mix (4Ps) is to ensure compliance with the newly enacted rules and regulations of the government and meet the ever-evolving requirements, and preferences of the target audience (Yusiana, Widodo & Hidayat, 2020). Supporting the growth of natural resources and creative processes, activities or practices can lead to environment-friendly manufacturing, sustainability as well as green marketing. Green marketing, as suggested by Sharma and Choubey (2022), has the potential to impact customer feedback and the financial performance of the company. Furthermore, Green marketing has the potential to enhance the image of the firm's brand-including assisting in mitigating the effects of unfavourable publicity and boosting the level of buyer loyalty. In addition, it has the potential to increase market share and return on investment as a form of sustainable competitive edge. Green marketing, as well as production, is viewed as manufacturing goods, and services that use processes that reduce the environmental effect that is dangerous, improves the preservation of energy including natural resources that are good for society, customers, and stakeholders and are economically sound (Sharma & Choubey, 2022). Thus, buyers are currently becoming aware of the environment which is depicted by the firms from whom they patronize their goods, and services. Hence, effectively communicating their sustainability initiatives through social media platforms can help firms to differentiate themselves from competitors, improve their reputation, and attract environmentally conscious customers (Amoako et al., 2022; Chan, 2013; Lepkowska-White et al., 2023).

P1. There is a positive relationship between social media green marketing communication and sustainability competitive advantage.

2.5. Ecological Marketing Orientation Communication and Sustainable Competitive Advantage

Ecological marketing is recognized as a marketing tool that deals with factors harming the ecology as well as pollution in a tactical manner. According to Kumar et al. (2012), ecological marketing is viewed as corporate marketing that has the responsibility of educating as well as directing buyers to use ecologically wise buying intentions. Ecological marketing is also concerned with how goods and their manufacturing process can turn ecologically friendly. Li et al. (2021) recognized that ecological marketing is a framework which expands a company strategy to sustainability including going beyond environmental issues. Moreover, ecological marketing is acknowledged by researchers as the willingness of firms to engage in environmentally safe production without any external pressures. Ecological marketing relies on pressures from legislation including stakeholders' influence to implement green initiatives to achieve sustainable competitive advantage (Kumar et al., 2012). Ecological management considers these approaches, for instance, eco supply chain, eco production, eco-building, eco advertising, reverse logistics, and others to attain a long-term competitive edge over their rivals in the marketplace. A company's performance is primarily related to sustainable competitive advantage as is a significant factor in perceiving goods and services' value (Barney et al., 2021b).

Moreover, literature suggest that firms use their ecological marketing activities to achieve a sustainable competitive edge in the marketplace. These activities include green packaging, green advertising, green product development among others to achieve s sustainable competitive advantage over competition (Maziriri, 2020; Reuter, Foerstl & Hartmann, 2010; Rosen, 2001). Researchers have identified the value of ecological marketing as a step towards catering to buyers' needs while appreciating the importance of it towards a firm's growth and expansion of businesses which may lead to long-term sustainability and competitiveness. It has become fashionable for businesses to be touted as being ecological as a way of identifying themselves with buyers. Ecological marketing, therefore, shows a paradigm shift strategy in many companies since it has changed the way through which businesses go about connecting with their customers. Ecological marketing practices assist businesses' bottom line and brand reputation growth by proving to potential buyers that the company is socially and environmentally responsible (Khalifeh et al.,

2020). Shahzad et al. (2020) argue that many businesses have embraced ecological marketing activities into their long-term strategies which are very important for sustainable development goals, sustainable company success, economic performance as well as competitive edge. Going green can therefore give firms a competitive advantage. Companies and businesses can explore several ecological marketing strategies, activities, and practices to outsmart their competitors in the industry to gain a competitive advantage. However, sustainable competitive advantage cannot be attained if it is not adequately communicated to consumers, hence the need to communicate a company's ecological activities which can affect consumers to be loyal (Lindridge et al., 2013). Therefore, we posit that:

P2: Companies' ecological marketing communication strategies and activities can lead to a sustainable competitive edge.

2.6. Social Media Corporate Social Responsibility Communication (CSR) and Sustainable Competitive Advantage

Corporate Social Responsibility (CSR) is seen as a crucial tool used by many organizations, companies and businesses that want to attract as well as gain the attention of their buyers and the general public. It can also be seen as global business agenda that posits that 'doing good' positively influences stakeholder groups, protects firms from negative publicity, positively shapes buyer's identifications (Einwiller et al., 2019), as well as indirectly enhances firm value (Bardos et al., 2020). The importance of CSR is constantly increasing as the aim of today's business is not only to be innovative (Lőrinczy et al., 2015) but also to be more accountable for their actions as well as being outstanding in every activity that the firms carry out (Jankalová, 2012). CSR practices usually mean utilizing a firm's resources to gain collective welfare through well-structured CSR strategies that can lead to an important source of long-term sustainable competitive advantage (Porter & Kramer, 2006). According to Dabija and Pop (2013), every company that wants to explore CSR strategies must understand the reasons why buyers prefer sustainable goods to meet their demand in terms of sustainability of goods and services. CSR is a concept that is constantly being revised (Carroll, 2021; Matten & Moon, 2020), and one that has been adapted to the economic, political, and social reality of each moment (Sarkar & Searcy, 2016). Firms show more interest in adopting CSR practices when they participate in the export market, which is positively reflected in their business performance (Arora & De, 2020). Aguinis et al. (2020) suggest that CSR should be considered as a strategy including the permanent commitment of companies, which is established not only as a response to market pressures, but also as an internalized response. CSR activities and practices are coerced by the firm's vision, mission, objectives, decisions, and motivations from management including other stakeholders and values. For instance, trust, loyalty, transparency, and responsibilities that are impactful to corporate governance.

Furthermore, CSR policies are a combination and harmonization of commitment including activities designed to analyze specific skills aimed at achieving a sustainable competitive edge in the marketplace. Thus, social media serve as an integrator of resources whilst CSR helps to build the strategic relationships by acting as a reinforcer of trust. This demonstrates that social media CSR will positive affect sustainable competitive advantage positively (Bown, Appiak & Okafor, 2020). This aligns with the argument by ElAlfy, Darwish and Weber (2020) that CSR helps to achieve SDGs communication on social media. Quairel-Lanoizelee (2011) also states that CSR practices could only provide sustainable competitive advantage if such practices are not imitable. Hence external communication about corporate social responsibility provides support for sustainable competitive advantage (Reilly & Larya,

2018). Several studies have examined the vital role that certain mediating variables such as corporate reputation (Saeidi et al., 2015), and customer satisfaction (Ali et al., 2020) can play in the relationship between CSR, performance, and sustainable competitive advantage. An organization's investment in CSR activities can also help to respond positively to shareholders' and stakeholders' concerns as well as enhance human and social conditions which will go a long way to improve their reputation and gain competitive advantage over their competitors. It is vital to state that appropriately communicating CSR on social media will help achieve a sustainability competitive advantage (Fernandez & Hartmann, 2022). Therefore, we propose that:

P3: Companies' CSR activities and practices when communicated online can help them achieve sustainable competitive advantage.

2.7. Caused Related Marketing Communication and Sustainable Competitive Advantage

Cause-related marketing (CRM) is any marketing activity promoted by companies as well as nonprofit organizations aimed at boosting sales both directly or indirectly. CRM may also be defined as the process of formulating as well as executing marketing activities that are characterized by an offer from the company to contribute to a particular amount to a designated cause when buyers involve themselves in revenue-providing exchanges that meet firms and individual objectives (Shen, Qian, & Chen, 2020). The concept of CRM using a condition that increases product sales for the company concomitances with fundraising for the non-profit organization. According to Folse et al. (2010), CRM is a marketing practice that combines a firm's charity, fundraising for a nonprofit institution as well as a social responsibility to promote the profitability of the company or business. Simply put, it is a marketing strategy in which a company aligns its brand and products with a particular cause like environmental sustainability and communicates this connection to its target market. Vlachos et al. (2009) propose that management choose to engage in cause-related marketing campaigns rather than other marketing strategies. CRM focuses on a particular cause that is connected with a company as a whole or with a specific product, goods or service of the business which is seen as transactional CRM. Some researchers asserted that CRM is a form of leveraged marketing communication, focusing on the brand to benefit from consumers' positive associations with a cause (Bergkvist & Taylor, 2016). Thus, CRM might not indicate the level of responsibility for a company's business activities (Jesse, 2021). Furthermore, literature has provided the significant impact of CRM effectiveness on business including its ability to differentiate firms from competitors and appeal to consumers who are interested in supporting social and environmental causes (Fan et al., 2022; Thomas, Kureshi, & Vatavwala, 2020).

Corporate CRM is aimed at enhancing business performance (Thomas et al., 2020). It also helps to achieve several substantial benefits. For instance, improving sales performance, strengthening corporate reputation as well as a brand image including expanding the target market of a company. Researchers have found that exposure to CRM ads might increase a consumer's desire to be more helpful and contribute to others, which then reduces self-indulgence in subsequent choices (Chang & Chu, 2020; Thomas et al., 2020). Wei, Ang and Liou (2020) propose that purchasers' assessment of or their beliefs around a cause can have a successful impact on CRM. Corporate CRM may act as a promotional tool for products and enhance brand image, and extenuate the risks of reputational losses. Thus, securing vital resources from stakeholders. Some scholars argue that brand image especially when coupled with other marketing activities can lead to sustainable competitive advantage that can later turn to increased sales performance and profitability (Wei et al., 2020). Furthermore, a good reputation is also a source of competitive advantage as it increases the level of trustworthiness of the company as well as consumers' trust thus limiting risk including transactional cost (Dowling & Moran, 2012). A good corporate reputation is a valuable intangible asset that helps firms to achieve sustainable competitive advantage in the marketplace (Salam & Jahed, 2023). Lastly, Companies' corporate reputation and marketing activities created through CRM generate as well as sustains their competitive edge. It is important to ensure that CRM communication should be authentic and transparent to ensure its effectiveness since the ability to communicate these practices effectively will help to achieve sustainability competitive advantage (Shen, Qian, & Chen, 2020). Therefore, we propose that:

P4: A company's CRM practices when communicated online are positively related to its sustainable competitive advantage.

2.8. Digital Marketing and Sustainable Competitive Advantage

The literature recognizes that there is a positive relationship between digital marketing and sustainability competitive advantage. This is because digital marketing can be used as a tool to communicate a firm's sustainability efforts to its target market, hence leading to a competitive advantage (de Zubielqui & Jones, 2022; Ghazie et al., 2018; Kumar, 2020; Pan, Bai & Ren, 2022). Consumers today are increasingly concerned about the impact of their purchasing decisions on the environment and are therefore more likely to do business with companies that demonstrate a commitment to sustainability (Kumar, 2020). Thus, by leveraging digital channels such as social media, email marketing and website content, firms should effectively communicate their sustainability initiatives to consumers and hence build trust and credibility with them (Veleva & Ttsvetanova, 2020). Sustainability competitive advantage can be attained via digital marketing since it provides access to real-time data and insights about the target market, it enhances the firm's reputation and customer loyalty (Meria et al., 2021; Kumar, 2020; Salam & Jahed, 2023). This drives profitability and growth in market share which enhances competitiveness in the long run. We propose that:

P5: There is a positive relationship between digital marketing and sustainability competitive advantage

3.0. DISCUSSION OF FRAMEWORK

The literature reviewed proposes that Sustainable development goals that are aligned with the company's sustainable marketing activities can be used to achieve a sustainable competitive advantage in any specific industry. The study is proposing that firms' sustainable marketing activities which consist social media green marketing communication positively affect sustainability competitive advantage (ElAlfy, Darwish & Weber, 2020) and ecological marketing orientation is also proposed to relate positively to sustainability competitive advantage (Maziriri, 2020; Reuter, Foerstl & Hartmann, 2010). Also, the study further proposed that social media corporate social responsibility communication positively impacts sustainability competitive advantage (Bown, Appiak & Okafor, 2020; Reilly & Larya, 2018). Additionally, caused-related marketing is said to relate positively to sustainability competitive advantage (Fan et al., 2022; Salam & Jahed, 2023; Thomas et al., 2020). Digital marketing is proposed to have a positive relationship with sustainability competitive advantage (de Zubielqui & Jones, 2022; Ghazie et al., 2018; Kumar, 2020; Pan et al., 2022). And that these sustainability practices should be well communicated to consumers to help

Figure 1. 2.9 Conceptual model
Source: Author's Construct (2023)

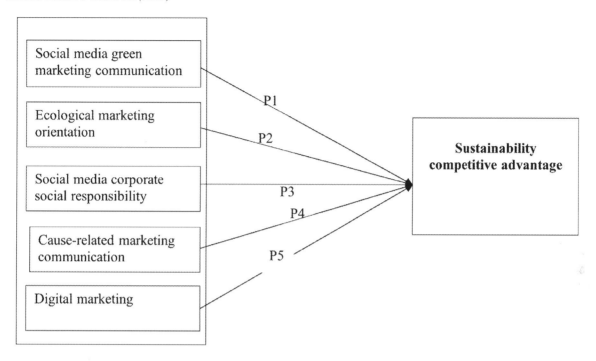

firms gain a sustainable competitive advantage (Maziriri, 2020; Reuter, Foerstl & Hartmann, 2010). These activities and factors can be used to develop a sustainable competitive edge through the effectiveness of strategy execution including management aggressiveness to influence buyers and stakeholders. Moreover, this article is proposing that shareholders and stakeholders can moderate the connection that exists between SDGs, sustainable marketing activities and sustainable competitive advantage.

4.0. RESEARCH LIMITATION AND FUTURE RESEARCH DIRECTION

This study has a few limitations that must be put into consideration as well as can guide future research; as this study did not address buyers' point of view, future studies can probe into purchasers' point of view to get a holistic view. Furthermore, this work is based on the literature review together with the conceptual model which has not been tested. Further studies could test the conceptual model in both developed and developing economies context.

5.0. THEORETICAL AND MANAGERIAL IMPLICATIONS

5.1 Theoretical Implications

First, moving digital marketing research forward, this paper provides an in-depth understanding of how companies can envision SDGs and marketing activities and propose how business owners or management can influence organizational goals by creating sustainability advantages in any given industry. Also, it could provide insights into how sustainability considerations are influencing marketing practices and consumer behaviour. Likewise, the findings serve as a useful guide for future studies in that the study shows that SDGs can moderate the relationship between sustainable marketing activities and sustainability advantage. The model developed recommends that the effective implementation of sustainable marketing activities plan is vital in creating value for companies. Organizations may have good corporate marketing activities or plans but have to ensure effective implementation to get the desired outcomes. Notwithstanding the growth in research on digital marketing, SDGs and marketing activities issues in the business world, limited studies have been conducted into how marketing activities and the effectiveness of strategy execution can affect how a firm's marketing activities influence its competitiveness. This paper makes an original contribution by recommending strategies for sustainable competitive advantage through the instrumentality of digital marketing tools, companies marketing activities and decisions as well as SDGs. This research could help inform public policy and promote sustainable business practices. For example, policymakers could use the insights from this research to develop guidelines and regulations that will encourage firms to adopt sustainable digital marketing strategies and promote sustainable economic growth and competitive advantage.

5.2 Managerial Implications

This study brings out the significance of policymakers and managers of organizations in recognizing the possible impact of stakeholder pressure in influencing a company's goals in society. Again, the findings of the research imply that entrepreneurial firms incorporating sustainability into digital marketing strategies can help them to improve their reputation and enhance their brand image. This indicates that consumers today are increasingly concerned about the impact of their purchasing decisions on the environment, and they are more likely to do business with companies that demonstrate a commitment to sustainability. By effectively communicating their sustainability efforts through digital channels, firms can build trust and credibility with their target audience. Thus, it can create opportunities for firms to develop new business models. For instance, firms can leverage digital technologies to create more sustainable supply chains or to develop new products and services that are environmentally friendly. This can help to differentiate firms from their competitors and capture new market opportunities. Finally, digital marketing allows firms to reduce their environmental footprint by eliminating the need for traditional marketing methods like printed advertisements and direct mail. Also, by using digital channels to reach their target audience, firms can reduce their reliance on paper and other materials that contribute to waste and pollution.

6.0. CONCLUSION

Sustainable development goals and sustainable marketing activities can give companies, businesses, and marketers an advantage in any specific industry. Social media green marketing communication, ecological marketing orientation, social media corporate social responsibility communication, and caused-related marketing are identified as the main activities of Digital marketing. Also, social media green marketing communication, ecological marketing orientation, social media corporate social responsibility communication, and caused-related marketing are said to have a positive relationship with sustainability competitive advantage. Digital marketing as a whole also drives sustainability competitive advantage.

Stakeholder pressure can also enhance the relationship between sustainable marketing activities and sustainable competitive advantage. How management uses digital marketing tools and SDGs to create effective strategies which are implemented effectively and efficiently can mediate the association between sustainable marketing activities and sustainable competitive advantage. This research therefore provides insights on the linkages between digital marketing activities and sustainability competitive advantage.

REFERENCES

Aguinis, H., Villamor, I., & Gabriel, K. P. (2020). Understanding employee responses to COVID-19: A behavioural corporate social responsibility perspective. *Management Research*, *18*(4), 421–438. doi:10.1108/MRJIAM-06-2020-1053

Al-Zyoud, M. F. (2018). Does social media marketing enhance impulse purchasing among female customers case study of Jordanian female shoppers? *The Journal of Business and Retail Management Research*, *13*(2). Advance online publication. doi:10.24052/JBRMR/V13IS02/ART-13

Ali, F., Ashfaq, M., Begum, S., & Ali, A. (2020). How "Green" thinking and altruism translates into purchasing intentions for electronics products: The intrinsic-extrinsic motivation mechanism. *Sustainable Production and Consumption*, *24*, 281–291. doi:10.1016/j.spc.2020.07.013

Amoako, G. K., Agbemabiese, G. C., Bonsu, G. A., & Sedalo, G. (2022). A Conceptual Framework: Creating Competitive Advantage Through Green Communication in Tourism and Hospitality Industry. *Green Marketing in Emerging Economies: A Communications Perspective*, 95-117.

Ancillai, C., Terho, H., Cardinali, S., & Pascucci, F. (2019). Advancing social media driven sales research: Establishing conceptual foundations for B-to-B social selling. *Industrial Marketing Management*, *82*, 293–308. doi:10.1016/j.indmarman.2019.01.002

Arora, P., & De, P. (2020). Environmental sustainability practices and exports: The interplay of strategy and institutions in Latin America. *Journal of World Business*, *55*(4), 101094. doi:10.1016/j.jwb.2020.101094

Asante, B. E., & Adu-Damoah, M. (2018). The impact of a sustainable competitive advantage on a firm's performance: Empirical evidence from Coca-Cola Ghana Limited. *Global Journal of Human Resource Management*, *6*(5), 30–46.

Bardos, K. S., Ertugrul, M., & Gao, L. S. (2020). Corporate social responsibility, product market perception, and firm value. *Journal of Corporate Finance*, *62*, 101588. doi:10.1016/j.jcorpfin.2020.101588

Barney, J. B., Ketchen, D. J. Jr, & Wright, M. (2021b). Resource-based theory and the value creation framework. *Journal of Management*, *47*(7), 1936–1955. doi:10.1177/01492063211021655

Bergkvist, L., & Taylor, C. R. (2016). Leveraged marketing communications: A framework for explaining the effects of secondary brand associations. *AMS Review*, *6*(3-4), 157–175. doi:10.100713162-016-0081-4

Borenstein, S., Bushnell, J., Wolak, F. A., & Zaragoza-Watkins, M. (2019). Expecting the unexpected: Emissions uncertainty and environmental market design. *The American Economic Review*, *109*(11), 3953–3977. doi:10.1257/aer.20161218

Bowen, G., Appiah, D., & Okafor, S. (2020). The influence of corporate social responsibility (CSR) and social media on the strategy formulation process. *Sustainability (Basel)*, *12*(15), 6057. doi:10.3390u12156057

Carroll, A. B. (2021). Corporate social responsibility: Perspectives on the CSR Construct's development and future. *Business & Society*, *60*(6), 1258–1278. doi:10.1177/00076503211001765

Chaffey, D., & Ellis-Chadwick, F. (2019). *Digital Marketing*. Pearson.

Chan, E. S. (2013). Managing green marketing: Hong Kong hotel managers' perspective. *International Journal of Hospitality Management*, *34*, 442–461. doi:10.1016/j.ijhm.2012.12.007

Chang, C. T., & Chu, X. Y. M. (2020). The give and take of cause-related marketing: Purchasing cause-related products licenses consumer indulgence. *Journal of the Academy of Marketing Science*, *48*(2), 203–221. doi:10.100711747-019-00675-5

Chuah, S. H., El-Manstrly, D., Tseng, M., & Ramayah, T. (2020). Sustaining customer engagement behaviour through corporate social responsibility: The roles of environmental concern and green trust. *Journal of Cleaner Production*, *262*, 121348. doi:10.1016/j.jclepro.2020.121348

Clarke, T. B., & Nelson, C. L. (2012). Classroom community, pedagogical effectiveness, and learning outcomes associated with Twitter use in undergraduate marketing courses. *Journal for Advancement of Marketing Education*, *20*(2).

Corral de Zubielqui, G., & Jones, J. (2020). How and when social media affects innovation in start-ups. A moderated mediation model. *Industrial Marketing Management*, *85*, 209–220. doi:10.1016/j.indmarman.2019.11.006

Dabija, D. C., & Pop, C. M. (2013). Green marketing-factor of competitiveness in retailing. [EEMJ]. *Environmental Engineering and Management Journal*, *12*(2), 393–400. doi:10.30638/eemj.2013.049

de Freitas Netto, S. V., Sobral, M. F. F., Ribeiro, A. R. B., & Soares, G. R. D. L. (2020). Concepts and forms of greenwashing: A systematic review. *Environmental Sciences Europe*, *32*(1), 1–12. doi:10.118612302-020-0300-3

de Zubielqui, C. G., & Jones, J. (2022). How and when does internal and external social media use for marketing impact B2B SME performance? *Journal of Business & Industrial Marketing*.

de Zubielqui, G. C., Fryges, H., & Jones, J. (2019). Social media, open innovation & HRM: Implications for performance. *Technological Forecasting and Social Change*, *144*, 334–347. doi:10.1016/j.techfore.2017.07.014

de Zubielqui, G. C., & Jones, J. (2020). How and when social media affects innovation in start-ups. A moderated mediation model. *Industrial Marketing Management*, *85*, 209–220. doi:10.1016/j.indmarman.2019.11.006

Dowling, G., & Moran, P. (2012). Corporate reputations: Built-in or bolted on?'. *California Management Review*, *54*(2), 25–42. doi:10.1525/cmr.2012.54.2.25

Dumitriu, D., Militaru, G., Deselnicu, D. C., Niculescu, A., & Popescu, M. A.-M. (2019). A Perspective Over Modern SMEs: Managing Brand Equity, Growth and Sustainability Through Digital Marketing Tools and Techniques. *Sustainability (Basel)*, *11*(7), 2111. doi:10.3390u11072111

Dwivedi, Y. K., Ismagilova, E., Hughes, D. L., Carlson, J., Filieri, R., Jacobson, J., Jain, V., Karjaluoto, H., Kefi, H., Krishen, A. S., Kumar, V., Rahman, M. M., Raman, R., Rauschnabel, P. A., Rowley, J., Salo, J., Tran, G. A., & Wang, Y. (2021). Setting the future of digital and social media marketing research: Perspectives and research propositions. *International Journal of Information Management*, *59*, 102168. doi:10.1016/j.ijinfomgt.2020.102168

Dwivedi, Y.K., Ismagilova, E., & Rana, N.P. (2021). *Social media adoption, usage and impact in business-to-business (B2B) context: a state-of-the-art literature review.*

Eccles, R. G., & Karbassi, L. (2018). The right way to support sustainable development goals. *Sloan Review*. https://sloanreview.mit.edu/article/the-right-way-to-support-the-uns-sustainabledevelopment-goals

Einwiller, S., Lis, B., Ruppel, C., & Sen, S. (2019). When CSR-based identification backfires: Testing the effects of CSR-related negative publicity. *Journal of Business Research*, *104*, 1–13. doi:10.1016/j.jbusres.2019.06.036

ElAlfy, A., Darwish, K. M., & Weber, O. (2020). Corporations and sustainable development goals communication on social media: Corporate social responsibility or just another buzzword? *Sustainable Development (Bradford)*, *28*(5), 1418–1430. doi:10.1002d.2095

Fan, X., Deng, N., Qian, Y., & Dong, X. (2022). Factors affecting the effectiveness of cause-related marketing: A meta-analysis. *Journal of Business Ethics*, *175*(2), 339–360. doi:10.100710551-020-04639-6 PMID:34024964

Fernández, P., Hartmann, P., & Apaolaza, V. (2022). What drives CSR communication effectiveness on social media? A process-based theoretical framework and research agenda. *International Journal of Advertising*, *41*(3), 385–413. doi:10.1080/02650487.2021.1947016

Folse, J. A. G., Niedrich, R. W., & Grau, S. L. (2010). Cause-relating marketing: The effects of purchase quantity and firm donation amount on consumer inferences and participation intentions'. *Journal of Retailing*, *86*(4), 295–309. doi:10.1016/j.jretai.2010.02.005

Hitchen, E. L., Nylund, P. A., Ferr'as, X., & Mussons, S. (2017). Social media: *Open innovation* in SMEs finds new support. *The Journal of Business Strategy*, *38*(3), 21–29. doi:10.1108/JBS-02-2016-0015

Huang, K. F., Dyerson, R., Wu, L. Y., & Harindranath, G. (2015). From temporary competitive advantage to sustainable competitive advantage. *British Journal of Management*, *26*(4), 617–636. doi:10.1111/1467-8551.12104

Jankalová, M. (2012). Business Excellence evaluation as the reaction to changes in the global business environment. *Procedia: Social and Behavioral Sciences*, *62*, 1056–1060. doi:10.1016/j.sbspro.2012.09.180

Jesse, H. (2021). Cause-related marketing (CRM) is when a company collaborates with an NPO for a good purpose, something that is now criticized by many as a greenwashing guise. Are they right? We get to the bottom of this question. DM Exco. https://dm-exco.com/stories/cause-related-marketing/

Job, M.L., Njihia, M., J., & Iraki, X. (2020). Reverse Logistics and competitive advantage: The mediating effect of operational performance among manufacturing firms in Kenya. *European Scientific Journal*.

Jones, P., Comfort, D., & Hillier, D. (2018). Common ground: The sustainable development goals and the marketing and advertising industry. *Journal of Public Affairs*, *18*(2), e1619. doi:10.1002/pa.1619

Jun, H., & Kim, M. (2021). From stakeholder communication to engagement for the sustainable development goals (SDGs): A case study of LG electronics. *Sustainability (Basel)*, *13*(15), 8624. doi:10.3390u13158624

Kaur, K., & Kumar, P. (2020). Social media usage in Indian beauty and wellness industry: A qualitative study. *The TQM Journal*, *33*(1), 17–32. doi:10.1108/TQM-09-2019-0216

Keong, L. S., & Dastane, O. (2019). Building a sustainable competitive advantage for Multi- Level Marketing (MLM) firms: An empirical investigation of contributing factors. *Journal of Distribution Science*, *17*(3), 5–19. doi:10.15722/jds.17.3.201903.5

Khater, D. (2021). A Procedural Paradigm for Green Project Management of Sustainable Development. In Towards Implementation of Sustainability Concepts in Developing Countries, 261–277. doi:10.1007/978-3-030-74349-9_20

Kim, R. Y. (2020). The impact of COVID-19 on consumers: Preparing for digital sales. *IEEE Engineering Management Review*, *48*(3), 212–218. doi:10.1109/EMR.2020.2990115

Kumar, D. (2020). The study of the significance of digital marketing tools in the promotion of e-commerce websites. *PalArch's Journal of Archaeology of Egypt*, *17*(9), 10411–10425. https://www.archives.palarch.nl/index.php/jae/article/view/7316

Kumar, V., Rahman, Z., Kazmi, A. A., & Goyal, P. (2012). Evolution of sustainability as a marketing strategy: Beginning of new era. *Procedia: Social and Behavioral Sciences*, *37*, 482–489. doi:10.1016/j.sbspro.2012.03.313

Le Blanc, D. (2015). Towards integration at last? The sustainable development goals as a network of targets. *Sustainable Development (Bradford)*, *23*(3), 176–187. doi:10.1002d.1582

Lepkowska-White, E., Parsons, A. L., Wong, B., & White, A. M. (2023). Building a socially responsible global community? Communicating B Corps on social media. *Corporate Communications*, *28*(1), 86–102. doi:10.1108/CCIJ-01-2022-0005

Li, T. T., Wang, K., Sueyoshi, T., & Wang, D. D. (2021). ESG: Research progress and future prospects. *Sustainability (Basel)*, *13*(21), 11663. doi:10.3390u132111663

Lindridge, A., MacAskill, S., Gnich, W., Eadie, D., & Holme, I. (2013). Applying an ecological model to social marketing communications. *European Journal of Marketing*, *47*(9), 1399–1420. doi:10.1108/EJM-10-2011-0561

Lőrinczy, M., Sroka, W., Jankal, R., Hittmár, Š., & Szántó, R. (2015). *Trends in Business Ethics and Corporate Social Responsibility in Central Europe*. Shaker Verlag.

Masocha, R. (2021). Green marketing practices: Green branding, advertisements and labelling and their nexus with the performance of SMEs in South Africa. *Journal of Sustainability Science and Management, 16*(1), 174–192. doi:10.46754/jssm.2021.01.015

Matten, D., & Moon, J. (2020). Reflections on the 2018-decade award: The meaning and dynamics of corporate social responsibility. *Academy of Management Review, 45*(1), 7–28. doi:10.5465/amr.2019.0348

Maziriri, E. T. (2020). Green packaging and green advertising as precursors of competitive advantage and business performance among manufacturing small and medium enterprises in South Africa. *Cogent Business & Management, 7*(1), 1719586. doi:10.1080/23311975.2020.1719586

Meria, L., Aini, Q., Santoso, N. P. L., Raharja, U., & Millah, S. (2021). Management of Access Control for Decentralized Online Educations using Blockchain Technology. *2021 Sixth International Conference on Informatics and Computing (ICIC)*, (pp. 1–6). IEEE. 10.1109/ICIC54025.2021.9632999

Muninger, M. I., Mahr, D., & Hammedi, W. (2022). Social media use: A review of innovation management practices. *Journal of Business Research, 143*, 140–156. doi:10.1016/j.jbusres.2022.01.039

Ogink, T., & Dong, J. Q. (2019). Stimulating innovation by user feedback on social media: The case of an online user innovation community. *Technological Forecasting and Social Change, 144*, 295–302. doi:10.1016/j.techfore.2017.07.029

Pan, M., Bai, M., & Ren, X. (2022). Does internet convergence improve manufacturing enterprises' competitive advantage? Empirical research based on the mediation effect model. *Technology in Society, 69*, 101944. doi:10.1016/j.techsoc.2022.101944

Quairel-Lanoizelée, F. (2011). Are competition and corporate social responsibility compatible? The myth of sustainable competitive advantage. *Society and Business Review, 6*(1), 77–98. doi:10.1108/17465681111105850

Reilly, A. H., & Larya, N. (2018). External communication about sustainability: Corporate social responsibility reports and social media activity. *Environmental Communication, 12*(5), 621–637. doi:10.1080/17524032.2018.1424009

Reuter, C., Foerstl, K. A. I., Hartmann, E. V. I., & Blome, C. (2010). Sustainable global supplier management: The role of dynamic capabilities in achieving competitive advantage. *The Journal of Supply Chain Management, 46*(2), 45–63. doi:10.1111/j.1745-493X.2010.03189.x

Rizvanović, B., Zutshi, A., Grilo, A., & Nodehi, T. (2023). Linking the potentials of extended digital marketing impact and start-up growth: Developing a macro-dynamic framework of start-up growth drivers supported by digital marketing. *Technological Forecasting and Social Change, 186*, 122128. doi:10.1016/j.techfore.2022.122128

Rosen, C. M. (2001). Environmental strategy and competitive advantage: An introduction. *California Management Review, 43*(3), 8–15. doi:10.2307/41166084

Sachs, J. D. (2012). From millennium development goals to sustainable development goals. *Lancet*, *379*(9832), 2206–2211. doi:10.1016/S0140-6736(12)60685-0 PMID:22682467

Saeidi, S. P., Sofian, S., Saeidi, P., Saeidi, S. P., & Saaeidi, S. A. (2015). How does corporate social responsibility contribute to firm financial performance? The mediating role of competitive advantage, reputation, and customer satisfaction. *Journal of Business Research*, *68*(2), 341–350. doi:10.1016/j.jbusres.2014.06.024

Salam, M. A., & Jahed, M. A. (2023). CSR orientation for competitive advantage in business-to-business markets of emerging economies: the mediating role of trust and corporate reputation. *Journal of Business & Industrial Marketing*.

Sarkar, S., & Searcy, C. (2016). Zeitgeist or chameleon? A quantitative analysis of CSR definitions. *Journal of Cleaner Production*, *135*, 1423–1435. doi:10.1016/j.jclepro.2016.06.157

Saura, J. R., Palos-sanchez, P., & Rodríguez Herráez, B. (2020). Digital Marketing for Sustainable Growth: Business Models and Online Campaigns Using Sustainable Strategies. *Sustainability (Basel)*, *12*(3), 1003. doi:10.3390u12031003

Scheyvens, R., Banks, G., & Hughes, E. (2016). The private sector and the SDGs: The need to move beyond 'business as usual'. *Sustainable Development (Bradford)*, *24*(6), 371–382. doi:10.1002d.1623

Schmeltz, L. (2012). Consumer-oriented CSR communication: Focusing on ability or morality? *Corporate Communications*, *17*(1), 29–49. doi:10.1108/13563281211196344

Shahzad, M., Qu, Y., Zafar, A. U., Rehman, S. U., & Islam, T. (2020). Exploring the influence of knowledge management process on corporate sustainable performance through green innovation. *Journal of Knowledge Management*, *24*(9), 2079–2106. doi:10.1108/JKM-11-2019-0624

Sharma, M., & Choubey, A. (2022). Green banking initiatives: A qualitative study on the Indian banking sector. *Environment, Development and Sustainability*, *24*(1), 293–319. doi:10.100710668-021-01426-9 PMID:33967597

Sheikh, A. A., Rana, N. A., Inam, A., Shahzad, A., & Awan, H. M. (2018). Is e-marketing a source of sustainable business performance? Predicting the role of top management support with various interaction factors. *Cogent Business Management*, *5*(1), 1516487. doi:10.1080/23311975.2018.1516487

Shen, L., Qian, J., & Chen, S. C. (2020). Effective communication strategies of sustainable hospitality: A qualitative exploration. *Sustainability (Basel)*, *12*(17), 6920. doi:10.3390u12176920

Sidek, S., Rosli, M. M., Khadri, N. A. M., Hasbolah, H., Manshar, M., & Abidin, N. M. F. N. Z. (2020). Fortifying Small Business Performance Sustainability in The Era of IR 4.0: E-Marketing As a Catalyst of Competitive Advantages and Business Performance. *J. Crit. Rev.*, *7*, 2143–2155.

Thomas, S., Kureshi, S., & Vatavwala, S. (2020). Cause-related marketing research (1988–2016): An academic review and classification. *Journal of Nonprofit & Public Sector Marketing*, *32*(5), 488–516. doi:10.1080/10495142.2019.1606757

Tirpude, S. R., & Kombade, S. W. T. (2018). *Proceedings of International Conference on Business Remodeling - Exploring New Initiatives In Key Business Functions*. Kottakkal Faruk Arts and Sciences.

Veleva, S. S., & Tsvetanova, A. I. (2020). Characteristics of digital marketing advantages and disadvantages. []. IOP Publishing.]. *IOP Conference Series. Materials Science and Engineering*, *940*(1), 012065. doi:10.1088/1757-899X/940/1/012065

Vlachos, P. A., Tsamakos, A., Vrechopoulos, A. P., & Avramidis, P. K. (2009). Corporate social responsibility: Attributions, loyalty, and the mediating role of trust. *Journal of the Academy of Marketing Science*, *37*(2), 170–180. doi:10.100711747-008-0117-x

Wang, Y., Hong, A., Li, X., & Gao, J. (2020a). Marketing Innovations during a global crisis: A study of China Firms' Response to COVID-19. *Journal of Business Research*, *116*, 214–220. doi:10.1016/j.jbusres.2020.05.029 PMID:32501308

Wei, S., Ang, T., & Liou, R. (2020). Does the global vs. local scope matter? Contingencies of cause-related marketing in a developed market. *Journal of Business Research*, *108*, 201–212. doi:10.1016/j.jbusres.2019.11.018

Yusiana, R., Widodo, A., & Hidayat, A. M. (2020, May). Green Marketing: Perspective of 4P's. In *First ASEAN Business, Environment, and Technology Symposium (ABEATS 2019)* (pp. 105-109). Atlantis Press.

Zafar, S., Aziz, A., & Hainf, M. (2020). Young Consumer Green Purchase Behavior. *International J. Mark. Res. Innov.*, *4*, 1–12.

Zhang, K., Liu, H., Li, Y., & Wu, X. (2023). Effects of social media usage on exploratory innovation, exploitative innovation and organizational agility: The moderating role of learning goal orientation. *Internet Research*. doi:10.1108/INTR-07-2021-0503

ADDITIONAL READINGS

Barbarossa, C., & De Pelsmacker, P. (2016). Positive and negative antecedents of purchasing eco-friendly products: A comparison between green and non-green consumers. *Journal of Business Ethics*, *134*(2), 229–247. doi:10.100710551-014-2425-z

Bhimani, H., Mention, A. L., & Barlatier, P. J. (2019). Social media and innovation: A systematic literature review and future research directions. *Technological Forecasting and Social Change*, *144*, 251–269. doi:10.1016/j.techfore.2018.10.007

Gil-Gomez, H., Guerola-Navarro, V., Oltra-Badenes, R., & Lozano-Quilis, J. A. (2020). Customer relationship management: Digital transformation and sustainable business model innovation. *Economic research-. Ekonomska Istrazivanja*, *33*(1), 2733–2750. doi:10.1080/1331677X.2019.1676283

Lukin, E., Krajnović, A., & Bosna, J. (2022). Sustainability strategies and achieving SDGs: A comparative analysis of leading companies in the automotive industry. *Sustainability (Basel)*, *14*(7), 4000. doi:10.3390u14074000

Nguyen, T. T. H., Yang, Z., Nguyen, N., Johnson, L. W., & Cao, T. K. (2019). Greenwash and green purchase intention: The mediating role of green skepticism. *Sustainability (Basel)*, *11*(9), 2653. doi:10.3390u11092653

Saura, J. R., Palos-Sanchez, P., & Rodríguez Herráez, B. (2020). Digital marketing for sustainable growth: Business models and online campaigns using sustainable strategies. *Sustainability (Basel)*, *12*(3), 1003. doi:10.3390u12031003

Sun, Y., Li, T., & Wang, S. (2022). "I buy green products for my benefits or yours": Understanding consumers' intention to purchase green products. *Asia Pacific Journal of Marketing and Logistics*, *34*(8), 1721–1739. doi:10.1108/APJML-04-2021-0244

Wang, H., Ma, B., & Bai, R. (2019). How does green product knowledge effectively promote green purchase intention? *Sustainability (Basel)*, *11*(4), 1193. doi:10.3390u11041193

Wei, C. F., Chiang, C. T., Kou, T. C., & Lee, B. C. (2017). Toward sustainable livelihoods: Investigating the drivers of purchase behavior for green products. *Business Strategy and the Environment*, *26*(5), 626–639. doi:10.1002/bse.1942

Zhuang, W., Luo, X., & Riaz, M. U. (2021). On the factors influencing green purchase intention: A meta-analysis approach. *Frontiers in Psychology*, *12*, 644020. doi:10.3389/fpsyg.2021.644020 PMID:33897545

KEY TERMS AND DEFINITIONS

Competitive advantage: It refers to any unique thing that gives a company an edge over its competitors.

Corporate social responsibility: It is the idea that firms integrate social and environmental concerns into their business operations

Digital marketing: It describes all marketing efforts that occur on the internet/via digital channels.

Ecological marketing: It is the promotion of environmentally friendly products, services, and initiatives.

Green marketing communication: It is the conscientious effort made by firms to inform, incite, persuade, and remind customers about green marketing initiatives.

Marketing communication: This refers to all the messages and media adopted to communicate with the target market about a products and brands.

Sustainability competitive advantage: This refers to a situation where a company's sustainability practices and initiatives create a competitive advantage that distinguishes it from its competitor and enhances its financial as well as market position in the long run.

Sustainability: This refers to the ability to fulfill the needs of current generations without compromising the needs of future generations whilst ensuring a balance between economic growth, environmental care, and social well-being.

Sustainable Development Goals: It is the blueprint for achieving better and more sustainable future for all.

Chapter 10
Design of Business Processes for Marketing Activity

Medea Tevdoradze
Georgian Technical University, Georgia

Samson Darchia
Georgian Technical University, Georgia

Tamta Rukhadze
Georgian Technical University, Georgia

ABSTRACT

As it is known, marketing plays a huge role in the activity of companies, which ensures the company's success in the market. Today the majority of companies have moved to process management, which because of some reason often is not applied to marketing activities and this has a negative impact on it. In order to correct the situation, this chapter serves the issues of design of business processes of marketing activities in the company. It is characterized by a marketing complex (4P model). Also, there are discussed holistic marketing features and marketing strategy issues, there are realized procedures which are necessary for management of marketing activities. But, the peculiarity of marketing activity is that, in addition to ERP-type programs, it is necessary to use a specialized marketing information system, which is due to the abundance and complexity of the models that must be used in the process of marketing evaluations. It is underlined that ERP-type and marketing information system must be used in the complex.

INTRODUCTION

As it is known, marketing plays the huge role in the activity of companies, which ensures the company's success in the market. Today the majority of companies have moved to process management, which because of some reasons often is not applied to marketing activities and this has a negative impact on it. In order to correct the situation, this article serves the issues of design of business processes of marketing activities in the company.

DOI: 10.4018/978-1-6684-8681-8.ch010

At the beginning of the presented article there are discussed the essence of marketing and its role. It is characterized marketing complex (4P model). Also, there are discussed holistic marketing features and marketing strategy issues.

The paper describes the concept of sustainable development from the point of view of the world, companies and marketing. It is characterized specific of sustainable marketing.

Moreover, in this article it is discussed the marketing information system which is responsible for processing of information for marketing. In this connection there are described necessity and character of marketing information, the sources of marketing information and their classification, classification of marketing information itself is presented. Then it is given the description of structure of the marketing information system, the assessment models which usually implemented in the marketing information system are presented. Also, there are characterized types of marketing information systems.

In addition to the above, the article describes the main problems of marketing activities. One of the problems is related to the fact that business processes are not implemented in marketing activities.

First of all, it should be noted that the introduction of business processes in the work of any department improves its results by approximately 30%-50% (Kasim et al., 2018; Gavala, 2022). This is also true for the marketing department. In addition, processes gain special importance when it comes to sustainable development, companies and sustainable marketing.

It should be said that the implementation of business processes in the company means the usage of appropriate information systems. As a rule, management of business processes is carried out by the mean of ERP-type programs. In the most of ERP-type programs, there are realized procedures which are necessary for management of marketing activities. But, the peculiarity of marketing activity is that, in addition to ERP-type programs, it is necessary to use a specialized marketing information system, which is due to the abundance and complexity of the models that must be used in the process of marketing evaluations. It is underlined that ERP-type and marketing information system must be used in the complex.

About busness processes, in the paper, it is offered the unified upper level business process of marketing, there are described the works of its stages, also various sub-processes of the developed business process. There are designed their models - diagrams using BPMN notation.

Using the developed diagrams, by the mean of the special software tool Bizagi BPMN Modeler, simulation modeling is carried out with different scenarios and different initial parameter values. The offered models can be used during the marketing business process design of any type of enterprise. By the mean of simulation, the results are obtained, which allow to evaluate and optimize the different (human and other) resources, usage of software tools, duration and cost of works in the activity of the marketing department. It is possible to select the best scenario, which is advantageous in the process of business process development, since the model must be built first - "as it is", and then - "as it must be".

1. THE ESSENCE AND ROLE OF MARKETING

The main condition for maintaining the presence of enterprises on the market is conducting marketing activities, which first of all means seeing of own business by customers. Marketing is an activity that brings buyers and sellers together. Marketing includes both advertising and buying and selling, transportation and storage, product nomenclature planning and market research, support to key the products, customer service, financing, insurance. In short, everything through which products or services are produced and sold, both in the global and local markets. When planning marketing, usually attention is paid to the so-called marketing 4P (Marketing Mix) model: Product, Price, Promotion and Place (Kotler & Keller, 2014).

Marketing is a management process, and its main function is customer's satisfaction, making forecasts and determining the profit of different activities, which, of course, is directed to the benefit of the organization.

It is necessary to underline, that, during development of marketing the next stage of its development was holistic marketing which was offered by Kotler. The main goal of holistic marketing is to focus on the customer in order to satisfy his needs. Holistic Marketing (Greek holos - whole) - is an approach to marketing in which all components of the process are considered, not as an individual, but as a set of elements. In its case, it is necessary to assess the impact of all the company's operations on all interested parties - customers, employees, distributors, dealers and suppliers, not just shareholders. Holistic marketing encourages a company to work with everyone: company employees, suppliers, distributors.

But it must be noted that today the world is striving towards sustainability – this is the world trend today. Sustainability is the concept that goods and services should be produced in ways that do not use resources that cannot be recovered and that harm the environment (Nijhof et al., 2022). What is sustainable development? Sustainable development is development that meets the needs of the present without compromising the ability of future generations to meet their own needs (United Nations,1987). The United Nations defines sustainability as the development of society when the requirements are met without compromising the interests of future generations. This in itself requires companies to follow the trend of sustainable development (Ozili, 2022).

And sustainable development entails the necessity of sustainable marketing. As a concept of sustainable development, sustainable marketing strives for a balance of economic benefit, social benefit and nature preservation, that is, it has three directions of work - economic, social and ecological (Kortam & Mahrous, 2020).

If traditional marketing is aimed at the constant growth of consumption, sustainable marketing seeks to meet demand in such a way as to increase the well-being of society and save natural resources for future generations. The majority of marketers are in favor of this trend, it has a positive effect on the image of companies, and the coronavirus has only proven it.

Sustainable marketing is environmentally oriented, economically successful, ethical and client-oriented. In this regard, marketing should:

1. To ensure the integration of sustainable business principles in the strategy of the company, region, country,
2. Must develop programs for the continuous growth of the company, region, country,
3. Must develop programs that will support companies that operate on the principles of sustainable development
4. To influence related business types to adapt the principles of sustainable development
5. To ensure the minimization of the cost of resources in business activities (optimization of costs)

Therefore, it can be said that there is a place to adapt the marketing complex to the created situation - to the traditional 4 P mix, issues such as personnel, processes, evidence related to environmental issues are added (Mir-Bernal & Sadaba, 2022).

But, all of the above is possible only if there is a strong, highly professional and well-organized marketing group. This work serves to establish a well-organized marketing department.

Marketing Process

Like PDCA cycle the marketing process includes main 4 stages: analysis, planning, realization and control (Weller, 2017).

Analysis - the planning process begins with a complete analysis of the current situation in the company. The company should also analyze the environment in which it has to operate - by this it will reveal its potential and dangers. It is necessary to analyze the company's strengths and weaknesses, what is needed to conduct marketing activities and to determine (anticipate) opportunities. Analysis provides information for all subsequent stages;

Planning - at the strategic planning stage, the company decides which steps to take for each business unit. Marketing planning includes marketing strategies that help the company achieve its strategic goals. In the mentioned process marketing planning, product or trademark planning is in the center of attention;

Realization - at this stage, strategic plans will be transferred to life, accordingly, the goals of the company are fulfilled. The employees of the organization are engaged in the implementation of the marketing plan, who work both inside and outside the company;

Control - control includes the analysis and evaluation of the results of the execution of company's plan, which is then connected with the adjustment of all its activities to achieve the main goal. The analysis represents all the necessary information and evaluation necessary for further activities.

Strategic Marketing Plan

At the beginning the strategic plan of business must be developed. It is base of all other plans. A company's overall strategy and its marketing strategy overlap in many ways. Marketing is concerned with the needs of customers and their satisfaction by the company. The mission of the company implies the same. In strategic planning, many items of marketing are used - market share, market development, growth. It is often difficult to separate strategic planning from marketing.

After selecting the overall strategy and determining of the competitive advantages, the company can begin to plan the marketing complex (Chernev & Kotler, 2018). Marketing complex is one of the essential concepts in modern marketing. They discus marketing complex as a set of marketing tools that are subject of control. It is a set that is used as unity to achieve the desired response of the target market. The marketing mix refers to everything that a company can do and that allows the company to influence the demand of goods. This means can be divided into four groups of variables: product, price, place, distribution methods and product promotion (called "Four P" – product, price, place, promotion).

The marketing mix also includes all the actual ways and methods that the company uses in the target market.

Since many unforeseen events may occur during the implementation of the marketing plan, it is necessary to control the current process. Marketing control involves evaluations of marketing strategies and actions adjustments for the achievement of the common goal.

It is necessary to underline that because of sustainable marketing it is necessary to expand marketing mix complex (Pomering, 2017).

Marketing Management Process and its Main Tasks

Marketing management is a complex process. It involves the planning, implementation and control of marketing events based on the analysis of situations created in the market in order to detect unfavorable situations in time and avoid unwanted consequence (Kotler & Keller, 2014).

Marketing management in enterprises of any field and sphere should solve the following tasks:

1. Find the number of customers who will completely buy the products produced by the enterprise in a given period;
2. Form a demand for the goods produced by the enterprise and put on the market for sale, which will be expanded and strengthened later
3. Promptly identify changes in the volume and structure of demand in order to influence them.

Heads and employees of sales divisions, heads and employees of advertising service, sales promotion specialists, marketing research specialists, price specialists are engaged in marketing management.

Marketing management is considered as a four-stage process: 1. analysis of market opportunities, 2. selection of target markets, 3. processing of the marketing complex, 4. implementation of marketing events.

Market Opportunity Analysis - typically, market opportunity analysis involves identifying of new markets and evaluating marketing opportunities based on the organization's goals and resources.

Selection of target markets - since the market consists of buyers and on them the product key and the company's profit depend, therefore it is necessary to take into account their needs and characteristics.

They differ from each other in terms of demographic characteristics, place of residence, needs, wishes, buying attitudes, buying behavior and many other characteristics.

In order to effectively cover a large market and better take into account the characteristics of consumers, manufacturers segment the market and thus manage to cover and match the needs and specificities of smaller segments.

Development of the marketing mix - to get the desired reaction from customers, the firm uses a set of variable marketing factors that can be controlled. In other words, it is a marketing complex. Among such factors we can list: goods, price, methods of distribution and stimulation. And finally comes the implementation of marketing events - marketing events can include: marketing planning system and marketing organization system. Planning system provides planning of marketing events.

The goal of each enterprise is to conduct its activities efficiently. This can be achieved with proper organization of the management process.

Proper organization of marketing activity plays an important role in achieving enterprise goals. As a rule, in developed countries, marketing activities are carried out by one person in small enterprises, and specialized marketing services are created in large enterprises.

Organization of marketing services is carried out on the basis of functional, commodity, geographical, market and commodity-market principles. Marketing services are mainly created according to functions. The advantage of these principles lies in their simplicity.

For the effectiveness of the marketing service of the enterprise, it is necessary to have a close relationship with the production, financial and personnel service, accounting, and scientific-research units. The creation and sale of a product according to the customer's demand is possible only through the joint work of all service.

2. MARKETING INFORMATION AND INFORMATION SISTEMS

Marketing Information and its Classification

One of the important issues in marketing management is obtaining information - about existing and potential markets, customers, suppliers and competitors. Marketing information is data, reports, facts, digitals, which are used in the evaluation and forecasting of commercial activities.

Marketing information should have the following qualities: value, completeness, reliability, truthfulness, purpose (universal and targeted), actuality, relevance and comparability, attainability and cost-effectiveness Marketing information can be classified according to different parameters: Depending on the area of coverage (internal and external), According to the order of admission (primary and secondary), According to the quality of processing (processed and unprocessed), According to the quality of estimation of object (general and local), According to the evaluation capabilities (quantitative and qualitative), According to the periodicity of generation (constant, variable and episodic), According to the period presented (retrospective, current, forecast), According to purpose (reference, recommendation, normative), According to the form of presentation (textual, tabular, matrix, graphic, numerical), According to the decision-making stage (determining, explanatory, planning, controlling) (Rukhadze et al., 2016).

Characterization of Marketing Information System

The marketing information system is responsible for the information support necessary for marketing management. This becomes especially important in the context of sustainable marketing, when a much wider range of information needs to be taken into account.

Marketing information system (MIS) – is a formalized sequence of actions aimed at obtaining, analyzing, storing and disseminating the information needed by those persons who are responsible for making decisions in the field of marketing (Rukhadze et al., 2016).

The marketing information system transforms the information received from various sources into the information needed by managers. The role of this system is to determine the need for information to make marketing decisions, its receiving, processing of it and presenting it to relevant managers in a timely manner.

Necessary data are obtained from the company's internal reporting, current marketing information, marketing research and data analysis.

The marketing information system is a system of relatively independent but closely related sub-blocks, which include primary data, data processing programs, provide the presentation of results and the formation of flows. There can be enumerated next sub-systems of marketing information system: Subsystem of marketing intelligence (surveillance), Marketing research subsystem, Marketing decision support subsystem, Marketing planning subsystem, Subsystem of marketing control, Marketing reporting subsystem, Operational subsystems of marketing (sales systems) (Rosário, 2021).

Along with this, it should be noted that the following methods and models are used for analysis in the mentioned system: regression, correlation, functional, discriminant, time series analysis methods; models of product competitiveness assessment, pricing, product promotion and distribution (sale).

The considered peculiarities of the organization of MIS allow us to conclude that the creation of effective marketing information systems requires a serious approach, and the large volume of marketing information requires the usage of modern computer technologies

One of its most important components of MIS are data processing tools. They include software tools, expert systems and decision support tools, as well as various integrated management systems that allow standardization of marketing decision-making procedures.

Among software tools, we can mention document processing programs and electronic spreadsheets. These tools provide the ability to manage and process one-dimensional data by using of an algorithm. They are acceptable for regularly performed calculations and some groups of operations. These tools are used for the realization of certain marketing functions and local tasks.

One of the factors of marketing activity' increasing effectiveness is the ability of its integration into the general mechanism of organizational management. A possible classification of integrated marketing information support systems can be next: Local functional systems, Small integrated systems, Medium integrated systems and Large integrated systems.

Some blocks which provide processing of marketing tasks are included in most integrated enterprise management systems (for example ERP-type of systems) that are available on the market. But compared to other functional blocks, such as finance and accounting, production, personnel, they are poorly processed and not sufficiently highlighted in the general management system.

As is known marketing blocks in such systems benefit from less demand. This is related to the fact that most marketing problems have qualitative character and relevant information cannot be processed algorithmically. To solve these problems, specialized software is needed, which is built on the basis of heuristics, which is related to the implementation of expert systems.

Expert system - is a set of specialized computer programs based on systematic accumulation of information, generalization and analysis of the knowledge of specialists-experts for use in the process of solving various types of tasks. An expert system in the best way should reflect the entire organization. It should work in the mode of simultaneous use, include and process information related to the production activity itself, as well as management and marketing activities. In general, an expert system includes the following components: database (knowledge base), a mechanism for decision making, and a user interface.

The database (knowledge base) represents the heart and base of the expert system. It should contain all the necessary marketing and other information, which should be clearly divided according to its direction, content, periodicity, necessity of use and other parameters. Accurate information, taken from the database, is the basis for decision making.

The mechanism for developing of decision is the main component of the enterprise's expert system. It is a complex of means that determines the order of their interpretation and use. A decision-making mechanism in the work process defines the conditions that affect the final result. The mechanism implies the existence of certain connections between certain blocks of information, it must be supported by well-developed software that responds to the basic requirements for expert systems.

Thanks to the continuity and synchronicity of the information entering the database, it becomes possible to accumulate, group, connect and systematize the incoming data. Based on them, it is possible to obtain stable statistical coefficients and temporal trends derived from them. According to the trends, medium and long-term forecasts are obtained. As a result, linking of current reports, forecasting and current operational planning tasks is achieved.

The user interface is a software complex that is designed to provide a simple and convenient relationship between the expert system and the user. It should be easily accessible and simple for everyone, since it means that a large number of users will work simultaneously in the system, starting from simple workers and ending with top managers.

Today, in marketing information systems they increasingly use artificial intelligence methods, in particular machine learning, which requires working with big data, as well as other scientific achievements (Shen, 2022).

Classification of Marketing Information Systems and Features of Use

The need to use a marketing information system in the enterprise is due to the increase in the general pace of the enterprise's development, its competitiveness, and the modernization of the quality of the products (Kotler, Kartajaya, & Setiawan, 2016). When using the marketing information system, the risk of bankruptcy in the process of managing the enterprise, the risk of not receiving ща the necessary information or the risk of falling into the hands of competitors are reduced. It is also very important for the enterprise to process the necessary data and evaluate the general picture quickly and efficiently.

Timely analysis of marketing information is impossible without the use of information technologies. First of all, this is due to the fact that the duration of the technological process have been reduced according to the release of products.

On the other hand, intensifying of competition and shortening the processing time of goods require precise actions. Enterprise activities cannot always be satisfied with standard application programs. Therefore, it is necessary to use specialized software that can be found in the market.

It should also be said that marketing companies themselves conduct expensive and in-depth marketing research. They need to have their own individual face and therefore they rarely use typical solutions. More often, they have their own sets of information-analytical programs, which are formed from both universal and custom-made special packages, including questionnaire data processing programs and statistical packages

Marketing information systems (MIS) themselves can be divided into two groups: based on the type and status of the user, and based on the need for use.

Based on the type and status of the user, they consider: managerial MIS (management and decision-making systems) and operational MIS (systems of operations, sales and marketing activities). Users of management and decision-making systems are managers, supervisors, experts, analysts. The second group includes operational systems for current sales and marketing activities, which are required for the realization of daily marketing activities.

Their use according to the need can be divided into the following groups: collection, data analysis, marketing planning, marketing decisions making, implementation of marketing events, control (internal and external).

In marketing researches, they use special programs designed to solve specific marketing tasks, basic software tools, application software packages that use a wide range of statistical methods or economic-mathematical methods, decision making support software tools and expert systems. One of the most important principles follows from all of the above: the combined use of software tools is appropriate.

It is very important to characterize middle and high integration systems, like are CRM and ERP-type systems.

Customer Relationship Management (CRM) — is a system of managing relationships with clients, collecting and organizing personal data. The main purpose of CRM is to form a process of communication with the client of the company, taking into account his needs or desires as much as possible through personalized offers and recommendations.

CRM takes into account and processes all user data that is recorded in a separate CRM card for each client. Collected information is used to create recommendations to the client, as well as to automate the company's work processes. CRM helps managers at every stage of the deal: processes documents according to the template, reminds about the need to repeat the call or issue an invoice, displays information about the company in complex reports. From here it can be concluded that it is worth choosing CRM if you need to automate the internal processes of the enterprise and control the work of managers.

Enterprise Resource Planning (ERP) — is a program for planning of company resources that allows to control every process of the organization and unite individual divisions of the company into a single mechanism. The main purpose of ERP is to collect and process all data about the company in a single array. The system allows to synchronize the activity of all divisions of the enterprise. The program unites different modules and tasks:

- Warehouse and logistics department,
- Production capacity,
- Table of orders and delivery service,
- Accountant,
- Department of marketing and advertising.

The implementation of the ERP system allows to form a complete information space for all employees of the enterprise, where information about the company's production and turnover will be stored. In other words, ERP is a system for managing the resource base and production capacity of an enterprise.

It is possible to use different approaches to informatization of marketing works, it is possible to use widespread general-purpose systems, specialized and expert systems, realization of marketing tasks in the integrated information system of the enterprise/organization. It is clear that proper planning and optimization of marketing work in the enterprise/organization, effective use of the marketing process itself and information systems and technologies are necessary (Tevdoradze et al., 2015).

As can be seen from the information presented in the previous paragraphs, marketing deals with a huge amount of information and uses many, complex methods, algorithms and approaches. By the way tt's activity should be characterized by promptness. That's why various types of information systems and technologies are widely used in the management of the marketing service and in solving of tasks. But this is still not enough. It becomes necessary to develop such an approach to the work of the marketing service as process-oriented management.

3. DESIGN AND MODELING OF MARKETING BUSINESS PROCESSES

Concept of Business Process

As it is known, today two approaches to management are distinguished in the organizations: traditional, which is based on the principles of division of labor, and process-oriented. There is no doubt that process-oriented management provides much better results than traditional management (Tevdoradze et al., 2014).

By definition a business process represents a repeating sequence of certain operations (functions), which is supplied with a resources at the entrance; resource are processed during the execution of the operations included in the business process, and as a result, a certain type of product is obtained at the output of business process, and this product necessarily has a customer. Different types of business processes are considered by their roles in organizational management and according to their functions.

Business processes have their own life cycle, which, like the PDCA cycle, consists of four stages:

1. Business process design,
2. Realization of the business process,
3. Observation during the realization of business processes and
4. Analysis of observation results and reaction in the case of their deviations.

Parameters of business processes play a very important role in their life cycle. Targeted (KPI) and non-targeted parameters can be discussed here. KPI indicators show us if business goals are achieved during the execution of a business process, while non-target parameters provide additional information about business processes - quantitative and qualitative.

In general, the processes of the organization, according to Potter's theory of the value chain, are divided into basic (main) and supporting (secondary) processes. These groups of processes are defined as follows:

- primary (main) processes are called basic and value-creating processes. These processes are carried out throughout the company, from the customer to the supplier;
- supporting (secondary) processes do not create added value. They are needed to ensure basic processes. Such supporting processes may be, for example, financial and personnel processes.

The number of processes in an organization can be enough large depending on the type of activity, and all are specialized in their own product.

It is clear that in order to release one of own products within the boundaries of the main business processes, high-quality supporting actions are also needed, which are carried out within the framework of the supporting processes. It is possible to attribute to them the selection of suppliers and partners and the establishment of mutually beneficial relations with them; staffing process; marketing and PR process; planning, analysis, management processes.

Appropriate software plays a huge role in the life cycle of business processes, which varies greatly depending on the stage of the life cycle. As it is known, when the organization starts implementation of business processes, it should also automatically to implement the corresponding software - and this type of software, which serves execution of business processes, is called ERP-type systems. ERP-type systems themselves serve to manage the execution of business processes, and in this type of systems, other specialized systems such as CRM and SCM are considered. By the way, as it is mentioned earlier, CRM (Custom Relationship Management) type of programs is closely related to solving of marketing tasks.

When a company begins transition to process oriented management and implements business processes, it deals with BPM (Business Processes Management) ideology, which includes not only business processes themselves, but also all questions in the connection with the life cycle of business processes - issues of their design, execution management, control as well as relevant software solutions.

Design, Improvement, and Modeling of Business Processes

The design of business processes begins with the identification of the strategy. It should be determined which market segments the company operates on, who are its target customers, which customer requirements are satisfied by the company's products and services, which differences from competitors should be formed. It is a mistake to think that marketing strategy issues have nothing to do with business processes, since a company's business processes exist to meet customer needs. That is why, before designing of business processes, the market requirements for the company's activities should be clearly defined.

At the next stage, the company's organizational concept is developed, which includes the description of the main processes and responsibility centers. The organizational concept provides a principled understanding of the structure of activities and it is the basis for further detailed description of business processes. Then, based on the organizational concept, the organizational structure is formed and the identification of the lower level processes is carried out.

The result of this work is the description and specifications of the organizational structure, which include the parameters of all the main business processes. Therefore, all the main activities of the company are developed quite completely, in order to make it possible to development of the regulations of specific processes, determinition of the performance indicators and official obligations of the employees.

It can be said that the results of business processes design are expressed in the following (Tevdoradze et al., 2017):

- A brief description of the marketing strategy (concept);
- Organizational concept (description of the main business processes and responsibility centers);
- Description of the organizational structure;
- Specification of basic business processes.

Also it can be mentioned the issues of business processes improving, the necessity of which arises over time during the execution of business processes. The fact is that business processes are characterized by degradation, which is related to the changes in the external world, technologies, competitors, customers, therefore it is necessary to improve business processes. Some methods are pointed out here: Fast, benchmarking, redesign and reengineering methods. The first three approaches can be grouped under the common name - optimization of business processes.

As it is known, in the process of designing and improving of business processes, modeling plays a huge role. Accurate modeling allows to study the functioning of the organization, its business processes in the best possible way and develop the business processes with the best indicators.

In the modeling of process, it is necessary to go through certain stages: creating of a work team, conducting a business analysis of the company in order to identify the disadvantages of the activity, selecting a business process model, determining the project rules (a document about business process modeling), selecting of modeling software, business process modeling, testing and implementation.

The composition of the works of the design and improvement stage, which includes business process modeling, is as follows:

- Identification of the processes and build of the initial model "as is". At this stage, the boundaries of the process and its main elements are identified, data are collected about the operation of the process. The model does not always correctly reflect the operation of the process, so the model at this stage can be called a "first draft" or an original "as is" model;

- Initial model verification, analysis and refinement. At this stage, contradictions and duplication of actions in the process, limitations of the process, relationships of the process will be determined, and the need to change the process will be determined. As a result, the final version of the "as is" model is formed;
- Develop of an "must be" model. After analyzing of the current situation, it is necessary to determine the desired state of the process. This desired state is represented as an "must be" model. This model shows how the process should look in the future, after all necessary improvements;
- Testing and deploying the "must be" model. This stage of modeling is associated with the implementation of the developed model in the practice of the organization. As a result of testing of the business process model, necessary changes are made to it;
- Improving of the "must be" model. As is known, the business process experiences deterioration during шеы operation. As a result, it becomes necessary to improve and make changes, so process models should be regularly developed and validated. This stage of modeling is associated with continuous

It can be underlined that the modeling of processes is quite complex. Therefore, it is necessary to use specialized tools . In addition, it should be noted that graphic modeling is widely used in the process of modeling of business processes.

Appropriate tools have been created for business processes planning and modeling, such as: ARIS, BizAgi BPM Modeler, ELMA BPM, Gliffy, System Architect, AllFusion, Oracle Designer, Rational Rose, Power Designer, Re-Think, Ithink Analyst, Workflow Modeler and others .

Various notations have also been developed that can be used for graphical presentation of business processes: WFD, DFD, RAD, STD, ERD, FDD, SADT, IDEF (IDEF0, IDEF1, IDEF2, IDEF3, IDEF4 and IDEF5), ARIS, BPMN, UML etc.

It can be uderlined that BPMN - notation and instrumental tool - Bizagi BPM Modeler are selected for marketing business process modeling.

General Description of Marketing Business Processes

In order to optimize marketing activities in modern companies, business process theory approaches are used more and more. The following arguments can be made in favor of this:

- each process has its own customer and concentration is carried out on each separate process, which contributes to better customer satisfaction;
- it is created the value of the final products in the processes;
  - determining of the boarders of the process, its suppliers and users, allows to ensure better interaction and understanding of the requirements, which must be satisfied;
  - during the management of a united process, which passes through many departments, and not a single department, the risk of sub-optimization is reduced;
- during the appointment of process owners who are responsible for the processes, it becomes possible to avoid the division of responsibility into fragments, which very often happens in specialized enterprises;

- management of processes gives us better conditions for the execution of works and control of resources.

As for the construction of business processes of the marketing service - here the issue can be raised in two ways: the formation of the main business processes of marketing (taking into account different aspects of the activity) and the construction of a unified business process of marketing.

During the formation of marketing business processes, it is possible to distinguish the following four main groups of tasks, and then build the corresponding business processes:

1. ensuring of economic indicators, development and management of trade directions, formation of a demanded assortment taking into account market trends and customer requirements, formation of working conditions and prices, providing sales support and training of sales staff;
2. formation of the target image of the company among existing and potential clients; providing information to target customers regarding price proposition, economic benefits and product features; providing of product promotion and sales marketing support;
3. studying the market situation and trends, studying the requirements of the target customers regarding the range of products and their characteristics; study of the conditions of operation and service; study of competitors and market opportunities, assessment of own resources; establishing a price proposal, elaboration of a development strategy, planning one's own actions;
4. evaluation of the company's activity in accordance with the mission announced in the market, evaluation of customer satisfaction; Determining ways to improve the competitiveness of the company's price offer.

Design of a Marketing Business Process

The input to this process is information received from the supporting planning and management processes of organization. The goals and objectives of the organization's marketing policy are derived precisely as a result of analysis and decisions making; the main directions of marketing activity and the ways of achieving of goals will be more clearly defined.

The first step of this process is to determine the objectives of the marketing campaign (Figure 1). Each company sets these goals individually, taking into account the following issues: goals in the field of quality; main directions of activity; established relationships with customers (potential customers), suppliers (potential suppliers) and other third parties; analysis of the situation in the goods and services market; innovative activities of the organization.

On the second stage of the process, a situational analysis is presented for each set of goals; also determining the weaknesses of the organization according to the directions of activity, assessments of perspectives are executed.

On the basis of the conducted analysis, a marketing strategy is developed and the main stages of its realization tactics are planned.

Realization tactics are represented by a set of documented procedures, which must be implemented both in the complex and individually, taking into account the separate directions of the organization's activities. The sub-processes of marketing business process implementation are presented in textual form below - all the main sub-processes of the marketing business process realization stage are discussed.

Based on the results of marketing activities, analysis is carried out using appropriate analysis methods and tools and then recommendations are developed for planning, new product creation, purchases, supplier selection, which is the final stage of the process.

As it is known, all processes depend on information. However, the "marketing" process, more than any other process, is effective only when both external and internal information is successfully processed in the organization. Analysis of specialized press and informational literature has an important place in the marketing and PR process.

This procedure is aimed to establish an objective picture of the company's place in the market in the field of goods and services, as well as the offer of goods and services.

For work with specialized and reference literature, it is most important to study and select information sources available on the market. Based on the analysis of the selected sources, a list of them is formed in order to continue working with them according to the business directions.

Figure 1. Unified business process of marketing
(Created by Authors)

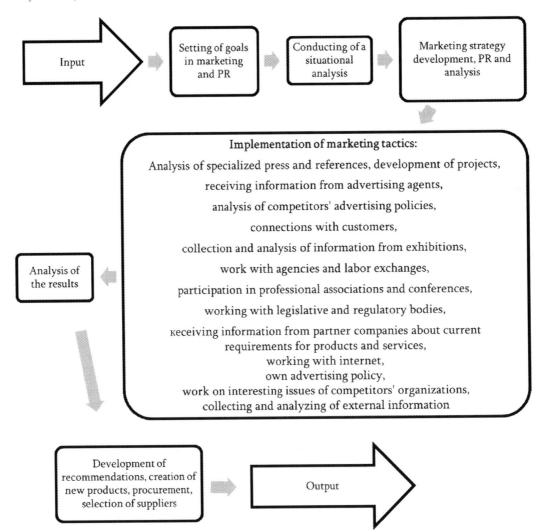

Design of Business Processes for Marketing Activity

In the process of working with selected sources, the issues of the amount of own information and the frequency of placement are actual, on the basis of which the plan for placing of own advertising products is developed.

But this does not mean that the organization works only with selected information sources. The market of services does not stand in one place, which makes it necessary to periodically familiarize with the news presented in the given service market. Evaluation of new information sources and analysis of the lists of publications with which the organization works, requires planned periodicity.

When working with advertising agencies, the most important thing is to establish trust and mutual relations. Only such type of a relationship contributes to long-term mutually beneficial cooperation, receiving useful recommendations and advices, receiving information about competitors, benefits and discounts.

Based on this relationship, it is possible to attract advertising agents to disseminate information about the organization in other additional ways.

The quality management system in accordance with the requirements of the international standard ISO 9001 has an important place in the organization of communication with the customer. The main task of this procedure are to communicate with customers, study their satisfaction, develop their expectations, and inform potential clients of the company's policies, goals, capabilities, and successful practices.

The requirements which are set by the legislative and normative framework can be requirements to products set at the state level. That's why for the companies that are engaged in the release of such kind of products, the mentioned procedure acquires especial relevance.

Actions of the given procedure (such as "connecting to the information-legal systems, using them and regularly updating them) are already proof of the existence of the list of necessary laws and the ability to work with them according to the ISO 9001:2000 standard.

The final result of this procedure is the monitoring and analysis of the performed events, making recommendations for the improvement of products and services advertising, and the creation of new ones. Each performed procedure should be evaluated by the performed actions and their effectiveness and compliance with the set goals should be determined.

In addition, according to the requirements of ISO 9001:2000, it is mandatory for the organization to implement corrective actions in order to eliminate the causes of non-conformity so that they do not happen again.

Therefore, these actions are mandatory for the organization and are part of the mandatory documented procedure "corrective actions". The given marketing process diagram is only one possible example.

DETERMINATION OF MARKETING BUSINESS-PROCESS SUB-PROCESSES

Goal Setting Sub-Process

The sub-process of defining of goals includes the following main activities: setting marketing goals, determining the main direction of activity, establishing relationships with customers and establishing relationships with suppliers (Figure 2). All these actions must be carried out in the context of sustainable marketing directions, which include three areas of operation: economic, social and environmental.

Situational Analysis Sub-Process

Situational analysis in marketing includes the following procedures, from which we can distinguish two main ones: internal and external situational analysis. Internal situational analysis consists of the following sub-processes: marketing, financial, production and personnel. The external situational analysis includes the analysis of the market, competitors and factors, which is presented (Figure 3).

Development of Marketing Strategy and Selection of Complexes Sub-Process

The marketing strategy development sub-process consists of the following procedures: selection of market segments, development of pricing methodology, planning of promotional activities and processing of existing products and creation of new ones (presented in Figure 4).

Realization of Marketing Events Sub-Process

Marketing includes many procedures, such as: 1. Analysis of specialized press and references, development of projects, 2. Obtaining of information from advertising agencies, 3. Analysis of competitors' advertising policies, 4. connections with customers, 5. Collection and analysis of information from exhibitions, 6. Work with recruiting agencies and labor exchanges, 7. Participation in professional associations and conferences, 8. Working with the legislative and normative base, 9. Obtaining of information from partner firms about current requirements for products and services, 10. Working with the Internet, 11. Own advertising policy, 12. Working with information of competing companies and 13. Collecting and analyzing of external information using mass media as a marketing research tool.

Figure 2. Setting of goals in marketing and PR
(Created by Authors)

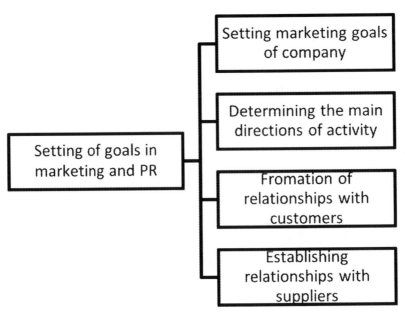

Figure 3. Situational analysis
(Created by Authors)

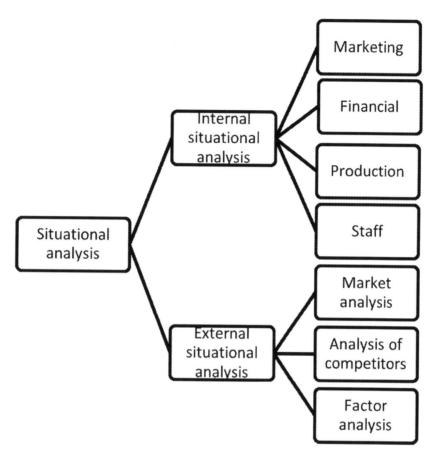

The main operations of the mentioned sub-processes are presented below:

1. **Analysis of specialized press and references and development of projects** consists of the following steps: making a useful press list; study of publications and materials; analysis of studied materials and planning of development of own advertising: where, when, how much and how often; establishing systematic work with advertising agents; creation of own advertising products; analysis of the results of advertising publications and advertisements;
2. **Obtaining of information from advertising agencies** includes the following actions: establishing a list of planning agencies; finding especially reliable partners; arranging of planned works with advertising agents; attracting advertising agents to spread the information of the organization; monitoring of performed works;
3. **The analysis of competitors' advertising policy** consists of the following operations: establishment of a list of competitive organizations for all directions; development of a plan-schedule for studying of the advertising activities of competitors; systematic compilation of digests according to the list of competitors; determination of recommendations based on the analysis; improving of advertising products and planning new ones; based on analysis conducting of corrective events in advertising work

Figure 4. Development of marketing strategy and selection of complexes
(Created by Authors)

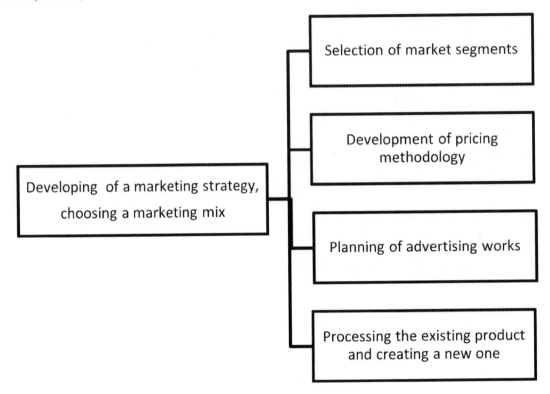

4. **Connection with customers** includes the following: creation and updating of a special customer base; development of programs and schedules of work with former and potential clients; regularly providing information sending by all means of connection; conducting of special promotion events for clients, offering of discounts; ensuring monitoring of work with clients; providing of corrective events and analysis of effectiveness
5. **Collection and analysis of information from the exhibitions** is a set of the following actions: drawing up a plan-schedule via the Internet; development of the program of participation in exhibitions; participation in the exhibition or gathering of information; analysis of information from exhibition, development of recommendations; analysis of the results of participation in the exhibition, recommendations for repeat participation and preparation;
6. **Work with recruiting agencies and labor exchanges** includes the following: formation of the list and address base of agencies and exchanges; development of cooperation program, regular informing of partners about the needs of the organization, according to personnel; joint work with partners regarding the formation of goals and objectives; analysis of cooperation results and recommendations for further cooperation relations;
7. **Participation in professional associations and conferences** implies the following: formation of the list of professional associations and the address base according to the various activities of the organization; development of a cooperation program and regular informing of partners about the organization's capabilities and wishes; entry into professional associations and participation in activities, attendance and presentations at meetings and conferences; analysis of the results of

cooperation and recommendations regarding the expansion of cooperation, corrections, improvement of new cooperation programs; attracting of participants;
8. **Working with the legislative and normative base** implies the following: formation of the list of sources of the legislative and normative base according to the activities of the organization; study of publications about projects, laws and normative channels; connecting to the information- legislative system, their use and regular updating; analysis of current and future changes and preparation of proposals regarding the adjustment of existing advertising products and the development of new ones;
9. **Obtaining of information from partner companies about current requirements for products and services** consists in the following: formation of the list and databases of loyal organizations, profile companies and customer companies; description of goals and development of cooperation program; attracting of partners to cooperation for determination of the demand for products and services; usage of recommendations from partners during product service adjustments and creation of new one;
10. **Working with the Internet** means the following: Launching a program for working with the Internet including the work with sites that are of interesting for the organization; analysis of work with the Internet and preparation of proposals; suggestions for adjusting and improving own site, taking into account the best practices; proposals for the correction of product service and the development of new ones;
11. **Own advertising policy** is a sequence of the following steps: formation of a list of mass information sources, including directories and professional magazines; development of the organization's advertising work program, which includes monitoring of advertising effectiveness; formulation of request with substantiation of advertising financing for one year; forming of proposals in order to improve the adjustment of advertising and to develop new ones;
12. **Working with information on competing companies** includes the following tasks: forming a database of competitors that need to be studied; conducting a systematic analysis of information about the techniques and technology of working with clients of competitors; development of a program for working with competitors' information; according to the results of the analysis, making recommendations for adjusting and improving of the advertisement and developing of new ones;
13. **Collecting and analyzing of external information using mass media as a marketing research tool** implies the following: placement of advertising information in mass media, which precedes the development of new products and services in order to study trends in the development of the consumer market; development of a system for monitoring of the demands for offered products and services; analysis of monitoring results; based on the results of the analysis, development of recommendations regarding the improvement of advertising adjustments and the design and development of new ones.

ANALYSIS OF RESULTS SUB-PROCESS

The last step of the marketing business process - the analysis of results consists of the following main operations: analysis of the market, competitors, product policy, price policy, sales policy and communication policy (Figure 5).

Figure 5. Analysis of results
(Created by Authors)

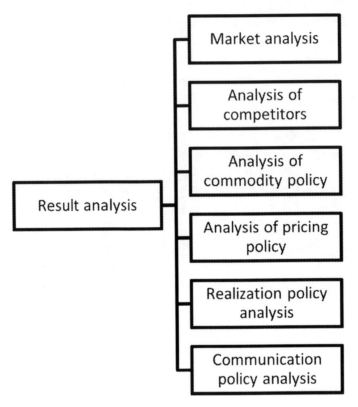

MARKETING BUSINESS PROCESS MODELING

For simulation of the marketing business process, it is used the Bizagi BPMN Modeler system. In this program, a model for the main business process of marketing is built graphically by mean of BPMN notation.

Parameters which are defined during model creation: time, process cost, labor salary. The main attention is paid to the parameters of time and cost, since it can be seen from the previous material that the time and cost parameters of the marketer-analyst's work are very important.

As it already was mentioned a unified marketing business process includes the following stages: Setting marketing goals, situation analysis, development of marketing strategy, implementation of marketing activities and analysis of results.

Initially, it is necessary to underline that depending on different types of programs which can be used during marketing process a simulation of a single marketing business process was carried out, which was realized with three scenarios: the first one assumes the usage of the ERP-type system in the marketing process, the second scenario assumes the usage of the CRM system in marketing work, and the third scenario - the usage of the analytical programs in the business process. The simulation of business process and results of the first scenario are shown in Fig.- 6,7,8,9,10 correspondently. Figures - 8,9 and 10 show results of simulation for different parameters: cost, time and labor cost.

SCENARIO ONE: PROCESS USING ERP SYSTEM

Figure 6. Diagram of marketing business process with usage of an ERP system
(Created by Authors)

Figure 7. Simulation of marketing business process with usage of ERP system
(Created by Authors)

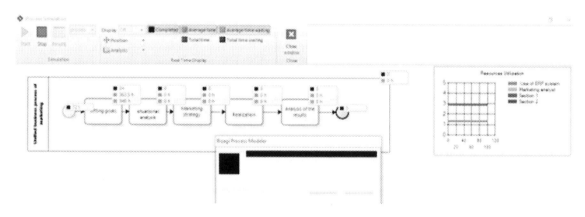

Figure 8. Results of marketing business process simulation with usage of ERP system-1.1
(Created by Authors)

Figure 9. Results of marketing business process simulation with usage of ERP system- 1.2
(Created by Authors)

Figure 10. Results of marketing business process simulation with usage of ERP system-1.3
(Created by Authors)

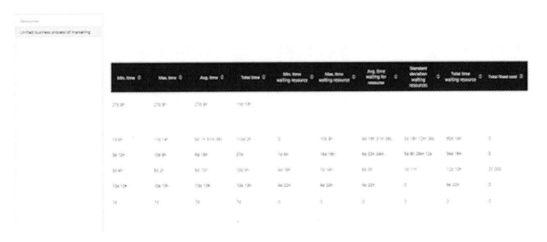

SCENARIO 2: PROCESS USING CRM SYSTEM

As it is mentioned above, the second scenario takes into account the usage of the CRM system in marketing work. The model based this scenario is presented on Figure 11, simulation of the business process - on Figure 12, and the results of simulation are shown on Figure 13, 14, 15.

SCENARIO 3: PROCESS USING ANALYTICAL SOFTWARE

The third scenario takes into account the usage of analytical software in marketing work. The model of this business process is presented on Figure 16, the simulation of the business process - on Figure 17, and the results of simulation - on Figures 18, 19, 20.

Figure 11. Diagram of marketing business process with usage of a CRM system
(Created by Authors)

Figure 12. Simulation of marketing business process with usage of CRM system
(Created by Authors)

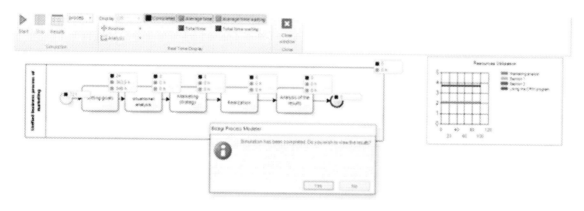

Figure 13. Result of simulation of marketing business process with usage of CRM system- 2.1
(Created by Authors)

Figure 14. Result of simulation of marketing business process with usage of CRM system 2.2
(Created by Authors)

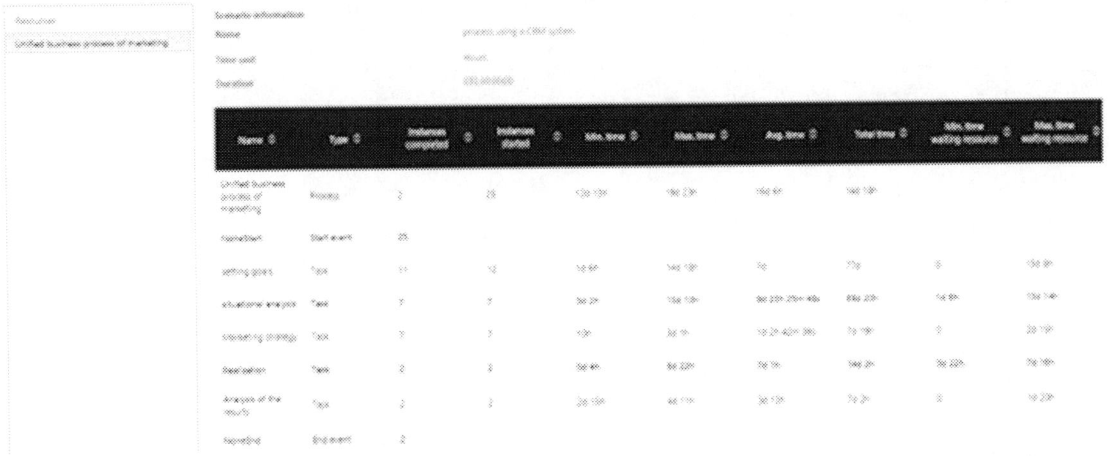

Figure 15. Result of simulation of marketing business process with usage of the CRM system 2.3
(Created by Authors)

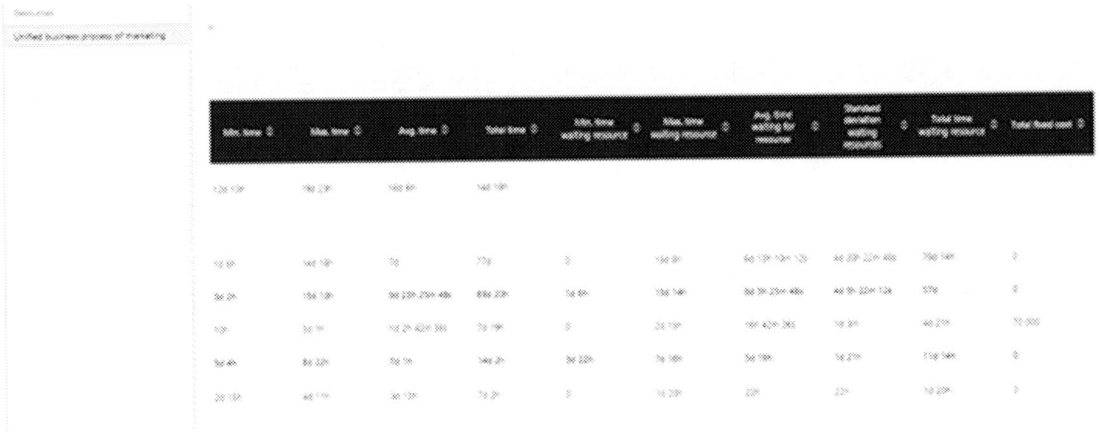

The differences between diagrams on Figures 6, 11 and 16 are in settings of parameters

Of course, it is possible to elaborate another style of diagram of marketing business process, for example, with usage of all types of programs. It is possible to set different means for parameters – their value depends on specific or organization of marketing service.

CONCLUSION

Taking into account that today there is a new concept - sustainable marketing, which works in three directions - economic, social and ecological directions, it can be said that serious changes are taking place in the organization of the marketing service itself. Without its successful, properly organized work, it is impossible to carry out the serious work that comes with the concept of sustainability.

Figure 16. Diagram of marketing business process with usage of an analytical software
(Created by Authors)

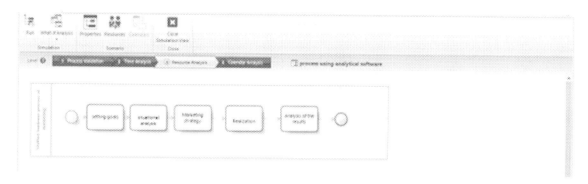

Figure 17. Simulation of marketing business process with usage of analytical software
(Created by Authors)

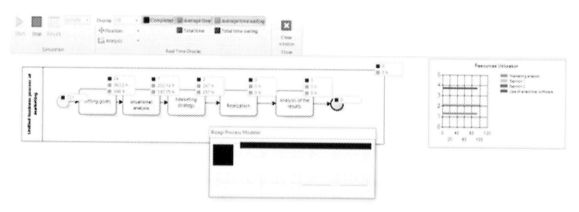

Figure 18. Result of simulation of marketing business process with usage of analytical program -3.1
(Created by Authors)

In this case, it becomes necessary to introduce business processes in marketing activities, which allow to obtain the maximum effect and reduce costs in the organization of marketing and the work of the company itself. Therefore, the issue presented in this paper - the development and modeling of the marketing business process is extremely relevant. Along with this, it is possible to take into account the

Design of Business Processes for Marketing Activity

Figure 19. Result of simulation of marketing business process with usage of analytical program -3.2
(Created by Authors)

Figure 20. Result of simulation of marketing business process with usage of analytical program -3.3
(Created by Authors)

realization of sustainable marketing tasks in the presented business process. Using the developed diagrams, by the mean of the special software tool Bizagi BPMN Modeler, simulation modeling is carried out with different scenarios and different initial parameter values. The offered models can be used during the marketing business process design of any type of enterprise. By the mean of simulation, the results are obtained, which allow to evaluate and optimize the different (human and other) resources, usage of software tools, duration and cost of works in the activity of the marketing department. It is possible to select the best scenario, which is advantageous in the process of business process development, since the model must be built first - "as it is", and then - "as it must be".

Resalts of simulation are very usfull for decission making person during the organizacion of marketing service in organization considering the concept of sustainable marketing.

REFERENCES

Chernev, A., & Kotler, P. (2018). *Strategic Marketing Management* (9th ed.). Cerebellum Press.

Gavala, G. (2022, March 2). 5 Business Process Management Statistics You Should Know. *Solutions Review*. https://solutionsreview.com/business-process-management/business-process-management-statistics-you-should-know/

Kasim, T., Haracic, M., & Haracic, M. (2018). The Improvement of Business Efficiency Through Business Process Management, *Economic Review. Journal of Economics and Business, 16*(1), 31–43.

Kortam, W., & Mahrous, A. A. (2020). Sustainable Marketing: A Marketing Revolution or A Research Fad. *Archives of Business Research, 8*(1), 172–181. doi:10.14738/abr.81.7747

Kotler, P., Kartajaya, H., & Setiawan, I. (2016). *Marketing 4.0*. John Wiley & Sons.

Kotler, P., & Keller, K. L. (2014). *Marketing Management* (15th ed.). Pearson.

Mir-Bernal, P., & Sadaba, T. (2022). The ultimate theory of the marketing mix: A proposal for marketers and managers. *International Journal of Entrepreneurship, 28*, 1–22.

Nijhof, A., Wins, A., Argyrou, A., & Chevrollier, N. (2022). Sustainable market transformation: A refined framework for analyzing causal loops in transitions to sustainability. *Environmental Innovation and Societal Transitions, 42*, 352–361. doi:10.1016/j.eist.2022.01.010

Ozili, P. K. (2022). Sustainability and Sustainable Development Research around the World. *Managing Global Transitions, 20*(3). doi:10.26493/1854-6935.20.259-293

Pomering, A. (2017). Marketing for Sustainability: Extending the Conceptualisation of the Marketing Mix to Drive Value for Individuals and Society at Large. *Australasian Marketing Journal, 25*(2), 157–165. doi:10.1016/j.ausmj.2017.04.011

Rosário, A. T. (2021). based guidelines for marketing information systems. [IJBSA]. *International Journal of Business Strategy and Automation, 2*(1), 1–16. doi:10.4018/IJBSA.20210101.oa1

Rukhadze, T., Tevdoradze, M., Bajiashvili, A., Lolashvili, N., & Saltkhutsishvili, M. (2016). Marketing management and its informational support. *Automated Management Systems, 2*(22).

Shen, Z. (2022). Big Data Analysis of Marketing User Intelligence Information Based on Deep Learning. *Mobile Information Systems, 2022*, 1–7. doi:10.1155/2022/2990649

Tevdoradze, M., Aptsiauri, D., Gudava, V., Rukhadze, T., Darchia, S., & Lobazhanidze, L. (2015). Use of information technology in financial management and marketing of the company. *International scientific conference Information and computer technologies, modeling, management dedicated to the 85th birthday of Academician Iv. Frangishvili. works*. GTU.

Tevdoradze, M., Chigladze, T., Bajiashvili, A., Ioseliani, G., Lolashvili, N. (2014). Process-oriented management of modern organization. *Intellect Magazine, 3*(50).

Tevdoradze, M., Lolashvilia, N., Bajiashvili, A., Rukhadze, T., Saltkhutsishvili, M., Chigladze, T. (2017). *The role of modeling in the design and optimization of business processes*. Monograph. GTU.

United Nations. (1987). United Nations general assembly: Development and international co-operation. Environment report of the world commission on environment and development. *Our common future. Released by the Brundtland commission.* UN. https://sustainabledevelopment.un.org/content/documents/5987our-common-future.pdf

Weller, J. (2017, June 23). Essential Guide to Strategic Planning. *Smart Sheet.* https://www.smartsheet.com/strategic-planning-guide

KEY TERMS AND DEFINITIONS

Business process: Represents a repeating sequence of certain operations (functions), which has entrance and exit. Itis supplied with a resources at the entrance; resource are processed during the execution of the operations included in the business process, and as a result, a certain type of product is obtained at the output of business process, and this product necessarily has a customer.

Business processes life cycle: Consists of four stages: 1. Business process design; 2. Realization of the business process; 3. Observation during the realization of business processes and 4. Analysis of observation results and reaction in the case of their deviations

Besigning a business process: This is obtaining its full description, including its operations, inputs, outputs, resources, parameters, process instructions

ERP (Enterprice Resourse Planning): The type of information systems manage the execution of business processes.

CRM (Custom Relationship Management): This is type of programs is closely related to solving of marketing tasks.

BPM (Business Processes Management): The ideology, which includes not only business processes themselves, but also all questions in the connection with the life cycle of business processes - issues of their design, execution management, control as well as relevant software solutions.

Section 3
Marketing and Digitalization for Achieving Sustainability: Country and Industry Context

Chapter 11
Digitalization of the Marketing Strategy as SMEs' Sustainable Development Guarantee

Natia Surmanidze
The University of Georgia, Georgia

Keti Tskhadadze
The University of Georgia, Georgia

Khatuna Tabagari
Guram Tavartkiladze Tbilisi Teaching University, Georgia

Sopiko Tevdoradze
Guram Tavartkiladze Tbilisi Teaching University, Georgia

Zurab Mushkudiani
Guram Tavartkiladze Tbilisi Teaching University, Georgia

ABSTRACT

The chapter reviews and analyzes in depth the role and importance of marketing digitalization strategies in small companies, using the example of Georgian handmade accessories (bag manufacturer), where the problematic aspects of access to finance are considered vital for developing countries' entrepreneurship. Qualitative research was conducted on 90 respondents, the results of which and the comparative analysis of desk research confirmed the hypothesis that digital marketing strategy is a significant factor for SMEs to reach sustainable development. Besides, if the strategy is long-term, the company gets a guarantee to grow its size and obtain high competitiveness. The research solved the most critical problem, how small companies can implement marketing activities cheaply and qualitatively, and effectively, forming a brand and a loyal customer.

INTRODUCTION

Small and medium enterprises (SMEs) are a significant part of the economy that helps the country to have high economic growth and sustainable development. Developed countries are trying to create a

DOI: 10.4018/978-1-6684-8681-8.ch011

stable environment for small businesses, such as loyal taxation, cheap credits, government support for exporting and trading, supporting innovations, etc. For example, 99% of registered business entities are small businesses in the U. S. which help local economies stability as the development of small entrepreneurship defines the direction of the country's economy in general.

Small and medium-sized enterprises (SMEs) employ fewer than 250 persons, have an annual turnover not exceeding EUR 50 million, and an annual balance sheet total not exceeding EUR 43 million. An enterprise is an entity engaged in economic activity, irrespective of its legal form. (EU, 2003). Digital transformation is "an evolutionary process that leverages digital capabilities and technologies to enable business models, operational processes, and customer experiences to create value" (Morakanyane et al., 2017). Sustainable development is "development that meets the needs of the present without compromising the ability of future generations to meet their own needs" (Emas, 2015). Digital marketing strategy involves an assessment of specific goals achievable through online channels (ama.org. 2022).

As for less developed countries, the above-said proportion is different, and they need to strengthen SMEs. Covid-19 became a strong challenge for small and medium entities as the need for digitalization has appeared as a major factor for survival. Spreading the Covid 19, it insulted first of all people's life, health, economic stability, business work, and in general world and each country's GDPs. There was a big question of how businesses will recover and how society will get used to it. Besides, not all society was emotionally ready to receive the new reality of the world order. The Covid pandemic impacted most of the fields in the world so acutely that some companies' scales were reduced or even closed in the worst case. There were lockdowns, stay-at-home policies, and social distances; part of the "old" entrepreneurs began diversifying their small businesses, on the other hand, there was always a second side to the medal and all these challenges boosted new ideas. There can be distinguished some activities by which small businesses tried to run their own business, namely trading with agricultural products, cakes and generally sweets, handmade designers, craftsmen activities, etc., and "new" entrepreneurs, tried to establish new businesses which would be affordable to everyone online: online services, delivering services, e-commerce, etc. Online consumption also was raised and formed in the world. Even though Covid Pandemic is more or less over, the past will not be back. There is a new reality, new business ideas, rules and new confront where digitalization became the main leader for companies in the competitive market.

Today traditional ways are not enough in the competitive and fast-developed market because nowadays digital era is in the world.

In the economy, there are two sides: consumption and production. Consumption can be formed via sophisticated, stable, and high-quality goods or/and services.

Even after overcoming the Pandemic, digital ways maintain their advanced position for producers and service suppliers, which made them make various creative marketing strategies in digital channels. Today it is easy to start a business, globalisation allows one to find a proper environment for business activity. Besides sustainable development is especially hard for SMEs, as they experience difficulties with maintaining finances.

According to official surveys, digital transformation creates a giant opportunity for entrepreneurs and generally small and medium-sized businesses. Digital platforms, web browsing, and web pages for business purposes become vital. High-quality web pages and delivering services are more consumed and demanded.

Developing or less developed countries also faced and still face these challenges. Georgia is a Post-Soviet country, and small businesses more or less are developed. But it seems these entrepreneurs or little companies stay within their small boundaries. There appear significant challenges and failures. First of all, most businesses do not have a marketing strategy (marketing plan), especially a long-term strategy. Unfortunately, the pandemic boosted entrepreneurs to run their businesses without deep knowledge, plans, and strategy, as they retired or wages were reduced, so, there appeared a gap: these "new" entrepreneurs needed to analyse the significance of the digital marketing strategy of SMEs as the guarantor of developed business. The idea of starting a business is also connected to security, finances, planning, etc. most entrepreneurs plan their business only locally and restrain to expand their scale of economy digitally. (Surmanidze, 2022)

When a small business is developed in the country, this helps society be courageous and strong. They can work with family members, relatives, and friends or even hire other foreign persons to increase their little company. So, this enlarges the number of employers and provides the reduction of unemployment.

The government should support small businesses in the country in different ways with tax relief, actual training, and supporting online businesses via TV, radio, social media, and online magazines to expand the marketing strategy, and increase the amount of consumption for their goods or/and services.

The work aims to figure out the need for digitalization for SMEs' sustainable development, especially long-term digital strategies, which become the guarantee for small entrepreneurship to succeed.

To reach the aim, the following objectives should be solved:

To analyse SME digitalization strategies before and after the pandemic.

To identify the need of having long-term digitalization strategies.

To study digital marketing strategies for companies that are small-sized.

To compare Georgian SMEs with companies in other countries.

To identify the role of maintaining finances in developing digital marketing strategies.

To conduct quantitative research on Georgian SMEs.

The independent variable in the study is a digital marketing strategy, and the dependent variable is sustainable development. The connection between variables is positive. According to this comes the hypothesis: digital marketing strategy is a significant factor for SMEs to reach sustainable development. Besides, if the strategy is long-term, the company gets a guarantee to grow its size and obtain high competitiveness.

According to the abovementioned issues the main mission and concept of the proposed chapter are to show what role the marketing strategy of digitalization plays for small business to provide their stable development in the competitive market.

LITERATURE REVIEW

Small enterprises are the core of economic growth and development; it also gives opportunities to people to run their own business in various fields; digitalization of companies is more competitive than the ones with traditional opportunities as digitalized companies have online payments, e-commerce platforms, online lending services, etc. there are also five forms of digital support for small business, as follows: digital market access, operations, credit, skill building and engagement (Friederici, 2022). Small and medium-sized enterprises play a significant role in national economies and the world; it also helps the economy create jobs, reduce the rate of unemployment, increase GDP value, and become a backbone of the country, etc. (OECD, 2017).

In the EU, there were 23.1 million small and medium-sized enterprises (SMEs) in 2021, 99% of all businesses. They employ about 50% of the GDPs of Europe (approximately $ 23 trillion) (European Commission, 2022) (Clark, 2022) (The World Bank, 2021).

In 2021, 99% of registered business entities (31.7 million small businesses) were small businesses in the U. S. which help local economies stability as the development of small entrepreneurship defines the direction of the country's economy in general (U.S. Chamber of Commerce 2021). Furthermore, for 2022, there was also 99% of the small business in total U. S. registered businesses (Oberlo, 2022). The share of SME contribution was 50% of the GDP ($ 23 trillion) of the U. S. in 2021 (U.S. SMALL BUSINESS ADMINISTRATION, 2021) (The World Bank, 2021).

Small enterprises are non-subsidiary firms with less than 50 employees in the E. U. with EUR 10 million turnovers or less than EUR 10 million balance-sheet valuations. Medium-sized enterprises have a staff of less than 250 with less than EUR 10 million turnovers and less than EUR 43 million balance sheets (Official Journal of the European Union, 2003). As for the U. S., there are less than 500 people with $ 10 million in assets, etc. (U.S. Small business administration, 2023).

The Covid Pandemic impacted the world economy, policy, health, business, etc. The income rate decreased, some even lost their jobs, and Covid 19 Pandemic interference with them to start or increase their businesses with small and medium-sized enterprises or expand them; Digital transformation is "an evolutionary process that leverages digital capabilities and technologies to enable business models, operational processes, and customer experiences to create value" (Morakanyane et al, 2017). According to research in China, digital transformation can overcome innovation challenges facing small and medium-sized enterprises. Furthermore, digital transformation can make it with improving the quality of innovation (Zhuo and Chen, 2023). According to the other significant research paper, digital transformation can upgrade innovation capacity with quality and quantity directions. The fundamental issues that positively impact digital transformation and innovation are Knowledge flow, technical personnel, R&D investment, and innovation awareness (Chen & Kim, 2023). According to recent research on digital transformation, it not only provides SME-s business sector creates a comparative advantage but eases access to customers and finances. At the same time, there are increased risks of a lack of skilled employers (Skare et al., 2023).

Sustainable development is "development that meets the needs of the present without compromising the ability of future generations to meet their own needs" (Global Sustainable Development Report (GSDR), 2015) (United Nations General Assembly, 1987). As SMEs are the root of Sustainable development in the countries' economy, it needs a marketing strategy. In the digital age, it means digital marketing strategy to keep competitiveness in the jeopardized business environment and country.

"Marketing strategy is an organization's integrated pattern of decisions that specify its crucial choices concerning products, markets, marketing activities, and marketing resources in the creation, communication, and delivery of products that offer value to customers in exchanges with the organization and thereby enables the organization to achieve specific objectives "(Varadarajan, 2010). Marketing strategy began its existence in 1960, and its objectives are to make a framework to assess the research about marketing strategy, create and execute the performance of the "state of knowledge," and make the research agenda to define the future possibilities of the marketing strategy that requires more than it has (Morgan et al, 2018). As the world developed, everything changed, but sometimes such issues pushed science to be more set than it is: The Pandemic.

After the spreading the Covid 19, small and medium-sized enterprises tried to survive at least; the Pandemic interrupted marketing strategies work traditionally; according to recently conducted research, companies tried to change the method of existing communication marketing during the Pandemic, and the concepts were identified by which companies need to have: knowledge and expertise, and IT-related resources, IT-related capabilities, dynamic capabilities, and environmental uncertainty (Behl et al., 2023). Covid 19 indeed impacted the transport system. The virus changed society's behavior and accelerated its understanding of informational technologies. According to the research conducted in 2022, the Pandemic boosted online commerce, the development of digital connections, delivery services, remote working, hybrid modes of jobs, souring the demand for delivery services of goods, development of customer interactions based on Big Data technologies, etc. (Strauli et al., 2022). According to other also conducted research, digital marketing strategy involves an assessment of specific goals achievable through online channels (ama.org, 2022), but the foremost challenges of small business sustainable transformation are the security of information technology (IT) and the lack of adequate labor market; furthermore, the number of employees, income, and skills to install the digital issues in their own business (Rupeika-Apoga & Petrovska, 2022). Furthermore, the key drivers of marketing innovation for small and medium-sized enterprises are institutional, resource, innovation, and performance measurement factors (Dwivedi & Pawsey, 2023). As the Pandemic influenced SMEs, they tried to change strategies digitally, and they need to know the following five steps, "passive acceptance," "connection," "immersion," "fusion," and "transformation," to achieve a proper strategy (Canhoto et al., 2021).

SMEs as a Powerful Institution in the Country's Economy

The role of small and medium entrepreneurship is significant in a country's economy, as it is responsible for reducing unemployment, growing added value, and raising social welfare. Besides, SMEs bring innovations. They are flexible, and it helps them to be stable against shocks. In the Georgian economy SMEs, sustainable development is a national strategy. Government supports SMEs by implementing various projects that contribute to their development and prove the competitiveness of the products they create for the international market.

As of 2022, almost 93% of enterprises in Georgia are in the form of individual enterprises or limited liability enterprises. Among them, the percentage share according to active status is even higher and is approximately 95%. The mentioned fact clarifies these companies' importance in ensuring the economy's sustainable development.

Small and medium-sized enterprises play a significant role in economies of any size but are particularly important in developing countries. Small and medium-sized enterprises are the most common form of business worldwide and contribute significantly to job creation and global economic development. According to the World Bank, they represent about 90% of businesses and more than 50% of significant employers globally. The sector's share in national incomes is exceptionally high. In particular, up to 40% of the GDP of developing countries comes from them. (World Bank, 2022) Statistical dynamics estimates that by 2030, 600 million jobs will be created globally by them, making the development of small and medium businesses a high priority for many governments worldwide. SMEs generate most jobs in emerging markets, which account for 7 out of 10 jobs. (World Employment Organization, 2022)

Georgia's parameters are different from world dynamics. About 60% of total output and added value comes from small companies. Moreover, for a country in the active phase of social problems, the small business sector creates about 63% of jobs. Regarding wages, medium-sized enterprises from the SME sector lead in average monthly wages and labor productivity per employee. (Geostat 2023)

The issue of access to finance is quite relevant in Georgia, proven by the lack of capital in the SME sector. Large enterprises have almost ten times more capital productivity than small and medium enterprises. However, medium-level enterprises are still in the lead regarding capital equipment. The share of the small category in the total export is 14.5%, and the share of the medium category is up to 26%. (Geostat 2023)

The given reasoning, supported by statistical indicators, confirms that the SME sector is a strong pillar of the Georgian economy. Focusing on long-term goals will allow the business to achieve sustainable development, primarily through marketing strategies. Even more so, businesses with difficulties accessing finance need to understand the benefits of taking a long-term marketing view in today's digital world. Traditional marketing, which may have been expensive for a small business, has now been replaced by digital marketing, which, from social networks to e-stores, allows businesses to reach more customers with less investment in marketing.

Finally, it will allow Sme's to increase productivity and create additional value and, therefore, more jobs, which will eventually be distributed among the layers of the population and make the prospect of eliminating social problems more tangible. Small and medium enterprises are rapidly adapting to the dynamic business world by moving to e-commerce and online transaction of goods and services. Technological developments have not only eased the process of selling and buying but have also helped entrepreneurs reduce advertising and marketing costs. Various e-commerce platforms make it easier for small and medium businesses to exist.

Business Process Digitalization Efficiency for Small and Medium Enterprises

In recent years, business digitalization has been developing quickly, although the dynamics in different sectors are different. Firms are increasingly equipping their staff with digital tools, although smaller firms are doing so more slowly than the sector's giants. (OECD, 2021) Digitization is a multifaceted process involving different technologies that serve different purposes and require recombining different strategic activities. (Zairis, 2022) Not all SMEs have the capacity to make this transformation. The smaller the firm, the less likely it is to introduce new digital practices and the more likely it is. Overall, the digitalization of SMEs is closely related to value creation within the firm and the sector in which it operates. (Cariolle, Carroll, 2020)

As SMEs digitize their business functions, they increasingly consider process outsourcing to compensate for weak in-house capabilities and cost considerations. For example, digital platforms (e.g., social networks, e-commerce markets, etc.) serve to optimize certain functions at a meager cost. (Suresh, 2022) Similarly, to manage digital security risks, SMEs usually rely on external consultants or security design features of their products and services.

In countries where technological progress has not yet been adequately penetrated and developed, the potential of technology in small and medium-sized businesses is quite limited. For example, in African countries, there is a 60% rate of Internet access among the population, which hinders small entrepreneurs' introduction of Internet-based services. At the same time, these entrepreneurs create jobs and the main wealth in these countries. (Agmeka, Wathoni, Santoso, 2019) Studies in African countries have shown that firms that use digital technologies have more workers, have higher sales and export rates, are more productive, and potentially earn more. A study of small and medium-sized firms in Africa revealed that companies that are open to technology operate more efficiently, which gives grounds for assuming that the crucial issues of increasing market efficiency and strengthening the economy go through digitalization. (Daud, Nurjannah, Mohyi, Ambarwati, Cahyono, Haryoko, Jihadi, 2022)

The role of digital marketing in sales growth and brand building is quite significant, as evidenced by a study conducted on Indonesian business entities, improved digitalization enhanced branding strategies. (Dumitriu, Militaru, Deselnicu, Niculescu, Popescu, 2019) Making a purchase decision in the digital environment is more powerful, and the formation of a brand in social media becomes more accessible in the case of small and medium entrepreneurs. Studies show that marketing management is moving to a new level with digitalization, where the dynamic is significantly positive. (Haudi, Rahadjeng, Santamoko, Putra, Purwoko, Nurjannah, Purwanto, 2022)

To ensure growth and sustainability, many modern small and medium-sized enterprises (SMEs) operating in the EU have made building a stronger brand one of their primary goals. To achieve this goal, the main task for them has become the use of digital marketing tools and techniques for brand formation, which implies an increase in investments in this direction in human capital or directly in technologies, refinement of the business model, and digitalization of marketing activities. (Khan, Bilal, Saif, Shehzad, 2020)

Research on customer relationship management in Indonesia concluded that digitalization provides even more potential for small and medium enterprises to become more competitive and increase efficiency using innovative technologies. With a CRM application, companies can use all customer information collected from various sources, such as through call centers, the Internet, field services, and marketing personnel. This consistent information intake provides better service and sales thanks to a wide variety of important information about these customers. Using CRM applications at various stages of business operations is essential and effective in order to state and achieve the company's specific goals correctly. These goals are acquiring new customers, increasing customer value, and maintaining customer loyalty. (Liu, Perry, Gadzinski, 2019)

Globalization has increased access to world markets for small businesses, but they must incorporate technology to manage supply chains effectively. By properly organizing the logistics, it is possible to gain customer loyalty. (Purwanto, 2022) Digital supply chain management by SMEs predicts excellent success in business processes. Using supply chain management as a digital marketing strategy enables business owners to increase customer satisfaction levels. High customer satisfaction will, in turn, increase customer loyalty. To achieve this goal, small and medium business owners and managers must improve their business management capabilities by smartly using digital technologies. (Indumathi, 2018)

The role of digital technologies is immeasurably remarkable in terms of simplifying payment systems. A study of small and medium businesses in Indonesia has proven that those businesses that manage their finances using digital technologies operate much more effectively in the market. The focus here is not only on payment systems but also fundraising and other processes a business needs to operate. The research highlighted the following the heads of firms in Indonesia need to raise awareness and deepen their knowledge regarding the digitization of financial management. (Juwaini, Chidir, Novitasari, Iskandar, Hutagalung, Pramono, Purwanto, 2022) On the other hand, the most crucial issue is that digital financial management of companies will bring more transparency, which will help form a reliable reputation.

Access to finance is the primary constraint to the growth of SMEs; it is the second most apparent obstacle that SMEs face, preventing them from expanding their business in emerging markets and developing countries.

Small and medium-sized enterprises have less access to bank loans than large firms. Instead, they rely on internal funds, or cash from IPrady contacts, to launch and run their early-stage ventures. The

International Finance Corporation (IFC) estimates that 65 million firms, or 40% of formal micro, small and medium enterprises (MSMEs) in developing countries, have unmet financing needs of $5.2 trillion annually—the level of global lending to SMEs. East Asia and the Pacific region have the largest share of global access to finance problems (46%), followed by Latin America and the Caribbean (23%) and Europe and Central Asia (15%). In particular, Latin America, the Caribbean, the Middle East, and North Africa regions have the highest share of the problem of access to finance compared to potential demand, which is approximately equal to 87% and 88%. About half of the formal SMEs do not have access to formal credit. The financing gap is even more significant when it includes micro and informal enterprises.

Since resources are constantly limited, managers must decide where and how much money to invest. There is no universal combination; logical reasoning and correct calculations are critical. (Syazali, Putra, Rinaldi, Utami, Widayanti, Umam, Jermsittiparsert, 2019) The fact is that digital technologies are constantly changing and developing; therefore, in the budgeting part, companies should carefully review the funds they have allocated in this direction and act according to the situation, for example, content marketing, optimization of search systems, management of the supply network, or the development of any other direction the company will need at a given time. (Suharto, Junaedi, Muhdar, Firmansyah, Sarana, 2022)

In the era of the digital economy, digital transformation has become a new approach for firms to gain competitive advantages in the face of intense and dynamic market competition. Companies in almost all industries have undergone or are currently undergoing digital transformation. (Brodny, 2022) Due to limited resources and capabilities, the digitization process of SMEs could be faster. Therefore it is crucial to determine the primary factors and ways that influence the digital transformation of SMEs. On success in order to optimize the allocation of resources. However, there needs to be more research on the digital transformation of SMEs. The results of the analysis of data collected from 180 Chinese SMEs show that technological and environmental factors have a positive impact on organizational capabilities and then contribute to the success of the digital transformation process of SMEs. (Zhang, Xu, Ma, 2022) Organizational capabilities play a mediating role in the transformation process. They are considering technological and environmental factors. Also, employees' professional and personal skills positively impact organizational capabilities and digital transformation.

The main challenges of digitization may be the difficulty of accessing the Internet, digital literacy, and cultural differences that small companies often face. For example, Alter Socks is a Georgian company with a different positioning strategy in social channels. The main difference is their page's content, represented by humorous posts. Since humor is an integral part of the culture, their social media channel is wholly dedicated to a niche readership, as cultural diversification only allows the company to cater to a global audience.

The problem of Internet access in Georgia still needs to be solved. However, high-quality, high-speed Internet still needs to be made available for many people. At the same time, the level of digital awareness could be better. Many companies choose the positioning strategy in social media channels because digital channels are more popular among Georgian consumers, and therefore they should be familiar with them.

The importance of developing digital technologies is mentioned in the UN Sustainable Development Goals, according to which the availability of information and communication technologies, the use of digital technologies, and the elimination of digital inequality are among the main factors for ensuring sustainable development.

Sustainable development of business companies implies an emphasis on economic development, social welfare and environmental protection at the same time. In order for the company to be able to transition to a new sustainable business model, it is necessary for the company's management team to have a good understanding of the existing sustainable vision and dynamic sustainability challenges. At the next stage, the ecosystem where the company operates should be studied, taking into account all environmental and social factors. At this time, the company needs to see its activities in a broader perspective. After understanding this vision, it is important to develop a business expansion plan and identify opportunities for innovation. At this time, the existence of digitization strategies becomes relevant. The most affordable option for a company, if it has access to finance, is to digitize its marketing. Digital marketing includes social media and its management process is associated with lower costs compared to other digital channels.

Design of the research

Desk research - secondary material, description, and analysis of valid statistical material from official sources. In the literature review section, the research concludes with recent articles published in high-impact factor scientific journals that make the paper relevant. In addition, the statistical material analysis showed the consumer's attitude towards digital technologies and presented the economic importance of small and medium entrepreneurship.

Qualitative research - qualitative research is an important part, within the framework of which preliminary information was collected through in-depth interviews with various representatives of the small and medium sectors operating in the Georgian market. Nineteen Georgian small and medium-sized enterprises are surveyed, characterized by the behavior of using digital technologies. The main activity of these companies is the production of Georgian handmade accessories. The research units are small Georgian companies producing imitation, artificial leather, and fabric bags. The unit of the study is only businesses with legal status. The sector is relatively small. In total, about 250 companies in this direction are active in the current period. The sampling allowed the research to be valid as 36% of the total market is studied. Responses were collected using the Zoom platform, and video recordings of the interviews were made, followed by transcripts based on them. The interview questions develop in two directions; on the one hand, the respondents' digital technology management strategies are generally studied, if they have a clear strategy in the direction of digital technology management, if they have appropriate persons who are responsible for this direction, if they were forced to digitize or if digital technologies naturally entered their activities.

On the other hand, the study examines the importance of digital marketing in businesses. Since small companies have the problem of access to finance and classical marketing is not available for them. Therefore social media is a powerful tool to establish a brand and form loyal customers. Due to the difficulty of access to finance and the difficult economic situation in Georgia, the search for critical markets for companies, brand formation, etc. It is delegated to cheaper means than traditional marketing elements. In order to increase validity in interpreting the results of the study, random sampling was carried out using the equal probability sampling method so that each element had an equal probability of being included in the sample.

Results

The results of the in-depth interviews are discussed below, compared with the official materials to cross-check the information provided by the respondents. Also, in some cases, the field's local or global statistical material has been used to make the conclusions valid. At the same time, analysis of the statistical dynamics of consumption by certain digital technology providers and comparison with the received answers adds significant value to the research. Accordingly, the process of generalizing the in-depth interview results is relevant in the background of analyzing the secondary data.

Respondents are highly dependent on digital channels, especially in sales promotion, as most of them do their advertising activities on social media. More than 50% of respondents (47 respondents) say that they use digital media channels for marketing activities and providing information to consumers. In particular, the information includes the products' exact characteristics and the necessary care recommendations.

Although some are also consumers of traditional marketing activities, social media is part of their marketing strategy. In particular, 23 respondents used traditional marketing, and 82 used digital marketing. It demonstrates that traditional marketing is developing parallel to digital:

The number of social media users is growing dynamically.

According to Statista's forecast, social media users are increasing by 6.7% annually, and the market is growing and potentially developing. Respondents who do not currently use social media intend to start actively digitizing their marketing shortly.

Most of the respondents are focused on local customers (73 respondents) because the business size is small, and only 17 of them are trying to capture the international market. Accordingly, their social media channels are intended mainly for Georgian users, although some simultaneously post information in Georgian and English. In addition, 47 respondents believe they will attract foreign users through Instagram more than through other visual channels.

Figure 1. Statista's 2023 social media consumption dynamics and forecast are as follows
Source: Statista 2023

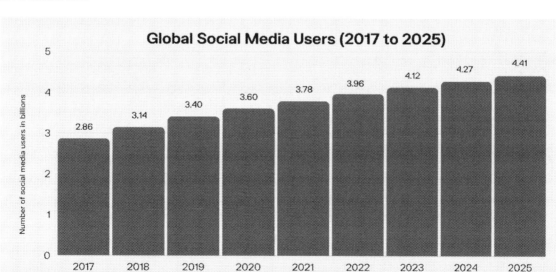

Most respondents (53) need more export potential due to business size and lack of financial resources. Therefore, Georgian brands at this stage use only popular social media tools that are famous in Georgia.

When identifying the advantages of digital media, most respondents highlighted the advantages of social media because these channels are interactive platforms, which allows them to speak directly to consumers. Although some companies also use TV advertising, it does not create a feeling of interactivity in the customer. Therefore they need to talk to the customer, listen to him and solve the problem.

Facebook has a particular feature - Ads Manager that helps a manager select his segment and test its adequacy, which is a good way for young companies to reach the right segment. Businesses can follow the advertising distribution process and analyze advertising effectiveness based on feedback. In addition, Facebook's algorithm embeds that the longer the boost lasts, the more opportunities are given to the advertisement to reach the masses.

In addition, Facebook allows people to form their communities. For example, in the case of 9 respondents, even though the business physically locates in Georgia, its formation as a brand occurs for the community outside the borders of Georgia through a Facebook group. They actively use the informative Facebook group, the smallest of which unites 16.1 thousand people from different countries. They built their community not about their brand but around their brand. In particular, the members of these groups get advice on modern trends, trendy items, care of various accessories, and other similar issues. Occasionally, their brand is announced in these groups, although this is not an annoying advertisement or even advertisement.

The effective management strategies of social media mean forming a community around the brand and making advertising offers to them in a non-irritating (non-viral) form has a prominent place. Experts believe that if the company perceives the public only as potential customers on social media, it will affect negatively because this is people's personal space. Therefore no one likes to be treated here as a customer entering the store. (Bovee and Thill, 2016)

Seventy-one respondents answer that influencers are part of social media. It is a powerful element of modern marketing, so it can benefit a start-up business by gaining quick exposure.

In some cases, specific products require a YouTube channel, as tutorials are vital today. Youtube is a user-generated platform. As a result, one thing is that the tutorials themselves have an audience, and the other thing is that the user created in the name of the brand itself becomes popular.

Businesses that focus on attracting customers start using the LinkedIn platform, which is an opportunity to establish business contacts directly. At the same time, the latest social channels like TikTok are becoming increasingly popular, and companies understand this very well, so they try to create valuable content on the platform.

Most of the respondents use Facebook and Instagram daily.

The dynamics of the top popularity of popular social media channels in Georgia are similar to the global dynamics. 60% (55) of respondents simultaneously post the same information on Facebook and Instagram pages.

Regarding digital technology management, 64 respondents stated they do not have a centralized digital technology management system. They implement and manage the appropriate technology based on the need to implement a specific operation. Some of them (37 respondents) use ERP systems in their daily activities, which help them in accounting, and accordingly, its information is provided to different departments. Some companies (41 respondents) have a marketing manager who communicates with the social media outsourcing company and gives orders based on marketing strategies.

Figure 2. The following are the statistics on the use of social media channels by global surveys
Source: Statista, 2023

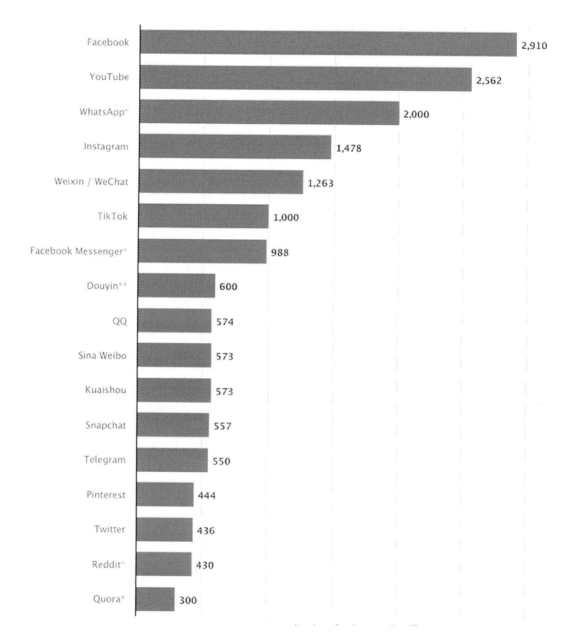

Similar respondents are large companies, so they have the resources to manage the process in a decentralized manner. In small companies, the marketing management process is mainly distributed in the upper management functions. At the same time, receiving services from outsourcing is popular. For example, those companies with a website (17 respondents) have entirely outsourced the management of the website.

Most respondents (72) will post information about their product on digital channels. Some (29 respondents) are developing information delivery on a blog model because they consider it necessary for their business. According to many experts, a blog helps a company indirectly stimulate sales. (Bovee, Thill, 2019) Each channel should be used according to its function. Conditionally, suppose the company has a website. In that case, it should perform a different function than a Facebook page because the management of the website requires much more money; therefore, if its role is not clearly defined, the issue of existence is questioned.

The inclusion of ratings indicates the extent to which a company has a CRM strategy and how adequately it understands the role of a satisfied customer. In the case of the respondents, most of them (65 respondents) have included the evaluation field, which can be evaluated positively because the modern consumer takes this into account when making a purchase decision. At the same time, an impression of transparency is created on the company's part and, accordingly, increases its credibility. A few companies (27 respondents) stated that they had been forced to enable rating fields in their delivery service provider applications because it is a requirement and standard. Where they have a choice, for example, in social media, they have disabled them. This fact cannot be considered optimistic because businesses need to understand the importance of CRM. Salesforce, the leader in integrating cloud technologies into business, says in its research that a 29% increase in sales can be achieved with the right CRM. (Bova, 2019)

In the research process, it was analyzed to what extent they provide feedback on evaluations and comments because the mentioned issue is a part of CRM on the one hand. On the other hand, it contributes to forming the company's image. If we compare the small and medium sectors, we will be convinced that it is much easier for small companies to establish feedback than for medium or large companies. The size of the company largely determines how flexibly it manages media channels. In the case of the respondents, large-sized businesses do not establish feedback because they need to pay more attention to familiarizing themselves with their content, and they need to have the appropriate human resources which will directly deal with this matter.

Furthermore, in some cases (43 respondents), they pay more attention to the evaluations than to the comments because their uncontrollable number of thousands requires a lot of resources and energy to answer. In this case, the leaders act with a particular strategy. In the case of reviews, they mostly react but prefer to remain silent regarding negative comments. Thirty-two respondents say that customers often complain about the price and find it difficult to explain the price's reasons and realism. If the products are primarily handmade, the price is correspondingly high, especially if they are made with natural materials. When respondents (34 respondents) see obscene comments, they immediately delete them. In our case, the product is high priced and accordingly.

Experts also consider this case a good action because obscene comments need to be deleted. On the contrary, the company should not delete negative comments but have a vision of satisfying the given user. Some companies (13 respondents) spend too much time on feedback. They constantly monitor the evaluations, and the presence of negative evaluations is an incentive for them to become stronger. However, there are cases when competitors or other interested parties try to damage the reputation of companies (11 respondents) by spreading false information. Someone may say that black PR is also PR, although the respondent companies do not want to establish themselves this way. That is why they constantly monitor the comments written on their page and periodically look for a group of strategic importance to them (for example, about fashion trends or among dissatisfied customers) to see if anything has been written about their brand in order to establish feedback.

Most respondents (59 respondents) say that digital channels determine the development and success of their company, and the vast majority of them consider that not only digital but also social media channels are of decisive importance in their effectiveness. At the same time, they believe that their company is constantly concerned with creating valuable content in the social environment. A study by the social media management platform Hootsuite found that 51-57% of social media users learn more skills on social media than at university. (Martin, M. 2022) Accordingly, there is a recommendation for companies to make social media channels as informative as possible.

Only a few surveyed companies (37 respondents) still need a digital technology management strategy. Moreover, they have decentralized management, as all departments act in their interests, as management strategies are set at a reasonably high level. They use management methods based on quick responses. Concerning digital technologies, the field itself is proliferating, and they are trying to keep up with the trends. Digitalization issues are of great importance to finance and marketing, as well as in other departments.

However, for some respondents (24 respondents), the strategy is there, and digital management is part of the strategy of every department, where it is written in detail what type of details should be emphasized.

As for a small part of the respondents (15 respondents), the strategy in their company is considered a means of solving tasks because they focus on the tasks necessary for increasing production and mobilizing finances.

In this case, the decentralized model, by its content, implies that the management goes through less bureaucracy before making a decision, and its importance in efficient time management is quite immense.

To analyze the correlation of digital technology management with time, the respondents answered questions about their digitalization plans in time. A small part of the respondents (36 respondents) has a strategy of long-term and short-term digitization and positioning in digital channels divided into two parts. Short-term is more called operational or steps towards the long term. They are focused on calculations for about one year because they must implement many changes permanently.

In the business world, the traditionally established views on periods, for example, a period of up to 1 year is short-term, 1-5 years are considered medium, and more than five years are considered long-term, do not necessarily work in the digital world. Considering that Facebook is only ten years old, the Internet has been around since 1983, and the Zoom platform was launched in 2011, it is clear that one year is a long time in the digital environment, and therefore the traditional understanding of time needs to be modified here.

At the same time, those companies trying to build a brand (63 respondents) focus on a long-term strategy because their main goal is to build a brand, and it will not be possible in the short term.

Moreover, 35 respondents have interconnected traditional and digital marketing, so they have long-term strategic plans. Regarding marketing activities, some (17 respondents) invested quite a lot in traditional marketing. Therefore, at the same time, they believe that they need to manage social media at least for the same period properly.

Significantly, the respondents observed a very healthy vision, and raising awareness among business entities regarding the digitalization of marketing is desirable.

Nine companies show significant behavior in digital transformation. In particular, they move to those channels that become popular. For example, Facebook and Instagram were popular before TikTok, and they use television more when the rating is high.

This issue is a joyous event because catching the right moment in a rapidly changing environment is the best way to position, stimulate sales and build a brand. Therefore, the company needs to follow the trends.

In the case of several companies (22 respondents), expansion became the main trigger of digitization. At first, when they started, there was no need for a website, but then the question of forming a brand arose, and the idea of a website came up. Collaboration systems were needed from the beginning, although at the initial stage, they had unlicensed accounts and replaced them with licensed ones.

At the same time, the strategies of those who expanded the segment to go from business users to the individual segment also changed significantly, which five companies did, having to invest more resources in technology.

The role of digital technologies is particularly relevant regarding the effective management of resources. Any business considering the need for efficient use of limited resources believes it can only survive with digital technologies.

This case is reasonable regarding the proper management of digital marketing when a community is formed around the brand and information about the brand is provided to them in a permanent, less annoying way—information and not an offer to buy. No matter how much a company wants to attract customers, digital marketing should not consider the entire social space as a potential customer because this space is not the only key market. Accordingly, proper management of reporting from advertising is necessary.

DISCUSSION

Significant decisions on digital technologies in Georgian companies are made at the top management level. Especially when discussing implementation, the issue is raised directly at the top level of the administrative decision.

The pandemic has further convinced the business sector of the need for digitization. Therefore, the respondents see how much easier their activities had become in the face of social distance and other restrictions when they moved to the virtual space and created offices, stores, meetings, etc. Accordingly, the pandemic made the world transition to digital technologies rapidly. Some respondent companies were founded during the pandemic, which shows how important the strategic management of digital technologies is for them.

The majority of respondents use social media tools in their activities. The forecast statistics of the mentioned platforms are increasing in dynamics, which gives grounds for assuming that the choice of the respondents is precisely on this digital technology with a good and promising future.

The respondents correctly perceived which channel their frequent use would bring them the maximum effect because the channels they listed coincided with the leading units of the most actively used platforms in the world statistics.

It should be noted here that Facebook has a chatbot, which is the best way for businesses to save resources (in particular, the call center). Therefore, their use should be further increased shortly.

Some companies have delegated the management of digital technologies in the marketing field to outsourcing companies, which is the correct calculation because the advantages of outsourcing, in general, are that it promotes the most effective use of limited resources. In addition, companies develop a strategy, and part of the execution is delegated, which further convinces us of the privilege of social media tools for the respondents.

There is a broad debate in the scientific literature about how important it is for effective management to use each digital channel in a targeted and correct way for success and effectiveness. The research showed that the respondents carefully considered the above, mainly when they decided to shut down the site because they had Facebook for the same function. Unlike managing the site, they administered it free of charge.

When understanding the importance of CRM, it is necessary to consider both the means of assessing the customer's side and establishing feedback on this assessment from the company's side. In the case of the respondents, they poorly understood this process because they had disabled the evaluation function. It should also be noted that they often need to manage to establish feedback. With modern research on the importance of CRM for the company, if companies do not start thinking about CRM management in time, they may not correctly identify the customer's wants and needs.

Expert research has established that companies should build their brand by creating content. Some respondents consider this and have a blog that they develop alongside other marketing activities. Companies are also trying to provide tutorials to their existing and potential customers about their product features and proper usage. Of course, first of all, it is a correct calculation because there will be fewer cases of misuse of given items, which may increase the number of dissatisfied customers. Also, video distribution channels like TikTok and YouTube (mostly) are viral, and in this regard, it is evident that they actively follow the trends.

Preferring a decentralized model of digital technology management means faster response and flexibility because, in a decentralized model, decisions are made at the level of departments and involve less bureaucracy. Accordingly, companies make decisions to support the proper functioning of digital technologies at the level of department managers, thereby implementing effective time management.

It should be noted here that when the company representatives recalled the digital transformation of their companies, they listed several factors that led to this. In particular, production expansion, market, and segment expansion, the Covid-19 pandemic, etc. They can no longer see a future without these technologies. This fact confirms the tremendous role of digital technologies in terms of the effective management of resources.

CONCLUSION

As a result of the research, it was revealed that the hypothesis is true. It is true that among digital technology management strategies, Georgian SME sector companies mainly apply digital technologies that stimulate marketing activities and more or less have a management strategy. However, a digital marketing management strategy was on their agenda at all stages of existence. They believe this saved their business from the restrictions imposed during the Covid-19 pandemic, brought their products to the international market, and increased sales and awareness. The advantage of digital marketing compared to classical marketing is the fact that positioning in digital media channels requires less financial investment than digitalization in other directions.

The mentioned sector and situation in Georgia are similar to the example of developing countries, which is caused by less access to finance in the SME sector, which is a severe problem for Georgia. For this purpose, several measures are implemented to create favorable conditions for income verification for small entrepreneurs. The smaller the company, the more urgent the issue. At this time, a digital marketing strategy is a guarantee to get better results with less money.

It will be helpful for companies to evaluate the efficiency of marketing digitalization strategy in two directions: the formation of loyalty and the increase in their brand awareness. Digitization of customer satisfaction management will be the best decision to measure loyalty formation.

The marketing digitalization process is bringing ethical and privacy issues to the companies. Companies will have to profoundly understand that the issue of consumer rights in the online space is gaining more relevance. Accordingly, they should familiarize themselves with the normative aspects surrounding the issue.

Strategy for data – A future-oriented business should aim to transform into a data-driven business where decisions are made based on relevant and accurate information. For this, it is necessary not only to collect data but also to visualize and process them.

Strategy for processes – Digitization of processes is a logical step in the development of any company. In a modern company, business processes are automated; Modern technologies help companies to reduce expenditures on routine processes, for example, chatbots; with the help of process mining, processes are constantly being observed and further refined.

Strategy on technology – Technology plays a central role in digital transformation. Using modern technologies in daily operations and customer relations opens up new opportunities and ways of development for business. The fastest way for companies to gain a competitive advantage is to incorporate more artificial intelligence into their business processes. Accordingly, the company should select the best technologies most suitable for its activities.

Strategy on the customer – The customer is the key to the success of any business. Therefore, it is critically important for a business to know its customers and have an established relationship policy with them, where CRM will be crucial.

Strategy on sales channels – when many other competitors offer a similar product or service to the market, a timely transformation of the company's products or services and digitization of sales channels is fundamental.

Strategy on security – One of the main challenges of the digital world and digital business is cyber security and ensuring business continuity. For this, cyber security norms should be observed according to international standards, and the assessment and maintenance of awareness of the cyber environment and employees should be ongoing.

Strategy on culture and employees – The people who directly create the product or service are as important as having the right strategy for a company. A company must have a well-established and sustainable digital culture in today's market. The company must ensure employees' involvement in the digital transformation process. They should be familiar with modern technologies, cyber hygiene rules and understand the importance of data collection and use.

A company can only have a sustainable development strategy with a digitalization strategy. The most affordable way to digitize, if there is a problem with access to finance, is the digitization of marketing. The most potent component of digital marketing is social media, the effective management of which has provided the company with opportunities for new market acquisition, loyalty, and brand building.

The research was conducted on small-scale craft enterprises. However, its results can be generalized for enterprises of the fourth category, which according to Georgian legislation, belong to small-scale enterprises. However, craft enterprises are specific, and therefore it will be more informative if the questionnaire is adapted to the specifics of the sector while studying other retail trade segments.

REFERENCES

Adam, M., Ibrahim, M., Ikramuddin, I., & Syahputra, H. (2020). The role of digital marketing platforms on supply chain management for customer satisfaction and loyalty in small and medium enterprises (SMEs) at Indonesia. *International Journal of Supply Chain Management, 9*(3), 1210–1220.

Agmeka, F., Wathoni, R. N., & Santoso, A. S. (2019). The influence of discount framing towards brand reputation and brand image on purchase intention and actual behaviour in e-commerce. *Procedia Computer Science, 161*, 851–858. doi:10.1016/j.procs.2019.11.192

ama.org, (2022). *Why You Need a Digital Marketing Strategy*. AMA.

Behl, Jayawardena, N., Nigam, A., Pereira, V., Shankar, A., & Jebarajakirthy, C. (2023). Investigating the revised international marketing strategies during COVID-19 based on resources and capabilities of the firms: A mixed msethod approach. *Journal of Business Research, 158*, 1–16. doi:10.1016/j.jbusres.2023.113662 PMID:36644446

Bova, T. 2019. 26 Sales Statistics That Prove Selling Is Changing. *Salesforce*. https://www.salesforce.com/blog/15-sales-statistics/

Bovee, C. L., & Thill, J. V. (2019). *Business Communication Essentials: Fundamental Skills for the Mobile-Digital-Social Workplace (What's New in Business Communication)* (8th ed.). Pearson.

Brodny, J., & Tutak, M. (2022). Magdalena Tutak, Digitalization of Small and Medium-Sized Enterprises and Economic Growth: Evidence for the EU-27 Countries. *Journal of Open Innovation, 8*(2), 67. doi:10.3390/joitmc8020067

Canhoto, Quinton, S., Pera, R., Molinillo, S., & Simkin, L. (2021). Digital strategy aligning in SMEs: A dynamic capabilities perspective. *The Journal of Strategic Information Systems, 30*(3), 1–17. doi:10.1016/j.jsis.2021.101682

Cariolle, J., & Carroll, D. 2020. Digital Technologies for Small and Medium Enterprises and job creation in Sub-Saharan Africa. Hal- 03004583, Ferdi https://hal.archives-ouvertes.fr/hal-03004583

Chen, K. (2023). The impact of digital transformation on innovation performance - The mediating role of innovation factors. *Heliyon, 9*, 1–11.

Daud, I., Nurjannah, D., Mohyi, A., Ambarwati, T., Cahyono, Y., Haryoko, A., & Jihadi, M. (2022). The effect of digital marketing, digital finance and digital payment on finance performance of Indonesian smes. *International Journal of Data and Network Science, 6*(1), 37–44. doi:10.5267/j.ijdns.2021.10.006

Dumitriu, D., Militaru, G., Deselnicu, D. C., Niculescu, A., & Popescu, M. A. M. (2019). A perspective over modern SMEs: Managing brand equity, growth and sustainability through digital marketing tools and techniques. *Sustainability (Basel), 11*(7), 2111. doi:10.3390u11072111

Dwivedi and Pawsey. (2023). Examining the drivers of marketing innovation in SMEs. *Journal of Business Research, 155*, 1–12.

Friederici. (2022). *The Digital Transformation of Small Business Support*. STRive Community.

Global Sustainable Development Report (GSDR). (2015). UN. https://sustainabledevelopment.un.org/content/documents/5839GSDR%202015_SD_concept_definiton_rev.pdf. [Online]

Haudi, H., Rahadjeng, E., Santamoko, R., Putra, R., Purwoko, D., Nurjannah, D., & Purwanto, A. (2022). The role of e-marketing and e-CRM on e-loyalty of Indonesian companies during Covid pandemic and digital era. *Uncertain Supply Chain Management*, 10(1), 217–224. doi:10.5267/j.uscm.2021.9.006

Indumathi, R. (2018). Influence of digital marketing on brand building. [IJMET]. *International Journal of Mechanical Engineering and Technology*, 9(7), 235–243.

Juwaini, A., Chidir, G., Novitasari, D., Iskandar, J., Hutagalung, D., Pramono, T., & Purwanto, A. (2022). The role of customer e-trust, customer e-service quality and customer e-satisfaction on customer e-loyalty. *International Journal of Data and Network Science*, 6(2), 477–486. doi:10.5267/j.ijdns.2021.12.006

Khan, A.S., Bilal, M., Saif, M., & Shehzad, M. (2020). Impact of Digital Marketing on Online Purchase Intention: Mediating Effect of Brand Equity & Perceived Value. *Inst. Bus. Manag*, 1-50.

Liu, S., Perry, P., & Gadzinski, G. (2019). The implications of digital marketing on WeChat for luxury fashion brands in China. *Journal of Brand Management*, 26(4), 395–409. doi:10.105741262-018-0140-2

Martin, M. (2022). 39 Facebook Stats That Matter to Marketers in 2022. *Hootsuite*. https://blog.hootsuite.com/facebook-statistics/

Masouras, A., Maris, G., & Kavoura, A. (2020). *Entrepreneurial Development and Innovation in Family Businesses and SMEs*. Business Science Reference.

Melovic, B., Jocovic, M., Dabic, M., Vulic, T. B., & Dudic, B. (2020). The impact of digital transformation and digital marketing on the brand promotion, positioning and electronic business in Montenegro. *Technology in Society*, 63, 101425. doi:10.1016/j.techsoc.2020.101425

Mihardjo, L., Sasmoko, S., Alamsjah, F., & Elidjen, E. (2019). The influence of digital customer experience and electronic word of mouth on brand image and supply chain sustainable performance. *Uncertain Supply Chain Management*, 7(4), 691–702. doi:10.5267/j.uscm.2019.4.001

Morakanyane. (2017). Conceptualizing Digital Transformation in Business Organizations: A Systematic Review of Literature. *Bled, 30th Bled eConference, Digital Transformation – From Connecting Things to Transforming Our Lives*. Contentful.

Morgan, Whitler, K. A., Feng, H., & Chari, S. (2018). RESEARCH IN MARKETING STRATEGY. *Journal of the Academy of Marketing Science*, 47(1), 4–29. doi:10.100711747-018-0598-1

OECD. (2017). *Meeting of the OECD Council at Ministerial Level*. OECD Publishing.

OECD. (2021). *The Digital Transformation of SMEs*. OECD. doi:10.1787/bdb9256a-en

Olson, E. M., Olson, K. M., Czaplewski, A. J., & Key, T. M. (2021). Business strategy and the management of digital marketing. *Business Horizons*, 64(2), 285–293. doi:10.1016/j.bushor.2020.12.004

Purwanto, A. (2022). How The Role of Digital Marketing and Brand Image on Food Product Purchase Decisions? An Empirical Study on Indonesian SMEs in the Digital Era. *Journal of Industrial Engineering & Management Research*, 3(6), 34–41. doi:10.7777/jiemar.v3i6.323

Rathnayaka, U. (2018). Role of digital marketing in retail fashion industry: A synthesis of the theory and the practice. *Journal of Accounting & Marketing, 7*(02). doi:10.4172/2168-9601.1000279

Rupeika-Apoga & Petrovska. (2022). Barriers to Sustainable Digital Transformation in Micro-, Small-, and Medium-Sized Enterprises. *Sustainability, 14*, 1–19.

Savitri, C., Hurriyati, R., Wibowo, L., & Hendrayati, H. (2022). The role of social media marketing and brand image on smartphone purchase intention. *International Journal of Data and Network Science, 6*(1), 185–192. doi:10.5267/j.ijdns.2021.9.009

Skare, de las Mercedes de Obesso, M., & Ribeiro-Navarrete, S. (2023). Digital transformation and European small and medium enterprises (SMEs): A comparative study using digital economy and society index data. *International Journal of Information Management, 68*, 1–16. doi:10.1016/j.ijinfomgt.2022.102594

Strauli, Tuvikene, T., Weicker, T., Kębłowski, W., Sgibnev, W., Timko, P., & Finbom, M. (2022). Beyond fear and abandonment: Public transport resilience during the COVID-19 pandemic. *Transportation Research Interdisciplinary Perspectives, 16*, 1–9. doi:10.1016/j.trip.2022.100711 PMID:36373146

Suharto, S., Junaedi, I., Muhdar, H., Firmansyah, A., & Sarana, S. (2022). Consumer loyalty of Indonesia e-commerce SMEs: The role of social media marketing and customer satisfaction. *International Journal of Data and Network Science, 6*(2), 383–390. doi:10.5267/j.ijdns.2021.12.016

Suresh, C. (2022). Recent trends in Digital Marketing in Today's Scenario, Recent Trends in Management & [), Germany: Weser Books]. *Social Sciences, 2*.

Surmanidze, N. (2022, July). Legislative Challenges of Georgian Entrepreneurship and Business Competitiveness. *Institutions and Economies, 14*(3), 1–24. doi:10.22452/IJIE.vol14no3.1

Syazali, M., Putra, F., Rinaldi, A., Utami, L., Widayanti, W., Umam, R., & Jermsittiparsert, K. (2019). Retracted: Partial correlation analysis using multiple linear regression: Impact on business environment of digital marketing interest in the era of industrial revolution 4.0. *Management Science Letters, 9*(11), 1880–1886.

United Nations. (1987). Development And International Economic Co-Operation: Environment. New York: United Nations, General Assembly.

Varadarajan. (2010). Strategic marketing and marketing strategy: domain, definition, fundamental issues and foundational premises. *Journal of the Academy of Marketing Science, 38*, 119-140.

Zairis, A. G. (2020). *The Effective Use of Digital Technology by SMEs. Entrepreneurial Development and Innovation in Family Businesses and SMEs*. Neapolis University.

Zhang, X., Xu, Y., & Ma, L. (2022). Research on Successful Factors and Influencing Mechanism of the Digital Transformation in SMEs. *Sustainability (Basel), 14*(5), 2549. doi:10.3390u14052549

Zhuo & Chen. (2023). Can digital transformation overcome the enterprise innovation dilemma: Effect, mechanism and effective boundary. *Technological Forecasting and Social Change, 190*, 1–13.

APPENDIX 1

Questionnaire:

What do you use digital channels for in your business?
What do you use traditional marketing activities for?
Which market is your digital marketing aim?
Which social media platforms do you use for marketing activities?
What kind of information do you post on social media channels?
How do you research customer satisfaction, and how do you manage the process?
What type of feedback do you provide on ratings in social media channels? On the comments? Indicate negative and positive separately.
What type of digital channel management strategy does your company have?
What is the time frame of your company's digital strategy?
Link the strategy timeline and marketing objective together:
Why did you decide to digitize your marketing?

Chapter 12
The Impact of Social Marketing and Corporate Social Responsibility on Energy Savings as a Competitive Strategy

Filiz Mızrak
Istanbul Medipol University, Turkey

Muhammed Fatih Cevher
Munzur University, Turkey

ABSTRACT

In today's globalizing world, corporate social responsibility has become a necessity for businesses. The corporate social responsibility approach, which is based on the principles of giving back to the society what it has taken from the society and observing the benefit of the society in the activities of the enterprise, has an important place in terms of promoting the products and services they produce in the market under the best conditions and strengthening the brand image. From this point of view, corporate social responsibility is seen as a valid practice to make a difference. However, businesses mostly carry out social marketing activities for this purpose. Thus, while trying to find solutions to social problems, they can obtain a competitive strategy. In this context, the aim of the study is to show that the energy crisis, which is one of the most serious problems of today, can be solved by raising awareness in consumers with corporate social response activities and social marketing methods.

INTRODUCTION

Businesses are organizations established primarily to generate income and achieve commercial goals. When we look at the historical process, at the beginning of the 20th century, while organizations posi-

DOI: 10.4018/978-1-6684-8681-8.ch012

tioned their purpose as only making profit and making their owners, partners, and shareholders happy, from the middle of the century they are also faced with the reality that they are responsible to their employees, other businesses, society, environment, and consumers. While businesses were fulfilling their social responsibilities in certain areas with legal regulations, later, they started to carry out various social responsibility projects with their own will and decisions, especially in the areas in which they operate, or to take part in the projects as supporters. The main factors that led businesses to this, were their desire to cope with the increasing competition and to keep their brands alive (Sharma, 2019).

Today, businesses have become organizations that are aware of their social responsibilities while considering their economic benefits, and that show interest in the developments and changes within the business as well as outside. According to this discourse, the business is no longer defined as an organization whose purpose is only to gain financial gain, but also as an organization that has social responsibilities towards its stakeholders as well as financial gain. Fulfilling social responsibilities will not directly satisfy the stakeholders of a business financially, but primarily spiritually, and as a result of the practices, it will positively change the society's perspective on the business and their perceptions about their brands. In addition, recent studies have revealed that social responsibility practices influence consumers' purchasing behavior (Zaman et al., 2022).

Recent developments in the field of marketing and new elements added to the definition of marketing have led to significant changes in the marketing strategies of companies in terms of differentiation from competitors. Now, the focus of the marketing concept is the concept of "being value-based". To demonstrate this value, there is a prevailing opinion that institutions should contribute to the society in an economic sense as well as in a social sense. By acting with this awareness, institutions give weight to corporate social responsibility activities and can provide great benefits in the long term thanks to these efforts (He & Harris, 2020).

Today, the whole world is facing with serious energy problems, including rapid consumption of energy resources, deterioration in the ecosystem, increasing energy prices and climate change. In the last few years, when the effects of the Covid-19 pandemic are added to all these problems, it is seen that the problems in the energy field continue to increase. While the world countries have been dealing with recovery activities with the decrease of the pandemic effect in 2022, the world agenda started to shake with the war between Russia and Ukraine this time. All these developments and the increase in energy demand have created a new crisis. The tension between Russia and Ukraine, which has been going on since February 2022, has not been resolved even after about seven months. Although this situation is evaluated from different perspectives such as geopolitical, strategic, economic and superiority strategies, it is seen that the issue of energy comes to the fore as a common problem of the whole world.

It was thought that the sanctions against Russia would weaken Russia and its economy in this process and cause it to end the occupation of Ukraine. While the USA and the UK increased their sanctions on Russian energy imports, they continued to have energy problems. Europe, and especially Germany, turned to natural gas as a carbon-free and more environmentally friendly fuel option, but the European Union met 40% of its natural gas imports from Russia, at the level of 80%. In addition to the natural gas shortage, it was seen that electricity problems were also on the agenda (Chew, 2022).

The effect of investments in Russian natural gas causes the search for alternative sources and increases oil and gas prices globally. On the other hand, it is seen that the sanctions could not prevent Moscow's progress in Ukraine and even revealed the discourse of nuclear war. All the global negatives and the Russia-Ukraine war once again brought up the seriousness of energy saving, renewable energy, climate change and environmental protection issues. Although different strategies are determined according to the countries in eliminating the energy problems experienced, efficient use of resources and saving is one of the main strategies (Dinçer et al., 2023).

In this scope, the purpose of this study is to evaluate the energy problem from a different perspective proposing the solutions and questioning if social marketing and corporate social responsibility can be effective solution. The role of companies in this process has been analyzed. Furthermore, from the strategic management framework, the competitive advantage that the companies can gain because of social marketing and corporate social responsibility activities have been discussed.

BACKGROUND

The Concept of Corporate Social Responsibility

According to the definition made by the European Commission (Green Declaration, 2001), corporate social responsibility is the concept in which companies voluntarily integrate social and environmental issues into their operations and interactions with their stakeholders. In line with this definition, being socially responsible means not only fulfilling official expectations, but also voluntarily investing more in human capital, the environment, and relations with shareholders. The World Bank, of which many states are members, defines corporate social responsibility as "a tool for the economic development of society, education, treatment of disaster wounds, protection of the environment, solving health problems and solving many more problems around governments" (Michael, 2003). According to The World Business Council for Sustainable Development, corporate social responsibility requires that the business behave honestly towards the society, that the management has a responsible attitude while arranging its relations with the stakeholders, that its employees, it requires their families and society to contribute to economic growth while improving the quality of life (Najam, 2013).

When we look at the definitions of corporate social responsibility in general, the common points emerge as being voluntary, honest, and responsible to their stakeholders, while at the same time having obligations. It is necessary to distinguish between the concepts of social responsibility and corporate social responsibility. The most important difference between the concept of social responsibility and the concept of corporate social responsibility is the presence of volunteerism and willingness in the concept of corporate social responsibility. General social responsibility is a concept that is mentioned and used within the framework of business ethics, such as not deceiving the consumer, being sensitive to and respecting their rights, acting in a sense of justice. Social responsibilities are fulfilled mostly due to the existence of certain sanctions and the necessity of protecting certain rights. In the sense of corporate social responsibility, on the other hand, the main purpose is not so simple and single-subjective, but the company, the voluntary committee and the consumers come together for this purpose. The company decides to implement a corporate social responsibility project by establishing a relationship with a brand or product. In line with this decision, it sets a goal and target and informs its stakeholders about the results after implementing the project (Islam et al., 2021).

The term corporate social responsibility was conceptually first used by economist Howard R. Bowen (1953) in his book "Social Responsibilities of the Businessman", which emphasizes that companies should adopt policies that align with the values of society. According to Bowen, while making decisions, businesses must consider the social consequences of these decisions. Bowen is known as the "Father of

Corporate Social Responsibility" for his work on the subject After Bowen's book, the concept has been popular among businesses since the 1960s and there has been an interest in the concept (Marens, 2008).

Corporate social responsibility has gone beyond being a strategic option after 1990 and has become a necessity for organizations. Organizations such as the United Nations, the European Union, the World Bank, the Economic Union and the Organization for Development have established units related to corporate social responsibility and have initiated legal regulations and training activities. They have worked for the dissemination of corporate social responsibility by establishing relevant standards and principles. For example, 2005 was declared as "Corporate Social Responsibility Year" by the European Union. The European Commission produces corporate social responsibility policies and tries to disseminate them, the World Bank creates budgets to solve social problems (Mazurkiewicz, 2004).

Relationship Between Corporate Social Responsibility and Marketing Management

Companies that produce goods or services are considered as one of the institutions that form the basis of the social system. Therefore, they are obliged to fulfill their responsibilities towards the society in which they live. In fact, businesses have accepted their responsibilities from the first day they were established to operate and maintain their existence. From this point of view, businesses need to carry out their activities by considering the goals of the society as well as their own, serving accordingly and adopting policies that are in line with the value judgments of the society. When businesses act according to the fact that they are a part of the system that surrounds them, they must adapt to the changes in this system to survive. In particular, businesses approach global environmental problems from a strategic perspective with the effect of the change in social values and aim to solve these problems with the most appropriate solution methods (Bardos, Ertugrul & Gao, 2020).

Recognizing the elements that threaten the environment and taking measures for environmental protection concern both individuals, businesses and those who govern the state. On the other hand, although environmentally friendly activities and actions are optional, the driving forces and motivations at their source may be different. Businesses, which have an important role in the pollution of the environment, have had to take care to protect the environment due to the importance of individuals to this issue, and at the same time, they have seen this situation as a competitive tool. Thus, the control of environmental pollution caused by businesses is connected to an automatic control mechanism created by consumers. Symbols and adjectives symbolizing environmental friendliness that businesses use in their products have started to be the reason for preference of customers (Abdelfattah & Aboud, 2020).

Today, businesses should see their activities in the direction of environmental awareness as a competitive opportunity instead of seeing them as an annoying cost item or an undelayable threat. If businesses use this tool well and turn it into an opportunity, both the reputation and image of the business will increase, and it will be able to reach a good market share by getting ahead of the competition. On the other hand, businesses will be considered successful businesses by the public only to the extent that they consider public health and are sensitive to environmental pollution. It is obvious that a business that only thinks about making a profit will no longer have a place in today's world. For this reason, it is both an obligation and an important tool for businesses to become an environmentally sensitive business (Caputo, 2021).

There are three approaches to environmental management. These are passive, active, and proactive approach. Since the passive approach considers the environment as a cost factor, it resists external change and ignores new opportunities. On the other hand, in businesses that adopt an active approach, environmental activities are carried out only because of compliance with the law. In businesses that adopt the proactive approach, environmental issues are important for businesses and are considered among their priority issues, and within the scope of the continuous development policy, it is aimed to internalize and adopt the environmental issue by all personnel in the business and to harmonize environmental issues with Total Quality Management (Ahmad et al., 2021).

Green marketing is the marketing application of environmentally conscious business. The most important reason for the emergence of green marketing is that consumer behavior has become more sensitive to the environment. This should be seen as a continuation of the process of adapting the marketing thought to the needs of the current era. One of the reasons for the emergence of green marketing is social marketing. Social marketing is a marketing model that not only pleases the consumers, but also tries to produce solutions according to the demands of the society. We can also consider the environment-friendly management approach in this category (Mogaji et al., 2022).

According to Kotler, in the social marketing model, businesses will satisfy the desires and needs of their customers more effectively than their competitors, while not neglecting the benefit of the society. The social marketing approach asks marketers to focus on social and moral considerations while carrying out their marketing activities. From this point of view, businesses should act in a way to ensure that the profit, customer requests and needs that are likely to conflict with each other, and the interests of the society are carried out in a balanced way with each other. Businesses, which are increasingly important in terms of providing more social benefits to the interest groups they are in, should focus on the social interest of the society and produce various strategies and policies for the solution of the problems experienced (Nurjaman, 2022).

Energy and Corporate Social Responsibility

In recent years, the necessity for international institutions, governments, business leaders and non-governmental organizations to address environmental and social issues with increasing sensitivity has been discussed intensively. By addressing climate change issues, companies can choose to incorporate energy and carbon reduction initiatives as part of a broader Corporate Social Responsibility policy or as a stand-alone policy facing new opportunities to make significant savings through energy efficiency. Both energy saving and energy efficiency have been recognized as positively related to CSR efforts. In addition, initiatives to reduce carbon dioxide (CO_2) emissions from energy consumption can be promoted through Corporate Social Responsibility as a catalyst to improve communication between energy professionals and other key stakeholders such as end users, financiers and authorities (Agudelo, Johannsdottir & Davidsdottir, 2020).

With the increase in production, the need for energy is increasing day by day, oil is 40% of the world's energy consumption. Since fuel companies meet this need and are used in transportation and heating, they are highly profitable and important both politically and economically. Therefore, their power is high and their lobbying ability is high. Fuel companies have started to receive a lot of criticism about their operations in recent years (Streimikiene, Simanaviciene & Kovaliov, 2009).

Fossil fuels and the impact of petroleum-based products on climate change are the leading criticisms of the fuel sector. Since oil increases greenhouse gas emissions, it also causes an increase in the temperature in the world and contributes negatively to the bad course of the environment, which is currently being discussed in the world. This issue, which started with intergovernmental cooperation and strengthened with the concept of sustainability, has also increased criticism against oil companies. The damage that oil causes to the world and the climate is clear, unequivocal, and inevitable. For this reason, many companies are switching from oil to renewable energy consumption, and governments are giving great support in this area (Kou, Yüksel & Dinçer, 2022).

Almost every company in the fuel sector produces social responsibility projects in the field of education, art, or the environment. For example, BP has social responsibility projects on the environment and road safety in general. The main projects are (BP, website);

BP Energy Forest Project: Within the scope of the project, eucalyptus, black locust and alyantus trees are planted in Adana. About 5,000 trees have been planted and the project has been operating since 2010.

Sustainable Development Project: It provides support and vocational training to entrepreneurs in the lands where the BTC Crude Oil pipeline project passes.

Energy Tree Project: BP Turkey has signed an important project in cooperation with the Turkish Science Centers Foundation in order to raise the awareness of children about "alternative energy". The "BP Energy Tree", established by BP Turkey at the Sisli Municipality Science Center, met with children on October 26, 2007. "BP Energy Tree", which works with the principle of converting solar and wind energy into electricity and aims to provide basic information on "alternative energy" to children, includes 4 120 W solar panels, 9 meters high 1500 W wind turbine, 12 V 200 Ah battery, digital solar control hardware, 1600 VA full Sine converter magazine units. The "BP Energy Tree", which consists of these units, has the capacity to operate equipment such as 42 inch LCD TV, laptop computer with clean energy for 8 hours without using mains electricity. The TV and laptop in the Science Center are powered by solar and wind-generated electricity from the BP Energy Tree.

Social Marketing

Social marketing emerged in the early 1970s when pioneering marketing scientists such as Philip Kotler, Sidney Levy and Gerald Zaltman defined it as a discipline (Kotler and Levy, 1969; Kotler and Zaltman, 1971). Product, planning, pricing, distribution, communication, and marketing research is thought to be the work of increasing the level of influence of ideas in the social sense by designing, implementing, and controlling a program (Kotler and Zaltman, 1971, 12). The American Marketing Association defines social marketing as the discipline that aligns with organizational activities the creation, communication, distribution and exchange of value propositions from customers to meet market needs, thus emphasizing the important role of the consumer/citizen and equating and enhancing it with an organizational role in this behavior change procedure (Rothschild, 2000).

Social marketing draws on many other fields such as psychology, sociology, anthropology and communication theory to understand how it affects human behavior. In a basic sense, it is also expressed as the adoption and adaptation of commercial marketing through social change programs, campaigns, by taking advantage of the theory and practice of commercial marketing (Menegaki, 2012). While commercial marketing aims to meet the expectations and goals of consumers and companies, social marketing aims to provide a better quality of life for society and its citizens (Dann, 2006).

Gordon (2011) draws attention to the fact that most of the social marketing ideas and practices are applied "downward", in other words, towards individual "consumers". However, social marketing aims to improve the socio-economic environment of the society beyond being an individual. Therefore, it should include politicians, administrators, and the whole society, far from individuality. Instead of blaming individuals, it should involve policy makers in improving the environment, eliminating inequalities, and solving the causes of health and social problems (Wymer, 2011). In addition, social marketing, which aims to influence social behavior and benefit not only the marketer but the whole society, is seen as a useful tool for government institutions and organizations (Dahl, 2010).

Although social marketing has been successful in changing many behaviors, it has been insufficient to maintain a long-term behavior change (Rodriguez & Diaz Meneses, 2015 and Brennan et al., 2016). In addition, it has been observed that social marketing applications made through public advertisements have a strong effect on awareness and attitude, but their power in changing behavior has decreased (McKenzie-Mohr, 2000).

Social marketing practices should focus on long-term initiatives to create behavior change. Behavior change can provide more benefits in the long run (Dessart & Van Bavel, 2017; Brennan et al, 2016). Therefore, social marketers should pay attention to the long-term perspective of understanding and interacting with their target audiences so that behavior change is sustainable (Hastings, 2003; Marques & Domegan, 2011; Issock, Roberts-Lombard & Mpinganjira, 2020).

It is seen that social marketing strategies are applied in the support and implementation of health services, in the issues that concern the society such as protecting the society and individuals from the problems that threaten, environmental problems and protecting the environment. In addition to this, it has been seen that it is applied more specifically to problems such as substance addiction, unhealthy diet and obesity such as alcohol, cigarettes and drugs. In the Covid-19 pandemic, which affected the whole world in 2020, social marketing activities were applied to protect individuals and society. Beyond all these, social marketing activities can also benefit by using them for climate protection, energy saving, reducing violence and accidents (Noiseux & Hostitler 2007; Cheng, Kotler & Lee, 2009; Batu & Atas 2017; Cismaru, Lavack & Markewich, 2009).

Marketing science, which is effective in involving the consumer in the change process, is controlled by the marketing mix elements in this persuasion process. In this respect, marketing mix elements play a central role in promoting behavior change in social marketing (House, 1995; Kotler et al., 2002).

It is seen that the marketing mix elements, which form the basis of the marketing process, also form the basis of social marketing, but differ in some parts. While the marketing mix elements (4Ps) are also the focal point in social marketing, it has been seen that it is possible to add public, partnership, policies, and Pure string elements to these elements (Coşkun, 2012). The commercial marketing mix and the social marketing mix elements are analyzed in the table below.

When the product, which is one of the marketing mix elements, is examined in terms of the social marketing mix, it appears as an offer, proposition, and desired behavior. This is the case when social marketing encourages a change in behavior by suggestion. The price of the product expresses the cost of participation in social marketing. It is also defined as the cost that the target market associates with adopting the new behavior. Place (accessibility) in social marketing means distribution in commercial marketing. It is defined as where and when the target market will perform the desired behavior, obtain relevant tangible objects, and receive related services. The promotional mix, on the other hand, refers to the persuasive communication that will mobilize the target audience in social marketing (Kotler & Lee, 2008).

In social marketing, the public is the target audience, policy makers and people involved in the implementation of the program. In the implementation of the program, businessmen, banks, partnership of public institutions, legislation and institutional framework express the policy. All institutions that provide financial support show their funding sources (Peattie and Peattie, 2009).

Social marketing practices, which aim to change the behavior of individuals and act together in solving the problems that concern the whole society in different subjects, can also have effects in the field of

Table 1. Commercial marketing mix and social marketing mix

Commercial Marketing Mix (7P)	Social Marketing Mix (8P)
1. Product/Service: Assortment, quality, design, features, brand name, packaging, dimensions, services, warranties, returns.	1. Product/Service: Offers, Behaviors to be adopted
2. Price: List price, discounts, allowances, payment term, credit terms.	2. Cost of participation: time and effort, discomfort, psychological barriers
3. Distribution/Location: Global channels, scope, assortment, locations, inventory, transportation	3. Distribution/Place: Product availability, channels to reach consumers for information and education.
4. Promotion: Sales promotion, advertising, sales force, public relations, direct marketing, internet.	4. Promotion: Social communication, visible and measurable results to build trust, a mayor's letter, booths, local press, mailing lists, community outreach, cell phone messages, banner ads, viral procedures, warranties, mass customization opportunities.
5. People: Participants, staff, customers to customers, co-creation	5. The Public: The target audience, secondary audiences, policy makers, and those involved in program approval or implementation. Social networking, citizen engagement, word of mouth, endorsement by celebrities and politicians, focus groups and combined analysis.
6. Physical facilities: Service environment, sound, sight, smell, taste, touch, proof of service.	6. Partnerships: Invitation to businesspeople, banks and universities.
7. Process: Service plan, process design, self-service technologies, online service delivery.	7. Policy: Legislation and institutional framework, reward structures, access to information and subsidies.
	8. Funding Sources: All organizations providing financial support, subsidies, donations

Source: Weinrich (2006) ve Peattie and Peattie (2009).

energy. There are also studies examining social marketing activities on energy (McKenzie-Mohr, 1994; Anda & Temmen, 2013; Sheau-Ting, Mohammed & Weng-Wai, 2013; Menegaki, 2012; Butler, Gordon, Roggeveen, Waitt, and Cooper, 2016; Gordon, Cooper, & Butler, 2018; Dursun & Belit, 2017; Issock, Roberts-Lombard & Mpinganjira, 2020).

Energy and Social Marketing

When the role of Russia in the global economy is examined, it is seen that it has 19% of the world's natural gas reserves, the largest wheat exporter and the second oil exporter in the world. When analyzed in terms of energy, it is seen that Russia's oil exports to the EU before the war were 25%, natural gas exports 40% and coal exports 42%. 70% of the thermal coal required to meet the electricity generation was exported from Russia. When all these data are examined, it is thought that the global energy crisis and its effects will continue for a while (Bağış, 2020).

In this crisis environment, the desire of countries and consumers to protect themselves against price increases and crises is increasing. Countries develop new strategies and allocate some funds to protect their citizens. Information on the funds allocated by selected EU countries, Norway and the United Kingdom in the September 2021-July 2022 period to protect households and companies from rising energy prices and their consequences on cost of living is shown in Table 2.

Although marketing science can lead people to buy, it can also help reduce people's consumption when used differently. Social marketing practices can influence consumers' energy-saving behavior and enable them to buy savings behavior, that is, to direct consumers to savings. Although little work has been done on energy saving in terms of marketing, it is thought that it has recently started to attract

Table 2. Funds allocated by selected EU countries

COUNTRIES	Precaution-1	Precaution-2	Precaution-3	Precaution-4	Precaution-5	Precaution-6
ENGLAND	General government support for cost of living.	Energy Bills Support Program is included in the package.	Hot house discount	Support for County Councils and Unitary Authorities in England	£650 direct one-time cost of living payment for households for vehicle-tested benefits	A retiree cost of living payment of £300 for retirees paid in conjunction with the Winter Fuel Payment
GERMANY	Heating subsidy for low-income households and individuals	One-time energy price allowance	Reduction of the energy tax on fuel for a period of three months	Inflation Aid Package: Provisions of lump-sum payments to students and pensioners, subsidies to electricity grids	Rent subsidy payments, welfare increases, child benefit increases and electricity price brakes	Credit guarantees to energy companies struggling with high gas prices
FRANCE	Freezing gas tariffs	Limit increase in regulated electricity tariffs	Inflation control	Business support	Aid package: gas and electricity price caps, general subsidies and 30 c/L petrol price subsidy	Gas and electricity price cap
SWEDEN	Electricity bill compensation subsidies	Reducing diesel and gasoline taxes	(100 € sent to 38 millionPeople)	Climate bonus for electric cars	Compensatory payment for electricity costs for households in the south and central Sweden	Housing assistance to protect families in need from rising energy prices
SPAIN	Royal Decree 17/2021	Social Thermal Bond, RDL 23/2021 item 3	Compensatory payment for fuel costs incurred for private individuals	Refund of 20 cents per liter of gasoline and diesel	Reducing the input costs of fossil fuel powered power plants	Royal Decree: Reduction of VAT for electricity from 10% to 5%
AUSTRALIA	Compensation of energy costs	Cost of living allowance for particularly vulnerable groups	Reducing natural gas and electricity tax	Price discounts on public transport	Compensation of agricultural diesel cost	
BELGIUM	Extension of the social energy tariff	€80 deduction from the bill for vulnerable citizens	Gas and Electricity Supplementary Fund (for those who cannot apply for social tariffs)	Energy package (including VAT reduction on electricity, €100 bonus per household and additional measures for low-income people)	Extension of VAT discount on electricity and social tariffs	Extension of VAT and social tariff reductions in electricity and fuel consumption taxes
CZECH-REPUBLIC	VAT exemption on electricity and gas	Assistance to households and entrepreneurs	Direct payments to low-income families, retirees, as well as discounts on energy bills	Direct payments to low-income families, retirees, as well as discounts on energy bills	Support for companies during the heating season - Includes subsidies to energy-intensive businesses and renewable energy surcharge	Trying to save utility company CEZ
DENMARK	Tax-free checks to back up against the cost of heating	Phase-out of fossil fuel heat sources	Tax-free checks for support against heating cost: 2nd round	Increasing the working allowance Lowering the electricity tax	Senior check & retirees lump-sums, SU disability benefits and single parents and increased student grants	Credit plan to consumers to spread energy bill payments over 5 years
NORWAY	Support program for households	Support program for primary producers in agriculture	Support program for voluntary organizations	Additional measures: increased housing support,	Additional measures 2-: Increasing transfers to municipalities for additional expenditures for financial social assistance to meet	Additional measures 3- and energy measures that may result in lower electricity bills in municipal residences.
HOLLAND	One-time energy allowance for low-income people	VAT reduction on energy reduced from 21% to 9%	Gasoline and diesel consumption tax is 21%	Extra energy-saving measures for low-income households	Mitigate the impact of high energy prices in the Caribbean part of the Netherlands	Compensation of households and companies for high energy prices

Source: Sgaravatti, Tagliapietra ve Zachmann (2021)

attention (Sheau-Ting, Mohammed, & Weng-Wai, 2013). It can be said that after the global energy crisis, especially since 2020, there is an awareness of countries' tendency to save. It is thought that social marketing will attract more attention in creating consumption awareness.

The subject of energy saving, which is one of the subjects that should be treated responsibly in consumption, is also in the field of interest of social marketing. Energy saving actually means reducing the consumption of environmentally harmful fuel, not limiting natural resources and not consuming more than the basic needs. By the 2050s, it is thought that the world economy will increase 4 times more than it is today, and therefore the amount of energy expenditure will increase. This increase in energy draws attention to the importance of the level of need for natural resources. Therefore, it is important to carry out studies on energy saving today (Dursun and Belit, 2017).

People are affected by external factors in many cases. The same is true in the case of people saving energy. It has been seen that people are more effective in creating the desired behavior in the best way, by internalizing the behavior. In their intention to engage in energy saving behavior, people's internalization of the situation and their determination can contribute to purposeful energy saving. Therefore, it would be advantageous to find ways to strengthen the internalization of energy-saving behavior. Reinforcing the behavior and making it a habit will greatly contribute to the desired result (Webb, Soutar, Gagne, Mazzarol, & Boeing, 2022).

The marketing of energy saving can be inculcated in the energy saving behavior of users. It is known that marketing strategies are effective in purchasing decisions of consumers. While commercial marketing is effective in purchasing, social marketing can be effective in adopting the desired behaviors in consumers. Social marketing has been accepted as an effective approach in creating behavior change and directing the desired behavior on consumers (Stead, Gordon, Angus, McDermott, 2007; Mah, Rothschild, & Deshpande, 2006).

CONCLUSION

With the phenomenon of globalization in today's world, the changes experienced in the social sense are also reflected in the commercial life, and the product, consumer-oriented marketing periods of the past have now left their place to the social responsibility-oriented period. In this period, the necessity of considering the interests of the society as well as the interests of the consumers and the interests of the enterprises emerged in the decisions of the enterprises. In this period, the relations that businesses establish with their social partners are important, and these relations must consider the interests of the social partners as well as their own. Otherwise, it will cause a decrease in the reputation of the business and therefore the profit it aims in the next period. As the social stakeholders of the enterprise, it is possible to count every segment with which it has relations, such as its employees, shareholders, society, suppliers, and customers. The concept of social responsibility is based on considering the interests of these social partners, which we count as their own interests, in the decisions of the business.

The changing world order has caused changes in the demands of both consumers, employees, and all other social stakeholders. In general, society and in particular, consumers expect businesses to show interest in social issues as well as producing quality products. At this point, it wants not to pollute the environment while carrying out production activities, even to contribute to the environment, to produce recyclable products, and to deal with issues such as energy, education, health, culture, and art. We see that the demands of consumers have changed, and they have climbed to the top in Maslow's hierarchy of needs. While the society, which tended to consumption with emotional elements in the first periods, considered the rational elements in consumption, today's consumer increasingly carries out consumption activities by giving importance to moral values. In the complex social structure, people who become more isolated try to fulfill their needs for belonging and self-actualization in different ways. Sometimes it does this by purchasing the product of the company that it thinks is doing a beneficial activity for the society, and sometimes it does this by being a member of a non-governmental organization.

Among all the problems humanity has been facing today, energy crisis is one of the most serious ones. A well-defined communication is required to raise awareness about energy conservation. While many consumers have a positive attitude towards energy savings, they are less aware of their own energy consumption trend and possible consequences. Although consumers consider themselves conscious in their use of energy, water and natural gas, it seems that they do not act for the purpose of saving, and even do not act consciously in the use of electrical appliances, water consumption and natural gas use in their daily lives (Pop, Dabija, Pelau and Dinu, 2022). At this point, it should be considered that consumers are influenced by each other. The promotion and dissemination of energy efficient applications will be effective in this regard with interaction among consumers.

Energy saving is seen as a goal that can be achieved with the awareness and behavior change that may occur in consumers, the effect of technological developments and the programs that can be a mixture of these two factors. The individual roles of consumers in the efficient use of energy should not be overlooked. As one of the parties taking an active role in social marketing campaigns, the analysis of consumer behavior, the determination of effective savings methods, and the creation and activation of intermediary programs in creating behavior change will contribute to all humanity both in the short term and in the long term (Gifford, 2014; Dursun and Belit, 2017).

Today, when social media users are heavily exposed to influencer marketing, it should not be forgotten that influencers play a major role in shaping the attitudes and behaviors of young people (Zatwarnicka-Madura, Nowacki & Wojciechowska, 2022). Social marketing campaigns to be made with the choice of reliable influencer in energy consumption and energy saving will be effective in directing young people to the desired behavior in this area. It has been seen that the use of relational marketing variables such as customer satisfaction, trust and loyalty can be effective in developing social marketing programs for energy efficiency. Social marketing should also draw on effective business marketing concepts such as relationship marketing, branding or perceived values (Issock, Roberts-Lombard & Mpinganjira, 2020).

Gordon, Roggeveen, Waitt, & Cooper (2016) contribute to energy savings/efficiency and environmental management by identifying how collective video storytelling can be used as an important part of multi-level and multi-component energy efficiency social marketing programs in their work. They have tried to make energy consumers reflective about their own lives and to encourage energy savings. They realized this with video narration as a social marketing application to save energy. It is thought that similar studies may be useful in providing energy savings in the future. As Wee & Choong (2019), who tried the gamification method to motivate users' energy saving behavior internally, emphasized in their study, gamification can also be used in social marketing applications. A fun and interesting campaign environment can be created to attract the attention of consumers and improve their energy saving behavior. If consumers are made to feel free and have the competence to fulfill their energy-saving tasks with carefully selected game design elements, their internal motivation can be achieved in this regard. In this design, if consumers are supported by competition and communication through social networks, energy saving will become a pleasurable situation for consumers.

To sum up, one of the most serious problems of today, energy crisis, can be solved with activities in the name of corporate social responsibility. Thus, especially big brands should improve some strategies to find solutions to this problem and at the same time gain competitive advantage in the market. Secondly, social marketing activities will encourage consumers to pay attention to the problem and be cautious while consuming energy. This study is thought to contribute to literature well as it attempts to summarize the latest literature on corporate social responsibility and social market and it provides suggestions on energy crisis problem.

REFERENCES

Abdelfattah, T., & Aboud, A. (2020). Tax avoidance, corporate governance, and corporate social responsibility: The case of the Egyptian capital market. *Journal of International Accounting, Auditing & Taxation, 38*, 100304. doi:10.1016/j.intaccaudtax.2020.100304

Agudelo, M. A. L., Johannsdottir, L., & Davidsdottir, B. (2020). Drivers that motivate energy companies to be responsible. A systematic literature review of Corporate Social Responsibility in the energy sector. *Journal of Cleaner Production, 247*, 119094. doi:10.1016/j.jclepro.2019.119094

Ahmad, N., Ullah, Z., Mahmood, A., Ariza-Montes, A., Vega-Muñoz, A., Han, H., & Scholz, M. (2021). Corporate social responsibility at the micro-level as a "new organizational value" for sustainability: Are females more aligned towards it? *International Journal of Environmental Research and Public Health, 18*(4), 2165. doi:10.3390/ijerph18042165 PMID:33672139

Anda, M., & Temmen, J. (2014). Smart metering for residential energy efficiency: The use of community based social marketing for behavioural change and smart grid introduction. *Renewable Energy, 67*, 119–127. doi:10.1016/j.renene.2013.11.020

Bağış, B. (2020). *Rusya-Ukrayna Savaşının Küresel Ekonomiye ve Türkiye'ye Etkileri*.

Bardos, K. S., Ertugrul, M., & Gao, L. S. (2020). Corporate social responsibility, product market perception, and firm value. *Journal of Corporate Finance, 62*, 101588. doi:10.1016/j.jcorpfin.2020.101588

Batu, M., & Atas, U. (2017). Social marketing campaign management; a comparative analysis of anti-smoking campaigns implemented in the United Kingdom and in Turkey. *Uluslararası Hakemli İletişim ve Edebiyat Araştırmaları Dergisi, 17*, 369–400.

Bowen, H. R. (1953). *Social Responsibilities of the Businessman*. New York: Harper & Brothers.

Brennan, L., Previte, J., & Fry, M. L. (2016). Social marketing's consumer myopia: Applying a behavioral ecological model to address wicked problems. *Journal of Social Marketing, 6*(3), 219–239. doi:10.1108/JSOCM-12-2015-0079

Butler, K., Gordon, R., Roggeveen, K., Waitt, G., & Cooper, P. (2016). Social marketing and value in behaviour? Perceived value of using energy efficiently among low-income older citizens. *Journal of Social Marketing, 6*(2), 144–168. doi:10.1108/JSOCM-07-2015-0045

Caputo, F. (2021). Towards a holistic view of corporate social responsibility. The antecedent role of information asymmetry and cognitive distance. *Kybernetes, 50*(3), 639–655. doi:10.1108/K-01-2020-0057

Cismaru, M., Lavack, A. M., & Markewich, E. (2009). Social marketing campaigns aimed at preventing drunk driving: A review and recommendations. *International Marketing Review*, *26*(3), 292–311. doi:10.1108/02651330910960799

Coşkun, G. (2012). Sosyal Pazarlama ve Sosyal Pazarlama Karması: Antalya Emniyet Müdürlüğü Komşu Kollama Projesi Örneği. *Celal Bayar Üniversitesi Sosyal Bilimler Dergisi*, *10*(02), 226–246.

Dahl, S. (2010). Current themes in social marketing research: Text-mining the past five years. *Social Marketing Quarterly*, *16*(2), 128–136. doi:10.1080/15245001003746790

Dann, S. (2006). Social marketing in the age of direct benefit and upstream marketing. *Third Australasian non-profit and social marketing conference.* Australian National University.

Dessart, F. J., & Van Bavel, R. (2017). Two converging paths: Behavioural sciences and social marketing for better policies. *Journal of Social Marketing*, *7*(4), 355–365. doi:10.1108/JSOCM-04-2017-0027

Díaz Meneses, G., & Rodríguez, L. I. (2015). Comparing short-and long-term breastfeeding models. *Journal of Social Marketing*, *5*(4), 338–356. doi:10.1108/JSOCM-11-2014-0084

Dinçer, H., Yüksel, S., Çağlayan, Ç., Yavuz, D., & Kararoğlu, D. (2023). Can Renewable Energy Investments Be a Solution to the Energy-Sourced High Inflation Problem? In *Managing inflation and supply chain disruptions in the global economy* (pp. 220–238). IGI Global.

Dursun, İ., & Belit, M. (2017). Bir Sosyal Pazarlama Hedefi Olarak Enerji Tasarrufu: Tasarruf Yöntemleri Kullanımına Yönelik Bir Ölçek Önerisi. *Ömer Halisdemir Üniversitesi İktisadi ve İdari Bilimler Fakültesi Dergisi*, *10*(3), 130-153.

Gordon, R. (2011). Critical social marketing: Definition, application and domain. *Journal of Social Marketing*, *1*(2), 82–99. doi:10.1108/20426761111141850

Gordon, R., Waitt, G., Cooper, P., & Butler, K. (2018). Storying energy consumption: Collective video storytelling in energy efficiency social marketing. *Journal of Environmental Management*, *213*, 1–10. doi:10.1016/j.jenvman.2018.02.046 PMID:29477845

Hastings, G. (2003). Relational paradigms in social marketing. *Journal of Macromarketing*, *23*(1), 6–15. doi:10.1177/0276146703023001006

He, H., & Harris, L. (2020). The impact of Covid-19 pandemic on corporate social responsibility and marketing philosophy. *Journal of Business Research*, *116*, 176–182. doi:10.1016/j.jbusres.2020.05.030 PMID:32457556

Islam, T., Islam, R., Pitafi, A. H., Xiaobei, L., Rehmani, M., Irfan, M., & Mubarak, M. S. (2021). The impact of corporate social responsibility on customer loyalty: The mediating role of corporate reputation, customer satisfaction, and trust. *Sustainable Production and Consumption*, *25*, 123–135. doi:10.1016/j.spc.2020.07.019

Issock, P. B. I., Roberts-Lombard, M., & Mpinganjira, M. (2020). The importance of customer trust for social marketing interventions: A case of energy-efficiency consumption. *Journal of Social Marketing*, *10*(2), 265–286. doi:10.1108/JSOCM-05-2019-0071

Kotler, P., & Lee, N. (2008). Social marketing: Influencing behaviors for good. *Sage (Atlanta, Ga.)*.

Kotler, P., & Levy, S. J. (1969). Broadening the concept of marketing. *Journal of Marketing, 33*(1), 10–15. doi:10.1177/002224296903300103 PMID:12309673

Kotler, P., & Zaltman, G. (1971). Social marketing- approach to planned social change. *Journal of Marketing, 35*(3), 3–12. doi:10.1177/002224297103500302 PMID:12276120

Kotler, P. R., & Roberto, N. N. & Lee, N. (2002). *Social Marketing: Improving the quality of life*. Northwestern University.

Kou, G., Yüksel, S., & Dinçer, H. (2022). Inventive problem-solving map of innovative carbon emission strategies for solar energy-based transportation investment projects. *Applied Energy, 311*, 118680. doi:10.1016/j.apenergy.2022.118680

Mah, M. W., Deshpande, S., & Rothschild, M. L. (2006). M.L. Rothschild Social marketing: A behaviour change technology for infection control. *American Journal of Infection Control, 34*(7), 452–457. doi:10.1016/j.ajic.2005.12.015 PMID:16945693

Marens, R. (2008). Recovering the past: Reviving the legacy of the early scholars of corporate social responsibility. *Journal of Management History, 14*(1), 55–72. doi:10.1108/17511340810845480

Marques, S., & Domegan, C. (2011). Relationship marketing and social marketing. In G. Hastings, K. Angus, & C. Bryant (Eds.), *The SAGE Handbook of Social Marketing* (pp. 44–60). SAGE. doi:10.4135/9781446201008.n4

Mazurkiewicz, P. (2004). Corporate environmental responsibility: Is a common CSR framework possible. *World Bank, 2*(1), 1-18.

McKenzie-Mohr, D. (2000). Promoting sustainable behavior: An introduction to community-based social marketing. *The Journal of Social Issues, 56*(3), 543–554. doi:10.1111/0022-4537.00183

Menegaki, A. N. (2012). A social marketing mix for renewable energy in Europe based on consumer stated preference surveys. *Renewable Energy, 39*(1), 30–39. doi:10.1016/j.renene.2011.08.042

Michael, B. (2003). Corporate social responsibility in international development: An overview and critique 1. *Corporate Social Responsibility and Environmental Management, 10*(3), 115–128. doi:10.1002/csr.41

Mogaji, E., Adeola, O., Adisa, I., Hinson, R. E., Mukonza, C., & Kirgiz, A. C. (2022). *Green marketing in emerging economies: Communication and brand perspective: An introduction*. Springer International Publishing. doi:10.1007/978-3-030-82572-0_1

Najam, A. (2013). World Business Council for Sustainable Development: The Greening of Business or a Greenwash? In Yearbook of International Cooperation on Environment and Development 2003-04 (pp. 69-81). Routledge.

Nurjaman, K. (2022). Overview Of The Application Of The Concept Of Green Marketing In Environment Conservation. *Eqien-Jurnal Ekonomi dan Bisnis, 11*(02), 649-655.

Peattie, K., & Peattie, S. (2009). Social marketing: A pathway to consumption reduction? *Journal of Business Research, 62*(2), 260–268. doi:10.1016/j.jbusres.2008.01.033

Peattie, K., & Peattie, S. (2011). The social marketing mix: a critical review. In G. Hastings, K. Angus, & C. Bryant (Eds.), *The SAGE Handbook of Social Marketing* (pp. 152–166). SAGE Publications. doi:10.4135/9781446201008.n11

Pop, R. A., Dabija, D. C., Pelău, C., & Dinu, V. (2022). Usage intentions, attitudes, and behaviors towards energy-efficient applications during the COVID-19 pandemic. *Journal of Business Economics and Management*, *23*(3), 668–689. doi:10.3846/jbem.2022.16959

Rothschild, M. L. (2000). Carrots, sticks, and promises: A conceptual framework for the management of public health and social issue behaviors. *Social Marketing Quarterly*, *6*(4), 86–114. doi:10.1080/15245004.2000.9961146

Sgaravatti, G., Tagliapietra, S., & Zachmann, G. (2021). National policies to shield consumers from rising energy prices. *Bruegel Datasets*. Bruegel. https://www.bruegel.org/dataset/national-policies-shield-consumers-rising-energy-prices

Sharma, E. (2019). A review of corporate social responsibility in developed and developing nations. *Corporate Social Responsibility and Environmental Management*, *26*(4), 712–720. doi:10.1002/csr.1739

Sheau-Ting, L., Mohammed, A. H., & Weng-Wai, C. (2013). What is the optimum social marketing mix to market energy conservation behaviour: An empirical study. *Journal of Environmental Management*, *131*, 196–205. doi:10.1016/j.jenvman.2013.10.001 PMID:24178312

Stead, M., Gordon, R., Angus, K., & McDermott, L. (2007). A systematic review of social marketing effectiveness. *Health Edu.*, *107* (2), 126-191.

Streimikiene, D., Simanaviciene, Z., & Kovaliov, R. (2009). Corporate social responsibility for implementation of sustainable energy development in Baltic States. *Renewable & Sustainable Energy Reviews*, *13*(4), 813–824. doi:10.1016/j.rser.2008.01.007

Tamvada, M. (2020). Corporate social responsibility and accountability: A new theoretical foundation for regulating CSR. *International Journal of Corporate Social Responsibility*, *5*(1), 1–14. doi:10.118640991-019-0045-8

Webb, D., Soutar, G. N., Gagné, M., Mazzarol, T., & Boeing, A. (2022). Saving energy at home: Exploring the role of behavior regulation and habit. *International Journal of Consumer Studies*, *46*(2), 621–635. doi:10.1111/ijcs.12716

Wee, S. C., & Choong, W. W. (2019). Gamification: Predicting the effectiveness of variety game design elements to intrinsically motivate users' energy conservation behaviour. *Journal of Environmental Management*, *233*, 97–106. doi:10.1016/j.jenvman.2018.11.127 PMID:30572268

Weinreich, N. K. (2006). *What is social marketing*. Weinreich Communications.

Wymer, W. (2011). Developing more effective marketing. *Journal of Social Marketing*, *1*(1), 17–31. doi:10.1108/20426761111104400

Zaman, R., Jain, T., Samara, G., & Jamali, D. (2022). Corporate governance meets corporate social responsibility: Mapping the interface. *Business & Society*, *61*(3), 690–752. doi:10.1177/0007650320973415

Zatwarnicka-Madura, B., Nowacki, R., & Wojciechowska, I. (2022). Influencer Marketing as a Tool in Modern Communication—Possibilities of Use in Green Energy Promotion amongst Poland's Generation Z. *Energies, 15*(18), 6570. https://www.bp.com/tr_tr/turkey/home/topluluk/toplumsal-projeler/gelisim-seninle.html and https://www.setav.org/rapor-rusya-ukrayna-savasinin-kuresel-ekonomiye-ve-turkiyeye-etkileri/ and https://www.rsis.edu.sg/rsis-publication/rsis/invasion-of-ukraine-eu-energy-crisis-to-sanction-or-not/#.Yy1ek3ZBzIW. doi:10.3390/en15186570

KEY TERMS AND DEFINITIONS

Consumer behavior: It is the study of how individual customers, groups or organizations select, buy, use, and dispose ideas, goods, and services to satisfy their needs and wants. It refers to the actions of the consumers in the marketplace and the underlying motives for those actions.

Green Marketing: It refers to the practice of developing and advertising products based on their real or perceived environmental sustainability.

Renewable Energy: Renewable energy is energy derived from natural sources that are replenished at a higher rate than they are consumed. For example: Sunlight and wind.

Stakeholders: Individual or group that has an interest in any decision or activity of an organization.

Total Quality Management: It is the continual process of detecting and reducing or eliminating errors in manufacturing, streamlining supply chain management, improving the customer experience, and ensuring that employees are up to speed with training. Total quality management aims to hold all parties involved in the production process accountable for the overall quality of the final product or service.

Chapter 13
The Threat of Unplanned Urban and Real Estate Expansion to Environmental Sustainability:
A Fresh Insight From Pakistan

Azeem Razzak
Technical University of Munich, Germany

Orhan Sanli
https://orcid.org/0000-0002-3366-8993
Aydin Adnan Menderes University, Turkey

Firdous Ahmad Malik
https://orcid.org/0000-0002-7815-0143
National Institute of Public finance and Policy, India

Maryum Sajid Raja
https://orcid.org/0009-0004-2556-3827
Southwest-Jiaotong University, China

Laeeq Razzak Janjua
WSB Merito University in Wroclaw, Poland

ABSTRACT

Urbanization is a complex and multifaceted process that positively and negatively impacts society and the environment. To promote sustainable and inclusive urban development, it is essential to adopt a holistic and interdisciplinary approach that takes into account social, economic, and environmental factors, as well as the needs and perspectives of local communities and stakeholders. By adopting sustainable real estate practices, Pakistan can create a more sustainable and prosperous future for all its citizens. Likewise, real estate firms that aim to promote environmental, social, and economic sustainability in their operations should consider adopting a sustainable marketing approach. Real estate organizations may

DOI: 10.4018/978-1-6684-8681-8.ch013

contribute to a more sustainable future while also benefiting their business by integrating sustainable practices into all facets of their operations and promoting sustainability to their clients and stakeholders. Sustainable marketing gives real estate companies a competitive edge and long-term profitability in addition to helping to safeguard the environment and society.

INTRODUCTION

Urbanization is a growing trend worldwide, with more people moving into cities and metropolitan areas than ever (The World Bank, 2022). This trend presents challenges for sustainable development, as cities are responsible for a significant portion of global carbon emissions and resource consumption (United Nations, 2018). Sustainable marketing can be critical in addressing these challenges, as it encourages businesses to adopt environmentally friendly practices and promote sustainable products and services (Kotler, Kartajaya, & Setiawan, 2018). By promoting sustainable lifestyles and encouraging consumers to make more conscious choices, sustainable marketing can help reduce the negative impact of urbanization on the environment and support the transition to a more sustainable future (Peattie & Belz, 2010).

Sustainable marketing can also be crucial in promoting sustainable lifestyles in urban areas. By encouraging consumers to adopt environmentally friendly behaviors, such as using public transportation or purchasing locally sourced products, sustainable marketing can help reduce the negative impact of urbanization on the environment (Dangelico & Pujari, 2010). In addition, sustainable marketing can help create a sense of community and shared responsibility for environmental issues, which can be particularly important in urban areas where people may feel disconnected from nature (Dhurup & Hislop, 2016). By creating campaigns that appeal to people's values and a sense of purpose, sustainable marketing can inspire people to take action and make a difference in their communities (Boulstridge & Carrigan, 2000).

Urbanization refers to people moving from rural areas to cities, leading to an increase in urban population and the growth of urban areas. This phenomenon has occurred for centuries but has accelerated in recent decades due to various factors, including industrialization, globalization, and modernization (United Nations, 2018). Urbanization has positive and negative effects on Society and the environment, and it is an essential topic for policymakers, academics, and the general public. One of the positive effects of urbanization is that it can lead to economic development and job creation. Urban areas are often the center of industry, commerce, and finance, and they can offer better employment opportunities than rural areas. Urbanization also increases productivity and innovation, as people and businesses are more likely to collaborate and exchange ideas in dense urban environments (Glaeser, 2014). Furthermore, urbanization can improve infrastructure, healthcare, education, and other public services, as cities have more resources and economies of scale to invest in these areas (United Nations, 2018).

However, urbanization also has adverse effects on Society and the environment. One of the most pressing issues is its strain on urban infrastructure and public services. As urban populations grow, cities may need help to provide all residents with essential services like housing, transportation, and sanitation (Peng, 2018). Urbanization can also exacerbate income inequality, as some residents may benefit from economic growth while others are left behind (Kleniewski, 2018). Additionally, urbanization can have negative environmental impacts, such as increased pollution, deforestation, and carbon emissions (Peng, 2018). To address these challenges, policymakers must adopt a holistic approach to urban development. It may include strategies to promote sustainable and inclusive urbanization, such as investing in public transport, green spaces, and affordable housing, strengthening social safety nets, and addressing the root causes of poverty and inequality (United Nations, 2018). Engaging local communities and stakeholders in urban planning is essential to ensure that development is responsive to their needs and preferences (Kleniewski, 2018).

Urbanization has become a global phenomenon, with more than half the world's population living in cities and urban areas (United Nations, 2018). This trend is expected to continue, with the global urban population projected to reach 68% by 2050 (United Nations, 2018). Rapid urbanization is particularly evident in developing countries, where urban populations are growing faster than developed countries (United Nations, 2018). One of the factors driving urbanization is industrialization, which has historically led to the growth of urban areas as people move from rural areas to cities in search of employment opportunities (Kleniewski, 2018). Globalization has also contributed to urbanization, as the movement of goods, services, and people across borders has increased the economic importance of cities as hubs of trade and commerce (Sassen, 2018). Modernization, including technological advancements and improvements in transportation and communication infrastructure, has also facilitated urbanization by making it easier for people to live and work in cities (Glaeser, 2014). While urbanization can positively affect economic growth and human development, it also poses significant sustainability and social equity challenges. For example, urbanization can contribute to air and water pollution, deforestation, and climate change, negatively impacting public health and the environment (Peng, 2018). In addition, urbanization can lead to social inequality and exclusion, as certain groups may be marginalized or displaced by urban development projects (Kleniewski, 2018). Similarly, to address these challenges, there has been increasing interest in sustainable urban development, which seeks to promote social, economic, and environmental sustainability in urban areas (United Nations, 2018). Sustainable urban development can involve a range of strategies, including improving access to essential services like housing, healthcare, and education, promoting renewable energy and resource efficiency, and investing in green infrastructure like parks and public transportation (Glaeser, 2014).

Urbanization Issues in Pakistan

Pakistan has undergone a significant transformation in recent years, shifting from a primarily rural economy to an increasingly urbanized one. As of 2021, approximately 36% of Pakistan's population lives in urban areas, and this is expected to rise to 50% by 2030. While urbanization can bring about economic growth and increased opportunities, it poses several challenges for Pakistan. The need for more suitable infrastructure in Pakistan is one of the main problems with urbanization. However, the rate of urbanization has yet to keep up with the infrastructure needed to serve these needs. As a result, many Pakistani urban areas need more cheap housing, shoddy public transit, and unreliable utility services. The effects of urban development on the environment are another issue associated with Pakistan's urbanization. Increased pollution and the deterioration of natural resources result from the construction of buildings, roads, and other infrastructure. The health and well-being of those who live in metropolitan areas have suffered as a result. For instance, some of the world's worst levels of air pollution are found in major Pakistani cities like Lahore and Karachi, which has contributed to a surge in respiratory ailments and other health issues. Inequalities in Pakistan's social and economic conditions are a result of urbanization. Many rural residents must move to urban regions for better career prospects and living conditions. These immigrants, however, frequently end up in low-paying occupations with little job security or access to essential services. Slums and other informal settlements have developed on the outskirts of cities, where residents lack access to necessities like clean water and sanitary facilities. The increasing likelihood of natural disasters in Pakistan is another problem urbanization brings. Buildings and infrastructure have been built in locations vulnerable to flooding, landslides, and other natural disasters because of the urban areas' rapid growth. The vulnerability of urban areas to these threats, which can cause significant loss of life and property, has increased due to improper planning and regulation. Pakistan must invest in infrastructure development, especially providing basic amenities and housing, and urban planning to address these problems. Moreover, policies that encourage inclusive economic growth should be used to combat poverty and inequality and promote ecologically friendly and sustainable urban development.

In terms of sustainability, there are several challenges facing urban areas in Pakistan. These include:

A. ***Environmental degradation:*** Rapid urbanization has increased pollution and environmental degradation, which can negatively impact public health and quality of life (Nathaniel et al., 2021).

B. ***Inadequate infrastructure:*** Many urban areas in Pakistan need adequate infrastructure, including essential services like water supply and sanitation, as well as transportation and communication networks (Ichimura, 2003; Janjua et al., 2021).

C. ***Informal settlements:*** As mentioned earlier, rapid urbanization has resulted in the growth of informal settlements and slums, which lack basic amenities and are often located in areas vulnerable to natural disasters and other hazards.

D. ***Inequity:*** Urbanization can exacerbate existing social and economic inequalities, as marginalized communities often have limited access to essential services and opportunities (Kanbur & Zhuang, 2013).

E. ***Water scarcity:*** Urbanization can pressure water resources, particularly in regions like Pakistan, where water scarcity is already a significant issue. Urban areas require a large amount of water for domestic, industrial, and agricultural use, which can lead to over-extraction of groundwater and depletion of surface water sources. It can have negative impacts on both human and ecological systems (Janjua et al., 2021)

F. ***Energy demand:*** As urban areas grow, so does the energy demand. It can increase greenhouse gas emissions, contributing to climate change. In Pakistan, the majority of energy is still generated from fossil fuels, which are not sustainable in the long term. There is a need for a shift toward renewable energy sources to meet urban areas' energy demands sustainably (Panait et al., 2022).

G. ***Planning and governance:*** Effective urban planning and governance are essential for sustainable urbanization. In Pakistan, there is a need for better coordination between different levels of government and stakeholders, as well as more robust legal frameworks and regulations to guide urban development. Additionally, public participation and community involvement in the planning process can help ensure that the needs and priorities of local communities are considered (Medeiros & van der Zwet, 2020).

H. ***Economic opportunities:*** Urbanization can bring about economic opportunities, often concentrated in certain areas or industries, leading to disparities between regions and communities. A sustainable approach to urbanization should promote inclusive economic growth by providing opportunities for small and medium-sized enterprises, supporting entrepreneurship, and investing in human capital development (Gross & Ouyang, 2021).

Overall, urbanization in Pakistan presents both opportunities and challenges for sustainable development. By adopting a holistic and integrated approach to urban development, which considers social, economic, and environmental factors, Pakistan can ensure that its cities and towns are sustainable and equitable places for all residents. Urbanization increases the flow of people into cities and contributes to overcrowding. As more people move into urban areas, the population density increases, leading to overcrowding. Overcrowding can be defined as a situation where the number of people living in an area exceeds the capacity of that area to support them, resulting in a range of negative social, economic, and environmental impacts. There are several ways in which urbanization contributes to overcrowding in cities. First, urbanization can result in the growth of informal settlements and slums, which lack basic amenities like water supply, sanitation, and electricity. These settlements are overcrowded, with multiple families often sharing small living spaces. Second, urbanization can lead to increased migration to cities, both from within the country and from other countries. It can result in rapid population growth in urban areas, which can outpace the capacity of those areas to provide services and infrastructure. Finally, urbanization can result in the concentration of economic activity and jobs in urban areas, attracting people from rural areas in search of employment opportunities. It can put additional pressure on urban infrastructure and services, leading to overcrowding.

There are many examples of how urbanization has contributed to overcrowding in cities worldwide, including in Pakistan. According to the Pakistan Bureau of Statistics, the population of Karachi, the largest city in Pakistan, has grown from 9.3 million in 1998 to an estimated 16.6 million in 2020. This rapid population growth has led to overcrowding in many city areas, particularly in informal settlements and slums. Overcrowding can have a range of negative impacts on urban areas, including increased traffic congestion, air and water pollution, and social and economic inequality. It is essential to take a holistic and integrated approach to urban development, which considers the social, economic, and environmental factors that contribute to city overcrowding. It could involve improving infrastructure and services in informal settlements, promoting affordable housing, and investing in public transportation and green spaces. Urbanization often involves converting agricultural land into urban areas as cities and towns expand to accommodate growing populations. Various factors, including economic growth, industrialization, and population growth, can drive this process. Conversion of agricultural land into urban areas can have a range of negative impacts on agricultural productivity and the environment more broadly (Raddad et al., 2010). For example, the loss of agricultural land can reduce the food supply, increasing food prices and food insecurity. It can also reduce biodiversity as buildings and infrastructure replace natural habitats.

Afghan Refugee and Urbanization in Pakistan

The Afghan War, which began in 1979 and continued until 2021, displaced millions of people from Afghanistan to neighboring countries, including Pakistan. According to the United Nations High Commissioner for Refugees (UNHCR), Pakistan has hosted one of the largest refugee populations in the world, with over 1.4 million registered Afghan refugees and an estimated 1.5 million unregistered Afghan refugees as of 2020. Refugees from non-endemic to endemic locations are more susceptible to local diseases than indigenous people because they have no immunity to native strains. The burden of communicable and non-communicable diseases has risen in Pakistan due to epidemiological change. While non-communicable disease (NCD: chronic disease) lasts a long time and is caused by various factors (genetic, physiological, environmental, and behavioral), infectious disease is an infection that can be transmitted to humans from a living or inanimate source. In Pakistan, no communicable diseases caused 51% of all deaths, while injuries caused the remaining 11%. Roughly 38% of deaths were attributed to communicable, maternal, prenatal, and nutritional diseases. Diabetes, chronic respiratory disease (CRD), cardiovascular disease, cancer, and their contributing risk factors are examples of NCDs. Several reasons contribute to the complex problem of migrants burdening big cities. In the case of Pakistan, the nation has, over the years, experienced a sizable influx of refugees, notably in the wake of the war on terror. As a result, there is a burden on urban infrastructure as migrants find it difficult to access necessities like water, sensitization, education, and healthcare. We shall examine the causes of this problem in this essay, emphasizing Afghan and KPK (Khyber Pakhtunkhwa) refugees from Pakistan.

Afghanistan has been embroiled in strife for many years, with ongoing wars, political unrest, and bloodshed driving many Afghans from their homes. Since the 1980s, Pakistan has been one of the leading destinations for Afghan refugees. Millions of Afghans have sought safety there. Most refugees have made their homes in populated places, especially in Peshawar, Karachi, and Quetta. Furthermore, primarily vulnerable Afghans want to move to the United States and other Western countries through refugee resettlement programs. Most of them live in and around Islamabad, the capital of Pakistan, in hotels, business guesthouses, and apartment complexes.

The lack of facilities and resources to support them is one of the key reasons why Afghan migrants have accumulated in Pakistan's urban areas and become a burden. Many refugees have difficulty accessing essential services like water, sanitation, and healthcare due to the refugee inflow, which has pressured the country's infrastructure. The situation is terrible in informal settlements, where refugees frequently reside in cramped, unhealthy conditions. Additionally, there are conflicts between refugees and host communities due to the high concentration of migrants in urban areas, which has intensified competition for resources and jobs. The lack of prospects for refugees has further increased their vulnerability and poverty as many turn to illegal labor or rely on help to get by. The absence of government assistance is another problem that has increased the load of Afghan refugees in Pakistan's urban centers. While the Pakistani government has helped refugees in some ways, it has not done enough to address the severity of the issue. Given the severity of the issue, many refugees have been forced to rely on the assistance of NGOs and international organizations, who have struggled to offer sufficient aid.

In the wake of the war on terror, Pakistan has moreover experienced a substantial migration of refugees from Khyber Pakhtunkhwa (KPK). Many KPK inhabitants were compelled to evacuate their homes and seek refuge in urban centers due to the violence and displacement brought on by the war against terror, which started in 2001. Many refugees are finding it difficult to access essential services like water, sanitation, and healthcare due to the KPK refugee surge, which has pressured municipal infrastructure. The situation is terrible in informal settlements, where refugees frequently reside in cramped, unhealthy conditions. For KPK refugees, the absence of government assistance has also been a significant problem, leaving many of them to rely on the assistance of NGOs and international organizations. It has caused a fragmented response, with several organizations operating in various capacities and offering varied assistance. The lack of integration policies is another problem that has increased the load of KPK refugees in Pakistan's urban centers. Language problems and cultural differences have made assimilating into urban neighborhoods difficult for many refugees. As a result, there has been increased marginalization and isolation, with many refugees feeling cut off from Society. Terrorism, political unrest, economic instability, and natural calamities like floods, earthquakes, and drought have all affected Pakistan. Some of these reasons result in the relocation of people from one location to another and directly impact the health of those living in the impacted areas. Additionally, people are more susceptible to diseases because of poverty, illiteracy, inadequate health care, and inadequate facilities. More than half of Pakistan's population lives in rural regions, where they are more at risk due to several additional factors, including lack of access to or affordability of medications due to low income, inadequate sanitation, and a shortage of healthcare workers.

Threat of Unplanned Urban Expansion to Environmental Sustainability

For the last 40 years, the ongoing conflict in Afghanistan's neighbour has impacted Pakistan in numerous ways. The large-scale emigration of Afghans affected a nation that was already in the process of expanding economically. People are occasionally displaced due to ongoing activities in border regions, mainly in nearby rural areas. It raises the risks to the indigenous population's health. On the other hand, migrants are also susceptible to local illnesses. No comprehensive information was available on the illness status of Afghan refugees and internally displaced people (IDPs) living in Pakistan in conflict-affected regions.

Since many years ago, Pakistan has struggled with terrorism, economic hardship, political unrest, destitution, and health issues. Health has been a significant problem among these issues. Disasters, including earthquakes, floods, and droughts, are common in Pakistan. Since the previous four decades, there has been a persistent influx of Afghan people seeking safety, sanctuary, and occasionally business opportunities in Pakistan due to the ongoing war in their country. Additionally, 1.8 million Pakistanis were internally or temporarily relocated due to counter-terrorism operations in 2015. The influx of Afghan refugees has put significant pressure on Pakistan's urban areas, particularly in cities like Karachi, Peshawar, and Quetta. Many refugees have settled in informal settlements and slums, which lack essential services and infrastructure, and often suffer from overcrowding and poor living conditions.

The presence of large numbers of refugees in urban areas has contributed to the urbanization of those areas, as the population of cities has grown in response to the influx of people. This process has put additional pressure on urban infrastructure and services, including housing, transportation, and water and sanitation. According to a report by the Pakistan Institute of Development Economics, the presence of refugees in Pakistan has contributed to the growth of informal settlements and slums, particularly in urban areas. The report notes that "in many cities and towns of Pakistan, refugees are increasingly clustering together and settling in congested areas, living in sub-standard conditions with inadequate infrastructure and limited access to basic services."

The urbanization induced by the Afghan War and the resulting displacement of people has had a range of negative impacts on Pakistan's urban areas, including increased traffic congestion, air and water pollution, and social and economic inequality. To address these issues, taking a holistic and integrated approach to urban development is essential, considering the social, economic, and environmental factors that contribute to urbanization in Pakistan. It could involve improving infrastructure and services in informal settlements, promoting affordable housing, and investing in public transportation and green spaces. Urbanization can negatively impact Pakistan's well-being, particularly regarding education, health, and access to essential services such as fresh water and sanitation. As urban areas in Pakistan continue to grow, access to education can become a challenge for many families. It can be due to poor schools and educational facilities in urban areas, particularly in low-income neighborhoods. According to a report by UNICEF, in urban areas of Pakistan, 6.5 million children aged 5 to 16 are out of school, representing 44% of the total out-of-school children in the country. Urbanization can also have negative impacts on health in Pakistan. As cities become crowded, the prevalence of air, noise, and water pollution can increase. It can lead to various health problems, including respiratory diseases, cardiovascular diseases, and mental health problems. According to a study conducted by the Pakistan Environmental Protection Agency, air pollution in urban areas of Pakistan is a significant contributor to premature deaths, with an estimated 135,000 deaths per year attributed to air pollution. As urban areas in Pakistan continue to grow, access to essential services such as fresh water and sanitation can become challenging for many families. According to a report by the Pakistan Council of Research in Water Resources, in urban areas of Pakistan, only 54% of households have access to piped water, and only 39% have access to improved sanitation facilities. It can lead to various health problems, including diarrheal diseases, a significant cause of morbidity and mortality among children under five in Pakistan.

Overall, the negative impacts of urbanization on well-being in Pakistan are significant and wide-ranging. To address these issues, taking a holistic and integrated approach to urban development is essential, considering the social, economic, and environmental factors that contribute to urbanization in Pakistan. It could involve investing in education and healthcare facilities, promoting clean energy and transportation, and improving access to essential services such as fresh water and sanitation.

- **Education**

As urban areas in Pakistan continue to grow, access to education can become a challenge for many families. It can be due to poor schools and educational facilities in urban areas, particularly in low-income neighborhoods. Children in these areas may have to travel long distances to attend school or may need access to schools at all, which can result in lower rates of enrolment and completion. In addition to physical barriers to education, urbanization can create social and economic barriers. For example, in many urban areas of Pakistan, there are significant disparities in educational opportunities between different socioeconomic groups. Children from low-income families may not have the same access to high-quality education as children from wealthier families, which can perpetuate cycles of poverty and inequality.

Moreover, urbanization can also impact the quality of education. As urban areas become more crowded and overpopulated, schools may become overcrowded, leading to larger class sizes and less individualized attention for students. It can make it more difficult for teachers to provide high-quality education and for students to succeed academically. According to a report by UNICEF, in urban areas of Pakistan, there is a significant need for investment in education infrastructure and services, particularly in low-income neighbourhoods. The report notes that improving access to education in these areas can help to address social and economic inequalities, reduce poverty and improve overall well-being. To address these issues, taking a holistic and integrated approach to urban development is essential, considering the social, economic, and environmental factors that contribute to urbanization in Pakistan. It could involve measures such as investing in education infrastructure and services, promoting access to affordable and high-quality education, and addressing social and economic inequalities to ensure that all children have the opportunity to succeed academically.

- **Health**

As cities in Pakistan continue to grow, the prevalence of air, noise, and water pollution can increase, leading to various health problems. Air pollution is a significant problem in many urban areas of Pakistan (Ali et al., 2019), particularly in cities like Lahore and Karachi. The sources of air pollution include emissions from vehicles, industry, and power generation. The primary pollutants include particulate matter (PM), nitrogen oxides (NOx), and sulfur dioxide (SO2). Exposure to these pollutants can lead to various health problems, including respiratory diseases, cardiovascular diseases, and lung cancer. According to a study conducted by the Pakistan Environmental Protection Agency, air pollution in urban areas of Pakistan is a significant contributor to premature deaths, with an estimated 135,000 deaths per year attributed to air pollution (Goossens et al., 2021).

Noise pollution is another problem in many urban areas of Pakistan, particularly in areas with high traffic volumes. Excessive noise can lead to various health problems, including hearing loss, stress, and sleep disturbances. According to a study conducted by the World Health Organization, exposure to excessive noise levels in urban areas of Pakistan is a significant problem, with noise levels exceeding recommended levels in many areas (Jariwala et al., 2017).

Water pollution is also a significant problem in many urban areas of Pakistan. According to a report by the Pakistan Council of Research in Water Resources, only 54% of households in urban areas of Pakistan have access to piped water, and many rely on contaminated water sources (Sohail et al., 2019). It can lead to various health problems, including diarrheal diseases, a significant cause of morbidity and mortality among children under five in Pakistan. Overall, the negative impacts of urbanization on health in Pakistan are significant and wide-ranging. It is essential to take a comprehensive and integrated approach to urban development to address these issues, considering the social, economic, and environmental factors that contribute to urbanization in Pakistan. It could involve promoting clean energy and transportation, improving access to safe drinking water and sanitation facilities, and reducing emissions from industrial and transportation sources.

- **Access to essential services such as fresh water and sanitation.**

As urban areas in Pakistan continue to grow, access to essential services such as fresh water and sanitation can become challenging for many families, particularly those in low-income neighborhoods. This can be due to a need for more infrastructure, such as piped water systems and sewage treatment plants, to support the growing population. According to a report by the Pakistan Council of Research in Water Resources, only 54% of households in urban areas of Pakistan have access to piped water, and many rely on contaminated water sources. This can lead to various health problems, including diarrheal diseases, a significant cause of morbidity and mortality among children under five in Pakistan. Similarly, access to sanitation facilities can also be a challenge in urban areas of Pakistan. According to the same report, only 39% of households in urban areas have access to improved sanitation facilities, such as flush toilets. In contrast, the remaining households rely on open defecation or other unimproved sanitation facilities (Fazal & Hotez, 2020).

The lack of access to essential services such as fresh water and sanitation can significantly impact the health and well-being of families living in urban areas of Pakistan. It can lead to various health problems, including waterborne diseases and poor hygiene, and perpetuate poverty and inequality cycles. It is essential to take a comprehensive and integrated approach to urban development to address these issues, considering the social, economic, and environmental factors that contribute to urbanization in Pakistan. It could involve improving access to piped water systems, investing in sanitation infrastructure, and promoting hygiene and sanitation education to ensure that all families have access to basic services essential for their health and well-being.

Essence of Sustainable Marketing in Real Estate

In the corporate world, sustainable marketing is a method that is gaining popularity. It is an approach to conducting business that promotes economic, social, and environmental sustainability in all business operations. Newly constructed buildings substantially affect the environment and Society, and sustainable marketing is particularly crucial in the real estate sector.

In the real estate sector, sustainable marketing can take many different shapes. One way is by promoting eco-friendly construction techniques like using eco-friendly materials and energy-saving equipment. It can incorporate energy-saving features like green spaces and landscaping and renewable energy sources like solar and wind energy. Sustainable marketing can also encourage renters to adopt environmentally friendly behaviors like recycling and promoting sustainable building operations (Warren-Myers, 2012).

Promoting social and economic sustainability is another way sustainable marketing can be applied to the real estate industry. This can entail supporting regional businesses, fostering neighborhood communities, and encouraging affordable housing. Also, real estate firms should encourage inclusion and diversity in their business areas. The LEED (Leadership in Energy and Environmental Design) certification program illustrates a sustainable marketing push in the real estate sector. This initiative encourages real estate firms to embrace sustainable practices across all business operations by providing a sustainable building design, construction, and operation framework. The program gives a recognized certification for buildings that satisfy specific sustainability criteria, helping to increase brand awareness and loyalty. Companies that use sustainable marketing in the real estate industry have a competitive advantage. Real estate firms can draw investors and environmentally aware buyers who are willing to pay more for sustainable properties by promoting sustainability. Long-term growth in revenue and profitability can be attributed to sustainable marketing's capacity to foster brand loyalty and raise customer happiness (Goering, 2009).

Companies must first comprehend the significance of sustainability and how it will affect their organization before executing sustainable marketing in the real estate sector. This calls for a change in perspective from one that prioritizes profit above all else to one that strikes a balance among economic, social, and environmental concerns. It also demands an investment in research and development to identify new sustainable construction practices and technology, as well as education and training for staff to encourage sustainable practices in their daily operations. Finally, corporations must connect with stakeholders, such as tenants, investors, and local communities, to promote sustainability and develop support for sustainable marketing strategies. It may involve collaboration with other firms and organizations with comparable sustainable objectives, outreach, and education initiatives. (Khan et al., 2021).

Initiative to Reduce Urbanization and Enhance Sustainability in Pakistan

The OROB (one road, one belt) Urban-Rural Infrastructure Development Demonstration Project, funded by the Asian Development Bank (ADB) and China, was designed to promote sustainable urbanization and rural development in China and other countries. The project focused on implementing an integrated approach to urbanization, which included policies and models to promote sustainable development in various areas, including land management, transportation, water supply, energy, and social services.

A critical policy that the project implemented was land management and planning strategies to guide urban growth and promote the protection of rural land and natural resources. In Pakistan, urbanization has led to the depletion of agricultural land, negatively impacting food security and livelihoods. Land management and planning strategies can protect agricultural land and promote sustainable urbanization. The project also focused on sustainable transportation systems, including expanding public transportation and promoting non-motorized transport options. In Pakistan, transportation significantly contributes to air pollution, negatively impacting human health. Promoting sustainable transportation options can reduce air pollution and improve public health.

In addition, the project supported the development of sustainable water supply and wastewater treatment systems and the promotion of sustainable energy systems to reduce greenhouse gas emissions and improve energy efficiency. In Pakistan, access to clean water and sanitation is a significant challenge, particularly in urban areas. Implementing sustainable water supply and wastewater treatment systems can help to improve access to clean water and sanitation while promoting sustainable energy systems to reduce the country's carbon footprint. Finally, the project included measures to improve the delivery of social services, including health care, education, and housing. In Pakistan, urbanization has led to significant disparities in access to these services between urban and rural areas. Improving the delivery of social services can help to address these disparities and improve the well-being of urban and rural communities.

1. *Land Use Management:* One of the critical policies implemented in the project was the development of land use management strategies that promote the protection of rural land and natural resources while guiding urban growth. In Pakistan, urbanization has led to the depletion of agricultural land, negatively impacting food security and livelihoods. The Pakistani government could help protect agricultural land and promote sustainable urbanization by implementing land management and planning strategies.
2. *Transportation:* The project also focused on sustainable transportation systems, including expanding public transportation and promoting non-motorized transport options. In Pakistan, transportation significantly contributes to air pollution, negatively impacting human health. Promoting sustainable transportation options could reduce air pollution and improve public health.
3. *Water Supply and Wastewater Treatment*: The project supported the development of sustainable water supply and wastewater treatment systems. In Pakistan, access to clean water and sanitation is a significant challenge, particularly in urban areas. Implementing sustainable water supply and wastewater treatment systems could improve clean water and sanitation access.
4. *Energy:* The project promoted sustainable energy systems to reduce greenhouse gas emissions and improve energy efficiency. In Pakistan, there is a need for sustainable energy systems to reduce the country's carbon footprint.
5. *Social Services:* The project also included measures to improve the delivery of social services, including health care, education, and housing. In Pakistan, urbanization has led to significant disparities in access to these services between urban and rural areas. Improving the delivery of social services addresses these disparities and improves the well-being of urban and rural communities.
6. *Community Participation:* The project emphasized the importance of community participation in decision-making processes related to urban development. By involving community members in planning and decision-making, the project could better reflect the needs and priorities of residents. In Pakistan, community participation could help ensure that urbanization policies and projects are tailored to the needs of different communities and include diverse perspectives.
7. *Private Sector Involvement:* The project also involved the private sector in infrastructure development, including through public-private partnerships (PPPs). Private sector involvement could help to leverage additional resources and expertise for urban development projects in Pakistan while also ensuring that projects are financially sustainable and aligned with the needs of the private sector.
8. *Disaster Risk Reduction:* The project included measures to address disaster risk reduction, including developing disaster risk management plans and improving infrastructure resilience. In Pakistan, natural disasters such as floods and earthquakes can significantly impact urban areas. Incorporating disaster risk reduction measures into urbanization policies and projects could mitigate the impacts of these disasters and promote resilience.

9. *Green Infrastructure:* The project also focused on developing green infrastructure, including parks and green spaces, to improve the liveability of urban areas. In Pakistan, urbanization has led to a decrease in green spaces and increased air pollution, negatively impacting public health and well-being. Incorporating green infrastructure into urbanization policies and projects could help improve urban areas' liveability and promote environmental sustainability.
10. *Financing Mechanisms:* Finally, the project included a range of financing mechanisms to support infrastructure development, including concessional loans and grants. Financing urban development projects in Pakistan can be challenging, particularly for lower-income communities. Developing financing mechanisms that are accessible to a wide range of communities could help to ensure that urbanization policies and projects are inclusive and equitable.
11. *Smart City Technologies:* The project included developing and deploying innovative city technologies, such as sensor networks and data analytics, to improve urban management and service delivery. In Pakistan, adopting innovative city technologies could help improve the efficiency and effectiveness of urban services, such as public transportation, waste management, and energy systems.
12. *Multi-Stakeholder Partnerships:* The project involved collaboration between multiple stakeholders, including government agencies, private sector partners, and community organizations. Multi-stakeholder partnerships could help to ensure that urbanization policies and projects are inclusive, transparent, and responsive to diverse needs and perspectives.
13. *Gender Mainstreaming:* The project included measures to promote gender mainstreaming, including developing gender-sensitive indicators for infrastructure projects and establishing gender equity funds. In Pakistan, gender mainstreaming in urbanization policies and projects could help to address gender-based inequalities and promote women's empowerment.
14. *Inclusive Economic Development:* The project included measures to promote inclusive economic development, such as developing industrial parks and promoting entrepreneurship and small and medium-sized enterprises (SMEs). In Pakistan, promoting inclusive economic development in urban areas could create job opportunities and support the growth of the informal sector.
15. *Land Use Planning:* The project included measures to improve land use planning, including the development of land use plans and regulations to guide urban development. In Pakistan, improving land use planning could help ensure that urbanization is managed sustainably and equitably, with appropriate consideration given to housing affordability, environmental sustainability, and social equity.

The OROB Urban-Rural, Infrastructure Development Demonstration Project, provides a valuable model for integrated urbanization policies and projects prioritizing sustainability, community participation, and equity. By incorporating these elements into urbanization policy in Pakistan, the country could address the challenges of urbanization and promote a more sustainable and inclusive future for all. By incorporating these elements into urbanization policy in Pakistan, the country could address the challenges of urbanization and promote a more sustainable and inclusive future for all.

CONCLUSION

In conclusion, urbanization is a complex and multifaceted process that positively and negatively impacts Society and the environment. It is essential to adopt a holistic and interdisciplinary approach that considers social, economic, and environmental factors and the needs and perspectives of local communities and stakeholders. The policymakers must adopt a comprehensive and inclusive approach to urban development, one that is grounded in principles of sustainability, equity, and community engagement. Similarly, Pakistan's urbanization has created both opportunities and difficulties. While it has helped the economy flourish and raised some people's living standards, it has also led to several social, environmental, and economic issues. In order to address these problems, the Pakistani government must give top priority to the creation of suitable infrastructure, environmentally friendly urban planning, and socially and economically inclusive policies. Efforts must also be taken to address the core causes of urbanization, such as rural poverty and a lack of job opportunities. Urbanization is a necessary process that is occurring in many countries around the world, including Pakistan. While urbanization can bring many benefits, such as improved access to employment and services, it can also create significant sustainability challenges. In Pakistan, these challenges include increased congestion and pollution, depletion of agricultural land, and negative impacts on well-being, including access to education, health care, and essential services such as fresh water and sanitation. The negative impacts of urbanization on sustainability in Pakistan are significant and complex, requiring a comprehensive and integrated approach to address them. It could involve promoting sustainable transportation options, investing in renewable energy, protecting and enhancing agricultural land, improving access to education and health care, and promoting infrastructure development for essential services such as fresh water and sanitation. Overall, addressing the sustainability challenges posed by urbanization in Pakistan will require a commitment to sustainable development, which considers the social, economic, and environmental factors that contribute to urbanization in the country. By working together to address these challenges, Pakistan can create a more sustainable and prosperous future for all its citizens. Likewise, real estate firms promoting environmental, social, and economic sustainability should adopt a sustainable marketing approach. Real estate organizations may contribute to a more sustainable future while also benefiting their business by integrating sustainable practices into all facets of their operations and promoting sustainability to their clients and stakeholders. Sustainable marketing gives real estate companies a competitive edge and long-term profitability in addition to helping to safeguard the environment and Society. Furthermore, the OROB Urban-Rural Infrastructure Development Demonstration Project is an example of how integrated approaches to urbanization can promote sustainable development and improve the well-being of communities. By implementing policies and models that prioritize sustainability in areas such as land management, transportation, water supply, energy, and social services, Pakistan could address the challenges of urbanization and promote a more sustainable and equitable future for all.

REFERENCES

Ali, R., Bakhsh, K., & Yasin, M. A. (2019). Impact of urbanization on CO2 emissions in an emerging economy: Evidence from Pakistan. *Sustainable Cities and Society, 48*, 101553. doi:10.1016/j.scs.2019.101553

Angel, S., Parent, J., Civco, D. L., Blei, A., & Potere, D. (2011). The dimensions of global urban expansion: Estimates and projections for all countries, 2000–2050. *Progress in Planning*, *75*(2), 53–107. doi:10.1016/j.progress.2011.04.001

Boulstridge, E., & Carrigan, M. (2000). Do consumers care about corporate responsibility? Highlighting the attitude–behavior gap. *Journal of Communication Management (London)*, *4*(4), 355–368. doi:10.1108/eb023532

Chen, W., & Chen, J. (2015). Urbanization and CO2 emissions: A review of empirical evidence. *Habitat International*, *48*, 11–21.

Cohen, B. (2006). Urbanization in developing countries: Current trends, future projections, and critical challenges for sustainability. *Technology in Society*, *28*(1-2), 63–80. doi:10.1016/j.techsoc.2005.10.005

Dangelico, R. M., & Pujari, D. (2010). Mainstreaming green product innovation: Why and how companies integrate environmental sustainability. *Journal of Business Ethics*, *95*(3), 471–486. doi:10.100710551-010-0434-0

Dhurup, M., & Hislop, D. (2016). Developing sustainable marketing strategies in the urban environment: A social marketing approach. *Journal of Cleaner Production, 112*.

Fazal, O., & Hotez, P. J. (2020). NTDs in the age of urbanization, climate change, and conflict: Karachi, Pakistan as a case study. *PLoS Neglected Tropical Diseases*, *14*(11), e0008791. doi:10.1371/journal.pntd.0008791 PMID:33180793

Glaeser, E. L. (2014). A world of cities: The causes and consequences of urbanization in poorer countries. *Journal of the European Economic Association*, *12*(5), 1154–1199. doi:10.1111/jeea.12100

Glaeser, E. L. (2014). Understanding cities. *Journal of Economic Literature*, *52*(3), 697–738.

Goering, J. (2009). Sustainable real estate development: The dynamics of market penetration. *Journal of Sustainable Real Estate*, *1*(1), 167–201. doi:10.1080/10835547.2009.12091794

Goossens, J., Jonckheere, A. C., Dupont, L. J., & Bullens, D. M. (2021). Air pollution and the airways: Lessons from a century of human urbanization. *Atmosphere (Basel)*, *12*(7), 898. doi:10.3390/atmos12070898

Gross, J., & Ouyang, Y. (2021). Types of urbanization and economic growth. *International Journal of Urban Sciences*, *25*(1), 71–85. doi:10.1080/12265934.2020.1759447

Ichimura, M. (2003, January). Urbanization, urban environment, and land use: challenges and opportunities. In *Asia-Pacific Forum for Environment and Development, Expert Meeting* (Vol. 23, pp. 1–14).

Janjua, L., Razzak, A., & Razzak, A. (2021). Lack of environmental policy and water governance: An alarming situation in Pakistan. [IJCEWM]. *International Journal of Circular Economy and Waste Management*, *1*(2), 29–40. doi:10.4018/IJCEWM.2021070104

Jariwala, H. J., Syed, H. S., Pandya, M. J., & Gajera, Y. M. (2017). Noise pollution & human health: A review. *Indoor and Built Environment*, *1*(1), 1–4.

Kanbur, R., & Zhuang, J. (2013). Urbanization and inequality in Asia. *Asian Development Review*, *30*(1), 131–147. doi:10.1162/ADEV_a_00006

Khan, S. A. R., Yu, Z., Panait, M., Janjua, L. R., & Shah, A. (Eds.). (2021). *Global corporate social responsibility initiatives for reluctant businesses*. IGI Global. doi:10.4018/978-1-7998-3988-0

Kleniewski, N. (2018). *Cities, change, and conflict: A political economy of urban life*. Routledge.

Kotler, P., Kartajaya, H., & Setiawan, I. (2018). *Marketing 4.0: Moving from Traditional to Digital*. John Wiley & Sons.

Medeiros, E., & van der Zwet, A. (2020). Sustainable and integrated urban planning and governance in metropolitan and medium-sized cities. *Sustainability (Basel)*, *12*(15), 5976. doi:10.3390u12155976

Nathaniel, S. P., Nwulu, N., & Bekun, F. (2021). Natural resources, globalization, urbanization, human capital, and environmental degradation in Latin American and Caribbean countries. *Environmental Science and Pollution Research International*, *28*(5), 6207–6221. doi:10.100711356-020-10850-9 PMID:32989704

Panait, M., Janjua, L. R., Apostu, S. A., & Mihăescu, C. (2022). Impact factors to reduce carbon emissions. Evidence from Latin America. *Kybernetes*, (ahead-of-print).

Peattie, S., & Belz, F. (2010). *Sustainability marketing: A global perspective*. John Wiley & Sons.

Peng, Y. (2018). The dark side of urbanization in China: Pollution and health problems. In *Handbook of China's Governance and Domestic Politics* (pp. 1–19). Springer.

Raddad, S., Salleh, A. G., & Samat, N. (2010). Determinants of agriculture land use change in Palestinian urban environment: Urban planners at local governments perspective. *American-Eurasian Journal of Sustainable Agriculture*, *4*(1), 30–38.

Sassen, S. (2018). *Globalization and its discontents: Essays on the new mobility of people and money*. The New Press.

Seto, K. C., Güneralp, B., & Hutyra, L. R. (2012). Global forecasts of urban expansion to 2030 and direct impacts on biodiversity and carbon pools. *Proceedings of the National Academy of Sciences of the United States of America*, *109*(40), 16083–16088. doi:10.1073/pnas.1211658109 PMID:22988086

Sohail, M. T., Mahfooz, Y., Azam, K., Yen, Y., Genfu, L., & Fahad, S. (2019). Impacts of urbanization and land cover dynamics on underground water in Islamabad, Pakistan. *Desalination and Water Treatment*, *159*, 402–411. doi:10.5004/dwt.2019.24156

The World Bank. (2022). *Urban population (% of the total population)*. The World Bank. https://data.worldbank.org/indicator/SP.URB.TOTL.IN.ZS

UN-Habitat. (2016). *World cities report 2016: Urbanization and Development–emerging futures*. United Nations Human Settlements Programme.

United Nations. (2018). *Sustainable Cities and Communities*. UN. https://www.un.org/sustainabledevelopment/cities/

United Nations. (2018). *World urbanization prospects: The 2018 revision*. Department of Economic and Social Affairs, Population Division.

United Nations. (2018). *World urbanization prospects: The 2018 revision*. Department of Economic and Social Affairs, Population Division.

Warren-Myers, G. (2012). The value of sustainability in real estate: A review from a valuation perspective. *Journal of Property Investment & Finance, 30*(2), 115–144. doi:10.1108/14635781211206887

Chapter 14
Sustainable Healthcare Reforming Model Based on Marketing:
Case of Georgia

Kakhaber Djakeli
International Black Sea University, Georgia

ABSTRACT

Discourse about sustainable marketing is not finished. The theme is very current, and it involves either business or government responsibility of sustainability, green marketing, and sustainable lifestyle. Sustainability marketing in healthcare reforming is oriented to societal goals and special type of approaches to society as a whole. The healthcare reforming must be totally devoted to people, but environmental and societal scanning is the business of societal marketing. What can be the special type of advantage of health marketing and reform marketing? If health reformers try to meet present goals of society and at the same time consider the environmental, green policies, societal problems, and meet the goals of next generation, such health reforming, they can be called sustainable health reforms.

INTRODUCTION

Health reforming needs appropriate concept of Marketing and without it any great idea can die (Jakeli et al., 2016). Consumer concerns about ethicality of business and nature-based values of any services, is well linked to the reformist concepts in health (Peterson, 2021). Marketing research for sustainable marketing development, offers deep understanding to the societal paradigms, with the questions about the past, present and the future demand (McDonagh et al., 2014). One of aspects of sustainability, for example the recycling policy of the country and the degree of recycling policy well represents the economic and social stability (Minton, 2013). Discourse about sustainable marketing is not finished. The theme is very actual and it involves either business or government responsibility of sustainability, green marketing and sustainable lifestyle (Kemper et al., 2019). Sustainability marketing in Health Care Re-

DOI: 10.4018/978-1-6684-8681-8.ch014

forming is oriented to Societal Goals and special type of approaches to society in a whole. The health care reforming must be totally devoted to people, but environmental and societal scanning is the business of Societal Marketing, what can be the special type of advantage of Health Marketing and Reform marketing. If health reformers try to meet present goals of Society and in the same time consider the environmental, green policies, societal problems, meet goals of next generation, such Health Reforming can be entitled as a Sustainable Health Reform. During the stages of the Reform Idea development, ecological studies, social dilemmas, mounting environmental problems, what will change the surface of Health Market, is the main aspects of sustainable marketing, with which, Health Reformers must be equipped (van Dam, 1996).

Interesting the way to go deeply into the concept of Sustainable Marketing is offered by different authors and researchers to the marketing practice. If the concept of the green marketing supports the development of long term sustainable products and services, and the social marketing concept tries to develop sustainable healthy behaviors, the third concept entitled as a critical marketing, committed to scan all marketing theory, turning it into more social concept, considering not only company and customer but the general publics (Gordon et al., 2011). This challenges direct any Health Reform, not only to the patients and healthcare providers but to the society and the government as a guarantors of human rights in the country.

To develop the Sustainable Health Reforming, the well-studied environmental questions have to be answered, using long term green marketing and some social marketing approaches, the health reform, must be understood as a phenomenon, inspiring new macroeconomic and supply demand on health related markets (Martin et al., 2011).

Taking into consideration environmental studies, health reformers will be more flexible to join society needs and demand (Murphy, 2005). The idea to construct the reform formula on the health needs of the country, will create sustainability and the success (Belz et al., 2009).

Health reformers must be committed that their reforms during long period will satisfy customer's ethical and socio needs, like it is main principle of sustainable marketing (Jung et al., 2020). Also we should not forget that the sustainable marketing with the invisible hand is the driving force of the Economy (Sheth, et al, 2021). While humanity is in the period of the war with natural environment and this questions the habitability of our world, sustainable marketing can abolish wrong market behavior, replacing it by best societal concept, what should be the heart of the business paradigm (Martin, 2014). It seems that sustainable marketing can not only be very effective methodology to be used by health reformers but it can be the rule how to assess the long term success of any approach in this direction. When we speak about the health reform concepts and strategies, sustainable marketing will turn them into comprehensive and wise, long term plans, affecting developing living goals of humanity, their environmental protection, culture, ethical goals and the ability to see far longer, then with some ordinary plans and methods used before.

Health Reforming Sustainability Concept

Some authors used to discuss the features and attributes of sustainable health systems and characters of successful health reforms. For example, they say that successful health systems have three attributes, healthy people, superior health systems and fairness in distribution of health care (Fineberg, 2012). National Health Reforms all times were and will continue to build main skeleton of country's success and future development. Health Reformers need, deepest knowledge base into the traditional economic models of the nation, approved social strategy and political will, beside main unique competences of the field of health and healthcare (McDonough, 2011). National health reforms must be built on the concept of environmental studies, green marketing and critical concepts of demand and supply, linked to the history of the country and its economic traditions. For example, the Health Reforming concepts of Georgia, cannot be understood as sustainable (Gigauri, 2021). The mission of all health reforms are more affordability and accessibility of health care for the population of the country. Sometimes countries find more rational not to start totally new health reform rather, widen some health segment reform to national boundaries (Elliott, 1996). Macroeconomic problems usually worsen the possibility of great achievements of Health Reform, for example in post-soviet countries, monopolies and cartels worsening health care reform opportunities (Sehngelia et al., 2016). It can be said that regional factor and inherited social capital, influence health reforms, especially in regions, having experienced planning economy and moved to market economy (Rechel et al., 2009). The healthcare accessibility affordability and the quality all times was and remains as a main goals of health challenges (Warner et al., 2020).

Three things must inspire health reformers: Economic Growth, economic failure, or need for Social sustainability. In future health reforms can be done by rules of social marketing, determining the environmental support and understanding to innovations in Health, Technology and health financing. If the health reform in China was inspired by Economic Growth, in Georgia in 1994 was inspired by Economic failure and in United States during the reign of Obama Administration the reform was inspired by demand for social stability. In different period Georgian health reforms were inspired either by Economic failure in 1994 or by Economic Growth in 2007 (Djakeli, 2013). During the Georgian health care reform in 1994, global budgeting approach, was not sustained and the people were insisted to bear all costs of medical services themselves (Verulava et al., 2017).

Many countries during their transitional periods, were hungry for affordable and accessible healthcare. It can be said that when country stays in the big transition, old autocratic, bureaucratic health systems cannot play they roles successfully, like it happened in many different countries starting from biggest China, to small countries like a Georgia. Before the reform, In China supply side of the health system was not only highly centralized but also ineffective, providing the health through hospital based structures (Liu et al., 2017). Some countries staying in the entrance of Economic growth facing great demand for health services. If Economic growth backs high demand for health, Economic failure increases demand for efficiency and social stability contributes countries to ensure equality based on solidarity. The adequate Electronic Health records (EHR) in Health Information Systems, will be relevant for any Sustainable Health Reforming (Fiscella, 2011). The proper implementation of Health Information Systems for right decisions must be the one of the main guiding principles for health reformers (Popescu et al, 2022). But in future the transformation of the civilization into ecology, green marketing concept and into renewable energetic sources will actualize the need to Health Reforming based on Sustainable Health Systems.

UNSUSTAINABLE HEALTHCARE REFORMS DONE IN GEORGIA

The First Health Reform in Georgia

After demise of Soviet Union, Georgia started its first health reform what was unsuccessful because of non-consideration of the environmental problems. First of all, why health reforming was urgent for

Georgia in 1994? The whole Soviet Health was the subject of Centrally Planning and Execution. With the destruction of Soviet Union, the Centrally Planning System had been ruling from the center was abolished. The state financing was also stalled. Georgian healthcare facilities, primary, secondary and the tertiary health organizations were stopped. So the Reforming was only solution to make Georgian Health to be directed to newly established medical market. In the Soviet past all citizens were assigned to some health facilities and this was territorial principles of planning used by old soviet health school (Ensor et al., 1997). The Semashko model was not efficient, it was expensive and could not be managed by rules of market economy. In 1994 country established the reform consul and made all possible changes. The First reformers of the health made several interesting steps to establish the basics for change. They formed:

- The law for healthcare and implemented the new understanding of the health politics,
- Decentralized the health,
- Established the basics for program-based funding,
- Prioritized the primary health care in the health concept of the country,
- Social health Insurance profile was set as a priority,
- Privatization of health facilities was set up as a priority,
- New model of accreditation of health providers, doctors and nurses,
- The education reform for health professionals.

For the financing of social health issues country established Social Medical Insurance company what was collecting money from the taxes. The citizens from their salaries were paying socially oriented taxes and this financial sources accumulated into State Budget was partially directing into special health care programs what were stewarded by different public bodies, either by Ministry of Labor, Health and Social Protection of Georgia or by Social Medical Insurance Company. Health Reformers also created Special Health Manipulation Standards and priced them. The Health Manipulation standards and their process were described in special restrictions of the State. These Health Standards would be used in calculation of health care treatment costs in different cases, but prices on the real health care market suddenly skyrocketed, made all these standards and stately confirmed prices, to lose their actuality. In 1996 the Health Care Market of Georgia was under shock as all markets of this country and Georgian government tried to find some methods to stop the inflation, fight against shadow markets, improve quality of life and so on. Despite many activities country failed into worst economic disaster and the health reform lost its temper. Neither government of the country nor health administrators were able to plan and implement something sustainable health system because they were busy to reshape the system without environmental analyses. In the period from 1994-1997 when Health Reform was already at the failure, leaders of the health were not informed about the new approaches of sustainable marketing and management what always starts from environmental analyses. Either the real health system or the health market was under the ruling of chaotic forces from shadow market been created by health reform of 1994-1997. The health administrators built some unreal health standards and priced them according the prices of past, motivated the biggest health shadow market for the Georgia. As some experts discovered almost all market gone to shadow in 1997 and these shadow market was only growing. Yes, we can say that first health reform of Georgia was based on unsustainable concept having not realized the environmental forces. That's why this reform even increased the risks for the patients.

Mistakes of First Health Reform

No environmental research or some survey was done to analyze the Political, Economic, Social and Technological changes of the country to clarify which way of the reform could be more beneficial for the rise of Quality Adjusted Life Years for Georgian people and patients. The doubtful is the knowledge of reformers to the concepts of Sustainable Marketing and even the basic marketing principles what are knowledge of SWOT and TOWS analyzes, environment scanning as a model of the Political, Economic, Social and Technological forces known as the PEST, model of the Porter's five forces and the approaches of industry analyzes. The reformers knew well the planned economy and not the market one. So traditionally they were on the side of their own knowledge and the education, what they received in different soviet universities. The Subjective approaches and the objective situation was not suited to each other. When the Reformers established the State Medical Insurance company (SMIC) to manage the Social Health Programs, they did not realize that the market was never considered by them in the period of planning and implementation of the reform concepts. Without the consideration of the markets they established system what could be only managed by strict orders, but they did not have any political powers of the strict order, because of failure of economics and the failure of the legal monetarist and fiscal mechanisms to manage the markets properly. In the period between 1994 to 2003 country leaders were pleadingly hesitating between the concepts of market economy and State Capitalism, knowing less about the first and guessing little about the second. More than 400 Health Facilities had been Privatized during 1995 – 2000 but many of them were immediately lost not only for health system of the country but for whole economy. Many health facilities found themselves in the hands of different businessmen who had no intention to continue healthcare business but rather to eliminate the health facility and construct a new private office or the living flat house. These unusual disruptions made professional doctors and nurses to lose their jobs and go to abroad. The number of hospital beds were reduced drastically from 57.300 to 44.481. The number of physicians what was near to 65000 in the country was drastically reduced (Collins, 2003). The main idea of the health reform was to guarantee to people the basic primary and hospital healthcare costs though state funded health care programs (Collins, 2006). But it was impossible to several main reasons:

- The healthcare prices were planned and managed by the country were unreal, inspiring health providers to establish the shadow market with shadow prices, having motivating the bribing and corruption,
- Because the most patients were paying out of their pockets (Balabanova et al., 2009) the out-of-pocket payments in the total health care expenditures reached 74.7% (World Health Organization, 2009) all these made legal and ethical issues for the system as well,
- The idea of the reform goals, tasks and the instruments created by the reformers of the Financial Protection for the healthcare of the citizens of Georgia became unrealistic and even dead (Kutzin et al., 2010).

The Second Heath Reform in Georgia

The government failed the first health reform, was changed by "Rose Revolution". The liberal ideas of "Rose Revolution", made Georgia to jump up and reform itself rapidly (Lawson et al., 2019). Because of the failure of the first 1994-1998 Health reform, in 2004 the new government of Georgia already started to think about the concepts of Health for the country. Why second health Reform was entitled as a "Bendukidzes"? Because it was prepared in the Ministry of Justice and the Ministry of Labor, Health and Social Affairs according the ideas of Vise Prime Minister of the Country – Mr. Kakha Bendukidze (Rinnert et al., 2015). Mr. Bendukidze originally Georgian, once was famous businessman who had made his fortune in Russia and directly involved in the ——shock therapy reforms in the 1990's, also developed his opinion about the reforms in Georgia. He admired the ideas of Milton Friedman and tried to develop Georgian Reforms in Education and in health care according his libertarian approaches (Schecter, 2011). One of very interesting books of Milton Friedman – "Capitalism and Freedom" (Friedman, 1982) became very popular among Georgian Health Reformers. Reform focused itself on poorer part of the country. Accordingly, reformers made health vouchers to be given to vulnerable people and pay the Insurance premium. The Health Voucher was a guarantee of the state funding for health insurance premium (Rukhadze, 2013). So more than half million Georgians received these vouchers from the state and people started to look for better health insurance services in private insurance companies (SDG, 2021). By This approach, the state established insurance culture and pumped insurance companies via vouchers and their holders. For each voucher state was funding insurance company selected by vulnerable person. One expert said that - in Georgia it was better to be poor (Hauschild et al., 2009). The Reform made poor people to have access to basic benefit package and some expensive surgery (UNICEF Report, 2010). But the fact that the health Reform was concentrated on the poor part of the population was great problem, for its sustainability. The second health reform in Georgia developed the objectives in these logical discourse:

- The privatization of state health facilities was done by first health reform, did not finish and the second health reform had the iron intention to continue the privatization of Soviet Health Properties,
- The vulnerable population was examined by state and organized by special data building process, giving to all vulnerable families some degrees,
- The vulnerable population were financed through Health Insurance Voucher, giving the chance to poorer people to exchange this voucher in any private health insurance company,
- The private insurance companies attracted vulnerable population who had received the State Funded health voucher,
- The reformers supported the idea of liberalism and even libertarianism, abolished much heavy regulation for private companies and established progressive free and soft regulation standards for health facilities. The state regulation was reduced to minimum.
- Public health was developed under governmental responsibility (UNICEF Report, 2010).

The public spending on health was increased from 0,6% to 1,8% from Gross Domestic Product in 2010. But because the fact that this health reform was done without carefully examination of Political, Economic, Social, Technological and Legal Environments of Healthcare it cannot be meant as sustainable. The second Health Reform not taking into consideration the concept of sustainable marketing, was shaking easily. It could not defend the healthcare market from monopolistic approaches of insurance companies, who tried to establish their own healthcare facilities to have more stake from the state funding. Due to many problems the author of this health reform – United National Movement lost Parliament Elections in 2012 and new political party – Georgian Dream came to power with new ideas for the National Health.

The Third Health Reform in Georgia

In 2013 Georgia started Universal Healthcare (UHC) reform program in Georgia because economic thoughts after total defeat of United National Movement went to the State Capitalism. New people coming to the power with their leader – Russian Made Georgian Billionaire Mr. Bidzina Ivanishvili could not stop themselves to represent their hate to Liberal Thinking and especially libertarianism. Defeated Georgian National Union with their leader – Misha Saakashvili, still were imagined by people of Georgia strong supporters of libertarian Reforms. Accordingly, Liberal thinking and libertarianism became some awful titles not only for defeated party but also to their reforms. Despite the fact that many reforms done by liberal thinkers were clever and made Georgians to increase their State Budget and GDP, the liberalism suffered heaviest losses in Georgia.

The Universal Healthcare systems were introduced by a lot of countries. Is was started by Social Insurance creators in Germany, entitled with the name of the founder – Chancellor Otto von Bismarck and exported to many countries like Great Britain, Sweden, Turkey, France, Canada and Australia (Abiiro, 2015). The Universal Health planned to cover two million persons in Georgia and this will be great and comprehensive healthcare, backed by doubled state budget (Verulava, 2017). With the Universal Healthcare model country announced to provide all people with needed health services:

- Visitations of family doctor,
- Access and affordability of emergency health services,
- Access and affordability to in-patient health,
- Access and affordability to planned surgical operations.

Health Reformers planned to rise the public expenditure. They made their best to increase the health spending from 1.6% of gross domestic product to 3% during 2012-2018 years (WHO, 2020). The Health Budget grew from 420 million GEL in 2013 to 1095 million GEL in 2018. The great increase of the state health expenditure what reached 2.9% of the Gross Domestic Product in 2017 encouraged leaders of the third health reform in Georgia to claim their victory over some externalities. For example, it was obvious that Out-of-pocket payments in total health expenditure was reduced to 7% (WHO, 2020). Universal Health Coverage model in Georgia has been challenged by factors of volatility of markets and the social troubles due to the Poverty in Georgia. Because the Foreign Direct Investments had been decreased in Georgia, including the healthcare sector, the state funding was under the question. The quality of Georgian health became very relevant (Verulava et al., 2017). During the COVID -19 the degree of vaccinated patents was less than 5 percent in 2021. Georgia suffered much losses from the COVID – 19 and the healthcare system was less prepared for this terrible pandemic diseases.

The Research Methodology

To increase the chances of next health reform in Georgia or in any other countries the idea of sustainability is the most vital. According the premise of this article, sustainability can come from the utilization of the Sustainable Marketing Concept. That's why to help reformers and to increase the effectiveness of the reform the research hypothesis is devoted to Sustainable Marketing. Having described the different health reform models and their implementation the researcher having developed the idea that any Health Reform needs sustainable marketing concept. This idea can be turned into hypothesis:

H0: The sustainable marketing concepts can increase the environmental suitability of the Health Reform concepts and its implementation making the reform more sustainable and effective. To confirm or deny this hypothesis the researchers developed the following research ideas. For the topic emphasized above we undertake some different research designs: a) Exploratory Marketing Research b) Descriptive Market Research design. These research designs allow to answer main research question correctly: Can sustainable marketing concept increase steadiness of the health reform?

a. The exploratory marketing research design is consisted by several different research techniques, first of all we apply to secondary literature review and analyzes to make us sure about the main research questions what is targeted to the research topic and the segment of the population what is taken into consideration when we speak about reform sustainability guaranteed by concepts of marketing. The secondary research is done to gather information about the past and current health reforms retailed and explained in this article above.

b. The descriptive research design - combines Delphi marketing research techniques what represents the study of the opinion of the Expert community about the steadiness of Health Reform. Each reform was studied by the expert community, gathered with the technique of Snow Ball. The Delphi methodology of the marketing research is a unique method eliciting and refining Expert judgment, based the expert answers in two stages. In Delphi Marketing Research Experts represent their knowledge and analyzing to the future sustainability chances of the Health Reforms. The panel of experts and repeated measurement and controlled feedbacks are the main aspects of the Delphi marketing research. It was tried to hold three main principles of Delphi Survey: a) anonymity, b) controlled feedback, and c) group response. The Principle of Anonymity, reduced the effect of the answers from well-known Experts. The Feedback, controlled by the experts through opportunity to change or optimize their opinion makes this research method to be more valuable for the analyzes. The Group response makes it is clear that the opinion of every Delphi Survey Panel is relevant and the group considers them well. It also ensures that the Group answers and opinions are well optimized through two stages of Delphi Survey.

Initial Questionnaire of Delphi Survey

Questions

I. Please make an estimate of the various demand levels for Health Reforms done in Georgia during the 1994-2023 Years. Which reform was fully based on sustainable marketing concept to satisfy needs, wants and demand of General Publics.

    1.2. What is your estimate, to the outcomes and core experiences what we gain from three Health Reforms done in Georgia from 1994 to 2023?

    1.3. In your estimation, what was the total enlisted strength, weaknesses, opportunities and treats of the three Health Reforms done in Georgia from 1994 to 2023?

    1.4. Which Health Reform you count as a main success oriented example for Georgia on the market of Health Reforms?

    1.5. What is the main sustainable oriented aspects of the Health Reforms established by the country?

    1.6. How would you assess the Health Reforms in future?

1.7. How would you assess the relevance of the Health Reform Sustainability to answer the questions to National Health System of the country satisfy general publics also attract and retain customers in Local Georgian Community?

1.8. How would you assess the relevance of Health Reforms Sustainability to attract and retain customers in Global/international Community?

1.9 Which geographical segmentation and targeting would be better to use to Implement Sustainable Health Reforms to Georgian community?

1.10. How demographic segments of Population would be better to use for targeting and positioning the Health Reforms ideas of Georgia?

1.11 What Suggestions and recommendations would you give to leaders of the Health Reforms to establish sustainable and strong Health Reforms fully answering the needs of society?

Marketing Research

Research was done in two stages, during the stage one experts received the questionnaire with 11 questions and they answered all questions. In next stage the sample of experts, once again received all answers and could make any changes in their own answers to optimize their decisions. The anonymity of experts was strongly guaranteed by the research team. The answers were assessed by research team and considered to see big picture about the research problem. The amount of sample was 12 experts, all participated in Health reforms of Georgia, having the background of health policy leaders, with modern knowledge in health economy, management and marketing.

Marketing Research Outcomes: Answers of Experts and the Analysis

The answers of experienced experts were much interesting and it identified the material for future Health Reform Planning. On the first question 66 percent of the sample in the first round and 71 percent in the second round estimated the demand levels for Health Reforms done in Georgia during the 1994-2023 Years, as very urgent, defining the first health reform as not satisfying the needs of population. The second health reform, experts recognized positive to satisfy the needs of citizens in the first round with 55%, and in the second round 61%. The third health reform – Universal Health Coverage national system, experts recognized as satisfying the needs and wants of citizens in the first round with 58 percent in the second round 63%.

About the second question to estimate, the outcomes and core experiences what we gain from three Health Reforms done in Georgia, 91% from experts answered that the first reform was done without any estimation of the Political, Economic, Social, and Technological Environments. So this reform was done wrongly. About the second health reform, 71% of the Experts said that it was done according the health models, successfully working only in the USA, especially in some American States, having totally different political, economic, social and technological backgrounds and the environments. The third Universal Health Coverage reform in Georgia by 88% of Experts were assessed as wise step, needed high sustainable country with steady growing economy.

In the third question, about the SWOT analyses of three health care reforms, 59% of experts found "nothing interesting and only waste of the time, no strengths at all" in first health care reform in Georgia.

But about the second health care reform 70% of experts represented their opinion that the strengths were in State-private partnership, weakness was about the administration of the sums received from the state budget, opportunities were assessed as zero because of dying liberalism in Georgia and threats were a lot, especially the monopolistic approaches of Insurance Companies, Economic problems and possible market failure. On four question 87% of experts as a main example for Health Reforms defined the Turkish Health Reforming about the Universal Health System, the health reforming in Germany and the reform in Nederland. About the question number five the sustainable oriented aspects of the Health Reforms more than 90% of all experts used very professional Strategic Marketing terminology about the previous PEST analyzes. The Scanning of the Environments and developing the reform concept accordingly was the decision of Experts. The next questions and especially the questions about the Sustainable Concept in Health Reform was answered by more than 88% experts in the prism of Sustainable Marketing concepts. Experts are confident that sustainable marketing concept, occupied on environmental analyses and working for the Affordability of Health Services in the link to Economic, Political, Technological and Social Forces, was the idea of Experts. On these answers and the literature analyses it was possible to establish the Sustainable Health Reform system based on the marketing. With these answers the main hypothesis of the research that Sustainable Marketing concept can make Health Reform more sustainable was confirmed positively.

How to Build Sustainable Healthcare Systems and What Is the Role of Marketing?

As a sustainable health system can be seen those, which offers: affordability, acceptability and adaptability for patients, government, employers, employs and insurers, and the support to the macro economy for the country (Fineberg, 2012). As a sustainable health system, Countries try to establish robust healthcare systems striving to strengthen their primary healthcare. The health reforming concepts traditionally were placed as a main followers of economy. What if humans change the concept and place health and its reforming, for the leadership of the country and its life. In some popular researches health systems were presenting through its control knobs – financing, regulation and behavior (Roberts et al., 2008). Some healthcare reforming models are using steps what are socially motivated like in a Costa Rica - restructuring the health government by the leading role of Social Security Administration, including households into multidisciplinary teams for sustainability (Spigel et al., 2020). The last health reforming of Turkey is known as successful and sustainable, having more emphasize either on prevention of diseases and increasing the power of Social Security Institution, with purchasing function (Ökem, 2015). The disastrous COVID-19 challenged and changed the course of marketing for a local period, what shows the high importance of environmental processes for the business in a whole (Gigauri et al., 2021). If some researchers divide health care policy into access, quality and the cost, for sustainable, marketing driven, health reform, importance of accessibility, affordability, quality, adaptability, innovation - ability and the evaluability can be higher.

Still countries follow the high defense budgets and some other risk covering policies not allowing them to increase health funding. Sustainable health is linked to the problem of poverty reduction and the community health initiatives (WHO, 2004). Sustainable systems do not like autocracy and the sustainability of health insists them to be more friendly with market (Bredesen, 2010). For Sustainable health care reforming the sustainable management approaches are in great need (Nicholson et al., 2013). The sustainable marketing is needed with some other methods and models. The sustainable marketing model must be more aggressively used in Health Reforms. When the marketing's role is denied for health reform that brings this process, in maximum, only to short running effectiveness. Actually marketing has great role in many aspects of health systems. For example, accessibility and affordability of health is marketing science in health. Irish health reformers established very interest Reference Pricing model. This was continuation of their health reform. When the Irish Health Minister announced the government's policy for generic drug substitution in 2011 they expected to deliver at least €50 million savings in 2014. The idea to make health service more affordable and accessible for population, belongs to sustainable marketing concept.

The Model of Sustainable health for the country must be based on deepest study of Political, Economic, Social, Technological, Environmental and Labor forces. The PEST and PESTEL analyzes with Segmentation Targeting, Differentiation and the Positioning must be main driving force of any Health Reforming. Itself the Concept of health reforming should have the Marketing Pillars:

- The concept of healthcare accessibility for different demographic, geographic, psychological and behavioral segments of the country population.
- The concept of healthcare affordability for different demographic, geographic, psychological and behavioral segments of the country population.
- The concept of healthcare adaptability for different demographic, geographic, psychological and behavioral segments of the country population.
- The concept of healthcare innovation for different demographic, geographic, psychological and behavioral segments of the country population.
- The concept of evaluability for different demographic, geographic, psychological and behavioral segments of the country population.
- The concept of healthcare quality for different demographic, geographic, psychological and behavioral segments of the country population.

Quality of Healthcare is the most vital and urgent milestone what must be considered by Health Reformers. When famous German Health Economist writes that, it is much difficult way to balance cost containment and solidarity in any health system (Graf von der Schulenburg, 2005), we must think about the new ways. The Health indicators measuring the success of health reforms does not exist (Lagomarsino et al., 2012), so we can create it. What will be the health reform indicators if not the same Accessibility of health Care system, Affordability, Evaluability, Adaptability, innovation and the Quality. This System we entitle as AAEAIQ and will describe its indicators in next paper. All aspects of healthcare increasing AAEAIQ must be done by reformers and measure their success through these indicators, even the helpline for diseases and especially rare ones is improving accessibility for healthcare (Babac et al., 2018) and such solutions must be guiding principle for sustainability of healthcare concept.

Current Situation and Need for Next Reforms

The Georgian Health in current situation is under the critics from patients. The main theme of critics is the quality of healthcare and the sustainability of the health system. Some researchers think that Emotional Intelligence of the medical staff must be improved for better quality of healthcare in Georgia (Karimi et al., 2021). When the satisfaction of Georgian patients was studied, the number of unsatisfied customers were 36%, what is really big number of people (Verulava et al., 2017). The another study found that, the healthcare prices for vulnerable population registered by the state are unaffordable and the customer awareness about the health system benefits is low (Verulava et al., 2019). Many studies show that affordability, accessibility and the quality of Georgian healthcare needs improvement.

RECOMMENDATIONS

The health reforming must cover all the socially important processes inspired or demanded by Health Care. Starting from Social Enterprises, all business and marketing process of the country must be critically explained through sustainability (Gigauri et al., 2021). Success of health reform is the result of social sustainability. The war, flood, environmental disasters, financial crisis worsens the situation in any health system (Kardas et al., 2022). In this paper the deeply analyze of three Health Reforms in Georgia through sustainable marketing concepts shows that the second heath reform was more sustainable than previous one. So it is clear why Rose Revolution reforms generated large per capita income grow in Georgia and how health reform inspired significant 25 percent decline in infant mortality (Lawson et al., 2019). According the rules of Sustainable Marketing, this third health Reform from 2013-2019 was much sustainable but not without mistakes. Having described different reforms, the main findings were in urgency of sustainable marketing research before of any Health Reform drafts. The Political, Economic, Social, Technological, Environmental and Labor analyzes of the past and future of the country - can show to health reformers the way to sustainable health system.

CONCLUSION

In conclusion it is possible to say that Georgia, once been under the Soviet Health Model, already experienced three waves of Health Reforms. The first health reform had been made during the 1994-1998 established the Program Financing, offering Basic Benefit Package to People, was unsuccessful. This health reform did not scan the environments, less interested about the Political, Economic, Social and Technological changes of the country and that's why suffered from the shadow markets, created by the state.

The second health reform done by Liberals from United Georgian National Movement during 2007-2012, was more oriented to reality of the Social, Political, Economic and technological forces. This health reform simply inspired State-Private partnership, giving vouchers to vulnerable part of the population, giving them the freedom of choice. This reform established the health insurance culture and made Georgians to think about their health insurance. Also this second reform encouraged Private Health Insurance organizations to be well equipped with marketing and management, try to attract and retain the customers and made them to increase their dominance on the markets. The second health reform established many good initiatives in the health markets and made Georgians to live better (Baumann, 2012). The third health Reform occupied with Universal Health Coverage Model, was successful especially in 2013 – 2019 years. Patients actually gained more interesting place in the whole health system of the country and they received much more services due to this much actual model. When we discuss the future Health Reforms it is clear that the main attention must be made to the sustainability of healthcare concept what is implemented in the country. The sustainability of healthcare is not possible without support from environmental forces. Macro and Micro environments must support the health. That means that the research done in environmental forces of the healthcare will benefit the health reform strategy and tactics (Yan et al., 2021). So the idea how can we guarantee the high satisfaction of patients and long run stability of Health Systems, lays down in Sustainable Marketing Concepts used by health reformers.

REFERENCES

Abiiro, G. A., & De Allegri, M. (2015). Universal Health Coverage from Multiple Perspectives: A Synthesis of Conceptual Literature and Global Debates. *BMC International Health and Human Rights*, *15*(1), 17. Advance online publication. doi:10.118612914-015-0056-9 PMID:26141806

Babac, A., Frank, M., Pauer, F., Litzkendorf, S., Rosenfeldt, D., Lührs, V., Biehl, L., Hartz, T., Storf, H., Schauer, F., Wagner, T. O. F., & Graf von der Schulenburg, J. (2018). Telephone health services in the field of rare diseases: A qualitative interview study examining the needs of patients, relatives, and health care professionals in Germany. *BMC Health Services Research*, *18*(1), 1–14. doi:10.118612913-018-2872-9 PMID:29426339

Balabanova, D., McKee, M., Koroleva, N., Chikovani, I., Goguadze, K., Kobaladze, T., Adeyi, O., & Robles, S. (2008). Navigating the health system: Diabetes care in Georgia. *Health Policy and Planning*, *24*(1), 46–54. doi:10.1093/heapol/czn041 PMID:19074492

Baumann, E. (2012). Post-Soviet Georgia: It's a long, long way to 'modern' social protection. *Economies et Sociétés*, *46*(2), 259–285.

Belz, F. M., & Peattie, K. (2009). *Sustainability marketing*. Wiley & Sons.

Bredesen, P. (2010). *Fresh Medicine: How to Fix, Reform, and Build a Sustainable Health Care System*. Grove/Atlantic, Inc.

Collins, T. (2003). The aftermath of health sector reform in the Republic of Georgia: Effects on People's Health. *Journal of Community Health*, *28*(2), 99–113. doi:10.1023/A:1022643329631 PMID:12705312

Collins, T. (2006). The Georgian Healthcare System: Is It Reaching the WHO Health System Goals? *The International Journal of Health Planning and Management*, *21*(4), 297–312. doi:10.1002/hpm.853 PMID:17175732

Djakeli, K. (2013). Analyzing success and failure of two health reforms in independent Georgia. *The Journal of Business*, *2*(2), 5–14.

Ensor, T., & Rittmann, J. (1997). Reforming health care in the republic of Kazakhstan. The International *Journal of Health Planning and Management, 12*(3). 219-234. https://doi.org/ doi:10.1002/(sici)1099-1751(199707/09)12:3<219::aid-hpm482>3.0.co;2-i

Fineberg, H. V. (2012). A successful and sustainable health system—How to get there from here. *The New England Journal of Medicine*, *366*(11), 1020–1027. doi:10.1056/NEJMsa1114777 PMID:22417255

Fiscella, K. (2011). Health care reform and equity: Promise, pitfalls, and prescriptions. *Annals of Family Medicine*, *9*(1), 78–84. doi:10.1370/afm.1213 PMID:21242565

Friedman, M. (1982). *Capitalism and Freedom*. The University of Chicago Press.

Gigauri, I., & Djakeli, K. (2021). Expecting Transformation of Marketing During the Post-Pandemic New Normal: Qualitative Research of Marketing Managers in Georgia. *International Journal of Sustainable Economies Management, 10*(2), 1–18. doi:10.4018/IJSEM.2021040101

Gigauri, I., & Djakeli, K. (2021). National Health Reforms in Georgia during 1994-2021 and their Success. *HOLISTICA–Journal of Business and Public Administration, 12*(2), 102–108. doi:10.2478/hjbpa-2021-0017

Gigauri, I., & Djakeli, K. (2021). Remote working challenges for Georgian social enterprises in the context of the current pandemic. *HOLISTICA–Journal of Business and Public Administration, 12*(3), 39–53. doi:10.2478/hjbpa-2021-0021

Gordon, R., Carrigan, M., & Hastings, G. (2011). A framework for sustainable marketing. *Marketing Theory, 11*(2), 143–163. doi:10.1177/1470593111403218

Graf von der Schulenburg, J. M. (2005). German health care system in transition: The difficult way to balance cost containment and solidarity. *The European Journal of Health Economics, 6*(2), 183–187. doi:10.100710198-005-0298-x PMID:15909198

Hauschild, T., & Berkhout, E. (2009). *Health-Care Reform in Georgia. A Civil-Society Perspective: Country Case Study. Oxfam Research Report*. Oxfam International.

Jakeli, T., & Djakeli, K. (2016). Health Reforms Need Marketing-Analyzing Current Georgian Healthcare Model through Reform Marketing Matrix (RMM). *The Journal of Business, 5*(2), 7–15. doi:10.31578/.v5i2.106

Jung, J., Kim, J. S., & Kim, H. K. (2020). Sustainable marketing activities of traditional fashion market and brand loyalty. *Journal of Business Research, 120*, 294-301. https://www.sciencedirect.com/science/article/pii/S0148296320302356 doi:10.1016/j.jbusres.2020.04.019

Kardas, P., Babicki, M., Krawczyk, J., & Mastalerz-Migas, A. (2022). War in Ukraine and the challenges it brings to the Polish healthcare system. *The Lancet Regional Health. Europe, 15*, 15. doi:10.1016/j.lanepe.2022.100365 PMID:35531498

Karimi, L., Leggat, S. G., Bartram, T., Afshari, L., Sarkeshik, S., & Verulava, T. (2021). Emotional intelligence: Predictor of employees' wellbeing, quality of patient care, and psychological empowerment. *BMC Psychology, 9*(1), 1–7. doi:10.118640359-021-00593-8 PMID:34088348

Kemper, J. A., & Ballantine, P. W. (2019). What do we mean by sustainability marketing? *Journal of Marketing Management, 35*(3-4), 277–309. doi:10.1080/0267257X.2019.1573845

Kutzin, J., Cashin, C., Jakab, M., Fidler, A., & Menabde, N. (2010). Implementing Health Financing Reform in CE/EECCA Countries: Synthesis and Lessons Learned. In *Implementing Health Financing Reform: Lessons from Countries in Transition*. World Health Organization, The European Observatory on Health Systems and Policies.

Lagomarsino, G., Garabrant, A., Adyas, A., Muga, R., & Otoo, N. (2012). Moving towards universal health coverage: Health insurance reforms in nine developing countries in Africa and Asia. *Lancet*, *380*(9845), 933–943. doi:10.1016/S0140-6736(12)61147-7 PMID:22959390

Lawson, R., Grier, K., & Absher, S. (2019). You say you want a (Rose) Revolution? The effects of Georgia's 2004 market reforms. *Economics of Transition and Institutional Change*, *27*(1), 301–323. doi:10.1111/ecot.12205

Liu, G. G., Vortherms, S. A., & Hong, X. (2017). China's health reform update. *Annual Review of Public Health*, *38*(1), 431–448. doi:10.1146/annurev-publhealth-031816-044247 PMID:28125384

Martin, D. M., & Schouten, J. (2011). *Sustainable Marketing*. Pearson Prentice Hall.

Martin, D. M., & Schouten, J. W. (2014). The answer is sustainable marketing, when the question is: What can we do? *Recherche et applications en marketing*, *29*(3), 107-109.

McDonagh, P., & Prothero, A. (2014). Sustainability marketing research: Past, present and future. *Journal of Marketing Management*, *30*(11-12), 11–12, 1186–1219. doi:10.1080/0267257X.2014.943263

McDonough, J. E. (2011). *Inside national health reform* (Vol. 22). Univ of California Press.

Minton, E., Lee, Ch., Orth, U., Kim, Ch., & Kahle, K. (2012). Sustainable Marketing and Social Media. *Journal of Advertising*, *41*(4), 69–84. doi:10.1080/00913367.2012.10672458

Murphy, E., P. (2005). Sustainable marketing. *Business & Professional Ethics Journal*, *24*(1-2), 171-198.

Nicholson, C., Jackson, C., & Marley, J. (2013). A governance model for integrated primary/secondary care for the health-reforming first world–results of a systematic review. *BMC Health Services Research*, *13*(1), 1–12. doi:10.1186/1472-6963-13-528 PMID:24359610

Ökem, Z. G., & Çakar, M. (2015). What have health care reforms achieved in Turkey? An appraisal of the "Health Transformation Programme". *Health Policy (Amsterdam)*, *119*(9), 1153–1163. doi:10.1016/j.healthpol.2015.06.003 PMID:26183890

Peterson, M., Minton, A. E., Liu, L. R., & Bartholomew, E. D. (2021). *Sustainable Marketing and Consumer Support for Sustainable Businsses* (Vol. 27). Sustainable Production and Consumption. doi:10.1016/j.spc.2020.10.018

Popescu, C., EL-Chaarani, H., EL-Abiad, Z., & Gigauri, I. (2022). Implementation of Health Information Systems to Improve Patient Identification. *International Journal of Environmental Research and Public Health*, *19*(22), 15236. doi:10.3390/ijerph192215236 PMID:36429954

Rechel, B., & McKee, M. (2009). Health reform in central and eastern Europe and the former Soviet Union. *Lancet*, *374*(9696), 1186–1195. doi:10.1016/S0140-6736(09)61334-9 PMID:19801097

Report, U. (2010). *Report of the Georgia National Nutrition Survey 2009 (UNICEF, 11 June 2010)*. Georgia Global Health Initiative Strategy.

Rinnert, D. (2015). The politics of civil service and administrative reforms in development—Explaining within-country variation of reform outcomes in Georgia after the Rose revolution. *Public Administration and Development*, *35*(1), 19–33. doi:10.1002/pad.1709

Roberts, M. J., Hsiao, W., Berman, P., & Reich, M. R. (2008). *Getting health reform right: a guide to improving performance and equity.* doi:10.1093/acprof:oso/9780195371505.001.0001

Rukhadze, T. (2013). An Overview of the Health Care System in Georgia: Expert Recommendations in the Context of Predictive, Preventive and Personalized Medicine. *The EPMA Journal.* http://www.epmajournal.com/content/4/1/8

Schecter, K. (2011). The privatization of the Georgian healthcare system. *Anthropology of East Europe Review, 29*(1), 16–22.

Sehngelia, L., Pavlova, M., & Groot, W. (2016). Impact of healthcare reform on universal coverage in Georgia: A systematic review. *Diversity and Equality in Health and Care, 13*(5). Advance online publication. doi:10.21767/2049-5471.100074

Sheth, J. N., & Parvatiyar, A. (2021). Sustainable marketing: Market-driving, not market-driven. *Journal of Macromarketing, 41*(1), 150–165. doi:10.1177/0276146720961836

Spigel, L., Pesec, M., Del Carpio, O. V., Ratcliffe, H. L., Brizuela, J. A. J., Montero, A. M., & Hirschhorn, L. R. (2020). Implementing sustainable primary healthcare reforms: Strategies from Costa Rica. *BMJ Global Health, 5*(8), e002674. doi:10.1136/bmjgh-2020-002674 PMID:32843571

Stamati, F., & Baeten, R. (2014). *Health care reforms and the crisis.* European Trade Union Institute.

Tracker, S. D. G. (n.d.). *Measuring progress towards the Sustainable Development Goals.* https://sdg-tracker.org/

van Dam, Y. K., & Apeldoorn, P. A. C. (1996). Sustainable Marketing. *Journal of Macromarketing, 16*(2), 45–56. doi:10.1177/027614679601600204

Verulava, T., Jorbenadze, R., & Barkalaia, T. (2017). Introduction of Universal Health Program in Georgia: Problems and Perspectives. *Georgian Medical News, 1*(262).

Verulava, T., Jorbenadze, R., Dangadze, B., & Eliava, E. (2019). Access to ambulatory medicines for the elderly in Georgia. *Home Health Care Management & Practice, 31*(2), 107–112. doi:10.1177/1084822318806316

Verulava, T., & Maglakelidze, T. (2017). Health financing policy in the south caucasus: Georgia, Armenia, Azerbaijan. *Soobshcheniia Akademii Nauk Gruzinskoi SSR, 11*(2), 143–150.

Warner, J. J., Benjamin, J. I., Churchwell, K., Firestone, G., Gardner, J. T., Johnson, J., Ng-Osorio, L., Rodriguez, J. C., Todman, L., Yaffe, K., Yancy, W. C., & Harrington, A. R. (2020). Advancing Healthcare Reform: The American Heart Association's 2020 Statement of Principles for Adequate, Accessible, and Affordable Health Care: A Presidential Advisory From the American Heart Association. *Circulation, 141*(10), 601–614. doi:10.1161/CIR.0000000000000759 PMID:32008369

World Health Organization. (2004). *Investing in the health of the poor: A strategy for sustainable health development and poverty reduction in the Eastern Mediterranean Region.* WHO.

World Health Organization. (2009). *Georgia Health System Performance Assessment.* World Bank, UNO, Health Assessment of Georgian Health System.

World Health Organization. (n.d.). https://georgia.un.org/sites/default/files/2020- 08/Georgia%205.pdf

Yan, C., Liao, H., Ma, Y., & Wang, J. (2021). The Impact of Health Care Reform Since 2009 on the Efficiency of Primary Health Services: A Provincial Panel Data Study in China. *Frontiers in Public Health*, *9*, 735654. Advance online publication. doi:10.3389/fpubh.2021.735654 PMID:34746081

Chapter 15
Circular Economy as a Sustainable Development Marketing Tool

Zbigniew Grzymala
SGH Warsaw School of Economics, Poland

ABSTRACT

The circular economy (also known as the circular economy and the circular economy) is one of the elements of the concept of sustainable development. Currently, it is most commonly described as an economy whose goal is to constantly maintain the highest value and utility of products, components, and materials in separate biological and technical cycles, and its task is ultimately to decouple economic development from the consumption of scarce resources. As humanity, we behave as if we have forgotten that we are part of the natural environment. The essence of assessing our progress has become the size of broadly understood consumption, which also pollutes our natural environment. In a sense, we have stopped observing nature, which can come to balance when it is out of balance. This chapter explores the circular economy as a sustainable development marketing tool.

INTRODUCTION

"Today, we understand better than our ancestors that the existence of all life on Earth – including our own – depends on the stability of the ecosystem. And if our ecosystem breaks down, even temporarily, the consequences for humanity will be catastrophic" (Mesarović, Pestel, 1977). One of the tools conducive to environmental protection is the circular economy.

The circular economy (also known as the circular economy and the circular economy) is one of the elements of the concept of sustainable development. Currently, it is most commonly described as an economy: "whose goal is to constantly maintain the highest value and utility of products, components and materials in separate biological and technical cycles, and its task is ultimately to decouple economic development from the consumption of scarce resources. This economy is designed not only to solve

DOI: 10.4018/978-1-6684-8681-8.ch015

problems of lack of resources, but also to be a source of growth, create new jobs and reduce negative environmental effects, including carbon dioxide emissions" (Ellen MacArthur Foundation, 2015).

The circular economy paradigm began to develop in the early 1970s, when scientists, politicians and entrepreneurs gathered around the Club of Rome began research on the future of the earth's natural environment, its limited raw material resources and the place occupied by humans in the ecosystem. The result of this research was the first report prepared for the Club of Rome entitled "Limits to Growth" (The Limits to Growth 1972). It was in this report that the idea of a circular economy emerged, where the authors of the report stated that: "Natural ecosystems can absorb many waste products of human activity and process them into substances usable, or at least harmless to other forms of life. However, when a waste product is released in large quantities, natural absorption mechanisms can become saturated. The waste products of human civilization can accumulate in a given environment until they finally become visible, annoying and even harmful. Therefore, larger consuming countries can learn how to recover and regenerate used materials. They can develop new methods to increase the durability of products made from scarce raw materials. They can introduce social and economic patterns of behavior that would meet needs while minimizing (rather than maximizing) the use and dissipation of the irreplaceable substances that man currently possesses" (Meadows, Meadows, Randers, Behrens, 1973).

As humanity, we behave as if we have forgotten that we are part of the natural environment. The essence of assessing our progress has become the size of broadly understood consumption, which also pollutes our natural environment. In a sense, we have stopped observing nature, which can come to balance when it is out of balance. As noted by JK Galbraith, "Environmental pollution resulting from both the production and consumption of goods, from the impact that a power plant has on the atmosphere, and the effects of neon lights on the eyes, from the impact of a steelworks on a nearby lake, and the effects of cars produced thanks to it, it is a pity such may be done individually or collectively" (Galbraith, 1979). Nature does not produce waste by itself. Used elements of nature then become part of it again. Nature shows us what a circular economy is all about. The environment, of course, became the model for inventiveness. Even the concept of jet engines is known in nature. In this way, by carefully observing and imitating it, we can adapt its mechanisms to our lives without destroying it.

The purpose of the chapter is not to moralize humanity and show its mistakes or to assess our behavior towards nature, but to get closer to discovering the existing mechanisms that will show us remedies that protect the natural environment and at the same time allow for economic functioning, so as to give nature the possibility of its regeneration and at the same time achieve our economic goals, including through proper waste management. By observing the already existing economy, the authors propose, as far as possible, the introduction of a closed-circuit mechanism inspired by nature. The author noted that the key to this is to expand the importance of waste management, both municipal and industrial.

LITERATURE REVIEW

Environmental Protection in the Concepts of Selected Economists

The importance of environmental protection has been recognized by many economists for a long time. For example, a representative of the classical school, Jean Baptiste Say (1767-1832), emphasized the relationship between economy and nature in the following way: "The height of common sense is the most profitable use of the forces of nature, and the height of insanity to fight them, is to waste our efforts in destroying the powers that nature would like to give us" (Say, 1960). A very clear emphasis on the importance of nature was also shown by the physiocrats. For example, François Quesnay (1694-1774), a French economic theorist, was a proponent of the natural order. He was also a biologist and a doctor by education, which allowed him to create a vision of a new economic system based on the laws of nature. According to F. Quesnay: "Nature is governed by its laws, which man learns in the process of experience in contact with nature and with the help of reason. The human individual has a considerable area of freedom of action limited by the conditions of natural human rights. By "*freedom* " one must understand the ability to reflect in order to make an informed decision in favor of action or inaction. The general idea of freedom in the economic process is based on an additional criterion which is essentially materialistic. Proper use of freedom means acts in accordance with the natural order and the laws of nature (Stankiewicz, 1998). Quesnay economic development also from the point of circulation of resources: Resources returning to circulation should be understood not only those that are wasted, but also sterile or inactive resources that become active and are used, for example, to create inputs for large agricultural enterprises, trade and handicrafts, which generate profit, or for land reclamation, the proceeds of which are returned to circulation every year. These active resources, well located, even give the state stability and secure large funds for the reproduction of significant wealth every year, maintaining the population in abundance, and to ensure the prosperity of the state and the power of the ruler (Stankiewicz, 1998, p. 136). Of course, one can accuse him of not being very interested in using the so-called non-renewable resources, which some other economists considered a limitation. However, from the perspective of the concept of sustainable development and its propagation, it is worth considering returning to these concepts to a greater or lesser extent.

Looking through the achievements of even modern economists, one can also notice concern for the natural environment. In addition to the quoted view of John Kenneth Galbraith, for example Milton Friedman, one of the supporters of monetarism, in his views tried to combine environmental protection and economic interest according to the principle: the polluter pays. He believed that "most economists agree that a much better method of pollution control than current regulation and supervision would be to introduce market discipline by imposing pollution levies ." For example, instead of requiring companies to build special treatment plants or adhere to legal standards for the purity of water discharged into a lake or river, a tax could be imposed on each specified unit of pollutants emitted. The company will then be incentivized to use the least expensive method of keeping pollutants low. And, just as importantly, there will be an objective account of the costs of pollution reduction. Even if the tax leads to a significant reduction, it will be a clear indication that the costs of this reduction are more profitable for the company than paying the tax, in other words, that the financial benefits it gained from freely emitting pollutants were small. On the other hand, if, even with a high tax, the emission remains large, it will indicate the opposite situation, but it will also provide substantial sums for compensation for the victims and repairing the damage. The tax rate itself can be changed when the cost-benefit relationship is established experimentally" (Friedman, Friedman, 1996).

H. Rogall, a supporter of development economics, believes that:

The destruction of the environment in the 21st century consists primarily in the abuse of natural resources. Environmental economics points to various socio-economic factors as the main reason for this. Their consequence is the creation of incorrect political and legal framework conditions in which the waste of energy and material becomes economically viable and the industrial system develops in the wrong direction. (Rogall, 2010)

Aspects of nature conservation can also be seen in the sharing economy (Poniatowska-Jaksch, Sobiecki, 2016). The sharing economy assumes that instead of buying a product, good or service, we rent or share it with others. The condition for running a sharing economy is not ownership of resources, but only access to them (Pietrewicz, Sobiecki, 2016). In this way, we inhibit the growth of individual consumerism, especially those goods that have been produced from non-renewable resources, and at the same time we build community. Figure 1 shows the essence of the sharing economy.

METHODOLOGY

The chapter uses a literature review as the basic method, including a review of examples of the use of the circular economy in selected countries. The Case Study method is used to illustrate the circular economy examples in practice. The circular economy enters both individual enterprises and in a broader aspect as a process of sustainable development in macroeconomic terms. Some of the presented examples of how all green pallets were created on the basis of the materials provided and individual interviews with the originator Krzysztof Witos. Similarly, the example of energy independence of a municipal company is mainly the result of an interview with Zbigniew Gieleciak - president of the sewage treatment plant in Tychy.

FINDINGS AND DISCUSSION

Waste management is traditionally considered as part of the urban economy by providing the so-called municipal service consisting in collecting both municipal and industrial waste from people and business entities. This service, if we do not want to experience the negative effects of waste decomposition, should be provided in a reliable and uninterrupted manner, of course in practice according to the adopted plan. Waste, especially the hazardous and long-term waste, is considered part of the costs of modern civilization and does not fit into the paradigm of sustainable development. From the company's point of view, waste can be managed in the simplest and cheapest way by storing it in appropriate landfills. They can be composted or thermally disposed of. Each type of waste management involves costs partly imposed by regional and central authorities on waste suppliers, hence the practice of illegal disposal of waste, even hazardous waste in a way that degrades the environment, can be observed in various countries, for example by burying it in less urbanized areas, dumping in the oceans or incineration without the use of dedicated installations.

The concept of environmental protection taking into account the development of modern civilization can be seen in various practical business projects. There is an extensive discussion on the circular economy in the company. Each company has its own specificity and the pursuit of the circular economy concept may be different. For example, the administrative office generates municipal waste. Some of them are defined as industrial activities. In Western Europe, including Poland, the national environmental protection services carry out inspections to check the collection of various types of waste and thus enforce activities in the spirit of the circular economy. In turn, catering businesses mainly produce biodegradable waste collected by waste management companies. Their management may vary from raw material input for biogas production to the production of compost for agricultural purposes. They can be incinerated with mixed waste, but this method of management should be used last. Companies generating hazardous waste require separate ways of managing this waste. In such cases, the most popular solution is thermal utilization of these wastes. Methods using saturated steam are also practiced. This technology assumes the disintegration of hazardous waste into particles that do not pose a threat to the environment. A separate approach to the circular economy, partly mentioned above, is the very process of managing the municipal and industrial waste that cannot be returned to the economy.

The clearest example is the way liquid and biodegradable waste is managed. This year, the author conducted an interview with Zbigniew Gieleciak, the president of the Tychy Energy Cluster and Centrum Gospodarki Wodno-Sciekowa SA in Tychy.

Interview With the President of the Tychy Energy Cluster and Centrum

Biogas production is not something new in Poland. However, the solution from Tych is innovative. According to Zbigniew Gieleciak in an interview, there were 350 biogas plants operating in Poland in 2021, including 109 at sewage treatment plants, 102 at municipal waste management plants and 140 agricultural biogas plants. The average coverage of the sewage treatment plant's needs for electricity was covered in 40% in the towns of the poviat of 100 thousand pe and 47% below PLN 100,000. None of these treatment plants in 2021 exceeded 100% coverage of needs on average during the year, except for the treatment plant in Tychy. Nearly 100% coverage was achieved by the treatment plants in Puck, Swarzewo Iława, Rzeszów and Mielec.

The project of modernization of the sludge part of the sewage treatment plant in Tychy-Urbanowice started in December 2006. Such good results are due to the additional use of industrial biodegradable waste for the production of biogas. „ In two WKF chambers built in the form of cylindrical reinforced concrete tanks with a diameter of 23 m each, a total volume of 11,000 m3 and at a temperature of approx. 38°C, methane fermentation of sewage sludge and organic waste is carried out. The auxiliary infrastructure also includes buffer tanks for collecting organic waste and an organic waste pasteurization station. The main purpose of the process is to transform the structure of sewage sludge into a stabilized waste, devoid of the tendency to putrefaction and pathogenic bacteria. The biogas produced in the fermentation process is used for the sewage treatment plant's own needs. The resulting biogas is directed to the biogas desulfurization plant. It consists of four adsorbers filled with bog iron ore. The presence of hydrogen sulphide in biogas resulting from the process of methane fermentation is inevitable. The need for desulphurization results from the need to reduce the emission of toxic components into the atmosphere, such as hydrogen sulphide or sulfur oxides formed after its combustion, and due to the corrosion properties and protection of the devices themselves. Desulfurized biogas is stored in two biogas tanks: one of the "wet" type with a capacity of 2000 m3 and one membrane tank with a capacity of 6370 m3. It is burned in three power generators: two with an electric power of 345 kW and a thermal power of 531 kW each, and one with an electric power of 400 kW and a thermal power of 394 kW, thus producing electricity and heat. The thermal energy generated in this way is used to heat the fermentation chambers to a constant temperature of 38o C and to heat the buildings at the sewage treatment plant. Water-sediment spiral exchangers are used to heat the sludge. The generated electricity is used to power the devices at the treatment plant, and its surplus is sold to the external power grid. Electricity generated in power generators is subject to the so-called green certificates, which are then sold on the Polish Power Exchange. Biogas from the treatment plant is also directed to power the bio-electric power plant at Wodny Park Tychy. After compression at the treatment plant, it flows through a gas pipeline over 6 km long, connecting the treatment plant and the Wodny Park (Photo 2). The role of the backup device is performed by a low-temperature gas boiler with a capacity of 895 kW of thermal energy, in which biogas is combusted in the event of a failure or downtime of the aggregates. The heat energy produced in the boiler is used to provide heat both for technological processes and heat for central heating purposes. Excess biogas is burned in a torch" (Technological process - RCGW SA - Regional Center for Water and Sewage Management SA).

According to the interlocutor:

- Electricity production 2006-2021; approx. 121.5 GWh – this amount of energy would power a town of approx. 10,000 inhabitants for 15 years.
- Amount of heat produced 2006 – 2021: approx. 539 TJ (consumption equivalent to over 15,000 single-family houses throughout the year).
- Equivalent amount of coal in a separate system (25 MJ/kg), approx. 79 thousand. Mg (1200 wagons).
- Avoided systemic CO_2 emissions approx. 90.5 thousand. Mg (only for electricity production).

The surplus is transferred through Tyski Klaster Energii to other municipal entities or sold to Tauron's network. The key to the success of the treatment plant in Tychy lies in the appropriate technology and know-how related to the added biodegradable waste. Tychy annually produces 5.8 - 6.6 million m3 of biogas, from which 15 thousand are produced. MWh of electricity, of which 3-5 thousand MWh, was a surplus over the needs of the treatment plant and the aqua park. The supply of electricity in 2006-2021 is shown in Figure 2.

Every year, there was an increase in the supply of energy from the sewage treatment plant. The exception was 2021, when the supply of biodegradable industrial waste decreased as a result of the pandemic. The surplus of electricity produced is first transferred by the Energy Cluster to other municipal enterprises in Tychy. In this way, these companies are largely independent of changes in the prices of energy supplied by the energy company Tauron. This also affects the lower prices of municipal services in this city compared to centers where such solutions have not been used.

The circular economy supporting sustainable development can be viewed from various points of view. For example, the flooding of land with plastic waste, which has also entered the aquatic environment, has become a worldwide problem. Microplastics contained in the oceans have become part of the food for the fauna living in them. In this way, it got into the nutritional circuit of humans as well. The author is not competent to speak in detail about the negative effects of consuming plastic, but it is certainly not beneficial to health. Ongoing discussions of scientists and practitioners, in which the author also participates, promote, on the one hand, the adoption of legislation prohibiting the production of plastic packaging in favor of those obtained from plant materials, including wood, on the other hand, the costs of obtaining such packaging are much higher and will contribute to further reduction of the forest area on the planet (cf. Table 1).

Only in Europe, Asia and Oceania there is a slight increase in forest area, but in relation to the entire planet, the saucer amounted to 4% in 2020 compared to 1990. However, from an economic and ecological point of view, a complete abandonment of plastics is impossible and not even advisable. For example, pallets for transporting loads, which are made of plastic, both save the world's resources of wood, from which wooden pallets are made, and due to the fact that the material is practically 100% recyclable, they can be reproduced for a very long time. At the same time, they do not pose a practical threat to the environment. Table 2 shows indicators of changes in population size and resources in the years 1990-2020.

Figure 1. Water park in Tychy
Source: Own

The data presented in Table 2 confirm the increase in the world's population. Over the last decade, the population has increased by almost 50%, energy consumption has increased by more than 60%, and CO2 emissions have increased by almost 50%. At that time, the area of forests and other energy resources decreased.

Against this background, the company All Green Pallets proposes solutions and puts resources at your disposal to conduct an economically effective and environmentally friendly return circulation of multiple pallets use, used in the processes of manufacturing, storage and transport of products. The pallets are made of polypropylene copolymer by structural injection. Approved for use in the production, storage and transport of food and packaged pharmaceuticals, in accordance with the requirements in force in

Figure 2. Increase in electricity production capacity in 2006-2021
Green color means electricity production, blue color- nergy consumption by the wastewater treatment plant, red color-level of energy self-sufficiency
Source: Data obtained from Zbigniew Gieleciak

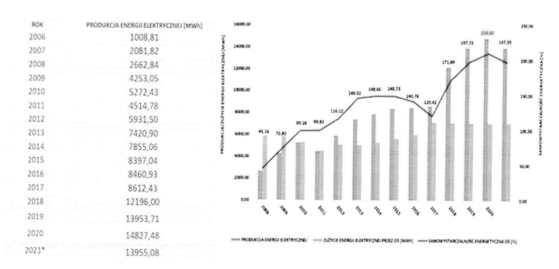

Table 1. Growing stock (billion m3) by region. FAO data, own calculations

Forest area (million ha)	1990	2000	2010	2020 [1)]	2020 - 1990 difference	
Africa	743	710	676	637	-106,2	-14,29%
Asia	585	587	611	623	37,3	6,37%
Europe	994	1 002	1 014	1 017	23,1	2,33%
North and Central America	755	752	754	753	-2,6	-0,34%
Oceania	185	183	181	185	0,3	0,15%
South America	974	923	870	844	-129,5	-13,30%
World	4 236	4 158	4 106	4 059	-177,5	-4,19%

Source: https://www.fao.org/forestry/en/ and Witos, Wójcik-Czerniawska, Szczepanik, and Grzymała (2022, p. 3)

the EU and the USA. The weight of AGP pallets is significantly lower than wooden equivalents: when a wooden EURO pallet weighs approx. 25 kg, the corresponding AGP-S pallet weighs approx. 11.7 kg and, just like a wooden pallet, can be used to store goods on high racks storage. The classic DHP pallet, with the dimensions of the carrier plate 800 × 600, weighs approx. 9 kg. The corresponding AGP-H pallet weighs approx. 3.3 kg. Details in the technical specifications (System of traceable pallets).

The quality and durability of the construction as well as the repeatability of dimensions and weight of individual types of AGP pallets allow them to be used in automated processes of picking, storage and

Table 2. World the gap in the years 1990-2020

WORLD	1990	2000	2010	2020	2020 / 1990
Rural population (million)	3,0	3,3	3,4	3,4	112,36%
urban population (million)	2,3	2,9	3,6	4,4	191,20%
population total (million)	5,3	6,1	7,0	7,8	146,23%
primary energy consumption (TWh)	95,5	110,2	141,3	156,7	164,01%
CO_2 emissions (billion Mt)	23,2	25,2	33,3	34,8	149,78%
Forest area (million ha)	4 236	4 158	4 106	4 059	95,81%
Growing stock (billion m^3)	560	556	555	557	99,42%
Carbon stock in biomass (Gt)	298	296	294	295	98,90%
Total carbon stock (Gt)	668	663	662	662	99,06%

Source: Witos, Wójcik-Czerniawska, Szczepanik, and Grzymała (2022, p. 5)

Figure 3. Green pallets
Source: Traceable Pallet System

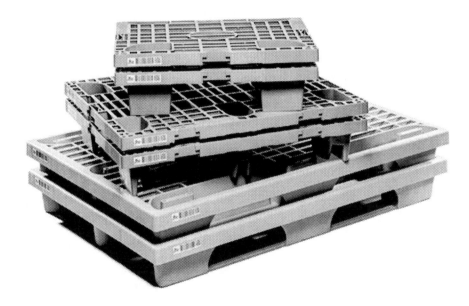

transport. The requirements of ergonomics, occupational health and safety are reflected in the design and weight of pallets. The pallets meet the criteria for women's manual handling. Unlike wooden pallets, AGP pallets do not get wet, they can be washed and disinfected. Identification allows you to automate data collection and transfer activities at every stage of the supply chain. The benefits of resource sharing are shared by all system participants. According to K. Witos, the transport of AGP pallets consumes 30% less fuel than the transport of comparable wooden pallets. Ergonomics, safety, economic and organizational efficiency of working with AGP pallets stand out from the solutions using traditional wooden pallets (Identifiable pallet system).

When asked which packaging, paper or plastic, is more environmentally friendly, most of us will most likely point to the former, explaining that: "paper degrades much faster in nature than plastic." How much resources and energy are needed to produce each of these packages, deliver to the recipient, how much waste is generated, where do they go, what happens to them? Can the packaging be used more than once, can it be recycled or recycled after use? The results of research in which answers to the above questions are sought, taking into account the product life cycle - Life Cycle Assessment (LCA) - are sometimes surprising. Our analysis of the pallet carbon footprint comparison - LCA on the environmental impact of wooden and plastic pallets shows that the production and use of AGP pallets can leave a carbon footprint three times smaller than that generated during the production and use of wooden pallets. Worn or damaged AGP pallets are recycled with full use of the originally used raw material. All Green Pallets are intended for intensive circulation. The specific shape and color, and above all, the unique number of the palette make it possible to monitor key events during its use. The entity in whose possession specific pallets remain bears full responsibility, among other things, for ensuring that no pallets or their parts end up "in a landfill". The system allows you to get closer to the goal of the "zero waste" concept in practice, and the method of settlement motivates Users to properly use environmentally friendly pallets. After decommissioning, used or damaged units are 100% used in the production of subsequent pallets (Traceable Pallet System).

A proposal for an outline of a circular economy model that protects the natural environment adapted to modern economics - practical public management (PPM).

In the author's opinion, it will be difficult to propose a universal circular economy model, especially with regard to municipal waste management, suitable for all inhabitants of the planet. Europeans, Americans and Asians react differently to certain solutions. Even among the inhabitants of a given continent, there are different preferences for solutions. For example, in Japan, in the town of Kamikatsu, there are no waste containers, because all waste is managed and segregated into several dozen fractions by residents. In 2003, the city authorities drew attention to the fact that waste heaps spoil the landscape, and burning pollutes the air, and have offered the residents to participate in an ecological experiment. It consisted in the production of the smallest amount of waste by members of society and its reprocessing on the largest possible scale. A "Zero Garbage Declaration" was announced, assuming that by 2020 Kamikatsu will become the first "waste-free" city without an incinerator or landfill. At the beginning, the declaration imposed on residents the obligation to sort garbage into 9 categories, later this list was extended to 34 items. Community members personally deliver waste and break it down to cartons placed in front of the collection point, separately magazines, leaflets, cardboard, PET bottles, caps, caps, whole light bulbs, broken fluorescent tubes, used cooking oil, disposable chopsticks, plastic packaging, fabrics, clothing, blankets and carpets, household appliances, lighters. Organic waste is not accepted, because every resident of Kamikatsu is obliged to compost it. Thanks to this, each month about 1000 kg of waste finds new owners and gains a second life. The town recycles up to 80% of its waste.

The above example shows that in Japan it is much easier to introduce ecological principles among residents who, it seems, "easier" accept the costs of recycling manifested in the acceptance of the costs of their own effort for the segregation of each fraction of waste. Of course, the awareness of the inhabitants of the cited town of Kamikatsu, who in practice use the so-called waste management hierarchy. This hierarchy, according to the European Directive 2008/98/EC of the European Parliament and of the Council

of 19 November 2008 on waste and repealing certain directives [Directive] in Article 4, stipulates that waste generation should be prevented first, and then waste prepared for reuse, then recycling and other recovery methods, and finally disposal.

on the other hand, optimizes the use of waste in an advanced way thanks to the adopted waste hierarchy: recycling takes precedence over energy recovery, which in turn has priority over landfilling. This model has proven to be highly effective as only 7% of all waste generated in Denmark ends up in landfill. A key element of Danish waste management is source separation. Paper, cardboard and glass sorting systems are generally accepted by society and are used on a large scale by both private individuals and businesses. Thus, 67% of all waste undergoes various forms of reuse and treatment, such as washing and refilling bottles, melting down cans and glass into new products or reusing residues from waste incineration in road construction, etc. Energy is recovered by burning the remaining waste in incineration plants to produce electricity and heat. The heat generated in this way covers approx. 20% of the needs of district heating systems in Denmark. Waste management in Denmark is regulated by several legal and economic instruments. Economic instruments seem to be particularly effective. The most important economic instrument is the packaging tax, which encourages waste avoidance. Packaging tax applies only to new packaging. Reused packaging is not taxed, so it is in the producer's interest to introduce reusable packaging (Adamczak, 2020).

In the Swedish model, it all started with the crisis in the 1970s, when oil prices rose by 400% and Sweden was on the brink of bankruptcy. It was then that the strategy of switching to renewable energy sources and ecological heating of houses was created. This required a combination of many activities, the beginning of which was the education of children and youth, and then appropriate legal regulations. Already in 2002, the landfilling of any flammable waste was banned, and in 2005, organic waste. In 2007, penal sanctions were introduced for littering and non-segregation of waste. The mentality of the society has also changed, and this is the result of the dissemination of knowledge related to ecological issues. It was important to develop a sense of common responsibility for the environment and regularity in action. In Sweden, sorting waste is natural. This rather non-segregation would be something strange, incomprehensible. Currently, 99.5% of all waste is recycled in Sweden and only 0.5% is landfilled. The role of the legislator was to create a system of incentives. In Sweden, there are special technologies used to recycle aluminium, glass, plastic and paper. As a result, 90% of all packaging is recycled. The system is uncomplicated and user-friendly. In every grocery store there is a vending machine where you can throw empty packages. When buying products in a package (carton, bottle, can) we will pay more at the checkout, but by throwing an empty package into the machine, which is deposited, we automatically receive a refund. An example of the modern development of the entire community towards the circular economy model is the Swedish city of Malmö, especially the Västra Hamnen district of the city, which was designed for 12 years by the joint forces of ecologists, architects and planners. Low-rise houses built of natural materials such as stone, wood and sand with walls and roofs covered with plants, which contribute to the creation of a favorable microclimate, were built there. The inhabitants of Västra Hamnen do not have to fight against smog, not only due to the location by the sea and a large number of vegetation, but also due to the reduction of car traffic in the district in favor of alternative bicycle transport and biofuel buses. The inhabitants of the blocks of flats were obliged to create at least ten so-called "Green Points" in the form of bird feeders, flower beds or vegetable gardens (BlogMorizon). The energy supplying this part of Malmö is obtained entirely from renewable sources thanks to the use of solar collectors, wind farms and thermal waters that heat radiators. In turn, biogas is obtained from biological waste, which is then transformed into electricity that powers city lanterns. Even summer air conditioning is powered by cold water from underground layers (BlogMorizon).

The key to convincing European and American society, including business, to apply the waste management hierarchy in one form or another must be properly implemented motivation, as shown by the examples of Denmark and Sweden. Appropriate legislation and modern waste management companies can generate such motivation. Therefore, in the proposed model, according to the author, the most important point or necessary condition is the openness of the municipal solid and liquid waste management company to the implementation and extension of the concept of the circular economy. A not isolated example of such an enterprise can be " BSR Berlin (Berliner Stadtreinigung), which is Germany's largest and one of Europe's leading municipal waste management companies" (Germany's most sustainable brands, 2015). The company belongs to the municipality of Berlin, which includes several subsidiaries: Berlin Recycling GmbH, BRAL Reststoff-Bearbeitungs GmbH, GBAV Gesellschaft für Boden- und Abfallverwertung mbH, Fuhrpark Business Service GmbH and MPS GmbH. With around 5,500 employees, BSR Berlin is the largest municipal company in Germany and one of the largest employers in Berlin. The company recycles Berlin household, biological and bulky waste and is also responsible for emptying recycling bins in some districts of the city. It also manages a Berlin combined heat and power plant, a biogas plant and 15 separate waste collection points (Wir sind BSR - Geschäftsbericht 2017). The company is positively perceived as an employer. The approach to waste management in many countries has changed from a kind of marginalization of people working in this industry to the pride of working in an environmentally friendly company that implements the principles of sustainable development. These types of enterprises integrate a significant part of the urban economy, including urban greenery management. Prospectively, they can arrange urban gardening projects, beekeeping, collecting water from rainfall, etc. closed-circuit projects.

The second point of such a model is the openness of the waste management company, and in principle it can be called ecological economy, to cooperation with private companies that will creatively join the process of recovering raw materials obtained during waste collection and thanks to their entrepreneurship will find appropriate management for each type of waste. bringing profit both to them and to the urban community and the ecological economy enterprise. The author called such a procedure Practical Public Management (PPM), which, unlike the well-known New Public Management (NPM), creates a symbiosis between the public and private economy, which allows the public and private ideas to complement each other. In other words, the public sector creates the idea, including the circular economy, and the private sector helps to implement it effectively. PPM is also significantly similar to the concept of Public Governance (PG) and it can be assumed that it is even its derivative, taking into account perhaps more practical solutions from the efficiency point of view. Of course, one can theoretically argue about this. The very idea of NPM was to apply solutions from the private sector, for example regarding the management and organization of enterprises, to the public sector, including entities providing municipal services by adopting a more entrepreneurial organizational and legal form for a municipal entity. Other tools of NPM were the introduction of management contracts, outsourcing, public- private partnership for the implementation of urban investments, creating a market where possible or only managing the urban economy and entrusting the provision of municipal services to private companies, etc. In other words, making the public sector similar to the private or exercising control over it. In the PPM approach (or supplemented by GUT), it is assumed that municipal enterprises have undergone such pro-entrepreneurial changes thanks to NPM and GUT that in the case of cooperation with the private sector they will show great initiative and openness to such cooperation. Thanks to such mutual penetration, the public sector has been privatized in a sense, and the private sector has been made public.

Appropriately motivating residents to accept sustainable development solutions requires showing both the benefits for the natural environment and their own. For example, in Poland, the positive movement for segregation of waste has decreased due to the lack of transparency of the system of fees for collection and management of waste. Regardless of how well a person segregates waste, even as well as the inhabitants of Kamikatsu, i.e., generating almost no waste, he pays the same as others who are less involved in the segregation process. In practice, most of the costs of collecting the introduced packaging and its management have also been transferred to the residents. This is expressed in the constantly increasing fee for the collection and management of waste. The so-called packagers, i.e. producers of packaged goods, bear the fee under extended producer responsibility, but in the case of Poland it is several times lower compared to, for example, Germany. Therefore, there is no such spirit of cooperation and commitment to pro-ecological activities. The existing waste management system in Poland does not yet contain too many PPM elements. First of all, this system is aimed at achieving the levels of segregated waste required by the European Union. Not much attention is paid to creating, for example, more efficient logistics for the collection of this waste, thanks to which the cost of the entire process would be lower. Of course, this is slowly changing. This can be clearly seen in wastewater treatment plants, where the sludge formed as a result of treatment processes is no longer a problem for the treatment plant, but a commodity that can be sold, for example, for agricultural or urban greenery purposes. The same is true for biodegradable municipal waste. As a rule, they are subjected to composting, and the compost is given or sold to the inhabitants. The already discussed example of the treatment plant in Tychy, where industrial biodegradable waste is used in the process of obtaining biogas, is also slowly spreading. A deposit-refund system is also slowly being introduced.

Returning to the model proposal, also in other European countries, including Poland, a special role is played by the municipal enterprise. The author's observations show that residents expect from the management board of such an enterprise and from the commune head the attitude of a leader who has a vision, looks for the best solutions, etc., as opposed to the behavior of a manager who usually avoids challenges and the risks associated with them.

CONCLUSION

In order to protect the natural environment and protect the positive achievements of modern civilization, it is postulated to adopt a circular economy model appropriate for a given country, based on the achievements of new public management and its evaluation for practical public management. This model in its universal proposal, which can then be adjusted accordingly for a given population group, consists in:

1. Recognition of the leading role of solid and liquid waste management companies in creating a circular economy model.
2. Such an enterprise should also strive for energy self-sufficiency, as is the case, among others, in the treatment plant in Tychy. Where possible, it should also use solar energy through the installation of solar panels and support the increasingly popular energy storage.
3. Instead of seeing waste, start seeing raw materials. For example, aluminum cans are basically pure raw material.
4. Regardless of the adopted organizational and legal form, this enterprise should cover a wider field of activity than just the collection of municipal or industrial waste. It should integrate with activities such as biogas production, urban greenery management, gardening projects, etc.
5. This enterprise should additionally cooperate and consolidate with other enterprises that manage waste in a practical way, e.g. for industrial purposes or to obtain electricity, heat or cold.

6. Non-renewable raw materials should be used to produce long-life and recyclable products in order to conserve natural resources, as the example of green pallets shows.
7. Residents should also be involved in the circular economy process in such a way that there is a relationship between the level of waste segregation and the fee paid by the resident, and thanks to a residents-friendly deposit system, for example on the Danish model.

REFERENCES

Adamczak, J. (2022). *Restructuring a municipal enterprise towards a circular economy on the example of the waste management industry*. Oficyna Wydawnicza SGH.

BlogMorizon.pl. (n.d.). https://www.morizon.pl/blog/vastra-hamnen-szwedzka-dzielnica-przyszlosci/

Directive 2008/98/EC of the European Parliament and of the Council of 19 November 2008 on waste and repealing certain directives, Journal device L 312/3

Ellen MacArthur Foundation. (2015). *Towards a Circular Economy: The Business Case for Accelerated Change*. https://www.ellenmacarthurfoundation.org/assets/downloads/PL-Towards-a-Circular-Economy-Business-Rationale-for-an-Accelerated-Transition-v.1.5.1.pdfm

Friedman, R., & Friedman, M. (1996). *Free Choice*. Panta Publishing House.

Galbraith, J. K. (1979). *Economics and Social Goals*. National Scientific Publishing House.

Germany's most sustainable brands. (2015). nachhaltigkeitspreis.de

Meadows, D. H., Meadows, D. L., Randers, J., & Behrens, W. W. (1973). *Limits to Growth*. National Economic Publishing House.

Mesarović, M., & Pestel, E. (1977). *Humanity at a turning point*. National Economic Publishing House.

Pietrewicz, J. W., & Sobiecki, R. (2016). Entrepreneurship sparing economy. In M. Poniatowska-Jaksch & R. Sobiecki (Eds.), *Sharing Economy* (p. 12). Oficyna Wydawnicza SGH.

Poniatowska-Jaksch, M., & Sobiecki, R. (Eds.). (2016). *Sharing Economy* (p. 8). Oficyna Wydawnicza SGH.

Rogall, H. (2010). *Theory and practice*. Wydawnictwo Zysk i S-ka.

Say, J. B. (1960). *A Treatise on Political Economy*. Polskie Wydawnictwo Naukowe.

Stankiewicz, W. (1998). *History of Economic Thought*. Polskie Wydawnictwo Ekonomiczne.

ENDNOTES

[1] A system of traceable returnable plastic pallets, source: All Green Pallets - All Green Pallets Polska, entry: 15/01/2023.

2. Wir sind BSR - Geschäftsbericht 2017.
3. Witos K, Wójcik-Czerniawska A, Szczepanik P, Grzymała Z, Carbon offset due to using plastic pallets, Contributed paper prepared for presentation at the 5th Symposium on Agri-Tech Economics for Sustainable Futures 19-20 September 2022, Harper Adams University, Newport, UK, p. 3,
4. https://www.bsr.de/assets/downloads/Gechaeftsbericht_2017.pdf
5. htttps://wethecrowd.pl/czem-jest-sharing-economy/ (access: 10.05.2020),
6. https://www.fao.org/forestry/en/
7. https://www.allgreenpallets.com/, accessed: 01/15/2023.
8. https://ulicaekologiczna.pl/przyjazne-srodowisko/kamikatsu-miasteczko-bez-koszy-smieci (access: 29.03.2020).

Chapter 16
Unethical Outsourcing and Marketing of International Clothing, Fashion Brands, and Global Supply Chains:
A Case Study of Bangladesh's RMG Industry

A. S. M. Anam Ullah
University of Wollongong, Australia

ABSTRACT

The exploitation of workers in global supply chains (GSCs) has been strengthened over the past 40 years, mainly since the emergence of globalization and neoliberalism. A primary ethical concern of outsourcing and marketing is labour exploitation in developing countries. In Bangladesh's RMG industry, workers are often paid low wages and forced to work long hours in unsafe conditions. Many international clothing brands have been criticized for outsourcing their production to factories that violate labor rights. As a result, unethical outsourcing and marketing of the global supply chains from Bangladesh's RMG industry has left millions of RMG workers in dire straits. Furthermore, this chapter focuses on theoretical interpretations and finds that globalization and neoliberalism exposed modern slavery in the global supply chain networks. Hence, this chapter suggests that international clothing and fashion brands must ethically outsource from a country like Bangladesh.

INTRODUCTION

The supply chains have contributed to modern slavery by degrading labor standards and work practices worldwide (New, 2015; Ishaya, Paraskevadakis, Bury & Bryde, 2023). In addition, the inherent difficulties of monitoring highly fragmented production processes also make developing countries and their

DOI: 10.4018/978-1-6684-8681-8.ch016

workers vulnerable to labor exploitation (see Alamgir & Banerjee, 2019; Saxena, 2022). Understanding from the current scholarship of the situation of global supply chains denotes that the growing social issue of modern slavery is becoming more extensive in the academic discourse. More specifically, the current research reveals that in Bangladesh and its extensive informal economic sectors, RMG workers have been severely exploited since the 1980s, the period of the industry's inception (Rahman, 2019; Crinis, 2019; Prentice, 2021).

Bangladesh's RMG industry employs more than six million workers who mainly migrated from the country's rural villages and took jobs from mostly non-compliant RMG factories at low wages (Rahman & Yadlapalli, 2021; Ullah, 2021). Most importantly, the precarious thing is that RMG workers often faced brutal death and injury in the Tazreen Fashions factory fires, and the Rana Plaza building collapsed (Syed & Ikra, 2022; Ullah, 2022a). These disastrous factory accidents were caused by the ignorance of the Government of Bangladesh and RMG factory owners to ensure workplace safety for RMG workers (Hasan, 2022; Moazzem, Preoty & Khan, 2022). At the same time, international apparel and fashion brands continued to outsource to developing countries like Bangladesh and its exploited RMG industry without ethical behaviour and providing no appropriate financial support to RMG workers (Siddiqi, 2019; Rahman, 2019; Huq, 2022; Saxena, 2022).

From this, Bangladesh's RMG industry faces ethical dilemmas in its supply chains, particularly with Western and European ones. This book chapter will focus on the unethical outsourcing of global clothing and fashion brands from a developing country such as Bangladesh. Scholars focused on global supply chains and negative publicity for many firms in the low-tech clothing, footwear, and toy industries — sweatshop labour. This book chapter's arguments on ethical outsourcing of supply chains transcend other essential issues of how globalisation and neoliberalism had severely squished the Corporate Social Responsibility (CSR) of global clothing and fashion brands and how they exploited RMG workers in Bangladesh since the 1980s when globalisation and neoliberalism came into force. Importantly, this book chapter will also look at the critical juncture of the literature review to understand how international treaties and organisations support extending globalization and global exploitation, mainly in the GSCs (see New, 2015; Ishaya, Paraskevadakis, Bury & Bryde, 2023).

The organization of this book chapter is as follows. Following the introductory section, this book chapter first understands the characteristics of international clothing and fashion brands and GSCs in the context of globalisation and neoliberalism. The second section will present the Objectives and research questions of the study. The third section will develop the theoretical arguments from the heuristic analysis—for example, the critical discourse for ethical and sustainable supply chain practices. The fourth section presents the literature reviews, drawing heavily on the modern RMG industry's growth that came through the rise of many international treaties and organisational development, such as NAFTA and WTO.

In addition, the fourth section also presents an analysis of the characteristics of international clothing and fashion brands and global supply chains and dilemmas of RMG workers in Bangladesh during globalisation and neoliberalism. The fifth section outlines the methodological choice of the book chapter. Following the methodological section, the next section, which is the empirical data presentation, will be in section six, and data analysis and critical discourse will be in section seven. Finally, it suggests how GSCs, and international clothing and fashion brands can become more ethical in outsourcing and marketing from less regulated developing countries, such as the RMG industry in Bangladesh, where workers are paid the world's lowest minimum wages with no or very meagre social benefits after analysis some empirical data from Bangladesh.

OBJECTIVES AND RESEARCH QUESTIONS OF THE STUDY

In this book chapter, ethnographically, I examine how Bangladesh has adopted the new politico-economic doctrine, i.e., globalization and neoliberalism, since the 1980s. Moreoever, it explores and examines how multinational corporations, mainly international clothing and fashion brands, found a new destination for cheap outsourcing by paying the world's lowest minimum wages and allowing workers to work in shoddy RMG factories in Bangladesh since the 1980s. This book chapter is also based on a critical understanding of academic and grey literature on globalisation and neoliberalism and unethical outsourcing and marketing of international clothing and fashion brands and how they have ignored to improve the livelihoods of RMG workers in Bangladesh, who are treated as modern slavery in the contemporary world. Hence, the following research questions are addressed in this book chapter:

1. What factors countenanced international clothing and fashion brands to outsource from a developing country, like Bangladesh, since the 1980s?
2. Why is Bangladesh's RMG industry shows a symbol of modern slavery and exploitation?
3. How can international clothing and fashion brands do ethical outsourcing, and why is it so essential for the suitability of the global clothing and fashion brands and Bangladesh's RMG industry?

THEORETICAL FRAMEWORK

First, this section will provide academic discourses on globalisation and neoliberalism and the scholarly debates on the WTO and NAFTA, which spread globalisation and neoliberalism worldwide. Second, it will discuss how these forces strengthened global supply chains and exploited workers in their supply chain networks since the 1980s through an unprecedented era of globalisation and neoliberalism. At the end of this section, the aim will be to connect these market forces and the evidence of unethical supply chain outsourcing and marketing in exploring the RMG industry and its workers in Bangladesh.

Several international scholars argue that establishing the WTO as a "trade liberalisation" project, in which free trade processes allowed compensation for those harmed, was a significant turning point in the conduct of trade under neoliberal globalism in a "trade-not-liberalisation" scheme. However, the situation is different in many developing countries where multinational corporations are doing business and exploiting the proletariat massively (see Crinis, 2019; Siddiqi, 2019; Alamgir & Banerjee, 2019). Bangladesh is a current example of this process (Ahmed, 2004; Mottaleb & Sonobe, 2011; Paul-Majumdar & Begum, 2000; Rahman, 2004). Indeed, from the beginning, the globalisation approach seemed to be a political project to establish new institutional arrangements at national and international levels (Chorev, 2005).

Since the abolition of the quota system, many developing countries have come under pressure from the neoliberal globalised trade system. This was reinforced when China was freed from quota restrictions to access the US market in 2009 (Asuyama et al., 2013). Nevertheless, due to the low wages of predominantly abundant rural low-skilled and low-educated female workers, Bangladesh has received Western and European capital investments over the past decade (see Paul-Majumder and Begum, 2000; Rahman, 2004; Haider, 2006). On the other hand, international scholars, globalisation has given rise to an ongoing debate between developed and developing countries regarding the adherence to international labour standards in international trade agreements (Truscott, Brust & Fesmire, 2007).

The sweatshop is a movable business that requires little capital, basic technology and cheap labour for formation (Bender & Greenwald, 2003, p. 7). In the 1980s and 1990s, economic globalisation leveraged by technological advancements led to the creation of more multinational companies (Cheek & Moore, 2003). Contemporary researchers also understand sweatshops as transnational. The contracting and subcontracting system that was once limited to a single nation or, more likely, a single city is now global (Bender & Greenwald, 2003). NAFTA and WTO agreements also significantly contributed to increasing globalization and neoliberalism (Cheek & Moore, 2003; Ullah, 2015).

To establish a global labour market, the mobility of labour is optional since the global market prices of goods shape the price of labour - lower labour costs in developing countries play a significant role. Consequently, they exert ever more tremendous pressure on wages in developed countries. The allocation of labour is achieved by the mobility of capital, which flows towards the basins of cheaper labour taking productivity levels into account. The situation has worsened in the last decade when capital in the developed countries has found investments in industry and new jobs uninteresting and reverted to financialization. Globalization in the developed countries has thus turned into an outflow of investment capital and jobs, the stagnation of wages and living standards of masses of workers, restrictions on social security and welfare systems, the rising indebtedness of individuals, companies and states, and unemployment tremendously high (see, for example, Harvey, 2007, 2016).

To analyse the concept of globalisation, most international scholars often referred to the process of international economic integration, while the organisational dimensions of globalisation were ignored (Chorev, 2005; Harvey, 2007; Rahman, 2013) formed NAFTA, leading to globalisation and neoliberalism (Chorev, 2005; Munck, 2010; Harvey, 2007). However, contemporary scholars, such as Anner (2020) and Rahman and Yadlapallai (2021), showed in their international research how global apparel brands and their supply chains intentionally targeted the abundant labour force in Bangladesh and exploited them. The endemic power of global capitalists, who intentionally targeted developing countries, is also best understood by Harvey (2007, 2016). For example, Harvey portrayed the characteristics of global clothing brands or Western and European capitalists who have internationally created global macro trade forces, i.e., globalisation and neoliberalism. He found an interesting argument; for example, Western and European capitalists or clothing brands targeted developing countries to exploit their abundant labour for job creation and to eliminate the income disparity between developed and developing countries. He suggested it was an intentional politico-economic agenda to leverage capitalism (see Harvey, 2007, 2016, 2022).

The economic globalisation theory and its impact on developing countries are essential to understanding the power nexus between global capitalists/GSCs and local Bangladeshi RMG employers (Alamgir & Banerjee, 2019). Undoubtedly, this reflects countries' consequences in post-economic global trade relations between developed and developing countries. Bangladesh is no exception to this dilemma, which could quickly identify in the country's garment industry. Researchers have now predicted and confirmed through their vigorous investigations that sweatshops and their activity will never disappear, but they can be controlled and substantial (Bender & Greenwald, 2003). So, what is more, needed now to keep the sector in a way to maintain its positive progress in Bangladesh now and in the future?

However, a significant criticism of globalization and neoliberalism is that in its current form, despite its overall welfare-producing nature, it has worsened inequality within and between countries, which is contrary to the promise of globalization. Interestingly, although scholars are deeply concerned about the real benefits of RMG workers who have moved to urban areas and worked in a small RMG factory over the last 40 years, RMG factory owners are still powerful mercenaries in the country. For example,

RMG traders have political power and occupy executive positions in the government (see Harvey, 2007; Rahman, 2013; Gilbert, 2018; Saxena, 2022).

Studying Bangladeshi sweatshops means examining many paradoxes. The economic roots of Bangladesh's sweatshops are international; however, its efforts are national (see, for example, Bender & Greenwald, 2003). Capitalists have exploited RMG workers as the country's weekly labour laws and regulations provided the scope to them (see Huq, 2022). Critically, theorising around the state in economic globalisation involves assessing its incapacity due to its weakness or continued strength, the power of global capital, or its ability to act with impunity (Connor & Haynes, 2013).

Nevertheless, global Western and European clothing brands intentionally ignored their Corporate Social Responsibilities (CSR) role. They violated International Labour Organization (ILO) and United Nations' human and international trade conventions and principles. As a result, while globalization and neoliberalism were supposed to reduce tensions between developed and developing countries by eradicating income inequalities, it has not been done. Hence, theoretically, it is understood that Western and European clothing and fashion brands and their GSCs intentionally ignore the proper CSR role during globalization and neoliberalism to be more competitive in the global apparel markets by producing RMG goods in most developing countries, mainly Bangladesh (see Ullah, 2022a; Uddin, Azmat, Fujimoto & Hossain, 2023).

LITERATURE REVIEWS

The Politico-Economic Significance of MFA, NAFTA, WTO, and RMG in Bangladesh

Multifiber Arrangement (MFA) is an international trade agreement involving apparel and textiles. The MFA was established in 1974 and imposed quotas on the amount of clothing and textiles that developing countries could export to developed countries. The agreement was administered in Switzerland under the General Agreement on Tariffs and Trade (GATT). Intended as a temporary agreement, the MFA expired on January 1, 1995, and was replaced by the Agreement on Textiles and Clothing under the World Trade Organization (WTO) (Anner, 2020; Hayes, 2021). The main objective was to expand trade and reduce barriers, such as the progressive liberalization of world trade in trade and textile products, while at the same time ensuring the orderly and equitable development of this trade and its avoidance of disruptive effects on imports in individual markets, production lines, and exporting countries (cited in Hasan, 2013).

The North American Free Trade Agreement (NAFTA) entered into force on 1 January 1994. USA President George H.W. Bush signed NAFTA on December 17, 1992, which Congress later ratified on November 20, 1993. NAFTA was signed into law. On 8 December 1993, President William J. Clinton signed the Law (Villareal & Fergusson, 2017). The vision and goal of NAFTA were to create more jobs (Paul-Majumdar & Begum, 2000; Mottaleb & Sonobe, 2011). NAFTA was a significant Free Trade Agreement (FTA) between the USA, Canada and Mexico. International scholars, such as Villareal and Fergusson (2017), suggest that the FTA of NAFTA was mainly designed to gear up the trade between the USA and Mexico. As a result, since 1993, Mexico has relied heavily on the United States as an export market until 2015. However, since 2005, the WTO lifted China's restriction on export, and Mexico's total exports to the United States decreased from 83% in 1993 to 81% in 2015 (Villareal & Fergusson,

2017). Nevertheless, international scholars, such as Chorev (2005) and Villareal and Fergusson (2017), suggest that NAFTA was mainly designed to rein China's export to the North American markets.

On the other hand, under the Marrakesh Agreement in January 1995, the World Trade Organisation (WTO) officially began to replace the GATT, established in 1947 (Chorev, 2005; Ullah, 2015; WTO, n.d.). As one of the youngest international organisations, WTO has made a functional shift in global trade and services. It has also played an essential role in the national and international political economy to speed up the process of globalisation (Chorev, 2005). Since its establishment, the WTO has been an alternative dispute or arbitration authority to rein international trade rules between its member states. As a result, WTO created a platform where all parties, mainly member governments, have found a scope to discuss and resolve trade issues with other member governments. WTO's central objective is to provide open lines of trade-related communication between its members. Hence, WTO has reduced trade barriers and increased trade among member countries. However, it has also maintained trade barriers when it makes sense to do so in a global context. The WTO tries to mediate between nations to benefit the global economy (Tarver, 2022). Counterargument by international scholars such as Ullah (2015) and Anderson (2016) suggests that due to WTO's free trade agreement between the state members, mainly in developing states and countries, such as Bangladesh, income inequality, workers' exploitation and even low taxes are evident (see also Alamgir & Banerjee, 2019).

Despite some critical arguments for NAFTA and WTO and their politico-economic agenda, other international scholars, still consider NAFTA and WTO as a supportive force to the growth and development of Bangladesh's RMG industry (see Ullah, 2015; Anner, 2020). Bangladesh's RMG industry was, in fact, utterly dependent on foreign investment. The 100 per cent export-oriented RMG industry has grown unprecedentedly over the last 20 years (Ullah, 2015; Anner, 2020). In 1978, only nine export-oriented garment manufacturing units earned an export income of about one million dollars (Mottaleb & Sonobe, 2011). Some of these units were small traditional tailoring shops for the domestic market. The four small pioneers of the RMG business were Riaz Garments, Paris Garments, Jewel Garments and Baishakhi Garments. Riaz Garments, as a pioneer, was founded in 1960 as a small tailoring garment called Riaz Store in Dhaka. It has only served the domestic market for about 15 years. In 1973 it changed its name to Riaz Garments Ltd. In 1978, it expanded its operations in the export market by selling 10,000 men's shirts worth Franc13 million to a Paris-based company in France. Riaz Garments Ltd was the first direct exporter of garments from Bangladesh (Chowdhury, Ahmed & Yasmin, 2014). By the end of 1982, there were only 47 garment manufacturing units. A breakthrough occurred in 1984-85 when the number of garment factories rose to 587. In 1999 the number of RMG factories increased to about 2,900. However, later international studies, such as Labowitz (2016), reveal that there are at least 7000 RMG factories in Bangladesh, most of which are non-compliant. However, the rise and subsequent success of the export-oriented garment industry in the 1970s gave a new social start to the reality of Bangladesh (see also Rock, 2003).

Characteristics of International Apparel Brands and Global Supply Chains and Dilemmas of RMG Workers in Bangladesh

Current research of international scholars, such as Crinis (2019), Syed (2020), Anner (2020), Rahman and Yadlapalli (2021), Ullah (2021) and Saxena (2022) carefully considered the characteristics of international apparel brands and their supply chains. For example, Syed (2020, p. 242) cited in his academic work Jason Brennan (2019), who portrayed international apparel brands and supply chains as:

X's boat capsizes in the sea. He will soon drown. "Y" comes along in a boat and says to "X," "I will save you from drowning, but only if you give me with 50% of your future earnings." X angrily agrees.

In the above situation, however, Y's position was not found as detrimental because Y at least helped X. Still, the question is, while X was in a critical situation, perhaps, Y took advantage of the situation, which is considered unethical. This example suggests that Western and European capitalists, their corporations, apparel brands, and supply chains are entangled in unethical outsourcing from a country like Bangladesh (see Crinis, 2019; Alamgir & Banerjee, 2019; Ullah, 2021; Reza & Du Plessis, 2022). While MFA, NAFTA, and WTO agreements helped a developing nation like Bangladesh boost its employment sectors, such as RMG, the discourse of extreme exploitation of RMG workers in the last Four decades is inevitable. Figure 1 incorporated data from the Clean Clothes Campaign to show how an RMG worker in Bangladesh devalued their labour power to the international apparel brands and supply chains.

Many international studies, such as Rahman (2013), Siddiqi (2019), Huq (2022) and Ullah (2022a,b), suggest that the unethical behaviour of international apparel brands and supply chains has led to disastrous factories such as Tazreen Fashion and Rana Plaza factory incident where thousands of RMG workers were killed. In addition, a thousand more were brutally injured in exchange for scant compensation from the Government of Bangladesh, domestic RMG employers and their global business partners, and chains supplying clothing to brands such as Walmart. While Bender and Greenwald (2003), decades ago, portrayed the nature of global sweatshops, surprisingly, contemporary research through international scholars denotes the same results (see Prentice, 2021). For example, Prentice's (2021) research shows that the global garment industry has long abused labour rights. Other international scholars found that Bangladeshi RMG workers symbolise modern slavery (Moazzem, Preoty & Khan, 2022).

According to Prentice (2021), while labour rights are severely violated in the GSCs, keeping lower minimum wages for RMG workers is also a key feature of global supply chains, as found in another study by Crinis (2019). Moreover, Prentice (2021), along with Alamgir and Banerjee (2019), it is intentional that GSCs create spaces of accumulation where labour is actively devalued. Moreover, academic discourse on global production hubs, mainly in developing countries, perhaps significantly focuses on social and spatial divisions of labour that regulate inequality and gender differences. Several international studies show that the Government of Bangladesh and RMG employers are deeply motivated to attract capital while denying workers fundamental rights in workplaces like the RMG. Moreover, rights to freedom of association and trade unionism are also shallow, while legislated national minimum wages are not living wages. Noncompliant factories are under operation to support GSCs resulting in factory fires and building collapses, such as the Tazreen Fashions and Rana Plaza, due to neglect of factory inspection and regulation (Ashraf & Prentice, 2019; Ullah, 2022a,b; Saxena, 2022).

The Impact of COVID-19 on the Bangladeshi Garment Sector

According to the World Bank (2020), RMG workers lost many factory jobs, and there is a significant risk of losing more jobs in the sector due to the direct impact of the COVID-19 pandemic. The World Bank report further states that the urban and rural poor will suffer the most. The World Bank speculated that the COVID-19 pandemic would reduce national and global demand for consumer products, especially in the garment sector, which might severely cause significant unemployment and deepening poverty in Bangladesh. According to the report by Uddin in Business Standard, the RMG sector faced enormous challenges, including shutting factories, leading to many RMG job retrenchments since the COVID-19

Figure 1. Breakdown of the costs of a t-shirt made in Bangladesh for Western and European consumers and sold at $29
Source: Author constructed based on Clean Clothes Campaign data.

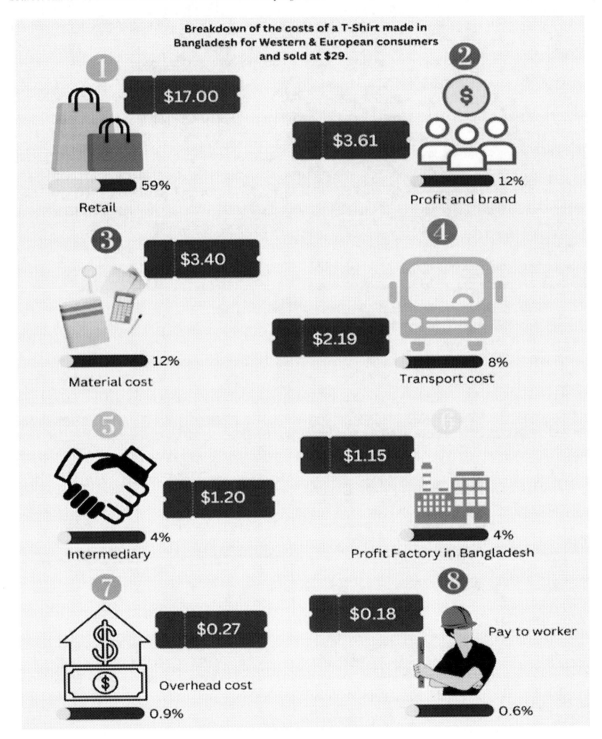

pandemic (Uddin, 2020). Moreover, Ullah (2020) found that the RMG sector was about to be ousted from its long-term global garment manufacturing position to an Asian competitor, Vietnam, before the pandemic, which is a worrying factor for Bangladesh.

Research by Rahman and Ishti (2020) suggested that the industry was seriously threatened because COVID-19 has affected it unprecedentedly. The crisis has put the Bangladesh Garment Manufacturers and Exporters Association (BGMEA) and RMG employers in an awkward situation. It has been difficult to close some factories since the COVID-19 pandemic (see Ullah & Amanullah, 2021; Ullah, 2021). For example, between 26 March 2020 to 30 May 2020, the Bangladeshi RMG sector was under a national closure process to stop the spread of COVID-19 (Kabir, Mapel & Usher, 2020). As a result, a significant number of RMG workers lost their jobs. International buyers also did not take any responsibility for financial support for RMG workers during the pandemic lockdown. Moreover, international brands cancelled pre-orders, closing many RMG factories in Bangladesh (Sen, Antara, Sen & Chowdhury, 2020). Bangladesh's leading newspaper, *The Daily Prothom Alo* (2020), published a touchy article on 2 May 2020 revealing how RMG workers suffered due to COVID-19. The report said:

Parents working in a garment factory located in Gazipur (near Dhaka) had to sell their newborn baby, as they could not pay the hospital bill of BDT 25 000 ($295). The father of the newborn baby said that they could not manage hospital bills as the garment factory, where both husband and wife used to work, was closed because of the COVID-19 pandemic. However, the local police rescued the baby and returned it to their parents. (cited in Kabir, Maple, & Usher, 2020, p. 47)

The Centre for Policy Dialogue (CPD) has revealed that around 357,000 RMG workers lost their work from January 2020 to September 2020 (cited in Russell, 2021). The CPD survey says that relatively small factories have been closed, at least 232, with at least 180 factories listed as BGMEA. The CPD report also revealed that most RMG factories needed to follow the correct retrenchment policy. Of the factories surveyed (610), only 3.6 per cent offered minimal compensation. *The Financial Express*, a leading English newspaper in Bangladesh, published a report on 6 August 2020 of the WTO Geneva office. The WTO's report stated that 45.8 per cent during the first quarter of 2020, which is 81 per cent of brands' order reduction experienced by the RMG in Bangladesh and mostly women workers lost their jobs, resulting in facing hurdles in their livelihoods (see Frenkel & Schuessler, 2021).

Study Design and Rationale for Methodological Choice

This study first conducted preliminary research for the literature review and from grey literature reviews, which helped the author create valid research questions for this study. In the empirical approach, the study conducted qualitative semi-structured interviews with relevant respondents, such as trade union organisations, NGOs and RMG workers. These respondents were selected to seek their views on the subject matter of the study.

Second, from a rational choice, a case study is a research method used to investigate a phenomenon in depth in its real-life context, where the researcher has little or no control over the situation. A case study is an appropriate design for exploring complex and relevant phenomena, focusing on understanding the meaning and nature of a phenomenon in a real-life context. Prospective researchers must understand that social science research design is more than a comprehensive analysis strategy, structure, and method. In a critical social context, when researchers are motivated to understand grounded situations, case studies and qualitative or semi-structured approaches allow researchers to explore the essential questions, mainly when "why" and "how" questions are involved (see Yin, 2003; Ghauri, 2004).

According to Lindsay (2004):

Qualitative data consist of words and observations, not numbers. As with all data, analysis and interpretation are required to bring order and understanding. This requires creativity, discipline and a systematic approach. (p. 487)

Therefore, this study has been justified from many aspects as it does not involve statistical sampling; instead, the author has presented the data in a narrative format (Yin, 2003).

Data Presentation

This section provides data from study respondents (see Figure 2), including RMG workers who voluntarily participated in several Focus Group Discussions (FGDs), to understand RMG workers' perspectives on working conditions and minimum wages in Bangladesh. Unethical business in Bangladesh's RMG industry is evident. While the suffering of RMG workers in Bangladesh is evident, it is also essential to know why Bangladeshi RMG workers have such tolerance. Therefore, stakeholders such as Bangladeshi trade union leaders, RMG employers and some NGOs participated in this study. This section provides information from ethnographic perspectives. So, the main points drawn from several interviews were:

1. Meagre minimum wages are a dilemma for the livelihood of RMG workers in Bangladesh;
2. RMG factory owners' negligence and greediness; and
3. Global supply chains' unethical business in Bangladesh.

Familiar anger among RMG workers surfaced when discussing working conditions and other minimum wages. My observations suggest a high concern among RMG workers for a decent wage rather than factory safety issues. Low wages and irregular payments put pressure on workers, sometimes leading to industrial lockouts. Workers feel that the government and employers can reduce these problems by taking appropriate initiatives. For example, government and RMG employers should reduce economic inequality by paying an appropriate wage, as income inequality is the primary determining factor. FGD1 respondent Ms Helen said, "a decent wage will reduce the gap between high-income earners and RMG workers in the sector. Workers must make a decent living first, then they can think about the rest, like working conditions" (Interview 1 December 2017).

While discussing the wages and working conditions of the RMG workers in the factory, I wanted to know why safety was not on their main agenda during the protests on many occasions. Thus, FGD respondent Mr Rohan added:

Because we need more jobs in this sector, the people of this country are poor. We are very concerned about poor people who work so hard. So, we want a job not to lose lives. However, we never get a decent level of wages. Our daily lives are more expensive than the minimum wage we receive. Even if they increase minimum wages after the extensive demonstration, it is much lower than expected. Our salaries should be at least BDTK. 8 to 9 thousand [the equivalent of USD 100+] a month to manage ourselves

Figure 2. The model of the methodological approach/strategies of data collection of the study

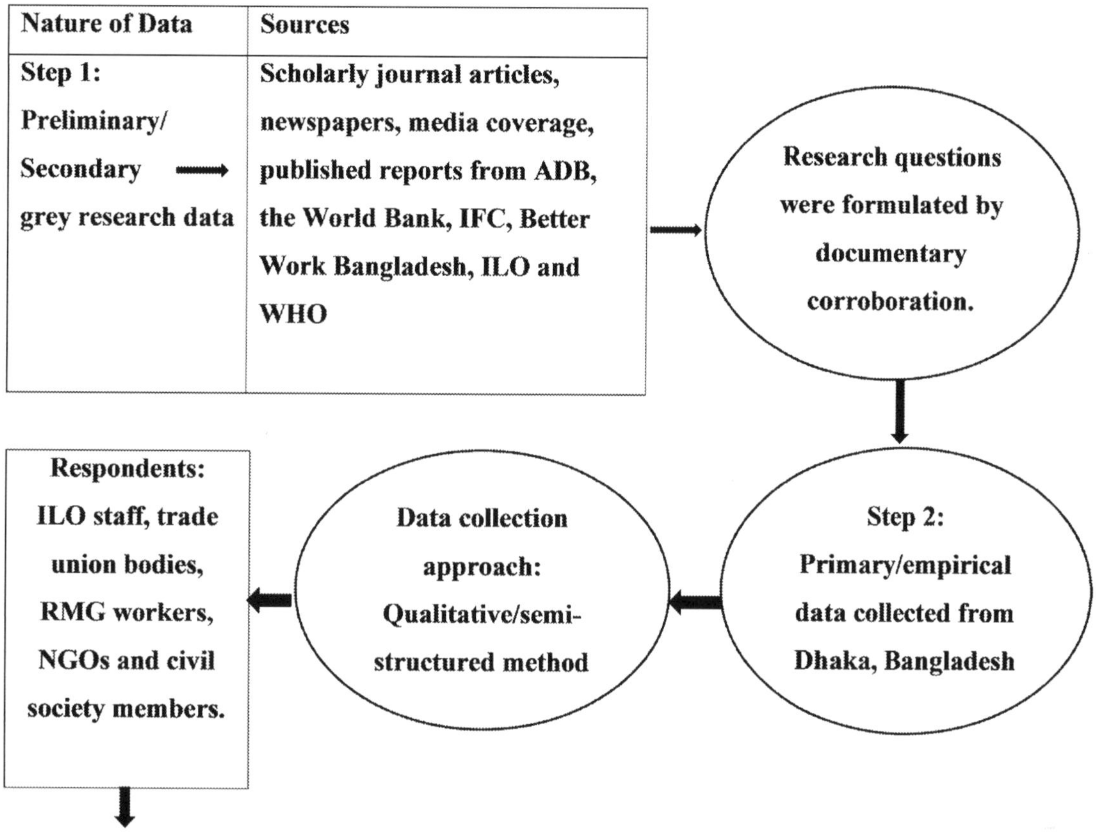

Nature of Data	Sources
Step 1: Preliminary/ Secondary grey research data	Scholarly journal articles, newspapers, media coverage, published reports from ADB, the World Bank, IFC, Better Work Bangladesh, ILO and WHO

Research questions were formulated by documentary corroboration.

Step 2: Primary/empirical data collected from Dhaka, Bangladesh

Data collection approach: Qualitative/semi-structured method

Respondents: ILO staff, trade union bodies, RMG workers, NGOs and civil society members.

How I reached the study respondents?
It was challenging fieldwork in Bangladesh. before reaching Bangladesh, collecting empirical data for the study was challenging. I initially contacted every possible respondent by email before I arrived in Bangladesh. However, arranging various interviews with respondents in different organisations was challenging in Bangladesh. Mainly, conducting RMG factory owners' interviews was another significant challenge. However, I eventually managed interviews with them using my strong communication skills and social network. The convenient part of my fieldwork was connecting trade union leaders/staff with BGMEA staff, RMG factory owners, government officers, and international organisation staff. However, FGDs were also challenging as they were found to be busy workers who usually stay most of their time in factory work. Through the generous support of local key informers and by using my social network, I finally managed several FGDs on the day RMG workers had off factory work.

Direction to future researchers: If a potential researcher wants to conduct fieldwork on a similar topic and target the same type of respondents, it would be wise to take extra precautions in advance. Researchers will need additional time and strong social networks to reach the target group in Bangladesh. In addition, potential researchers must develop practically sound methods or research tools and questions when designing any study method for fieldwork in Bangladesh.

Data sorting and analysis process followed in this study: After collecting empirical data, Nvivo11 was used to categorise themes and sub-themes, and then data was presented in a narrative format. Finally, the discussion and analyses were done by following a triangulation process for the authentication of the study.

Ethical issues: The author of this research study has received ethical approval by following all ethical codes from the University of Wollongong, Australia. This book chapter de-identifies participants as presenting their opinions and information by ensuring privacy.

properly. Our house rent is very high, and the food cost is very high too. So, we need to survive first, then think about the OHS. (Interview 1 December 2017)

Another striking point when discussing the low wages of RMG workers was that the factory owners are greedy and have little respect for the workers. Hence, another FGD respondent Ms Selina added: "the owners are greedy and want to make the most out of RMG workers' exploitation, and they do not care about us at all" (Interview 1 December 2017). On my further investigation on this issue, I had a question for an RMG factory owner, and Mr Max revealed:

After several recent significant incidents, particularly the Rana Plaza building collapse in April 2013, some buyers and international and national stakeholders of RMG in Bangladesh have extended their helping hand to regulate the industry through factory monitoring programs. However, the price remains the main factor for overall workers' well-being and Occupational Health and Safety (OHS) practice, which remained unchanged. (Interview 10 December 2010)

So, from the above excerpt, RMG employers are not happy with the international clothing buyers' pricing on RMG goods. However, another RMG employer (factory owner), Mr Kent, stated like Mr Max and added:

Western clothing retailers are very concerned about their competition, and Bangladesh is their most favourable destination. However, in most cases, international buyers want to do business in Bangladesh at a fraction of the cost of production, and more profit is in their business agenda, which needs to change. (Interview 4 December 2017)

Hence, it is understandable that RMG employers in Bangladesh want to push their basic responsibilities to the global apparel buyers who came to do business in Bangladesh in the 1980s with a specific agenda: profiting. In the current global trade system, it is perhaps a dilemma for a country like Bangladesh to change its pricing strategy. However, the minimum wages, bonuses and well-being of workers must be ensured despite the external pressure of the industry. Therefore, it was also essential to understand what other stakeholders of the RMG industry in Bangladesh think about the claim of RMG employers. Hence, Mr Alex, a senior trade union leader, who has over 50 years of experience in trade unionism in Bangladesh, added:

RMG employers are deeply motivated to make more profit using fewer workers and less time, so workers must work under extreme pressure, and an average worker works 15/16 hours or more per day. So, the mindset of long-term investment and a long-term business relationship must be present here, such as the classical business concept. (Interview 4 December 2017)

So, from the above quote of the trade union leader, it is reflective that RMG employers in Bangladesh are motivated to extra profit like their Western and European trading partners, known as global capitalists. Again, the NGO respondent, Mr Ben, blamed international clothing brands and GSCs for their unethical business. For example, he noted:

International buyers flock to Bangladesh for poor wages, low regulation and other benefits. Buyers were interested in earning higher returns than investing in the Bangladeshi RMG sector. As a result, they willingly ignore the safety of RMG factories and the minimum wages of RMG workers. (Interview 11 December 2017)

So, here is the evidence of unethical business in the RMG sector of Bangladesh since the 1980s in the era of globalization and neoliberalism. The next section will discuss the research findings and explore the links between the theoretical framework and whether the suffering of RMG workers is a response to globalization and neoliberalism.

DISCUSSIONS OF THE FINDINGS

Since the 1980s, Bangladesh, as a developing country, established a close nexus with Western and European capitalists who were searching for a favourable destination for secure capital investments. On the other hand, as inspired by several scholars, such as Crinis (2019) and Alamgir and Banerjee (2019), it can also be said that Western and European capitalists were looking to make more profits by exploiting the abundant workforce of Bangladesh (see also Ullah, 2020). Bangladeshi RMG employers and the Government of Bangladesh welcomed Western and European capitalists and corporatisation, such as Walmart and many other clothing and fashion brands. Although FDIs emerged in Bangladesh in the last 40 years, the ultimate development of Bangladesh's RMG workers never happened besides financial support to manage their livelihoods (see Siddiqi, 2019; Saxena, 2022).

On the other hand, while RMG workers were severely killed in a factory fire at Tazreen Fashions, a Western giant corporation, Walmart, has made extensive profits from exploiting RMG workers in Bangladesh. This corporation's revenues roared up to $595.6 billion for FY22, which is higher than Bangladesh's national GDP (e.g., Bangladesh's GDP in 2021 was $416.26 billion, less than 0.02% of the global economy). So now the question is if Walmart pays the correct wage to workers in the overseas manufacturing hubs or GSCs, such as Bangladeshi RMG workers, the total profit rate would significantly decrease. Still, it would be a more ethical business (see, for example, Butler, 2013; Bentonville, 2022).

The current study denotes that Western and European clothing and fashion brands and their supply chains intentionally overlooked the safety and minimum wage conditions of RMG workers in Bangladesh in the last few decades (see Alamgir & Banerjee, 2019; Prentice, 2021; Al Mamun & Hoque, 2022). While Western and European clothing brands finally took some responsibility after the catastrophic Rana Plaza building collapse, the actual pricing for production was not changed (see Anner, 2020; Rahman & Yadlapalli, 2021).

My analysis also suggests that international clothing and fashion brands' monitoring arrangements through Accord and Alliance were just a piecemeal strategy for their CSR role. It is denoted that the reason to see Accord and Alliance in Bangladesh is to save their reputation with global consumers that they lost for the Rana Plaza disaster. As a result, the ultimate suffering of RMG workers has not been stopped instead situation is more critical for their livelihoods during the current global economic recession and post-COVID-19 situation (see Ullah, 2021).

Bangladesh's RMG industry currently has around USD 45-50 billion turnover. The nation manages its micro and macro economy through the sector's low-skilled employment generation (see Rahman & Ishty, 2020). Nevertheless, these changes have mainly happened in Bangladesh's economic activity due to the robust efforts of nearly 6 million rural migrant RMG workers. However, the Government of Bangladesh, RMG employers, and even international apparel brands and their GSCs have never taken workers' well-being more seriously since the industry growth (see, for example, Islam & MacPhail, 2011; Ullah, 2021; Ullah, 2022a,b, Saxena, 2022; Huq, 2022). As a result, RMG workers are compromising working conditions with low minimum wages and living in unsanitary urban slums in and around stations in Dhaka. In addition, health, education, housing and recreational facilities for RMG workers are inadequate or, to some extent, unavailable.

The interview with RMG employers brought up the low cost of production, which is a valid point. However, while visiting their (RMG employers') offices in several posh urban slums of Dhaka, this was not reflected in the same way as they cited their limitations in offering high wages and maintaining good working conditions due to the low production price of international garment buyers.

RMG business has secured political posts of RMG employers in major political parties in Bangladesh, and most BGMEA former leaders occupy different ministries and city mayor's positions (Rahman & Rahman, 2020). Political parties collect big donation from those RMG exploiters who also supports global exploiters who came to do business in Bangladesh by exploiting RMG workers. As a result, both Government of Bangladesh, RMG employers and Western and European clothing and fashion brands and their GSCs are involved in unethical business in Bangladesh.

RMG employers in Bangladesh are also a wealthy capitalist class due to RMG business. Hence, RMG employers' luxurious lifestyle and social status reflect that pricing is not the only major issue in paying better wages to RMG workers. Instead, it was understood that both RMG employers in Bangladesh and their international trading partners have the mentality of making more profits by exploiting RMG workers (see Gilbert, 2018).

On the other hand, during a crucial time, such as the COVID-19 pandemic, Western and European clothing brands did not provide enough support to the RMG workers in Bangladesh. When the lockdown began in Bangladesh in March 2020, RMG workers lost jobs putting them in severe hardship, but they received no financial support from international clothing brands then. Many had to take out loans to survive. Because most women workers earned low wages (in some cases well below the government-mandated minimum wage) when they returned to work, they struggled to repay loans and support their families.

Also, some employers pay wages late, exacerbating women's economic problems as they are forced to buy food on credit, resulting in higher costs. In addition, financial problems for some workers were exacerbated by the loss of overtime pay, which women depend on to earn enough income to survive. For other women, overtime pay was lost due to reduced production and fewer orders. For others, they must work unpaid overtime to meet production targets (see Bhattacharya, 2019). This is the plight of RMG workers and the actual characteristics of global apparel brands and Bangladeshi RMG factory owners.

This current study shows how multinational corporations, mainly international clothing and fashion brands, through global supply chains network, unethically outsource from Bangladesh and do marketing to increase their market shares while RMG workers are severely exploited. In addition, multinational corporations commenced business and outsourcing from a low-regulated country like Bangladesh in the 1980s in the emergence of the new macroeconomic market force, i.e., globalisation and neoliberalism.

Limitations and Directions for Future Studies

I do not see any potential limitations in this study. However, potential researchers who intend to do a similar study should consider conducting interviews with international clothing and fashion brands and their supply chains involved in outsourcing from developing countries like Bangladesh.

Recommendations for International Clothing, Fashion Brands

1. The company that has been working with factories in Bangladesh must set up its standards for labor rights, trade union rights, working conditions and environmental sustainability.
2. International clothing and fashion brands and supply chains must respect ILO, UN, and WTO trade conventions offshore.
3. International clothing and fashion brands and supply chains must ensure decent prices for goods produced in Bangladeshi RMG manufacturing hubs.
4. International clothing and fashion brands and supply chains must establish a long-term business relationship with Bangladesh and establish their standard manufacturing hubs to eradicate exploitation and ensure workers' safety.

Recommendations for RMG Employers in Bangladesh

1. RMG employers should ensure that workers are paid fair wages sufficient to meet their basic needs. These include timely and accurate payments, overtime pay, and health care and insurance benefits.
2. RMG employers should provide RMG workers with a safe and healthy working environment. Proper ventilation, lighting and temperature control in factories, and appropriate safety equipment for workers are a must.
3. RMG employers should respect workers' rights to freedom of association, collective bargaining and a safe workplace. Allow workers to form unions or other organizations and express their concerns without fear of reprisal.
4. RMG employers should implement policies to prevent discrimination in the workplace based on gender. In addition, RMG workers should be treated fairly and equally regardless of their background.
5. RMG employers should provide RMG workers with training and skill development opportunities to improve their skills and advance their careers.

Recommendations for the Government of Bangladesh

1. The Government of Bangladesh should enforce the Labor Act of 2006 (amended in 2013) and ILO conventions to protect the rights of RMG workers, including minimum wage requirements, working hours, overtime pay and workplace safety.
2. The Government of Bangladesh should improve factory inspections by building the capacity of local monitoring agencies, DIFE, to ensure that factories comply with Labor Acts and regulations, including workplace safety standards.
3. The Government of Bangladesh should encourage collective bargaining between workers and employers so that workers can have a voice in their workplace and negotiate for better wages and working conditions.

4. The Government of Bangladesh should provide social protection programs, including health care, education and social security benefits, to support RMG workers and their families.

CONCLUSION

Ethical business is a concept that refers to the application of ethical principles and values in conducting business activities. It involves doing business responsibly and sustainably while complying with legal and regulatory requirements. In other words, ethical business practices prioritize social and environmental considerations in addition to economic ones and seek to create value for all stakeholders involved in the business.

Adopting fair and honest practices in all operations is an important aspect of ethical business. This means businesses must avoid fraudulent or deceptive practices, such as misrepresenting products or services, engaging in insider trading, or failing to disclose relevant information to stakeholders. In addition, this means that businesses must respect their customers' and employees' privacy and confidentiality and ensure they are not exploited or discriminated against.

Another important aspect of ethical business is considering business activities' social and environmental impact. This involves considering the potential impact of business operations on local communities, ecosystems, and the planet. Businesses must strive to reduce their negative environmental impacts, such as pollution or resource depletion, and work towards sustainable practices, such as reducing carbon emissions, using renewable energy or recycling waste.

In addition to these considerations, ethical business involves treating all stakeholders fairly and respectfully. This includes employees, customers, suppliers and shareholders, the wider community and society. Businesses must ensure fair working conditions and wages, maintain safe and healthy workplaces, and promote diversity and inclusion. They must be transparent in their dealings with stakeholders and seek to build trust and long-term relationships.

Therefore, global apparel and fashion brands and their supply chains, Bangladeshi RMG factory owners and employers, the Government of Bangladesh and other key stakeholders in the Bangladesh RMG sector must work together for the industry's sustainability. More specifically, for Western and European apparel and fashion brands and their supply chains, ethically outsourcing RMG products from Bangladesh is a top responsibility for the future sustainability of the supply chain business.

The Declaration of Conflicting Interests for the Current Article

The author of this study declared no potential conflict of interest concerning the research, authorship, and publication of this book chapter.

Funding

The author(s) received no financial support for this book chapter research, authorship, and publication. However, the original research was conducted with the Australian Government Research Training Program Scholarship for the author's PhD project.

ACKNOWLEDGMENT

I am deeply indebted to the Bangladeshi trade unionists and RMG workers whose unconditional support made this research paper complete.

REFERENCES

Ahamed, F. (2013). Could monitoring and surveillance be useful to establish social compliance in the ready-made garment (RMG) industry of Bangladesh. *International Journal of Management and Business Studies*, *3*(3), 88–100.

Ahmed, F. E. (2004). The rise of the Bangladesh garment industry: Globalisation, women workers, and voice. *NWSA Journal*, *16*(2), 34–45. doi:10.2979/NWS.2004.16.2.34

Al Mamun, M. A., & Hoque, M. M. (2022). The impact of paid employment on women's empowerment: A case study of female garment workers in Bangladesh. *World Development Sustainability*, *1*(100026), 1–11. doi:10.1016/j.wds.2022.100026

Alamgir, F., & Banerjee, S. B. (2019). Contested compliance regimes in global production networks: Insights from the Bangladesh garment industry. *Human Relations*, *72*(2), 272–297. doi:10.1177/0018726718760150

Anderson, K. (2016). Contributions of the GATT/WTO to global economic welfare: Empirical evidence. *Journal of Economic Surveys*, *30*(1), 56–92. doi:10.1111/joes.12087

Anner, M. (2020). Squeezing workers' rights in global supply chains: Purchasing practices in the Bangladesh garment export sector in comparative perspective. *Review of International Political Economy*, *27*(2), 320–347. doi:10.1080/09692290.2019.1625426

Anner, M., Bair, J., & Blasi, J. (2013). Toward joint liability in global supply chains: Addressing the root causes of labour violations in international subcontracting networks. *Comparative Labor Law & Policy Journal*, *35*(1), 1–44.

Appelbaum, R. P. (2008). Giant transnational contractors in East Asia: Emergent trends in global supply chains. *Competition & Change*, *12*(1), 69–87. doi:10.1179/102452908X264539

Ashraf, H., & Prentice, R. (2019). Beyond factory safety: Labor unions, militant protest, and the accelerated ambitions of Bangladesh's export garment industry. *Dialectical Anthropology*, *43*(1), 93–107. doi:10.100710624-018-9539-0

Asuyama, Y., Chhun, D., Fukunishi, T., Neou, S., & Yamagata, T. (2013). Firm dynamics in the Cambodian garment industry: Firm turnover, productivity growth and wage profile under trade liberalization. *Journal of the Asia Pacific Economy*, *18*(1), 51–70. doi:10.1080/13547860.2012.742671

Bender, D. E., & Greenwald, R. A. (2003). *Sweatshop USA: The American sweatshop in historical and global perspective*. Psychology Press.

Bentonville, A. (2022). *Walmart Inc. Provides Update for Second Quarter and Fiscal Year 2023.* Retrieved from https://corporate.walmart.com/newsroom/2022/07/25/walmart-inc-provides-update-for-second-quarter-and-fiscal-year-2023

Beresford, M. (2009). The Cambodian clothing industry in the post-MFA environment: A review of developments. *Journal of the Asia Pacific Economy, 14*(4), 366–388. doi:10.1080/13547860903169357

Bhattacharjee, S. S. (2019). Fast fashion, production targets, and gender-based violence in Asian garment supply chains. In S. B. Saxena (Ed.), *Labor, Global Supply Chains, and the Garment Industry in South Asia* (pp. 207–227). Routledge. doi:10.4324/9780429430039-12

Blecker, R. A., & Esquivel, G. (2010). NAFTA, Trade and Development (Robert A. Blecker and Gerardo Esquivel). CESifo Forum, 11(4), 17-30.

Butler, S. (2013). One in six Walmart factories in Bangladesh fail safety review. *The Guardian.* Retrieved from https://www.theguardian.com/business/2013/nov/18/walmart-bangladesh-factories-fail-safety-review

Cheek, W. K., & Moore, C. E. (2003). Apparel sweatshops at home and abroad: Global and ethical issues. *Journal of Family and Consumer Sciences, 95*(1), 9–19.

Chen, J. Y., & Baddam, S. R. (2015). The effect of unethical behavior and learning on strategic supplier selection. *International Journal of Production Economics, 167,* 74–87. doi:10.1016/j.ijpe.2015.05.003

Chorev, N. (2005). The institutional project of neo-liberal globalism: The case of the WTO. *Theory and Society, 34*(3), 317–355. doi:10.100711186-005-6301-9

Chowdhury, M., Ahmed, R., & Yasmin, M. (2014). Prospects and problems of RMG Industry: A study on Bangladesh. *Prospects, 5*(7), 103–118.

Crinis, V. (2019). Corporate social responsibility, human rights and clothing workers in Bangladesh and Malaysia. *Asian Studies Review, 43*(2), 295–312. doi:10.1080/10357823.2019.1588850

Frenkel, S. J., & Schuessler, E. S. (2021). From Rana Plaza to COVID-19: Deficiencies and opportunities for a new labour governance system in garment global supply chains. *International Labour Review, 160*(4), 591–609. doi:10.1111/ilr.12208 PMID:34230680

Ghauri, P. (2004). Designing and conducting case studies in international business research. In Handbook of qualitative research methods for international business. Edward Elgar. doi:10.4337/9781781954331.00019

Gilbert, P. R. (2018). Class, complicity, and capitalist ambition in Dhaka's elite enclaves. *Focaal: Tijdschrift voor Antropologie, 81*(81), 43–57. doi:10.3167/fcl.2018.810104

Harvey, D. (2007). *A brief history of neoliberalism.* Oxford University Press.

Harvey, D. (2016). *Neoliberalism is a political project.* Jacobin Magazine.

Harvey, D. (2022). The double consciousness of capital. *Socialist Register, 58.*

Hasan, J. (2013). *The Competitiveness of Ready Made Garments 2 Industry of Bangladesh in Post MFA era: How 3 does the industry behave to face the 4 competitive challenge?* Academic Press.

Hasan, M. T. (2022). *Everyday life of ready-made garment kormi in Bangladesh*. Palgrave Macmillan. doi:10.1007/978-3-030-99902-5

Hayes, A. (2021). Multifiber Arrangement (MFA). In *Investopedia*. Retrieved from https://www.investopedia.com/terms/m/multi-fiber-arrangement.asp

Hiba, J. C., Jentsch, M., & Zink, K. J. (2021). Globalization and working conditions in international supply chains. *Zeitschrift für Arbeitswissenschaft*, *75*(2), 146–154. doi:10.100741449-021-00258-7 PMID:34188355

Huq, C. (2019). Opportunities and limitations of the accord: Need for a worker organizing model. In S. B. Saxena (Ed.), *Labor, Global Supply Chains, and the Garment Industry in South Asia* (pp. 63–83). Routledge. doi:10.4324/9780429430039-4

Huq, C. (2022). Interdisciplinary perspectives on global labor governance: Organizing, legal mobilization and decolonization. *Mich. J. Int'l L.*, *43*(43.2), 423–503. doi:10.36642/mjil.43.2.interdisciplinary

Huq, S. M., Nekmahmud, M., & Aktar, M. S. (2016). Unethical practices of advertising in Bangladesh: A case study on some selective products. *International Journal of Economics. Finance and Management Sciences*, *4*(1), 10–19.

Ishaya, B. J., Paraskevadakis, D., Bury, A., & Bryde, D. (2023). A systematic literature review of modern slavery through benchmarking global supply chain. *Benchmarking*. Advance online publication. doi:10.1108/BIJ-09-2022-0554

Kabeer, N. (2019). The evolving politics of labor standards in Bangladesh: Taking stock and looking forward. In S. B. Saxena (Ed.), *Labor, global supply chains, and the garment industry in South Asia* (pp. 231–259). Routledge. doi:10.4324/9780429430039-13

Kabir, H., Maple, M., Islam, M., & Usher, K. (2022b). The paradoxical impacts of the minimum wage implementation on ready-made garment (RMG) Workers: A qualitative study. *The Indian Journal of Labour Economics : the Quarterly Journal of the Indian Society of Labour Economics*, *65*(2), 1–25. doi:10.100741027-022-00375-9 PMID:35937940

Kabir, H., Maple, M., Islam, M. S., & Usher, K. (2022a). A qualitative study of the working conditions in the readymade garment industry and the impact on workers' health and well-being. *Environmental and Occupational Health Practice*.

Krueger, R. A., & Casey, M. A. (2014). *Focus groups: A practical guide for applied research*. Sage publications.

Kurland, N. B., Baucus, M., & Steckler, E. (2022). Business and society in the age of COVID-19: Introduction to the special issue. *Business and Society Review*, *127*(S1), 147–157. doi:10.1111/basr.12265

Labowitz, S. (2016). *New data on the number of factories in Bangladesh*. Retrieved from https://bhr.stern.nyu.edu/blogs/-data-on-number-of-factories-bd

Labowitz, S., & Baumann-Pauly, D. (2014). *Business as usual is not an option: Supply chains sourcing after Rana Plaza*. Stern Center for Business and Human Rights. http://stern. Nyu. Edu/sites/default/files/assets/documents/con_047408.Pdf

Martínez-Jurado, P. J., & Moyano-Fuentes, J. (2014). Lean management, supply chain management and sustainability: A literature review. *Journal of Cleaner Production*, *85*, 134–150. doi:10.1016/j.jclepro.2013.09.042

Mefford, R. N. (2011). The economic value of a sustainable supply chain. *Business and Society Review*, *116*(1), 109–143. doi:10.1111/j.1467-8594.2011.00379.x

Moazzem, K. G. (2019). Behaviour of the buyers and suppliers in the post-Rana Plaza period: A decent work perspective. In S. B. Saxena (Ed.), *Labor, Global Supply Chains, and the Garment Industry in South Asia* (pp. 149–171). Routledge. doi:10.4324/9780429430039-9

Moazzem, K. G., Preoty, H. M., & Khan, A. M. (2022). *Institutionalisation of Labour Rights Practices in the RMG Sector under UNGP Framework: Are Public Agencies Playing Their Due Role?* Academic Press.

Mottaleb, K. A., & Sonobe, T. (2011). An inquiry into the rapid growth of the garment industry in Bangladesh. *Economic Development and Cultural Change*, *60*(1), 67–89. doi:10.1086/661218

Munck, R. P. (2010). Globalization and the labour movement: Challenges and responses. *Global Labour Journal*, *1*(2), 218–232. doi:10.15173/glj.v1i2.1073

New, S. J. (2015). Modern slavery and the supply chain: The limits of corporate social responsibility? *Supply Chain Management*, *20*(6), 697–707. doi:10.1108/SCM-06-2015-0201

Oka, C. (2018). Brands as labour rights advocates? Potential and limits of brand advocacy in global supply chains. *Business Ethics (Oxford, England)*, *27*(2), 95–107. doi:10.1111/beer.12172

Oka, C., Egels-Zandén, N., & Alexander, R. (2020). Buyer engagement and labour conditions in global supply chains: The Bangladesh accord and beyond. *Development and Change*, *51*(5), 1306–1330. doi:10.1111/dech.12575

Paul-Majumder, P., & Begum, A. (2000). *The gender imbalances in the export oriented garment industry in Bangladesh*. World Bank, Development Research Group/Poverty Reduction and Economic Management Network.

Prentice, R. (2021). Labour rights from labour wrongs? Transnational compensation and the spatial politics of labour rights after Bangladesh's rana plaza garment factory collapse. *Antipode*, *53*(6), 1767–1786. doi:10.1111/anti.12751

Rahman, S. (2019). Post-Rana Plaza responses: Changing role of the Bangladesh Government. In S. B. Saxena (Ed.), *Labor, global supply chains, and the garment industry in South Asia: Bangladesh after Rana Plaza* (pp. 131–148). Routledge. doi:10.4324/9780429430039-8

Rahman, S., & Ishty, S. I. (2020). *COVID-19 and the ready-made garment sector*. Retrieved from https://www.policyforum.net/covid-19-and-the-ready-made-garment-sector/

Rahman, S., & Rahman, K. M. (2020). Multi-actor initiatives after Rana Plaza: Factory managers' views. *Development and Change*, *51*(5), 1331–1359. doi:10.1111/dech.12572

Rahman, S., & Yadlapalli, A. (2021). *Years after the Rana Plaza tragedy, Bangladesh's garment workers are still bottom of the pile.* Retrieved from https://theconversation.com/years-after-the-rana-plaza-tragedy-bangladeshs-garment-workers-are-still-bottom-of-the-pile-159224

Reza, N., & Du Plessis, J. J. (2022). The Garment Industry in Bangladesh, Corporate Social Responsibility of Multinational Corporations, and The Impact of COVID-19. *Asian Journal of Law and Society, 9*(2), 255–285. doi:10.1017/als.2022.9

Russell, M. (2021). More than 350K jobs have been lost in Bangladesh RMG sector. *Just-Style.* Retrieved from https://www.just-style.com/news/more-than-350k-jobs-have-been-lost-in-bangladesh-rmg-sector_id140579.aspx

Saxena, S. B. (2022). Developing country responses to demands for improved labor standards: case studies from the garment and textiles industry in Asia. In K. A. Elliott (Ed.), *Handbook on globalisation and labour standards* (pp. 258–273). Edward Elgar Publishing. doi:10.4337/9781788977371.00020

Sen, S., Antara, N., Sen, S., & Chowdhury, S. (2020). The apparel workers are in the highest vulnerability due to COVID-19: A study on the Bangladesh Apparel Industry. *Asia Pacific Journal of Multidisciplinary Research., 8*(3), 1–7.

Siddiqi, D. M. (2019). Spaces of exception: National interest and the labor of sedition. In S. B. Saxena (Ed.), *Labor, Global Supply Chains, and the Garment Industry in South Asia* (pp. 100–114). Routledge. doi:10.4324/9780429430039-6

Syed, R. F. (2020). Ethical business strategy between east and west: An analysis of minimum wage policy in the garment global supply chain industry of Bangladesh. *Asian Journal of Business Ethics, 9*(2), 241–255. doi:10.100713520-020-00108-5

Syed, R. F., & Ikra, M. (2022). *Industrial killing in Bangladesh: State policies, common-law nexus, and international obligations. Employee Responsibilities and Rights Journal.*

Syed, R. F., & Mahmud, K. T. (2022). Factors influencing work-satisfaction of global garments supply chain workers in Bangladesh. *International Review of Economics, 69*(4), 507–524. doi:10.100712232-022-00403-6

Tabb, W. K. (2005). Sweated labor then and now. *International Labor and Working Class History, 67,* 164–173. doi:10.1017/S014754790500013X

Tarver, E. (2022). World Trade Organization (WTO): What It Is and What It Does. *Investopedia.* Retrieved from https://www.investopedia.com/terms/w/wto.asp

The Financial Express. (2020). *Pandemic triggers big job losses in BD's RMG sector: WTO.* thefinancialexpress.com.bd

Truscott, M. H., Brust, P. J., & Fesmire, J. M. (2007). Core international labour standards and the world trade organization. *Journal of Business Cases & Applications, 1,* 1–6.

Uddin, J. (2020). Vietnam overtakes Bangladesh in RMG export. *The Business Standard.* Retrieved from https://tbsnews.net/economy/rmg/vietnam-surpasses-bangladesh-rmg-export-118897

Uddin, M. J., Azmat, F., Fujimoto, Y., & Hossain, F. (2022). Exploitation in Bangladeshi ready-made garments supply chain: A case of irresponsible capitalism? *International Journal of Logistics Management.*

Uddin, M. J., Azmat, F., Fujimoto, Y., & Hossain, F. (2023). Exploitation in Bangladeshi ready-made garments supply chain: A case of irresponsible capitalism? *International Journal of Logistics Management, 34*(1), 164–188. doi:10.1108/IJLM-12-2021-0565

Ullah, A. (2020). The moral obligation of the global supply chains during the pandemic. *The Business Standard.* Retrieved from https://www.tbsnews.net/thoughts/moral-obligation-global-supply-chains-during-pandemic-124840

Ullah, A., & Amanullah, A. (2021). Vaccinating RMG workers in Bangladesh: Why it's urgent and how international brands can help. *The Business Standard.* Retrieved from https://www.tbsnews.net/thoughts/vaccinating-rmg-workers-bangladesh-why-its-urgent-and-how-international-brands-can-help

Ullah, A. A. (2021). Covid-19: The role of global clothing brands/retailers in vaccinating and providing financial aid to the RMG workers in Bangladesh. *Middle East Journal of Business, 16*(2), 5–11.

Ullah, A. A. S. M. (2015). Garment industry in Bangladesh: An era of globalization and neo-liberalization. *Middle East Journal of Business, 10*(2), 14–26. doi:10.5742/MEJB.2015.92634

Ullah, A. A. S. M. (2022a). Tazreen Fashions, Rana Plaza, FR Tower and then Hashem Food, what next: The ineffective OHS regulatory processes of the Bangladesh Government. *Middle East Journal of Business, 17*(1), 9–25.

Ullah, A. A. S. M. (2022b). An analysis of Marxism in industrial relations theory in light of capitalism, neoliberalism and globalisation: A petite critical review from Bangladesh's RMG perspectives. *Middle East Journal of Business, 17*(2), 5–18.

Villareal, M., & Fergusson, I. F. (2017). *The North American Free Trade Agreement.* NAFTA.

World Bank. (2020). *Bangladesh must ramp up COVID-19 action to protect its people, revive economy.* Retrieved from https://www.worldbank.org/en/news/press-release/2020/04/12/bangladesh-must-act-now-to-lessen-covid-19-health-impacts

WTO. (n.d.). *GATT and the goods council.* Retrieved from https://www.wto.org/english/tratop_e/gatt_e/gatt_e.htm

Yin, R. K. (2003). *Case Study Research: Design and methods* (3rd ed.). Sage.

Section 4
Green, Digital, and Sustainable Marketing for Sustainable Development

Chapter 17
Green Marketing:
Sustainability Is Already a Reality in Marketing

Łukasz Jacek Marecki
SGH Warsaw School of Economics, Poland

ABSTRACT

The marketing industry is struggling. The new consumers opt for green marketing products and strategies, more aware of the environment. After having grown 100% in the first quarter compared to the same period of the previous year, orders decreased significantly from March 2020 in large markets such as Spain, Germany, Italy, France, and EEUDE. It was a drop that affected the promotional marketing industry worldwide as a result of the coronavirus, which is why many companies are betting on green marketing. In the particular case of Sprout World, a pioneering company in sustainable merchandising with its plantable pencils, for example, the demand for writing products simply disappeared. And with this, it was experienced that the promotional products market was stagnating in the last year. Something that was also accompanied by a change of mentality in the consumer towards measures and products with a necessary environmental touch. Financial troubles are frequently a result of disasters, but businesses must carefully decide where to make savings.

INTRODUCTION

Green marketing refers to the practice of promoting environmentally-friendly products or services in order to satisfy the needs of consumers while minimizing the negative impact on the environment. It involves incorporating sustainability and social responsibility into a company's overall marketing strategy. Green marketing aims to not only generate profit but also benefit society as a whole, by addressing pressing environmental issues such as climate change, deforestation, and pollution. As consumers become increasingly aware of these issues, they are more likely to make purchasing decisions based on a company's environmental record. Therefore, green marketing can be an effective way for companies to differentiate themselves from competitors and gain a competitive advantage. However, it is significant for companies

DOI: 10.4018/978-1-6684-8681-8.ch017

to guarantee that their green marketing privileges are accurate and backed by credible evidence, to avoid being accused of "greenwashing" or misleading consumers (Dangelico and Vocalelli, 2017).

Businesses must undoubtedly make savings in these tough economic times, but not just in advertising. Sustainability is an issue that affects the entire world, just like money or perhaps the coronavirus, and it won't go away just because there is a pandemic. In fact, we are observing a demand for more recycled alternatives from both users and consumers. From a business standpoint, it makes little sense to continue using conventional products if the recipients no longer wish to use them (conventional promotional products are typically polluting due to their high plastic content and bad quality). Sustainability is a permanent trend. People started to consider more carefully after the most recent financial crisis in 2009. But shortly thereafter, they started ordering low-cost items from China once more, and the buying mania took over. I consider the current situation to be a stark wake-up call. We need to step back from this consumerism craze and begin making thoughtful, environmentally responsible purchases. And we're observing an increase in the number of consumers who comprehend why it's preferable to buy fewer items and choose superior, environmentally friendly goods that the recipient will truly use.

Since people have grown more conscious of how human activity affects the environment, the concept of sustainability has become very popular. Customers are increasingly looking for eco-friendly goods and services as they become more conscious of how their shopping habits affect the environment (Szabo and Webster, 2020). Green marketing, which entails advertising goods and services with little to no impact on the environment, has emerged as a result of this. Companies are beginning to understand the value of sustainability and their potential role in supporting it. Since businesses increasingly realise the value of sustainability in their operations, green marketing has emerged as a dominant trend in today's business world. Meeting present-day demands without sacrificing the capacity for future generations to do the same is the idea behind sustainability. In this proposal, we will discuss how sustainability has become a reality in marketing, and the benefits that companies can derive from embracing green marketing practices.

Sustainability has become a critical issue in the business world as companies progressively recognize the need to minimize their environmental impact while meeting the needs of their stakeholders. In order to be sustainable, corporate practises must take into account economic, social, and environmental factors. Customers are looking for goods and services that have a minimal adverse environmental effect as a result of growing consumer awareness of the effects of their purchase decisions on the environment in recent years. Green marketing, which entails promoting goods and services that are environmentally and socially responsible, has emerged as a result of this.

LITERATURE REVIEW

The Important Role of Green Marketing

Green marketing is becoming progressively important in today's business landscape for several reasons. Firstly, consumers are becoming more ecologically aware and are seeking products and services that align with their values. Companies that embrace sustainability and incorporate it into their marketing strategies are better positioned to meet this demand and differentiate themselves from competitors. Secondly, green marketing can help companies build a positive reputation as socially and environmentally responsible businesses. This can lead to increased consumer loyalty, enhanced brand equity, and better relationships with stakeholders such as employees, investors, and regulators. Thirdly, sustainable practices such as reducing waste, using renewable energy, and improving resource efficiency can help companies reduce costs and increase profitability. By communicating these initiatives to consumers through green marketing, companies can further enhance their financial performance. Fourthly, governments are implementing regulations to promote sustainable practices, and companies that fail to comply may face legal and financial penalties (Papadas, Avlonitis and Carrigan, 2017). Green marketing can demonstrate a company's commitment to sustainability, which can help them meet regulatory requirements and avoid penalties. Finally, green marketing can contribute to a more sustainable future by raising awareness about environmental and social issues and inspiring consumers to adopt more sustainable behaviors. By promoting sustainable products and practices, companies can play a role in creating a more sustainable future.

Green marketing is important for several reasons: Consumers are increasingly concerned about the environmental impact of products and services they use and are willing to pay a premium for products that are environmentally and socially responsible. Green marketing allows companies to communicate their sustainability efforts to consumers, meet their demand for sustainable products, and differentiate themselves in the market. Green marketing can help companies build a reputation as socially and environmentally responsible businesses. A positive reputation can lead to increased consumer loyalty, enhanced brand equity, and better relationships with stakeholders.

Sustainable practices such as reducing waste, using renewable energy, and improving resource efficiency can help companies reduce costs and increase profitability (Kemper and Ballantine, 2019). Green marketing can communicate these initiatives to consumers, which can lead to increased sales and brand loyalty. Governments are implementing regulations to promote sustainable practices, and companies that fail to comply may face legal and financial penalties. Green marketing can demonstrate a company's commitment to sustainability, which can help them meet regulatory requirements and avoid penalties. Sustainability is becoming an increasingly important aspect of business, and companies that fail to incorporate sustainability into their operations risk being left behind. By embracing green marketing, companies can future-proof their businesses, gain a competitive advantage, and contribute to a more sustainable future.

By promoting their sustainability efforts, companies can build a positive brand image as socially and environmentally responsible businesses. This can increase consumer loyalty and enhance brand equity. Consumers are increasingly seeking products and services that align with their values, including sustainability. By promoting sustainable products and practices, companies can attract environmentally conscious consumers and increase sales. Sustainable practices such as reducing waste, using renewable energy, and improving resource efficiency can help companies reduce costs and increase profitability. By promoting these initiatives through green marketing, companies can further enhance their financial performance. Companies that embrace sustainability and incorporate it into their marketing strategies can distinguish themselves from competitors and increase a competitive advantage in the marketplace.

By representative a promise to sustainability, companies can build better relationships with stakeholders such as employees, investors, and regulators. Green marketing can help companies mitigate the risks associated with environmental and social issues. By promoting sustainable products and practices, companies can demonstrate their commitment to addressing these issues and avoid reputational damage or financial losses.

Green marketing is important because it meets consumer demand for sustainable products, builds brand reputation, reduces costs, ensures compliance with regulations, and contributes to a more sustainable future. Companies that embrace sustainability and incorporate it into their marketing strategies are better positioned to succeed in today's business landscape and can play a role in creating a more sustainable future. Green marketing has become a prevalent trend in the modern business landscape, as companies seek to differentiate themselves from competitors by showcasing their commitment to sustainability. This includes a range of practices, such as using eco-friendly packaging, sourcing sustainable materials, and implementing energy-efficient operations. In addition to meeting the needs of environmentally conscious consumers, green marketing can also benefit companies by reducing costs, improving brand image, and attracting and retaining employees who are passionate about sustainability (Groening, Sarkis and Zhu, 2018).

In this article, we will discuss how sustainability has become a reality in marketing, and the benefits that companies can derive from embracing green marketing practices. We will explore the challenges associated with green marketing, such as the need for credible and accurate claims, and the importance of aligning marketing strategies with overall business objectives. Ultimately, our goal is to deliver a comprehensive considerate of the role that green marketing can play in driving business success while promoting sustainability (Nguyen et al., 2019).

Green Marketing for Sustainable Development

Green marketing has gained increasing consideration in current years due to the rising awareness of environmental matters and the necessity for businesses to adopt sustainable practices. Green marketing, which focuses on promoting environmentally sustainable products and practices, has emerged as an important strategy for businesses in recent years.

One important theme in green marketing is the use of eco-labels and certifications to communicate the environmental impact of products and services. These labels, such as the Energy Star label or the Forest Stewardship Council (FSC) certification, provide a clear and credible way for companies to communicate their environmental efforts to consumers. Sustainable product design can reduce waste, decrease carbon emissions, and improve customer loyalty and brand reputation. Green product design can lead to reduced environmental impact, increased customer loyalty, and improved brand reputation. The use of eco-labels has been found to positively influence consumers' purchasing decisions and willingness to pay a premium for environmentally friendly products (Laroche et al., 2001).

Another important theme in green marketing is the use of cause-related marketing, where companies align themselves with environmental causes to promote their products and services. This can be an effective way for companies to appeal to environmentally conscious consumers, while also supporting important environmental initiatives. However, it is significant for companies to guarantee that their environmental claims are exact and transparent, to avoid accusations of greenwashing (Liu & Jindal, 2016).

One of the chief challenges in green marketing is the possible for greenwashing, where companies make untrue or exaggerated environmental claims to mislead consumers (Bansal & Sharma, 2011). One important theme in green marketing is the usage of eco-labels and certifications, such as Energy Star or Fair Trade, to signal the environmental paybacks of a product or service. These labels can increase consumers' willingness to pay a premium for eco-friendly goods and are seen as more credible than companies' self-reported environmental claims. However, the use of eco-labels is not without controversy, as some labels lack standards or are too broad in scope (Bartiaux et al., 2013).

Another important theme in green marketing is the role of corporate social responsibility (CSR) in promoting sustainability. CSR initiatives, such as reducing carbon emissions or supporting community programs, can improve a company's reputation and attract environmentally conscious consumers. Though, it is vital for companies to confirm that their CSR efforts are transparent, consistent, and allied with their business goals. A third theme in green marketing is the importance of sustainable product design and innovation. This involves designing products that are more environmentally friendly throughout their lifecycle, from sourcing raw materials to disposal (Charter & Clark, 2007).

One of the foremost trials in green marketing is the latent for greenwashing, where companies make false or exaggerated environmental rights to appeal to consumers. Greenwashing can damage a company's reputation and credibility and undermine consumers' trust in environmentally friendly products. It is therefore essential for companies to ensure that their environmental claims are accurate, transparent, and backed up by credible evidence. Green marketing has become an significant aspect of marketing strategy for businesses looking to promote sustainability and appeal to environmentally conscious consumers. The use of eco-labels, CSR initiatives, and sustainable product design can all be effective strategies for promoting sustainability. However, it is vital for companies to confirm that their environmental claims are credible and transparent, and to avoid the pitfalls of greenwashing.

One key theme in green marketing is the use of environmental certifications and standards to communicate the environmental influence of goods and services. According to Charter and Polonsky (1999), guarantees such as the Forest Stewardship Council (FSC) and Leadership in Energy and Environmental Design (LEED) provide a credible and transparent way for companies to communicate their environmental efforts to consumers. Peattie and Charter (2003) suggest that these certifications can also provide a competitive advantage for businesses in attracting environmentally-conscious consumers.

Another theme in green marketing is the use of cause-related marketing, where companies align themselves with environmental causes to promote their products and services. Ottman (2011) argues that cause-related marketing can be an effective way for companies to appeal to environmentally-conscious consumers, while also supporting important environmental initiatives. However, it is significant for companies to certify that their environmental claims are accurate and transparent, to avoid accusations of greenwashing (Hartmann & Apaolaza-Ibáñez, 2020).

A third theme in green marketing is the importance of social norms and values in shaping consumer behavior. Consumers' willingness to pay for green products is influenced by their attitudes towards the environment and their perceptions of social norms. Companies are more likely to adopt sustainable practices when there is a cultural norm or expectation of environmental responsibility. One challenge in green marketing is the potential for greenwashing, where companies make false or exaggerated environmental claims to mislead consumers. Peattie (2001) suggests that this can damage a company's reputation and credibility, and it is important for companies to ensure that their environmental claims are backed up by credible evidence and standards.

Green marketing has become a significant aspect of marketing strategy for businesses looking to appeal to environmentally-conscious consumers and promote sustainability. However, it is important for companies to ensure that their environmental claims are accurate and credible, and to align their marketing goals with broader business objectives. The use of eco-labels, cause-related marketing, and green product design can all be effective strategies for promoting sustainability.

METHODOLOGY

The term "secondary data" refers to information that has previously been gathered from resources and made easily accessible for use in research by academics. It belongs to the group of information that has already been obtained. Secondary data is information that has already been acquired by another source, the government's publications, encompassing books, websites, scholarly papers, internal records, in-depth conversations, fieldwork, trials, etc. Sources may include government agencies, industry associations, non-governmental organizations, and academic institutions.

DISCUSSION

Green marketing, which mentions to the raise of environmentally-friendly products, services, and practices, has become an increasingly important area of focus for businesses in recent years. With consumers becoming more environmentally-conscious, companies are under pressure to adopt sustainable practices and promote their environmental initiatives through their marketing activities (T. H. O. Nguyen et al., 2019).

The last financial crisis in 2009 had a significant impact on consumer behavior, with many people turning to cheap goods from China and engaging in a frenzy of consumerism. However, the current disaster has served as a wake-up call, reminding us of the importance of making conscious and sustainable purchasing decisions. By way of the world becomes progressively aware of the influence of human actions on the environment and the need to transition to more sustainable practices, there is a growing demand for goods and services that align with these values. This shift in consumer behavior has created new opportunities for businesses that embrace sustainability and incorporate it into their operations and marketing strategies. In this context, green marketing has become increasingly important, enabling companies to communicate their sustainability efforts to consumers and differentiate themselves in the marketplace. In this essay, we will explore the importance of green marketing and sustainability in today's business landscape and provide insights and recommendations for companies looking to embrace sustainability and promote it through their marketing strategies.

One of the key movements in green marketing is the use of certifications and standards to communicate the environmental influence of products and services. For example, the Forest Stewardship Council (FSC) certification is used to indicate that wood and paper products are sourced from responsibly managed forests. Similarly, the LEED certification is used to indicate that buildings are designed and constructed with sustainable materials and practices. These certifications provide a credible and transparent way for companies to communicate their sustainability efforts to consumers.

Consumerism has been a main driver of economic growth over the past few decades, with people buying more and more products, often without much consideration for the environmental impact of their choices. However, this trend has started to shift, as more and more consumers become aware of the need for sustainable and environmentally friendly products. There is a growing recognition that buying less and opting for better, more sustainable products is not only better for the environment but also more fulfilling and satisfying for consumers. Consumers are increasingly realizing that they can make a difference by making conscious and sustainable purchasing decisions (Pomering, 2017). They are keen to pay more for goods that are made sustainably and ethically, and they are actively seeking out companies that share their values.

This shift in consumer behavior presents both challenges and opportunities for businesses. On the one hand, companies that continue to focus solely on profits and ignore sustainability are likely to lose market share and face reputational damage. On the other hand, companies that embrace sustainability and incorporate it into their operations and marketing strategies are likely to thrive and gain a competitive advantage. To succeed in this new business landscape, companies need to understand the importance of sustainability and green marketing, and they need to be proactive in making changes to their operations and products. They need to engage with customers, listen to their concerns and feedback, and actively promote their sustainability efforts. By doing so, they can build trust and loyalty with customers, differentiate themselves from competitors, and contribute to a more sustainable and responsible world.

Another trend in green marketing is the use of cause-related marketing, where companies align themselves with environmental causes to promote their products and services. For example, Patagonia's "1% for the Planet" initiative donates 1% of its sales to environmental organizations. This type of marketing can be effective in appealing to environmentally-conscious consumers, but it is significant for companies to guarantee that their environmental claims are precise and clear.

An environmentally friendly product is a product that is designed, manufactured, packaged, and distributed in an environmentally responsible way. It is a product that has a negligeable impact on the environment and is sustainable over the long term. Environmentally friendly products are typically made from renewable materials, recycled materials, or materials that can be easily and safely disposed of after use. Green marketing and environmentally friendly products are important because they help to decrease the environmental impact of production and consumption. By promoting the use of sustainable products, businesses and consumers can aid to reduce waste, preserve natural resources, and defend the environment for future generations. Green marketing may also be a potent weapon for companies trying to stand out from their rivals and attract customers who are becoming more environmentally conscious.

However, it's important to note that not all products marketed as "green" or "environmentally friendly" are actually sustainable or environmentally responsible. Greenwashing, or the practice of making false or exaggerated environmental claims, is a problem in the industry. Consumers should be cautious and do their research to guarantee that the products they purchase are truly environmentally approachable.

The Current State of Sustainability in Marketing and Identifying Trends and Challenges in Marketing

As consumers become more concerned about the environment and seek sustainable goods and services, sustainability has emerged as a key marketing feature. The current state of sustainability in marketing is that it has become an essential component of most marketing strategies. Companies are incorporating sustainability into their marketing messaging and making efforts to improve their sustainability practices (Amoako et al., 2020).

One trend in sustainable marketing is the focus on transparency and authenticity. Consumers want to know where their products come from, how they were made, and their environmental impact. Companies are responding by providing more information about their sustainability practices and certifications, such as Fair Trade, organic, or recycled content. Authenticity in marketing has become increasingly important, as consumers can quickly spot greenwashing or false sustainability claims. Another trend is the emphasis on circular economy practices, where products are intended to be recycled, secondhand, or repurposed at the end of their lifecycle. Many companies are working towards zero-waste manufacturing and reducing their carbon footprint. Sustainable packaging has also become a significant focus, with many companies opting for biodegradable, compostable, or reusable packaging materials.

Challenges in sustainable marketing include the high cost of sustainable practices and communicating sustainability efforts effectively. Sustainable products are often more expensive to produce, and companies must decide whether to absorb the additional costs or pass them on to consumers. Communicating sustainability efforts can be challenging, as consumers may not be familiar with the specific certifications or terminology used. Overall, the trend towards sustainability in marketing is a positive development, as it encourages companies to adopt more sustainable practices and provides consumers with more sustainable options. However, companies must be genuine in their sustainability efforts and communicate them effectively to avoid accusations of greenwashing.

The benefits of green marketing for: businesses, including improving brand image, reducing costs, and attracting environmentally-conscious consumers.

Green marketing, which involves promoting environmentally-friendly products, practices, and messages, can provide a range of benefits for businesses. The following are a few of the primary advantages of green marketing: Businesses that intends to ensure and promote everything through green marketing can enhance the perception of their brands. This could make them stand out from rival businesses and boost client loyalty. By decreasing waste, boosting energy efficiency, and extending the life of items, green marketing can also result in cost savings. For example, companies can reduce their environmental impact and save money by switching to renewable energy sources, optimizing their supply chains, and using sustainable materials (Diez-Martín, Blanco-González and Román, 2019). By promoting sustainability, companies can attract environmentally-conscious customers who are eager to pay a best for eco-friendly products and services. This can help to increase sales and market share, especially in industries where sustainability is a key factor in consumer purchasing decisions. Green marketing can also help businesses to comply with environmental regulations and avoid fines or legal action. By adopting sustainable practices and promoting them through marketing, companies can demonstrate their commitment to environmental responsibility and avoid negative publicity. Green marketing can also drive innovation and create new growth opportunities for businesses. By investing in sustainable technologies and practices, companies can grow new products and services that meet the altering wants of consumers and the environment.

Overall, green marketing can provide a range of benefits for businesses, from improving brand image and reducing costs to attracting environmentally-conscious consumers and driving innovation. By embracing sustainability and promoting it through marketing, companies can create a more sustainable and profitable future for themselves and the planet.

The Effect of Green Marketing on Consumer Behavior and Decision-Making

Green marketing has an important impact on consumer behavior and decision-making, as more consumers are becoming environmentally-conscious and looking for eco-friendly goods and services. Increased awareness and concern for the environment: which means green marketing campaigns can increase consumer consciousness and concern for the environment, making them more likely to consider the environmental impact of their purchasing decisions. Shift towards eco-friendly products that is green marketing can also encourage consumers to shift towards eco-friendly goods and services, as they become more aware of the environmental influence of their choices. Increased readiness to pay a premium means Customers who are environmentally-conscious may be eager to pay a premium for eco-friendly products, especially if they perceive them to be of higher quality or more ethical (Chung, 2020). Greater loyalty to sustainable brands that companies that have a strong reputation for sustainability and promote it effectively through green marketing can build greater loyalty among environmentally-conscious consumers.

To effectively communicate their environmental initiatives to consumers, companies should: Companies should be transparent and authentic about their environmental initiatives, avoiding greenwashing or false sustainability claims. Companies should use clear and simple messaging that resonates with consumers and clearly communicates the environmental benefits of their products or services. Companies should highlight any certifications or third-party endorsements that validate their environmental initiatives and demonstrate their commitment to sustainability. Companies should usage a variety of message channels, counting social media, email marketing, and packaging, to reach consumers and communicate their environmental initiatives effectively. Companies should engage consumers in sustainability initiatives, such as recycling programs or carbon offsetting, to build greater loyalty and show their commitment to sustainability (Shabbir et al., 2020).

Overall, green marketing can have a important impact on consumer performance and decision-making, as more consumers prioritize environmental sustainability in their purchasing decisions. By effectively communicating their environmental initiatives to consumers, companies can build greater loyalty and differentiate themselves in the marketplace.

Case Studies of Successful Green Marketing Campaigns and Their Impact on Business Performance

Patagonia's "Don't Buy This Jacket" campaign: In 2011, outdoor apparel brand Patagonia launched a campaign urging consumers not to purchase their products if they really needed them. The campaign emphasized the environmental influence of clothing production and fortified consumers to reduce their consumption. The campaign was highly successful, generating widespread media coverage and boosting brand loyalty among environmentally-conscious consumers. Patagonia also reported an increase in sales and profits following the campaign.

IKEA's sustainable living campaign: In 2020, furniture retailer IKEA launched a campaign encouraging consumers to live more sustainably. The campaign included a series of videos and social media posts highlighting sustainable living practices, such as reducing waste, conserving water, and using renewable energy. The campaign was well-received by consumers and helped to reinforce IKEA's reputation as a sustainability leader. The campaign also helped to drive sales of sustainable products, such as LED light bulbs and water-saving faucets.

Unilever's sustainable brands initiative: In 2010, consumer goods company Unilever launched an initiative to make all of their brands more sustainable. The initiative included a commitment to decrease the environmental impact of their products and to promote sustainable living to consumers. The initiative was successful in driving growth for Unilever's sustainable brands, such as Dove and Ben & Jerry's. Unilever also reported significant cost savings from sustainability initiatives, such as reducing water and energy use in their manufacturing processes.

Toyota's Prius campaign: In 2004, car manufacturer Toyota launched a campaign promoting their hybrid car, the Prius. The campaign emphasized the environmental benefits of the Prius, such as reduced emissions and increased fuel efficiency. The campaign was highly successful, boosting sales of the Prius and helping to establish Toyota as a leader in eco-friendly vehicles. The success of the campaign also helped to drive innovation in the automotive industry, with other manufacturers following Toyota's lead in developing hybrid and electric vehicles.

Overall, these successful green marketing campaigns demonstrate the potential for sustainability to drive growth and improve business performance. By promoting sustainability and engaging consumers in sustainable practices, companies can differentiate themselves in the marketplace and build greater loyalty among environmentally-conscious consumers.

The Role of Certification Schemes and Standards in Ensuring Credibility and Transparency

Accurately measuring and reporting on the environmental impact of goods and services is essential for several reasons: By accurately measuring and reporting on their environmental impact, companies can demonstrate their commitment to corporate social responsibility and sustainability. Consumers are increasingly interested in purchasing products and services with a reduced environmental impact, and accurate measurement and reporting can help companies meet this demand. Accurate measurement and reportage can help companies classify areas where they can advance their environmental performance, such as reducing carbon emissions or water use. Some industries are subject to regulatory requirements related to environmental impact, and accurate measurement and reporting can help companies comply with these requirements (Chandran and Bhattacharya, 2021).

Certification schemes and standards play an important role in ensuring credibility and transparency in environmental reporting. These schemes and standards provide a framework for measuring and reporting on environmental impact, and help to ensure that claims of sustainability are valid and meaningful. Some examples of certification schemes and standards include: A program run by the U.S. Environmental Protection Agency that certifies energy-efficient products, such as appliances and electronics.

- **Forest Stewardship Council (FSC):** A certification program for forest products, which ensures that the products come from responsibly managed forests.
- **LEED:** A rating system for buildings that measures their environmental performance, including energy use, water efficiency, and indoor air quality.
- **Fairtrade:** A certification program for products, such as coffee and chocolate, that ensures that the producers are paid fairly and work in safe and healthy conditions.

By adhering to certification schemes and standards, companies can demonstrate their commitment to transparency and credibility in their environmental reporting. This can help to build trust among consumers and stakeholders, and position the company as a leader in sustainability.

Best Practices for Integrating Sustainability Into Overall Marketing Strategies

Here are some best practices for integrating sustainability into overall marketing strategies and aligning marketing goals with broader business objectives: Companies should classify the sustainability issues that are most applicable to their business and investors. This will help to guarantee that sustainability initiatives are aligned with business goals and priorities. Companies should set clear, measurable sustainability goals that are aligned with broader business objectives. This will help to ensure that sustainability initiatives are integrated into overall business strategies and are not viewed as separate or disconnected from other business activities.

Companies should involve with stakeholders, such as clients, employees, suppliers, and savers, to understand their sustainability expectations and priorities. This will help to ensure that sustainability initiatives are relevant and meaningful to stakeholders. Companies should communicate their sustainability initiatives and progress effectively to stakeholders. This may include using sustainability reports, social media, and other channels to share information about sustainability goals, progress, and impact. Companies should incorporate sustainability considerations into product development processes. This may include using sustainable materials, designing products for durability and recyclability, and minimizing waste and emissions throughout the product lifecycle.

Companies should measure and report on their sustainability performance using credible and transparent metrics. This will help to demonstrate progress and build trust with stakeholders. Companies should foster a culture of sustainability throughout the organization. This may include training employees on sustainability practices, providing incentives for sustainable behavior, and incorporating sustainability into performance evaluations.

By following these best practices, companies can integrate sustainability into their overall marketing strategies and align marketing goals with broader business objectives. This can help to drive growth, build brand reputation, and contribute to a more sustainable future.

The Forthcoming of Green Marketing and Sustainability in the Business Landscape

The future of green marketing and sustainability in the business landscape is likely to be shaped by several trends and factors: Consumers are increasingly interested in purchasing products and services with a reduced environmental impact. This is likely to drive companies to invest more in green marketing and sustainability initiatives to meet this demand. Governments are increasingly regulating business activities related to sustainability, such as carbon emissions and waste management. This is likely to create new opportunities for companies to differentiate themselves through sustainable practices and marketing.

Advancements in technology, such as renewable energy and sustainable materials, are likely to create new opportunities for companies to innovate and differentiate themselves in the market. Supply chain transparency is becoming increasingly important, with consumers and stakeholders expecting companies to disclose information about their suppliers and their environmental and social practices. This is likely to create new challenges and opportunities for companies to improve the sustainability of their supply chains and communicate this to stakeholders. Collaboration and partnerships between companies, governments, and non-governmental organizations are likely to become more important in driving sustainability initiatives and addressing complex sustainability challenges (Lam and Li, 2019).

In terms of opportunities, companies that are able to effectively communicate their sustainability initiatives and differentiate themselves through sustainable practices are likely to see increased consumer demand and loyalty. Additionally, companies that are able to innovate and create new sustainable products and services may be able to capture new market opportunities. However, there are also potential challenges, such as increased competition, regulatory requirements, and the need for accurate measurement and reporting of environmental impact. Additionally, companies may face reputational risks if their sustainability claims are perceived as greenwashing or not credible. Overall, the future of green marketing and sustainability in the business landscape presents both opportunities and challenges, and companies that are able to effectively navigate these trends are likely to be well-positioned for success.

One challenge in green marketing is the potential for greenwashing, where companies make false or exaggerated environmental claims to mislead consumers. This can damage a company's reputation and credibility, and it is significant for companies to guarantee that their environmental claims are backed up by credible evidence and standards. Overall, green marketing is becoming an increasingly important feature of marketing strategy for businesses looking to appeal to environmentally-conscious consumers and promote sustainability. However, it is important for companies to confirm that their environmental rights are accurate and credible, and to align their marketing goals with broader business objectives.

Recommendations

Here are some actionable insights and recommendations for companies looking to embrace green marketing and promote sustainability in their operations:

- **Develop a Sustainability Strategy**

Companies should develop a clear sustainability strategy that outlines their sustainability goals and priorities, and identifies the sustainability problems that are most applicable to their business and investors. This strategy should be aligned with broader business objectives and should include clear targets, timelines, and performance indicators. Developing a clear sustainability strategy is essential for companies looking to embrace green marketing and promote sustainability in their operations. Businesses should determine which sustainability concerns are most important to their operations and stakeholder groups. Concerns including carbon emissions, energy use, wastewater treatment, and social impact may be included in this. Companies should set clear and measurable sustainability goals that align with their business objectives and stakeholder expectations. Companies should prioritize actions to achieve their sustainability goals based on their impact, feasibility, and alignment with business objectives (Papadas et al., 2019). This may involve identifying quick wins that can deliver immediate benefits, as well as longer-term initiatives that require more investment and effort. Companies should develop an implementation plan that outlines the actions, responsibilities, timelines, and resources needed to achieve their sustainability goals. This plan should be combined into the company's overall business strategy and should be regularly studied and updated. Companies should monitor and report on their progress towards their sustainability goals using credible and transparent metrics. This can help to identify areas for improvement, communicate progress to stakeholders, and build trust and credibility.

- **Integrate Sustainability Into All Aspects of the Business**

Sustainability should be integrated into all aspects of the business, from product development and supply chain management to marketing and communication. By doing so, it may be tried to make sure that sustainability is not seen as a distinct or unrelated activity but rather as a crucial component of the business's overall strategy. Throughout the whole life cycle of a product, from obtaining raw materials and manufacture to usage and disposal, businesses should take the environment into consideration when developing new products and services. Using eco-friendly materials, cutting down on packaging waste, and creating products that are both energy-efficient and recyclable are a few ways to do this. To guarantee that suppliers adhere to sustainability requirements and encourage sustainable practices, businesses should collaborate with them. Businesses should include sustainable practices into their daily operations, such as limiting waste, employing renewable energy sources, and consuming less energy and water. Companies should incorporate sustainability into their marketing and communication efforts to build brand reputation and engage with environmentally-conscious consumers. This may involve using sustainable packaging, promoting sustainable practices and certifications, and highlighting the environmental benefits of products and services. Companies should engage employees in sustainability initiatives and foster a culture of sustainability throughout the organization. This may involve providing training on sustainable practices, incorporating sustainability into performance evaluations, and recognizing and rewarding sustainable behavior.

- **Engage With Stakeholders**

Companies should engage with their stakeholders, including customers, employees, suppliers, and investors, to understand their sustainability expectations and priorities. This can help to ensure that sustainability initiatives are relevant and meaningful to stakeholders, and can build trust and loyalty among these groups. Companies should communicate their sustainability initiatives and progress effectively to stakeholders. This may include using sustainability reports, social media, and other channels to share information about sustainability goals, progress, and impact. Companies should also be transparent about their sustainability performance and avoid making misleading or exaggerated claims (Chang et al., 2019). Companies should identify their stakeholders and understand their interests, concerns, and priorities. This may involve conducting surveys, focus groups, or other forms of research to gather feedback and insights. Companies should communicate regularly with stakeholders to keep them informed about sustainability initiatives and progress. This may involve sharing updates through newsletters, reports, or social media channels. Companies should listen to stakeholder feedback and respond in a timely and transparent manner. This may involve setting up a feedback mechanism, such as a hotline or email address, and responding promptly to inquiries and concerns. Companies should collaborate with stakeholders to co-create sustainable solutions and initiatives. This may involve partnering with suppliers to reduce waste, or working with community organizations to promote sustainability education.

- **Invest in Sustainable Practices and Technologies**

Companies should invest in sustainable performs and technologies that reduce their environmental impact, such as renewable energy, energy-efficient equipment, and sustainable materials. This can help to reduce costs, increase efficiency, and improve brand reputation. Companies should behavior a sustainability assessment to classify areas where they can improve their environmental performance. This may involve measuring greenhouse gas emissions, water usage, waste production, and other environmental metrics. Companies should set measurable sustainability goals and develop a sustainability strategy to achieve them. This may involve setting targets for dropping greenhouse gas emissions, growing renewable energy usage, and reducing waste. Companies can invest in sustainable technologies such as energy-efficient lighting and HVAC systems, smart building technologies, and water-saving devices to reduce their environmental impact. Companies can invest in sustainable materials such as recycled paper, biodegradable packaging, and non-toxic cleaning products to reduce their environmental impact. Companies can adopt circular economy principles such as designing products for reuse, recycling, or repurposing to reduce waste and promote a more sustainable use of resources.

- **Measure and Report on Sustainability Performance**

Companies should measure and report on their sustainability performance using credible and transparent metrics. This can help to demonstrate progress, identify areas for improvement, and build trust with stakeholders. Companies should identify relevant sustainability metrics to measure their environmental, social, and governance (ESG) performance. This may include greenhouse gas emissions, water usage, waste production, employee diversity and inclusion, and ethical business practices. Companies should collect and analyze data to measure their sustainability performance. This may involve collecting data from multiple sources such as internal systems, suppliers, and third-party certifications. Companies should set targets to improve their sustainability performance and track progress towards these targets over time. This can help to identify areas where they can improve their sustainability performance and drive continuous improvement.

- **Foster a Culture of Sustainability**

Companies should foster a culture of sustainability throughout the organization by providing training and incentives for sustainable behavior, incorporating sustainability into performance evaluations, and creating opportunities for employee engagement and involvement in sustainability initiatives. By following these insights and recommendations, companies can embrace green marketing and promote sustainability in their operations. This can help to differentiate themselves in the market, meet growing consumer demand for sustainable products and services, and contribute to a more sustainable future. A sustainability strategy provides a roadmap for the company's sustainability initiatives. It should outline the company's sustainability goals, objectives, and targets and provide a framework for measuring progress. Companies can demonstrate their commitment to sustainability by integrating it into their mission, vision, and values. This will help to communicate the importance of sustainability to all stakeholders, including employees, customers, and investors. Employee education and training is crucial to fostering a culture of sustainability. Companies should provide regular training and education to employees on sustainability topics, including energy efficiency, waste reduction, and sustainable practices. Companies can encourage employees to participate in sustainability initiatives by providing incentives, recognizing and rewarding sustainable behavior, and providing opportunities for employee engagement. Companies can incorporate sustainability into their business operations by implementing sustainable practices such as energy efficiency, waste reduction, and water conservation. By making sustainability part of the day-to-day operations, companies can reduce their environmental impact and promote a culture of sustainability. Companies can promote sustainability by engaging with suppliers and customers on sustainability issues. This can include setting sustainability standards for suppliers, promoting sustainable products to customers, and collaborating with stakeholders to develop sustainable solutions.

CONCLUSION

In conclusion, sustainability has become a critical factor for companies looking to differentiate themselves in the market and meet growing consumer demand for sustainable products and services. Green marketing, or the promotion of sustainable products and practices, has emerged as a powerful tool for companies to communicate their environmental initiatives to consumers and build a reputation as a socially and environmentally responsible business. To succeed in green marketing, companies must develop a clear sustainability strategy, integrate sustainability into all aspects of the business, engage with stakeholders, invest in sustainable practices and technologies, and measure and report on sustainability performance. By doing so, companies can improve their environmental performance, build trust and credibility with stakeholders, and contribute to a more sustainable future. The shift towards sustainability in marketing is not just a passing trend, but a fundamental change in the way that companies operate and communicate with consumers. This shift has been driven by a combination of factors, including increasing consumer demand for environmentally and socially responsible products and services, the need to mitigate environmental risks and comply with regulations, and the recognition that sustainability can lead to long-term business success (Chou et al., 2020).

In conclusion, the marketing industry is undergoing a shift towards sustainability and green marketing strategies. Consumers are increasingly aware of the environmental impact of their purchasing decisions and are opting for products and services that align with their values. This shift has created new opportunities for businesses that embrace sustainability and incorporate it into their operations and marketing strategies. However, the COVID-19 pandemic has had a significant impact on the marketing industry, with orders decreasing in large markets such as Spain, Germany, Italy, France, and EEUDE. Despite these challenges, the importance of green marketing and sustainability remains relevant and necessary for businesses looking to position themselves for success in today's business landscape. By developing clear sustainability strategies, integrating sustainability into all aspects of the business, engaging with stakeholders, investing in sustainable practices and technologies, and measuring and reporting on sustainability performance, companies can effectively promote their sustainability efforts and differentiate themselves in the marketplace. As the world continues to grapple with environmental challenges, green marketing and sustainability will only become more important in the years to come.

Green marketing has emerged as a key strategy for companies to communicate their sustainability initiatives to consumers, differentiate themselves in the market, and build a reputation as a socially and environmentally responsible business. However, green marketing alone is not enough. To succeed in sustainability, companies must integrate it into all aspects of their operations, including product development, supply chain management, and communication with stakeholders (Jung, Kim and Kim, 2020).

To do so, companies need to develop a clear sustainability strategy that outlines their goals and commitments, identify the areas of their operations that have the greatest environmental impact, and take action to reduce their environmental footprint. This may involve investing in sustainable technologies, sourcing materials from responsible suppliers, and adopting circular business models that minimize waste and maximize resource efficiency.

Overall, sustainability is already a reality in marketing, and companies that embrace green marketing and promote sustainability in their operations are well-positioned to succeed in the evolving business landscape. The importance of sustainability in company has recently become more widely recognised, notably in marketing. Companies who don't meet the rising demand from customers for goods and services that are environmentally and socially friendly run the risk of forfeiting market share and having their reputations tarnished.

Green marketing has emerged as a powerful tool for companies to communicate their sustainability efforts to consumers and build a reputation as a socially and environmentally responsible business. Through green marketing, companies can differentiate themselves in the market, attract environmentally-conscious consumers, and reduce costs by implementing sustainable practices throughout their operations.

However, to succeed in green marketing, companies must take a holistic approach to sustainability. This involves developing a clear sustainability strategy, integrating sustainability into all aspects of the business, engaging with stakeholders, investing in sustainable practices and technologies, and measuring and reporting on sustainability performance. By embracing sustainability in marketing and throughout their operations, companies can not only improve their environmental performance but also build trust and credibility with stakeholders. This can help them to differentiate themselves in the market, meet growing consumer demand for sustainable products and services, and contribute to a more sustainable future.

At the same time, companies must engage with their stakeholders, including consumers, employees, suppliers, and regulators, to build trust and credibility and ensure that their sustainability initiatives align with stakeholder expectations. They must also measure and report on their sustainability performance to demonstrate accountability and transparency. In conclusion, sustainability is already a reality in marketing, and companies that embrace green marketing and promote sustainability in their operations are well-positioned to succeed in the evolving business landscape. As consumers continue to demand more socially and environmentally responsible products and services, companies that prioritize sustainability will have a competitive advantage and be better positioned for long-term success.

REFERENCES

Amoako, G. K., Dzogbenuku, R. K., Doe, J., & Adjaison, G. K. (2020). Green marketing and the SDGs: Emerging market perspective. *Marketing Intelligence & Planning*, *40*(3), 310–327. doi:10.1108/MIP-11-2018-0543

Bansal, P., & Sharma, B. (2011). The evolution of green marketing and the road ahead. *Journal of Business Research*, *65*(8), 1193–1200.

Bartiaux, F., Gram-Hanssen, K., Fonseca, P., Ozawa, C., & Cappelletti, G. (2013). Labeling schemes in energy efficiency and sustainability: Is there a credible third party certification behind the label? *Energy Policy*, *61*, 907–917.

Chandran, C., & Bhattacharya, P. (2021). *Hotel's best practices as strategic drivers for environmental sustainability and green marketing*. doi:10.4324/9781003181071-5

Chang, K. W., Hsu, C.-L., Hsu, Y.-T., & Chen, M.-C. (2019). How green marketing, perceived motives and incentives influence behavioral intentions. *Journal of Retailing and Consumer Services*, *49*, 336–345. doi:10.1016/j.jretconser.2019.04.012

Charter, M., & Clark, T. (2007). Sustainable innovation: Key conclusions from sustainable innovation conferences 2003–2006. *International Journal of Innovation and Sustainable Development*, *2*(3-4), 273–286.

Charter, M., & Polonsky, M. (1999). Green marketing: A global perspective on theory and practice. *Journal of Business Research*, *45*(3), 177–184.

Chou, S.-F., Horng, J.-S., Sam Liu, C.-H., & Lin, J.-Y. (2020). Identifying the critical factors of customer behavior: An integration perspective of marketing strategy and components of attitudes. *Journal of Retailing and Consumer Services*, *55*, 102113. doi:10.1016/j.jretconser.2020.102113

Chung, K. H. (2020). Green marketing orientation: Achieving sustainable development in green hotel management. *Journal of Hospitality Marketing & Management*, *29*(6), 722–738. doi:10.1080/19368623.2020.1693471

Dangelico, R. M., & Vocalelli, D. (2017). 'Green Marketing': An analysis of definitions, strategy steps, and tools through a systematic review of the literature. *Journal of Cleaner Production*, *165*, 1263–1279. doi:10.1016/j.jclepro.2017.07.184

Diez-Martín, F., Blanco-González, A., & Román, C. P. (2019). Research Challenges in Digital Marketing: Sustainability. *Sustainability (Basel)*, *11*(10), 2839. doi:10.3390u11102839

Fuller, D. A., & Tian, R. G. (2006). Social norms and consumers' willingness to pay for green electricity. *Energy Policy*, *34*(18), 36–43.

Green Marketing vs. Sustainable Marketing. (2022). Available at: https://www.clickinsights.asia/post/green-marketing-vs-sustainable-marketing

Groening, C., Sarkis, J., & Zhu, Q. (2018). Green marketing consumer-level theory review: A compendium of applied theories and further research directions. *Journal of Cleaner Production*, *172*, 1848–1866. doi:10.1016/j.jclepro.2017.12.002

Hartmann, P., & Apaolaza-Ibáñez, V. (2020). An update on the green washing phenomenon: Evidence from online stores. *Journal of Business Research*, *107*, 97–109.

Jung, J., Kim, S. H., & Kim, K. H. (2020). Sustainable marketing activities of traditional fashion market and brand loyalty. *Journal of Business Research*, *120*, 294–301. doi:10.1016/j.jbusres.2020.04.019

Kemper, J. A., & Ballantine, P. W. (2019). What do we mean by sustainability marketing? *Journal of Marketing Management*, *35*(3–4), 277–309. doi:10.1080/0267257X.2019.1573845

Lam, J. S. L., & Li, K. X. (2019). Green port marketing for sustainable growth and development. *Transport Policy*, *84*, 73–81. doi:10.1016/j.tranpol.2019.04.011

Laroche, M., Bergeron, J., & Barbaro-Forleo, G. (2001). Targeting consumers who are willing to pay more for environmentally friendly products. *Journal of Consumer Marketing*, *18*(6), 503–520. doi:10.1108/EUM0000000006155

Lee, M., & Park, S. Y. (2011). Cause-related marketing and consumers' responses to firms' ethical behavior: The moderating role of corporate social responsibility. *Journal of Business Ethics*, *103*(3), 435–451.

Liu, M. T., & Jindal, R. P. (2016). Green marketing: A review and research agenda. *International Journal of Management Reviews*, *18*(4), 504–521.

Moravcikova, D., Krizanova, A., Kliestikova, J., & Rypakova, M. (2017). Green Marketing as the Source of the Competitive Advantage of the Business. *Sustainability (Basel)*, *9*(12), 2218. doi:10.3390u9122218

Nguyen, H., Nguyen, N., Nguyen, B., Lobo, A., & Vu, P. (2019). Organic Food Purchases in an Emerging Market: The Influence of Consumers' Personal Factors and Green Marketing Practices of Food Stores. *International Journal of Environmental Research and Public Health*, *16*(6), 1037. doi:10.3390/ijerph16061037 PMID:30909390

Nguyen, T. H. O., Yang, Z., Nguyen, N., Johnson, L. W., & Cao, T. K. (2019). Greenwash and Green Purchase Intention: The Mediating Role of Green Skepticism. *Sustainability (Basel)*, *11*(9), 2653. doi:10.3390u11092653

Ottman, J. A. (2011). *The new rules of green marketing: Strategies, tools, and inspiration for sustainable branding.* Berrett-Koehler Publishers.

Papadas, K., Avlonitis, G. J., & Carrigan, M. (2017). Green marketing orientation: Conceptualization, scale development and validation. *Journal of Business Research*, *80*, 236–246. doi:10.1016/j.jbusres.2017.05.024

Papadas, K., Avlonitis, G. J., Carrigan, M., & Piha, L. (2019). The interplay of strategic and internal green marketing orientation on competitive advantage. *Journal of Business Research*, *104*, 632–643. doi:10.1016/j.jbusres.2018.07.009

Peattie, S. (2001). Golden goose or wild goose? The hunt for the green consumer. *Business Strategy and the Environment*, *10*(4), 187–199. doi:10.1002/bse.292

Peattie, S., & Charter, M. (2003). *Sustainable marketing*. Pearson Education.

Pomering, A. (2017). Marketing for Sustainability: Extending the Conceptualisation of the Marketing Mix to Drive Value for Individuals and Society at Large. *Australasian Marketing Journal (Amj)*, *25*(2), 157–165. doi:10.1016/j.ausmj.2017.04.011

Sarkis, J., & Cordeiro, J. J. (2012)... . *Sustainability*, *12*(21), 8977. doi:10.3390u12218977

Szabo, S., & Webster, J. (2020). Perceived Greenwashing: The Effects of Green Marketing on Environmental and Product Perceptions. *Journal of Business Ethics*. Advance online publication. doi:10.100710551-020-04461-0

The Triple Bottom Line: What It Is & Why It's Important. (2020). Available at: https://online.hbs.edu/blog/post/what-is-the-triple-bottom-line

Chapter 18
Internet Marketing as an Effective Instrument for the Development of Companies in the Era of Sustainable Marketing

Kristina Jganjgava
Ivane Javakhishvili Tbilisi State University, Georgia

ABSTRACT

This chapter presents the results of studying the possibilities of using internet marketing technologies in the activities of modern companies focused primarily on the use of IT technologies and identifying related problems. The constituent elements of marketing activities performed using internet technologies are characterized, and the possibilities for the development of modern business structures focused mainly on digital marketing are described. The role of internet marketing in the promotion of goods and services by companies on the market is revealed, its effectiveness is assessed, and the possibilities for increasing the marketing competence of enterprises in the implementation of internet technologies are outlined.

INTRODUCTION

Internet marketing is considered the direction of marketing. In its implementation, all components of traditional marketing are used, but in the Internet environment. The components of the marketing mix include price, product, promotion (search engine marketing and Internet marketing communications), and distribution.

Internet marketing (online marketing) can also be considered a part of e-commerce that includes several varieties, in particular:

- Search marketing;
- Hidden marketing;

DOI: 10.4018/978-1-6684-8681-8.ch018

- Guerrilla marketing;
- Viral marketing;
- Marketing in social networks;
- Affiliate (partnership) marketing.

The popularity of e-commerce and, in particular, internet marketing is related to empowerment access to Internet resources. Not a single marketing campaign is currently complete without this commerce.

Internet marketing is increasingly used by companies belonging to different business sectors. In the modern world, the Internet has steadily entered all aspects of society. This led to the fact that its networks annually cover an increasing number of users whose activity is growing. One of the important uses of the Internet is for business activities. The Internet is currently being used to improve the efficiency of business through the development of effective Internet marketing.

The available progressive technologies have made it possible to create Internet marketing, which becomes one of the main tools for the development of each enterprise.

More and more enterprises are actively integrating various interactive and digital tools into the business. Existing experience in Internet marketing at the level of any enterprise, especially in the field of e-commerce and e-business, has proved that with the right management of this tool, can be expanded the boundaries of the activities of any business and as well achieving Sustainable Development of modern companies.

THEORETICAL ASPECTS OF INTERNET MARKETING

Internet marketing is one of the important tasks in the formation of strategies in marketing, on the solution of that the efficiency of the enterprise depends.

Since the Internet as a communication medium is constantly progressing and becoming more complex, and with it, the possibilities of promoting a company in the virtual space are expanding, there is a need for a new direction in the structure of general marketing, that would describe the features of achieving marketing goals on the Internet. When specialists are writing articles and searching for information about this area of scientific knowledge, a number of terms are used (Internet marketing, online marketing, electronic marketing, web, digital marketing).

Based on the analysis of literary sources, it can be concluded that all of the above terms include marketing on the Internet, however, some, in particular, "electronic marketing", involve the use of other tools, such as SMS mailing lists and telephone help services. The main emphasis is placed on the use of all media channels connected to the Internet. There is a wide variety of definitions of internet marketing.

Eley and Tilley (2009) define Internet Marketing as "advertising activities on the Internet, including by email". Chaffey et al. (2009), when formulating a definition, depart from the pure advertising functions of Internet marketing. According to them, online marketing is the achievement of marketing goals using digital technologies. Baines et al. (2017) believe that online marketing is the use of the Internet and other forms of electronic communication.

According to Alekseeva et al. (2019), "Internet marketing is becoming the most important source of increasing business profitability. This involves conducting an in-depth study of the values, needs, experience, and other important characteristics of the client, as well as choosing the best communication channels on the Web".

Chaffey (2008) defines internet marketing as "Applying Digital technologies that form online channels (Web, e-mail, databases, plus mobile/wireless & digital TV) to contribute to marketing activities aimed at achieving profitable acquisition and retention of customers (within a multi-channel buying process and customer lifecycle) through improving our customer knowledge (of their profiles, behavior, value, and loyalty drivers), then delivering integrated targeted communications and online services that match their individual needs." Chaffey's definition reflects the relationship marketing concept, it emphasizes that it should not be technology that drives Electronic marketing, but the business model.

INTERNET MARKETING TOOLS AS THE BASIS OF THE COMPANY'S EFFICIENT ACTIVITIES

In Internet marketing, there are fundamentally new ways and tools to attract the target audience. Internet marketing is an extremely fast-developing sphere: what was relevant a year ago may no longer work and produce no results. Therefore, it is important to study in detail the features of each tool, follow the trends in Internet marketing, and improve the effectiveness of individual tools.

Internet marketing dates back to the 90s of the 20th century when the first sites began to appear informing Internet users about the services and products of their company. Internet marketing refers to the theory and methodology organization of marketing in the hypermedia space of the Internet. The Internet allows us to move from mass marketing to one-to-one marketing. The main Internet marketing tools that companies currently use to attract the attention of the target audience are:

- Contextual advertising;
- Search promotion;
- Promotion in social media;
- Targeted advertising;
- Lead generation.

Each tool is discussed separately as follows.

1. Contextual advertising is a type of advertising on the Internet, in which advertising the ad is shown in accordance with the content, and context of the web page, that is, the ad is shown only by the user whose interests coincide with the content of the ad. This is the main difference between contextual advertising, it is "unobtrusive", the user sees only what he is interested in himself. Contextual advertising is advertising blocks (text or graphics), which are located on the top or side fields of search engines and thematic portals. Payment for contextual advertising is made for clicks, then there is a payment is charged only if the user goes to the company's website. The most common contextual advertising system is - "Google. Adwords".

Contextual advertising is available for viewing only to those users who enter certain keywords into the search, thus showing interest in a particular type of product or service. Together with search results the user also sees contextual advertising that matches his request.

That is why contextual advertising is such an effective tool for Internet marketing. Another advantage of contextual advertising is that it attracts A "hot" target audience on the site is possible in a very short period of time because the number of impressions depends only on the literacy of the contextual campaign settings, the set CPC, and the number of competitors. Factors such as when the site was created, the number of third-party links to the site, etc. do not affect the position in contextual advertising, which means that by setting up contextual advertising, the site can appear on the first page of search results. A company can set up and place contextual advertising on its own, or through specialized contextual advertising agencies that have a ticket in the basic systems.

2. Search promotion (search engine optimization of the site, SEO - Search Engine Optimization) is a set of measures to increase the position of a site in the results of search engines for pre-selected queries. The statistics of visits to search engines are such that 90% of users view only the first page of search results. 98% of users go on the first three links of the search results, then the downward trend – to the tenth link on the first page of the issue is reached by 20-50% of users. Only 10-20% visit the second page of the search engine results. Being at the TOP-10 of search results will provide the company with stable traffic and potential customers to the site. Many visitors who come to the site through search results become customers of the company, as they themselves found the company's website when they were interested in a particular service.

Between search promotion and contextual advertising, one can spend parallel, they are indeed similar in their impact on the user, but the difference in principles of customization is colossal. If with the help of contextual advertising, a company can be advertised on the first page of search engine results per day advertising settings, search promotion for the same queries will take 3-15 months of systematic work with an SEO specialist to bring the company's website to the first search results page. Search promotion is influenced by more than five hundred factors, and on different search engines, these are different factors that affect the position in the search results. But search engine optimization is necessary for all companies that want to set up a stable flow of traffic to the site. Firstly, the company does not pay for clicks to the site from search results, but SEO is more loyal than contextual advertising. Then, if the company's website is at the TOP-3 of search results, then the conversion (percentage of users who went to the site) is about 90%, and in contextual advertising, the average conversion is 8-12%. But search engine promotion includes regular work on the site, constant improvement, and optimization.

3. Promotion in social media (Social Media Marketing, SMM) is a set of activities in social networks to promote the company's services and products, as well as to increase brand awareness and customer loyalty. Thanks to social networks, it has become possible to build long-term relationships with customers. Promotion in social networks allows companies to specifically influence the target audience, and choose platforms where this audience is more represented and the most appropriate ways to communicate with them.

In addition, an important lever for managing SMM is cooperation with "opinion leaders". Usually, these are people whose opinion is authoritative for one or another audience. As a rule, well-known bloggers, journalists, etc. are opinion leaders. Since their recommendations and reviews can cause a surge of interest in the products of the company, it is very important to constantly maintain a relationship with the opinion leaders of potential consumers. Any information obtained by "word of mouth" from interlocutors in a social network makes a greater impression than impersonal traditional advertising.

Social media marketing is a long-term process that requires correct and extremely careful use. SMM technologies do not require large investments, but at the same time, they do not have an instant effect and do not guarantee a quick solution to the tasks. The wrong approach to managing social media marketing can lead to undesirable consequences: aggressive advertising, a decrease in user interest in the company's products, and a decrease in sales and profits.

4. Targeted ads are text, display, or multimedia ads that are shown only to those Internet users who meet a certain set of requirements set by the advertiser. One of the most promising areas is targeting social networks, which collected the most complete and reliable information about Internet users. The main advantage of targeted advertising is the ability to convey an advertising message only to those who might really be interested in it. On the one hand, this ensures greater advertising effectiveness, which is especially relevant when paying for clicks, and on the other hand, it allows you to reduce the negative impact of the advertising effect due to the fact that the offered goods and services are more likely to be really needed by the user at the time of the ad-budget. Correctly configured targeting will also improve the quality of the site's landing pages from the point of view of the search engine, as users will interact more actively with them, providing a positive impact on the behavioral factor. Targeted ads are likewise easier to track and manage. If known in advance what criteria the referred users must meet, it will be more effortless, if necessary, to adjust the advertising campaign in order to free up wasted funds and transfer them to more promising areas.
5. Lead generation is one of the most popular and sought-after internet marketing techniques. Judging by the tendencies the popularity of lead generation will only continue to grow.

Lead generation is the process of attracting potential clients (leads). Two objects are needed to organize the process of lead generation on the Internet:

- The source of traffic that will be processed into leads.
- Website or converter that will process traffic into leads.

A lead generation channel is a method by which traffic (a stream of unique visitors) is attracted to a website (converter). As for converters, that is, sites that turn incoming traffic into leads. Landing is a one-page site, the main task of which is to turn a potential client into a lead. In this way, good landings have no equal. Converters also include more traditional types of sites, such as online stores, business card sites, corporate sites, etc.

The most important advantage of lead generation is its manageability. Armed with a sales funnel and a conversion that shows how many leads eventually turn into customers, a company has a manageable sales mechanism, and thus a managed business. Moreover, by changing certain indicators in the sales funnel, it became possible to adjust the cost of a lead (CPL), and hence the final cost per customer acquisition (CAC) at a value that would be beneficial to the company.

Thus, lead generation makes online marketing predictable and manageable, which allows marketers to organize and work very flexibly with the involvement of clients. Proper organization of lead generation can turn the costs into advertising in controlled investments.

The use of these methods of Internet marketing is the key to the successful promotion of the company, and this, in turn, will provide the necessary level of the company's competitiveness in the market, attract target consumers and rationalize the advertising budget, using only effective advertising channels.

INTERNET MARKETING AS A KEY ELEMENT OF NEW GENERATION MARKETING COMMUNICATIONS

In the age of rapidly advancing technology and vast availability of information, it is undeniable that the world we live in is changing rapidly. The rapid pace of development of science, globalization, and the transition to the information society and the digital economy have contributed to a significant transformation of potential consumers and their behavior. The development of consumer distrust of classic marketing tools makes it difficult for marketers to determine an effective set of the marketing communications mix. Various communication tools compete with each other to attract consumers every day. Digitization has changed businesses, and communications have moved from the real world to the virtual world. Currently, the increasing role of Internet communications and the transition to Internet marketing can be observed, which has radically transformed the traditional marketing mix, its main directions, and tools. As a result, there is no doubt about the need to know the history of the development of Internet marketing, its capabilities, and its features.

Internet marketing is marketing that provides interaction with customers and business partners using digital information and communication technologies and electronic devices. In a broader sense, marketing means the implementation of marketing activities using digital information and communication technologies (Danko & Kitova, 2013).

Internet marketing includes online marketing, but it allows communication with potential consumers not only online, but also offline (advertising displays on the street, QR codes, mobile applications, SMS / MMS, video walls, and interactive kiosks). With the help of these forms of advertising, the target audience penetrates the online environment through the offline environment.

Internet marketing is one of the most effective elements of the marketing communications mix today and shows no signs of slowing down or stopping. Therefore, leading companies and their marketers are focusing their efforts on the formation of digital communications with their consumers.

What does Internet marketing give modern companies? The main advantage of digital communications in marketing is the ability to maximize results at optimal cost, which is ensured by the advertiser's ability to control interest in their products and services for counting the counter of transitions to the site, counting the ways to go to the site, etc. Internet marketing implies high rationality: it has become possible to convey information to more people in a shorter period. At the same time, traditional marketing tools still involve a high level of cost, while internet marketing can achieve results at the lowest cost - sometimes the only cost of internet marketing is time. Interaction with consumers in social media, content marketing, and SEO indeed takes time for a miracle to happen. If a company wants faster results, it can use tactics that require investments. While a company cannot say exactly how many people saw their billboard on the street, digital technology makes it possible to perform such measurements.

Another great opportunity for Internet marketing is targeting. Companies can be sure that advertising messages will be received by their target audience. The technology allows businesses to customize everything so that the information reaches those consumers who are searching the Internet for topics related to business, for the right people.

Nowadays companies do not spend money on advertising, which will not reach the consumer who is interested in the product. The future is for marketing strategies that narrow the audience and eliminate ineffective impressions.

The global network has changed the communication between the consumer and the company. In the digital age, the orientation of companies has changed: now they seek not so much to maximize profit, but much to satisfy the customer's need, to be sure that their product has value in the market and will be in demand. If in traditional marketing approach to the consumer was of a general nature, and otherwise was impossible, then in internet marketing one can notice a trend toward an individual approach. Internet marketing allows companies to use the interests and preferences of the consumer to tailor the marketing message to their needs. Personalization is the most important resource in Internet marketing. One has only to remember how Coca-Cola released personalized bottles with names on them. According to the Wall Street Journal, this campaign led to a 2% increase in sales and an increase in the consumption of the drink from 1.7 billion to 1.9 billion servings per day (Esterl, 2014).

INTERNET MARKETING TOOLS: OPTIONS AND EFFECTIVENESS

Internet marketing is an important component of e-commerce. It is usually implemented through Internet integration, information management, organization of customer service, sales, etc. E-commerce and Internet marketing have become popular due to the expansion of access to the Web, they are an integral part of any marketing campaign. Some areas of using Internet marketing as one of the important components of modern company marketing are shown in Table 1.

The benefits of Internet marketing are evaluated by consumers based on three factors - price, time, and direct contact and they need to be considered together. Only the simultaneous presence of these factors will push the consumer (corporation or individual) to purchase something via the Internet or use the corresponding program, Internet project, etc. (Kenzina & Mandzhiev, 2016). It is the choice that characterizes the effectiveness and relevance of the proposed product or Internet product.

A rationally built system such as informing, organizing sales, and promotion allows consumers to choose and order goods or services without leaving home or office. They can get the maximum amount of information about goods and services, primarily of a comparative nature. The need to communicate

Table 1. The main directions using of Internet marketing

Marketing Complex	Areas of Using Internet Marketing
Product	Sales and after-sales service organization. Creation of added value of goods. Development of new products.
Price	Participation in the formation of a flexible system of discounts
Place	Internet sales. Internet payment.
Promotion	Building a system of promotion through the Internet. Internet branding. Public relations.
Segmentation	Identification of target segments and formation of a system of interaction with various audiences on the principle of "everyone is special".
Marketing research	Studying consumers. Research of competitors. Market analysis.

Source: Author based on Saakyan and Karpenko (2016)

with intermediaries is also eliminated, that is, the buyer is spared the influence of persuasive and emotional factors.

The effectiveness of Internet sales is evidenced by the variety of options around the world. For example, the grandiose activity of the radical innovation company Amazon, which began with a startup for the sale of books in 1994, its creator J. Bezos organized a small company under the brand Cadabra, which was later renamed Amazon, and become the largest organizer of online sales of books in the world. In 2018, Amazon reached a capitalization of trillion dollars, and the profit of this Internet giant (that's what they call the company in recent years) amounted to 52.9 billion dollars, being its founder recognized as one of the richest people in the world (Pakhunov, 2018).

For companies seeking to sell their products via the Internet, there are a number of advantages. For example:

- The ability to quickly respond to changing market conditions: quickly change the range, prices, and descriptions of goods and services;
- Analyze the reaction of buyers to certain offers, which allows companies to receive additional information about their needs and immediately make the necessary adjustments to advertising; be able to save on the delivery and dissemination of information.

The marketing competence of any company occurs on several levels, in particular at the strategic and tactical levels. Therefore, there are strategic and tactical marketing competencies. Strategic marketing competence is focused on the macro-environment of the company, ensuring long-term and strong interactions with partners, consumers, distributors, and other market entities. Tactical marketing competence is defined as the ability to timely and promptly respond to changes and solve current marketing problems. The marketing competence of both industrial and IT companies is focused primarily on securing competitive advantages, including in the Internet space, and in the future - to achieve leadership positions in the market by expanding market share. Marketing Competence needs not only constant development but also rational use. In this connection, an important role in its transformation into business processes is assigned not only to the marketing department of the company but also to the entire administrative management.

USE OF ARTIFICIAL INTELLIGENCE IN DIGITAL MARKETING

Nowadays using of Artificial Intelligence (AI) in digital marketing has become an almost indispensable means of modern promotion (Yau, Saad & Chong, 2021; Vlačić et al., 2021). Many organizations are implementing digital best practices into their work. A growing number of business leaders agree that the use of Artificial Intelligence allows companies to maintain a competitive edge. AI has the capability to create simulation models and personalize purchasing processes through recommendations based on machine learning technologies and interaction with virtual assistants (Verma et al., 2021). Many brands have adopted Artificial Intelligence to connect with their customers (Chatterjee et al., 2019), just like Amazon uses AI to recommend products based on their previous purchases, views and searches.

Currently customers have already discovered exceptional results, combining the abilities of marketers and the capabilities of artificial intelligence. However, previous survey results demonstrated consumers fear that chatbots may give false information (Arsenijevic & Jovic, 2019). AI can be used to cut production costs. AI managers write texts based on databases, given topics or analysis of similar materials. Also, it can suggest topics for copywriters, prepare reports, write drafts of the text. AI has the potential to revolutionize digital marketing by automating routines, personalizing campaigns and helping to make data-driven decisions. Moreover, it is capable of effectively solving many problems, from customer segmentation to content creation and ad optimization (Vlačić et al., 2021). However, for best results, marketers need to understand the limitations of Artificial Intelligence and use it in conjunction with other tools and techniques.

Artificial Intelligence is a very powerful tool, but it is not a panacea. To make informed decisions, digital marketers should be able to work with information and clearly understand their target audience and goals. AI can help in analyzing data, interpret communication, predict consumer behavior, and produce responses (Dimitrieska, Stankovska, & Efremova, 2018). Nevertheless, its careful implementation is advised to avoid vagueness of the results (Jarek & Mazurek, 2019). In Digital Marketing, the possibilities of AI should be used by creative and insightful people for achieving sustainable marketing goals.

CONCLUSION

Thus, summarizing the chapter, the following findings can be formulated.

1. Modern information and telecommunication technologies open up new opportunities and prospects for consumers and organizations, increasing their mobility and computerization. These factors are most significant for the development of Internet marketing. Internet marketing can rightfully be characterized as a set of tools, technologies, and techniques implemented on the Internet, aimed at drawing attention to a product or service, popularizing the product on the Web, and its effective promotion to target audiences for selling and maximizing profits.
2. In modern conditions, the number of tools that are used in the practice of Internet marketing is constantly growing. This is due to the development of the advertising business and strengthening the trend of moving advertising to the Web. The main and effective tools of Internet marketing are contextual and banner advertising, search engine promotion, promotion in social networks, and email marketing. Each of the presented tools has its own advantages and disadvantages, but they are endowed with their own characteristics and specifics, that certainly should be taken into account when choosing the most effective tools for each individual project.
3. The marketing competence of the company, representing a set of knowledge formed within its framework, increases with the use of new technologies, primarily such as computerization, satellite communications, fiber optics, and, of course, Internet marketing technologies. Therefore, allocate strategic and tactical marketing competence. Strategic marketing competence is focused on the macro environment of the company, ensuring long-term and strong interactions with partners, consumers, distributors, and other market entities. Tactical Marketing Competence is defined as the ability to promptly and promptly respond to changes in the company's macro- and microenvironment in order to solve current marketing problems.
4. Sustainable development tendencies should be taken into account by companies while developing Internet marketing strategies. Consumers' concerns about environmental and ethical marketing are growing demanding responsible behavior from companies (Gigauri & Djakeli, 2021) and anticipating sustainable marketing activities also in the digital space. Thus, marketing tendencies towards

sustainable production and consumption, communicating sustainable lifestyle, sustainable branding, and focusing on value creation (Martín-Cervantes et al., 2022) paves the way for sustainable digital marketing.

REFERENCES

Alekseeva, N., Stroganova, O., & Vasilenok, V. (2019). Identifying trends in the development of marketing in the digital age. *Proceedings of the International Conference on Digital Technologies in Logistics and Infrastructure (ICDTLI 2019)*. 10.2991/icdtli-19.2019.4

Arsenijevic, U., & Jovic, M. (2019). Artificial intelligence marketing: chatbots. In 2019 international conference on artificial intelligence: applications and innovations (IC-AIAI) (pp. 19-193). IEEE. doi:10.1109/IC-AIAI48757.2019.00010

Baines, P., Fill, C., Rosengren, S., & Antonetti, P. (2017). *Fundamentals of Marketing*. Oxford University Press.

Chaffey, D. (2008). *Internet Marketing: Strategy, Implementation and Practice, 3/E*. Pearson Education.

Chaffey, D., Ellis-Chadwick, F., Mayer, R., & Johnston, K. (2009). *Internet Marketing*. Pearson Education.

Chatterjee, S., Ghosh, S. K., Chaudhuri, R., & Nguyen, B. (2019). Are CRM systems ready for AI integration? A conceptual framework of organizational readiness for effective AI-CRM integration. *The Bottom Line (New York, N.Y.)*, 32(2), 144–157. doi:10.1108/BL-02-2019-0069

Danko, T.P., & Kitova, O.V. (2013). Issues of Digital Marketing Development. *Problems of Modern Economy*, 3(47).

Dimitrieska, S., Stankovska, A., & Efremova, T. (2018). Artificial intelligence and marketing. *Entrepreneurship*, 6(2), 298–304.

Eley, B., & Tilley, S. (2009). *Online Marketing Inside Out*. SitePoint.

Esterl, M. (2014). 'Share a coke' credited with a pop in sales. Marketing campaign that put first names on bottles reversed downward slide. *The Wall Street Journal*. Retrieved January 25, 2023 from https://www.wsj.com/articles/share-a-coke-credited-with-a-pop-in-sales-1411661519

Gigauri, I., & Djakeli, K. (2021). Expecting Transformation of Marketing During the Post-Pandemic New Normal: Qualitative Research of Marketing Managers in Georgia. *International Journal of Sustainable Economies Management*, 10(2), 1–18. doi:10.4018/IJSEM.2021040101

Jarek, K., & Mazurek, G. (2019). Marketing and Artificial Intelligence. *Central European Business Review*, 8(2).

Kenzina, Ts., & Mandzhiev, B. (2016). Internet marketing as a tool for enterprise development. *Young Scientist*, 27(2), 18-20.

Martín-Cervantes, P. A., del Carmen Valls Martínez, M., & Gigauri, I. (2022). Sustainable Marketing. In *Encyclopedia of Creativity, Invention, Innovation and Entrepreneurship*. Springer. doi:10.1007/978-1-4614-6616-1_200101-1

Pakhunov, K. (2018). Amazon throws a challenge. *Expert*, 37. Retrieved January 29, 2023 from https://expert.ru/expert/2018/37/amazon-brosaet-vyizov/

Sahakyan, A. I., & Karpenko, T. V. (2016). *Internet marketing as a modern direction in the development of companies. scientific forum*. Retrieved January 26, 2023 from https://www.scienceforum.ru/2016/1528/22456

Verma, S., Sharma, R., Deb, S., & Maitra, D. (2021). Artificial intelligence in marketing: Systematic review and future research direction. *International Journal of Information Management Data Insights*, *1*(1), 100002. doi:10.1016/j.jjimei.2020.100002

Vlačić, B., Corbo, L., Silva, S. C., & Dabić, M. (2021). The evolving role of artificial intelligence in marketing: A review and research agenda. *Journal of Business Research*, *128*, 187–203. doi:10.1016/j.jbusres.2021.01.055

Yau, K.-L. A., Saad, N. M., & Chong, Y.-W. (2021). Artificial Intelligence Marketing (AIM) for Enhancing Customer Relationships. *Applied Sciences (Basel, Switzerland)*, *11*(18), 8562. doi:10.3390/app11188562

Chapter 19
The Role of Artificial Intelligence in Modern Finance and Sustainable Marketing

Agnieszka Jadwiga Wójcik-Czerniawska
SGH Warsaw School of Economics, Poland

ABSTRACT

Artificial intelligence (AI) is reshaping marketing and is becoming a capable assistant supporting many facets of the industry. Artificial intelligence plays a vital role in modern finance and sustainable marketing. AI can be utilized to improve sustainability and enhance financial services. The chapter begins with the assertion that contemporary finance and market viability are crucial components of every economy. The most recent disruptive technology is artificial intelligence (AI), which has the greatest potential to change marketing. International practitioners are trying to recognize the best AI results for their marketing functions. To build a more secure business and economic environment and lower human mistakes, the chapter demonstrates how artificial intelligence may combine contemporary finance and market sustainability with tech skills.

INTRODUCTION

An emerging field of technology science called artificial intelligence may be used to study, create, and extend the conceptual framework and technological applications of human intelligence. It is the nexus of technological science, social science, and basic sciences. Artificial intelligence is essentially a simulation of how people's awareness and thought processes work with information. It is a technological approach of emulation, expansion, and companies can expand on the examination of the nature of intelligence to create a novel class of autonomous robots that responds in a manner comparable to human intellect.

In recent years, artificial intelligence has achieved significant advances in robotics, language image recognition, expert systems, and other fields. It is widely used in artificial intelligence applications like as robotics, economic and political decision-making, control mechanisms, developing a model, and

DOI: 10.4018/978-1-6684-8681-8.ch019

others. Artificial intelligence can substitute financial employees in the sectors of finance and taxation to handle extremely repetitive accounting difficulties (Wang et al., 2020).

It can realize cross-business and cross-post technical operations, intensely dig up the relevant data of solidified businesses, fortify the transition of financial functions, save labor costs, start reducing the false alarm rate of manual operations, enhance the productivity of fiscal and tax work, and enhance the accuracy of risk management and internal control.

The accuracy of the aforementioned techniques and models will be greatly enhanced by the development of artificial intelligence technology, enabling more effective risk assessments. In the management of credit risk, artificial intelligence can optimise prediction model and fix measurement between many factors; and in downside risk, artificial intelligence can incorporate emergency situations into vulnerability assessment via a successful teaching method. For example, artificial intelligence automatically mines message, information, photos, and others to get artificial intelligence for in-depth insight, exploring, and labelling risk cautions (Murgai, 2018).

The rise of artificial intelligence is stealing our money. It makes sense that there has been a lot of interest recently in the emergence of artificial intelligence in banking and other industries. While there is still more to be done, emerging technologies related to artificial intelligence have made enormous strides and offer great potential for use in the finance industry and other parts of the economy. The era of artificial intelligence has just begun, and we are at its dawn. In just the last few decades, financial technology has made significant advances, some of which were made feasible by the application of artificial intelligence to the financial sector. Past human-dominated economic transactions and endeavours have been replaced, supplemented, or abolished by artificial intelligence and smart machines.

Trading, financial analysis, risk assessment, investment management, financial services, and other facets of the financial industry have all seen substantial changes as a result of the advent of artificial intelligence. Many of these innovations and improvements have been successful and beneficial to society. They have reduced the cost of financing for firms and entrepreneurs, increased the variety of financial resources and artificial Intelligencelable to investors, and simplified banking and investing for individuals. However, despite the notable advancement and promise that artificial intelligence in banking offers, it also poses substantial risks and problems (Lin, 2016).

"Artificial intelligence" is becoming more and more common, although there is no one, clear meaning. This project aims to make machines intelligent, because intelligence is the quality that enables an organism to react accurately and predictably to its environment. In terms of technology, artificial intelligence is the process of combining a variety of business operations, systems, and routine tasks with cloud computing, wireless connections, robotics, computers, and the creation of online content. Computers with artificial intelligence already exist and will do so in the future. Future marketing campaigns must support the expansion and development of artificial intelligence. Businesses employ artificial intelligence software to automate processes, lower costs, accelerate turnaround times, and boost productivity. Teams now moving toward marketing artificial intelligence software are at a significant advantage to get on board as technology is advancing at an unparalleled rate.

Applications of AI are being employed in fields as diverse as marketing, banking, finance, agriculture, healthcare, security, robots, and transportation, as well as chatbots, artificial intelligence, and manufacturing. AI applications have started to become a fundamental aspect of cities in recent years. Cities' transportation networks are run by AIs in the form of self-driving vehicles. Robots manage daily activities such as running stores and eating establishments that are fundamental to urban life. They also maintain city infrastructure. Invisible intelligence platforms control many aspects of urban life, from air quality monitoring to waste collection and from traffic to safety (Yigitcanlar & Cugurullo, 2020).

In their study on the technological and digital development in advertising, experts have been examining how advancements in technology impact how effectively businesses can handle customer desires and supply offers at a quick pace (Crittenden et al., 2019). In the field of market analysis, studies that examine the impact and use of various technologies on marketing effectiveness are frequently available. Even while current study demands have prompted a closer analysis of AI-related themes and their significance in marketing, the focus on research placed at the interface of Artificial Intelligence (AI) and brand management has only recently increased.

For the sake of this evaluation, we use the description of AI as "computational agents that behave intelligently" in light of the foregoing. This idea differs from prior ones, which held that AI only referred to computers that would have intellect comparable to that of humans. In this regard, we accept the description of marketing AI as "the creation of artificial entities that, given the knowledge, they possess about consumers, rivals, and the primary organization, advise and/or perform actions to obtain the greatest marketing outcome" (Dwivedi et al., 2021).

From a tactical standpoint, AI in marketing is becoming increasingly important. A rising lot of corporations, like Google, Rare Carat, Spotify, and Under Armour, are enhancing their productivity by using AI-based technologies (include Microsoft Cognitive Services, Amazon Lex, Google Assistant). This approach increases customer touch throughout advertising networks while improving market forecasts and management (Lin, 2019).

By supporting in division, directing, and placing, artificial intelligence may support venders in directing and scheduling marketing struggles (STP).

In addition to STP, AI can aid marketers in envisioning a company's strategic approach. In the banking and finance, art marketing, retail, and tourism industries, sentiment analysis and machine learning methods can be utilised to find profitable consumer segments. Additionally, a combination of learning algorithms, causality forests, and data optimization technique may be used to compress the traumatised consumers. An artificial intelligence-powered advertising analytics platform may evaluate how successfully a product is created to reach customer requests and how pleased consumers are as a result. The use of topic modelling improves the system's capacity for service delivery and innovation. To understand the product recommendation systems and synchronise marketing strategies with efficient product management, preference weights are provided to product characteristics during product searches. Deep learning can tailor point-of-interest suggestions and encourage travel. Artificial intelligence provides the aptitude to tailor products to the demands of the client. AI has a significant positive impact on corporate financing since it can better precisely detect and assess credit risks. By improving loan screening and reducing the financial risk, AI advances like machine learning might assist companies increase their worth (Moloi and Marwala, 2020).

Buying is a calculation-intensive process that considers a number of variables before arriving at the final price. The real-time price variation caused by changing demand makes pricing more complicated. A multiarmed bandit method based on artificial intelligence is capable of real-time dynamic pricing adjustment. In a setting where prices are continually changing, like on an e-commerce site, a machine learning algorithm using Bayesian inference may swiftly adjust sales prices to match those of the competition. According to Dekimpe (2020), the best reply pricing systems use customer preferences, rivalry tactics, and supplier networks to optimise dynamic pricing.

Both suppliers and buyers benefit from the distribution process' calibration and mechanization. In contrast to its usefulness for distribution centers, AI offers opportunities for customer interaction in service situations. Artificial intelligence-programmed service robots are helpful for superficial behavior. Incarnated robots may greet and converse with customers, but a human touch must also be there in the service area for a satisfying user experience. The additional opportunity to increase productivity and efficiency comes from using artificial intelligence to streamline service activities.

Promotion management includes a variety of activities such as media planning, media scheduling, controlling marketing movements, and search engine optimization. Digital marketing tactics are replacing more traditional tactile ones in advertising. Digital marketing and social media activities have become more popular as a result of the global digital revolution. The client decides the timetable, venue, and content in today's technologically advanced world. Based on user preferences and profiles, AI provides message personalisation and customisation. Content analytics may increase the usefulness and impact of messages. Customer preferences may be tracked in real-time using emotional AI algorithms. Internet-based social media content offers new possibilities for marketers to customise their advertising campaigns to the tastes of their target market.

LITERATURE REVIEW

1. Role of Artificial Intelligence in Modern Finance

Big data technology gives social progress a fresh drive. With the advancement of financial reform, more and more finance data has been included in the big data information database. The growth of digital information poses significant problems to financial advancement and management. The use of big data in sponsorship translates new technology into efficiency, puts an end to the conventional period of artificial Intelligence sessions for accounting generals, heralds the technology age of real-time processes in finance, and modifies the practice manner in finance.

The financial planning division could deliver trustworthy data assessment for firm capital spending and advise companies to improve scientific financial decisions through the measurement of economic big data, enabling businesses to meet the demands of financial expansion and international financial interdependence. Big data analysis of investment breaks down traditional data analysis of finance channels, broadens financial data information channels, and is more favorable to achieving the objective of financial integration (Fernández, 2019).

The development of a big data practice center allows for the collection of comprehensive data from the Internet and hardware assets. The data is chosen, categorized, and analyzed using the management system formed in the financial management information forum, and then the smart data recognition role of big data machinery is used for statistics storing evidence, inquiry, and other in-depth dispensation. Businesses should adopt big data technology management as the foundation of financial managing, alter the notion of business management, achieve a better informational level of financial administration, and enhance the mentoring of data theory and real-world task services for financial organization staff. We will promote data exchange and efficient reserve use, enhance corporate financial management systems, develop a financial management information platform, and fully exploit management's collaborative efforts. To prevent the disclosure of confidential information and individual information in big data analysis, data security must be strengthened.

We begin by outlining some of the major fields of the financial sector where artificial intelligence is having the most influence and adding the most value above conventional methods.

Credit Scoring

Credit scoring is one of the key uses of machine learning in the finance sector. Loaning money is a commercial that many monetary institutions, including big banks and lesser fintech companies, are engaged in. And to achieve it, they must suitably evaluate the creditworthiness of a certain person or business.

Traditionally, analysts would conduct interviews with individuals to obtain the necessary information before making such choices. In contrast to earlier scoring systems, artificial intelligence enables a quicker and more precise evaluation of a potential borrower using more sophisticated techniques. Advanced classification algorithms are then used to calculate the final score, which defines whether the applicant will be granted the loan. These explanatory variables include demographic information, salary, assets, previous creditworthiness, trading history within the same company, and numerous other factors (Waliszewski & Warchlewska, 2020).

The ability for generating impartial judgments is another benefit of AI-based scoring systems; there is no human aspect, includes the mood of the bank worker on a particular day or other things impacting the decision. Additionally, it could help those without a long credit history by enabling them to prove their consistency and capacity to pay back the loan in any case.

Fraud Prevention

One crucial sector where machine learning could have a big impact is fraud detection. Any fraudulent behavior, including credit card fraud, money laundering, etc., is referred to as fraud. Due to the increase in e-popularity, market's growth in the volume of online transactions, and third-party integrations, the former has been expanding tremendously in recent years.

In the past, corporations employed sets of hardcoded rubrics shaped by domain experts to battle deception. The risk comes from impostors learning the rules and then being able to abuse the system, though. AI-based solutions, on the other hand, may change over time and adjust to new patterns discovered in the data, so that is not the case.

Many machine learning algorithms are adept at detecting fraudulent transactions and specialize in anomaly identification. A warning can be triggered by such an algorithm by sorting through hundreds of transaction-related data (the customer's location, historical attitude, expenditure trends, etc.).

The market is constantly looking for improvements, even while many traditional machine learning techniques like regression models, assistance vector machines, and decision tree algorithm may already give adequate results. More sophisticated systems that are better equipped to handle big quantities of information make that possible (the quantity of data and conceivable traits). Given its capacity to handle unstructured data and recognize patterns without a lot of feature engineering, Deep Neural Networks, in addition to Kaggle competition winners like XGBoost or LightGBM, excel in fraud detection (Musleh Al-Sartawi et al., 2022).

Algorithm Trading

The adage "time is money" is perhaps never more true than in trading, as quicker research leads to quicker pattern recognition, which results in better trades and judgments. It is already too late to take action, and the opportunity has passed by the time a pattern is recognized and the market reacts.

That is why so much time and money are spent on algorithmic trading, which involves sophisticated computers that make quick choices and carry out transactions on their own based on recognized patterns. Given that they are not affected by emotions, such algorithms are capable of outperforming human traders by a wide margin. According to research by Mordor Intelligence, between 60 and 73% of all US equities trades were handled by AI-supported systems in 2020 (Lewinson, 2022).

Automated trading platforms from several fields incorporate contemporary breakthroughs in machine learning techniques. While some of these systems may concentrate on making (quite good) predictions about asset returns, other elements may take a more conservative approach depends on econometrics and asset division theory.

Utilizing alternate data sources to outperform rivals is a strategy that is getting a lot of momentum right now. The most recent approaches in Natural Language Processing (NLP) enable effective emotion detection from bases includes news articles, Twitter, Reddit, etc. The advancements in object recognition can help in the examination of satellite photos (Horowitz et al., 2018).

Individual data science practitioners who strive to create their trading platforms, either on their local PCs or in the cloud, are becoming more and more interested in algorithmic trading. More and more individuals are prepared to give it a try as a result of recent modifications in how simple it is to make trades and the expanding accessibility of various brokers' APIs.

Data scientists can also take part in data science challenges, where the objective is to forecast stock market returns using the supplied data and possibly other, alternative data. The business might be characterized as an AI-driven hedge fund that collects the forecasts made by participants and allows them to profit from Numeraire's earnings.

Robo-Advisory

More individuals are becoming fascinated with passive funds as a result of how inflation is impacting our savings and the reality that it is no longer beneficial to retain money in a savings account. And this is precisely the situation where Robo-advisors are useful. They are financial advisory services where AI compiles portfolio suggestions based on the unique goals (short- and long-term), risk attitudes, and disposable income of the investors. Everything is taken care of for the investor; they just need to choose the assets to invest in, buy them, and then maybe rebalance the portfolio after some time. The investor simply needs to deposit the cash each month (or automate the transfer). All of those things are done to make sure the client is headed in the greatest direction for success.

The key benefits of these systems are that they are simple for clients to use and don't require any financial expertise. Naturally, price is a significant factor as well; Robo-advisors are frequently less expensive than hiring a human asset manager (Trivedi and Patel, 2020).

Personalized Banking Experience

The banking sector is making an effort to employ AI to provide each consumer with a tailored banking experience. One possible example is chatbots, which are becoming more difficult to differentiate from actual human advisors. They can comprehend the customer's purpose and try to steer them in the appropriate route using cutting-edge NLP approaches. They might assist users with changing their passwords, checking their balances, scheduling transactions, etc.

Additionally, these chatbots frequently can detect the consumer's emotions and modify their response accordingly. To try to address the matter as quickly as possible and prevent additional aggravation, it would sound right to link the customer to a human adviser if they see that they are furious. Smart chatbots' expanding capabilities also make it possible to cut costs by lightening the strain on contact centers.

But there are other personalized financial experiences than chatbots. Numerous organizations use the huge amounts of information they possess to study the spending habits of the public and offer specialized financial counsel that may aid in the achievement of their objectives. These services may include suggestions for lowering monthly spending or even helping the client see those expenditures in a clear, understandable manner, such as the three areas where you spent the greatest amount this month. The institutions may also inform you if there are recurrent transfers scheduled for your account but insufficient funds are now available. All of those services are only the top of what modern financial institutions can offer their clients (Manta, 2020).

Process Automation

Finally, AI has a lot to offer in terms of automation. The efficiency of repetitive, time-consuming operations that were previously managed by staff can be greatly improved by using sophisticated optical character recognition (OCR). Digitizing papers, completing forms, or retrieving relevant data from papers are a few examples.

For the KYC (Know Your Customer) procedure, many financial firms either utilize specialized software or develop in-house solutions. To prevent fraud, it is common in the financial industry to demand some sort of ID. The procedure is made incredibly simple by many neo-brokers and fintech firms; all you have to do is use your phone to scan your ID, followed by a selfie to confirm that it matches the ID. An AI-based approach looks for a match in the backdrop while also ensuring that the ID is authentic and that the picture does not include anything unsettling. Deep Learning and architectures like Convolutional Neural Networks (CNNs) exhibit highly promising results when applied to photos.

Role of Artificial Intelligence in Sustainable Marketing

History's profit-driven environment forces marketers to often achieve really high standards. Over my more than seven years as a marketers in the market, people frequently found themselves drawn into the realm of profit, profit, and more profit.

The "rewards" that managers get for reaching certain objectives help to highlight the profit-centric nature of conventional marketing even more. But as the public becomes more aware of business sustainability, advertisers are beginning to question the traditional approach to marketing.

Advertising and company go hand in hand, thus they are significant. Marketing is engaged in every stage of a company, from ideation to manufacture to selling. Venders are every business's strongest evangelists and spokespersons. People marketing experience has been intriguing. People are expert in digital marketing, and They have found great satisfaction in assisting companies in building their brands online (Raiter, 2021).

Numerous changes or shifts in marketing have been observed globally throughout the innovation. The change we're making to sustainable marketing is what I've discovered to be most important. Given the usually alarming effects of corporations on society and the environment, a more sustainable marketing strategy is necessary. If consumers adopt a culture of waste or choose to make more environmentally friendly purchases, it has a significant impact on marketers.

The need to boost corporate impact has never been more urgent. For many entrepreneurs, choosing not to use sustainable marketing is no longer an option. A new approach is necessary for the world. However, one must be aware of what sustainability marketing comprises and how it ties into the greater sustainability framework before partaking in it.

One of the most trustworthy descriptions of sustainability is provided by the World Council on Economic Development (WCED) is "development that serves the requirements of young ones without sacrificing the needs of future generations (Sustainable Development, 2023)". The three main sectors of economic, environmental, and social growth are frequently shown together. To combat poverty, businesses should increase income while preserving the environment. This calls for long-term thinking and taking into account ideas like social fairness, natural resource conservation, and human rights.

Although knowledge is beneficial, practice is superior. To an outsider, assigning a marketer the task of engaging in sustainable marketing may seem straightforward. Sustainable marketing tactics sometimes take a back seat when managers and CEOs are expecting to hear how much money they made in the previous quarter at an executive meeting.

And for that reason, implementing sustainable marketing should be done gradually. Marketers can't always entirely shift an organization's course in one single stroke, but there are methods to guide them in the direction of sustainable marketing (Nahr et al., 2021).

According to marketing expert Richard Varey, marketing communication is "a cultural activity that has a cultural relevance" (Varey, 2002). One of a marketer's most effective tools is the brand message. Imagine a future where marketers use their superpowers to influence customer behavior by developing branding and marketing that encourage customers to make more environmentally friendly purchases.

The ability to observe how the marketing techniques contributed to affect consumer behavior and foster new consuming cultures is one of the most interesting aspects of being a marketer. Investigating how to use marketing communications to raise your spirits more sustainable social activities is a great place to start when involved sustainable marketing.

In marketing, artificial intelligence is a significant area. It is referred described as the advertising industry's ultimate horizon. Given its broad definition, "artificial intelligence" has been applied to characterise a wide range of technologies. Anything that attempts to mimic human intelligence is referred to as artificial intelligence. Artificial intelligence includes a broad range of abilities, like voice, photo identification, computer vision, and keyword queries. Marketers love to wax eloquent about cutting-edge, contemporary technology. They use artificial intelligence for voice and image identification. Furthermore, it facilitates drones monitoring of remote areas and prevents advertising data leakage (Ahmed et al., 2021).

Traditional marketing strategies, such as outbound marketing initiatives, are no longer as effective at gaining and keeping clients. Artificial intelligence is essential to achieving a sustainable competitive edge in a constantly linked, real-time world where advertisers must deliver continual, personalised, insight-driven client interactions on a per-individual level. Products that have involved artificial intelligence and implemented the appropriate schemes for scaling are effective in establishing a competitive edge that is very challenging to match. Artificial intelligence is about providing the ideal mixture of material and perspective, not about technology.

METHODOLOGY

The current research paper uses investigative methods to conduct an exploratory study. To accomplish effective, sustainable investments in financial markets and sustainable marketing, this fundamental and qualitative research seeks to uncover and promote managing new financial approaches through digital technologies and artificial intelligence. The paper seeks to promote cutting-edge methods for creating financial systems by utilizing smart cities, artificial intelligence, and blending facilities in modern finance and marketing. The goal of the study paper is to demonstrate how artificial intelligence may be used to combine finance and market sustainability with technological advancements, speed up the digital transformation of finance, and reduce human error while creating a more secure commercial and economic environment.

DISCUSSION

Businesses that provide exceptional customer experiences will benefit from the Fourth Industrial Revolution, in which intelligence will rule supreme. The organisation is thought to be taking integrated data about clients and products throughout all networks and products in the Fourth Industrial Revolution to better comprehend its end-user awareness and visibility via all purposeful areas. AI has been important in large data analytics for forecasting and delivering guided engagements that satisfy user prospects. The authors offer a thorough viewpoint on applying AI to regain client experience through this study (Mogaji et al., 2020). Using AI and analytical insights is the key to creating customer experiences that foster loyalty and long-term customers. Event-based architectures, along with AI and predictive analytics, are the way of the future. There is no set destination as we enter the Fourth Industrial Revolution, but all businesses must set out on their trip.

Disruptive technologies like the internet of things, big data analytics, blockchain, and artificial intelligence have changed how businesses operate today. The most recent problematic technology, artificial intelligence (AI), has enormous potential for the industrial, pharmaceutical, healthcare, agricultural, logistical, and digital marketing sectors. Many professionals and educators are looking throughout the world for the best AI solutions that their businesses may use. However, there is a lack of bibliometric data that demonstrates a detailed research pattern for AI in marketing (Chintalapati & Pandey, 2021).

AI has the potential to significantly increase corporate productivity. This encompasses the emergence of digital platforms, the acceleration of technological diffusion, and the convergence of many technologies. AI is predictable to meaningfully reduce costs by mechanizing all vital company processes, counting account management, marketing, accounting, and human resource management. For example, the luxurious process of studying dozens of applicant profiles all through staff recruitment can be automatic by utilizing AI technology. AI is essential to data analytics and performance assessment. With the help of AI, marketers can monitor the success of their campaigns, from general messaging to specific social media posts. By utilising thousands of data points, marketers can optimize their set of measures in accordance with the goals and metrics that are important to the company.

The time it receipts to hire somebody can be abridged from ten weeks to two, and the time it takings to select applicants can be condensed from two to almost instantly. Moreover, AI can replace the labor-intensive human assessment of financial records or inventory, subsequent in important cost reductions. For example, the automation of accounting facilities in Brazil is predictable to reduce the cost of bureaucracy faced by medium-sized businesses, such as tax filing costs. These progressions are probably successful to spur the growth of informal businesses, which can explanation for up to two-thirds of the GDP in some lower-income nations.

Marketing teams struggle to analyze the vast amounts of data that arrive every second and draw conclusions from them. Using predictive analytics, which uses a variety of machine-learning algorithms, models, and databases to forecast future behavior, AI enables marketing organizations to make the most of the data. For marketing teams, being able to predict what kinds of things consumers will be shopping for and when can help them position advertisements more effectively. Marketers who use predictive marketing analytics can better understand what customers are saying, believing, and thinking about their products and brands in real-time (Mogaji & Nguyen, 2021).

Since customers want businesses to comprehend and meet their requirements and expectations, Businesses may better understand their target market and personalise the consumer experience with the help of AI marketing. AI enables data processing at a rate many times faster than human communication, ensures accuracy and security, and frees teams to focus on tactical objectives to build successful AI-powered movements. Due to AI's ability to fold and track strategic data in real-time, marketers may make decisions now rather than wait until the movement has come to an end. They may select what to do next, assembling the options in an intelligent and objective manner based on the data-driven reports.

Founded on AL models' dimensions to recognize signals and seize fundamental relationships in big data, AI methods are used in investment administration and the buy-side activity of the industry for investment collection and investment policies, as well as for the optimization of operational workflows and risk management. Superior investment firms or asset firms with the means to invest in such technology may be the only ones allowed to deploy AI approaches. When used to trading, AI upsurges the difficulty of traditional algorithmic interchange since the algorithms uninterruptedly develop into computer-programmed that can classify and fulfil trades without human intervention as they learn from data inputs.

With minimal market impact, AI algorithms can increase liquidity management and the execution of large orders in highly digital markets, such as equities and FX marketplaces, by improving size, length, and order size in some sort of dynamic manner based on market conditions. To speed up execution and generate efficacies, traders can also use AI for risk assessment and order flow administration (Pau, 1991). Similar to non-AI models and algos, a high number of finance professionals using the same Ml techniques could perhaps principal to herding behavior and one-way marketplaces, increasing jeopardies for system liquidity and steadiness, especially under pressure.

Although AI Algo trading can boost liquidity in normal circumstances, it can also result in convergence and, as a result, in periods of illiquidity and flash crashes during stressful situations. Large simultaneous sales or purchases could enhance market volatility and open up new security risks. Convergence of trading methods raises the possibility of self-perpetuating feedback loops, which may therefore result in abrupt price changes. Convergence also makes it easier for attackers to persuade agents operating similarly, which raises the danger of cyberattacks.

All forms of algorithmic trading carry the aforementioned dangers, but using AI magnifies them due to its learning capacity and dynamic adapting to altering situations in a completely autonomous way. AI models, for instance, can recognize signals, comprehend the effects of driving, alter their behavior, and learn to forge ahead based on the simplest of signals. It is tricky to mitigate these risks due to the complexity of AI algorithms and models and the difficulty in understanding and replicating their decision-making processes. If there is machine cooperation, AI approaches could exacerbate unlawful trading performs intended to effect the markets and create it harder for supervisors to spot such performs. Self-learning and deep-learning AI models' dynamic adaptive characteristics enable this (Verma et al., 2021). These models have the capacity to understand how they are interdependent on one another and adapt to the behaviour and actions of other market participants or other AI models, potentially leading to a collusive outcome without any human intervention and possibly even without the user being aware of it.

AI lending models may inferior credit underwriting costs and make it easier to spread credit to consumers with "thin file" histories, potentially hopeful financial inclusion. The usage of AI can increase data dispensation efficiency for the evaluation of potential borrowers' trustworthiness, enhance the decision-making procedure for underwriting, and boost lending portfolio administration. Additionally, it may be possible to offer creditworthiness to clients who have the little credit history or who have been "unscored," facilitating the funding of SMEs and perhaps advancing access to financial services for underbanked groups. Despite having huge promise, AI-based models and the usage of inadequate data (such as those about race or gender) in lending might upsurge the risk of unequal effect on credit results and the possibility of biased, biased, or unjust loaning. AI-driven models not only unintentionally create or maintain biases, but they also make it more challenging to identify discrimination in credit distribution and make it challenging to interpret and explain the model's results to rejected potential borrowers. Credit provided by BigTech that takes advantage of their contact to enormous amounts of client data exacerbates these problems, raising concerns about potential anti-competitive behavior and market structure in the technology area of facility offering (e.g. cloud).

The application of AI approaches to block chain-based finance may increase the competence improvements that may be achieved in DLT-based systems and expand the functionality of smart contracts. By enabling the fundamental code to be constantly efficient in response to market conditions, AI can boost the autonomy of smart contracts. The usage of AI in DLT systems also adds, if not intensifies, difficulties with traditional investment instruments based on AI, including trouble in overseeing networks and platforms created on impervious AI models and a lack of understandability of AI decision-making mechanisms. Currently, AI is primarily used to identify coding errors and manage risks associated with smart contracts. However, it should be emphasized that contracts have been around for a very long time and only require basic software code, predating the development of AI applications. Many of the alleged advantages of the use of AI in DLT systems are currently only theoretical, and the majority of smart contracts that are used in a practical sense have no connection to AI methods (Xie, 2019).

RECOMMENDATIONS

By enhancing the excellence of services provided and providing competences for financial service workers, the expanded implementation of AI in financial products can offer significant benefits to financial customers and market participants. In addition, AI-based applications in finance may create new difficulties (such as those involving a lack of explainability) or increase dangers already present in the financial marketplaces (e.g. related to data management and use). The use of AI in finance must be in line with advancing financial stability, safeguarding financial consumers, and advancing market integrity and effectiveness, according to regulators and regulators. To encourage and promote the use of accountable AI, emerging dangers from the deployment of intelligent systems need to be detected and mitigated. To solve a number of the alleged mismatches of current preparations with AI applications, existing supervisory and regulatory criteria may need to be explained and occasionally changed.

Dependent on the importance of the use and the potential influence on the customer, regulatory and oversight requirements for AI approaches could be examined within a background and proportionate framework. This is probably going to promote AI use while not needlessly restricting innovation. To strengthen consumer protection through AI applications in finance, policymakers should think about focusing more intently on greater data management by financial sector enterprises. Privacy protection, personal privacy, information concentration, and potential effects on the industry's competitive dynamics are a few of the most significant risks mentioned in this note. Other risks include the potential for accidental bias and judgement against certain sections of the population as well as data points (Chen et al., 2012). Data is crucial for ML model training, validation, and evaluation as well as determining how well these models can continue to forecast the future in the face of extreme events.

The adoption of specific requirements or best practices for data management in AI-based approaches could be reflected in policymaking. These could have to do with the accuracy of the data, the suitability of the dataset chosen in light of the intended application of the AI model, and safeguards that guarantee the model's resilience in terms of avoiding potential biases. Two examples of best practices to reduce the danger of discrimination include appropriate sense examination of model results against benchmark datasets and additional tests based on whether restricted classes may be derived from other attributes in the data. The verification of the model's variables' suitability could eliminate a source of potential biases (Vlačić et al., 2021). Conceptual drifts could be tracked and corrected using tools that could be created. Authorities may take into account imposing additional transparency requirements and opt-out choices for the usage of individual data.

The application of AI approaches in the delivery of monetary services, which may have an impact on the client outcome, might be disclosed, and policymakers might adopt disclosure regulations. For banking consumers to make educated decisions between competing products, they must be aware of the usage of Techniques in the product delivery process as well as any prospective interactions with an AI system rather than a human being. Such disclosure should clearly state the capabilities and constraints of the AI system. Authorities may take into account introducing suitability standards for AI-driven financial services, comparable to those that apply to the selling of investment produces. These conditions would make it easier for financial service providers to decide whether potential customers have a clear knowledge of how the usage of AI marks the product distribution process (Huang & Rust, 2020).

The alleged inconsistency of AI's lack of comprehensibility with current laws and regulations should be addressed by regulators. To address the issues brought on by the usage of AI-based models, financial services businesses may need to keep informed and modify the frameworks already in use for classic governance and risk management. Superintendents may need to shift their attention from the documentary evidence of the model's development phase and how it arrives at its predictions of expected and actual results, and they may want to look into more technical approaches to risk management, like argumentative model pressure testing or outcome-based metrics (Gensler and Bailey, 2020).

To assist the foster trust in AI-driven systems, policymakers can reflect mandating transparent model authority outlines and ascribing accountability to people. To strengthen current arrangements for activities that involve AI, financial facilities workers may need to establish explicit governance frameworks that precisely outline lines of accountability for the development and misinterpretation of AI-based system applications across the whole of their lifespan, from development to implementation. Internal model governance outlines may need to be modified to better account for the risks associated with AI use, as well as to include targeted consumer goals and a determination of if and how such results are achieved utilizing AI technologies. The proper certification and check trails of the aforementioned steps might help supervisors monitor such activities.

Future academics will face new strategic imperatives when semantic information and machine learning for deeper consumer insights are developed. Algorithms for reasoning that are psychologically motivated and inspired by the brain would increase the predictability of customer behavior. Intelligent sentiment mining systems will be created using a combination of engineering techniques and psychological theories speaking the cognitive and moving needs of customers. In the future, improved sentiment classification will be possible thanks to hybrid machine learning algorithms (Tripathy et al., 2016). The use of AI in marketing will increase with the development of optimization models based on current advertising theories.

The complexity and precision of projected behavior are increased by the obvious and concealed use of emotional jargons on social media. Linguistic decorations for deep education may aid in the detection of sarcasm and enhance the predictability of sentiment. Future researchers would benefit from the development of small computer transcript and anaphora resolution for dealing with dynamic sentiment investigation (Poria et al., 2015). Knowledge-based systems' marketplace suitability is increased through co-creation, thus future researchers should work to develop cooperative market intelligence. For large data sentiment analysis using Twitter datasets, upcoming researchers should focus on high-inflection languages and reflect emotive lexicons (Giatsoglou et al., 2017).

CONCLUSION

The digital revolution is transforming how people work, live, and communicate. The development and ongoing advancement of digital technology have had a significant impact on the transition occurring within the telecommunications business. Among them is artificial intelligence. It is a modern technological advancement that, when used in conjunction with industrial technology, aids in overcoming numerous human faults and outperforming human performance in various domains. IT software is getting better at object detection and outpacing people in terms of scalability. Speech recognition algorithms may now be able to identify the language of phone conversations and voicemails with an accuracy on par with that of humans. A straight phone app makes it possible to translate across languages in real time.

Straight connections to Google Maps or other search engines are thinkable with glasses. These are all already a part of our daily life. Solutions based on artificial intelligence have the potential to significantly alter fields as diverse and important as schooling, science, medicine, finance, accountancy, auditing, and transportation and energy. It is a foundational technology rather than a single technology. Systems based on artificial intelligence can also promote regional development that is speedy, viable, and sustainable (Davenport et al., 2019). Regional economic imbalances that exist around the globe can be significantly reduced. Because of this, artificial intelligence can assist in effectively implementing regional development policy goals, regardless of the geographic location, the language that is spoken, or the primary industry sectors. To improve business operations and openness and raise the market's standing in the eyes of investors, public authorities in many nations and areas mandate the use of XBRL.

Based on the results we discovered, we discovered that almost all of the participants are in favor of using AI in advertising and assume its expertise to complete the work in higher quality and speed as well as its inevitable momentum of replacing the majority of human jobs, including factory workers, truck drivers, and many other jobs that do not require innovative thinking. Additionally, there aren't many differences in the views of participants from various backgrounds; almost all of them valued and valued AI in marketing more than they did issues or worries. Therefore, it is very important for us to investigate and learn about the benefits of marketing that are made possible by AI.

The economic sector with the biggest potential for growth has been identified as the marketing industry. It is a place where development is possible, particularly through technology. Modern technology has improved efficiency as marketing strategies have grown and changed through time. Thanks to technical improvements that allow companies to harvest vast quantities of items and use digital marketing to increase sectors' prospects to promote and wholesale products to customers, digital marketing has the prospective to have a noteworthy impact on people.

Moreover, the fusion of big data and academic study of smart apps has led to innovations in digital marketing. As a result, information about each person and their interests are kept on file for use during marketing activities. This study sought to ascertain the advantages of digital marketing, namely the use of market artificial intelligence and automation to enhance market outcomes (Huang & Rust, 2020). The impact of digital marketing on business performance was also taken into account. According to the survey, market automation and artificial technology have a favorable effect on digital marketing. As with any sort of technology, a substantial improvement was seen in the marketing firms under investigation, and the findings were consistent with prior research (Rust, 2020). Marketers have high expectations that automation will gradually replace the majority of marketing processes and that AI will continue to develop automation parameters. Today's marketers are eager to learn new ways to make digital marketing more effective so they can speak directly to every client and understand their needs.

Finding out how AI is used in digital marketing and what results from it will shed light on this technology and its present uses. The results of this study will shed additional light on the advantages of market automation and AI technology in the marketing industry. Explaining how artificial intelligence is used to sell to customers and achieve marketing purposes is essential given the expansion of online businesses throughout the world and the increasing usage of digital marketing by firms to promote their goods and services. The results demonstrate that AI is the cutting-edge technique of marketing, which sorts digital marketing operative. Digital marketers who employ AI have reported significant advancements in their marketing tactics. In order to stay competitive and support successful business outcomes, marketing managers must now grasp the competences of artificial intelligence.

The development of technology in marketing systems and structures is essential for the forthcoming of marketing. The marketing industry is predicted to be fully taken over by AI technology in order to produce experiences that are specifically suited for each customer and propel marketing to absurdly high levels. Since artificial intelligence and market automation are becoming increasingly common, every marketing manager should want to implement them into their systems. The economic impact of AI technology is anticipated to increase Gross domestic product through investment returns. With the gradual replacement of human marketing jobs like communication by technology, other tasks are becoming simpler to complete and more effective. Every consumer interacts with the AI in the most human way possible thanks to the virtual assistant's mode of operation. While this development should be properly watched, it is evident that digital marketing is steadily improving.

By providing automatic credit scoring based on operators' online information, asset advice-giving, and trade using monetary data, or insurance guaranteeing, AI may one day facilitate decentralized applications in decentralized finance (or "Defi"). The construction of fully autonomous chains might theoretically be achieved by AI-based contracts that seem to be self-learned1 and alter dynamically without human involvement. By substituting directly on-chain AI inference for off-chain third-party information providers, the adoption of AI could encourage greater disintermediation.

However, it should be emphasized that AI-based structures may not always solve the "garbage in, garbage out" problem or the issue of inadequate or poor-quality data contributions seen in blockchain-based systems. Depending on the magnitude of the DeFi market, this in turn creates considerable dangers for investors, marketplace integrity, and system stability. The multiple dangers present in the DeFi marketplace could also be amplified by AI. Without a single controlling access point or supremacy framework that chains accountability and obedience with oversight standards, autonomous DeFi networks would become even more difficult to regulate. With cumulative cross-disciplinary influences and synthesis of AI, data science, machine knowledge, finance, and marketing, AI in finance has been an important research way over decades. With the rapid development of new age group AI and data science and their applicability to varied financial applications, this trend has been further strengthened in recent years. The part of artificial intelligence in modern finance and sustainable marketing are presented in-depth and densely in this review. We examine and offer commentary on the data-driven approaches used in financial applications in particular. The review also sparks conversation about the unresolved problems, potential future prospects. This review heavily draws from other similar studies that only concentrate on particular AI techniques or money-related issues.

REFERENCES

Ahmad, T., Zhang, D., Huang, C., Zhang, H., Dai, N., Song, Y., & Chen, H. (2021). Artificial intelligence in the sustainable energy industry: Status Quo, challenges, and opportunities. *Journal of Cleaner Production, 289*, 125834. doi:10.1016/j.jclepro.2021.125834

Chen, C., Chiang, & Storey. (2012). Business Intelligence and Analytics: From Big Data to Big Impact. *Management Information Systems Quarterly, 36*(4), 1165. doi:10.2307/41703503

Chintalapati, S., & Pandey, S. K. (2021). Artificial intelligence in marketing: A systematic literature review. *International Journal of Market Research, 64*(1), 38–68. doi:10.1177/14707853211018428

Corporate Finance Institute. (2022). *Machine Learning (in Finance)*. https://corporatefinanceinstitute.com/resources/data-science/machine-learning-in-finance/

Davenport, T., Guha, A., Grewal, D., & Bressgott, T. (2019). How artificial intelligence will change the future of marketing. *Journal of the Academy of Marketing Science, 48*(1), 24–42. doi:10.100711747-019-00696-0

Dayan, A. (2021). *4 Practical Ways to Use AI in Marketing (& Why You Need To)*. Business 2 Community. https://www.business2community.com/online-marketing/4-practical-ways-to-use-ai-in-marketing-why-you-need-to-02420037

Dwivedi, Y. K., Ismagilova, E., Hughes, D. H., Carlson, J., Filieri, R., Jacobson, J., Jain, V., Karjaluoto, H., Kefi, H., Krishen, A. S., Kumar, V., Rahman, M. M., Raman, R., Rauschnabel, P. A., Rowley, J., Salo, J., Tran, G. A., & Wang, Y. (2021). Setting the future of digital and social media marketing research: Perspectives and research propositions. *International Journal of Information Management, 59*, 102168. doi:10.1016/j.ijinfomgt.2020.102168

Fernández, A. (2019). Artificial intelligence in financial services. *Banco de Espana Article, 3*, 19.

Gensler, G., & Bailey, L. (2020). Deep Learning and Financial Stability. SSRN *Electronic Journal*. doi:10.2139/ssrn.3723132

Giatsoglou, M., Vozalis, M. G., Diamantaras, K., Vakali, A., Sarigiannidis, G., & Chatzisavvas, K. C. (2017). Sentiment analysis leveraging emotions and word embeddings. *Expert Systems with Applications, 69*, 214–224. doi:10.1016/j.eswa.2016.10.043

Horowitz, M. C., Allen, G. C., Saravalle, E., Cho, A., Frederick, K., & Scharre, P. (2018). *Artificial intelligence and international security*. Center for a New American Security.

Huang, M. H., & Rust, R. T. (2020). A strategic framework for artificial intelligence in marketing. *Journal of the Academy of Marketing Science, 49*(1), 30–50. doi:10.100711747-020-00749-9

Lewinson, E. (2022, January 5). Artificial Intelligence in Finance: Opportunities and Challenges. *Medium*. https://towardsdatascience.com/artificial-intelligence-in-finance-opportunities-and-challenges-cee94f2f3858

Lin, T. C. (2016). Compliance, technology, and modern finance. *Brook. J. Corp. Fin. & Com. L., 11*, 159.

Lin, T. C. (2019). Artificial intelligence, finance, and the law. *Fordham Law Review, 88*, 531.

Manta, O. (2020). Financing and Fiscality in the context of artificial intelligence at the global level. *European Journal of Marketing and Economics, 3*(1), 39–62. doi:10.26417/ejme.v3i1.p31-47

Mogaji, E., & Nguyen, N. P. (2021). Managers' understanding of artificial intelligence in relation to marketing financial services: Insights from a cross-country study. *International Journal of Bank Marketing, 40*(6), 1272–1298. doi:10.1108/IJBM-09-2021-0440

Mogaji, E., Soetan, T. O., & Kieu, T. A. (2020). The implications of artificial intelligence on the digital marketing of financial services to vulnerable customers. *Australasian Marketing Journal, 29*(3), 235–242. doi:10.1016/j.ausmj.2020.05.003

Moloi, T., & Marwala, T. (2020). *Artificial intelligence in economics and finance theories*. Springer. doi:10.1007/978-3-030-42962-1

Murgai, A. (2018). Transforming digital marketing with artificial intelligence. International Journal of Latest Technology in Engineering, Management &. *Applied Sciences (Basel, Switzerland), 7*(4), 259–262.

Musleh Al-Sartawi, A. M., Hussainey, K., & Razzaque, A. (2022). The role of artificial intelligence in sustainable finance. *Journal of Sustainable Finance & Investment*, 1–6. doi:10.1080/20430795.2022.2057405

Nahr, J. G., Nozari, H., & Sadeghi, M. E. (2021). Green supply chain based on the artificial intelligence of things (IoT). *International Journal of Innovation in Management, Economics, and Social Sciences*, *1*(2), 56–63.

Pau, L. (1991). Artificial intelligence and financial services. *IEEE Transactions on Knowledge and Data Engineering*, *3*(2), 137–148. doi:10.1109/69.87994

Poria, S., Cambria, E., Hussain, A., & Huang, G. B. (2015). Towards an intelligent framework for multimodal affective data analysis. *Neural Networks*, *63*, 104–116. doi:10.1016/j.neunet.2014.10.005 PMID:25523041

Raiter, O. (2021). Segmentation of Bank Consumers for Artificial Intelligence Marketing. *International Journal of Contemporary Financial Issues*, *1*(1), 39–54.

Rust, R. T. (2020). The future of marketing. *International Journal of Research in Marketing*, *37*(1), 15–26. doi:10.1016/j.ijresmar.2019.08.002

Sustainable Development. (2023). International Institute for Sustainable Development. https://www.iisd.org/mission-and-goals/sustainable-development

Tripathy, A., Agrawal, A., & Rath, S. K. (2016). Classification of sentiment reviews using n-gram machine learning approach. *Expert Systems with Applications*, *57*, 117–126. doi:10.1016/j.eswa.2016.03.028

Trivedi, S., & Patel, N. (2020). The Role of Automation and Artificial Intelligence in Increasing the Sales Volume: Evidence from M, S, and, MM Regressions. *SSRN*, *3*(2), 1–19. doi:10.2139srn.4180379

Varey, R. J. (2002). Marketing communication: Principles and practice. *Routledge eBooks*. https://ci.nii.ac.jp/ncid/BA5525018X

Verma, S., Sharma, R., Deb, S., & Maitra, D. (2021). Artificial intelligence in marketing: Systematic review and future research direction. *International Journal of Information Management Data Insights*, *1*(1), 100002. doi:10.1016/j.jjimei.2020.100002

Vlačić, B., Corbo, L., Costa e Silva, S., & Dabić, M. (2021). The evolving role of artificial intelligence in marketing: A review and research agenda. *Journal of Business Research*, *128*, 187–203. doi:10.1016/j.jbusres.2021.01.055

Waliszewski, K., & Warchlewska, A. (2020). Attitudes towards artificial intelligence in the area of personal financial planning: A case study of selected countries. *Entrepreneurship and Sustainability Issues*, *8*(2), 399–420. doi:10.9770/jesi.2020.8.2(24)

Wang, N., Liu, Y., Liu, Z., & Huang, X. (2020, June). Application of artificial intelligence and big data in modern financial management. In *2020 International Conference on Artificial Intelligence and Education (ICAIE)* (pp. 85-87). IEEE. 10.1109/ICAIE50891.2020.00027

Xie, M. (2019). Development of Artificial Intelligence and Effects on Financial System. *Journal of Physics: Conference Series*, *1187*(3), 032084. doi:10.1088/1742-6596/1187/3/032084

Yigitcanlar, T., & Cugurullo, F. (2020). The sustainability of artificial intelligence: An urbanistic viewpoint from the lens of smart and sustainable cities. *Sustainability (Basel)*, *12*(20), 8548. doi:10.3390u12208548

Chapter 20
Why Do We Need Sustainable Digital Marketing?

Nino Tchanturia
Guram Tavartkiladze Tbilisi Teaching University, Georgia

Rusudan Dalakishvili
Davit Agmashenebeli National Defence Academy of Georgia, Georgia

ABSTRACT

The conventional approach to business is not eco-friendly, and as the issue of climate change intensifies, consumers are becoming increasingly aware of the environmental impact of their preferred companies. Therefore, businesses need to evaluate their impact on the environment. Consumers are becoming more informed about how their purchases affect the environment and more selective about which companies they buy from. According to a survey by IBM, 57% of respondents are willing to alter their buying habits to decrease environmental impact. People want to contribute to ecological preservation, and one way to do so is by using their purchasing power. As a company, it is crucial to provide customers with the opportunity to support environmental sustainability by purchasing your products. This is where sustainable marketing can be beneficial.

INTRODUCTION

In order to communicate with customers and demonstrate environmentally friendly production, companies must use a sustainable digital marketing plan. Which means, on the one hand, offering sustainable marketing and satisfying customers and businesses in ways that protect the environment, and on the other hand, using digital marketing, digital tactics, and channels to connect with customers, since customers spend the most time in the digital world.

Sustainable marketing is a component of sustainable development, which is confirmed by the World Commission's Brundtland Report as development that meets the needs of the present in order to meet the needs of future generations. The goal of sustainable marketing is to maintain productivity and efficiency by substituting resources with more valuable alternatives to avoid harming ecosystems or impacting natural resources (Kortam & Mahrous, 2020).

DOI: 10.4018/978-1-6684-8681-8.ch020

Sustainable marketing is seen as a component of the broader field of sustainable development because of its impact on promoting sustainability (Essam & Mahrous, 2019).

The Earth is facing various environmental and social problems such as ecosystem degradation, endangered species, global warming, and resource depletion. Today's development is not sustainable, humanity must adopt a new paradigm of sustainable development that integrates economic, social, and environmental dimensions and meets the needs of present and future generations. A green economy that focuses on sustainable production and consumption patterns can address these challenges by incorporating social and environmental considerations into everyday economic activity. Such an approach can improve overall welfare and equity (Danciu & Marketing, 2013).

Marketing has been a part of the problem of creating unsustainable habits but can also be a part of the solution by making sustainable alternatives desirable. Sustainable marketing can foster more sustainable levels and patterns of consumption by creating sustainable value for consumers while respecting social and environmental limits. The current development pattern based on excessive production and consumption has negative consequences on the economy, society, and environment, necessitating a shift towards sustainable development (Danciu & Marketing, 2013).

The evolution of marketing and sustainability over several decades, with the term "sustainable marketing" being introduced only recently. Marketing has evolved from a product-driven approach to a consumer-centric focus, and now we are witnessing the emergence of a value-driven era, Marketing 3.0. The current socio-economic landscape is shaped by technology and globalization, and consumers expect organizations to provide solutions that make the world a better place to live. Despite contributing to economic growth, marketing has also attracted considerable criticism (Seretny & Seretny, 2012).

The fundamental principle of sustainable marketing is to minimize the harmful impact on the environment while creating lasting value for consumers and society by promoting socially and environmentally responsible products, services, and practices. In today's world, consumers are increasingly concerned about environmental and social issues and are looking for products and services that align with their values. Sustainable marketing offers companies a way to satisfy their needs, as well as promote the brand and build a positive reputation (Rotschedl & Čermáková, 2014).

One of the main principles of sustainable marketing is an emphasis on transparency and honesty. Companies that implement sustainable marketing should be open and transparent, including in terms of environmental impact and social responsibility. Another important aspect of sustainable marketing is the use or production of environmentally friendly products and services. Companies can develop products that are made from sustainable materials, such as recycled or biodegradable materials. They can also offer services that promote sustainability, such as energy-efficient appliances or green transportation (Pogrebova, Konnikov, & Yuldasheva, 2017).

In addition to environmentally friendly products and services, sustainable marketing also includes the use of green advertising. This may include promoting the environmental benefits of a product or service, using sustainable messaging and imagery in advertisements, or highlighting a company's commitment to sustainability (Katrandjiev, n.d.).

Sustainable marketing focuses on long-term impact. Companies that implement sustainable marketing practices must ensure that throughout the life cycle of their products or services, from production to disposal, the impact on the environment and society is not negative. to consider their activities in terms of sustainability (Pogrebova et al., 2017).

The usage of sustainable packaging is one illustration of sustainable marketing. To lessen their influence on the environment, several businesses employ packing materials that decompose or can be composted. For instance, several food businesses employ disposable and biodegradable bamboo or sugarcane packaging.

Another example of sustainable marketing is the use of environmentally friendly raw materials. For example, some clothing brands use recycled plastic bottles or other sustainable materials. They can also use eco-friendly paints or water-saving techniques to reduce their environmental impact.

Sustainable marketing can also involve social responsibility. Companies that implement sustainable marketing practices can donate a portion of their profits to environmental or social causes, or support local communities through volunteer work or charitable donations (Gordon, Carrigan, & Hastings, 2011).

One potential challenge for companies implementing sustainable marketing strategies is cost. Sustainable activities can cost more than traditional ones, which can affect the company. However, many companies find that the long-term benefits of sustainable marketing, including improved brand reputation and customer loyalty, outweigh the initial costs (Osburg, Davies, Yoganathan, & McLeay, 2021).

Therefore, sustainable marketing is an increasingly important strategy for modern companies that want to meet the growing demand for environmentally and socially responsible products and services. By focusing on transparency, environmentally friendly products and practices, green advertising and social responsibility, companies can create a positive brand image that promotes sustainability and a better world.

EVOLUTION OF SUSTAINABLE MARKETING

Marketing and sustainability are not new concepts, but the term "sustainable marketing" has only recently entered the business world. As mentioned above, sustainable marketing is a form of marketing that focuses on the long-term well-being of society and the environment. The concept of sustainable marketing emerged in response to growing concerns about the impact of business activities on the environment and society (Kumar, Rahman, & Kazmi, 2013).

The evolution of sustainable marketing began in the 1970s. During this period, companies began to realize the need to consider the impact of their business activities on the environment. As a result, they started developing environmentally friendly products and services (History, 2007).

In the 1980s and 1990s, companies began to focus more on sustainability and social responsibility. This was due to the increase in the impact of business activities on society and the environment. Companies have begun to incorporate sustainability into their business strategies, and sustainable marketing has emerged as a key component of these strategies (Polonsky, 1994a)

The 21st century has ushered in a new era of marketing kno.wn as Marketing 3.0. This era is characterized by a focus on values and emotions, not just demographics. Marketing 3.0 involves engaging with customers at a deeper level and building meaningful relationships based on shared values. Sustainable marketing has become an integral part of Marketing 3.0 as companies strive to align their values with the values of their customers (Kotler, Kartajaya, & Setiawan, 2011).

One of the main drivers of sustainable marketing is consumer demand for more sustainable products and services. Consumers are increasingly thinking about the impact of their purchasing decisions on the environment and society. They want to buy sustainable and socially responsible products and services. As a result, companies that can demonstrate their commitment to sustainability and social responsibility are more likely to gain customer loyalty. In the early 2000s, sustainable marketing continued to evolve as consumer demand for environmentally friendly products and services increased. This led to increased green advertising campaigns that emphasized the environmental benefits of products such as energy-efficient appliances and hybrid cars ("Ethical Consumers Among the Millennials: A Cross-National Study on JSTOR," n.d.).

The expanding understanding of the significance of sustainability and social responsibility in the business world has been another driver of sustainable marketing. Companies are becoming aware that their capacity to do business in a sustainable and socially responsible manner is essential to their long-term success. This applies to both their own operations as well as those of their partners and suppliers (Polonsky, 1994b).

As customer preferences have changed and environmental and social concerns have grown, sustainable marketing has also evolved. One significant development is the move toward circular economy models, which place more emphasis on material reuse and recycling than traditional linear models that concentrate on extraction, production, and disposal (Gazzola, Pavione, Pezzetti, & Grechi, 2020).

Many companies now use sustainable materials in their products, such as recycled plastic or organic cotton. They are also exploring new business models, such as leasing or renting products, to further encourage the production of raw materials for sustainable consumption (Shrivastava & Hart, 1995).

Sustainable marketing has also begun to emphasize social responsibility more and more. Companies are now expected to have a minimal impact on the environment and actively support social issues, such helping out the community where they operate or fostering diversity and inclusion (Batat & Khochman, 2021).

Social responsibility has also become an increasingly important aspect of sustainable marketing. Society expects companies to minimize their environmental impact and actively contribute to social projects, such as supporting local communities or promoting diversity and inclusion (Hepburn, 2015).

Another trend in sustainable marketing is using technology to promote sustainability. For example, some companies use blockchain technology to track the environmental and social impact of their supply chains, while others use artificial intelligence to optimize energy use or reduce waste (Bhalerao, 2021).

Finally, sustainable marketing has evolved to highlight more holistic approaches to sustainability that go beyond just environmental or social issues. For example, some companies are now exploring the concept of "regenerative" business models that seek to create positive impacts on the environment and society, rather than just reducing negative impacts (Guinot, 2020).

THE BENEFITS OF SUSTAINABILITY OF BUSINESS

Sustainability is an essential aspect of modern business that strives to act responsibly and reduce its negative impact on the environment. In recent years, sustainability has become a critical focus for many organizations as they realize the benefits of adopting sustainable practices (Schaltegger, Hörisch, & Freeman, 2017).

Economic Benefits

Sustainability practices can lead to significant economic benefits for businesses. By adopting sustainable practices, businesses can reduce operating costs by reducing waste and minimizing the use of natural resources. These practices can also lead to increased efficiency, productivity, and innovation. For example, businesses that adopt sustainable practices can develop new products or services that cater to environmentally oriented customers, which can create new revenue streams (Atz, van Holt, Douglas, & Whelan, 2020).

Social Benefits

Sustainability practices can also have significant social benefits. By implementing sustainable practices, businesses can improve their reputation and brand image, which can lead to increased customer loyalty and trust. Sustainability practices can also lead to increased employee engagement and retention, as employees feel proud to work for a socially responsible organization. In addition, businesses that adopt sustainable practices can contribute to the well-being of their communities by supporting local suppliers and philanthropic activities (Wu, Subramanian, Abdulrahman, Liu, & Pawar, 2017).

Environmental Benefits

Sustainability practices can have a significant positive impact on the environment. By reducing their carbon footprint and minimizing the use of natural resources, businesses can help mitigate the effects of climate change and protect the planet's natural resources. In addition, sustainability practices can lead to a more sustainable supply chain by reducing waste and encouraging the use of renewable materials. This can help future generations access the resources they need to thrive (Wu et al., 2017).

Sustainability is a critical aspect of modern business that offers significant benefits to organizations, including economic, social, and environmental benefits. By adopting sustainable practices, businesses can reduce their operating costs, improve their reputation and contribute to the well-being of their communities. In addition, sustainability practices can help protect the environment by reducing waste, minimizing the use of natural resources, and mitigating the effects of climate change ("The Comprehensive Business Case for Sustainability," n.d.).

FIVE PRINCIPLES OF SUSTAINABLE MARKETING

Sustainable marketing refers to the ethical and environmentally responsible practices adopted by businesses in order to promote sustainable development. The purpose of sustainable marketing is to strike a balance between economic, social, and environmental objectives. In this part, we will discuss the five principles of sustainable marketing and their benefits to businesses and society.

Principle 1: Consumer Education

Consumer education is the fundamental rule of sustainable marketing. This principle calls for educating customers about how their purchase decisions affect the social and environmental landscape. The goal is to give customers the information they need to make decisions that support sustainable development. Businesses can improve their brand reputation, cultivate a more sustainable market, and increase customer trust by educating consumers (Kotler et al., 2011).

Principle 2: Product Innovation

Product innovation is the second rule of sustainable marketing. This idea entails creating environmentally friendly products that satisfy consumer demands while reducing harm to the environment. Sustainable product innovation can assist companies in growing their market share, decreasing their environmental impact, and enhancing consumer perception (Kotler et al., 2011).

Principle 3: Social Responsibility

The third principle of sustainable marketing is social responsibility. Socially responsible businesses consider the well-being of their employees, customers, suppliers, and society as a whole. Social responsibility can help businesses build trust with stakeholders, increase customer loyalty, and strengthen their brand reputation (Belz & Binder, 2017).

Principle 4: Environmental Stewardship

The fourth principle of sustainable marketing is to protect the environment. This principle involves proactive measures by businesses to reduce their impact on the environment. Environmental stewardship may include measures such as reducing greenhouse gas emissions, conserving natural resources, and using renewable energy sources. Environmental stewardship can help businesses reduce their environmental footprint, comply with regulations, and enhance their reputation with customers and stakeholders (Iles, 2008).

Principle 5: Stakeholder Engagement

The fifth principle of sustainable marketing is stakeholder engagement. This principle involves engaging with stakeholders such as customers, suppliers, employees, and the community to understand their needs and concerns. By engaging with stakeholders, businesses can build trust, gain valuable insights, and develop more effective sustainability strategies. Stakeholder engagement can help businesses improve their reputation, increase customer loyalty, and enhance their social and environmental impact (Bal et al., 2013).

Businesses can concurrently accomplish economic, social, and environmental goals by using sustainable marketing strategies. Businesses can grow their market share, improve their reputation, foster stakeholder confidence, and support sustainable development by implementing sustainable marketing strategies. Consumer education, product innovation, social responsibility, environmental stewardship, and stakeholder involvement, the five sustainable marketing principles covered in this chapter, are essential for creating a long-lasting company.

MOVING ON SUSTAINABLE MARKETING

Sustainable marketing is becoming increasingly important for companies to remain competitive in today's market. By incorporating sustainability into the overall business strategy, adopting sustainable product development, communicating sustainability efforts, and implementing sustainable supply chain management, companies can improve their financial performance and have a positive impact on society and the environment:

- **Incorporate Sustainability into Business Strategy:** The first step towards sustainable marketing is to incorporate sustainability into the overall business strategy. This can be achieved by setting sustainability goals, identifying the environmental and social impact of the company's activities, and assessing the sustainability of the products and services offered. Several studies have shown that companies that adopt a sustainability strategy are more likely to have a positive impact on society and the environment (García-Sánchez, Frías-Aceituno, & Rodríguez-Domínguez, 2013).
- **Adopt Sustainable Product Development:** Another important aspect of sustainable marketing is adopting sustainable product development. This means designing environmentally friendly and socially responsible products. Companies can achieve this by using environmentally friendly materials, reducing waste, and implementing energy-efficient manufacturing processes. Several studies have shown that consumers are willing to pay a premium for sustainable products, indicating that sustainable product development can lead to increased profitability (Kate, Sahu, Pandey, Mishra, & Sharma, 2022).
- **Communicate Sustainability Efforts:** It is also important for companies to communicate their sustainability efforts to consumers. This can be achieved by using eco-labels and certifications, providing transparent information about the environmental and social impact of products, and engaging with consumers on social media. Several studies have shown that consumers are more likely to buy products from companies that communicate their sustainability efforts (Peng, Liu, Corstanje, & Meersmans, 2021).
- **Implement Sustainable Supply Chain Management:** Adopting sustainable supply chain management is also important for sustainable marketing. This involves selecting suppliers based on their environmental and social performance, reducing transportation and logistics, carbon footprint and implementing sustainable packaging practices. Research shows that sustainable supply chain management can lead to improved financial performance and increased customer loyalty (Benzidia, Makaoui, & Bentahar, 2021).

Address Sustainability in Digital Marketing

Sustainability has become a central issue in modern society, where consumers and businesses alike recognize the importance of preserving the environment for future generations. Digital marketing is a crucial tool for businesses trying to promote their products and services to a global audience, but it also has a significant impact on the environment. In this article, we discuss how businesses can address sustainability in digital marketing.

Importance of Sustainability in Digital Marketing

Digital marketing has become increasingly popular in recent years due to its ability to reach a global audience quickly and efficiently. However, it also has a significant impact on the environment, primarily through energy consumption and e-waste generation. Businesses must consider the environmental impact of their digital marketing efforts to ensure long-term sustainability.

One way businesses can address sustainability in digital marketing is by using renewable energy sources to power their digital marketing operations. For example, a business can use solar panels or wind turbines to generate the energy needed to power its website or social media platforms. Research has shown that renewable energy sources are becoming increasingly cost-effective (Şahin, 2020), and at the same time, they can significantly reduce the impact of harmful substances (Gaustad, Utgård, & Fitzsimons, 2020).

Another way businesses can address digital marketing sustainability is by reducing their e-waste generation. E-waste is an important environmental issue that is important to society to address. One solution to this problem is for businesses to adopt a "circular economy" approach that focuses on extending the life cycle of products and reducing waste. For example, businesses can offer repair services or encourage customers to recycle old devices (Carvalho, Moreira, Dias, Rodrigues, & Costa, 2020).

Businesses can also address sustainability in digital marketing by using more sustainable materials in their products and packaging. This approach not only benefits the environment but also appeals to consumers who are increasingly environmentally conscious. For example, companies can use biodegradable materials for their product packaging or switch to eco-friendly inks for printed marketing materials (Zhuang, Luo, & Riaz, 2021).

Finally, businesses can address sustainability in digital marketing by encouraging their customers to adopt sustainable behaviors. For example, a company can promote environmentally friendly habits, such as reducing water consumption or using public transportation, through their social media platforms or email marketing campaigns (Zhuang et al., 2021). This approach not only benefits the environment but also creates a positive image for the company, as consumers increasingly prefer to support businesses that align with their values.

In conclusion, sustainability is crucial for businesses involved in digital marketing. By using renewable energy sources, reducing e-waste, using sustainable materials, and promoting sustainable behavior, businesses can reduce their environmental impact and create a positive image among consumers. As consumers become increasingly environmentally conscious, talking about sustainability in digital marketing is not only an ethical choice but also a strategic one.

Sustainable digital marketing practices have a number of benefits for businesses. These include cost savings, improved brand reputation, increased customer loyalty, and reduced environmental impact. By using sustainable digital marketing techniques, businesses can reduce energy consumption and carbon emissions, resulting in cost savings on energy bills and reduced greenhouse gas emissions. Additionally, by demonstrating a commitment to sustainability, businesses can improve brand reputation and increase customer loyalty, which can lead to increased sales and profitability (Loeser, Recker, Brocke, Molla, & Zarnekow, 2017).

Challenges in Implementation

While sustainable digital marketing has many advantages, there are also some difficulties that companies must overcome in order to put these strategies into practice successfully. The lack of awareness and expertise regarding ethical digital marketing strategies is one of the main problems. Many companies might not understand the potential advantages of sustainable digital marketing or may not know how to put these strategies into practice successfully (Fraj, Martínez, & Matute, 2011).

The complexity of ethical digital marketing strategies is another difficulty. For small and medium-sized firms, implementing sustainable digital marketing involves a considerable investment in technology and training. Additionally, because of how quickly technology is developing, it can be difficult for businesses to keep up with the most recent digital marketing strategies and tools (Carfora, Scandurra, & Thomas, 2021).

Environmental Impact

Sustainable digital marketing practices can have a significant positive impact on the environment. By reducing energy consumption and carbon emissions, businesses can help mitigate the effects of climate change. In addition, sustainable digital marketing practices can reduce the use of paper and other physical marketing materials, which can help prevent deforestation and reduce waste.

However, it is important to note that digital marketing affects the environment. Energy consumption associated with data centers, servers, and other digital infrastructure can be voluminous. Therefore, it is important for businesses to adopt sustainable digital marketing practices that minimize energy consumption and carbon emissions (Sovacool, Upham, & Monyei, 2022).

THE SUSTAINABLE DIGITAL MARKETING MIX

The concept of sustainability has gained significant attention in recent years, and businesses are increasingly adopting sustainable practices. Sustainable digital marketing, in particular, has become a critical area of concern for businesses as they strive to reduce their environmental impact and maintain profitability.

The traditional marketing mix, which includes product, price, promotion, and place, has been the cornerstone of marketing strategy for decades. However, with the advent of digital marketing, the marketing mix has evolved to include additional elements such as process, people, and physical evidence. A sustainable digital marketing mix adds another layer to the marketing mix by incorporating sustainability considerations into each element of the traditional marketing mix (Zhong, Song, Yang, Fang, & Liu, 2021):

- **Product:** The product is where the sustainable digital marketing mix begins. By utilizing environmentally friendly materials, minimizing production waste, and guaranteeing that the product is recyclable or biodegradable, businesses can incorporate sustainability into their products. Businesses can also tell customers about a product's sustainability by giving them details like its carbon footprint or environmental certifications (Wan, Tian, Fu, & Zhang, 2021).
- **Price:** A key element of the marketing mix is pricing, and sustainable pricing can aid companies in achieving their sustainability objectives. Businesses can encourage customers to buy sustainable products by using pricing tactics like eco-pricing, in which the cost of the product reflects its environmental impact. Businesses can also reward customers for choosing sustainable products with discounts or loyalty programs (Sun et al., 2021).

Promoting the sustainability of the product or service is the main goal of sustainable digital marketing promotion. To inform customers about their sustainability efforts, businesses can use digital marketing channels, including social media, email marketing, and search engine optimization. Businesses can also utilize cause-related marketing or partnerships with environmental groups to publicize their sustainability initiatives (Wen et al., 1998):

- **Place:** The distribution methods used to get the good or service to the customer are referred to as the "place." Sustainable distribution methods can lessen the negative effects of a company's operations on the environment. Businesses can use digital channels, like e-commerce, to do away with physical stores and cut down on emissions from transportation. Additionally, companies can lessen their carbon footprint by using sustainable logistics and delivery methods like bike couriers or electric vehicles (Roldán Fernández, Burgos Payán, & Riquelme Santos, 2021).
- **Process:** The term "process" refers to a company's internal procedures, including supply chain management, production, and purchasing. Businesses can lessen their environmental effect and achieve their sustainability goals by using sustainable procedures. Businesses can use sustainable production techniques, including reusing materials, cutting waste, and employing renewable energy sources. Businesses can also employ sustainable supply chain management techniques and engage with sustainable suppliers (Duan et al., 2020).
- **People:** The term "people" refers to the company's clients and workers. Sustainable digital marketing initiatives should take the effects on people into account. Businesses can encourage employees and clients to lead sustainable lifestyles by educating them about sustainability, pushing them to take public transit or carpool, and offering rewards for sustainable behavior. Businesses can also enforce fair labor laws to guarantee that no child or forced labor is used in the production of their goods (Vastola & Russo, 2021).
- **Physical Evidence:** The tangible components of a business, such as a store's layout or a product's packaging, are referred to as physical evidence. Businesses can lessen their environmental effect and demonstrate their sustainability efforts by using sustainable physical evidence. Businesses can utilize sustainable store designs that include natural lighting, energy-efficient heating and cooling systems, eco-friendly packaging, and a reduction in the usage of single-use plastics (Chai, Simayi, & Yang, 2021).

In conclusion, a sustainable digital marketing mix provides businesses with a framework to incorporate sustainability into their marketing strategy. By considering sustainability in all elements of the marketing mix, businesses can reduce their environmental impact, promote sustainability efforts to consumers, and differentiate themselves in the marketplace. A sustainable digital marketing mix is not only good for the planet but can also lead to increased profitability with consumers who are increasingly concerned about sustainability. As businesses continue to prioritize sustainability, incorporating a sustainable digital marketing mix into their marketing strategy will become even more important for long-term success.

CONCLUSION

In conclusion, because of the substantial environmental impact of digital marketing, sustainability has emerged as a critical problem. To lessen their environmental impact and keep their profitability, businesses must implement sustainable methods in digital marketing. Practices for sustainable digital marketing have several benefits, such as lower costs, enhanced brand reputation, higher consumer loyalty, and little environmental effect. However, there are obstacles to their implementation, such as a lack of knowledge and experience, as well as the complexity of ethical digital marketing strategies. By lowering energy use, carbon emissions, and waste, sustainable digital marketing strategies can have a significant positive impact on the environment. The sustainable digital marketing mix adds a new dimension to the marketing strategy by including sustainability considerations into each component of the traditional marketing mix. Future studies should concentrate on creating realistic, efficient, and sustainable digital marketing strategies that can be successfully applied by companies of all sizes.

REFERENCES

Atz, U., van Holt, T., Douglas, E., & Whelan, T. (2020). *The return on sustainability investment (ROSI): Monetizing financial benefits of sustainability actions in companies. In Sustainable Consumption and Production* (Vol. 2). Circular Economy and Beyond. doi:10.1007/978-3-030-55285-5_14/TABLES/12

Bal, M., Bryde, D., Fearon, D., Ochieng, E., & Brydejmu, D. J. A. (2013). Stakeholder Engagement: Achieving Sustainability in the Construction Sector. *Sustainability (Basel)*, 6(2), 695–710. doi:10.3390u5020695

Batat, W., & Khochman, I. (2021). *Is Luxury Compatible With Corporate Social Responsibility (CSR)*. doi:10.4018/978-1-7998-5882-9.ch010

Belz, F. M., & Binder, J. K. (2017). Sustainable Entrepreneurship: A Convergent Process Model. *Business Strategy and the Environment*, 26(1), 1–17. doi:10.1002/bse.1887

Benzidia, S., Makaoui, N., & Bentahar, O. (2021). The impact of big data analytics and artificial intelligence on green supply chain process integration and hospital environmental performance. *Technological Forecasting and Social Change*, 165, 120557. doi:10.1016/j.techfore.2020.120557

Carfora, A., Scandurra, G., & Thomas, A. (2021). Determinants of environmental innovations supporting small- and medium-sized enterprises sustainable development. *Business Strategy and the Environment*, 30(5), 2621–2636. doi:10.1002/bse.2767

Carvalho, L. C., Moreira, S. B., Dias, R., Rodrigues, S., & Costa, B. (2020). *Circular Economy Principles and Their Influence on Attitudes to Consume Green Products in the Fashion Industry*. doi:10.4018/978-1-5225-9885-5.ch012

Chai, Z., Simayi, Z., & Yang, Z. (2021). *Examining the Driving Factors of the Direct Carbon Emissions of Households in the Ebinur Lake Basin Using the Extended STIRPAT Model*. doi:10.3390/su13031339

Danciu, V., & Marketing, M. (2013). The contribution of sustainable marketing to sustainable development. *Challenges for the Knowledge Society*, 8(2), 385–400.

Duan, W., Zou, S., Chen, Y., Nover, D., Fang, G., & Wang, Y. (2020). Sustainable water management for cross-border resources: The Balkhash Lake Basin of Central Asia, 1931–2015. *Journal of Cleaner Production*, 263, 121614. doi:10.1016/j.jclepro.2020.121614

Essam, R., & Mahrous, A. A. (2019). A Qualitative Study of Cause-Related Marketing Campaigns and Consumers' Purchase Intention of On-Demand Ride Services in Egypt. SSRN *Electronic Journal*. https://doi.org/ doi:10.2139/SSRN.3464859

Ethical Consumers Among the Millennials. A Cross-National Study on JSTOR. (n.d.). Retrieved April 30, 2023, from https://www.jstor.org/stable/41684017

Fraj, E., Martínez, E., & Matute, J. (2011). *Green marketing strategy and the firm's performance: the moderating role of environmental culture.* doi:10.1080/0965254X.2011.581382

García-Sánchez, I. M., Frías-Aceituno, J. V., & Rodríguez-Domínguez, L. (2013). Determinants of corporate social disclosure in Spanish local governments. *Journal of Cleaner Production, 39*, 60–72. doi:10.1016/j.jclepro.2012.08.037

Gaustad, T., Utgård, J., & Fitzsimons, G. J. (2020). When accidents are good for a brand. *Journal of Business Research, 107*, 153–161. doi:10.1016/j.jbusres.2018.10.040

Gazzola, P., Pavione, E., Pezzetti, R., & Grechi, D. (2020). Trends in the Fashion Industry. The Perception of Sustainability and Circular Economy: A Gender/Generation Quantitative Approach. *Sustainability, 12*(7), 2809. doi:10.3390/su12072809

Gordon, R., Carrigan, M., & Hastings, G. (2011). *A framework for sustainable marketing.* doi:10.1177/1470593111403218

Guinot, J. (2020). Changing the economic paradigm: Towards a sustainable business model. *International Journal of Sustainable Development and Planning, 15*(5), 603–610. doi:10.18280/ijsdp.150502

Hepburn, S. J. (2015). *In Patagonia (Clothing): A Complicated Greenness.* doi:10.2752/175174113X13718320331035

History, J. (2007). *Sustainable development – Historical roots of the concept.* doi:10.1080/15693430600688831

Iles, A. (2008). Shifting to green chemistry: The need for innovations in sustainability marketing. *Business Strategy and the Environment, 17*(8), 524–535. doi:10.1002/bse.547

Kate, A., Sahu, L. K., Pandey, J., Mishra, M., & Sharma, P. K. (2022, January 1). Green catalysis for chemical transformation: The need for the sustainable development. In *Current Research in Green and Sustainable Chemistry.* Elsevier B.V. doi:10.1016/j.crgsc.2021.100248

Katrandjiev, H. (n.d.). *Ecological Marketing, Green Marketing, Sustainable Marketing: Synonyms or an Evolution of Ideas?* Academic Press.

Kortam, W., & Mahrous, A. A. (2020). Sustainable Marketing: A Marketing Revolution or A Research Fad. *Archives of Business Research, 8*(1), 172–181. doi:10.14738/abr.81.7747

Kotler, P., Kartajaya, H., & Setiawan, I. (2011). *Marketing 3.0: From Products to Customers to the Human Spirit.* doi:10.1002/9781118257883

Kumar, V., Rahman, Z., & Kazmi, A. A. (2013). *Sustainability Marketing Strategy: An Analysis of Recent Literature.* doi:10.1177/0972150913501598

Loeser, F., Recker, J., vom Brocke, J., Molla, A., & Zarnekow, R. (2017). How IT executives create organizational benefits by translating environmental strategies into Green IS initiatives. *Information Systems Journal, 27*(4), 503–553. doi:10.1111/isj.12136

Osburg, V. S., Davies, I., Yoganathan, V., & McLeay, F. (2021). Perspectives, Opportunities and Tensions in Ethical and Sustainable Luxury: Introduction to the Thematic Symposium. *Journal of Business Ethics, 169*(2), 201–210. doi:10.100710551-020-04487-4 PMID:33132467

Peng, J., Liu, Y., Corstanje, R., & Meersmans, J. (2021). Promoting sustainable landscape patterns for landscape sustainability. *Landscape Ecology*, *36*(7), 1839–1844. doi:10.100710980-021-01271-1

Pogrebova, O. A., Konnikov, E. A., & Yuldasheva, O. U. (2017). Fuzzy model assessing the index of development of sustainable marketing of the company. *Proceedings of 2017 20th IEEE International Conference on Soft Computing and Measurements, SCM 2017*, 694–696. 10.1109/SCM.2017.7970693

Polonsky, M. J. (1994). An Introduction To Green Marketing. *Electronic Green Journal*, *1*(2). Advance online publication. doi:10.5070/G31210177

Roldán Fernández, J. M., Burgos Payán, M., & Riquelme Santos, J. M. (2021). Profitability of household photovoltaic self-consumption in Spain. *Journal of Cleaner Production*, *279*, 123439. doi:10.1016/j.jclepro.2020.123439

Rotschedl, J., & Čermáková, A. (2014). *Proceedings of the 11th International Academic Conference, Reykjavik, Iceland, 24-27 June 204*. International Institute of Social and Economic Sciences (IISES).

Şahin, U. (2020). Projections of Turkey's electricity generation and installed capacity from total renewable and hydro energy using fractional nonlinear grey Bernoulli model and its reduced forms. *Sustainable Production and Consumption*, *23*, 52–62. doi:10.1016/j.spc.2020.04.004

Schaltegger, S., Hörisch, J., & Freeman, R. E. (2017). *Business Cases for Sustainability: A Stakeholder Theory Perspective*. doi:10.1177/1086026617722882

Seretny, M., & Seretny, A. (2012). Sustainable Marketing -A New Era in the Responsible Marketing Development. *Foundations of Management*, *4*(2), 63–76. doi:10.2478/fman-2013-0011

Shrivastava, P., & Hart, S. (1995). Creating sustainable corporations. *Business Strategy and the Environment*, *4*(3), 154–165. doi:10.1002/bse.3280040307

Sovacool, B. K., Upham, P., & Monyei, C. G. (2022). The "whole systems" energy sustainability of digitalization: Humanizing the community risks and benefits of Nordic datacenter development. *Energy Research & Social Science*, *88*, 102493. doi:10.1016/j.erss.2022.102493

Sun, X., Li, D., Li, B., Sun, S., Geng, J., Ma, L., & Qi, H. (2021). Exploring the effects of haze pollution on airborne fungal composition in a cold megacity in Northeast China. *Journal of Cleaner Production*, *280*, 124205. doi:10.1016/j.jclepro.2020.124205

Technology: A Pathway Towards Sustainability. (n.d.). Retrieved April 30, 2023, from https://www.proquest.com/openview/329f4d51a0b62d5023f1af7dbaed1e12/1?pq-origsite=gscholar&cbl=38744

The Comprehensive Business Case for Sustainability. (n.d.). Retrieved April 30, 2023, from https://hbr.org/2016/10/the-comprehensive-business-case-for-sustainability

Vastola, V., & Russo, A. (2021). Exploring the effects of mergers and acquisitions on acquirers' sustainability orientation: Embedding, adding, or losing sustainability. *Business Strategy and the Environment*, *30*(2), 1094–1104. doi:10.1002/bse.2673

Wan, B., Tian, L., Fu, M., & Zhang, G. (2021). Green development growth momentum under carbon neutrality scenario. *Journal of Cleaner Production*, *316*, 128327. doi:10.1016/j.jclepro.2021.128327

Wen, M., Zhang, T., Li, L., Chen, L., Hu, S., Wang, J., Liu, W., Zhang, Y., & Yuan, L. (1998). Assessment of Land Ecological Security and Analysis of Influencing Factors in Chaohu Lake Basin, China from 1998–2018. *Sustainability (Basel)*, *13*(1), 358. doi:10.3390u13010358

Wu, L., Subramanian, N., Abdulrahman, M. D., Liu, C., & Pawar, K. S. (2017). Short-term versus long-term benefits: Balanced sustainability framework and research propositions. *Sustainable Production and Consumption*, *11*, 18–30. doi:10.1016/j.spc.2016.09.003

Zhong, W., Song, J., Yang, W., Fang, K., & Liu, X. (2021). Evolving household consumption-driven industrial energy consumption under urbanization: A dynamic input-output analysis. *Journal of Cleaner Production*, *289*, 125732. doi:10.1016/j.jclepro.2020.125732

Zhuang, W., Luo, X., & Riaz, M. U. (2021). On the Factors Influencing Green Purchase Intention: A Meta-Analysis Approach. *Frontiers in Psychology*, *12*, 644020. doi:10.3389/fpsyg.2021.644020 PMID:33897545

KEY TERMS AND DEFINITIONS

Consumer Demand: Refers to the level of desire or needs that exists among consumers for a particular product or service at a given time. It is a measure of the quantity of a product or service that consumers are willing and able to purchase at a certain price point. Consumer demand is influenced by various factors, including changes in consumer preferences, economic conditions, market trends, and product availability. Understanding consumer demand is important for businesses because it can help them determine the level of production and pricing needed to meet customer needs and maximize profitability.

Consumer Preferences: Refer to the choices and priorities of individual consumers in the marketplace. These preferences are shaped by various factors such as personal values, needs, wants, and beliefs, as well as external factors such as marketing, advertising, and cultural influences. Understanding consumer preferences is important for businesses because it can help them develop products, services, and marketing strategies that better meet the needs and wants of their target customers.

Digital Marketing Refers: To the use of various digital channels and technologies to promote products or services to potential customers. It includes a wide range of tactics, such as search engine optimization (SEO), social media marketing, email marketing, pay-per-click (PPC) advertising, and content marketing. Digital marketing has become increasingly important in recent years as more consumers turn to digital channels to research products, compare prices, and make purchasing decisions. The demand for digital marketing has grown as businesses seek to reach these consumers and compete in an increasingly crowded marketplace. Digital marketing allows businesses to target specific demographics and measure the effectiveness of their marketing efforts in real-time, providing valuable insights into consumer behavior and preferences. As a result, businesses are investing more resources into digital marketing to drive sales, increase brand awareness, and build customer loyalty.

Green Advertising: Includes promoting the environmental benefits of a product or service, using sustainable messaging and imagery in ads, or highlighting the company's commitment to sustainability.

Green Products: Refer to goods and services that are produced and marketed with a focus on their environmental sustainability. These products are designed to have a lower impact on the environment compared to traditional products, often by using sustainable materials, reducing waste, and minimizing energy use in production and distribution. Green products can range from household items such as cleaning supplies and personal care products to larger consumer goods such as cars and appliances. The use of green products is becoming increasingly popular as consumers become more environmentally conscious and seek out products that align with their values. Green products can also be certified by third-party organizations to ensure that they meet specific environmental standards, providing additional assurance to consumers.

Sustainable Digital Marketing: Can be described as the various methods used to promote an environmentally conscious business online in a sustainable and ethical manner. It involves marketing a company's sustainable and ethical products or services, as well as eco-friendly practices, in a way that is beneficial for both the business, the planet, and society in the long term.

Sustainable Marketing: Sustainable marketing is a marketing strategy that focuses on promoting socially and environmentally responsible products, services, and practices.

Sustainable Materials: Are materials that are produced, used, and disposed of in a way that minimizes their negative impact on the environment and human health. They are typically made from renewable or recycled resources and are designed to be long-lasting and biodegradable. The use of sustainable materials is becoming increasingly important in many industries as a way to reduce waste, conserve resources, and mitigate the effects of climate change.

Compilation of References

Abdelfattah, T., & Aboud, A. (2020). Tax avoidance, corporate governance, and corporate social responsibility: The case of the Egyptian capital market. *Journal of International Accounting, Auditing & Taxation, 38*, 100304. doi:10.1016/j.intaccaudtax.2020.100304

Abiiro, G. A., & De Allegri, M. (2015). Universal Health Coverage from Multiple Perspectives: A Synthesis of Conceptual Literature and Global Debates. *BMC International Health and Human Rights, 15*(1), 17. Advance online publication. doi:10.118612914-015-0056-9 PMID:26141806

Accenture. (2019). *More than Half of Consumers Would Pay More for Sustainable Products Designed to Be Reused or Recycled, Accenture Survey Finds.* Newsroom. https://newsroom.accenture.com/news/more-than-half-of-consumers-would-pay-more-for-sustainable-products

Accenture. (2022). Almost One-Third of Europe's Largest Listed Companies Have Pledged to Reach Net-Zero by 2050, Accenture Study Finds. *Travel Perk.* https://www.travelperk.com/blog/business-sustainability-statistics/

Adamczak, J. (2022). *Restructuring a municipal enterprise towards a circular economy on the example of the waste management industry.* Oficyna Wydawnicza SGH.

Adam, M., Ibrahim, M., Ikramuddin, I., & Syahputra, H. (2020). The role of digital marketing platforms on supply chain management for customer satisfaction and loyalty in small and medium enterprises (SMEs) at Indonesia. *International Journal of Supply Chain Management, 9*(3), 1210–1220.

Agmeka, F., Wathoni, R. N., & Santoso, A. S. (2019). The influence of discount framing towards brand reputation and brand image on purchase intention and actual behaviour in e-commerce. *Procedia Computer Science, 161*, 851–858. doi:10.1016/j.procs.2019.11.192

Agudelo, M. A. L., Johannsdottir, L., & Davidsdottir, B. (2020). Drivers that motivate energy companies to be responsible. A systematic literature review of Corporate Social Responsibility in the energy sector. *Journal of Cleaner Production, 247*, 119094. doi:10.1016/j.jclepro.2019.119094

Aguilar, F. J. (1967). *Scanning the business environment.* Macmillan.

Aguinis, H., Villamor, I., & Gabriel, K. P. (2020). Understanding employee responses to COVID-19: A behavioural corporate social responsibility perspective. *Management Research, 18*(4), 421–438. doi:10.1108/MRJIAM-06-2020-1053

Ahamed, F. (2013). Could monitoring and surveillance be useful to establish social compliance in the ready-made garment (RMG) industry of Bangladesh. *International Journal of Management and Business Studies, 3*(3), 88–100.

Ahi, P., & Searcy, C. (2013). A comparative literature analysis of definitions for green and sustainable supply chain management. *Journal of Cleaner Production, 52*, 329–341. doi:10.1016/j.jclepro.2013.02.018

Ahmad, N., Ullah, Z., Mahmood, A., Ariza-Montes, A., Vega-Muñoz, A., Han, H., & Scholz, M. (2021). Corporate social responsibility at the micro-level as a "new organizational value" for sustainability: Are females more aligned towards it? *International Journal of Environmental Research and Public Health*, *18*(4), 2165. doi:10.3390/ijerph18042165 PMID:33672139

Ahmad, S. Z., Abu Bakar, A. R., & Ahmad, N. (2019). Social media adoption and its impact on firm performance: The case of the UAE. *International Journal of Entrepreneurial Behaviour & Research*, *25*(1), 84–111. doi:10.1108/IJEBR-08-2017-0299

Ahmad, S. Z., Ahmad, N., & Abu Bakar, A. R. (2018). Reflections of entrepreneurs of small and medium-sized enterprises concerning the adoption of social media and its impact on performance outcomes: Evidence from the UAE. *Telematics and Informatics*, *35*(1), 6–17. doi:10.1016/j.tele.2017.09.006

Ahmad, S., & Khan, M. (2019). Tesla: Disruptor or Sustaining Innovator. *Journal of Case Research*, *10*(1).

Ahmad, T., Zhang, D., Huang, C., Zhang, H., Dai, N., Song, Y., & Chen, H. (2021). Artificial intelligence in the sustainable energy industry: Status Quo, challenges, and opportunities. *Journal of Cleaner Production*, *289*, 125834. doi:10.1016/j.jclepro.2021.125834

Ahmed, F. E. (2004). The rise of the Bangladesh garment industry: Globalisation, women workers, and voice. *NWSA Journal*, *16*(2), 34–45. doi:10.2979/NWS.2004.16.2.34

Ahmed, R. R., Streimikiene, D., Berchtold, G., Vveinhardt, J., Channar, Z. A., & Soomro, R. H. (2019). Effectiveness of online digital media advertising as a strategic tool for building brand sustainability: Evidence from FMCGs and services sectors of Pakistan. *Sustainability (Basel)*, *11*(12), 3436. doi:10.3390u11123436

Aiolfi, S., Bellini, S., & Pellegrini, D. (2021). Data-driven digital advertising: Benefits and risks of online behavioral advertising. *International Journal of Retail & Distribution Management*, *49*(7), 1089–1110. doi:10.1108/IJRDM-10-2020-0410

Aires, L. (2011). *Paradigma qualitativo e práticas de investigação educacional*. Universidade Aberta.

Ajwani-Ramchandani, R., Figueira, S., De Oliveira, R. T., Jha, S., Ramchandani, A., & Schuricht, L. (2021). Towards a circular economy for packaging waste by using new technologies: The case of large multinationals in emerging economies. *Journal of Cleaner Production*, *281*, 125139. doi:10.1016/j.jclepro.2020.125139

Akhzar, P. (2021). *Advantages of Using Intelligent Packaging for Your E-Commerce Business*. Calcurates. https://calcurates.com/advantages-of-using-intelligent-packaging

Akkaya, M. (2021). Understanding the impacts of lifestyle segmentation & perceived value on brand purchase intention: An empirical study in different product categories. *European Research on Management and Business Economics*, *27*(3), 100155. doi:10.1016/j.iedeen.2021.100155

Aksin-Sivrikaya, S., & Bhattacharya, C. B. (2017). Where digitalization meets sustainability: Opportunities and challenges. *CSR, Sustainability*. Ethics & Governance. doi:10.1007/978-3-319-54603-2_3

Al Mamun, M. A., & Hoque, M. M. (2022). The impact of paid employment on women's empowerment: A case study of female garment workers in Bangladesh. *World Development Sustainability*, *1*(100026), 1–11. doi:10.1016/j.wds.2022.100026

Alamgir, F., & Banerjee, S. B. (2019). Contested compliance regimes in global production networks: Insights from the Bangladesh garment industry. *Human Relations*, *72*(2), 272–297. doi:10.1177/0018726718760150

Compilation of References

Alam, S. M. S., & Islam, K. M. Z. (2021). Examining the role of environmental corporate social responsibility in building green corporate image and green competitive advantage. *Int J Corporate Soc Responsibility, 6*(8), 8. doi:10.118640991-021-00062-w

Alekseeva, N., Stroganova, O., & Vasilenok, V. (2019). Identifying trends in the development of marketing in the digital age. *Proceedings of the International Conference on Digital Technologies in Logistics and Infrastructure (ICDTLI 2019).* 10.2991/icdtli-19.2019.4

Al-Haddad, S., Awad, A., Albate, D., Almashhadani, I., & Dirani, W. (2020). Factors affecting green cosmetics purchase intention. *Journal of Management Information & Decision Sciences, 23*(4).

Ali, F., Ashfaq, M., Begum, S., & Ali, A. (2020). How "Green" thinking and altruism translates into purchasing intentions for electronics products: The intrinsic-extrinsic motivation mechanism. *Sustainable Production and Consumption, 24,* 281–291. doi:10.1016/j.spc.2020.07.013

Ali, R., Bakhsh, K., & Yasin, M. A. (2019). Impact of urbanization on CO2 emissions in an emerging economy: Evidence from Pakistan. *Sustainable Cities and Society, 48,* 101553. doi:10.1016/j.scs.2019.101553

Al-Zyoud, M. F. (2018). Does social media marketing enhance impulse purchasing among female customers case study of Jordanian female shoppers? *The Journal of Business and Retail Management Research, 13*(2). Advance online publication. doi:10.24052/JBRMR/V13IS02/ART-13

ama.org, (2022). *Why You Need a Digital Marketing Strategy.* AMA.

Amado, J. (2017). *Manual de investigação Qualitativa em Educação (3ª ed).* Imprensa da Universidade de Coimbra/Coimbra University Press.

Amallia, B. A., Effendi, M. I., & Ghofar, A. (2021). The effect of green advertising, trust, and attitude on green purchase intention: An evidence from Jogjakarta, Indonesia. *International Journal of Creative Business and Management, 1*(1), 66–79. doi:10.31098/ijcbm.v1i1.4553

Amberg, N., & Fogarassy, C. (2019). Green consumer behavior in the cosmetics market. *Resources, 8*(3), 137. doi:10.3390/resources8030137

Ambler, T., & Barrow, S. J. (1996). The Employer Brand. *Journal of Brand Management, 4*(3), 185–206. doi:10.1057/bm.1996.42

Amit, G. (2022). 10 Advantages Of Being A Sustainable Business. Available at: https://www.ismartrecruit.com/blog-advantages-sustainable-business

Amoako, G. K., Agbemabiese, G. C., Bonsu, G. A., & Sedalo, G. (2022). A Conceptual Framework: Creating Competitive Advantage Through Green Communication in Tourism and Hospitality Industry. *Green Marketing in Emerging Economies: A Communications Perspective,* 95-117.

Amoako, G. K., Dzogbenuku, R. K., Doe, J., & Adjaison, G. K. (2022). Green marketing and the SDGs: Emerging market perspective. *Marketing Intelligence & Planning, 40*(3), 310–327. doi:10.1108/MIP-11-2018-0543

Ancillai, C., Terho, H., Cardinali, S., & Pascucci, F. (2019). Advancing social media driven sales research: Establishing conceptual foundations for B-to-B social selling. *Industrial Marketing Management, 82,* 293–308. doi:10.1016/j.indmarman.2019.01.002

Anda, M., & Temmen, J. (2014). Smart metering for residential energy efficiency: The use of community based social marketing for behavioural change and smart grid introduction. *Renewable Energy, 67,* 119–127. doi:10.1016/j.renene.2013.11.020

Anderson, K. (2016). Contributions of the GATT/WTO to global economic welfare: Empirical evidence. *Journal of Economic Surveys, 30*(1), 56–92. doi:10.1111/joes.12087

Andries, P., & Stephan, U. (2019). Environmental innovation and firm performance: How firm size and motives matter. *Sustainability (Basel), 11*(13), 3585. doi:10.3390u11133585

Angel, S., Parent, J., Civco, D. L., Blei, A., & Potere, D. (2011). The dimensions of global urban expansion: Estimates and projections for all countries, 2000–2050. *Progress in Planning, 75*(2), 53–107. doi:10.1016/j.progress.2011.04.001

Anner, M. (2020). Squeezing workers' rights in global supply chains: Purchasing practices in the Bangladesh garment export sector in comparative perspective. *Review of International Political Economy, 27*(2), 320–347. doi:10.1080/09692290.2019.1625426

Anner, M., Bair, J., & Blasi, J. (2013). Toward joint liability in global supply chains: Addressing the root causes of labour violations in international subcontracting networks. *Comparative Labor Law & Policy Journal, 35*(1), 1–44.

Anwar, Y., & El-Bassiouny, N. (2019). Marketing and the sustainable development goals (SDGs): A review and research agenda. The Future of the UN Sustainable Development Goals: Business Perspectives for Global Development in 2030, 187-207.

Apostu, S. A., Gigauri, I., Panait, M., & Martín-Cervantes, P. A. (2023). Is Europe on the Way to Sustainable Development? Compatibility of Green Environment, Economic Growth, and Circular Economy Issues. *International Journal of Environmental Research and Public Health, 20*(2), 1078. doi:10.3390/ijerph20021078 PMID:36673838

Apostu, S. A., Mukli, L., Panait, M., Gigauri, I., & Hysa, E. (2022). Economic Growth through the Lenses of Education, Entrepreneurship, and Innovation. *Administrative Sciences, 12*(3), 74. doi:10.3390/admsci12030074

Appelbaum, R. P. (2008). Giant transnational contractors in East Asia: Emergent trends in global supply chains. *Competition & Change, 12*(1), 69–87. doi:10.1179/102452908X264539

Arora, P., & De, P. (2020). Environmental sustainability practices and exports: The interplay of strategy and institutions in Latin America. *Journal of World Business, 55*(4), 101094. doi:10.1016/j.jwb.2020.101094

Arsenijevic, U., & Jovic, M. (2019). Artificial intelligence marketing: chatbots. In 2019 international conference on artificial intelligence: applications and innovations (IC-AIAI) (pp. 19-193). IEEE. doi:10.1109/IC-AIAI48757.2019.00010

Asante, B. E., & Adu-Damoah, M. (2018). The impact of a sustainable competitive advantage on a firm's performance: Empirical evidence from Coca-Cola Ghana Limited. *Global Journal of Human Resource Management, 6*(5), 30–46.

Ashraf, H., & Prentice, R. (2019). Beyond factory safety: Labor unions, militant protest, and the accelerated ambitions of Bangladesh's export garment industry. *Dialectical Anthropology, 43*(1), 93–107. doi:10.100710624-018-9539-0

Asuyama, Y., Chhun, D., Fukunishi, T., Neou, S., & Yamagata, T. (2013). Firm dynamics in the Cambodian garment industry: Firm turnover, productivity growth and wage profile under trade liberalization. *Journal of the Asia Pacific Economy, 18*(1), 51–70. doi:10.1080/13547860.2012.742671

Athwal, N., Wells, V. K., Carrigan, M., & Henninger, C. E. (2019). Sustainable luxury marketing: A synthesis and research agenda. *International Journal of Management Reviews, 21*(4), 405–426. doi:10.1111/ijmr.12195

Atluri, V., Dietz, M., & Henke, N. (2017). Competing in a world of sectors without borders. McKinsey Quarterly, July, 2017. https://www.mckinsey.com/capabilities/quantumblack/our-insights/competing-in-a-world-of-sectors-without-borders

Compilation of References

Atz, U., van Holt, T., Douglas, E., & Whelan, T. (2020). *The return on sustainability investment (ROSI): Monetizing financial benefits of sustainability actions in companies. In Sustainable Consumption and Production* (Vol. 2). Circular Economy and Beyond. doi:10.1007/978-3-030-55285-5_14/TABLES/12

Atz, U., Van Holt, T., Douglas, E., & Whelan, T. (2021). *The Return on Sustainability Investment (ROSI): Monetizing financial benefits of sustainability actions in companies. Sustainable Consumption and Production* (Vol. II). Circular Economy and Beyond.

Aysha, S. B. MohdSalleh, Z. Abdul Kadir, S. Sanif (2016). The Relationship between Organizational Communication and Employees Productivity with New Dimensions of Effective Communication Flow, *Journal of Business and Social Review in Emerging Economies.*

Babac, A., Frank, M., Pauer, F., Litzkendorf, S., Rosenfeldt, D., Lührs, V., Biehl, L., Hartz, T., Storf, H., Schauer, F., Wagner, T. O. F., & Graf von der Schulenburg, J. (2018). Telephone health services in the field of rare diseases: A qualitative interview study examining the needs of patients, relatives, and health care professionals in Germany. *BMC Health Services Research*, *18*(1), 1–14. doi:10.118612913-018-2872-9 PMID:29426339

Bağış, B. (2020). *Rusya-Ukrayna Savaşının Küresel Ekonomiye ve Türkiye'ye Etkileri.*

Baines, P., Fill, C., Rosengren, S., & Antonetti, P. (2017). *Fundamentals of Marketing.* Oxford University Press.

Bakker, S., Maat, K., & Van Wee, B. (2014). Stakeholders' interests, expectations, and strategies regarding the development and implementation of electric vehicles: The case of the Netherlands. *Transportation Research Part A, Policy and Practice*, *66*, 52–64. doi:10.1016/j.tra.2014.04.018

Bakri, A. A. (2017). The impact of social media adoption on competitive advantage in the small and medium enterprises. *International Journal of Business Innovation and Research*, *13*(2), 255–269. doi:10.1504/IJBIR.2017.083542

Balabanova, D., McKee, M., Koroleva, N., Chikovani, I., Goguadze, K., Kobaladze, T., Adeyi, O., & Robles, S. (2008). Navigating the health system: Diabetes care in Georgia. *Health Policy and Planning*, *24*(1), 46–54. doi:10.1093/heapol/czn041 PMID:19074492

Bal, M., Bryde, D., Fearon, D., Ochieng, E., & Brydejmu, D. J. A. (2013). Stakeholder Engagement: Achieving Sustainability in the Construction Sector. *Sustainability (Basel)*, *6*(2), 695–710. doi:10.3390u5020695

Bansal, P., & Sharma, B. (2011). The evolution of green marketing and the road ahead. *Journal of Business Research*, *65*(8), 1193–1200.

Barbu, A., Catană, Ș.-A., Deselnicu, D. C., Cioca, L.-I., & Ioanid, A. (2022). Factors Influencing Consumer Behavior toward Green Products: A Systematic Literature Review. *International Journal of Environmental Research and Public Health*, *19*(24), 16568. doi:10.3390/ijerph192416568 PMID:36554445

Bardos, K. S., Ertugrul, M., & Gao, L. S. (2020). Corporate social responsibility, product market perception, and firm value. *Journal of Corporate Finance*, *62*, 101588. doi:10.1016/j.jcorpfin.2020.101588

Barney, J. B., Ketchen, D. J. Jr, & Wright, M. (2021b). Resource-based theory and the value creation framework. *Journal of Management*, *47*(7), 1936–1955. doi:10.1177/01492063211021655

Bartiaux, F., Gram-Hanssen, K., Fonseca, P., Ozawa, C., & Cappelletti, G. (2013). Labeling schemes in energy efficiency and sustainability: Is there a credible third party certification behind the label? *Energy Policy*, *61*, 907–917.

Batat, W., & Khochman, I. (2021). *Is Luxury Compatible With Corporate Social Responsibility (CSR).* doi:10.4018/978-1-7998-5882-9.ch010

Batu, M., & Atas, U. (2017). Social marketing campaign management; a comparative analysis of anti-smoking campaigns implemented in the United Kingdom and in Turkey. *Uluslararası Hakemli İletişim ve Edebiyat Araştırmaları Dergisi, 17*, 369–400.

Baumann, E. (2012). Post-Soviet Georgia: It'sa long, long way to 'modern' social protection. *Economies et Sociétés, 46*(2), 259–285.

Baumgartner, R. J. (2013). Managing corporate sustainability and CSR: A Conceptual Framework combining values, strategies and instruments contributing to sustainable development. *Corporate Social Responsibility and Environmental Management, 21*(5), 258–271. doi:10.1002/csr.1336

Baumgartner, R. J., & Rauter, R. (2017). Strategic perspectives of corporate sustainability management to develop a sustainable organization. *Journal of Cleaner Production, 140*, 81–92. doi:10.1016/j.jclepro.2016.04.146

Becker-Olsen, K., & Moynihan, K. (2013). Sustainable Marketing. In S. O. Idowu, N. Capaldi, L. Zu, & A. D. Gupta (Eds.), *Encyclopedia of Corporate Social Responsibility*. Springer. doi:10.1007/978-3-642-28036-8_105

Bedante, G. N. (2004). O comportamento de consumo sustentável e suas relações com a consciência ambiental e a intenção de compra de produtos ecologicamente embalados. Master Dissertation. Universidade Federal do Rio Grande do Sul.

Behl, Jayawardena, N., Nigam, A., Pereira, V., Shankar, A., & Jebarajakirthy, C. (2023). Investigating the revised international marketing strategies during COVID-19 based on resources and capabilities of the firms: A mixed msethod approach. *Journal of Business Research, 158*, 1–16. doi:10.1016/j.jbusres.2023.113662 PMID:36644446

Belz, F. M., & Binder, J. K. (2017). Sustainable Entrepreneurship: A Convergent Process Model. *Business Strategy and the Environment, 26*(1), 1–17. doi:10.1002/bse.1887

Belz, F. M., & Peattie, K. (2009). *Sustainability marketing*. Wiley & Sons.

Belz, F.-M., & Peattie, K. (2012). *Sustainability Marketing*. Wiley & Sons.

Bender, D. E., & Greenwald, R. A. (2003). *Sweatshop USA: The American sweatshop in historical and global perspective*. Psychology Press.

Bentonville, A. (2022). *Walmart Inc. Provides Update for Second Quarter and Fiscal Year 2023*. Retrieved from https://corporate.walmart.com/newsroom/2022/07/25/walmart-inc-provides-update-for-second-quarter-and-fiscal-year-2023

Benzidia, S., Makaoui, N., & Bentahar, O. (2021). The impact of big data analytics and artificial intelligence on green supply chain process integration and hospital environmental performance. *Technological Forecasting and Social Change, 165*, 120557. doi:10.1016/j.techfore.2020.120557

Beresford, M. (2009). The Cambodian clothing industry in the post-MFA environment: A review of developments. *Journal of the Asia Pacific Economy, 14*(4), 366–388. doi:10.1080/13547860903169357

Berger, B. (2008, November 17). Employee/Organizational Communications. *Institute for Public Relations*.

Bergkvist, L., & Taylor, C. R. (2016). Leveraged marketing communications: A framework for explaining the effects of secondary brand associations. *AMS Review, 6*(3-4), 157–175. doi:10.100713162-016-0081-4

Berrone, P., & Gomez-Mejia, L. R. (2009). Environmental performance and executive compensation: An integrated agency-institutional perspective. *Academy of Management Journal, 52*(1), 103–126. doi:10.5465/amj.2009.36461950

Bhattacharjee, S. S. (2019). Fast fashion, production targets, and gender-based violence in Asian garment supply chains. In S. B. Saxena (Ed.), *Labor, Global Supply Chains, and the Garment Industry in South Asia* (pp. 207–227). Routledge. doi:10.4324/9780429430039-12

Biermann, F., Kanie, N., & Kim, R. E. (2017). Global governance by goal-setting: The novel approach of the UN Sustainable Development Goals. *Current Opinion in Environmental Sustainability*, *26*, 26–31. doi:10.1016/j.cosust.2017.01.010

Bilal, M., Mehmood, S., & Iqbal, H. M. (2020). The beast of beauty: Environmental and health concerns of toxic components in cosmetics. *Cosmetics*, *7*(1), 13. doi:10.3390/cosmetics7010013

Blagoeva-Yarkova, Y. I. (2012). The Role of Local Cultural Institutions for Local Sustainable Development. The Case-study of Bulgaria. *Trakia Journal of Sciences*, *10*(4), 42–52.

Blecker, R. A., & Esquivel, G. (2010). NAFTA, Trade and Development (Robert A. Blecker and Gerardo Esquivel). CESifo Forum, 11(4), 17-30.

BlogMorizon.pl. (n.d.). https://www.morizon.pl/blog/vastra-hamnen-szwedzka-dzielnica-przyszlosci/

Bocken, N. (2021). Sustainable Business Models. In W. Leal Filho, A. M. Azul, L. Brandli, A. Lange Salvia, & T. Wall (Eds.), *Decent Work and Economic Growth. Encyclopedia of the UN Sustainable Development Goals*. Springer., doi:10.1007/978-3-319-95867-5_48

Bocken, N. M. P., Short, S. W., Rana, P., & Evans, S. (2014). A literature and practice review to develop sustainable business model archetypes. *Journal of Cleaner Production*, *65*, 42–56. doi:10.1016/j.jclepro.2013.11.039

Bombiak, E., & Marciniuk-Kluska, A. (2018). Green human resource management as a tool for the sustainable development of enterprises: Polish young company experience. *Sustainability (Basel)*, *10*(6), 1739. doi:10.3390u10061739

Bom, S., Jorge, J., Ribeiro, H., & Marto, J. (2019). A step forward on sustainability in the cosmetics industry: A review. *Journal of Cleaner Production*, *225*, 270–290. doi:10.1016/j.jclepro.2019.03.255

Borchardt, M., Ndubisi, N. O., Jabbour, C. J. C., Grebinevych, O., & Pereira, G. M. (2020). The evolution of base of the pyramid approaches and the role of multinational and domestic business ventures: Value-commitment and profit-making perspectives. *Industrial Marketing Management*, *89*, 171–180. doi:10.1016/j.indmarman.2019.05.013

Borenstein, S., Bushnell, J., Wolak, F. A., & Zaragoza-Watkins, M. (2019). Expecting the unexpected: Emissions uncertainty and environmental market design. *The American Economic Review*, *109*(11), 3953–3977. doi:10.1257/aer.20161218

Borrego, C., Lopes, M., Ribeiro, I., Carvalho, A., & Miranda, A. I. (2010). As alterações climáticas: Uma realidade transformada em desafio. *Revista Captar: Ciência e Ambiente para Todos*, *2*(2), 1–16.

Boston Consulting Group. (2022). *More than 80% of companies plan to increase their investments in sustainability*. BCG. https://www.prnewswire.com/news-releases/more-than-60-of-companies-prioritize-esg-in-their-digital-transformations-301514352.html# Bruno.

Boulstridge, E., & Carrigan, M. (2000). Do consumers care about corporate responsibility? Highlighting the attitude–behavior gap. *Journal of Communication Management (London)*, *4*(4), 355–368. doi:10.1108/eb023532

Bova, T. 2019. 26 Sales Statistics That Prove Selling Is Changing. *Salesforce*. https://www.salesforce.com/blog/15-sales-statistics/

Bovee, C. L., & Thill, J. V. (2019). *Business Communication Essentials: Fundamental Skills for the Mobile-Digital-Social Workplace (What's New in Business Communication)* (8th ed.). Pearson.

Bowen, H. R. (1953). Social Responsibilities of the Businessman. New York: Harper & Brothers.

Bowen, G., Appiah, D., & Okafor, S. (2020). The influence of corporate social responsibility (CSR) and social media on the strategy formulation process. *Sustainability (Basel)*, *12*(15), 6057. doi:10.3390u12156057

Bredesen, P. (2010). *Fresh Medicine: How to Fix, Reform, and Build a Sustainable Health Care System.* Grove/Atlantic, Inc.

Brennan, L., Previte, J., & Fry, M. L. (2016). Social marketing's consumer myopia: Applying a behavioral ecological model to address wicked problems. *Journal of Social Marketing, 6*(3), 219–239. doi:10.1108/JSOCM-12-2015-0079

Brida, J. G., Disegna, M., & Scuderi, R. (2013). Visitors of two types of museums: A segmentation study. *Expert Systems with Applications, 40*(6), 2224–2232. doi:10.1016/j.eswa.2012.10.039

Bridges, C. M., & Wilhelm, W. B. (2008). Going beyond green: The "why and how" of integrating sustainability into the marketing curriculum. *Journal of Marketing Education, 30*(1), 33–46. doi:10.1177/0273475307312196

Brockgreitens, J., & Abbas, A. (2016). Responsive food packaging: Recent progress and technological prospects. *Comprehensive Reviews in Food Science and Food Safety, 15*(1), 3–15. doi:10.1111/1541-4337.12174 PMID:33371571

Brodny, J., & Tutak, M. (2022). Magdalena Tutak, Digitalization of Small and Medium-Sized Enterprises and Economic Growth: Evidence for the EU-27 Countries. *Journal of Open Innovation, 8*(2), 67. doi:10.3390/joitmc8020067

Brown, K. (2019). Museums and local development: An introduction to museums, sustainability and wellbeing. *Museum International, 71*(3-4), 1–13. doi:10.1080/13500775.2019.1702257

Buckland, M. K. (1991). Information as thing. *Journal of the American Society for Information Science, 42*(5), 351–360. doi:10.1002/(SICI)1097-4571(199106)42:5<351::AID-ASI5>3.0.CO;2-3

Butler, P. (2013). Smart and interactive Packaging developments for enhanced communication at the packaging/user interface. In N. Farmer, Trends in Packaging of Food, Beverages and Other Fast-Moving Consumer Goods (FMCG) (pp. 261-286). Science Direct. doi:10.1533/9780857098979.261

Butler, S. (2013). One in six Walmart factories in Bangladesh fail safety review. *The Guardian.* Retrieved from https://www.theguardian.com/business/2013/nov/18/walmart-bangladesh-factories-fail-safety-review

Butler, K., Gordon, R., Roggeveen, K., Waitt, G., & Cooper, P. (2016). Social marketing and value in behaviour? Perceived value of using energy efficiently among low-income older citizens. *Journal of Social Marketing, 6*(2), 144–168. doi:10.1108/JSOCM-07-2015-0045

Calu, A., Negrei, C., Calu, D. A., & Avram, V. (2015). Reporting of Non-Financial Performance Indicators – a Useful Tool for a Sustainable Marketing Strategy. *Amfiteatru Economic, 17*(40), 977–993.

Canhoto, Quinton, S., Pera, R., Molinillo, S., & Simkin, L. (2021). Digital strategy aligning in SMEs: A dynamic capabilities perspective. *The Journal of Strategic Information Systems, 30*(3), 1–17. doi:10.1016/j.jsis.2021.101682

Cantele, S., & Zardini, A. (2018). Is sustainability a competitive advantage for small businesses? An empirical analysis of possible mediators in the sustainability–financial performance relationship. *Journal of Cleaner Production, 182,* 166–176. doi:10.1016/j.jclepro.2018.02.016

Cantele, S., & Zardini, A. (2020). What drives small and medium enterprises towards sustainability? Role of interactions between pressures, barriers, and benefits. *Corporate Social Responsibility and Environmental Management, 27*(1), 126–136. doi:10.1002/csr.1778

Caputo, F. (2021). Towards a holistic view of corporate social responsibility. The antecedent role of information asymmetry and cognitive distance. *Kybernetes, 50*(3), 639–655. doi:10.1108/K-01-2020-0057

Carfora, A., Scandurra, G., & Thomas, A. (2021). Determinants of environmental innovations supporting small- and medium-sized enterprises sustainable development. *Business Strategy and the Environment, 30*(5), 2621–2636. doi:10.1002/bse.2767

Compilation of References

Cariolle, J., & Carroll, D. 2020. Digital Technologies for Small and Medium Enterprises and job creation in Sub-Saharan Africa. Hal- 03004583, Ferdi https://hal.archives-ouvertes.fr/hal-03004583

Carré, P. (2021). Naturalness in the production of vegetable oils and proteins. *OCL. Oilseeds & Fats Crops and Lipids, 28*, 10. doi:10.1051/ocl/2020065

Carrigan, M., & Attalla, A. (2001). The myth of the ethical consumer - do ethics matter in purchase behaviour? *Journal of Consumer Marketing, 18*(7), 560–578. doi:10.1108/07363760110410263

Carroll, A. B. (2021). Corporate social responsibility: Perspectives on the CSR Construct's development and future. *Business & Society, 60*(6), 1258–1278. doi:10.1177/00076503211001765

Carroll, A. B., & Hoy, F. (1984). Integrating corporate social policy into strategic management. *The Journal of Business Strategy, 4*(3), 48–57. doi:10.1108/eb039031

Carson, D., Gilmore, A., Perry, C., & Gronhaug, K. (2001). *Qualitative marketing research*. Sage.

Carvalho, L. C., Moreira, S. B., Dias, R., Rodrigues, S., & Costa, B. (2020). *Circular Economy Principles and Their Influence on Attitudes to Consume Green Products in the Fashion Industry*. doi:10.4018/978-1-5225-9885-5.ch012

Cassman, K. G., & Grassini, P. (2020). A global perspective on sustainable intensification research. *Nature Sustainability, 3*(4), 262–268. doi:10.103841893-020-0507-8

Castro, G. D. R., Fernandez, M. C. G., & Colsa, A. U. (2021). Unleashing the convergence amid digitalization and sustainability towards pursuing the Sustainable Development Goals (SDGs): A holistic review. *Journal of Cleaner Production, 280*, 122204. doi:10.1016/j.jclepro.2020.122204

Chaffey, D. (2008). *Internet Marketing: Strategy, Implementation and Practice, 3/E*. Pearson Education.

Chaffey, D., & Ellis-Chadwick, F. (2019). *Digital Marketing*. Pearson.

Chaffey, D., Ellis-Chadwick, F., Mayer, R., & Johnston, K. (2009). *Internet Marketing*. Pearson Education.

Chai, Z., Simayi, Z., & Yang, Z. (2021). *Examining the Driving Factors of the Direct Carbon Emissions of Households in the Ebinur Lake Basin Using the Extended STIRPAT Model*. doi:10.3390/su13031339

Chams, N., & García-Blandón, J. (2019). On the importance of sustainable human resource management for the adoption of sustainable development goals. *Resources, Conservation and Recycling, 141*, 109–122. doi:10.1016/j.resconrec.2018.10.006

Chandran, C., & Bhattacharya, P. (2021). *Hotel's best practices as strategic drivers for environmental sustainability and green marketing*. doi:10.4324/9781003181071-5

Chan, E. S. (2013). Managing green marketing: Hong Kong hotel managers' perspective. *International Journal of Hospitality Management, 34*, 442–461. doi:10.1016/j.ijhm.2012.12.007

Chang, C. T., & Chu, X. Y. M. (2020). The give and take of cause-related marketing: Purchasing cause-related products licenses consumer indulgence. *Journal of the Academy of Marketing Science, 48*(2), 203–221. doi:10.100711747-019-00675-5

Chang, K. W., Hsu, C.-L., Hsu, Y.-T., & Chen, M.-C. (2019). How green marketing, perceived motives and incentives influence behavioral intentions. *Journal of Retailing and Consumer Services, 49*, 336–345. doi:10.1016/j.jretconser.2019.04.012

Chankova, D. & V., V. (2020). Leadership and deliberative democracy in the changing world: compatible or reconcilable paradigms. *Perspectives of Law and Public Administration, 9*(2).

Chan, M. M. W., & Chiu, D. K. W. (2022). Alert Driven Customer Relationship Management in Online Travel Agencies: Event-Condition-Actions rules and Key Performance Indicators. In A. Naim & S. Kautish (Eds.), *Building a Brand Image Through Electronic Customer Relationship Management*. IGI Global. doi:10.4018/978-1-6684-5386-5.ch012

Chan, R. Y. (2004). Consumer responses to environmental advertising in China. *Marketing Intelligence & Planning*, 22(4), 427–437. doi:10.1108/02634500410542789

Chan, T. T. W., Lam, A. H. C., & Chiu, D. K. W. (2020). From Facebook to Instagram: Exploring user engagement in an academic library. *Journal of Academic Librarianship*, 46(6), 102229. doi:10.1016/j.acalib.2020.102229 PMID:34173399

Chan, V. H. Y., Ho, K. K. W., & Chiu, D. K. W. (2022). Mediating effects on the relationship between perceived service quality and public library app loyalty during the COVID-19 era. *Journal of Retailing and Consumer Services*, 67, 102960. doi:10.1016/j.jretconser.2022.102960

Charoensukmongkol, P., & Sasatanun, P. (2017). Social media use for CRM and business performance satisfaction: The moderating roles of social skills and social media sales intensity. *Asia Pacific Management Review*, 22(1), 25–34. doi:10.1016/j.apmrv.2016.10.005

Charter, M., Peattie, K., Ottman, J., & Polonsky, M. J. (2006). *Marketing and sustainability*. CSFD. https://cfsd.org.uk/smart-know-net/smart-know-net.pdf

Charter, M., & Clark, T. (2007). Sustainable innovation: Key conclusions from sustainable innovation conferences 2003–2006. *International Journal of Innovation and Sustainable Development*, 2(3-4), 273–286.

Charter, M., & Polonsky, M. (1999). Green marketing: A global perspective on theory and practice. *Journal of Business Research*, 45(3), 177–184.

Chatterjee, S., Ghosh, S. K., Chaudhuri, R., & Nguyen, B. (2019). Are CRM systems ready for AI integration? A conceptual framework of organizational readiness for effective AI-CRM integration. *The Bottom Line (New York, N.Y.)*, 32(2), 144–157. doi:10.1108/BL-02-2019-0069

Chatterjee, S., & Kumar Kar, A. (2020). Why do small and medium enterprises use social media marketing and what is the impact: Empirical insights from India. *International Journal of Information Management*, 53, 102103. doi:10.1016/j.ijinfomgt.2020.102103

Chatterjee, S., Sreen, N., Rana, J., Dhir, A., & Sadarangani, P. H. (2022). Impact of ethical certifications and product involvement on consumers' decision to purchase ethical products at price premiums in an emerging market context. *International Review on Public and Nonprofit Marketing*, 19(4), 737–762. doi:10.100712208-021-00288-1

Cheek, W. K., & Moore, C. E. (2003). Apparel sweatshops at home and abroad: Global and ethical issues. *Journal of Family and Consumer Sciences*, 95(1), 9–19.

Chen, K. (2023). The impact of digital transformation on innovation performance - The mediating role of innovation factors. *Heliyon*, 9, 1–11.

Chen, C., Chiang, & Storey. (2012). Business Intelligence and Analytics: From Big Data to Big Impact. *Management Information Systems Quarterly*, 36(4), 1165. doi:10.2307/41703503

Cheng, J., Yuen, A. H., & Chiu, D. K. (2022). Systematic review of MOOC research in mainland China. *Library Hi Tech*. Advance online publication. doi:10.1108/LHT-02-2022-0099

Cheng, W., Tian, R., & Chiu, D. K. W. (2023). Travel vlogs influencing tourist decisions: Information preferences and gender differences. *Aslib Journal of Information Management*. Advance online publication. doi:10.1108/AJIM-05-2022-0261

Chen, J. Y., & Baddam, S. R. (2015). The effect of unethical behavior and learning on strategic supplier selection. *International Journal of Production Economics*, *167*, 74–87. doi:10.1016/j.ijpe.2015.05.003

Chen, Q., Zhang, Y., Liu, H., Zhang, W., & Evans, R. (2023). Dialogic communication on local government social media during the first wave of COVID-19: Evidence from the health commissions of prefecture-level cities in China. *Computers in Human Behavior*, *143*(3), 107715. doi:10.1016/j.chb.2023.107715 PMID:36846271

Chen, S. C., & Lin, C. P. (2019). Understanding the effect of social media marketing activities: The mediation of social identification, perceived value, and satisfaction. *Technological Forecasting and Social Change*, *140*, 22–32. doi:10.1016/j.techfore.2018.11.025

Chen, W., & Chen, J. (2015). Urbanization and CO2 emissions: A review of empirical evidence. *Habitat International*, *48*, 11–21.

Chen, X., & Wei, S. (2020). The impact of social media use for communication and social exchange relationship on employee performance. *Journal of Knowledge Management*, *24*(6), 1289–1314. doi:10.1108/JKM-04-2019-0167

Chen, Y. S., & Chang, C. H. (2012). Enhance green purchase intentions. *Management Decision*, *50*(3), 502–520. doi:10.1108/00251741211216250

Chen, Y., Chiu, D. K. W., & Ho, K. K. W. (2018). Facilitating the learning of the art of Chinese painting and calligraphy at Chao Shao-an Gallery. *Micronesian Educators*, *26*, 45–58.

Chen, Y.-S. (2010). The drivers of green brand equity: Green brand image, green satisfaction, and green trust. *Journal of Business Ethics*, *93*(2), 307–319. doi:10.100710551-009-0223-9

Chernev, A., & Kotler, P. (2018). *Strategic Marketing Management* (9th ed.). Cerebellum Press.

Cheung, T. Y., Ye, Z., & Chiu, D. K. W. (2021). Value chain analysis of information services for the visually impaired: A case study of contemporary technological solutions. *Library Hi Tech*, *39*(2), 625–642. doi:10.1108/LHT-08-2020-0185

Cheung, V. S. Y., Lo, J. C. Y., Chiu, D. K. W., & Ho, K. K. W. (2023). Predicting Facebook's influence on travel products marketing based on the AIDA model. *Information Discovery and Delivery*, *51*(1), 66–73. doi:10.1108/IDD-10-2021-0117

Chin, G. Y. L., & Chiu, D. K. W. (2023). RFID-based Robotic Process Automation for Smart Museums with an Alert-driven Approach. In R. Tailor (Ed.), *Application and Adoption of Robotic Process Automation for Smart Cities*. IGI. Global.

Chin, J., Jiang, B. C., Mufidah, I., Persada, S. F., & Noer, B. A. (2018). The investigation of consumers' behavior intention in using green skincare products: A pro-environmental behavior model approach. *Sustainability (Basel)*, *10*(11), 3922. doi:10.3390u10113922

Chintalapati, S., & Pandey, S. K. (2021). Artificial intelligence in marketing: A systematic literature review. *International Journal of Market Research*, *64*(1), 38–68. doi:10.1177/14707853211018428

Chiu, D. K. W., & Ho, K. K. W. (2022a). Special selection on contemporary digital culture and reading. *Library Hi Tech*, *40*(5), 1204–1209. doi:10.1108/LHT-10-2022-516

Chiu, D. K. W., & Ho, K. K. W. (2022b). Editorial: 40th anniversary: contemporary library research. *Library Hi Tech*, *40*(6), 1525–1531. doi:10.1108/LHT-12-2022-517

Cho, A., Lo, P., & Chiu, D. K. W. (2017). *Inside the World's Major East Asian Collections: One Belt, One Road, and Beyond*. Chandos Publishing.

Choi, E., & Lee, K. C. (2019). Effect of trust in domain-specific information of safety, brand loyalty, and perceived value for cosmetics on purchase intentions in mobile e-commerce context. *Sustainability (Basel)*, *11*(22), 6257. doi:10.3390u11226257

Chorev, N. (2005). The institutional project of neo-liberal globalism: The case of the WTO. *Theory and Society*, *34*(3), 317–355. doi:10.100711186-005-6301-9

Chou, S.-F., Horng, J.-S., Sam Liu, C.-H., & Lin, J.-Y. (2020). Identifying the critical factors of customer behavior: An integration perspective of marketing strategy and components of attitudes. *Journal of Retailing and Consumer Services*, *55*, 102113. doi:10.1016/j.jretconser.2020.102113

Chowdhury, M., Ahmed, R., & Yasmin, M. (2014). Prospects and problems of RMG Industry: A study on Bangladesh. *Prospects*, *5*(7), 103–118.

Christensen, C. M. (2013). *The innovator's dilemma: when new technologies cause great firms to fail*. Harvard Business Review Press.

Chuah, S. H., El-Manstrly, D., Tseng, M., & Ramayah, T. (2020). Sustaining customer engagement behaviour through corporate social responsibility: The roles of environmental concern and green trust. *Journal of Cleaner Production*, *262*, 121348. doi:10.1016/j.jclepro.2020.121348

Chung, A. C. W., & Chiu, D. K. (2016). OPAC Usability Problems of Archives: A Case Study of the Hong Kong Film Archive. [IJSSOE]. *International Journal of Systems and Service-Oriented Engineering*, *6*(1), 54–70. doi:10.4018/IJSSOE.2016010104

Chung, C., Chiu, D. K. W., Ho, K. K. W., & Au, C. H. (2020). Applying social media to environmental education: Is it more impactful than traditional media? *Information Discovery and Delivery*, *48*(4), 255–266. doi:10.1108/IDD-04-2020-0047

Chung, K. H. (2020). Green marketing orientation: Achieving sustainable development in green hotel management. *Journal of Hospitality Marketing & Management*, *29*(6), 722–738. doi:10.1080/19368623.2020.1693471

Çıldır, Z., & Karadeniz, C. (2014). Museum, Education and visual culture practices: Museums in Turkey. *American Journal of Educational Research*, *2*(7), 543–551. doi:10.12691/education-2-7-18

Cinelli, P., Coltelli, M. B., Signori, F., Morganti, P., & Lazzeri, A. (2019). Cosmetic packaging to save the environment: Future perspectives. *Cosmetics*, *6*(2), 26. doi:10.3390/cosmetics6020026

Cismaru, M., Lavack, A. M., & Markewich, E. (2009). Social marketing campaigns aimed at preventing drunk driving: A review and recommendations. *International Marketing Review*, *26*(3), 292–311. doi:10.1108/02651330910960799

Clarke, T. B., & Nelson, C. L. (2012). Classroom community, pedagogical effectiveness, and learning outcomes associated with Twitter use in undergraduate marketing courses. *Journal for Advancement of Marketing Education*, *20*(2).

Claudy, M. C., Peterson, M., & Pagell, M. (2016). The Roles of Sustainability Orientation and Market Knowledge Competence in New Product Development Success. *Journal of Product Innovation Management*, *33*, 72–85. doi:10.1111/jpim.12343

Clegg, A. (2007). *Unlock the power of brands*. Marketing Week Edelman Trust Barometer (2023). https://www.edelman.com/trust/2023/Trust-Barometer/navigating-a-polarized-world

Cohen, B. (2006). Urbanization in developing countries: Current trends, future projections, and critical challenges for sustainability. *Technology in Society*, *28*(1-2), 63–80. doi:10.1016/j.techsoc.2005.10.005

Collins, T. (2003). The aftermath of health sector reform in the Republic of Georgia: Effects on People's Health. *Journal of Community Health*, *28*(2), 99–113. doi:10.1023/A:1022643329631 PMID:12705312

Collins, T. (2006). The Georgian Healthcare System: Is It Reaching the WHO Health System Goals? *The International Journal of Health Planning and Management*, *21*(4), 297–312. doi:10.1002/hpm.853 PMID:17175732

Corporate Finance Institute. (2022). *Machine Learning (in Finance)*. https://corporatefinanceinstitute.com/resources/data-science/machine-learning-in-finance/

Corral de Zubielqui, G., & Jones, J. (2020). How and when social media affects innovation in start-ups. A moderated mediation model. *Industrial Marketing Management*, *85*, 209–220. doi:10.1016/j.indmarman.2019.11.006

Coşkun, G. (2012). Sosyal Pazarlama ve Sosyal Pazarlama Karması: Antalya Emniyet Müdürlüğü Komşu Kollama Projesi Örneği. *Celal Bayar Üniversitesi Sosyal Bilimler Dergisi*, *10*(02), 226–246.

Costa, J., & Fonseca, J. P. (2022). The Impact of Corporate Social Responsibility and Innovative Strategies on Financial Performance. *Risks*, *10*(5), 103. doi:10.3390/risks10050103

Crinis, V. (2019). Corporate social responsibility, human rights and clothing workers in Bangladesh and Malaysia. *Asian Studies Review*, *43*(2), 295–312. doi:10.1080/10357823.2019.1588850

Csorba, L. M., & Boglea, V. A. (2011). Sustainable cosmetics: A major instrument in protecting the consumer's interest. *Regional and Business Studies*, *3*(1, Suppl.), 167–176.

Culture, Sports and Tourism Bureau. (2022). *Culture and the arts*. CSTB. https://www.cstb.gov.hk/en/policies/culture/culture-and-the-arts.html

Dabija, D. C., & Pop, C. M. (2013). Green marketing-factor of competitiveness in retailing. [EEMJ]. *Environmental Engineering and Management Journal*, *12*(2), 393–400. doi:10.30638/eemj.2013.049

Dahl, S. (2010). Current themes in social marketing research: Text-mining the past five years. *Social Marketing Quarterly*, *16*(2), 128–136. doi:10.1080/15245001003746790

Dai, C., & Chiu, D. K. W. (2023). (in press). Impact of COVID-19 on reading behaviors and preferences: Investigating high school students and parents with the 5E instructional model. *Library Hi Tech*. doi:10.1108/LHT-10-2022-0472

Danciu, V. (2013). The contribution of sustainable marketing to sustainable development. *Management & Marketing*, *8*(2), 385.

Danciu, V., & Marketing, M. (2013). The contribution of sustainable marketing to sustainable development. *Challenges for the Knowledge Society*, *8*(2), 385–400.

Dangelico, R. M., & Pujari, D. (2010). Mainstreaming green product innovation: Why and how companies integrate environmental sustainability. *Journal of Business Ethics*, *95*(3), 471–486. doi:10.100710551-010-0434-0

Dangelico, R. M., & Vocalelli, D. (2017). 'Green Marketing': An analysis of definitions, strategy steps, and tools through a systematic review of the literature. *Journal of Cleaner Production*, *165*, 1263–1279. doi:10.1016/j.jclepro.2017.07.184

Danko, T.P., & Kitova, O.V. (2013). Issues of Digital Marketing Development. *Problems of Modern Economy*, *3*(47).

Dann, S. (2006). Social marketing in the age of direct benefit and upstream marketing. *Third Australasian non-profit and social marketing conference*. Australian National University.

Das, A. (2020). Low Carbon Growth, Climate Change and Sustainable Development Nexus: The Tale of Hong Kong. *Journal of Environmental Engineering and Its Scope*, *2*(3), 1–10.

Daud, I., Nurjannah, D., Mohyi, A., Ambarwati, T., Cahyono, Y., Haryoko, A., & Jihadi, M. (2022). The effect of digital marketing, digital finance and digital payment on finance performance of Indonesian smes. *International Journal of Data and Network Science*, *6*(1), 37–44. doi:10.5267/j.ijdns.2021.10.006

Davenport, T., Guha, A., Grewal, D., & Bressgott, T. (2019). How artificial intelligence will change the future of marketing. *Journal of the Academy of Marketing Science*, *48*(1), 24–42. doi:10.100711747-019-00696-0

Davey, L. (2022). 15 Green Marketing Examples to Inspire You in 2022. *Givz.* https://www.givz.com/blog/green-marketing-examples

Dawar, N., & Bagga, C. K. (2015). A Better Way to Map Brand Strategy. Figure out where you are on the distinctiveness-centrality spectrum. *Harvard Business Review*, (June), 90–97. https://hbr.org/2015/06/a-better-way-to-map-brand-strategy

Dayan, A. (2021). *4 Practical Ways to Use AI in Marketing (& Why You Need To)*. Business 2 Community. https://www.business2community.com/online-marketing/4-practical-ways-to-use-ai-in-marketing-why-you-need-to-02420037

de Freitas Netto, S. V., Sobral, M. F. F., Ribeiro, A. R. B., & Soares, G. R. D. L. (2020). Concepts and forms of greenwashing: A systematic review. *Environmental Sciences Europe*, *32*(1), 1–12. doi:10.118612302-020-0300-3

de Zubielqui, C. G., & Jones, J. (2022). How and when does internal and external social media use for marketing impact B2B SME performance? *Journal of Business & Industrial Marketing*.

de Zubielqui, G. C., Fryges, H., & Jones, J. (2019). Social media, open innovation & HRM: Implications for performance. *Technological Forecasting and Social Change*, *144*, 334–347. doi:10.1016/j.techfore.2017.07.014

Delmas, M. A., & Burbano, V. C. (2011). The drivers of greenwashing. *California Management Review*, *54*(1), 64–87. doi:10.1525/cmr.2011.54.1.64

Deng, S., & Chiu, D. K. W. (2023). Analyzing Hong Kong Philharmonic Orchestra's Facebook Community Engagement with the Honeycomb Model. In M. Dennis & J. Halbert (Eds.), *Community Engagement in the Online Space*. IGI. Global. doi:10.4018/978-1-6684-5190-8.ch003

Deng, W., Chin, G. Y.-l., Chiu, D. K. W., & Ho, K. K. W. (2022). Contribution of Literature Thematic Exhibition to Cultural Education: A Case Study of Jin Yong's Gallery. *Micronesian Educators*, *32*, 14–26.

Dennissen, M., Benschop, Y., & van den Brink, M. (2020). Rethinking diversity management: An intersectional analysis of diversity networks. *Organization Studies*, *41*(2), 219–240. doi:10.1177/0170840618800103

Dessart, F. J., & Van Bavel, R. (2017). Two converging paths: Behavioural sciences and social marketing for better policies. *Journal of Social Marketing*, *7*(4), 355–365. doi:10.1108/JSOCM-04-2017-0027

Dhurup, M., & Hislop, D. (2016). Developing sustainable marketing strategies in the urban environment: A social marketing approach. *Journal of Cleaner Production*, *112*.

Díaz Meneses, G., & Rodríguez, L. I. (2015). Comparing short-and long-term breastfeeding models. *Journal of Social Marketing*, *5*(4), 338–356. doi:10.1108/JSOCM-11-2014-0084

Diez-Martin, F., Blanco-Gonzalez, A., & Prado-Roman, C. (2019). Research challenges in digital marketing: Sustainability. *Sustainability (Basel)*, *11*(10), 2839. doi:10.3390u11102839

Dimitrieska, S., Stankovska, A., & Efremova, T. (2018). Artificial intelligence and marketing. *Entrepreneurship*, *6*(2), 298–304.

Compilation of References

Dinçer, H., Yüksel, S., Çağlayan, Ç., Yavuz, D., & Kararoğlu, D. (2023). Can Renewable Energy Investments Be a Solution to the Energy-Sourced High Inflation Problem? In *Managing inflation and supply chain disruptions in the global economy* (pp. 220–238). IGI Global.

Ding, S. J., Lam, E. T. H., Chiu, D. K. W., Lung, M. M., & Ho, K. K. W. (2021). Changes in reading behavior of periodicals on mobile devices: A comparative study. *Journal of Librarianship and Information Science*, *53*(2), 233–244. doi:10.1177/0961000620938119

Directive 2008/98/EC of the European Parliament and of the Council of 19 November 2008 on waste and repealing certain directives, Journal device L 312/3

Djakeli, K. (2013). Analyzing success and failure of two health reforms in independent Georgia. *The Journal of Business*, *2*(2), 5–14.

Donaldson, T., & Walsh, J. P. (2015). Toward a theory of business. *Research in Organizational Behavior*, *35*, 181–20. doi:10.1016/j.riob.2015.10.002

Doppelt, B. (2012). *The power of sustainable thinking: How to create a positive future for the climate, the planet, your organization and your life*. Routledge. doi:10.4324/9781849773232

Dowling, G., & Moran, P. (2012). Corporate reputations: Built-in or bolted on?'. *California Management Review*, *54*(2), 25–42. doi:10.1525/cmr.2012.54.2.25

Draskovic, N. (2007). The marketing role of packaging: A review. *International Journal of Management Cases*, *9*(3-4), 315–323. doi:10.5848/APBJ.2007.00034

Duan, W., Zou, S., Chen, Y., Nover, D., Fang, G., & Wang, Y. (2020). Sustainable water management for cross-border resources: The Balkhash Lake Basin of Central Asia, 1931–2015. *Journal of Cleaner Production*, *263*, 121614. doi:10.1016/j.jclepro.2020.121614

Dumitriu, D., Militaru, G., Deselnicu, D. C., Niculescu, A., & Popescu, M. A.-M. (2019). A Perspective Over Modern SMEs: Managing Brand Equity, Growth and Sustainability Through Digital Marketing Tools and Techniques. *Sustainability (Basel)*, *11*(7), 2111. doi:10.3390u11072111

Durif, F., Boivin, C., & Julien, C. (2010). In search of a green product definition. *Innovative Marketing*, *6*(1), 25-33.

Dursun, İ., & Belit, M. (2017). Bir Sosyal Pazarlama Hedefi Olarak Enerji Tasarrufu: Tasarruf Yöntemleri Kullanımına Yönelik Bir Ölçek Önerisi. *Ömer Halisdemir Üniversitesi İktisadi ve İdari Bilimler Fakültesi Dergisi*, *10*(3), 130-153.

Dwivedi and Pawsey. (2023). Examining the drivers of marketing innovation in SMEs. *Journal of Business Research*, *155*, 1–12.

Dwivedi, Y.K., Ismagilova, E., & Rana, N.P. (2021). *Social media adoption, usage and impact in business-to-business (B2B) context: a state-of-the-art literature review*.

Dwivedi, Y. K., Ismagilova, E., Hughes, D. L., Carlson, J., Filieri, R., Jacobson, J., Jain, V., Karjaluoto, H., Kefi, H., Krishen, A. S., Kumar, V., Rahman, M. M., Raman, R., Rauschnabel, P. A., Rowley, J., Salo, J., Tran, G. A., & Wang, Y. (2021). Setting the future of digital and social media marketing research: Perspectives and research propositions. *International Journal of Information Management*, *59*, 102168. doi:10.1016/j.ijinfomgt.2020.102168

Dwyer, D. B., Falkai, P., & Koutsouleris, N. (2018). Machine Learning Approaches for Clinical Psychology and Psychiatry. *Annual Review of Clinical Psychology*, *7*(14), 91–118. doi:10.1146/annurev-clinpsy-032816-045037 PMID:29401044

Eccles, R. G., & Karbassi, L. (2018). The right way to support sustainable development goals. *Sloan Review*. https://sloanreview.mit.edu/article/the-right-way-to-support-the-uns-sustainabledevelopment-goals

Ehnert, I. (2009). *Sustainable human resource management*. Physica-Verlag. doi:10.1007/978-3-7908-2188-8

Einwiller, S., Lis, B., Ruppel, C., & Sen, S. (2019). When CSR-based identification backfires: Testing the effects of CSR-related negative publicity. *Journal of Business Research*, *104*, 1–13. doi:10.1016/j.jbusres.2019.06.036

El Alfy, A., Darwish, K. M., & Weber, O. (2020). Corporations and sustainable development goals communication on social media: Corporate social responsibility or just another buzzword? *Sustainable Development (Bradford)*, *28*(5), 1418–1430. doi:10.1002d.2095

El Alfy, A., Palaschuk, N., El-Bassiouny, D., Wilson, J., & Weber, O. (2020). Scoping the evolution of corporate social responsibility (CSR) research in the sustainable development goals (SDGS) era. *Sustainability (Basel)*, *12*(14), 5544. doi:10.3390u12145544

Eley, B., & Tilley, S. (2009). *Online Marketing Inside Out*. SitePoint.

Elkington, J. (2018). 25 Years Ago I Coined the Phrase "Triple Bottom Line." Here's Why It's Time to Rethink It. *Harvard Business Review*. https://hbr.org/2018/06/25-years-ago-i-coined-the-phrase-triple-bottom-line-heres-why-im-giving-up-on-it

Elkington, J. (1994). Towards the Sustainable Corporation: Win-Win-Win Business Strategies for Sustainable Development. *California Management Review*, *36*(2), 90–100. doi:10.2307/41165746

Ellen MacArthur Foundation. (2015). *Towards a Circular Economy: The Business Case for Accelerated Change*. https://www.ellenmacarthurfoundation.org/assets/downloads/PL-Towards-a-Circular-Economy-Business-Rationale-for-an-Accelerated-Transition-v.1.5.1.pdfm

Ensor, T., & Rittmann, J. (1997). Reforming health care in the republic of Kazakhstan. The International *Journal of Health Planning and Management, 12*(3). 219-234. https://doi.org/ doi:10.1002/(sici)1099-1751(199707/09)12:3<219::aid-hpm482>3.0.co;2-i

Essam, R., & Mahrous, A. A. (2019). A Qualitative Study of Cause-Related Marketing Campaigns and Consumers' Purchase Intention of On-Demand Ride Services in Egypt. SSRN *Electronic Journal*. https://doi.org/ doi:10.2139/SSRN.3464859

Esteban-Sanchez, P., de la Cuesta-Gonzalez, M., & Paredes-Gazquez, J. D. (2017). Corporate social performance and its relation with corporate financial performance: International evidence in the banking industry. *Journal of Cleaner Production*, *162*, 1102–1110. doi:10.1016/j.jclepro.2017.06.127

Esterl, M. (2014). 'Share a coke' credited with a pop in sales. Marketing campaign that put first names on bottles reversed downward slide. *The Wall Street Journal*. Retrieved January 25, 2023 from https://www.wsj.com/articles/share-a-coke-credited-with-a-pop-in-sales-1411661519

Ethical Consumers Among the Millennials. A Cross-National Study on JSTOR. (n.d.). Retrieved April 30, 2023, from https://www.jstor.org/stable/41684017

European Parliament. (2015). *Circular economy: definition, importance and benefits*. European Parliament. https://www.europarl.europa.eu/news/en/headlines/economy/20151201STO05603/circular-economy-definition-importance-and-benefits#:~:text=The%20circular%20economy%20is%20a,reducing%20waste%20to%20a%20minimum

Eurostat. (2022). *Packaging waste statistics*. Eurostat. https://ec.europa.eu/eurostat/statistics-explained/index.php?title=Packaging_waste_statistics

Ezeamuzie, N. M., Rhim, A. H. R., Chiu, D. K. W., & Lung, M. M. (2022). (in press). Mobile Technology Usage by Foreign Domestic Helpers: Exploring Gender Differences. *Library Hi Tech*. Advance online publication. doi:10.1108/LHT-07-2022-0350

Fallah Shayan, N., Mohabbati-Kalejahi, N., Alavi, S., & Zahed, M. A. (2022). Sustainable Development Goals (SDGs) as a Framework for Corporate Social Responsibility (CSR). *Sustainability (Basel)*, *14*(3), 1222. doi:10.3390u14031222

Fang, Z., Zhao, Y., Warner, R. D., & Johnson, S. K. (2017). Active and intelligent packaging in meat industry. *Trends in Food Science & Technology*, *61*, 60–71. doi:10.1016/j.tifs.2017.01.002

Fan, K. Y. K., Lo, P., Ho, K. K. W., So, S., Chiu, D. K. W., & Ko, K. H. T. (2020). Exploring the mobile learning needs amongst performing arts students. *Information Discovery and Delivery*, *48*(2), 103–112. doi:10.1108/IDD-12-2019-0085

Fan, X., Deng, N., Qian, Y., & Dong, X. (2022). Factors affecting the effectiveness of cause-related marketing: A meta-analysis. *Journal of Business Ethics*, *175*(2), 339–360. doi:10.100710551-020-04639-6 PMID:34024964

FAO. (n.d.). *Home*. Food and Agriculture Organization of the United Nations. www.fao.org

Fazal, O., & Hotez, P. J. (2020). NTDs in the age of urbanization, climate change, and conflict: Karachi, Pakistan as a case study. *PLoS Neglected Tropical Diseases*, *14*(11), e0008791. doi:10.1371/journal.pntd.0008791 PMID:33180793

Feng, P., & Ngai, C. (2020). Doing more on the corporate sustainability front: A longitudinal analysis of CSR reporting of global fashion companies. *Sustainability (Basel)*, *12*(6), 2477. doi:10.3390u12062477

Fernandes, C. I., Ferreira, J. J., Lobo, C. A., &Raposo, M. (2020). The impact of market orientation on the internationalisation of SMEs. *Review of International Business and Strategy*.

Fernández, A. (2019). Artificial intelligence in financial services. *Banco de Espana Article*, *3*, 19.

Fernández, P., Hartmann, P., & Apaolaza, V. (2022). What drives CSR communication effectiveness on social media? A process-based theoretical framework and research agenda. *International Journal of Advertising*, *41*(3), 385–413. doi:10.1080/02650487.2021.1947016

Fineberg, H. V. (2012). A successful and sustainable health system—How to get there from here. *The New England Journal of Medicine*, *366*(11), 1020–1027. doi:10.1056/NEJMsa1114777 PMID:22417255

Fiscella, K. (2011). Health care reform and equity: Promise, pitfalls, and prescriptions. *Annals of Family Medicine*, *9*(1), 78–84. doi:10.1370/afm.1213 PMID:21242565

Floreddu, P. B., & Cabiddu, F. (2016). Social media communication strategies. *Journal of Services Marketing*, *34*(1), 1–5.

Folse, J. A. G., Niedrich, R. W., & Grau, S. L. (2010). Cause-relating marketing: The effects of purchase quantity and firm donation amount on consumer inferences and participation intentions'. *Journal of Retailing*, *86*(4), 295–309. doi:10.1016/j.jretai.2010.02.005

Fong, K. C. H., Au, C. H., Lam, E. T. H., & Chiu, D. K. W. (2020). Social network services for academic libraries: A study based on social capital and social proof. *Journal of Academic Librarianship*, *46*(1), 102091. doi:10.1016/j.acalib.2019.102091

Fonseca-Santos, B., Corrêa, M. A., & Chorilli, M. (2015). Sustainability, natural and organic cosmetics: Consumer, products, efficacy, toxicological and regulatory considerations. *Brazilian Journal of Pharmaceutical Sciences*, *51*(1), 17–26. doi:10.1590/S1984-82502015000100002

Foroudi, P., Marvi, R., Cuomo, M. T., Bagozzi, R., Dennis, C., & Jannelli, R. (2022). Consumer Perceptions of Sustainable Development Goals: Conceptualization, Measurement and Contingent Effects. *British Journal of Management*, *00*, 1–27. doi:10.1111/1467-8551.12637

Fraj, E., Martínez, E., & Matute, J. (2011). *Green marketing strategy and the firm's performance: the moderating role of environmental culture*. doi:10.1080/0965254X.2011.581382

Franca, C. C. V., & Ueno, H. M. (2020). Green cosmetics: Perspectives and challenges in the context of green chemistry. *Desenvolvimento e Meio Ambiente*, *53*, 53. doi:10.5380/dma.v53i0.62322

Frank-Martin, B., & Peattie, K. J. (2009). *Sustainability marketing: a global perspective*. Wiley.

Frenkel, S. J., & Schuessler, E. S. (2021). From Rana Plaza to COVID-19: Deficiencies and opportunities for a new labour governance system in garment global supply chains. *International Labour Review*, *160*(4), 591–609. doi:10.1111/ilr.12208 PMID:34230680

Friederici. (2022). *The Digital Transformation of Small Business Support*. STRive Community.

Friedman, M. (1982). *Capitalism and Freedom*. The University of Chicago Press.

Friedman, R., & Friedman, M. (1996). *Free Choice*. Panta Publishing House.

Fu, J., & Lu, X. (2020). *Sustainable Energy and Green Finance for a Low-carbon Economy: Perspectives from the Greater Bay Area of China*. Springer. doi:10.1007/978-3-030-35411-4

Fuller, D. A., & Tian, R. G. (2006). Social norms and consumers' willingness to pay for green electricity. *Energy Policy*, *34*(18), 36–43.

Fung, R. H. Y., Chiu, D. K. W., Ko, E. H. T., Ho, K. K., & Lo, P. (2016). Heuristic usability evaluation of university of Hong Kong Libraries' mobile website. *Journal of Academic Librarianship*, *42*(5), 581–594. doi:10.1016/j.acalib.2016.06.004

Furtado, B. A., & Sampaio, D. O. (2020). Cosméticos sustentáveis: Quais fatores influenciam o consumo destes produtos? *International Journal of Business Marketing*, *5*(1), 36–54.

Gaber, H. R., Wright, L. T., & Kooli, K. (2019). Consumer attitudes towards Instagram advertisements in Egypt: The role of the perceived advertising value and personalization. *Cogent Business & Management*, *6*(1), 1618431. doi:10.1080/23311975.2019.1618431

Galbraith, J. K. (1979). *Economics and Social Goals*. National Scientific Publishing House.

Garavaglia, E., Marcaletti, F., & Iñiguez-Berrozpe, T. (2021). Action research in age management: The quality of ageing at work model. *Work, Aging and Retirement*, *7*(4), 339–351. doi:10.1093/workar/waaa025

García-Salirrosas, E. E., & Rondon-Eusebio, R. F. (2022). Green Marketing Practices Related to Key Variables of Consumer Purchasing Behavior. *Sustainability (Basel)*, *14*(14), 8499. doi:10.3390u14148499

García-Sánchez, I. M., Frías-Aceituno, J. V., & Rodríguez-Domínguez, L. (2013). Determinants of corporate social disclosure in Spanish local governments. *Journal of Cleaner Production*, *39*, 60–72. doi:10.1016/j.jclepro.2012.08.037

Garg, S., & Sharma, V. (2017). Green Marketing: An Emerging Approach to Sustainable Development. *International Journal of Applied Agricultural Research*, *12*(2), 177–184.

Gartner. (2019). *4 Hidden forces that will shape marketing in 2019*. Gartner Research. https://www.gartner.com/en/marketing/insights/articles/4-hidden-forces-that-will-shape-marketing-in-2019

Gaustad, T., Utgård, J., & Fitzsimons, G. J. (2020). When accidents are good for a brand. *Journal of Business Research*, *107*, 153–161. doi:10.1016/j.jbusres.2018.10.040

Gavala, G. (2022, March 2). 5 Business Process Management Statistics You Should Know. *Solutions Review*. https://solutionsreview.com/business-process-management/business-process-management-statistics-you-should-know/

Gazzola, P., Pavione, E., Pezzetti, R., & Grechi, D. (2020). Trends in the Fashion Industry. The Perception of Sustainability and Circular Economy: A Gender/Generation Quantitative Approach. *Sustainability*, *12*(7), 2809. doi:10.3390/su12072809

Geissdoerfer, M., Vladimirova, D., & Evans, S. (2018). Sustainable business model innovation: A review. *Journal of Cleaner Production*, *198*, 401–416. doi:10.1016/j.jclepro.2018.06.240

Gensler, G., & Bailey, L. (2020). Deep Learning and Financial Stability. SSRN *Electronic Journal*. doi:10.2139/ssrn.3723132

Gerard, P., & Leyland, P. (1996). Packaging, marketing, logistics and the environment: Are there trade-offs? *International Journal of Physical Distribution & Logistics Management*, *26*(6), 60–72. doi:10.1108/09600039610125206

Germany's most sustainable brands. (2015). nachhaltigkeitspreis.de

Geyskens et al., (1999). A meta – analysis of satisfaction in marketing channel relationships. *Journal of Marketing Research*, 36 (2), ;

Ghaani, M., Cozzolino, C. A., Castelli, G., & Farris, S. (2016). An overview of the intelligent packaging technologies in the food sector. *Trends in Food Science & Technology*, *51*, 1–11. doi:10.1016/j.tifs.2016.02.008

Ghauri, P. (2004). Designing and conducting case studies in international business research. In Handbook of qualitative research methods for international business. Edward Elgar. doi:10.4337/9781781954331.00019

Ghazali, E., Soon, P. C., Mutum, D. S., & Nguyen, B. (2017). Health and cosmetics: Investigating consumers' values for buying organic personal care products. *Journal of Retailing and Consumer Services*, *39*, 154–163. doi:10.1016/j.jretconser.2017.08.002

Ghosh, S., & Rajan, J. (2019). The business case for SDGs: An analysis of inclusive business models in emerging economies. *International Journal of Sustainable Development and World Ecology*, *26*(4), 344–353. doi:10.1080/13504509.2019.1591539

Giatsoglou, M., Vozalis, M. G., Diamantaras, K., Vakali, A., Sarigiannidis, G., & Chatzisavvas, K. C. (2017). Sentiment analysis leveraging emotions and word embeddings. *Expert Systems with Applications*, *69*, 214–224. doi:10.1016/j.eswa.2016.10.043

Gigauri, I. (2020). Implications Of Covid-19 For Human Resources; Management SSRG. *International Journal of Economics and Management Studies*, *7*(11).

Gigauri, I. (2021a). New Economic Concepts Shaping Business Models in Post-Pandemic Era. *International Journal of Innovative Technologies in Economy*, *1*(33). doi:10.31435/rsglobal_ijite/30032021/7393

Gigauri, I. (2021b). Corporate Social Responsibility and COVID-19 Pandemic Crisis: Evidence from Georgia. [IJSECSR]. *International Journal of Sustainable Entrepreneurship and Corporate Social Responsibility*, *6*(1), 30–47. doi:10.4018/IJSECSR.2021010103

Gigauri, I., & Djakeli, K. (2021). Expecting Transformation of Marketing During the Post-Pandemic New Normal: Qualitative Research of Marketing Managers in Georgia. [IJSEM]. *International Journal of Sustainable Economies Management*, *10*(2), 1–18. doi:10.4018/IJSEM.2021040101

Gigauri, I., & Djakeli, K. (2021). National Health Reforms in Georgia during 1994-2021 and their Success. *HOLISTICA–Journal of Business and Public Administration*, *12*(2), 102–108. doi:10.2478/hjbpa-2021-0017

Gigauri, I., & Djakeli, K. (2021). Remote working challenges for Georgian social enterprises in the context of the current pandemic. *HOLISTICA–Journal of Business and Public Administration*, *12*(3), 39–53. doi:10.2478/hjbpa-2021-0021

Gigauri, I., & Vasilev, V. (2022). Corporate Social Responsibility in the Energy Sector: Towards Sustainability. In S. A. R. Khan, M. Panait, F. Puime Guillen, & L. Raimi (Eds.), *Energy Transition. Industrial Ecology*. Springer. doi:10.1007/978-981-19-3540-4_10

Gilbert, P. R. (2018). Class, complicity, and capitalist ambition in Dhaka's elite enclaves. *Focaal: Tijdschrift voor Antropologie*, *81*(81), 43–57. doi:10.3167/fcl.2018.810104

Gil-Gomez, H., Guerola-Navarro, V., Oltra-Badenes, R., & Lozano-Quilis, J. A. (2020). Customer relationship management: digital transformation and sustainable business model innovation. *Economic research-Ekonomskaistraživanja*, *33*(1), 2733-2750.

Gil-Soto, E., Armas-Cruz, Y., Morini-Marrero, S., & Ramos-Henríquez, J. M. (2019). Hotel guests' perceptions of environmental friendly practices in social media. *International Journal of Hospitality Management*, *78*, 59–67. doi:10.1016/j.ijhm.2018.11.016

Gironda, J. T., & Korgaonkar, P. K. (2018). iSpy? Tailored versus invasive ads and consumers' perceptions of personalized advertising. *Electronic Commerce Research and Applications*, *29*, 64–77. doi:10.1016/j.elerap.2018.03.007

Glaeser, E. L. (2014). A world of cities: The causes and consequences of urbanization in poorer countries. *Journal of the European Economic Association*, *12*(5), 1154–1199. doi:10.1111/jeea.12100

Glaeser, E. L. (2014). Understanding cities. *Journal of Economic Literature*, *52*(3), 697–738.

Gleim, M. R., Smith, J. S., Andrews, D., & Cronin, J. J. Jr. (2013). Against the green: A multi-method examination of the barriers to green consumption. *Journal of Retailing*, *89*(1), 44–61. doi:10.1016/j.jretai.2012.10.001

Global Sustainable Development Report (GSDR). (2015). UN. https://sustainabledevelopment.un.org/content/documents/5839GSDR%202015_SD_concept_definiton_rev.pdf. [Online]

Globe Newswire. (2022). Active and Intelligent Packaging Market Overview. *Globe Newswire*. https://www.globenewswire.com/en/news-release/2022/06/27/2469410/0/en/Active-and-Intelligent-Packaging-Market-Worth-USD-26-8-Billion-by-2028-at-6-51-CAGR-Report-by-Market-Research-Future-MRFR.html

Gobbo, J. A. Jr, & Olsson, A. (2010). The transformation between exploration and exploitation applied to inventors of packaging innovations. *Technovation*, *30*(5-6), 322–331. doi:10.1016/j.technovation.2010.01.001

Goering, J. (2009). Sustainable real estate development: The dynamics of market penetration. *Journal of Sustainable Real Estate*, *1*(1), 167–201. doi:10.1080/10835547.2009.12091794

Goh, S. K., & Balaji, M. (2016). Linking green skepticism to green purchase behavior. *Journal of Cleaner Production*, *131*, 629–638. doi:10.1016/j.jclepro.2016.04.122

Golmohammadi, A., Gauri, D. K., & Mirahmad, H. (2023). Social Media Communication and Company Value: The Moderating Role of Industry Competitiveness. *Journal of Service Research*, *26*(1), 120–135. doi:10.1177/10946705211072429

Goossens, J., Jonckheere, A. C., Dupont, L. J., & Bullens, D. M. (2021). Air pollution and the airways: Lessons from a century of human urbanization. *Atmosphere (Basel)*, *12*(7), 898. doi:10.3390/atmos12070898

Gordon, R. (2011). Critical social marketing: Definition, application and domain. *Journal of Social Marketing*, *1*(2), 82–99. doi:10.1108/20426761111141850

Gordon, R., Carrigan, M., & Hastings, G. (2011). A framework for sustainable marketing. *Marketing Theory*, *11*(2), 143–163. doi:10.1177/1470593111403218

Gordon, R., Waitt, G., Cooper, P., & Butler, K. (2018). Storying energy consumption: Collective video storytelling in energy efficiency social marketing. *Journal of Environmental Management*, *213*, 1–10. doi:10.1016/j.jenvman.2018.02.046 PMID:29477845

Graf von der Schulenburg, J. M. (2005). German health care system in transition: The difficult way to balance cost containment and solidarity. *The European Journal of Health Economics*, *6*(2), 183–187. doi:10.100710198-005-0298-x PMID:15909198

Green Marketing vs. Sustainable Marketing. (2022). Available at: https://www.clickinsights.asia/post/green-marketing-vs-sustainable-marketing

Griffin, L. (2023). 5 best practices for a sustainable marketing strategy. *Tech Target*. https://www.techtarget.com/searchcustomerexperience/tip/Best-practices-for-a-sustainable-marketing-strategy

Groening, C., Sarkis, J., & Zhu, Q. (2018). Green marketing consumer-level theory review: A compendium of applied theories and further research directions. *Journal of Cleaner Production*, *172*, 1848–1866. doi:10.1016/j.jclepro.2017.12.002

Gronroos, C. (1994). From marketing mix to relationship marketing. *Management Decisions*, *32* (2)

Gross, J., & Ouyang, Y. (2021). Types of urbanization and economic growth. *International Journal of Urban Sciences*, *25*(1), 71–85. doi:10.1080/12265934.2020.1759447

Gruner, R. L., Vomberg, A., Homburg, C., & Lukas, B. A. (2019). Supporting New Product Launches With Social Media Communication and Online Advertising: Sales Volume and Profit Implications. *Journal of Product Innovation Management*, *36*(2), 172–195. doi:10.1111/jpim.12475

Guinot, J. (2020). Changing the economic paradigm: Towards a sustainable business model. *International Journal of Sustainable Development and Planning*, *15*(5), 603–610. doi:10.18280/ijsdp.150502

Han, J. H., Ho, C. H., & Rodrigues, E. T. (2005). Intelligent packaging. *Innovations in food packaging*, 138-155. doi:10.1016/B978-012311632-1/50041-3

Harahap, A., Zuhriyah, A., & Rahmayanti, H. (2018). Relationship between knowledge of green product, social impact and perceived value with green purchase behavior. E3S Web of Conferences, Hwang, J. K., Kim, E.-J., Lee, S.-M., & Lee, Y.-K. (2021). Impact of susceptibility to global consumer culture on commitment and loyalty in botanic cosmetic brands. *Sustainability*, *13*(2), 892.

Hartley, D. M., Reisinger, H. S., & Perencevich, E. N. (2020). When infection prevention enters the temple: Intergenerational social distancing and Covid-19. *Infection Control and Hospital Epidemiology*, *41*(7), 868–869. doi:10.1017/ice.2020.100 PMID:32234091

Hartmann, P., & Apaolaza-Ibáñez, V. (2020). An update on the green washing phenomenon: Evidence from online stores. *Journal of Business Research*, *107*, 97–109.

Harvey, D. (2007). *A brief history of neoliberalism*. Oxford University Press.

Harvey, D. (2016). *Neoliberalism is a political project*. Jacobin Magazine.

Harvey, D. (2022). The double consciousness of capital. *Socialist Register*, *58*.

Hasan, J. (2013). *The Competitiveness of Ready Made Garments 2 Industry of Bangladesh in Post MFA era: How 3 does the industry behave to face the 4 competitive challenge?* Academic Press.

Hasan, M. T. (2022). *Everyday life of ready-made garment kormi in Bangladesh*. Palgrave Macmillan. doi:10.1007/978-3-030-99902-5

Hastings, G. (2003). Relational paradigms in social marketing. *Journal of Macromarketing, 23*(1), 6–15. doi:10.1177/0276146703023001006

Haudi, H., Rahadjeng, E., Santamoko, R., Putra, R., Purwoko, D., Nurjannah, D., & Purwanto, A. (2022). The role of e-marketing and e-CRM on e-loyalty of Indonesian companies during Covid pandemic and digital era. *Uncertain Supply Chain Management, 10*(1), 217–224. doi:10.5267/j.uscm.2021.9.006

Hauschild, T., & Berkhout, E. (2009). *Health-Care Reform in Georgia. A Civil-Society Perspective: Country Case Study. Oxfam Research Report*. Oxfam International.

Hayes, A. (2021). Multifiber Arrangement (MFA). In *Investopedia*. Retrieved from https://www.investopedia.com/terms/m/multi-fiber-arrangement.asp

He, H., & Harris, L. (2020). The impact of Covid-19 pandemic on corporate social responsibility and marketing philosophy. *Journal of Business Research, 116*, 176–182. doi:10.1016/j.jbusres.2020.05.030 PMID:32457556

Hepburn, S. J. (2015). *In Patagonia (Clothing): A Complicated Greenness*. doi:10.2752/175174113X13718320331035

Heras-Saizarbitoria, I., Urbieta, L., & Boiral, O. (2022). Organizations' engagement with sustainable development goals: From cherry-picking to SDG-washing? *Corporate Social Responsibility and Environmental Management, 29*(2), 316–328. doi:10.1002/csr.2202

Hess, P. N. (2016). *Economic Growth and Sustainable Development*. Routledge. doi:10.4324/9781315722467

Hiba, J. C., Jentsch, M., & Zink, K. J. (2021). Globalization and working conditions in international supply chains. *Zeitschrift für Arbeitswissenschaft, 75*(2), 146–154. doi:10.100741449-021-00258-7 PMID:34188355

History, J. (2007). *Sustainable development – Historical roots of the concept*. doi:10.1080/15693430600688831

Hitchen, E. L., Nylund, P. A., Ferr'as, X., & Mussons, S. (2017). Social media: *Open innovation* in SMEs finds new support. *The Journal of Business Strategy, 38*(3), 21–29. doi:10.1108/JBS-02-2016-0015

Hitesh, B. (2021). Sustainable Marketing – Strategy, Importance and Principles. *Marketing 91*. https://www.marketing91.com/sustainable-marketing/

Hitka, M., Balazova, Z., Gražulis, V., & Lejskova, P. (2018). Differences in employee motivation in selected countries of CEE (Slovakia, Lithuania and the Czech Republic). *Inžinerinė ekonomika*.

Ho, K. K. W., Takagi, T., Ye, S., Au, C. K., & Chiu, D. K. W. (2018) The Use of Social Media for Engaging People with Environmentally Friendly Lifestyle – A Conceptual Model. *SIG Green Pre ICIS Workshop*. AISEL. https://aisel.aisnet.org/sprouts_proceedings_siggreen_2018/2/

Ho, C. Y., Chiu, D. K. W., & Ho, K. K. W. (2023). Green Space Development in Academic Libraries: A Case Study in Hong Kong. In V. Okojie & M. Igbinovia (Eds.), *Global Perspectives on Sustainable Library Practices* (pp. 142–156). IGI. Global.

Holland, M. (2022). SEC's proposed climate rule a game-changer for sustainability. *Tech Target*. https://www.techtarget.com/searchcio/news/252515034/SECs-proposed-climate-rule-a-game-changer-for-sustainability

Hollensbe, E., Wookey, Ch., Hickey, L., George, G., & Nichols, C. V. (2014). Organizations with Purpose. *Academy of Management Journal*, *57*(5), 1227–1234. doi:10.5465/amj.2014.4005

Hooper-Greenhill, E. (1994). *Museums and their visitors*. Routledge.

Ho, R. C., & Rezaei, S. (2018). Social Media Communication and Consumers Decisions: Analysis of the Antecedents for Intended Apps Purchase. *Journal of Relationship Marketing*, *17*(3), 204–228. doi:10.1080/15332667.2018.1492322

Horowitz, M. C., Allen, G. C., Saravalle, E., Cho, A., Frederick, K., & Scharre, P. (2018). *Artificial intelligence and international security*. Center for a New American Security.

Huang, C. (2012). *The impact of local environmental quality on international tourism demand: The case of China*. University of San Francisco.

Huang, K. F., Dyerson, R., Wu, L. Y., & Harindranath, G. (2015). From temporary competitive advantage to sustainable competitive advantage. *British Journal of Management*, *26*(4), 617–636. doi:10.1111/1467-8551.12104

Huang, M. H., & Rust, R. T. (2020). A strategic framework for artificial intelligence in marketing. *Journal of the Academy of Marketing Science*, *49*(1), 30–50. doi:10.100711747-020-00749-9

Huang, P. S., Paulino, Y., So, S., Chiu, D. K. W., & Ho, K. K. W. (2021). Editorial - COVID-19 Pandemic and Health Informatics (Part 1). *Library Hi Tech*, *39*(3), 693–695. doi:10.1108/LHT-09-2021-324

Huang, P.-S., Paulino, Y. C., So, S., Chiu, D. K. W., & Ho, K. K. W. (2022). Guest editorial: COVID-19 Pandemic and Health Informatics Part 2. *Library Hi Tech*, *40*(2), 281–285. doi:10.1108/LHT-04-2022-447

Huang, P.-S., Paulino, Y. C., So, S., Chiu, D. K. W., & Ho, K. K. W. (2023). Guest editorial: COVID-19 Pandemic and Health Informatics Part 3. *Library Hi Tech*, *41*(1), 1–6. doi:10.1108/LHT-02-2023-585

Hui, S. C., Kwok, M. Y., Kong, E. W. S., & Chiu, D. K. W. (2023). (in press). Information Security and Technical Issues of Cloud Storage Services: A Qualitative Study on University Students in Hong Kong. *Library Hi Tech*. doi:10.1108/LHT-11-2022-0533

Hung, S. W., Li, C. M., & Lee, J. M. (2019). Firm growth, business risk, and corporate social responsibility in Taiwan's food industry. *Agricultural Economics*, *65*(8), 366–374.

Huq, C. (2019). Opportunities and limitations of the accord: Need for a worker organizing model. In S. B. Saxena (Ed.), *Labor, Global Supply Chains, and the Garment Industry in South Asia* (pp. 63–83). Routledge. doi:10.4324/9780429430039-4

Huq, C. (2022). Interdisciplinary perspectives on global labor governance: Organizing, legal mobilization and decolonization. *Mich. J. Int'l L.*, *43*(43.2), 423–503. doi:10.36642/mjil.43.2.interdisciplinary

Huq, S. M., Nekmahmud, M., & Aktar, M. S. (2016). Unethical practices of advertising in Bangladesh: A case study on some selective products. *International Journal of Economics. Finance and Management Sciences*, *4*(1), 10–19.

Ibrahim, B., & Aljarah, A. (2018). Dataset of relationships among social media marketing activities, brand loyalty, revisit intention. Evidence from the hospitality industry in Northern Cyprus. *Data in Brief*, *21*, 1823–1828. doi:10.1016/j.dib.2018.11.024 PMID:30519601

Ichimura, M. (2003, January). Urbanization, urban environment, and land use: challenges and opportunities. In *Asia-Pacific Forum for Environment and Development, Expert Meeting* (Vol. 23, pp. 1–14).

Iles, A. (2008). Shifting to green chemistry: The need for innovations in sustainability marketing. *Business Strategy and the Environment*, *17*(8), 524–535. doi:10.1002/bse.547

Ilicic, J., & Webster, C. M. (2011). Effects of multiple endorsements and consumer–celebrity attachment on attitude and purchase intention [AMJ]. *Australasian Marketing Journal*, *19*(4), 230–237. doi:10.1016/j.ausmj.2011.07.005

IMD. (2022). Why all businesses should embrace sustainability. IMD. https://www.imd.org/research-knowledge/articles/why-all-businesses-should-embrace-sustainability/

Indumathi, R. (2018). Influence of digital marketing on brand building. [IJMET]. *International Journal of Mechanical Engineering and Technology*, *9*(7), 235–243.

Ishaya, B. J., Paraskevadakis, D., Bury, A., & Bryde, D. (2023). A systematic literature review of modern slavery through benchmarking global supply chain. *Benchmarking*. Advance online publication. doi:10.1108/BIJ-09-2022-0554

Islam, T., Islam, R., Pitafi, A. H., Xiaobei, L., Rehmani, M., Irfan, M., & Mubarak, M. S. (2021). The impact of corporate social responsibility on customer loyalty: The mediating role of corporate reputation, customer satisfaction, and trust. *Sustainable Production and Consumption*, *25*, 123–135. doi:10.1016/j.spc.2020.07.019

Issock, P. B. I., Roberts-Lombard, M., & Mpinganjira, M. (2020). The importance of customer trust for social marketing interventions: A case of energy-efficiency consumption. *Journal of Social Marketing*, *10*(2), 265–286. doi:10.1108/JSOCM-05-2019-0071

Jain, M., Sharma, G. D., & Srivastava, M. (2019). Can sustainable investment yield better financial returns: A comparative study of ESG indices and MSCI indices. *Risks*, *7*(1), 15. doi:10.3390/risks7010015

Jakeli, T., & Djakeli, K. (2016). Health Reforms Need Marketing-Analyzing Current Georgian Healthcare Model through Reform Marketing Matrix (RMM). *The Journal of Business*, *5*(2), 7–15. doi:10.31578/.v5i2.106

Janjua, L., Razzak, A., & Razzak, A. (2021). Lack of environmental policy and water governance: An alarming situation in Pakistan. [IJCEWM]. *International Journal of Circular Economy and Waste Management*, *1*(2), 29–40. doi:10.4018/IJCEWM.2021070104

Jankalová, M. (2012). Business Excellence evaluation as the reaction to changes in the global business environment. *Procedia: Social and Behavioral Sciences*, *62*, 1056–1060. doi:10.1016/j.sbspro.2012.09.180

Janßen, D., & Langen, N. (2017). The bunch of sustainability labels–Do consumers differentiate? *Journal of Cleaner Production*, *143*, 1233–1245. doi:10.1016/j.jclepro.2016.11.171

Jarek, K., & Mazurek, G. (2019). Marketing and Artificial Intelligence. *Central European Business Review*, *8*(2).

Jariwala, H. J., Syed, H. S., Pandya, M. J., & Gajera, Y. M. (2017). Noise pollution & human health: A review. *Indoor and Built Environment*, *1*(1), 1–4.

Järlström, M., Saru, E., & Vanhala, S. (2018). Sustainable human resource management with salience of stakeholders: A top management perspective. *Journal of Business Ethics*, *152*(3), 703–724. doi:10.100710551-016-3310-8

Jesse, H. (2021). Cause-related marketing (CRM) is when a company collaborates with an NPO for a good purpose, something that is now criticized by many as a greenwashing guise. Are they right? We get to the bottom of this question. DM Exco. https://dm-exco.com/stories/cause-related-marketing/

Jessica, La. (2022). Sustainable Marketing Basics: 5 Strategies for Greener E-Commerce. *Spiralytics*. https://www.spiralytics.com/blog/sustainable-marketing-strategies-for-greener-ecommerce/

Jiang, T., Lo, P., Cheuk, M. K., Chiu, D. K. W., Chu, M. Y., Zhang, X., Zhou, Q., Liu, Q., Tang, J., Zhang, X., Sun, X., Ye, Z., Yang, M., & Lam, S. K. (2019) 文化新語:兩岸四地傑出圖書館、檔案館及博物館傑出工作者訪談 [New Cultural Dialog: Interviews with Outstanding Librarians, Archivists, and Curators in Greater China]. Hong Kong: Systech publications.

Jiang, X., Chiu, D. K. W., & Chan, C. T. (2023). Application of the AIDA model in social media promotion and community engagement for small cultural organizations: A case study of the Choi Chang Sau Qin Society. In M. Dennis & J. Halbert (Eds.), *Community Engagement in the Online Space* (pp. 48–70). IGI Global. doi:10.4018/978-1-6684-5190-8.ch004

Job, M.L., Njihia, M., J., & Iraki, X. (2020). Reverse Logistics and competitive advantage: The mediating effect of operational performance among manufacturing firms in Kenya. *European Scientific Journal*.

Jog, D., & Singhal, D. (2020). Greenwashing understanding among Indian consumers and its impact on their green consumption. *Global Business Review*, 0972150920962933. doi:10.1177/0972150920962933

Johnstone, M.-L., & Tan, L. P. (2015). Exploring the gap between consumers' green rhetoric and purchasing behaviour. *Journal of Business Ethics*, *132*(2), 311–328. doi:10.100710551-014-2316-3

Jones, P., Comfort, D., & Hillier, D. (2018). Common ground: The sustainable development goals and the marketing and advertising industry. *Journal of Public Affairs*, *18*(2), e1619. doi:10.1002/pa.1619

Joshi, Y., & Rahman, Z. (2015). Factors affecting green purchase behaviour and future research directions. *International. Strategic Management Review*, *3*(1-2), 128–143.

Joshi, Y., & Rahman, Z. (2017). Investigating the determinants of consumers' sustainable purchase behaviour. *Sustainable Production and Consumption*, *10*, 110–120. doi:10.1016/j.spc.2017.02.002

Joung, S. H., Park, S. W., & Ko, Y. J. (2014). Willingness to pay for eco-friendly products: Case of cosmetics. *Asia Marketing Journal*, *15*(4), 33–49. doi:10.53728/2765-6500.1565

Joyce, A., & Paquin, R. L. (2016). The triple layered business model canvas: A tool to design more sustainable business models. *Journal of Cleaner Production*, *135*, 1474–1486. doi:10.1016/j.jclepro.2016.06.067

Jung, J., Kim, S. J., & Kim, K. H. (2020). Sustainable marketing activities of traditional fashion market and brand loyalty. *Journal of Business Research*, *120*, 294–301. doi:10.1016/j.jbusres.2020.04.019

Jun, H., & Kim, M. (2021). From stakeholder communication to engagement for the sustainable development goals (SDGs): A case study of LG electronics. *Sustainability (Basel)*, *13*(15), 8624. doi:10.3390u13158624

Juwaini, A., Chidir, G., Novitasari, D., Iskandar, J., Hutagalung, D., Pramono, T., & Purwanto, A. (2022). The role of customer e-trust, customer e-service quality and customer e-satisfaction on customer e- loyalty. *International Journal of Data and Network Science*, *6*(2), 477–486. doi:10.5267/j.ijdns.2021.12.006

Kabeer, N. (2019). The evolving politics of labor standards in Bangladesh: Taking stock and looking forward. In S. B. Saxena (Ed.), *Labor, global supply chains, and the garment industry in South Asia* (pp. 231–259). Routledge. doi:10.4324/9780429430039-13

Kabir, H., Maple, M., Islam, M. S., & Usher, K. (2022a). A qualitative study of the working conditions in the readymade garment industry and the impact on workers' health and well-being. *Environmental and Occupational Health Practice*.

Kabir, H., Maple, M., Islam, M., & Usher, K. (2022b). The paradoxical impacts of the minimum wage implementation on ready-made garment (RMG) Workers: A qualitative study. *The Indian Journal of Labour Economics : the Quarterly Journal of the Indian Society of Labour Economics*, *65*(2), 1–25. doi:10.100741027-022-00375-9 PMID:35937940

Kadry, A. K. (2022). The Metaverse revolution and its impact on the future of advertising industry. *Journal of Design Sciences and Applied Arts*, *3*(2), 347–358. doi:10.21608/jdsaa.2022.129876.1171

Kahraman, A., & Kazançoğlu, İ. (2019). Understanding consumers' purchase intentions toward natural-claimed products: A qualitative research in personal care products. *Business Strategy and the Environment*, *28*(6), 1218–1233. doi:10.1002/bse.2312

Kaliyadan, F., Al Dhafiri, M., & Aatif, M. (2021). Attitudes toward organic cosmetics: A cross-sectional population-based survey from the Middle East. *Journal of Cosmetic Dermatology*, *20*(8), 2552–2555. doi:10.1111/jocd.13909 PMID:33355981

Kalpana, S., Priyadarshini, S. R., Leena, M. M., Moses, J. A., & Anandharamakrishnan, C. (2019). Intelligent packaging: Trends and applications in food systems. *Trends in Food Science & Technology*, *93*, 145–157. doi:10.1016/j.tifs.2019.09.008

Kanbur, R., & Zhuang, J. (2013). Urbanization and inequality in Asia. *Asian Development Review*, *30*(1), 131–147. doi:10.1162/ADEV_a_00006

Kapoor, P. S., Balaji, M. S., & Jiang, Y. (2021). Effectiveness of sustainability communication on social media: Role of message appeal and message source. *International Journal of Contemporary Hospitality Management*, *33*(3), 949–972. doi:10.1108/IJCHM-09-2020-0974

Kardas, P., Babicki, M., Krawczyk, J., & Mastalerz-Migas, A. (2022). War in Ukraine and the challenges it brings to the Polish healthcare system. *The Lancet Regional Health. Europe*, *15*, 15. doi:10.1016/j.lanepe.2022.100365 PMID:35531498

Karimi, L., Leggat, S. G., Bartram, T., Afshari, L., Sarkeshik, S., & Verulava, T. (2021). Emotional intelligence: Predictor of employees' wellbeing, quality of patient care, and psychological empowerment. *BMC Psychology*, *9*(1), 1–7. doi:10.118640359-021-00593-8 PMID:34088348

Kasim, T., Haracic, M., & Haracic, M. (2018). The Improvement of Business Efficiency Through Business Process Management, *Economic Review*. *Journal of Economics and Business*, *16*(1), 31–43.

Kate, A., Sahu, L. K., Pandey, J., Mishra, M., & Sharma, P. K. (2022, January 1). Green catalysis for chemical transformation: The need for the sustainable development. In *Current Research in Green and Sustainable Chemistry*. Elsevier B.V. doi:10.1016/j.crgsc.2021.100248

Katrandjiev, H. (n.d.). *Ecological Marketing, Green Marketing, Sustainable Marketing: Synonyms or an Evolution of Ideas?* Academic Press.

Kaur, B., Gangwar, V. P., & Dash, G. (2022). Green Marketing Strategies, Environmental Attitude, and Green Buying Intention: A Multi-Group Analysis in an Emerging Economy Context. *Sustainability (Basel)*, *14*(10), 6107. doi:10.3390u14106107

Kaur, K., & Kumar, P. (2020). Social media usage in Indian beauty and wellness industry: A qualitative study. *The TQM Journal*, *33*(1), 17–32. doi:10.1108/TQM-09-2019-0216

Keeble, B. R. (1988). The Brundtland report: 'Our common future'. *Medicine and War*, *4*(1), 17–25. doi:10.1080/07488008808408783

Keidanren (Japan Business Federation). (2016). *Toward Realization of the New Economy and Society, Reform of the Economy and Society by the Deepening of 'Society 5.0'*. Keidanren. https://www.keidanren.or.jp/en/policy/2016/029.html

Kemper, J. A., & Ballantine, P. W. (2019). What do we mean by sustainability marketing? *Journal of Marketing Management*, *35*(3-4), 277–309. doi:10.1080/0267257X.2019.1573845

Kendall, M. (2021). Sustainable Marketing: What It Is, Why It Matters, & How to Get It Right. *Unstack*. https://www.unstack.com/sustainable-marketing-what-it-is-why-it-matters-how-to-get-it-right

Kenzina, Ts., & Mandzhiev, B. (2016). Internet marketing as a tool for enterprise development. *Young Scientist, 27*(2), 18-20.

Keong, L. S., & Dastane, O. (2019). Building a sustainable competitive advantage for Multi- Level Marketing (MLM) firms: An empirical investigation of contributing factors. *Journal of Distribution Science, 17*(3), 5–19. doi:10.15722/jds.17.3.201903.5

Kerry, J., & Butler, P. (Eds.). (2008). *Smart packaging technologies for fast moving consumer goods*. John Wiley & Sons. doi:10.1002/9780470753699

Khaled, R., Ali, H., & Mohamed, E. K. A. (2021). The Sustainable Development Goals and corporate sustainability performance: Mapping, extent and determinants. *Journal of Cleaner Production, 311*(May), 127599. doi:10.1016/j.jclepro.2021.127599

Khan, A.S., Bilal, M., Saif, M., & Shehzad, M. (2020). Impact of Digital Marketing on Online Purchase Intention: Mediating Effect of Brand Equity & Perceived Value. *Inst. Bus. Manag*, 1-50.

Khan, S. A. R., Yu, Z., Panait, M., Janjua, L. R., & Shah, A. (Eds.). (2021). *Global corporate social responsibility initiatives for reluctant businesses*. IGI Global. doi:10.4018/978-1-7998-3988-0

Khater, D. (2021). A Procedural Paradigm for Green Project Management of Sustainable Development. In Towards Implementation of Sustainability Concepts in Developing Countries, 261–277. doi:10.1007/978-3-030-74349-9_20

Kim, D., Kim, E. A., & Shoenberger, H. (2023). The next hype in social media advertising: Examining virtual influencers' brand endorsement effectiveness. *Frontiers in Psychology, 14*, 485. doi:10.3389/fpsyg.2023.1089051 PMID:36949930

Kim, H. Y., & Chung, J. E. (2011). Consumer purchase intention for organic personal care products. *Journal of Consumer Marketing, 28*(1), 40–47. doi:10.1108/07363761111101930

Kim, K. H., & Kim, E. Y. (2020). Fashion marketing trends in social media and sustainability in fashion management. *Journal of Business Research, 11*(7), 1–2. doi:10.1016/j.jbusres.2020.06.001

Kim, R. Y. (2020). The impact of COVID-19 on consumers: Preparing for digital sales. *IEEE Engineering Management Review, 48*(3), 212–218. doi:10.1109/EMR.2020.2990115

Kim, S., & Seock, Y. K. (2009). Impacts of health and environmental consciousness on young female consumers' attitude towards and purchase of natural beauty products. *International Journal of Consumer Studies, 33*(6), 627–638. doi:10.1111/j.1470-6431.2009.00817.x

Kleniewski, N. (2018). *Cities, change, and conflict: A political economy of urban life*. Routledge.

Klineberg, S. L., McKeever, M., & Rothenbach, B. (1998). Demographic predictors of environmental concern: It does make a difference how it's measured. *Social Science Quarterly, 79*(4), 734–753.

Klöckner, C. A. (2013). A comprehensive model of the psychology of environmental behaviour - A meta-analysis. *Global Environmental Change, 23*(5), 1028–1038. doi:10.1016/j.gloenvcha.2013.05.014

Kollmuss, A., & Agyeman, J. (2002). Mind the gap: Why do people act environmentally and what are the barriers to pro-environmental behavior? *Environmental Education Research, 8*(3), 239–260. doi:10.1080/13504620220145401

Kong, H. M., Witmaier, A., & Ko, E. (2021). Sustainability and social media communication: How consumers respond to marketing efforts of luxury and non-luxury fashion brands. *Journal of Business Research*, *131*, 640–651. doi:10.1016/j.jbusres.2020.08.021

Kortam, W., & Mahrous, A. A. (2020). Sustainable Marketing: A Marketing Revolution or A Research Fad. *Archives of Business Research*, *8*(1), 172–181. doi:10.14738/abr.81.7747

Kotler, P. R., & Roberto, N. N. & Lee, N. (2002). *Social Marketing: Improving the quality of life*. Northwestern University.

Kotler, P., Kartajaya, H., & Setiawan, I. (2011). *Marketing 3.0: From Products to Customers to the Human Spirit*. doi:10.1002/9781118257883

Kotler, P. (2011). Reinventing marketing to manage the environmental imperative. *Journal of Marketing*, *75*(4), 132–135. doi:10.1509/jmkg.75.4.132

Kotler, P. T., & Armstrong, G. (2020). *Principles of marketing* (18th ed.). Person.

Kotler, P., Kartajaya, H., Hooi, D. H., & Liu, S. (2002). *Rethinking Marketing: Sustainable Marketing Enterprise in Asia*. Pearson Education Canada.

Kotler, P., Kartajaya, H., & Setiawan, I. (2016). *Marketing 4.0*. John Wiley & Sons.

Kotler, P., Kartajaya, H., & Setiawan, I. (2018). *Marketing 4.0: Moving from Traditional to Digital*. John Wiley & Sons.

Kotler, P., & Keller, K. L. (2014). *Marketing Management* (15th ed.). Pearson.

Kotler, P., & Lee, N. (2008). Social marketing: Influencing behaviors for good. *Sage (Atlanta, Ga.)*.

Kotler, P., & Levy, S. J. (1969). Broadening the concept of marketing. *Journal of Marketing*, *33*(1), 10–15. doi:10.1177/002224296903300103 PMID:12309673

Kotler, P., & Levy, S. J. (1971). Demarketing, yes, demarketing. *Harvard Business Review*, *79*, 74–80.

Kotler, P., & Zaltman, G. (1971). Social Marketing: An Approach to Planned Social Change. *Journal of Marketing*, *35*(3), 3–12. doi:10.1177/002224297103500302 PMID:12276120

Kou, G., Yüksel, S., & Dinçer, H. (2022). Inventive problem-solving map of innovative carbon emission strategies for solar energy-based transportation investment projects. *Applied Energy*, *311*, 118680. doi:10.1016/j.apenergy.2022.118680

Kozik, N. (2020). Sustainable packaging as a tool for global sustainable development. In *SHS Web of Conferences*, 74, 04012. EDP Sciences. 10.1051hsconf/20207404012

Kramar, R. (2014). Beyond strategic human resource management: Is sustainable human resource management the next approach? *International Journal of Human Resource Management*, *25*(8), 1069–1089. doi:10.1080/09585192.2013.816863

Krueger, R. A., & Casey, M. A. (2014). *Focus groups: A practical guide for applied research*. Sage publications.

Kumar, D. (2020). The study of the significance of digital marketing tools in the promotion of e-commerce websites. *PalArch's Journal of Archaeology of Egypt*, *17*(9), 10411–10425. https://www.archives.palarch.nl/index.php/jae/article/view/7316

Kumar, V., Rahman, Z., & Kazmi, A. A. (2013). *Sustainability Marketing Strategy: An Analysis of Recent Literature*. doi:10.1177/0972150913501598

Kumar, V., Rahman, Z., Kazmi, A. A., & Goyal, P. (2012). Evolution of sustainability as a marketing strategy: Beginning of new era. *Procedia: Social and Behavioral Sciences*, *37*, 482–489. doi:10.1016/j.sbspro.2012.03.313

Kurland, N. B., Baucus, M., & Steckler, E. (2022). Business and society in the age of COVID-19: Introduction to the special issue. *Business and Society Review*, *127*(S1), 147–157. doi:10.1111/basr.12265

Kusá. (2021). *Alena & Urmínová, Marianna*. Innovative Approaches in Marketing Communication in Sustainable Fashion Business. doi:10.34190/EIE.20.183

Kuswandi, B., Wicaksono, Y., Abdullah, A., Heng, L. Y., & Ahmad, M. (2011). Smart packaging: Sensors for monitoring of food quality and safety. *Sensing and Instrumentation for Food Quality and Safety*, *5*(3), 137–146. doi:10.100711694-011-9120-x

Kutzin, J., Cashin, C., Jakab, M., Fidler, A., & Menabde, N. (2010). Implementing Health Financing Reform in CE/EECCA Countries: Synthesis and Lessons Learned. In *Implementing Health Financing Reform: Lessons from Countries in Transition*. World Health Organization, The European Observatory on Health Systems and Policies.

Kyu Kim, Y., Yim, M. Y. C., Kim, E., & Reeves, W. (2020). Exploring the optimized social advertising strategy that can generate consumer engagement with green messages on social media. *Journal of Research in Interactive Marketing*, *15*(1), 30–48. doi:10.1108/JRIM-10-2019-0171

Labowitz, S. (2016). *New data on the number of factories in Bangladesh*. Retrieved from https://bhr.stern.nyu.edu/blogs/-data-on-number-of-factories-bd

Labowitz, S., & Baumann-Pauly, D. (2014). *Business as usual is not an option: Supply chains sourcing after Rana Plaza*. Stern Center for Business and Human Rights. http://stern. Nyu. Edu/sites/default/files/assets/documents/con_047408.Pdf

Lagomarsino, G., Garabrant, A., Adyas, A., Muga, R., & Otoo, N. (2012). Moving towards universal health coverage: Health insurance reforms in nine developing countries in Africa and Asia. *Lancet*, *380*(9845), 933–943. doi:10.1016/S0140-6736(12)61147-7 PMID:22959390

Lai, C. K., & Cheng, E. W. (2016). Green purchase behavior of undergraduate students in Hong Kong. *The Social Science Journal*, *53*(1), 67–76. doi:10.1016/j.soscij.2015.11.003

Lam, A. H. C., Ho, K. K. W., & Chiu, D. K. W. (2023). Instagram for student learning and library promotions? A quantitative study using the 5E Instructional Model. *Aslib Journal of Information Management*, *75*(1), 112–130. doi:10.1108/AJIM-12-2021-0389

Lam, E. T. H., Au, C. H., & Chiu, D. K. W. (2019). Analyzing the use of Facebook among university libraries in Hong Kong. *Journal of Academic Librarianship*, *45*(3), 175–183. doi:10.1016/j.acalib.2019.02.007

Lam, J. S. L., & Li, K. X. (2019). Green port marketing for sustainable growth and development. *Transport Policy*, *84*, 73–81. doi:10.1016/j.tranpol.2019.04.011

Laroche, M., Bergeron, J., & Barbaro-Forleo, G. (2001). Targeting consumers who are willing to pay more for environmentally friendly products. *Journal of Consumer Marketing*, *18*(6), 503–520. doi:10.1108/EUM0000000006155

Lawson, R., Grier, K., & Absher, S. (2019). You say you want a (Rose) Revolution? The effects of Georgia's 2004 market reforms. *Economics of Transition and Institutional Change*, *27*(1), 301–323. doi:10.1111/ecot.12205

Le Blanc, D. (2015). Towards integration at last? The sustainable development goals as a network of targets. *Sustainable Development (Bradford)*, *23*(3), 176–187. doi:10.1002d.1582

Lebelo, K., Masinde, M., Malebo, N., & Mochane, M. J. (2021). The surveillance and prediction of food contamination using intelligent systems: A bibliometric analysis. *British Food Journal*, *124*(4), 1149–1169. doi:10.1108/BFJ-04-2021-0366

Lee, M., & Park, S. Y. (2011). Cause-related marketing and consumers' responses to firms' ethical behavior: The moderating role of corporate social responsibility. *Journal of Business Ethics*, *103*(3), 435–451.

Lee, S. J., & Rahman, A. M. (2014). Intelligent packaging for food products. In J. H. Han (Ed.), *Innovations in food packaging* (pp. 171–209). Academic Press. doi:10.1016/B978-0-12-394601-0.00008-4

Lee, Y.-H., & Chen, S.-L. (2019). Effect of green attributes transparency on wta for green cosmetics: Mediating effects of CSR and green brand concepts. *Sustainability (Basel)*, *11*(19), 5258. doi:10.3390u11195258

Lei, S. Y., Chiu, D. K. W., Lung, M. M., & Chan, C. T. (2021). Exploring the aids of social media for musical instrument education. *International Journal of Music Education*, *39*(2), 187–201. doi:10.1177/0255761420986217

Lemus-Aguilar, I., Morales-Alonso, G., Ramirez-Portilla, A., & Hidalgo, A. (2019). Sustainable Business Models through the Lens of Organizational Design: A Systematic Literature Review. *Sustainability (Basel)*, *11*(19), 5379. doi:10.3390u11195379

Leopold, H. (2019). Innovation through culture and communication. *E&I Elektrotechnik und Informationstechnik*, *136*(3), 225–225. doi:10.100700502-019-0730-z

Lepkowska-White, E., Parsons, A. L., Wong, B., & White, A. M. (2023). Building a socially responsible global community? Communicating B Corps on social media. *Corporate Communications*, *28*(1), 86–102. doi:10.1108/CCIJ-01-2022-0005

Leung, T. N., Luk, C. K. L., Chiu, D. K. W., & Ho, K. K. W. (2022). User perceptions, academic library usage, and social capital: A correlation analysis under COVID-19 after library renovation. *Library Hi Tech*, *40*(2), 304–322. doi:10.1108/LHT-04-2021-0122

Lewinson, E. (2022, January 5). Artificial Intelligence in Finance: Opportunities and Challenges. *Medium*. https://towardsdatascience.com/artificial-intelligence-in-finance-opportunities-and-challenges-cee94f2f3858

Liao, H.-T., Zhao, M., & Sun, S.-P. (2020). A literature review of Museum and Heritage on Digitization, digitalization, and Digital Transformation. *Proceedings of the 6th International Conference on Humanities and Social Science Research (ICHSSR2020)*. Atlantis Press. 10.2991/assehr.k.200428.101

Li, K. K., & Chiu, D. K. W. (2022). A Worldwide Quantitative Review of the iSchools' Archival Education. *Library Hi Tech*, *40*(5), 1497–1518. doi:10.1108/LHT-09-2021-0311

Lim, X. J., Radzol, A. M., Cheah, J., & Wong, M. W. (2017). The impact of social media influencers on purchase intention and the mediation effect of customer attitude. *Asian Journal of Business Research*, *7*(2), 19–36. doi:10.14707/ajbr.170035

Lindridge, A., MacAskill, S., Gnich, W., Eadie, D., & Holme, I. (2013). Applying an ecological model to social marketing communications. *European Journal of Marketing*, *47*(9), 1399–1420. doi:10.1108/EJM-10-2011-0561

Lin, T. C. (2016). Compliance, technology, and modern finance. *Brook. J. Corp. Fin. & Com. L.*, *11*, 159.

Lin, T. C. (2019). Artificial intelligence, finance, and the law. *Fordham Law Review*, *88*, 531.

Liobikienė, G., & Bernatonienė, J. (2017). Why determinants of green purchase cannot be treated equally? The case of green cosmetics: Literature review. *Journal of Cleaner Production*, *162*, 109–120. doi:10.1016/j.jclepro.2017.05.204

Li, S. M., Lam, A. H. C., & Chiu, D. K. W. (2023). Digital transformation of ticketing services: A value chain analysis of POPTICKET in Hong Kong. In J. D. Santos & I. V. Pereira (Eds.), *Management and Marketing for Improved Retail Competitiveness and Performance*. IGI. Global.

Compilation of References

Li, S., Xie, Z., Chiu, D. K. W., & Ho, K. K. W. (2023). Sentiment Analysis and Topic Modeling Regarding Online Classes on the Reddit Platform: Educators versus Learners. *Applied Sciences (Basel, Switzerland)*, *13*(4), 2250. doi:10.3390/app13042250

Li, T. T., Wang, K., Sueyoshi, T., & Wang, D. D. (2021). ESG: Research progress and future prospects. *Sustainability (Basel)*, *13*(21), 11663. doi:10.3390u132111663

Liu, G. G., Vortherms, S. A., & Hong, X. (2017). China's health reform update. *Annual Review of Public Health*, *38*(1), 431–448. doi:10.1146/annurev-publhealth-031816-044247 PMID:28125384

Liu, L., Chen, R., & He, F. (2015). How to promote purchase of carbon offset products: Labeling vs. calculation? *Journal of Business Research*, *68*(5), 942–948. doi:10.1016/j.jbusres.2014.09.021

Liu, M. T., & Jindal, R. P. (2016). Green marketing: A review and research agenda. *International Journal of Management Reviews*, *18*(4), 504–521.

Liu, S., Perry, P., & Gadzinski, G. (2019). The implications of digital marketing on WeChat for luxury fashion brands in China. *Journal of Brand Management*, *26*(4), 395–409. doi:10.105741262-018-0140-2

Liu, X., Wang, C., Shishime, T., & Fujitsuka, T. (2012). Sustainable consumption: Green purchasing behaviours of urban residents in China. *Sustainable Development (Bradford)*, *20*(4), 293–308. doi:10.1002d.484

Liu, Y., Chiu, D. K. W., & Ho, K. K. W. (2023). Short-Form Videos for Public Library Marketing: Performance Analytics of Douyin in China. *Applied Sciences (Basel, Switzerland)*, *13*(6), 3386. doi:10.3390/app13063386

Li, X., He, X., & Zhang, Y. (2020). The impact of social media on the business performance of small firms in China. *Information Technology for Development*, *26*(2), 346–368. doi:10.1080/02681102.2019.1594661

Li, Y., Chu, F., Côté, J. F., Coelho, L. C., & Chu, C. (2020). The multi-plant perishable food production routing with packaging consideration. *International Journal of Production Economics*, *221*, 107472. doi:10.1016/j.ijpe.2019.08.007

Loeser, F., Recker, J., vom Brocke, J., Molla, A., & Zarnekow, R. (2017). How IT executives create organizational benefits by translating environmental strategies into Green IS initiatives. *Information Systems Journal*, *27*(4), 503–553. doi:10.1111/isj.12136

Lo, P., Allard, B., Anghelescu, H. G. B., Xin, Y., Chiu, D. K. W., & Stark, A. J. (2020). Transformational Leadership and Library Management in World's Leading Academic Libraries. *Journal of Librarianship and Information Science*, *52*(4), 972–999. doi:10.1177/0961000619897991

Lo, P., Chan, H. H. Y., Tang, A. W. M., Chiu, D. K. W., Cho, A., Ho, K. K. W., See-To, E., & He, J. (2019). Visualising and Revitalising Traditional Chinese Martial Arts – Visitors' Engagement and Learning Experience at the 300 Years of Hakka KungFu. *Library Hi Tech*, *37*(2), 273–292. doi:10.1108/LHT-05-2018-0071

Lo, P., Cho, A., Law, B. K. K., Chiu, D. K. W., & Allard, B. (2017). Progressive trends in electronic resources management among academic libraries in Hong Kong. *Library Collections, Acquisitions & Technical Services*, *40*(1-2), 28–37. doi:10.1080/14649055.2017.1291243

Lo, P., Hsu, W.-E., Wu, S. H. S., Travis, J., & Chiu, D. K. W. (2021). *Creating a Global Cultural City via Public Participation in the Arts: Conversations with Hong Kong's Leading Arts and Cultural Administrators*. Nova Science Publishers.

Lőrinczy, M., Sroka, W., Jankal, R., Hittmár, Š., & Szántó, R. (2015). *Trends in Business Ethics and Corporate Social Responsibility in Central Europe*. Shaker Verlag.

Low, M. P. (2016). Corporate Social Responsibility and the Evolution of Internal Corporate Social Responsibility in 21st Century. *Asian Journal of Social Sciences and Management Studies, 3*(1), 56–74. doi:10.20448/journal.500/2016.3.1/500.1.56.74

Luo, X., & Bhattacharya, C. B. (2006). Corporate Social Responsibility, Customer Satisfaction, and Market Value. *Journal of Marketing, 70*(4), 1–18. doi:10.1509/jmkg.70.4.001

Lu, S. S., Tian, R., & Chiu, D. K. W. (2023). (in press). Why do people not attend public library programs in the current digital age? *Library Hi Tech*. doi:10.1108/LHT-04-2022-0217

Lydekaityte, J., & Tambo, T. (2020). Smart packaging: Definitions, models and packaging as an intermediator between digital and physical product management. *International Review of Retail, Distribution and Consumer Research, 30*(4), 377–410. doi:10.1080/09593969.2020.1724555

M+ Museum. (2021) *M+Sustainable Document*. M+ Museum. https://webmedia.mplus.org.hk/documents/M_Sustainability_Document_EN_Accessible_Version.pdf

Maccarrone, P., & Contri, A. M. (2021). Integrating Corporate Social Responsibility into Corporate Strategy: The Role of Formal Tools. *Sustainability (Basel), 13*(22), 12551. doi:10.3390u132212551

Machová, R., Ambrus, R., Zsigmond, T., & Bakó, F. (2022). The Impact of Green Marketing on Consumer Behavior in the Market of Palm Oil Products. *Sustainability (Basel), 14*(3), 1364. doi:10.3390u14031364

Macke, J., & Genari, D. (2019). Systematic literature review on sustainable human resource management. *Journal of Cleaner Production, 208*, 806–815. doi:10.1016/j.jclepro.2018.10.091

Mah, M. W., Deshpande, S., & Rothschild, M. L. (2006). M.L. Rothschild Social marketing: A behaviour change technology for infection control. *American Journal of Infection Control, 34*(7), 452–457. doi:10.1016/j.ajic.2005.12.015 PMID:16945693

Mahmoudi, M., & Parviziomran, I. (2020). Reusable packaging in supply chains: A review of environmental and economic impacts, logistics system designs, and operations management. *International Journal of Production Economics, 228*, 107730. doi:10.1016/j.ijpe.2020.107730

Majeed, M. U., Aslam, S., Murtaza, S. A., Attila, S., & Molnár, E. (2022). Green Marketing Approaches and Their Impact on Green Purchase Intentions: Mediating Role of Green Brand Image and Consumer Beliefs towards the Environment. *Sustainability (Basel), 14*(18), 11703. doi:10.3390u141811703

Major Sustainability. (2022). Sustainability Marketing Strategy: Engaging Consumers in Responsible Consumption. *Major Sustainability*. https://majorsustainability.smeal.psu.edu/five-principles-of-sustainability-marketing/

Mak, M. Y. C., Poon, A. Y. M., & Chiu, D. K. W. (2022). Using Social Media as Learning Aids and Preservation: Chinese Martial Arts in Hong Kong. In S. Papadakis & A. Kapaniaris (Eds.), *The Digital Folklore of Cyberculture and Digital Humanities* (pp. 171–185). IGI Global. doi:10.4018/978-1-6684-4461-0.ch010

Malhotra, N., Hall, J., Shaw, M., & Oppenheim, P. (2006). *Marketing research: an applied orientation. Frenchs Forest*. Pearson Education Australia. doi:10.1108/S1548-6435(2006)2

Malik, A. Z., Thapa, S., & Paswan, A. K. (2023). Social media influencer (SMI) as a human brand – a need fulfillment perspective. *Journal of Product and Brand Management, 32*(2), 173–190. doi:10.1108/JPBM-07-2021-3546

Mandal, P. C. (2019). Public Policy Issues in Direct and Digital Marketing – Concerns and Initiatives: Public Policy in Direct and Digital Marketing. [IJPADA]. *International Journal of Public Administration in the Digital Age, 6*(4), 54–71. doi:10.4018/IJPADA.2019100105

Compilation of References

Mandarić, D., Hunjet, A., & Vuković, D. (2022). The Impact of Fashion Brand Sustainability on Consumer Purchasing Decisions. *J. Risk Financial Manag.*, *15*(4), 176. doi:10.3390/jrfm15040176

Manta, O. (2020). Financing and Fiscality in the context of artificial intelligence at the global level. *European Journal of Marketing and Economics*, *3*(1), 39–62. doi:10.26417/ejme.v3i1.p31-47

Manta, O., Panait, M., Hysa, E., Rusu, E., & Cojocaru, M. (2022). Public procurement, a tool for achieving the goals of sustainable development. *Amfiteatru Economic*, *61*(24), 861–876. doi:10.24818/EA/2022/61/861

Marcel, M., & Dragan, M. (2014, June). Sustainable marketing for sustainable development. In *Proceedings of the 11th International Academic Conference in Reykjavik* (pp. 230-248). ACM.

Marens, R. (2008). Recovering the past: Reviving the legacy of the early scholars of corporate social responsibility. *Journal of Management History*, *14*(1), 55–72. doi:10.1108/17511340810845480

Marketing, S. (2014). *Schouten* (International Edition). Sustainable Marketing. D. M. J. Pearson New.

Marques, S., & Domegan, C. (2011). Relationship marketing and social marketing. In G. Hastings, K. Angus, & C. Bryant (Eds.), *The SAGE Handbook of Social Marketing* (pp. 44–60). SAGE. doi:10.4135/9781446201008.n4

Martek, I., Hosseini, M. R., Shrestha, A., Edwards, D. J., & Durdyev, S. (2019). Barriers inhibiting the transition to sustainability within the Australian construction industry: An investigation of technical and social interactions. *Journal of Cleaner Production*, *211*, 281–292. doi:10.1016/j.jclepro.2018.11.166

Martin, D. M., & Schouten, J. W. (2014). The answer is sustainable marketing, when the question is: What can we do? *Recherche et applications en marketing*, *29*(3), 107-109.

Martin, M. (2022). 39 Facebook Stats That Matter to Marketers in 2022. *Hootsuite*. https://blog.hootsuite.com/facebook-statistics/

Martín-Cervantes, P. A., del Carmen Valls Martínez, M., & Gigauri, I. (2022a). Sustainable Marketing. In *Encyclopedia of Creativity, Invention, Innovation and Entrepreneurship*. Springer. doi:10.1007/978-1-4614-6616-1_200101-1

Martin, D. M., & Schouten, J. (2011). *Sustainable Marketing*. Pearson Prentice Hall.

Martin, D., & Schouten, J. (2014). *Sustainable marketing*. Pearson Prentice Hall.

Martínez-Jurado, P. J., & Moyano-Fuentes, J. (2014). Lean management, supply chain management and sustainability: A literature review. *Journal of Cleaner Production*, *85*, 134–150. doi:10.1016/j.jclepro.2013.09.042

Martínez, M. D. C. V., Martín-Cervantes, P. A., & del Mar Miralles-Quirós, M. (2022b). Sustainable development and the limits of gender policies on corporate boards in Europe. A comparative analysis between developed and emerging markets. *European Research on Management and Business Economics*, *28*(1), 100168. doi:10.1016/j.iedeen.2021.100168

Martin, K. D., & Murphy, P. E. (2017). The role of data privacy in marketing. *Journal of the Academy of Marketing Science*, *45*(2), 135–155. doi:10.100711747-016-0495-4

Masocha, R. (2021). Green marketing practices: Green branding, advertisements and labelling and their nexus with the performance of SMEs in South Africa. *Journal of Sustainability Science and Management*, *16*(1), 174–192. doi:10.46754/jssm.2021.01.015

Mason, W. R. (1958). A theory of packaging in the marketing mix. *Business Horizons*, *1*(3), 91–95. doi:10.1016/0007-6813(58)90082-X

Masouras, A., Maris, G., & Kavoura, A. (2020). *Entrepreneurial Development and Innovation in Family Businesses and SMEs*. Business Science Reference.

Matten, D., & Moon, J. (2020). Reflections on the 2018-decade award: The meaning and dynamics of corporate social responsibility. *Academy of Management Review*, *45*(1), 7–28. doi:10.5465/amr.2019.0348

Matthes, J., & Wonneberger, A. (2014). The skeptical green consumer revisited: Testing the relationship between green consumerism and skepticism toward advertising. *Journal of Advertising*, *43*(2), 115–127. doi:10.1080/00913367.2013.834804

Maziriri, E. T. (2020). Green packaging and green advertising as precursors of competitive advantage and business performance among manufacturing small and medium enterprises in South Africa. *Cogent Business & Management*, *7*(1), 1. doi:10.1080/23311975.2020.1719586

Mazurkiewicz, P. (2004). Corporate environmental responsibility: Is a common CSR framework possible. *World Bank*, *2*(1), 1-18.

McDonagh, P., & Prothero, A. (2014). Sustainability marketing research: Past, present and future. *Journal of Marketing Management*, *30*(11-12), 1186–1219. doi:10.1080/0267257X.2014.943263

McDonough, J. E. (2011). *Inside national health reform* (Vol. 22). Univ of California Press.

McKenzie-Mohr, D. (2000). Promoting sustainable behavior: An introduction to community-based social marketing. *The Journal of Social Issues*, *56*(3), 543–554. doi:10.1111/0022-4537.00183

McKinsey. (2021). *How companies capture the value of sustainability: Survey findings*. McKinsey. https://www.mckinsey.com/capabilities/sustainability/our-insights/how-companies-capture-the-value-of-sustainability-survey-findings

Meadows, D. H., Meadows, D. L., Randers, J., & Behrens, W. W. (1973). *Limits to Growth*. National Economic Publishing House.

Medeiros, E., & van der Zwet, A. (2020). Sustainable and integrated urban planning and governance in metropolitan and medium-sized cities. *Sustainability (Basel)*, *12*(15), 5976. doi:10.3390u12155976

Mefford, R. N. (2011). The economic value of a sustainable supply chain. *Business and Society Review*, *116*(1), 109–143. doi:10.1111/j.1467-8594.2011.00379.x

Melović, B., Cirović, D., Backovic-Vulić, T., Dudić, B., & Gubiniova, K. (2020). Attracting green consumers as a basis for creating sustainable marketing strategy on the organic market—Relevance for sustainable agriculture business development. *Foods*, *9*(11), 1552. doi:10.3390/foods9111552 PMID:33120944

Melovic, B., Jocovic, M., Dabic, M., Vulic, T. B., & Dudic, B. (2020). The impact of digital transformation and digital marketing on the brand promotion, positioning and electronic business in Montenegro. *Technology in Society*, *63*, 101425. doi:10.1016/j.techsoc.2020.101425

Menegaki, A. N. (2012). A social marketing mix for renewable energy in Europe based on consumer stated preference surveys. *Renewable Energy*, *39*(1), 30–39. doi:10.1016/j.renene.2011.08.042

Meng, Y., Chu, M. Y., & Chiu, D. K. W. (2023). The impact of COVID-19 on museums in the digital era: Practices and Challenges in Hong Kong. *Library Hi Tech*, *41*(1), 130–151. doi:10.1108/LHT-05-2022-0273

Menon, A., Menon, A., Chowdhury, J., & Jankovich, J. (1999). Evolving paradigm for environmental sensitivity in marketing programs: A synthesis of theory and practice. *Journal of Marketing Theory and Practice*, *7*(2), 1–15. doi:10.1080/10696679.1999.11501825

Mensah, J., & Casadevall, S. R. (2019). Sustainable development: Meaning, history, principles, pillars, and implications for human action: Literature review. *Cogent Social Sciences*, *5*(1), 1653531. doi:10.1080/23311886.2019.1653531

Meria, L., Aini, Q., Santoso, N. P. L., Raharja, U., & Millah, S. (2021). Management of Access Control for Decentralized Online Educations using Blockchain Technology. *2021 Sixth International Conference on Informatics and Computing (ICIC)*, (pp. 1–6). IEEE. 10.1109/ICIC54025.2021.9632999

Mesarović, M., & Pestel, E. (1977). *Humanity at a turning point*. National Economic Publishing House.

Metz, P., Burek, S., Hultgren, T. R., Kogan, S., & Schwartz, L. (2016). The Path to Sustainability-Driven Innovation: Environmental sustainability can be the foundation for increasing competitive advantage and the basis for effective innovation. *Research Technology Management*, *59*(3), 50–61. doi:10.1080/08956308.2016.1161409

Michael, B. (2003). Corporate social responsibility in international development: An overview and critique 1. *Corporate Social Responsibility and Environmental Management*, *10*(3), 115–128. doi:10.1002/csr.41

Mihardjo, L., Sasmoko, S., Alamsjah, F., & Elidjen, E. (2019). The influence of digital customer experience and electronic word of mouth on brand image and supply chain sustainable performance. *Uncertain Supply Chain Management*, *7*(4), 691–702. doi:10.5267/j.uscm.2019.4.001

Mikušová, M. (2017). To be or not to be a business responsible for sustainable development? Survey from small Czech businesses. *Economic Research –. Ekonomska Istrazivanja*, *30*(1), 1318–1338. doi:10.1080/1331677X.2017.1355257

Minton, E., Lee, Ch., Orth, U., Kim, Ch., & Kahle, K. (2012). Sustainable Marketing and Social Media. *Journal of Advertising*, *41*(4), 69–84. doi:10.1080/00913367.2012.10672458

Mio, C., Panfilo, S., & Blundo, B. (2020). Sustainable development goals and the strategic role of business: A systematic literature review. *Business Strategy and the Environment*, *29*(8), 3220–3245. doi:10.1002/bse.2568

Mir-Bernal, P., & Sadaba, T. (2022). The ultimate theory of the marketing mix: A proposal for marketers and managers. *International Journal of Entrepreneurship*, *28*, 1–22.

Mir, S. N. (2016). Social marketing and its efficacy in creating responsible and respectful societies, *International Journal of Economics. Commerce and Management*, *4*(3), 525–534.

Moazzem, K. G., Preoty, H. M., & Khan, A. M. (2022). *Institutionalisation of Labour Rights Practices in the RMG Sector under UNGP Framework: Are Public Agencies Playing Their Due Role?* Academic Press.

Moazzem, K. G. (2019). Behaviour of the buyers and suppliers in the post-Rana Plaza period: A decent work perspective. In S. B. Saxena (Ed.), *Labor, Global Supply Chains, and the Garment Industry in South Asia* (pp. 149–171). Routledge. doi:10.4324/9780429430039-9

Mogaji, E., Adeola, O., Adisa, I., Hinson, R. E., Mukonza, C., & Kirgiz, A. C. (2022). *Green marketing in emerging economies: Communication and brand perspective: An introduction*. Springer International Publishing. doi:10.1007/978-3-030-82572-0_1

Mogaji, E., & Nguyen, N. P. (2021). Managers' understanding of artificial intelligence in relation to marketing financial services: Insights from a cross-country study. *International Journal of Bank Marketing*, *40*(6), 1272–1298. doi:10.1108/IJBM-09-2021-0440

Mogaji, E., Soetan, T. O., & Kieu, T. A. (2020). The implications of artificial intelligence on the digital marketing of financial services to vulnerable customers. *Australasian Marketing Journal*, *29*(3), 235–242. doi:10.1016/j.ausmj.2020.05.003

Mohammad, N., & Baharun, R. (2018). Predicting the Purchase Intention for Organic Product: A Review and Conceptual Framework. *Advanced Science Letters*, *24*(6), 3849–3853. doi:10.1166/asl.2018.11496

Mohebbi, B. (2014). The art of packaging: An investigation into the role of colour in packaging, marketing, and branding. *International Journal of Organizational Leadership*, *3*(2), 92–102. doi:10.33844/ijol.2014.60248

Moldavanova, A. (2014). Two narratives of Intergenerational Sustainability. *American Review of Public Administration*, *46*(5), 526–545. doi:10.1177/0275074014565390

Moloi, T., & Marwala, T. (2020). *Artificial intelligence in economics and finance theories*. Springer. doi:10.1007/978-3-030-42962-1

Montoro Rios, F. J., Luque Martinez, T., Fuentes Moreno, F., & Cañadas Soriano, P. (2006). Improving attitudes toward brands with environmental associations: An experimental approach. *Journal of Consumer Marketing*, *23*(1), 26–33. doi:10.1108/07363760610641136

Montoro-Ríos, F. J., & Rey-Pino, J. M. (2021). Business Marketing Practices: Main Cause of Overconsumption. In W. Leal Filho, A. M. Azul, L. Brandli, P. G. Özuyar, & T. Wall (Eds.), *Responsible Consumption and Production. Encyclopedia of the UN Sustainable Development Goals*. Springer., doi:10.1007/978-3-319-71062-4_121-1

Morakanyane. (2017). Conceptualizing Digital Transformation in Business Organizations: A Systematic Review of Literature. *Bled, 30th Bled eConference, Digital Transformation – From Connecting Things to Transforming Our Lives*. Contentful.

Morales, P. A., True, S., & Tudor, R. K. (2020). Insights, challenges and recommendations for research on sustainability in marketing. *Journal of Global Scholars of Marketing Science*, *30*(4), 394–406. doi:10.1080/21639159.2020.1803757

Moravcikova, D., Krizanova, A., Kliestikova, J., & Rypakova, M. (2017). Green Marketing as the Source of the Competitive Advantage of the Business. *Sustainability (Basel)*, *9*(12), 2218. doi:10.3390u9122218

Morgan, R., & Hunt, S. (1994). The commitment – trust theory of relationship marketing. *Journal of Marketing*, *58*(3), 20–38. doi:10.1177/002224299405800302

Morgan, Whitler, K. A., Feng, H., & Chari, S. (2018). RESEARCH IN MARKETING STRATEGY. *Journal of the Academy of Marketing Science*, *47*(1), 4–29. doi:10.100711747-018-0598-1

Mottaleb, K. A., & Sonobe, T. (2011). An inquiry into the rapid growth of the garment industry in Bangladesh. *Economic Development and Cultural Change*, *60*(1), 67–89. doi:10.1086/661218

Mousa, M., Massoud, H. K., & Ayoubi, R. M. (2020). Gender, diversity management perceptions, workplace happiness and organisational citizenship behaviour. *Employee Relations*, *42*(6), 1249–1269. doi:10.1108/ER-10-2019-0385

Mozas-Moral, A., Fernández-Uclés, D., Medina-Viruel, M. J., & Bernal-Jurado, E. (2021). The role of the SDGs as enhancers of the performance of Spanish wine cooperatives. *Technological Forecasting and Social Change*, *173*(9), 121176. doi:10.1016/j.techfore.2021.121176

Müller, P., & Schmid, M. (2019). Intelligent Packaging in the Food Sector: A Brief Overview. *Foods*, *8*(1), 16. doi:10.3390/foods8010016 PMID:30621006

Mumani, A., & Stone, R. (2018). State of the art of user packaging interaction (UPI). *Packaging Technology & Science*, *31*(6), 401–419. doi:10.1002/pts.2363

Munck, R. P. (2010). Globalization and the labour movement: Challenges and responses. *Global Labour Journal*, *1*(2), 218–232. doi:10.15173/glj.v1i2.1073

Muninger, M. I., Mahr, D., & Hammedi, W. (2022). Social media use: A review of innovation management practices. *Journal of Business Research, 143*, 140–156. doi:10.1016/j.jbusres.2022.01.039

Murgai, A. (2018). Transforming digital marketing with artificial intelligence. International Journal of Latest Technology in Engineering, Management &. *Applied Sciences (Basel, Switzerland), 7*(4), 259–262.

Murphy, E., P. (2005). Sustainable marketing. *Business & Professional Ethics Journal, 24*(1-2), 171-198.

Murphy, T. (2023). Why is sustainable marketing important? *Tech Target.* https://www.techtarget.com/searchcustomer-experience/feature/Why-is-sustainable-marketing-important#:~:text=Sustainable%20marketing%20can%20improve%20how,with%20regulations%20and%20increase%20profits

Murphy, P. E. (2005). Sustainable marketing. *Business & Professional Ethics Journal, 24*(1/2), 171–198. doi:10.5840/bpej2005241/210

Musleh Al-Sartawi, A. M., Hussainey, K., & Razzaque, A. (2022). The role of artificial intelligence in sustainable finance. *Journal of Sustainable Finance & Investment*, 1–6. doi:10.1080/20430795.2022.2057405

Nadanyiova, M., Gajanova, L., & Majerova, J. (2020). Green Marketing as a Part of the Socially Responsible Brand's Communication from the Aspect of Generational Stratification. *Sustainability (Basel), 12*(17), 7118. doi:10.3390u12177118

Nahr, J. G., Nozari, H., & Sadeghi, M. E. (2021). Green supply chain based on the artificial intelligence of things (IoT). *International Journal of Innovation in Management, Economics, and Social Sciences, 1*(2), 56–63.

Najam, A. (2013). World Business Council for Sustainable Development: The Greening of Business or a Greenwash? In Yearbook of International Cooperation on Environment and Development 2003-04 (pp. 69-81). Routledge.

Nathaniel, S. P., Nwulu, N., & Bekun, F. (2021). Natural resources, globalization, urbanization, human capital, and environmental degradation in Latin American and Caribbean countries. *Environmental Science and Pollution Research International, 28*(5), 6207–6221. doi:10.100711356-020-10850-9 PMID:32989704

Nekmahmud, M., & Fekete-Farkas, M. (2020). Why Not Green Marketing? Determinates of Consumers' Intention to Green Purchase Decision in a New Developing Nation. *Sustainability (Basel), 12*(19), 7880. doi:10.3390u12197880

Nemes, N., Scanlan, S. J., Smith, P., Smith, T., Aronczyk, M., Hill, S., Lewis, S. L., Montgomery, A. W., Tubiello, F. N., & Stabinsky, D. (2022). An Integrated Framework to Assess Greenwashing. *Sustainability (Basel), 14*(8), 4431. doi:10.3390u14084431

Neureiter, A., & Matthes, J. (2022). Comparing the effects of greenwashing claims in environmental airline advertising: Perceived greenwashing, brand evaluation, and flight shame. *International Journal of Advertising*, 1–27. doi:10.1080/02650487.2022.2076510

New, S. J. (2015). Modern slavery and the supply chain: The limits of corporate social responsibility? *Supply Chain Management, 20*(6), 697–707. doi:10.1108/SCM-06-2015-0201

Ng, T. C. W., Chiu, D. K. W., & Li, K. K. (2022). Motivations of choosing archival studies as major in the i-School: Viewpoint between two universities across the Pacific Ocean. *Library Hi Tech, 40*(5), 1483–1496. doi:10.1108/LHT-07-2021-0230

Nguyen, H., Nguyen, N., Nguyen, B., Lobo, A., & Vu, P. (2019). Organic Food Purchases in an Emerging Market: The Influence of Consumers' Personal Factors and Green Marketing Practices of Food Stores. *International Journal of Environmental Research and Public Health, 16*(6), 1037. doi:10.3390/ijerph16061037 PMID:30909390

Nguyen, T. H. O., Yang, Z., Nguyen, N., Johnson, L. W., & Cao, T. K. (2019). Greenwash and Green Purchase Intention: The Mediating Role of Green Skepticism. *Sustainability (Basel)*, *11*(9), 2653. doi:10.3390u11092653

Nicholson, C., Jackson, C., & Marley, J. (2013). A governance model for integrated primary/secondary care for the health-reforming first world–results of a systematic review. *BMC Health Services Research*, *13*(1), 1–12. doi:10.1186/1472-6963-13-528 PMID:24359610

Nidumolu, R., Prahalad, C. K., & Rangaswami, M. R. (2009). Why sustainability is now the key driver of innovation. *Harvard Business Review*, *87*(9), 56–64.

Ni, J., Chiu, D. K. W., & Ho, K. K. W. (2022). Information search behavior among Chinese self-drive tourists in the smartphone era. *Information Discovery and Delivery*, *50*(3), 285–296. doi:10.1108/IDD-05-2020-0054

Nijhof, A., Wins, A., Argyrou, A., & Chevrollier, N. (2022). Sustainable market transformation: A refined framework for analyzing causal loops in transitions to sustainability. *Environmental Innovation and Societal Transitions*, *42*, 352–361. doi:10.1016/j.eist.2022.01.010

Nikolaou, I. E., Tsalis, T. A., & Evangelinos, K. I. (2019). A framework to measure corporate sustainability performance: A strong sustainability-based view of firm. *Sustainable Production and Consumption*, *18*, 1–18. doi:10.1016/j.spc.2018.10.004

Nkamnebe, A. D. (2011). Sustainability marketing in the emerging markets: imperatives, challenges, and agenda setting. *International Journal of Emerging Markets*.

Nurjaman, K. (2022). Overview Of The Application Of The Concept Of Green Marketing In Environment Conservation. *Eqien-Jurnal Ekonomi dan Bisnis*, *11*(02), 649-655.

OECD. (2017). *Meeting of the OECD Council at Ministerial Level*. OECD Publishing.

OECD. (2021). *The Digital Transformation of SMEs*. OECD. doi:10.1787/bdb9256a-en

Ogink, T., & Dong, J. Q. (2019). Stimulating innovation by user feedback on social media: The case of an online user innovation community. *Technological Forecasting and Social Change*, *144*, 295–302. doi:10.1016/j.techfore.2017.07.029

Oka, C. (2018). Brands as labour rights advocates? Potential and limits of brand advocacy in global supply chains. *Business Ethics (Oxford, England)*, *27*(2), 95–107. doi:10.1111/beer.12172

Oka, C., Egels-Zandén, N., & Alexander, R. (2020). Buyer engagement and labour conditions in global supply chains: The Bangladesh accord and beyond. *Development and Change*, *51*(5), 1306–1330. doi:10.1111/dech.12575

Ökem, Z. G., & Çakar, M. (2015). What have health care reforms achieved in Turkey? An appraisal of the "Health Transformation Programme". *Health Policy (Amsterdam)*, *119*(9), 1153–1163. doi:10.1016/j.healthpol.2015.06.003 PMID:26183890

Okuah, O., Scholtz, B. M., & Snow, B. (2019). A grounded theory analysis of the techniques used by social media influencers and their potential for influencing the public regarding environmental awareness. *ACM International Conference Proceeding Series*. ACM. 10.1145/3351108.3351145

Ölander, F., & Thøgersen, J. (1995). Understanding of consumer behaviour as a prerequisite for environmental protection. *Journal of Consumer Policy*, *18*(4), 345–385. doi:10.1007/BF01024160

Olson, E. M., Olson, K. M., Czaplewski, A. J., & Key, T. M. (2021). Business strategy and the management of digital marketing. *Business Horizons*, *64*(2), 285–293. doi:10.1016/j.bushor.2020.12.004

Ordonez-Ponce, E., Clarke, A., & MacDonald, A. (2021). Business contributions to the sustainable development goals through community sustainability partnerships. *Sustainability Accounting. Management and Policy Journal, 12*(6), 1239–1267. doi:10.1108/SAMPJ-03-2020-0068

Orîndaru, A., Popescu, M. F., Ceescu, S. C., Botezatu, F., Florescu, M. S., & Runceanu-Albu, C. C. (2021). Leveraging COVID-19 Outbreak for Shaping a More Sustainable Consumer Behavior. *Sustainability (Basel), 13*(11), 5762. doi:10.3390u13115762

Osburg, V. S., Davies, I., Yoganathan, V., & McLeay, F. (2021). Perspectives, Opportunities and Tensions in Ethical and Sustainable Luxury: Introduction to the Thematic Symposium. *Journal of Business Ethics, 169*(2), 201–210. doi:10.100710551-020-04487-4 PMID:33132467

Ottman, J. A. (1992). Industry's response to green consumerism. *The Journal of Business Strategy, 13*(4), 3–7. doi:10.1108/eb039498 PMID:10120307

Ottman, J. A. (2011). *The new rules of green marketing: Strategies, tools, and inspiration for sustainable branding.* Berrett-Koehler Publishers.

Outlook. (2023). *Sustainable Marketing: A Key Priority for Management Professionals Explains Dr. Adya Sharma, Director of SCMS Pune.* Microsoft. https://www.outlookindia.com/outlook-spotlight/sustainable-marketing-a-key-priority-for-management-professionals-explains-dr-adya-sharma-director-of-scms-pune-news-245162

Ozili, P. K. (2022). Sustainability and Sustainable Development Research around the World. *Managing Global Transitions, 20*(3). doi:10.26493/1854-6935.20.259-293

Paço, A., & Raposo, M. (2009). "Green" segmentation: An application to the Portuguese consumer market. *Marketing Intelligence & Planning, 27*(3), 364–379. doi:10.1108/02634500910955245

Pakhunov, K. (2018). Amazon throws a challenge. *Expert, 37*. Retrieved January 29, 2023 from https://expert.ru/expert/2018/37/amazon-brosaet-vyizov/

Palazzo, M., Gigauri, I., Panait, M. C., Apostu, S. A., & Siano, A. (2022). Sustainable Tourism Issues in European Countries during the Global Pandemic Crisis. *Sustainability (Basel), 14*(7), 3844. doi:10.3390u14073844

Palazzo, M., Vollero, A., & Siano, A. (2023). Intelligent packaging in the transition from linear to circular economy: Driving research in practice. *Journal of Cleaner Production, 135984*, 135984. doi:10.1016/j.jclepro.2023.135984

Panait, M., Janjua, L. R., Apostu, S. A., & Mihăescu, C. (2022). Impact factors to reduce carbon emissions. Evidence from Latin America. *Kybernetes*, (ahead-of-print).

Panait, M., Hysa, E., Raimi, L., Kruja, A., & Rodriguez, A. (2022). Guest editorial: Circular economy and entrepreneurship in emerging economies: opportunities and challenges. *Journal of Entrepreneurship in Emerging Economies, 14*(5), 673–677. doi:10.1108/JEEE-10-2022-487

Pan, M., Bai, M., & Ren, X. (2022). Does internet convergence improve manufacturing enterprises' competitive advantage? Empirical research based on the mediation effect model. *Technology in Society, 69*, 101944. doi:10.1016/j.techsoc.2022.101944

Papadas, K., Avlonitis, G. J., & Carrigan, M. (2017). Green marketing orientation: Conceptualization, scale development and validation. *Journal of Business Research, 80*, 236–246. doi:10.1016/j.jbusres.2017.05.024

Papadas, K., Avlonitis, G. J., Carrigan, M., & Piha, L. (2019). The interplay of strategic and internal green marketing orientation on competitive advantage. *Journal of Business Research, 104*, 632–643. doi:10.1016/j.jbusres.2018.07.009

Park, J. Y., Perumal, S. V., Sanyal, S., Ah Nguyen, B., Ray, S., Krishnan, R., Narasimhaiah, R., & Thangam, D. (2022). Sustainable Marketing Strategies as an Essential Tool of Business. *American Journal of Economics and Sociology*, *81*(2), 359–379. doi:10.1111/ajes.12459

Patak, M., Branska, L., & Pecinova, Z. (2021). Consumer intention to purchase green consumer chemicals. *Sustainability (Basel)*, *13*(14), 7992. doi:10.3390u13147992

Pau, L. (1991). Artificial intelligence and financial services. *IEEE Transactions on Knowledge and Data Engineering*, *3*(2), 137–148. doi:10.1109/69.87994

Paul-Majumder, P., & Begum, A. (2000). *The gender imbalances in the export oriented garment industry in Bangladesh.* World Bank, Development Research Group/Poverty Reduction and Economic Management Network.

Peattie, K. (2001). Towards Sustainability: The Third Age of Green Marketing. *The Marketing Review*, *2*(2), 129–146. doi:10.1362/1469347012569869

Peattie, K., & Belz, F. M. (2010). Sustainability marketing—An innovative conception of marketing. *Marketing Review St. Gallen*, *27*(5), 8–15. doi:10.100711621-010-0085-7

Peattie, K., & Peattie, S. (2009). Social marketing: A pathway to consumption reduction? *Journal of Business Research*, *62*(2), 260–268. doi:10.1016/j.jbusres.2008.01.033

Peattie, K., & Peattie, S. (2011). The social marketing mix: a critical review. In G. Hastings, K. Angus, & C. Bryant (Eds.), *The SAGE Handbook of Social Marketing* (pp. 152–166). SAGE Publications. doi:10.4135/9781446201008.n11

Peattie, S. (2001). Golden goose or wild goose? The hunt for the green consumer. *Business Strategy and the Environment*, *10*(4), 187–199. doi:10.1002/bse.292

Peattie, S., & Belz, F. (2010). *Sustainability marketing: A global perspective.* John Wiley & Sons.

Peattie, S., & Peattie, K. (2003). Ready to fly solo? Reducing social marketing's dependence on commercial marketing theory. *Marketing Theory*, *3*(3), 365–385. doi:10.1177/147059310333006

Pedersen, C. S. (2018). The un Sustainable Development Goals (SDGs) are a Great Gift to Business! *Procedia CIRP*, *69*(May), 21–24. doi:10.1016/j.procir.2018.01.003

Peel-Yates, V. (2022). *5 Sustainability Social Media Campaigns that Rocked.* The Sustainable Agency. https://thesustainableagency.com/blog/sustainability-social-media-campaigns-that-rocked/

Penagos-Londoño, G. I., Ruiz-Moreno, F., Sellers-Rubio, R., Del Barrio-García, S., & Casado-Díaz, A. B. (2022). Consistency of Experts' Product Reviews: An Application to Wine Guides. *Wine Economics and Policy*, *11*(2), 51–60. doi:10.36253/wep-12400

Peng, J. (2022). Research on digitalization of the museum industry in china- based on SWOT-pest model. *Asian Journal of Social Science Studies*, *7*(1), 31. doi:10.20849/ajsss.v7i1.982

Peng, J., Liu, Y., Corstanje, R., & Meersmans, J. (2021). Promoting sustainable landscape patterns for landscape sustainability. *Landscape Ecology*, *36*(7), 1839–1844. doi:10.100710980-021-01271-1

Peng, Y. (2018). The dark side of urbanization in China: Pollution and health problems. In *Handbook of China's Governance and Domestic Politics* (pp. 1–19). Springer.

Peters, J., & Simaens, A. (2020). Integrating Sustainability into Corporate Strategy: A Case Study of the Textile and Clothing Industry. *Sustainability (Basel)*, *12*(15), 6125. doi:10.3390u12156125

Peterson, M., Minton, E. A., Liu, R. L., & Bartholomew, D. E. (2021). Sustainable Marketing and Consumer Support for Sustainable Businsses. *Sustainable Production and Consumption*, 27, 157–168. doi:10.1016/j.spc.2020.10.018

Pham, T. H., Nguyen, T. N., Phan, T. T. H., & Nguyen, N. T. (2019). Evaluating the purchase behaviour of organic food by young consumers in an emerging market economy. *Journal of Strategic Marketing*, 27(6), 540–556. doi:10.1080/0965254X.2018.1447984

Piergiovanni, L., & Limbo, S. (2010). *Food packaging: Materiali, tecnologie e soluzioni*. Springer Science & Business Media., doi:10.1007/978-88-470-1457-2

Pietrewicz, J. W., & Sobiecki, R. (2016). Entrepreneurship sparing economy. In M. Poniatowska-Jaksch & R. Sobiecki (Eds.), *Sharing Economy* (p. 12). Oficyna Wydawnicza SGH.

Plastic Soup Foundation. (n.d.). *Individual SDG's*. PSF. https://www.plasticsoupfoundation.org/en/plastic-problem/sustainable-development/individual-sdgs/

Pogrebova, O. A., Konnikov, E. A., & Yuldasheva, O. U. (2017). Fuzzy model assessing the index of development of sustainable marketing of the company. *Proceedings of 2017 20th IEEE International Conference on Soft Computing and Measurements, SCM 2017*, 694–696. 10.1109/SCM.2017.7970693

Polonsky, M. J. (1994). An Introduction To Green Marketing. *Electronic Green Journal*, 1(2). Advance online publication. doi:10.5070/G31210177

Pomering, A. (2017). Marketing for Sustainability: Extending the Conceptualisation of the Marketing Mix to Drive Value for Individuals and Society at Large. *Australasian Marketing Journal*, 25(2), 157–165. doi:10.1016/j.ausmj.2017.04.011

Poniatowska-Jaksch, M., & Sobiecki, R. (Eds.). (2016). *Sharing Economy* (p. 8). Oficyna Wydawnicza SGH.

Popescu, C., EL-Chaarani, H., EL-Abiad, Z., & Gigauri, I. (2022). Implementation of Health Information Systems to Improve Patient Identification. *International Journal of Environmental Research and Public Health*, 19(22), 15236. doi:10.3390/ijerph192215236 PMID:36429954

Pop, R. A., Dabija, D. C., Pelău, C., & Dinu, V. (2022). Usage intentions, attitudes, and behaviors towards energy-efficient applications during the COVID-19 pandemic. *Journal of Business Economics and Management*, 23(3), 668–689. doi:10.3846/jbem.2022.16959

Pop, R.-A., Săplăcan, Z., & Alt, M.-A. (2020). Social media goes green - The impact of social media on green cosmetics purchase motivation and intention. *Information (Basel)*, 11(9), 447. doi:10.3390/info11090447

Poria, S., Cambria, E., Hussain, A., & Huang, G. B. (2015). Towards an intelligent framework for multimodal affective data analysis. *Neural Networks*, 63, 104–116. doi:10.1016/j.neunet.2014.10.005 PMID:25523041

Porter, M. E., & Kramer, M. R. (2002). The competitive advantage of corporate philanthropy. *Harvard Business Review*, 80, 56–68. PMID:12510538

Poyatos-Racionero, E., Ros-Lis, J. V., Vivancos, J. L., & Martinez-Manez, R. (2018). Recent advances on intelligent packaging as tools to reduce food waste. *Journal of Cleaner Production*, 172, 3398–3409. doi:10.1016/j.jclepro.2017.11.075

Prates, C., Pedrozo, E., & Silva, T. (2015). Corporate social responsibility: A case study in subsidiaries from Brazil and China. *Journal of Technology Management & Innovation*, 10(3), 131–142. doi:10.4067/S0718-27242015000300014

Prentice, R. (2021). Labour rights from labour wrongs? Transnational compensation and the spatial politics of labour rights after Bangladesh's rana plaza garment factory collapse. *Antipode*, 53(6), 1767–1786. doi:10.1111/anti.12751

Priyanka, C. N., & Parag, D. N. (2013). Intelligent and active packaging. *International Journal of Engineering and Management Sciences*, *4*(4), 417–418.

Purvis, B., Mao, Y., & Robinson, D. (2018). Three pillars of sustainability: In Search of Conceptual Origins. *Sustainability Science*, *14*(3), 681–695. doi:10.100711625-018-0627-5

Purwanto, A. (2022). How The Role of Digital Marketing and Brand Image on Food Product Purchase Decisions? An Empirical Study on Indonesian SMEs in the Digital Era. *Journal of Industrial Engineering & Management Research*, *3*(6), 34–41. doi:10.7777/jiemar.v3i6.323

PwC. (2019). *Creating a strategy for a better world*. PwC. doi:10.2307/j.ctvc77cxj.37

Qalati, S. A., Yuan, L. W., Khan, M. A. S., & Anwar, F. (2021). A mediated model on the adoption of social media and SMEs' performance in developing countries. *Technology in Society*, *64*, 101513. doi:10.1016/j.techsoc.2020.101513

Qin, X., Godil, D. I., Sarwat, S., Yu, Z., Khan, S. A. R., & Shujaat, S. (2022). Green practices in food supply chains: Evidence from emerging economies. *Operations Management Research : Advancing Practice Through Research*, *15*(1), 62–75. doi:10.100712063-021-00187-y

Quairel-Lanoizelée, F. (2011). Are competition and corporate social responsibility compatible? The myth of sustainable competitive advantage. *Society and Business Review*, *6*(1), 77–98. doi:10.1108/17465681111105850

Quoquab, F., Mohamed Sadom, N. Z., & Mohammad, J. (2020). Sustainable Marketing. In S. Seifi (Ed.), *The Palgrave Handbook of Corporate Social Responsibility*. Palgrave Macmillan., doi:10.1007/978-3-030-22438-7_76-1

Raddad, S., Salleh, A. G., & Samat, N. (2010). Determinants of agriculture land use change in Palestinian urban environment: Urban planners at local governments perspective. *American-Eurasian Journal of Sustainable Agriculture*, *4*(1), 30–38.

Radi, A. S., & Shokouhyar, S. (2021). Toward consumer perception of cellphones sustainability: A social media analytics. *Sustainable Production and Consumption*, *25*, 217–233. doi:10.1016/j.spc.2020.08.012

Rahman, S., & Ishty, S. I. (2020). *COVID-19 and the ready-made garment sector*. Retrieved from https://www.policyforum.net/covid-19-and-the-ready-made-garment-sector/

Rahman, S., & Yadlapalli, A. (2021). *Years after the Rana Plaza tragedy, Bangladesh's garment workers are still bottom of the pile*. Retrieved from https://theconversation.com/years-after-the-rana-plaza-tragedy-bangladeshs-garment-workers-are-still-bottom-of-the-pile-159224

Rahman, S. (2019). Post-Rana Plaza responses: Changing role of the Bangladesh Government. In S. B. Saxena (Ed.), *Labor, global supply chains, and the garment industry in South Asia: Bangladesh after Rana Plaza* (pp. 131–148). Routledge. doi:10.4324/9780429430039-8

Rahman, S., & Rahman, K. M. (2020). Multi-actor initiatives after Rana Plaza: Factory managers' views. *Development and Change*, *51*(5), 1331–1359. doi:10.1111/dech.12572

Raimo, N., De Turi, I., Ricciardelli, A., & Vitolla, F. (2021). Digitalization in the cultural industry: Evidence from Italian museums. *International Journal of Entrepreneurial Behaviour & Research*, *28*(8), 1962–1974. doi:10.1108/IJEBR-01-2021-0082

Raiter, O. (2021). Segmentation of Bank Consumers for Artificial Intelligence Marketing. *International Journal of Contemporary Financial Issues*, *1*(1), 39–54.

Rajnoha, R., Lesnikova, P., & Korauš, A. (2016). From financial measures to strategic performance measurement system and corporate sustainability: Empirical evidence from Slovakia. *Economics & Sociology (Ternopil)*, *9*(4), 134–152. doi:10.14254/2071-789X.2016/9-4/8

Rajput, N., Sharma, U., Kaur, B., Rani, P., Tongkachok, K., & Dornadula, V. H. R. (2022). Current global green marketing standard: Changing market and company branding. *International Journal of System Assurance Engineering and Management*, *13*(S1, Suppl 1), 727–735. doi:10.100713198-021-01604-y

Randstad, (2013). *Results Randstad Award 2013*. Randstad. www.randstadt.com

Rathnayaka, U. (2018). Role of digital marketing in retail fashion industry: A synthesis of the theory and the practice. *Journal of Accounting & Marketing*, *7*(02). doi:10.4172/2168-9601.1000279

Rawat, S. R., & Garga, P. (2012). Understanding consumer behaviour towards green cosmetics. *Available at SSRN 2111545*. doi: 10.2139/ssrn.2111545

Rawof, W. (2021). *Ethical and Sustainable Cosmetics and Their Importance on Consumer Purchase Behavior* (Publication Number Paper 746) [Undergraduate Honors Theses, ETSU.], https://dc.etsu.edu/honors/746

Rechel, B., & McKee, M. (2009). Health reform in central and eastern Europe and the former Soviet Union. *Lancet*, *374*(9696), 1186–1195. doi:10.1016/S0140-6736(09)61334-9 PMID:19801097

Reilly, A. H., & Hynan, K. A. (2014). Corporate communication, sustainability, and social media: It's not easy (really) being green. *Business Horizons*, *57*(6), 747–758. doi:10.1016/j.bushor.2014.07.008

Reilly, A. H., & Larya, N. (2018). External Communication About Sustainability: Corporate Social Responsibility Reports and Social Media Activity. *Environmental Communication*, *12*(5), 621–637. doi:10.1080/17524032.2018.1424009

Ren, S., Tang, G., & Jackson, S. E. (2018). Green human resource management research in emergence: A review and future directions. *Asia Pacific Journal of Management*, *35*, 769–803. doi:10.100710490-017-9532-1

Report, U. (2010). *Report of the Georgia National Nutrition Survey 2009 (UNICEF, 11 June 2010)*. Georgia Global Health Initiative Strategy.

Restuccia, D., Spizzirri, U. G., Parisi, O. I., Cirillo, G., Curcio, M., Iemma, F., Puoci, F., Vinci, G., & Picci, N. (2010). New EU regulation aspects and global market of active and intelligent packaging for food industry applications. *Food Control*, *21*(11), 1425–1435. doi:10.1016/j.foodcont.2010.04.028

Reuter, C., Foerstl, K. A. I., Hartmann, E. V. I., & Blome, C. (2010). Sustainable global supplier management: The role of dynamic capabilities in achieving competitive advantage. *The Journal of Supply Chain Management*, *46*(2), 45–63. doi:10.1111/j.1745-493X.2010.03189.x

Reyes-Rodríguez, J. F. (2021). Explaining the business case for environmental management practices in SMEs: The role of organisational capabilities for environmental communication. *Journal of Cleaner Production*, *318*, 128590. doi:10.1016/j.jclepro.2021.128590

Reza, N., & Du Plessis, J. J. (2022). The Garment Industry in Bangladesh, Corporate Social Responsibility of Multinational Corporations, and The Impact of COVID-19. *Asian Journal of Law and Society*, *9*(2), 255–285. doi:10.1017/als.2022.9

Ribeiro, J. A., & Veiga, R. T. (2011). Proposição de uma escala de consumo sustentável. *Revista ADM*, *46*(1), 45–60.

Richardson, N. (2022). How new sustainability typologies will reshape traditional approaches to loyalty. *Ital. J. Mark.*, 289–315. doi:10.1007/s43039-022-00047-y

Rinnert, D. (2015). The politics of civil service and administrative reforms in development—Explaining within-country variation of reform outcomes in Georgia after the Rose revolution. *Public Administration and Development*, *35*(1), 19–33. doi:10.1002/pad.1709

Rizvanović, B., Zutshi, A., Grilo, A., & Nodehi, T. (2023). Linking the potentials of extended digital marketing impact and start-up growth: Developing a macro-dynamic framework of start-up growth drivers supported by digital marketing. *Technological Forecasting and Social Change*, *186*, 122128. doi:10.1016/j.techfore.2022.122128

Roberts, M. J., Hsiao, W., Berman, P., & Reich, M. R. (2008). *Getting health reform right: a guide to improving performance and equity*. doi:10.1093/acprof:oso/9780195371505.001.0001

Rodrigues, M., & Franco, M. (2019). The Corporate Sustainability Strategy in Organisations: A Systematic Review and Future Directions. *Sustainability (Basel)*, *11*(22), 6214. doi:10.3390u11226214

Rogall, H. (2010). *Theory and practice*. Wydawnictwo Zysk i S-ka.

Roldán Fernández, J. M., Burgos Payán, M., & Riquelme Santos, J. M. (2021). Profitability of household photovoltaic self-consumption in Spain. *Journal of Cleaner Production*, *279*, 123439. doi:10.1016/j.jclepro.2020.123439

Romero, V., Khury, E., Aiello, L. M., Foglio, M. A., & Leonardi, G. R. (2018). Diferenças entre cosméticos orgânicos e naturais: Literatura esclarecedora para prescritores. *Surgical & Cosmetic Dermatology*, *10*(3), 188–193. doi:10.5935 cd1984-8773.20181031087

Rosário, A. T. (2021). based guidelines for marketing information systems. [IJBSA]. *International Journal of Business Strategy and Automation*, *2*(1), 1–16. doi:10.4018/IJBSA.20210101.oa1

Rosen, C. M. (2001). Environmental strategy and competitive advantage: An introduction. *California Management Review*, *43*(3), 8–15. doi:10.2307/41166084

Rosethorn, H. (2009). *The Employer Brand. Keeping Faith with the Deal*. Gower Publishing Limited.

Rothschild, M. L. (2000). Carrots, sticks, and promises: A conceptual framework for the management of public health and social issue behaviors. *Social Marketing Quarterly*, *6*(4), 86–114. doi:10.1080/15245004.2000.9961146

Rotschedl, J., & Čermáková, A. (2014). *Proceedings of the 11th International Academic Conference, Reykjavik, Iceland, 24-27 June 204*. International Institute of Social and Economic Sciences (IISES).

Rudawska, E. (2019). Sustainable marketing strategy in food and drink industry: a comparative analysis of B2B and B2C SMEs operating in Europe. *Journal of Business & Industrial Marketing*.

Rukhadze, T. (2013). An Overview of the Health Care System in Georgia: Expert Recommendations in the Context of Predictive, Preventive and Personalized Medicine. *The EPMA Journal*. http://www.epmajournal.com/content/4/1/8

Rukhadze, T., Tevdoradze, M., Bajiashvili, A., Lolashvili, N., & Saltkhutsishvili, M. (2016). Marketing management and its informational support. *Automated Management Systems*, *2*(22).

Rundh, B. (2013). Linking Packaging to Marketing: How Packaging is Influencing the Marketing Strategy. *British Food Journal*, *115*(11), 1547–1563. doi:10.1108/BFJ-12-2011-0297

Rundh, B. (2016). The role of packaging within marketing and value creation. *British Food Journal*, *118*(10), 2491–2511. doi:10.1108/BFJ-10-2015-0390

Rupeika-Apoga & Petrovska. (2022). Barriers to Sustainable Digital Transformation in Micro-, Small-, and Medium-Sized Enterprises. *Sustainability*, *14*, 1–19.

Compilation of References

Russell, M. (2021). More than 350K jobs have been lost in Bangladesh RMG sector. *Just-Style*. Retrieved from https://www.just-style.com/news/more-than-350k-jobs-have-been-lost-in-bangladesh-rmg-sector_id140579.aspx

Rust, R. T. (2020). The future of marketing. *International Journal of Research in Marketing*, *37*(1), 15–26. doi:10.1016/j.ijresmar.2019.08.002

Sachs, J. D. (2012). From millennium development goals to sustainable development goals. *Lancet*, *379*(9832), 2206–2211. doi:10.1016/S0140-6736(12)60685-0 PMID:22682467

Saeidi, S. P., Sofian, S., Saeidi, P., Saeidi, S. P., & Saaeidi, S. A. (2015). How does corporate social responsibility contribute to firm financial performance? The mediating role of competitive advantage, reputation, and customer satisfaction. *Journal of Business Research*, *68*(2), 341–350. doi:10.1016/j.jbusres.2014.06.024

Sahakyan, A. I., & Karpenko, T. V. (2016). *Internet marketing as a modern direction in the development of companies. scientific forum*. Retrieved January 26, 2023 from https://www.scienceforum.ru/2016/1528/22456

Şahin, U. (2020). Projections of Turkey's electricity generation and installed capacity from total renewable and hydro energy using fractional nonlinear grey Bernoulli model and its reduced forms. *Sustainable Production and Consumption*, *23*, 52–62. doi:10.1016/j.spc.2020.04.004

Salam, M. A., & Jahed, M. A. (2023). CSR orientation for competitive advantage in business-to-business markets of emerging economies: the mediating role of trust and corporate reputation. *Journal of Business & Industrial Marketing*.

Sanclemente-Téllez, J.C. (2017). Marketing and Corporate Social Responsibility (CSR). Moving between broadening the concept of marketing and social factors as a marketing strategy, *Spanish Journal of Marketing - ESIC*, *21*(1), 4-25, doi:10.1016/j.sjme.2017.05.001

Sarkar, S., & Searcy, C. (2016). Zeitgeist or chameleon? A quantitative analysis of CSR definitions. *Journal of Cleaner Production*, *135*, 1423–1435. doi:10.1016/j.jclepro.2016.06.157

Sarkis, J., & Cordeiro, J. J. (2012)... *Sustainability*, *12*(21), 8977. doi:10.3390u12218977

Sassen, S. (2018). *Globalization and its discontents: Essays on the new mobility of people and money*. The New Press.

Saura, J. R., Palos-sanchez, P., & Rodríguez Herráez, B. (2020). Digital Marketing for Sustainable Growth: Business Models and Online Campaigns Using Sustainable Strategies. *Sustainability (Basel)*, *12*(3), 1003. doi:10.3390u12031003

Savitri, C., Hurriyati, R., Wibowo, L., & Hendrayati, H. (2022). The role of social media marketing and brand image on smartphone purchase intention. *International Journal of Data and Network Science*, *6*(1), 185–192. doi:10.5267/j.ijdns.2021.9.009

Saxena, S. B. (2022). Developing country responses to demands for improved labor standards: case studies from the garment and textiles industry in Asia. In K. A. Elliott (Ed.), *Handbook on globalisation and labour standards* (pp. 258–273). Edward Elgar Publishing. doi:10.4337/9781788977371.00020

Say, J. B. (1960). *A Treatise on Political Economy*. Polskie Wydawnictwo Naukowe.

Schaltegger, S., Hörisch, J., & Freeman, R. E. (2017). *Business Cases for Sustainability: A Stakeholder Theory Perspective*. doi:10.1177/1086026617722882

Schaltegger, S., & Burritt, R. (2018). Business cases and corporate engagement with sustainability: Differentiating ethical motivations. *Journal of Business Ethics*, *147*(2), 241–259. doi:10.100710551-015-2938-0

Schecter, K. (2011). The privatization of the Georgian healthcare system. *Anthropology of East Europe Review*, *29*(1), 16–22.

Scheyvens, R., Banks, G., & Hughes, E. (2016). The private sector and the SDGs: The need to move beyond 'business as usual'. *Sustainable Development (Bradford), 24*(6), 371–382. doi:10.1002d.1623

Schmeltz, L. (2012). Consumer-oriented CSR communication: Focusing on ability or morality? *Corporate Communications, 17*(1), 29–49. doi:10.1108/13563281211196344

Schramade, W. (2017). Investing in the UN Sustainable Development Goals. *The Bank of America Journal of Applied Corporate Finance, 29*(2), 87–99. doi:10.1111/jacf.12236

SDGs. (n.d.). *The 17 Goals*. United Nations. https://sdgs.un.org/goals

Sdrolia, E., & Zarotiadis, G. (2019). A comprehensive review for green product term: From definition to evaluation. *Journal of Economic Surveys, 33*(1), 150–178. doi:10.1111/joes.12268

Šebestová, J., & Sroka, W. (2020). Sustainable development goals and SMEs decisions: Czech Republic vs. Poland. [JEECAR]. *Journal of Eastern European and Central Asian Research, 7*(1), 39–50.

Sehngelia, L., Pavlova, M., & Groot, W. (2016). Impact of healthcare reform on universal coverage in Georgia: A systematic review. *Diversity and Equality in Health and Care, 13*(5). Advance online publication. doi:10.21767/2049-5471.100074

Sen, S., Antara, N., Sen, S., & Chowdhury, S. (2020). The apparel workers are in the highest vulnerability due to COVID-19: A study on the Bangladesh Apparel Industry. *Asia Pacific Journal of Multidisciplinary Research., 8*(3), 1–7.

Seretny, M., & Seretny, A. (2012). Sustainable Marketing -A New Era in the Responsible Marketing Development. *Foundations of Management, 4*(2), 63–76. doi:10.2478/fman-2013-0011

Seto, K. C., Güneralp, B., & Hutyra, L. R. (2012). Global forecasts of urban expansion to 2030 and direct impacts on biodiversity and carbon pools. *Proceedings of the National Academy of Sciences of the United States of America, 109*(40), 16083–16088. doi:10.1073/pnas.1211658109 PMID:22988086

Sgaravatti, G., Tagliapietra, S., & Zachmann, G. (2021). National policies to shield consumers from rising energy prices. *Bruegel Datasets*. Bruegel. https://www.bruegel.org/dataset/national-policies-shield-consumers-rising-energy-prices

Shahzad, M., Qu, Y., Zafar, A. U., Rehman, S. U., & Islam, T. (2020). Exploring the influence of knowledge management process on corporate sustainable performance through green innovation. *Journal of Knowledge Management, 24*(9), 2079–2106. doi:10.1108/JKM-11-2019-0624

Shamim, K., Ahmad, S., & Alam, M. A. (2022). Consumer understanding of food date labels: Preventing food wastage. *British Food Journal, 124*(10), 3116–3132. doi:10.1108/BFJ-06-2021-0672

Sharma, E. (2019). A review of corporate social responsibility in developed and developing nations. *Corporate Social Responsibility and Environmental Management, 26*(4), 712–720. doi:10.1002/csr.1739

Sharma, M., & Choubey, A. (2022). Green banking initiatives: A qualitative study on the Indian banking sector. *Environment, Development and Sustainability, 24*(1), 293–319. doi:10.100710668-021-01426-9 PMID:33967597

Sheau-Ting, L., Mohammed, A. H., & Weng-Wai, C. (2013). What is the optimum social marketing mix to market energy conservation behaviour: An empirical study. *Journal of Environmental Management, 131*, 196–205. doi:10.1016/j.jenvman.2013.10.001 PMID:24178312

Sheikh, A. A., Rana, N. A., Inam, A., Shahzad, A., & Awan, H. M. (2018). Is e-marketing a source of sustainable business performance? Predicting the role of top management support with various interaction factors. *Cogent Business Management, 5*(1), 1516487. doi:10.1080/23311975.2018.1516487

Shen, L., Qian, J., & Chen, S. C. (2020). Effective communication strategies of sustainable hospitality: A qualitative exploration. *Sustainability (Basel)*, *12*(17), 6920. doi:10.3390u12176920

Shen, Z. (2022). Big Data Analysis of Marketing User Intelligence Information Based on Deep Learning. *Mobile Information Systems*, *2022*, 1–7. doi:10.1155/2022/2990649

Sheth, J., & Parvatiyar, A. (1995). Ecological imperatives and the role of marketing. *Environmental marketing: Strategies, practice, theory, and research*, 3-20.

Sheth, J. N., & Parvatiyar, A. (2021). Sustainable marketing: Market-driving, not market-driven. *Journal of Macromarketing*, *41*(1), 150–165. doi:10.1177/0276146720961836

Short, D., & Stovell, R. J. (1966). Packaging for people. *Human Factors*, *8*(4), 307–315. doi:10.1177/001872086600800406

Shrivastava, P., & Hart, S. (1995). Creating sustainable corporations. *Business Strategy and the Environment*, *4*(3), 154–165. doi:10.1002/bse.3280040307

Shukla, P. S., & Nigam, P. V. (2018). E-shopping using mobile apps and the emerging consumer in the digital age of retail hyper personalization: An insight. *Pacific Business Review International*, *10*(10), 131–139.

Siddiqi, D. M. (2019). Spaces of exception: National interest and the labor of sedition. In S. B. Saxena (Ed.), *Labor, Global Supply Chains, and the Garment Industry in South Asia* (pp. 100–114). Routledge. doi:10.4324/9780429430039-6

Sidek, S., Rosli, M. M., Khadri, N. A. M., Hasbolah, H., Manshar, M., & Abidin, N. M. F. N. Z. (2020). Fortifying Small Business Performance Sustainability in The Era of IR 4.0: E-Marketing As a Catalyst of Competitive Advantages and Business Performance. *J. Crit. Rev.*, *7*, 2143–2155.

Sikdar, S. K. (2019). Fractured state of decisions on sustainability: An assessment. *Sustainable Production and Consumption*, *19*, 231–237. doi:10.1016/j.spc.2019.04.004

Silva, S. (2021). Corporate contributions to the Sustainable Development Goals: An empirical analysis informed by legitimacy theory. *Journal of Cleaner Production*, *292*, 125962. doi:10.1016/j.jclepro.2021.125962

Simon-Kucher. (2021). *Global Sustainability Study 2021 - Consumers are key players for a sustainable future*. Simon-Kucher.

Sividas, E., & Dwyer, F. (2000). An examination of organizational factors influencing new product success in internal and alliance-based processes. *Journal of Marketing*, *64*(1), 31–49. doi:10.1509/jmkg.64.1.31.17985

Skare, de las Mercedes de Obesso, M., & Ribeiro-Navarrete, S. (2023). Digital transformation and European small and medium enterprises (SMEs): A comparative study using digital economy and society index data. *International Journal of Information Management*, *68*, 1–16. doi:10.1016/j.ijinfomgt.2022.102594

Skibiński, A., Sipa, M., & Gorzeń-Mitka, I. (2016). An intergenerational cooperation in the organization-view from the age perspective. *Procedia: Social and Behavioral Sciences*, *235*, 412–419. doi:10.1016/j.sbspro.2016.11.051

Sohail, M. T., Mahfooz, Y., Azam, K., Yen, Y., Genfu, L., & Fahad, S. (2019). Impacts of urbanization and land cover dynamics on underground water in Islamabad, Pakistan. *Desalination and Water Treatment*, *159*, 402–411. doi:10.5004/dwt.2019.24156

Sohail, M., Sun, D. W., & Zhu, Z. (2018). Recent developments in intelligent packaging for enhancing food quality and safety. *Critical Reviews in Food Science and Nutrition*, *58*(15), 2650–2662. doi:10.1080/10408398.2018.1449731 PMID:29513558

Song, L., Zhan, X., Zhang, H., Xu, M., Liu, J., & Zheng, C. (2022). How much is global business sectors contributing to sustainable development goals? *Sustainable Horizons*, *1*, 100012. doi:10.1016/j.horiz.2022.100012

Sovacool, B. K., Upham, P., & Monyei, C. G. (2022). The "whole systems" energy sustainability of digitalization: Humanizing the community risks and benefits of Nordic datacenter development. *Energy Research & Social Science*, *88*, 102493. doi:10.1016/j.erss.2022.102493

Spigel, L., Pesec, M., Del Carpio, O. V., Ratcliffe, H. L., Brizuela, J. A. J., Montero, A. M., & Hirschhorn, L. R. (2020). Implementing sustainable primary healthcare reforms: Strategies from Costa Rica. *BMJ Global Health*, *5*(8), e002674. doi:10.1136/bmjgh-2020-002674 PMID:32843571

Stachová, K., Stacho, Z., & Vicen, V. (2017). Efficient involvement of human resources in innovations through effective communication. *Business: Theory and Practice*, *18*(0), 33–42. doi:10.3846/btp.2017.004

Stamati, F., & Baeten, R. (2014). *Health care reforms and the crisis*. European Trade Union Institute.

Stankiewicz, W. (1998). *History of Economic Thought*. Polskie Wydawnictwo Ekonomiczne.

Starbucks. (2018). *Starbucks Announces Global Greener Stores Commitment*. Starbucks. https://stories.starbucks.com/press/2018/starbucks-announces-global-greener-stores-commitment/

Statista. (2021). *Umfrage zu Gründen für das Wegwerfen von Lebensmitteln in Deutschland 2021*. Statista. https://de.statista.com/statistik/daten/studie/486235/umfrage/umfrage-zu-gruenden-fuer-das-wegwerfen-von-lebensmitteln-in-deutschland/

Statista. (2023). *Number of internet and social media users worldwide as of January 2023*. Statista. https://www.statista.com/statistics/617136/digital-population-worldwide/#:~:text=Of this total%2C 4.76 billion,population%2C were social media users.

Statista. (2023a). *Influencer marketing market size worldwide from 2016 to 2022*. Statista. https://www.statista.com/statistics/1092819/global-influencer-market-size/

Statista. (2023b). *Share of consumers who follow at least one virtual influencer in the United States as of March 2022, by age group*. Statista. https://www.statista.com/statistics/1304080/consumers-follow-virtual-influencers-age-us/

Stead, M., Gordon, R., Angus, K., & McDermott, L. (2007). A systematic review of social marketing effectiveness. *Health Edu.*, *107*(2), 126-191.

Stefanova, D. (2016). Features of PR strategy and its implementation in stages. *Rhetoric and Communications Journal*, *24*. Advance online publication. doi:10.13140/RG.2.2.19020.85128

Stephen, A. (2001). The Contemporary Museum and leisure: Recreation as a museum function. *Museum Management and Curatorship*, *19*(3), 297–308. doi:10.1080/09647770100601903

Strauli, Tuvikene, T., Weicker, T., Kębłowski, W., Sgibnev, W., Timko, P., & Finbom, M. (2022). Beyond fear and abandonment: Public transport resilience during the COVID-19 pandemic. *Transportation Research Interdisciplinary Perspectives*, *16*, 1–9. doi:10.1016/j.trip.2022.100711 PMID:36373146

Strehlau, V. I., Claro, D. P., & Laban Neto, S. A. (2015). A vaidade impulsiona o consumo de cosméticos e de procedimentos estéticos cirúrgicos nas mulheres? Uma investigação exploratória. *Revista de Administração (São Paulo)*, *50*(1), 73–88. doi:10.5700/rausp1185

Streimikiene, D., Simanaviciene, Z., & Kovaliov, R. (2009). Corporate social responsibility for implementation of sustainable energy development in Baltic States. *Renewable & Sustainable Energy Reviews*, *13*(4), 813–824. doi:10.1016/j.rser.2008.01.007

Compilation of References

Suen, R. L. T., Tang, J., & Chiu, D. K. W. (2020). Virtual reality services in academic libraries: Deployment experience in Hong Kong. *The Electronic Library*, *38*(4), 843–858. doi:10.1108/EL-05-2020-0116

Suharto, S., Junaedi, I., Muhdar, H., Firmansyah, A., & Sarana, S. (2022). Consumer loyalty of Indonesia e-commerce SMEs: The role of social media marketing and customer satisfaction. *International Journal of Data and Network Science*, *6*(2), 383–390. doi:10.5267/j.ijdns.2021.12.016

Sullivan, J. (2004). The 8 Elements of a Successful Employment Brand. *ER Daily*. https://www.ere.net/the-8-elements-of-a-successful-employment-brand/

Sung, Y. Y. C., & Chiu, D. K. W. (2022). E-book or print book: Parents' Current View in Hong Kong. *Library Hi Tech*, *40*(5), 1289–1304. doi:10.1108/LHT-09-2020-0230

Sun, X., Chiu, D. K. W., & Chan, C. T. (2022). Recent Digitalization Development of Buddhist Libraries: A Comparative Case Study. In S. Papadakis & A. Kapaniaris (Eds.), *The Digital Folklore of Cyberculture and Digital Humanities* (pp. 251–266). IGI Global. doi:10.4018/978-1-6684-4461-0.ch014

Sun, X., Li, D., Li, B., Sun, S., Geng, J., Ma, L., & Qi, H. (2021). Exploring the effects of haze pollution on airborne fungal composition in a cold megacity in Northeast China. *Journal of Cleaner Production*, *280*, 124205. doi:10.1016/j.jclepro.2020.124205

Sun, Y., Luo, B., Wang, S., & Fang, W. (2021). What you see is meaningful: Does green advertising change the intentions of consumers to purchase eco-labeled products? *Business Strategy and the Environment*, *30*(1), 694–704. doi:10.1002/bse.2648

Sun, Y., & Shi, B. (2022). Impact of Greenwashing Perception on Consumers' Green Purchasing Intentions: A Moderated Mediation Model. *Sustainability (Basel)*, *14*(19), 12119. doi:10.3390u141912119

Sun, Y., & Wang, S. (2020). Understanding consumers' intentions to purchase green products in the social media marketing context. *Asia Pacific Journal of Marketing and Logistics*, *32*(4), 860–878. doi:10.1108/APJML-03-2019-0178

Suppakul, P. (2012). Intelligent packaging. In D. W. Sun (Ed.), *Handbook of Frozen Food Processing and Packaging* (pp. 837–860). CRC Press.

Suresh, C. (2022). Recent trends in Digital Marketing in Today's Scenario, Recent Trends in Management & [), Germany: Weser Books]. *Social Sciences*, *2*.

Surmanidze, N. (2022, July). Legislative Challenges of Georgian Entrepreneurship and Business Competitiveness. *Institutions and Economies*, *14*(3), 1–24. doi:10.22452/IJIE.vol14no3.1

Sustainable Development Goals (n.d). *Goal 12: Ensure sustainable consumption and production patterns*. United Nations. https://www.un.org/sustainabledevelopment/sustainable-consumption-production/

Sustainable Development. (2023). International Institute for Sustainable Development. https://www.iisd.org/mission-and-goals/sustainable-development

Syazali, M., Putra, F., Rinaldi, A., Utami, L., Widayanti, W., Umam, R., & Jermsittiparsert, K. (2019). Retracted: Partial correlation analysis using multiple linear regression: Impact on business environment of digital marketing interest in the era of industrial revolution 4.0. *Management Science Letters*, *9*(11), 1880–1886.

Syed, R. F. (2020). Ethical business strategy between east and west: An analysis of minimum wage policy in the garment global supply chain industry of Bangladesh. *Asian Journal of Business Ethics*, *9*(2), 241–255. doi:10.100713520-020-00108-5

Syed, R. F., & Ikra, M. (2022). *Industrial killing in Bangladesh: State policies, common-law nexus, and international obligations. Employee Responsibilities and Rights Journal*.

Syed, R. F., & Mahmud, K. T. (2022). Factors influencing work-satisfaction of global garments supply chain workers in Bangladesh. *International Review of Economics*, *69*(4), 507–524. doi:10.100712232-022-00403-6

Szabo, S., & Webster, J. (2021). Perceived Greenwashing: The Effects of Green Marketing on Environmental and Product Perceptions. *Journal of Business Ethics*, *171*(4), 719–739. doi:10.100710551-020-04461-0

Tabb, W. K. (2005). Sweated labor then and now. *International Labor and Working Class History*, *67*, 164–173. doi:10.1017/S014754790500013X

Tajudeen, F. P., Jaafar, N. I., & Ainin, S. (2018). Understanding the impact of social media usage among organizations. *Information & Management*, *55*(3), 308–321. doi:10.1016/j.im.2017.08.004

Tajvidi, R., & Karami, A. (2021). The effect of social media on firm performance. *Computers in Human Behavior*, *115*, 1–10. doi:10.1016/j.chb.2017.09.026

Taleb, N. (2019). *Antifragile; InfoDar.* Sofiq.

Tamashiro, H. R. S., da Silveira, J. A. G., Mantovani, D. M. N., & de Abreu Campanário, C. R. A. (2014). Aspectos determinantes do consumo de produtos cosméticos verdes. *RAI Revista de Administração e Inovação*, *11*(1), 238–262. doi:10.5773/rai.v11i1.1206

Tamvada, M. (2020). Corporate social responsibility and accountability: A new theoretical foundation for regulating CSR. *International Journal of Corporate Social Responsibility*, *5*(1), 1–14. doi:10.118640991-019-0045-8

Tarver, E. (2022). World Trade Organization (WTO): What It Is and What It Does. *Investopedia*. Retrieved from https://www.investopedia.com/terms/w/wto.asp

Taylor, N., Barker, K., & Simpson, M. (2003). Achieving "sustainable business": A study of perceptions of environmental best practice by SMEs in South Yorkshire. *Environment and Planning. C, Government & Policy*, *21*(1), 89–105. doi:10.1068/c0219

Technology: A Pathway Towards Sustainability. (n.d.). Retrieved April 30, 2023, from https://www.proquest.com/openview/329f4d51a0b62d5023f1af7dbaed1e12/1?pq-origsite=gscholar&cbl=38744

Tevdoradze, M., Aptsiauri, D., Gudava, V., Rukhadze, T., Darchia, S., & Lobazhanidze, L. (2015). Use of information technology in financial management and marketing of the company. *International scientific conference Information and computer technologies, modeling, management dedicated to the 85th birthday of Academician Iv. Frangishvili. works.* GTU.

Tevdoradze, M., Chigladze, T., Bajiashvili, A., Ioseliani, G., Lolashvili, N. (2014). Process-oriented management of modern organization. *Intellect Magazine*, **3**(50).

Tevdoradze, M., Lolashvilia, N., Bajiashvili, A., Rukhadze, T., Saltkhutsishvili, M., Chigladze, T. (2017). *The role of modeling in the design and optimization of business processes.* Monograph. GTU.

Thangam, D., & Chavadi, C. (2023). Impact of Digital Marketing Practices on Energy Consumption, Climate Change, and Sustainability. *Climate and Energy*, *39*(7), 11–19. doi:10.1002/gas.22329

The Comprehensive Business Case for Sustainability. (n.d.). Retrieved April 30, 2023, from https://hbr.org/2016/10/the-comprehensive-business-case-for-sustainability

The Financial Express. (2020). *Pandemic triggers big job losses in BD's RMG sector: WTO.* thefinancialexpress.com.bd

The Good Grade. (2022). *11 Sustainability Influencers Inspiring Us To Do A Little Better Every Day.* The Good Grade. https://www.thegoodtrade.com/features/sustainability-influencers/

Compilation of References

The Triple Bottom Line: What It Is & Why It's Important . (2020). Available at: https://online.hbs.edu/blog/post/what-is-the-triple-bottom-line

The World Bank. (2022). *Urban population (% of the total population)*. The World Bank. https://data.worldbank.org/indicator/SP.URB.TOTL.IN.ZS

Thøgersen, J. (2021). Consumer behavior and climate change: Consumers need considerable assistance. *Current Opinion in Behavioral Sciences*, *42*, 9–14. doi:10.1016/j.cobeha.2021.02.008

Thomas, S., Kureshi, S., & Vatavwala, S. (2020). Cause-related marketing research (1988–2016): An academic review and classification. *Journal of Nonprofit & Public Sector Marketing*, *32*(5), 488–516. doi:10.1080/10495142.2019.1606757

Tirpude, S. R., & Kombade, S. W. T. (2018). *Proceedings of International Conference on Business Remodeling - Exploring New Initiatives In Key Business Functions*. Kottakkal Faruk Arts and Sciences.

Tollin, K., & Christensen, L. B. (2019). Sustainability marketing commitment: Empirical insights about its drivers at the corporate and functional level of marketing. *Journal of Business Ethics*, *156*(4), 1165–1185. doi:10.100710551-017-3591-6

TOMS. (2021). *Overall B Impact Score*. BC Corporation. https://www.bcorporation.net/en-us/find-a-b-corp/company/toms

Tooranloo, H. S., Azadi, M. H., & Sayyahpoor, A. (2017). Analyzing factors affecting implementation success of sustainable human resource management (SHRM) using a hybrid approach of FAHP and Type-2 fuzzy DEMATEL. *Journal of Cleaner Production*, *162*, 1252–1265. doi:10.1016/j.jclepro.2017.06.109

Tracker, S. D. G. (n.d.). *Measuring progress towards the Sustainable Development Goals*. https://sdg-tracker.org/

TravelPerk. (2023). *Are companies becoming more sustainable?* Travel Perk. https://www.travelperk.com/blog/business-sustainability-statistics/

Tripathy, A., Agrawal, A., & Rath, S. K. (2016). Classification of sentiment reviews using n-gram machine learning approach. *Expert Systems with Applications*, *57*, 117–126. doi:10.1016/j.eswa.2016.03.028

Trivedi, J., Soni, S., & Kishore, A. (2020). Exploring the Role of Social Media Communications in the Success of Professional Sports Leagues: An Emerging Market Perspective. *Journal of Promotion Management*, *27*(2), 306–331. doi:10.1080/10496491.2020.1829774

Trivedi, K., Trivedi, P., & Goswami, V. (2018). Sustainable marketing strategies: Creating business value by meeting consumer expectation. [IJMESS]. *International Journal of Management, Economics and Social Sciences*, *7*(2), 186–205.

Trivedi, S., & Patel, N. (2020). The Role of Automation and Artificial Intelligence in Increasing the Sales Volume: Evidence from M, S, and, MM Regressions. *SSRN*, *3*(2), 1–19. doi:10.2139srn.4180379

Tröester, R., & Hiete, M. (2018). Success of voluntary sustainability certification schemes–a comprehensive review. *Journal of Cleaner Production*, *196*, 1034–1043. doi:10.1016/j.jclepro.2018.05.240

Truscott, M. H., Brust, P. J., & Fesmire, J. M. (2007). Core international labour standards and the world trade organization. *Journal of Business Cases & Applications*, *1*, 1–6.

Tse, H. L., Chiu, D. K., & Lam, A. H. (2022). From Reading Promotion to Digital Literacy: An Analysis of Digitalizing Mobile Library Services With the 5E Instructional Model. In A. Almeida & S. Esteves (Eds.), *Modern Reading Practices and Collaboration Between Schools, Family, and Community* (pp. 239–256). IGI Global. doi:10.4018/978-1-7998-9750-7.ch011

Uddin, J. (2020). Vietnam overtakes Bangladesh in RMG export. *The Business Standard*. Retrieved from https://tbsnews.net/economy/rmg/vietnam-surpasses-bangladesh-rmg-export-118897

Uddin, M. J., Azmat, F., Fujimoto, Y., & Hossain, F. (2022). Exploitation in Bangladeshi ready-made garments supply chain: A case of irresponsible capitalism? *International Journal of Logistics Management*.

Ullah, A. (2020). The moral obligation of the global supply chains during the pandemic. *The Business Standard*. Retrieved from https://www.tbsnews.net/thoughts/moral-obligation-global-supply-chains-during-pandemic-124840

Ullah, A., & Amanullah, A. (2021). Vaccinating RMG workers in Bangladesh: Why it's urgent and how international brands can help. *The Business Standard*. Retrieved from https://www.tbsnews.net/thoughts/vaccinating-rmg-workers-bangladesh-why-its-urgent-and-how-international-brands-can-help

Ullah, A. A. (2021). Covid-19: The role of global clothing brands/retailers in vaccinating and providing financial aid to the RMG workers in Bangladesh. *Middle East Journal of Business*, *16*(2), 5–11.

Ullah, A. A. S. M. (2015). Garment industry in Bangladesh: An era of globalization and neo-liberalization. *Middle East Journal of Business*, *10*(2), 14–26. doi:10.5742/MEJB.2015.92634

Ullah, A. A. S. M. (2022a). Tazreen Fashions, Rana Plaza, FR Tower and then Hashem Food, what next: The ineffective OHS regulatory processes of the Bangladesh Government. *Middle East Journal of Business*, *17*(1), 9–25.

Ullah, A. A. S. M. (2022b). An analysis of Marxism in industrial relations theory in light of capitalism, neoliberalism and globalisation: A petite critical review from Bangladesh's RMG perspectives. *Middle East Journal of Business*, *17*(2), 5–18.

UN. (n.d.). *Sustainable Development Goals*. United Nations. https://www.un.org/sustainabledevelopment/

UNESCO. (2022, September 5). *Culture & Sustainable Development*. UNESCO. https://en.unesco.org/culture-development

UN-Habitat. (2016). *World cities report 2016: Urbanization and Development–emerging futures*. United Nations Human Settlements Programme.

United Nations. (1987). Development And International Economic Co-Operation: Environment. New York: United Nations, General Assembly.

United Nations. (1987). United Nations general assembly: Development and international co-operation. Environment report of the world commission on environment and development. *Our common future. Released by the Brundtland commission*. UN. https://sustainabledevelopment.un.org/content/documents/5987our-common-future.pdf

United Nations. (2018). *Sustainable Cities and Communities*. UN. https://www.un.org/sustainabledevelopment/cities/

United Nations. (2018). *World urbanization prospects: The 2018 revision*. Department of Economic and Social Affairs, Population Division.

Urbancová, H. (2017). *Age management in organisations*. Wolters Kluwer.

Urbancová, H. (2019). Organisation of Working Time for Senior Workers in Agricultural Companies with a Focus on Age Management. *Studies in Agricultural Economics (Budapest)*, *121*, 161–165.

Urbancová, H., & Vrabcová, P. (2020). Age management as a human resources management strategy with a focus on the primary sector of the Czech Republic. *Agricultural Economics*, *66*, 251–259.

van Dam, Y. K., & Apeldoorn, P. A. C. (1996). Sustainable Marketing. *Journal of Macromarketing*, *16*(2), 45–56. doi:10.1177/027614679601600204

Van der Waal, J. W., & Thijssens, T. (2020). Corporate involvement in Sustainable Development Goals: Exploring the territory. *Journal of Cleaner Production*, *252*, 119625. doi:10.1016/j.jclepro.2019.119625 van Zanten, J. A., & van Tulder, R. (2021). Improving companies' impacts on sustainable development: A nexus approach to the SDGS. *Business Strategy and the Environment*, *30*(8), 3703–3720. doi:10.1002/bse.2835

Vangelov, N. (2023). Ambient Advertising in Metaverse Smart Cities. *Smart Cities and Regional Development (SCRD). Journal*, *7*(1), 43–55. doi:10.25019crdjournal.v7i1.175

Varadarajan. (2010). Strategic marketing and marketing strategy: domain, definition, fundamental issues and foundational premises. *Journal of the Academy of Marketing Science, 38*, 119-140.

Varey, R. J. (2002). Marketing communication: Principles and practice. *Routledge eBooks*. https://ci.nii.ac.jp/ncid/BA5525018X

Vasilev, V. (2020). From a crisis of confidence to effective crisis management in the public administration. *KNOWLEDGE - International Journal, 43*.

Vasilev, V., & Stefanova, D. (2021). Complex communication barriers in the organization in a crisis context. *International Journal (Toronto, Ont.)*, *49*(1). https://ikm.mk/ojs/index.php/kij/article/view/4617

Vastola, V., & Russo, A. (2021). Exploring the effects of mergers and acquisitions on acquirers' sustainability orientation: Embedding, adding, or losing sustainability. *Business Strategy and the Environment*, *30*(2), 1094–1104. doi:10.1002/bse.2673

Vayena, E., Blasimme, A., & Cohen, I. G. (2018). Machine learning in medicine: Addressing ethical challenges. *PLoS Medicine*, *15*(11), e1002689. doi:10.1371/journal.pmed.1002689 PMID:30399149

Veleva, S. S., & Tsvetanova, A. I. (2020). Characteristics of digital marketing advantages and disadvantages. [ ). IOP Publishing.]. *IOP Conference Series. Materials Science and Engineering*, *940*(1), 012065. doi:10.1088/1757-899X/940/1/012065

Verma, S., Sharma, R., Deb, S., & Maitra, D. (2021). Artificial intelligence in marketing: Systematic review and future research direction. *International Journal of Information Management Data Insights*, *1*(1), 100002. doi:10.1016/j.jjimei.2020.100002

Verulava, T., Jorbenadze, R., & Barkalaia, T. (2017). Introduction of Universal Health Program in Georgia: Problems and Perspectives. *Georgian Medical News, 1*(262).

Verulava, T., Jorbenadze, R., Dangadze, B., & Eliava, E. (2019). Access to ambulatory medicines for the elderly in Georgia. *Home Health Care Management & Practice*, *31*(2), 107–112. doi:10.1177/1084822318806316

Verulava, T., & Maglakelidze, T. (2017). Health financing policy in the south caucasus: Georgia, Armenia, Azerbaijan. *Soobshcheniia Akademii Nauk Gruzinskoi SSR*, *11*(2), 143–150.

Veseli-Kurtishi, T. (2018). Social media as a tool for the sustainability of small and medium businesses in Macedonia. *European Journal of Sustainable Development*, *7*(4), 262–262. doi:10.14207/ejsd.2018.v7n4p262

Vila-Lopez, N., & Küster-Boluda, I. (2020). A bibliometric analysis on packaging research: Towards sustainable and healthy packages. *British Food Journal*, *123*(2), 684–701. doi:10.1108/BFJ-03-2020-0245

Villareal, M., & Fergusson, I. F. (2017). *The North American Free Trade Agreement*. NAFTA.

Vlachos, P. A., Tsamakos, A., Vrechopoulos, A. P., & Avramidis, P. K. (2009). Corporate social responsibility: Attributions, loyalty, and the mediating role of trust. *Journal of the Academy of Marketing Science*, *37*(2), 170–180. doi:10.100711747-008-0117-x

Vlačić, B., Corbo, L., Silva, S. C., & Dabić, M. (2021). The evolving role of artificial intelligence in marketing: A review and research agenda. *Journal of Business Research*, *128*, 187–203. doi:10.1016/j.jbusres.2021.01.055

Vock, M. (2022). Luxurious and responsible? Consumer perceptions of corporate social responsibility efforts by luxury versus mass-market brands. *Journal of Brand Management, 29*(6), 569–583. doi:10.105741262-022-00281-x

Voipio, V., Elfvengren, K., & Korpela, J. (2020). In the bowling alley: Acceptance of an intelligent packaging concept in European markets. *International Journal of Value Chain Management, 11*(2), 180–197. doi:10.1504/IJVCM.2020.106825

Vollero, A., Siano, A. & Bertolini, A. (2022). Ex ante assessment of sustainable marketing investments. *Italian Journal of Marketing,* 271-287. doi:10.1007/s43039-022-00052-1

vom Brocke, J., & Rosemann, M. (2013). *Metodologia de pesquisa.* AMGH Editora.

Voola, R., Bandyopadhyay, C., Voola, A., Ray, S., & Carlson, J. (2022). B2B marketing scholarship and the UN sustainable development goals (SDGs): A systematic literature review. *Industrial Marketing Management, 101,* 12–32. doi:10.1016/j.indmarman.2021.11.013

Voorveld, H. A. M. (2019). Brand Communication in Social Media: A Research Agenda. *Journal of Advertising, 48*(1), 14–26. doi:10.1080/00913367.2019.1588808

Vrabcová, P. (2021). Udržitelné podnikání: dobrovolné nástroje (nejen) zemědělských a lesnických podniků. Praha: Grada Publishing, 192 s.

Vrabcová, P., & Urbancová, H. (2022). Holistic Human Resource Management as a Tool for the Intergenerational Cooperation and Sustainable Business. *Agricultural Economics, 68*(4), 117–126.

Vrabcová, P., Urbancová, H., & Hudáková, M. (2022). Strategic Trends of Organizations in the Context of New Perspectives of Sustainable Competitiveness. *Journal of Competitiveness, 14*(2), 174–193. doi:10.7441/joc.2022.02.10

Vrabcová, P., Urbancová, H., & Petříček, M. (2021). Knowledge and its transfer–key prerequisite for long-term competitive advantage and sustainable business. *Knowledge Management Research and Practice,* 1–11.

Wai, I. S. H., Ng, S. S. Y., Chiu, D. K. W., Ho, K. K., & Lo, P. (2018). Exploring undergraduate students' usage pattern of mobile apps for education. *Journal of Librarianship and Information Science, 50*(1), 34–47. doi:10.1177/0961000616662699

Waliszewski, K., & Warchlewska, A. (2020). Attitudes towards artificial intelligence in the area of personal financial planning: A case study of selected countries. *Entrepreneurship and Sustainability Issues, 8*(2), 399–420. doi:10.9770/jesi.2020.8.2(24)

Wan, B., Tian, L., Fu, M., & Zhang, G. (2021). Green development growth momentum under carbon neutrality scenario. *Journal of Cleaner Production, 316,* 128327. doi:10.1016/j.jclepro.2021.128327

Wang, H., Ma, B., & Bai, R. (2019). How does green product knowledge effectively promote green purchase intention? *Sustainability (Basel), 11*(4), 1193. doi:10.3390u11041193

Wang, J., Deng, S., Chiu, D. K. W., & Chan, C. T. (2022). Social network customer relationship management for orchestras: A case study on Hong Kong Philharmonic Orchestra. In N. B. Ammari (Ed.), *Social customer relationship management (Social-CRM) in the era of Web 4.0* (pp. 250–268). IGI Global. doi:10.4018/978-1-7998-9553-4.ch012

Wang, N., Liu, Y., Liu, Z., & Huang, X. (2020, June). Application of artificial intelligence and big data in modern financial management. In *2020 International Conference on Artificial Intelligence and Education (ICAIE)* (pp. 85-87). IEEE. 10.1109/ICAIE50891.2020.00027

Wang, W., Lam, E. T. H., Chiu, D. K. W., Lung, M. M., & Ho, K. K. W. (2021). Supporting Higher Education with Social Networks: Trust and Privacy vs. Perceived Effectiveness. *Online Information Review, 45*(1), 207–219. doi:10.1108/OIR-02-2020-0042

Wang, X., Pacho, F., Liu, J., & Kajungiro, R. (2019). Factors Influencing Organic Food Purchase Intention in Developing Countries and the Moderating Role of Knowledge. *Sustainability (Basel)*, *11*(1), 209–221. doi:10.3390u11010209

Wang, Y., Hong, A., Li, X., & Gao, J. (2020a). Marketing Innovations during a global crisis: A study of China Firms' Response to COVID-19. *Journal of Business Research*, *116*, 214–220. doi:10.1016/j.jbusres.2020.05.029 PMID:32501308

Ward, B. (2013). *Progress for a small planet*. Routledge. doi:10.4324/9781315066202

Warner, J. J., Benjamin, J. I., Churchwell, K., Firestone, G., Gardner, J. T., Johnson, J., Ng-Osorio, L., Rodriguez, J. C., Todman, L., Yaffe, K., Yancy, W. C., & Harrington, A. R. (2020). Advancing Healthcare Reform: The American Heart Association's 2020 Statement of Principles for Adequate, Accessible, and Affordable Health Care: A Presidential Advisory From the American Heart Association. *Circulation*, *141*(10), 601–614. doi:10.1161/CIR.0000000000000759 PMID:32008369

Warren-Myers, G. (2012). The value of sustainability in real estate: A review from a valuation perspective. *Journal of Property Investment & Finance*, *30*(2), 115–144. doi:10.1108/14635781211206887

Webb, D., Soutar, G. N., Gagné, M., Mazzarol, T., & Boeing, A. (2022). Saving energy at home: Exploring the role of behavior regulation and habit. *International Journal of Consumer Studies*, *46*(2), 621–635. doi:10.1111/ijcs.12716

Weber, M. (2008). The business case for corporate social responsibility: A company-level measurement approach for CSR. *European Management Journal*, *26*(4), 247–261. doi:10.1016/j.emj.2008.01.006

Wee, S. C., & Choong, W. W. (2019). Gamification: Predicting the effectiveness of variety game design elements to intrinsically motivate users' energy conservation behaviour. *Journal of Environmental Management*, *233*, 97–106. doi:10.1016/j.jenvman.2018.11.127 PMID:30572268

Wei, A.-P., Peng, C.-L., Huang, H.-C., & Yeh, S.-P. (2020). Effects of Corporate Social Responsibility on Firm Performance: Does Customer Satisfaction Matter? *Sustainability (Basel)*, *12*(18), 7545. doi:10.3390u12187545

Weinreich, N. K. (2006). *What is social marketing*. Weinreich Communications.

Wei, S., Ang, T., & Liou, R. (2020). Does the global vs. local scope matter? Contingencies of cause-related marketing in a developed market. *Journal of Business Research*, *108*, 201–212. doi:10.1016/j.jbusres.2019.11.018

Weller, J. (2017, June 23). Essential Guide to Strategic Planning. *Smart Sheet*. https://www.smartsheet.com/strategic-planning-guide

Welsh, D. T., Ordóñez, L. D., Snyder, D. G., & Christian, M. S. (2015). The slippery slope: How small ethical transgressions pave the way for larger future transgressions. *The Journal of Applied Psychology*, *100*(1), 114–127. doi:10.1037/a0036950 PMID:24865577

Wen, M., Zhang, T., Li, L., Chen, L., Hu, S., Wang, J., Liu, W., Zhang, Y., & Yuan, L. (1998). Assessment of Land Ecological Security and Analysis of Influencing Factors in Chaohu Lake Basin, China from 1998–2018. *Sustainability (Basel)*, *13*(1), 358. doi:10.3390u13010358

Wijekoon, R., & Sabri, M. F. (2021). Determinants that influence green product purchase intention and behavior: A literature review and guiding framework. *Sustainability (Basel)*, *13*(11), 6219. doi:10.3390u13116219

Wong, A. K.-k., & Chiu, D. K. W. (2023). Digital Transformation of Museum Conservation Practices: A Value Chain Analysis of Public Museums in Hong Kong. In R. Pettinger, B. B. Gupta, A. Roja, & D. Cozmiuc (Eds.), *Handbook of Research on the Digital Transformation Digitalization Solutions for Social and Economic Needs* (pp. 226–242). IGI. Global. doi:10.4018/978-1-6684-4102-2.ch010

Wood, H. W. (1985). The United Nations World Charter for Nature: The Developing Nations' Initiative to Establish Protections for the Environment. *Ecology Law Quarterly*, *12*(4), 977–996.

World Bank. (2020). *Bangladesh must ramp up COVID-19 action to protect its people, revive economy.* Retrieved from https://www.worldbank.org/en/news/press-release/2020/04/12/bangladesh-must-act-now-to-lessen-covid-19-health-impacts

World Economic Forum. (2021). *The global eco-wakening: how consumers are driving sustainability.* WEF. https://www.weforum.org/agenda/2021/05/eco-wakening-consumers-driving-sustainability/

World Health Organization. (2004). *Investing in the health of the poor: A strategy for sustainable health development and poverty reduction in the Eastern Mediterranean Region.* WHO.

World Health Organization. (2009). *Georgia Health System Performance Assessment.* World Bank, UNO, Health Assessment of Georgian Health System.

World Health Organization. (n.d.). https://georgia.un.org/sites/default/files/2020- 08/Georgia%205.pdf

WTO. (n.d.). *GATT and the goods council.* Retrieved from https://www.wto.org/english/tratop_e/gatt_e/gatt_e.htm

Wu, M., Lam, A. H. C., & Chiu, D. K. W. (2023) Transforming and Promoting Reference Services with Digital Technologies: A Case Study on Hong Kong Baptist University Library. In: B. Holland (Ed.) Handbook of Research on Advancements of Contactless Technology and Service Innovation in Library and Information Science. IGI. Global. doi:10.4018/978-1-6684-7693-2.ch007

Wu, L., Subramanian, N., Abdulrahman, M. D., Liu, C., & Pawar, K. S. (2017). Short-term versus long-term benefits: Balanced sustainability framework and research propositions. *Sustainable Production and Consumption*, *11*, 18–30. doi:10.1016/j.spc.2016.09.003

Wymer, W. (2011). Developing more effective marketing. *Journal of Social Marketing*, *1*(1), 17–31. doi:10.1108/20426761111104400

Wymer, W., & Polonsky, M. J. (2015). The limitations and potentialities of green marketing. *Journal of Nonprofit & Public Sector Marketing*, *27*(3), 239–262. doi:10.1080/10495142.2015.1053341

Xie, M. (2019). Development of Artificial Intelligence and Effects on Financial System. *Journal of Physics: Conference Series*, *1187*(3), 032084. doi:10.1088/1742-6596/1187/3/032084

Xie, Z., Chiu, D. K. W., & Ho, K. K. W. (2023). (in press). The Role of Social Media as Aids for Accounting Education and Knowledge Sharing: Learning Effectiveness and Knowledge Management Perspectives in Mainland China. *Journal of the Knowledge Economy.* doi:10.100713132-023-01262-4

Xu, C., Lam, A. H. C., & Chiu, D. K. W. (2023). Antique Bookstores Marketing Strategies as Urban Cultural Landmark: A Case Analysis for Suzhou Antique Bookstore. In M. Rodrigues & M. A. M. Carvalho (Eds.), *Exploring Niche Tourism Business Models, Marketing, and Consumer Experience.* I.G.I. Global.

Xue, B., Lam, A. H. C., & Chiu, D. K. W. (2023). Redesigning Library Information Literacy Education with the BOPPPS Model: A Case Study of the HKUST. In R. Taiwo, B. Idowu-Faith, & S. Ajiboye (Eds.), *Transformation of Higher Education Through Institutional Online Spaces.* IGI Global.

Yamane, T., & Kaneko, S. (2021). Impact of raising awareness of Sustainable Development Goals: A survey experiment eliciting stakeholder preferences for corporate behavior. *Journal of Cleaner Production*, *28*(5), 125291. doi:10.1016/j.jclepro.2020.125291

Compilation of References

Yam, K. L., Takhistov, P. T., & Miltz, J. (2005). Intelligent packaging: Concepts and applications. *Journal of Food Science*, *70*(1), R1–R10. doi:10.1111/j.1365-2621.2005.tb09052.x

Yan, C., Liao, H., Ma, Y., & Wang, J. (2021). The Impact of Health Care Reform Since 2009 on the Efficiency of Primary Health Services: A Provincial Panel Data Study in China. *Frontiers in Public Health*, *9*, 735654. Advance online publication. doi:10.3389/fpubh.2021.735654 PMID:34746081

Yao, L., Lei, J., Chiu, D. K. W., & Xie, Z. (2023). Adult Learners' Perception of Online Language English Learning Platforms in China. In A. Garcés-Manzanera & M. E. C. García (Eds.), *New Approaches to the Investigation of Language Teaching and Literature*. IGI Global.

Yastrow, S. (2003). *Brand Harmony: Achieving Dynamic Results by Orchestrating Your Customer's Total Experience*. Select Books Inc.

Yau, K.-L. A., Saad, N. M., & Chong, Y.-W. (2021). Artificial Intelligence Marketing (AIM) for Enhancing Customer Relationships. *Applied Sciences (Basel, Switzerland)*, *11*(18), 8562. doi:10.3390/app11188562

Yigitcanlar, T., & Cugurullo, F. (2020). The sustainability of artificial intelligence: An urbanistic viewpoint from the lens of smart and sustainable cities. *Sustainability (Basel)*, *12*(20), 8548. doi:10.3390u12208548

Yildirim, K. (2021). The determinants of purchase intention and willingness to pay for cosmetics and personal care products. *Marketing i menedžment innovacij*.

Yıldırım, S. (2021). Do green women in fluencers spur sustainable consumption patterns? Descriptive evidences from social media in fluencers. *Ecofeminism and Climate Change*, *2*(4), 198–210. doi:10.1108/EFCC-02-2021-0003

Yin, R. K. (2003). *Case Study Research: Design and methods* (3rd ed.). Sage.

Yip, K. H. T., Chiu, D. K. W., Ho, K. K. W., & Lo, P. (2021). Adoption of Mobile Library Apps as Learning Tools in Higher Education: A Tale between Hong Kong and Japan. *Online Information Review*, *45*(2), 389–405. doi:10.1108/OIR-07-2020-0287

Yi, Y., & Chiu, D. K. W. (2023). Public information needs during the COVID-19 outbreak: A qualitative study in mainland China. *Library Hi Tech*, *41*(1), 248–274. doi:10.1108/LHT-08-2022-0398

Yu, H. H. K., Chiu, D. K. W., & Chan, C. T. (2023). Resilience of symphony orchestras to challenges in the COVID-19 era: Analyzing the Hong Kong Philharmonic Orchestra with Porter's five force model. In W. Aloulou (Ed.), *Handbook of Research on Entrepreneurship and Organizational Resilience During Unprecedented Times* (pp. 586–601). IGI Global.

Yu, P. Y., Lam, E. T. H., & Chiu, D. K. W. (2023). Operation management of academic libraries in Hong Kong under COVID-19. *Library Hi Tech*, *41*(1), 108–129. doi:10.1108/LHT-10-2021-0342

Yusiana, R., Widodo, A., & Hidayat, A. M. (2020, May). Green Marketing: Perspective of 4P's. In *First ASEAN Business, Environment, and Technology Symposium (ABEATS 2019)* (pp. 105-109). Atlantis Press.

Zafar, S., Aziz, A., & Hainf, M. (2020). Young Consumer Green Purchase Behavior. *International J. Mark. Res. Innov.*, *4*, 1–12.

Zahid, M. M., Ali, B., Ahmad, M. S., Thurasamy, R., & Amin, N. (2018). Factors affecting purchase intention and social media publicity of green products: The mediating role of concern for consequences. *Corporate Social Responsibility and Environmental Management*, *25*(3), 225–236. doi:10.1002/csr.1450

Zairi, M. (2000). Social responsibility and impact on society. *The TQM Magazine*, *12*(3), 172–178. doi:10.1108/09544780010320278

Zairis, A. G. (2020). *The Effective Use of Digital Technology by SMEs. Entrepreneurial Development and Innovation in Family Businesses and SMEs*. Neapolis University.

Zaman, R., Jain, T., Samara, G., & Jamali, D. (2022). Corporate governance meets corporate social responsibility: Mapping the interface. *Business & Society, 61*(3), 690–752. doi:10.1177/0007650320973415

Zatwarnicka-Madura, B., Nowacki, R., & Wojciechowska, I. (2022). Influencer Marketing as a Tool in Modern Communication—Possibilities of Use in Green Energy Promotion amongst Poland's Generation Z. *Energies, 15*(18), 6570. https://www.bp.com/tr_tr/turkey/home/topluluk/toplumsal-projeler/gelisim-seninle.html and https://www.setav.org/rapor-rusya-ukrayna-savasinin-kuresel-ekonomiye-ve-turkiyeye-etkileri/ and https://www.rsis.edu.sg/rsis-publication/rsis/invasion-of-ukraine-eu-energy-crisis-to-sanction-or-not/#.Yy1ek3ZBzIW. doi:10.3390/en15186570

Zeng, T. (2022). Impacts of consumers' perceived risks in eco-design packaging on food wastage behaviors. *British Food Journal, 124*(8), 2512–2532. doi:10.1108/BFJ-05-2021-0603

Zhang, B., Zhang, Y., & Zhou, P. (2021). Consumer Attitude towards Sustainability of Fast Fashion Products in the UK. *Sustainability (Basel), 13*(4), 1646. doi:10.3390u13041646

Zhang, K., Liu, H., Li, Y., & Wu, X. (2023). Effects of social media usage on exploratory innovation, exploitative innovation and organizational agility: The moderating role of learning goal orientation. *Internet Research*. doi:10.1108/INTR-07-2021-0503

Zhang, X., Lo, P., So, S., Chiu, D. K. W., Leung, T. N., Ho, K. K. W., & Stark, A. (2021). Medical students' attitudes and perceptions towards the effectiveness of mobile learning: A comparative information-need perspective. *Journal of Librarianship and Information Science, 53*(1), 116–129. doi:10.1177/0961000620925547

Zhang, X., Xu, Y., & Ma, L. (2022). Research on Successful Factors and Influencing Mechanism of the Digital Transformation in SMEs. *Sustainability (Basel), 14*(5), 2549. doi:10.3390u14052549

Zhong, W., Song, J., Yang, W., Fang, K., & Liu, X. (2021). Evolving household consumption-driven industrial energy consumption under urbanization: A dynamic input-output analysis. *Journal of Cleaner Production, 289*, 125732. doi:10.1016/j.jclepro.2020.125732

Zhuang, W., Luo, X., & Riaz, M. U. (2021). On the Factors Influencing Green Purchase Intention: A Meta-Analysis Approach. *Frontiers in Psychology, 12*, 644020. doi:10.3389/fpsyg.2021.644020 PMID:33897545

Zhuang, Y., Jiang, N., Wu, Z., Li, Q., Chiu, D. K., & Hu, H. (2014). Efficient and robust large medical image retrieval in mobile cloud computing environment. *Information Sciences, 263*, 60–86. doi:10.1016/j.ins.2013.10.013

Zhuo & Chen. (2023). Can digital transformation overcome the enterprise innovation dilemma: Effect, mechanism and effective boundary. *Technological Forecasting and Social Change, 190*, 1–13.

Ziolo, M., Bak, I., & Cheba, K. (2021). The role of sustainable finance in achieving Sustainable Development Goals: Does it work? *Technological and Economic Development of Economy, 27*(1), 45–70. doi:10.3846/tede.2020.13863

Zuo, Y., Lam, A. H. C., & Chiu, D. K. W. (2023). Digital protection of traditional villages for sustainable heritage tourism: A case study on Qiqiao Ancient Village, China. In A. Masouras, C. Papademetriou, D. Belias, & S. Anastasiadou (Eds.), *Sustainable Growth Strategies for Entrepreneurial Venture Tourism and Regional Development*. IGI Global. doi:10.4018/978-1-6684-6055-9.ch009

About the Contributors

Iza Gigauri is based at St. Andrew the First-Called Georgian University in Tbilisi, Georgia. She has a Ph.D. in Business Administration from Ivane Javakhishvili Tbilisi State University, Georgia. She holds an MBA from Business School Netherlands and an MBA from American University for Humanities Tbilisi Campus. She graduated from Ilia State University (Georgia) and Ruhr-University Bochum (Germany). She delivers lectures and teaches seminars at all three levels of higher education. She has more than 70 scientific publications in international journals and books, participated in more than 30 international scientific conferences. She is a member of the editorial and reviewer boards of more than 35 international journals within Emerald Publishing, IGI Global, Inderscience, Frontiers, MDPI, Taylor & Francis, and Springer. Her research interests include marketing, corporate responsibility and business ethics, sustainable development, organizational behavior, leadership, human resource management, entrepreneurship and social entrepreneurship.

Maria Palazzo (PhD) is Associate Professor at Universitas Mercatorum, Rome, Italy. She was a Research Fellow at the Department of Political, Social and Communication Studies (DSPSC), University of Salerno (Italy). Since 2015, she has been a member of the 'Sustainability Communication Centre' (SCC) at the DSPSC. She was a former Lecturer at University of Bedfordshire, School of Business (London, Luton, UK), a Visiting Scholar at the University of Granada (Granada, Spain), and a Visiting Lecturer at the Universidad del Norte, Escuela de Negocios (Barranquilla, Colombia). Her research focuses on corporate and marketing communication, branding, corporate social responsibility, tourism, community relations, and sustainability. Her articles have been published in Journal of Cleaner Production, Current Issues in Tourism, Journal of Retailing and Consumer Services, International Journal of Contemporary Hospitality Management, Qualitative Market Research: An International Journal, Journal of Brand Management and in other academic outlets.

Maria Antonella Ferri is Chair and Full Professor of Management at Universitas Mercatorum, where she teaches Strategy, Marketing and Management. She got a PhD in Business Management at The University Ca' Foscari of Venice; she became researcher at the University of Rome "La Sapienza" and then Associate Professor at the Parthenope University of Naples. She is interested in strategic sustainability, social responsibility, management and marketing. She published several books and articles on these items on national and international journals such as TQM journal and Journal of Business Research.

* * *

Anuradha A. is working as a Professor, in the Department of MBA, Cambridge Institute of Technology, K.R. Puram, Bangalore. She has done her post graduation and Ph.D., under The University of Madras and has a teaching experience of 23 years. She worked under various affiliated institutions of Madras University, Anna University, Visvesvaraya Technological University and Christ deemed to be University. Her area of research includes Economics and Marketing. Currently she is guiding research scholars under VTU.

George Kofi Amoako, BSc (Hons, KNUST), MBA (Marketing, UG), PhD (LondonMet), Chartered Marketer-CIM-UK, is an Associate Professor at the Marketing Department of Ghana Communication Technology University Accra, an academic and a practicing Chartered Marketer (CIM_UK) with specialization in, Sustainability, Branding, CSR, and Strategic Marketing. He was educated in Kwame Nkrumah University of Science and Technology in Kumasi Ghana and at the University of Ghana and the London School of Marketing (UK).. He has considerable research, teaching, consulting, and practice experience in the application of Marketing Theory and principles to everyday marketing challenges and management and Organizational issues. He is a Chartered Marketer with The Chartered Institute of Marketing-UK. He has consulted for Public Sector and Private organizations both in Ghana and UK. George has published extensively in international peer-reviewed academic journals and presented many papers at international conferences.

George Oppong Appiagyei Ampong is an Associate Professor in Management and Dean of the Business School at Ghana Communication Technology University in Ghana. He holds Ph.D. in Business Administration and PGCert in International Higher Education Academic Practice. His research interest includes Business and Sustainability strategies, entrepreneurship and SME development, organizational leadership, etc. His research has been published in reputable journals such as VINE Journal of Information and Knowledge Management Systems, Journal of Hospitality and Tourism Insights, and Journal of Technological Forecasting & Social Change, among others.

Gifty Agyeiwah Bonsu is currently a contract staff working with Ghana Revenue Authority in kaneshie Taxpayer Service Center, Kaneshie-Accra, Ghana. Gifty graduated with Bachelor's Degree in Business Administration (Marketing Option) with a second class upper division. Her academic performance, dedication to studies and punctuality earned her a good reputation so much that she became the course representative of a class from 2016-2017. After her degree, she was encouraged by her Head of Department, Prof George Kofi Amoako to understudy and tutored on how to learn and write papers and ever since have been part of academic papers published in Scopus and B- ranked journals. Gifty is hard working and very organised.

Chandan Chavadi is the Dean & Professor of the Presidency Business School, Presidency College, Bengaluru. A PhD from Karnatak University, Dharwad, and an MBA (Mktg.) He holds a primary degree in B.E. (E&C). He has two years of corporate experience before his moving to academics. He has been in academics for the last 21 years. He has 32 papers & 2 book reviews to his credit, published in reputed journals and magazines such as ABDC-C journals, Web of Science, Scopus, UGC Care list and other indexed journals. Under Google scholar indices, he has total citations of 90, h-index of 6 & i10-index of 4. His paper has been accepted for publication in the IIM –A Vikalpa. Five of his research papers were recently published in the IIM Kozhikode Society And Management Review journal, IIM-Shillong

About the Contributors

Journal of Management Science, Business Perspective & Research journal of K J Somaiya Institute of Management, the MDI journal "Vision", and IIM-Lucknow journal "Metamorphosis". He is the recipient of Labdhi Bhandari Best Paper Award for the 7th IIM-A International Marketing Conference held on 11th to 13th Jan 2017. He is a recognized PhD Guide in Management for Bangalore City University.

Yitong Chen is a current postgraduate student in the MSc Library and Information Management programme at the University of Hong Kong. She obtained a Bachelor of Commerce degree majored in Accounting and Information Systems from the University of Auckland. Yitong Chen has worked as a part-time tutor for two years in the field of Accounting and Information System.

Dickson K. W. Chiu received the B.Sc. (Hons.) degree in Computer Studies from the University of Hong Kong in 1987. He received the M.Sc. (1994) and Ph.D. (2000) degrees in Computer Science from the Hong Kong University of Science and Technology (HKUST). He started his own computer consultant company while studying part-time. He has also taught at several universities in Hong Kong. His teaching and research interest is in Library & Information Management, Service Computing, and E-learning with a cross-disciplinary approach involving library and information management, e-learning, e-business, service sciences, and databases. The results have been widely published in over 300 international publications (most of them have been indexed by SCI/-E, SSCI, and EI, such as top journals MIS Quarterly, Computer & Education, Government Information Quarterly, Decision Support Systems, Information Sciences, Knowledge-Based Systems, Expert Systems with Application, Information Systems Frontiers, IEEE Transactions, including many taught master and undergraduate project results and around 20 edited books. He received a best paper award at the 37th Hawaii International Conference on System Sciences in 2004. He is an Editor (-in-chief) of Library Hi Tech, a prestigious journal indexed by SSCI. He is the Editor-in-chief Emeritus of the International Journal on Systems and Service-Oriented0 Engineering (founding) and International Journal of Organizational and Collective Intelligence, and serves on the editorial boards of several international journals. He co-founded several international workshops and co-edited several journal special issues. He also served as a program committee member for around 300 international conferences and workshops. Dr. Chiu is a Senior Member of both the ACM and the IEEE and a life member of the Hong Kong Computer Society. According to Google Scholar, he has over 6,200 citations, h-index=41, i-10 index=142, ranked worldwide 1st in "LIS," "m-learning," and "e-services." He received nearly 1,000 citations in 2022.

Isaac Sewornu Coffie obtained his Doctor of Philosophy Degree from the University of Ghana with a specialization in social marketing. He is currently an adjunct lecturer at Accra Technical University. His teaching and research interests are social marketing, corporate social responsibility, entrepreneurship and SME development.

Catarina Delgado, Ph.D., is an assistant professor at the Faculty of Economics, University of Porto (FEP.UP), and a researcher at CEF.UP and LIAAD/ INESC TEC. Her research interests are primarily in the areas of responsible consumers, responsible e-commerce, sustainable and responsible supply chains, ecotourism, ESG/ CSR disclosure, quality management/ kaizen/ lean six sigma, and scientometrics. Her teaching focus is on Operations and Logistics (operations management, supply chain management, operational research), Quality Management and Continuous Improvement (Kaizen, Lean, Six Sigma), and Social Responsibility and Sustainability Reporting. Author of the book "Supply Chain Social

About the Contributors

Sustainability for Manufacturing" (Springer, 2020), her academic work has been published in several leading international scientific journals, such as Journal of Cleaner Production, International Journal of Production Economics, Sustainability, Journal of Manufacturing Technology Management, JASIST, Informetrics, Scientometrics, and Social Responsibility Journal.

Antoinette Gabrah is a Ph.D. candidate at the University of Professional Studies Accra. She holds an MPhil in Marketing from the University of Ghana. She is currently a lecturer at Academic City University College Accra Ghana and an adjunct faculty at Akenten Appiah-Minka University of Skills Training and Entrepreneurial Development in Kumasi Ghana. Antoinette has published in Scopus Indexed journals. Her research interest includes e-business, services marketing, and digital marketing strategies.

Razvan Ionescu is an entrepreneur in the IT industry since 2010. Holds a bachelor's degree in Public Administration from the Dimitrie Cantemir Christian University in Bucharest as well as a master's degree in Economics from the Petroleum-Gas University of Ploiesti. His research interests include Financial Markets, Behavioral Finance, Corporate Governance and Corporate Social Responsibility, Financial Technology.

Firdous Ahmad Malik, an Indian citizen by birth, is a full time PhD fellow at Babasaheb Bhimrao Ambedkar University Lucknow, India. His research area of interest is financial behaviour of poorest of the poor, financial inclusion, and financial literacy. He holds a MPhil degree in Economics from Babasaheb Bhimrao Ambedkar University Lucknow, a Master's degree in Economics from Kashmir University. He has published papers in springer, Elsevier, Taylor Francis and other Scopus indexed journals. Specialization: Microfinance, Development Economics, Urban-Rural Poverty, Monetary Economics, Public Finance, Inclusive Education.

Thirupathi Manickam, M.Com, M.Phil, B.Ed, TN-SET, KSET, Ph.D., is presently working as an Assistant professor in the Department of Professional Studies at Christ University, Bangalore. It is one of the leading institution in Bangalore, Karnataka, and the institution is Accreditated by NIRF, NBA and NAAC Accredited university. He has more than 7 years of teaching and Research experience. He has 44 citations and 3 h-Index. He has published 22 research papers in Scopus, Web of Science, UGC-CARE, and UGC-approved and leading International journals and 11 presented papers in national and international conferences. He has also participated in over 40 seminars, conferences, FDP & workshops at the National and International Levels. His areas of expertise are Financial Accounting, Corporate Accounting, Financial Management, Management Accounting, Taxation, Digital Marketing and Technology Management.

Zurab Mushkudiani is from the Republic of Georgia. He has a PhD. in Business Administration. He has been teaching for 16 years at the university and public high schools. In addition to teaching, Dr. Zurab Mushkudiani has been working as a PR specialist in Kutaisi City Council since 2002. He regularly takes active participation in different professional, educational, scientific and cultural projects, conferences, training, seminars and workshops throughout the world. He attended an English language intensive course in Edinburgh Language Academy (UK) and Training of Trainers Summer Institute (TOTSI) in the USA.. Right now he is attending Education Policy and Leadership Master program at AU.

About the Contributors

Elikem Chosniel Ocloo is a Senior Lecturer in the Marketing Department and currently, the Head of the Marketing Department. He holds a Bachelor of Arts Degree in Geography and Resource Development (Major) with First Class Honours from the University of Ghana and a Master's degree in Business Administration (Marketing option) from the University of Leicester, United Kingdom, and a Doctor of Philosophy (Ph.D.) degree from Jiangsu University, China in Management Science and Engineering (Marketing). He has acquired experience in both academia and industry and is an ardent seeker of innovation and creative ways to solve societal and business marketing problems. He is an Associate Member of the Chartered Institute of Marketing Ghana (CIMG). Dr. Ocloo has publications in International Journals and other journals with Scopus indexing, SSCI-Indexed, and ESCI-Indexed and presented papers in both local and international conferences. He has a special interest in current business trends in Digitalisation and 4th Industrial Revolution concepts. His current research interests include E-commerce/Digitalisation, Health Marketing, SMEs Development, Social Marketing, and Marketing Management.

Cătălin Popescu is Professor of Management at Petroleum-Gas University from Ploiesti, Romania. His research and consulting interest include general management, engineering management, project management, quantitative methods for business and management, human resource management, operations management, energy and environmental management, feasibility studies and petroleum economics. He received in 1991 a degree in Engineering, a degree in Management (2000) and a PhD (2001) in Automated Systems concern Modelling and simulation of production systems, from the University of Oil and Gas from Ploiesti, Romania. He became PhD Advisor for Engineering and Management domain with a habilitation thesis entitled: Researches and contributions to the development of managerial tools for the sustainable management of conventional and non-conventional resources of energy and for the innovation in education and research. Dr. Popescu has published over 220 articles and conference papers, 9 books, 8 book chapters and he was involved in more than 33 scientific research grants and international projects. His international experience includes presentations in more than 27 countries.

Maryum Sajid Raja is a PhD candidate in Technology Management at South West Jiaotong University. Her research interests lie in the intersection of sustainable development, information and communication technology (ICT), and logistics. Maryum's passion for sustainable development and its impact on technology and logistics drive her to pursue a PhD in Technology Management. Her research focuses on finding ways to integrate sustainable practices into technology and logistics industries, thereby contributing to the overall sustainable development of society. Maryum is dedicated to her work and is committed to making a positive impact on the world through her research.

Ana Rodrigues has a degree in Management from Universidade do Minho at School of Economics and Management. In 2022 she finished her Masters in Sales Management by the Universidade do Porto.

José Duarte da Rocha Santos received his PhD in Management from Vigo University. He also holds MSc in Marketing and a bachelor's degree in Business Sciences. Between 1987 and 2002, he played various roles in sales, marketing, and management of companies in the information technology sector. From 2003 to 2018, he performed the functions of a management and marketing consultant. Since 1999, he has been a professor in higher education in Portugal in the fields of management and marketing. He is currently a marketing professor at the Accounting and Business School of the Polytechnic of Porto (ISCAP/P.PORTO). He is also a senior researcher at the CEOS.PP - Centre for Organizational and Social Studies of the Polytechnic of Porto, Portugal. His main research areas are Strategic Marketing and Digital Marketing Strategies.

Gopalakrishnan Subramaniyan is Head, Research and Development Cell, Project Director (ICSSR) & Associate Professor, Department of Commerce & Management, Acharya Institute of Graduate Studies, Bangalore. He has completed a Major Research Project on "Solid Waste Management" funded by ICSSR (Indian Council of Social Sciences Research). Has 25 years of experience including 12 years of industry and 13 years of teaching Management and Commerce subjects. He has International experience of 1 year working in Nigeria as an Assistant Professor, University of UYO, Nigeria. Published more than 30 articles in refereed journals with 56 citations, h-INDEX -3 and i10 INDEX – 1. He is also the Editor and Reviewer for Elsevier and other Journals.

Natia Surmanidze has a Ph.D. in economics, is a research associate at the University of Georgia, is a professor (associate) at Guram Tavartkiladze Tbilisi Educational University, and is a guest lecturer at Ilia State University. A member of the editorial board Noble International Journal of Social Sciences Research and Journal of Economics and Management Sciences. She authorized about 30 scientific articles and reports published with a high impact factor, including in international scientific journals and conference collections indexed in the Scopus database. She is also the author of a monograph.

Khatuna Tabagari is a Doctor of Economics, an assistant professor at Guram Tavartkiladze Tbilisi Teaching University, Group Chief at the Service Department of LEPL Revenue Service, an editorial board member at European Business & Management(EBM), ISSN Print: 2575-579X; ISSN Online: 2575-5811, a researcher at Iran Research Department of Georgian Neighborhood Institute of Social and Political Science Faculty of Ivane Javakhishvili Tbilisi State University. She is a co-author of the monograph published in 2021 and more than 25 articles and conferences.

Sopiko Tevdoradze is a Doctor of Business Administration, Vice-Rector for Academic Process at Guram Tavartkiladze Teaching University, Professor, Head of Bachelor's Program in Tourism. She received her higher education and academic degree at Tbilisi State University of Economic Relations: - 2004-2006 (MBA) specialization: commerce and marketing of resort-hotel complexes and international tourism; - 2006-2009 (Ph.D.) specialty: tourism. She authorizes over 20 scientific articles, one textbook, and several lecture courses. To improve her qualifications, she has undergone training in various directions. She has participated in several international conferences. Sopiko Tevdoradze has published scientific works in the field of the Tourism Industry. In particular, on modern aspects of international tourism, Peculiarities of International tourism market service and Georgian tourism potential integration possibilities into the global tourism market, Digital challenges in the tourism industry, and Branding in tourism using digital marketing. Publications dealing with social, economic, and legal aspects of globalization and international business development.

Dhanabalan Thangam is presently working as Assistant Professor in Presidency Business School, Bengaluru, India. Earlier he was worked as Post-Doctoral researcher in Konkuk School of Business, Konkuk University, Seoul, Korea South. He received his Ph.D. degree in Management from Alagappa University, Tamilnadu, India. His current research interests are marketing, small business management and artificial intelligence in management fields.

About the Contributors

Keti Tskhadadze holds a Ph.D. degree in Economics from Ivane Javakhishvili Tbilisi State University (TSU), a Master's degree in Economics from International School of Economics at TSU (ISET) and a Bachelor's degree in Business Administration from the University of Georgia. Currently she works as the Head of the Business Analytics program, Professor and International Accreditation Manager at the University of Georgia. She has completed number of trainings in the USA, Czech Republic, Italy, Romania, Slovenia, Kenya in the field of Business and Economics. She has published several research papers (both in Georgia and abroad) and has meaningful experience in scientific work, consulting, designing and conducting trainings in the field of Economics. All the above mentioned gives competence to Keti Tskhadadze to teach the following courses: Microeconomics, Macroeconomics, Public Finance, Managerial economics, the Basics of Business and Economics Forecast, International Economics Policy.

Valentin Vasilev is a "professor" of "National Security" ("Crisis Situations and Human Resource Management") at the Higher School of Security and Economics /HSSE/, city of Plovdiv and head of the "Center for Leadership and Public Policies" at the same educational institution. In the period from 2000 to 2021, he was part of the South-West University "Neofit Rilski", Blagoevgrad. He is the author of more than a hundred publications in scientific publications in Bulgaria and abroad, as well as seven monographic publications in the field of human resources management, crisis situations; the team form of work; motivation and organizational behavior; public management and public policies and others. Professor Vasilev has extensive practical experience in the public sector, such as: Deputy Mayor of Blagoevgrad Municipality /2007-2010/; Public Mediator /Ombudsman/ of the Municipality of Blagoevgrad.

Agnieszka Wójcik-Czerniawska is Associate Professor at Warsaw School of Economics (SGH) in Poland. The PhD of Economics field Management, MBA in Spanish- ICEX-CECO- Madryt. Visiting Professor at many foreign Universities in Europe (Italy, Spain) and World (Peru, Kenya), The area of research are connected with: modern finance, finance technology, digital currency, financial isolation. The participant in many international conferences in all around the world.

Index

A

Accessibility 28, 59-60, 245, 271, 273, 280-282, 360

Advertising 22-24, 29-31, 33-34, 36-38, 40-41, 48-50, 57, 60-62, 66, 137, 144-145, 147, 150-151, 156, 161, 173, 175, 183-185, 190, 193, 197, 203-205, 207, 223, 227-228, 232, 254, 285, 321, 327, 344-349, 351-352, 357-358, 361-362, 367-368, 373, 375, 385

Affordability 260, 266, 271, 273, 277, 280-282

age management 92-93, 96-97, 101-103, 105, 107-109, 111

Artificial Intelligence 23-24, 120, 196, 234, 351-359, 361-363, 367-371, 375, 382

B

Branding 16, 18, 65, 103, 108, 112-113, 117, 120, 122-123, 125, 168, 172, 185, 224, 249, 342, 353, 362

Business Performance 38, 134-135, 137, 140, 142-143, 145, 148, 171, 176-177, 185-186, 334, 368

Business process 171, 189-190, 197-202, 207-216, 223

Business processes life cycle 189, 216

Business Processes Management (BPM) 198, 200, 216

Business Sustainability Perception 129

C

case study 39, 68-69, 83, 85-87, 89-91, 110, 164, 181, 184, 268, 284, 291, 303, 311, 319, 321, 324, 371

Cause-Related Marketing 170, 174, 177, 182-184, 186-187, 329-330, 332, 342, 380, 382

Certification Systems 45

Circular Economy 6, 9, 13, 16, 25, 34, 38, 44, 101, 154, 165-166, 268, 288-289, 291-293, 297-301, 332, 338, 375, 379, 382-383

Communications 112-113, 116-117, 119-121, 124-126, 130, 132, 138, 147, 172, 181, 184, 186, 253, 344, 346, 349, 352, 362

Companies 1-4, 6-8, 10-11, 19-26, 28-31, 34, 36, 43, 48, 50, 73, 75, 95-96, 99, 101, 103, 105-106, 108, 111, 120, 123, 131, 133-134, 137-140, 143, 145, 147, 149-152, 154, 156-157, 159-161, 163-165, 170-180, 187, 189-191, 196, 200, 203-204, 207, 218-220, 222-226, 228-234, 236, 240-244, 246, 250, 256, 264, 267-268, 276, 280, 290-291, 293, 299-300, 306, 326-341, 344-347, 349-352, 354-355, 357-359, 362, 368, 372-375, 377-382

Competitive advantage 22-23, 26, 34, 38-39, 94, 96-97, 101, 103, 111, 133-134, 136, 143, 153, 167, 170-181, 183-186, 188, 234, 241, 250, 264, 326, 328, 330-331, 341-343

Competitive Strategy 239

Consumer behavior 19-24, 29, 34, 37-38, 46, 48, 50-51, 61, 66, 129, 154, 243, 249, 254, 330-331, 333, 352, 362, 385

Consumer Demand 19, 138, 328, 336, 339-340, 374, 385

Consumer Preferences 2, 22, 26, 385

Consumers' Perception Of Sustainability 137, 139-140, 148

Contemporary Finance 355

Corporate social responsibility 14, 18, 22, 28, 34-37, 39-40, 66, 84, 94, 96-97, 103, 110, 143-144, 146, 170, 176, 178, 180-183, 185-188, 239-243, 250-253, 269, 304, 320, 322-323, 329, 335, 342, 382

Cosmetics 2, 7, 41-54, 56-67, 140

COVID-19 Pandemic 2, 14, 31, 36, 71, 87, 97, 115, 233, 237, 240, 245, 251, 253, 309, 311, 316, 340

CSR 22-23, 33, 35-36, 39-40, 64, 66, 84, 92, 94-97, 100-101, 105, 107-108, 123, 136-137, 143-144, 174, 176-177, 182-183, 186, 243, 252-253, 304, 307, 315, 329-330, 382

Customer Relationship Management (CRM) 143, 177-178, 184, 196-198, 208, 210-212, 216, 218, 224, 230, 233-234, 353

Customers 3-4, 6-7, 9, 13, 23-24, 26-29, 42-44, 46-52, 57-58, 94, 96, 100, 103, 106-107, 114-115, 120,

Index

122, 124, 130-132, 134, 137, 149-151, 153, 155-156, 159, 161-162, 164-165, 170-171, 173, 175, 181, 188, 190-194, 199, 201, 203-204, 206, 221, 223-224, 226-228, 230, 232-234, 242-244, 248, 254, 279, 281-282, 318, 327, 332-333, 338-340, 346-349, 351, 358, 362-368, 370, 372, 374, 376-377, 379-380, 383, 385

Czech Republic 92-93, 96, 98, 100, 110-111

D

Determinants of Green Purchasing 41

Digital marketing 23, 31, 37, 68, 150, 166, 168, 170-173, 178-188, 218-224, 226-227, 231-238, 341, 344-345, 351-353, 358, 362-363, 368, 370, 372, 378-382, 385-386

Digital Marketing Refers 385

Digitalization 2-3, 18, 68, 71, 84, 88-90, 116, 171, 218-220, 223-224, 231, 233-235, 384

diversity management 92-93, 96, 106, 108-110

E

Eco-label 47, 67

Ecological marketing 170, 174-176, 178, 180, 188, 383

Ecological marketing orientation 170, 175, 178, 180

Energy Savings 239, 249

Enterprice Resoursce Planning (ERP) 189, 197, 209-210, 216, 228

Environment 1-2, 4-9, 11, 13-14, 16, 19, 22-23, 25-26, 29, 31, 33-34, 37, 42-47, 49-52, 54, 58-59, 61-63, 66-67, 69-70, 72, 74-75, 77, 80, 83-84, 90-91, 93-96, 99-101, 103, 105-108, 113, 116, 120-121, 124-125, 130, 133-134, 138, 145, 147, 149-153, 155-158, 160-165, 174-175, 178, 180, 183, 186-188, 191-192, 216, 219, 221, 224, 231, 234, 237, 240-246, 248-249, 252, 255-257, 259, 263, 267-269, 272, 275, 288-293, 297-300, 317, 320, 326-327, 330-333, 337, 343-344, 349, 352, 355-356, 361-363, 372-386

Environmental Marketing 18, 39, 288

Environmentally Friendly Product 326, 332

ESG 25, 30, 151, 156-157, 166, 184, 338

Evaluability 280-281

F

Fair Trade 21, 41, 58, 61, 329, 332

Financial Crisis 282, 326-327, 331

Food 1-3, 5, 8-11, 14-17, 28, 39, 43, 51, 66, 110, 147, 168, 236, 259, 264-265, 293-294, 314, 316, 324, 342, 374

G

Georgia 1, 14, 18, 36, 189, 218-219, 222-223, 225-226, 228, 233, 271, 274-287, 344, 353, 372

Global Supply Chains 303-305, 308-309, 312, 316, 319-324

Governance 25, 71, 84, 151, 156, 176, 250, 253, 255, 258, 268-269, 285, 299, 320-321, 338, 366-367

Green Advertising 22, 38, 48-50, 61, 66, 175, 185, 372-373, 375, 385

Green Cosmetics 41-54, 56-61, 63-67, 140

Green Labels 41, 47

Green Marketing 18, 20-23, 36-38, 50, 65, 147, 150-151, 153, 155, 161, 164-165, 167-170, 174-175, 178, 180-182, 185, 187-188, 243, 252, 254, 271-273, 326-334, 336-337, 339-343, 383-384

Green Marketing Communication 174-175, 178, 180, 188

Green Products 20, 34, 42-44, 48, 50, 52, 66, 146, 156, 188, 330, 382, 385-386

Green Purchasing 39, 41-42, 48, 50, 53, 64, 159

H

Health Reforming 271-273, 280-282

Health Systems 271-273, 280-281, 283-284

Human Resource Management 92-93, 95-97, 100, 102-103, 106-114, 117, 121-122, 125, 181, 363

I

Industry 1-2, 4, 6-10, 14, 17, 34, 36, 39, 41-43, 62, 65, 77, 89, 101, 103, 109-110, 139-140, 144, 151, 154, 158, 167-168, 172, 176, 178, 180-181, 184, 187, 237, 256, 262, 264, 275, 299, 301, 303-306, 308-309, 311-312, 314-316, 318-324, 326, 331-332, 334, 340, 355-356, 361-362, 364, 366-369, 382-383

Innovation 3, 11, 13, 15, 35, 37, 72, 90, 100-101, 105, 107, 110, 112-113, 115, 136, 143-144, 153-154, 159, 165-168, 171, 182-183, 185-187, 215, 221-222, 226, 235-237, 256, 268, 280-281, 330, 333-334, 341, 351, 354, 357, 362, 366, 371, 375, 377

Intelligent packaging 1-2, 5-11, 13-17

International Clothing and Fashion Brands 303-305, 315-317

International Practitioners 355

Internet 23, 29-31, 82, 113, 118, 122, 130-131, 134, 138-139, 146, 172-173, 185, 187-188, 204, 206-

207, 223-225, 231, 344-346, 348-354, 358, 363
Internet Marketing 173, 344-346, 348-350, 352-354

L

Loyal customer 218

M

Market Viability 355
Marketing 1-4, 7, 9, 11, 14-40, 48, 50, 53, 59-60, 62-66, 68, 85, 88, 90, 92-93, 96, 98, 103, 105, 112-114, 122-123, 125-126, 132, 140, 143-147, 149-157, 159-204, 206-216, 218-229, 231-246, 248-256, 263-264, 267-269, 271-286, 288, 304-305, 316, 326-337, 339-358, 361-364, 367-380, 382-386
Marketing communication 7, 26, 29, 126, 140, 174-178, 180, 188, 362, 371
Marketing Competence 344, 351-352
Marketing Efforts 26, 145, 156, 172-173, 188, 378, 385
Marketing Functions 195, 355
Marketing strategies 18-23, 26, 33, 36, 68, 90, 113, 149-153, 157, 160-161, 164, 168, 170, 172-173, 176-177, 180, 192, 219-221, 223, 228, 235, 240, 245, 248, 264, 268, 327-329, 331-332, 335-336, 340, 349, 352, 357, 362, 368, 374, 377, 379-382, 385
Modern Finance 355, 358, 363, 369-370
modern trends in HR 92
Municipal and Industrial Waste 288, 291-292
Municipal Enterprise 300-301

N

Natural Cosmetics 44, 50, 52-53, 59, 67
Niche Art Museum 68

O

Online Communities 68, 80-82, 148
Organic Cosmetics 44, 49, 53, 59-60, 63-64, 67

P

Pakistan 34, 255, 257-269
PEST analysis 68, 72, 80-81, 83
Pollution 9, 19, 29-30, 42, 46, 59, 70, 73, 77, 99, 151, 153-154, 175, 180, 242, 255-259, 261-269, 289-290, 318, 326, 384

R

Re-Inovation 112

Renewable Energy 159, 240, 244, 250-252, 254, 257-258, 264, 267, 298, 318, 328, 333-334, 336-338, 377, 379, 381

S

SDG 3, 9-11, 16, 18, 25, 69-70, 150, 276
SME sector 218, 222-223, 233
Social Influence 50-51, 57-58, 60, 67, 82
Social Marketing 18, 21-22, 26, 37-38, 153-154, 167-168, 184, 239, 241, 243-246, 248-253, 268, 272-273
Social Media 23-25, 30-31, 35-37, 40, 65-66, 74, 81, 85-88, 90, 116, 120, 130-132, 134-148, 150, 162, 170-171, 173, 175-178, 180-185, 187, 218, 220, 224-232, 234, 237-238, 249, 285, 334-335, 338, 346-349, 358, 363, 367, 370, 378-380, 385
Social Media Communication 129-131, 134-142, 144-145
Social Media Influencers 31, 129-130, 139-142, 145
Stakeholders 1, 3-5, 22-26, 30, 33-34, 93-94, 96-97, 99, 101-102, 107-110, 114, 117, 122-124, 132-133, 135-138, 150, 156, 160, 163-164, 173, 175-177, 179, 240-241, 243, 248, 254-258, 264, 266-267, 312, 314, 318, 327-328, 335-340, 377
survey 6, 28, 61, 64, 98, 102-103, 108, 110, 133, 138-139, 142, 145, 147, 275, 278, 285, 311, 351, 368, 372
Sustainability 1, 6-10, 13-14, 16, 18-31, 33-40, 42-44, 46-49, 59, 62-66, 68-84, 88-89, 92-97, 99, 101, 108-109, 111, 114, 117, 122, 126, 129-130, 132-133, 135-170, 172-178, 180-188, 191, 212, 215, 224, 226, 235, 237, 243, 250, 254-258, 263-264, 266-273, 276-285, 317-319, 322, 326-330, 332-343, 355, 361-363, 371-385
Sustainability competitive advantage 170, 172, 174-175, 177-178, 180-181, 188
Sustainability Perception Of Business 135-136, 148
Sustainability Performance 33-34, 38, 69, 114, 137, 140, 145, 148, 336, 338-341
Sustainable Development 1-3, 6, 9, 11-13, 15-18, 24-26, 33-36, 39-40, 59, 64, 68-71, 73-76, 79-80, 82-84, 86, 89, 93, 99, 102, 106, 109-112, 114, 117, 125, 129, 132-133, 137, 144-147, 149-151, 153-154, 165-167, 169, 174, 176, 178, 180, 183-184, 186, 188, 190-191, 215, 218-223, 225, 234, 236, 241, 244, 252, 256, 258, 264, 267, 286, 288, 290-291, 293, 299, 329, 341, 344-345, 352, 362, 371-373, 376-377, 382-383
Sustainable Development Goals 1-3, 6, 9, 11-12, 16-18, 24-26, 33-35, 39-40, 69-70, 84, 109, 111, 129,

Index

132, 144-147, 149-150, 165, 169, 174, 176, 178, 180, 183-184, 186, 188, 225, 286
Sustainable Digital Marketing 180, 353, 372, 379-382, 386
Sustainable Digital Marketing Mix 372, 380-381
Sustainable Marketing 1-3, 11, 15, 18-23, 25-30, 33-35, 37, 39-40, 64, 149-153, 155-157, 159-168, 170, 172, 174, 178-181, 190-192, 194, 203, 212, 214-215, 255-256, 263-264, 267-268, 271-272, 274-278, 280-286, 332, 342-344, 352, 354-355, 361-363, 369, 372-378, 382-384, 386
Sustainable Materials 22, 140, 329, 331, 333, 336, 338, 373-375, 379, 385-386
Sustainable real estate marketing 255

T

Technology 13-16, 44, 69, 71-72, 74-75, 81, 83, 86, 90, 110, 116, 120, 122, 129, 131, 145-146, 149, 156, 164, 167, 170, 173, 185, 187, 207, 215, 222-224, 226-228, 231-234, 236-237, 252, 264, 268, 273, 292-293, 306, 336, 346, 349, 355-358, 362-365, 367-368, 370, 373, 375, 379-380, 384
three pillars of sustainable development 68, 76, 83
Total Quality Management 106, 243, 254

U

Unethical Outsourcing and Marketing 303, 305
Urbanization 6, 255-259, 261-270, 385

V

Visual culture 68-70, 73-75, 77-83, 85

W

Workers' Exploitation 308, 314

Recommended Reference Books

IGI Global's reference books are available in three unique pricing formats:
Print Only, E-Book Only, or Print + E-Book.

Order direct through IGI Global's Online Bookstore at
www.igi-global.com or through your preferred provider.

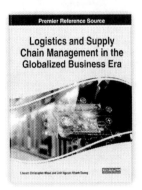

ISBN: 9781799887096
EISBN: 9781799887119
© 2022; 413 pp.
List Price: US$ **250**

ISBN: 9781799874157
EISBN: 9781799874164
© 2022; 334 pp.
List Price: US$ **240**

ISBN: 9781668440230
EISBN: 9781668440254
© 2022; 320 pp.
List Price: US$ **215**

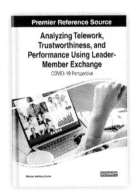

ISBN: 9781799889502
EISBN: 9781799889526
© 2022; 263 pp.
List Price: US$ **240**

ISBN: 9781799885283
EISBN: 9781799885306
© 2022; 587 pp.
List Price: US$ **360**

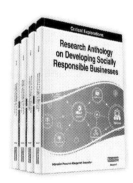

ISBN: 9781668455906
EISBN: 9781668455913
© 2022; 2,235 pp.
List Price: US$ **1,865**

Do you want to stay current on the latest research trends, product announcements, news, and special offers?
Join IGI Global's mailing list to receive customized recommendations, exclusive discounts, and more.
Sign up at: **www.igi-global.com/newsletters**.

Publisher of Timely, Peer-Reviewed Inclusive Research Since 1988

www.igi-global.com | Sign up at www.igi-global.com/newsletters | facebook.com/igiglobal | twitter.com/igiglobal | linkedin.com/igiglobal

Ensure Quality Research is Introduced to the Academic Community

Become an Evaluator for IGI Global Authored Book Projects

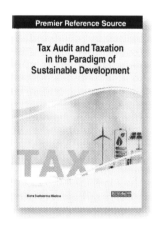   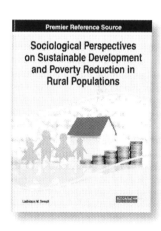

The overall success of an authored book project is dependent on quality and timely manuscript evaluations.

Applications and Inquiries may be sent to:
development@igi-global.com

Applicants must have a doctorate (or equivalent degree) as well as publishing, research, and reviewing experience. Authored Book Evaluators are appointed for one-year terms and are expected to complete at least three evaluations per term. Upon successful completion of this term, evaluators can be considered for an additional term.

If you have a colleague that may be interested in this opportunity, we encourage you to share this information with them.

Easily Identify, Acquire, and Utilize Published Peer-Reviewed Findings in Support of Your Current Research

IGI Global OnDemand

Purchase Individual IGI Global OnDemand Book Chapters and Journal Articles

For More Information:
www.igi-global.com/e-resources/ondemand/

Browse through 150,000+ Articles and Chapters!

Find specific research related to your current studies and projects that have been contributed by international researchers from prestigious institutions, including:

- Accurate and Advanced Search
- Affordably Acquire Research
- Instantly Access Your Content
- Benefit from the InfoSci Platform Features

"It really provides an excellent entry into the research literature of the field. It presents a manageable number of highly relevant sources on topics of interest to a wide range of researchers. The sources are scholarly, but also accessible to 'practitioners'."

- Ms. Lisa Stimatz, MLS, University of North Carolina at Chapel Hill, USA

Interested in Additional Savings?

Subscribe to

IGI Global OnDemand *Plus*

Learn More

Acquire content from over 128,000+ research-focused book chapters and 33,000+ scholarly journal articles for as low as US$ 5 per article/chapter (original retail price for an article/chapter: US$ 37.50).

7,300+ E-BOOKS.
ADVANCED RESEARCH.
INCLUSIVE & AFFORDABLE.

IGI Global e-Book Collection

- **Flexible Purchasing Options** (Perpetual, Subscription, EBA, etc.)
- Multi-Year Agreements with **No Price Increases** Guaranteed
- **No Additional Charge** for Multi-User Licensing
- No Maintenance, Hosting, or Archiving Fees
- Continually Enhanced & Innovated **Accessibility Compliance Features** (WCAG)

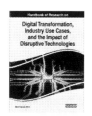

Handbook of Research on Digital Transformation, Industry Use Cases, and the Impact of Disruptive Technologies
ISBN: 9781799877127
EISBN: 9781799877141

Handbook of Research on New Investigations in Artificial Life, AI, and Machine Learning
ISBN: 9781799886860
EISBN: 9781799886877

Handbook of Research on Future of Work and Education
ISBN: 9781799882756
EISBN: 9781799882770

Research Anthology on Physical and Intellectual Disabilities in an Inclusive Society (4 Vols.)
ISBN: 9781668435427
EISBN: 9781668435434

Innovative Economic, Social, and Environmental Practices for Progressing Future Sustainability
ISBN: 9781799895909
EISBN: 9781799895923

Applied Guide for Event Study Research in Supply Chain Management
ISBN: 9781799889694
EISBN: 9781799889717

Mental Health and Wellness in Healthcare Workers
ISBN: 9781799888130
EISBN: 9781799888147

Clean Technologies and Sustainable Development in Civil Engineering
ISBN: 9781799898108
EISBN: 9781799898122

Request More Information, or Recommend the IGI Global e-Book Collection to Your Institution's Librarian

For More Information or to Request a Free Trial, Contact IGI Global's e-Collections Team: eresources@igi-global.com | 1-866-342-6657 ext. 100 | 717-533-8845 ext. 100

Printed in the United States
by Baker & Taylor Publisher Services